Social Justice and Culturally–Affirming Education in K–12 Settings

Jonathan Chitiyo
University of Pittsburgh, Bradford, USA

Zachary Pietrantoni
Florida International University, USA

A volume in the Advances in Early Childhood and K–12 Education (AECKE) Book Series

Published in the United States of America by
IGI Global
Information Science Reference (an imprint of IGI Global)
701 E. Chocolate Avenue
Hershey PA, USA 17033
Tel: 717-533-8845
Fax: 717-533-8661
E-mail: cust@igi-global.com
Web site: http://www.igi-global.com

Library of Congress Cataloging-in-Publication Data

Names: Chitiyo, Jonathan, 1985- editor. | Pietrantoni, Zachary, 1985-
   editor.
Title: Social justice and culturally-affirming education in K-12 settings /
   edited by Jonathan Chitiyo, Zachary Pietrantoni.
Description: Hershey, PA : Information Science Reference, 2023. | Includes
   bibliographical references and index. | Summary: "The purpose of this
   edited book is to bring together social scientists, scholars and other
   education practitioners to write chapters about social justice and
   inclusive education issues in k-12 settings. Chapters will provide an
   in-depth analysis of the factors that affect the education of
   marginalized populations, educational legislation, inclusive education,
   special education, and models or frameworks that deal with social
   justice and inclusive education"-- Provided by publisher.
Identifiers: LCCN 2022043777 (print) | LCCN 2022043778 (ebook) | ISBN
   9781668463864 (hardcover) | ISBN 9781668463901 (paperback) | ISBN
   9781668463871 (ebook)
Subjects: LCSH: Social justice and education--Case studies. | Inclusive
   education--Case studies.
Classification: LCC LC192.2 .S625 2023 (print) | LCC LC192.2 (ebook) |
   DDC 370.117--dc23/eng/20221102
LC record available at https://lccn.loc.gov/2022043777
LC ebook record available at https://lccn.loc.gov/2022043778

This book is published in the IGI Global book series Advances in Early Childhood and K-12 Education (AECKE) (ISSN: 2329-5929; eISSN: 2329-5937)

British Cataloguing in Publication Data
A Cataloguing in Publication record for this book is available from the British Library.

For electronic access to this publication, please contact: eresources@igi-global.com.

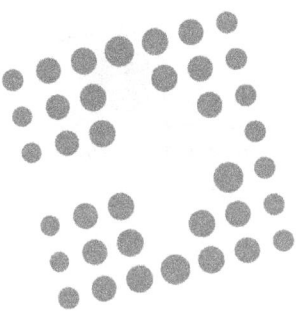

Advances in Early Childhood and K-12 Education (AECKE) Book Series

Jared Keengwe
University of North Dakota, USA

ISSN:2329-5929
EISSN:2329-5937

MISSION

Early childhood and K-12 education is always evolving as new methods and tools are developed through which to shape the minds of today's youth. Globally, educational approaches vary allowing for new discussions on the best methods to not only educate, but also measure and analyze the learning process as well as an individual's intellectual development. New research in these fields is necessary to improve the current state of education and ensure that future generations are presented with quality learning opportunities.

The **Advances in Early Childhood and K-12 Education (AECKE)** series aims to present the latest research on trends, pedagogies, tools, and methodologies regarding all facets of early childhood and K-12 education.

COVERAGE

- Bullying in the Classroom
- Standardized Testing
- Performance Assessment
- Learning Outcomes
- Literacy Development
- STEM Education
- K-12 Education
- Poverty and Education
- Head Start and Pre-K Programs
- Urban K-12 Education

IGI Global is currently accepting manuscripts for publication within this series. To submit a proposal for a volume in this series, please contact our Acquisition Editors at Acquisitions@igi-global.com or visit: http://www.igi-global.com/publish/.

Titles in this Series

For a list of additional titles in this series, please visit: www.igi-global.com/book-series/advances-early-childhood-educa-tion/76699

Preparing Pre-Service Teachers to Integrate Technology in K-12 Classrooms Standards and Best Practices
C. Lorraine Webb (Texas A&M University, San Antonio, USA) and Amanda L. Lindner (Texas A&M University, San Antonio, USA)
Information Science Reference • © 2022 • 340pp • H/C (ISBN: 9781668454787) • US $215.00

Cutting-Edge Language and Literacy Tools for Students on the Autism Spectrum
Katharine P. Beals (Drexel University, USA)
Information Science Reference • © 2022 • 298pp • H/C (ISBN: 9781799894421) • US $215.00

Handbook of Research on Family Literacy Practices and Home-School Connections
Kathy R. Fox (University of North Carolina Wilmington, USA) and Laura E. Szech (University of North Carolina Wilmington, USA)
Information Science Reference • © 2022 • 353pp • H/C (ISBN: 9781668445693) • US $270.00

Rethinking Inclusion and Transformation in Special Education
Maria Efstratopoulou (United Arab Emirates University, UAE)
Information Science Reference • © 2022 • 348pp • H/C (ISBN: 9781668446805) • US $215.00

Best Practices for Trauma-Informed School Counseling
Angela M. Powell (Lone Star College, USA)
Information Science Reference • © 2022 • 331pp • H/C (ISBN: 9781799897859) • US $215.00

Disciplinary Literacy as a Support for Culturally and Linguistically Responsive Teaching and Learning
Leslie Haas (Xavier University of Louisiana, USA) and Jill T. Tussey (Buena Vista University, USA)
Information Science Reference • © 2022 • 391pp • H/C (ISBN: 9781668442159) • US $215.00

Handbook of Research on Using Motor Games in Teaching and Learning Strategy
Pedro Gil-Madrona (University of Castilla-La Mancha, Spain)
Information Science Reference • © 2022 • 511pp • H/C (ISBN: 9781799896210) • US $270.00

Modern Reading Practices and Collaboration Between Schools, Family, and Community
Ana Patrícia Almeida (Universidade Aberta, Portugal) and Sandrina Esteves (ISEC Lisboa, Portugal)
Information Science Reference • © 2022 • 304pp • H/C (ISBN: 9781799897507) • US $215.00

701 East Chocolate Avenue, Hershey, PA 17033, USA
Tel: 717-533-8845 x100 • Fax: 717-533-8661
E-Mail: cust@igi-global.com • www.igi-global.com

Table of Contents

Section 2
Equity-Based Education

Section 3
Inclusive Education

Section 4
Educator Training

Detailed Table of Contents

Section 1
Marginalized and Vulnerable Students

This chapter explores the intersection of race, culture, and language, so teachers can provide racially, linguistically, and culturally responsive teaching for diverse learners, as classrooms around the world are increasingly diverse. There has been an urgent call for teacher training to move beyond colorblindness to serve racially, linguistically, and culturally diverse learners in an equitable, antiracist, and socially-just climate. The purpose of this chapter is to present teaching materials framed by a cosmopolitan lens that help teachers examine who they are as a racial, linguistic, and cultural being to help super diverse learners in this global era.

Two Spirit, transgender, intersex, non-binary, and gender non-conforming (2STING) teachers face significant additional stress in their careers. Research shows intolerable conditions for many teachers, even those in states with long-standing anti-discrimination policies in place. Educators reported experiencing harassment at work, hostile colleagues, hostile families, and doxing and social media bullying. Twenty-five percent of participants interviewed for a recent study had left their careers in education within a month of the study completion. Transgender and gender-diverse educators reported shocking rates of non-suicidal self-injury, suicidal ideation, and suicide attempts. All learning communities must change the culture surrounding these issues to help keep our LGB and 2STING educators and students alive.

    Lori Leibowitz, Baylor University, USA
    Leanne Howell, Baylor University, USA
    Nicholas R. Werse, Baylor University, USA

The underrepresentation of linguistically diverse gifted learners continues to be a pervasive issue in schools across the United States. Many leaders in the field recognize the problem of this inequitable access to gifted education programs. In light of this persistent challenge, the present chapter critically examines the barriers that gifted multilanguage learners (ML) face that can hinder or prevent their access to gifted and talented programs to identify promising solutions and actionable changes. To achieve these ends, the following chapter unfolds in two parts. First, the authors examine four avenues through which gifted ML students may be identified and referred to gifted and talented programs to critically consider potential obstacles they face and solutions to those obstacles. Second, the authors then present the "talent development" model, combined with insights from Culturally Relevant Teaching, as a way to construct classroom environments that make the identification of gifted ML students more likely.

    Antoinette Gagné, OISE, University of Toronto, Canada
    Thursica Kovinthan Levi, OISE, University of Toronto, Canada

Students with refugee experiences face several social and academic challenges in the Canadian school system. Supportive relationships and school spaces where educators, parents, and peers act as cultural brokers to help students navigate challenges can contribute to reducing experiences of educational inequality for children with refugee experiences. This duoethnography maps these relationships during a year-long identity text project with Grade 6 students in an ESL/ELD classroom by two educator researchers. Using an intersectional lens, the authors identify gaps and highlight promising pathways and practices for the integration of students with refugee backgrounds, including 1) working towards the greater interconnectedness of service and referrals between welcome centres, schools and service organizations; 2) knowledge exchange surrounding different education pathways and practices and the opportunities afforded by these for the integration of students with refugee experiences; 3) individually tailored educational support and services; and 4) translanguaging pedagogy.

    Selvinaz Saçan, Aydın Adnan Menderes University, Turkey
    Serap Öztürk, Ministry of Family and Social Policies, Turkey

Children enter the child protection system as a result of neglect or abuse. Due to their past experiences, these children's academic and social-emotional skills lag behind their peers. This situation can result in social exclusion, academic failure, absenteeism, and dropping out of school. The school stands out with its supportive value for children in the child protection system. However, in cases where school personnel do not have sufficient information about the child protection system, policies, and the characteristics of these children, the school cannot fulfill its protective-preventive and supportive role. However, a positive school experience has a protective, preventive, developing, and curative potential, especially for at-risk children.

Section 2
Equity-Based Education

Chapter 6

Elizabeth D. Cramer, Florida International University, USA
Sharde Theodore, Florida International University, USA
Aniva Lumpkins, Florida International University, USA
Chauntea S. Cummings, Florida International University, USA
Helen Rose Flores, Florida International University, USA

The purpose of this chapter is to provide an overview of a framework for equity-based multi-tiered systems of support (MTSS), practical strategies for its implementation, and resources to be used by stakeholders when implementing these supports. Special education referral and placement have historically been contingent upon subjective decisions fraught with discriminatory practices that affect racially, ethnically, and linguistically diverse (RELD) students. Through a social justice and culturally responsive lens, this chapter provides an in-depth analysis of existing MTSS systems and ways that inequities in schools can be mediated. Equitable practices are then described across academic and socioemotional supports. The chapter includes: (1) focus on an equity-based MTSS framework for RELD students; (2) implementation of equity-based approaches across three tiers; (3) equity-based assessment and progress monitoring; (4) recommendations for implementation; and (5) future research directions to ensure equity-based supports for RELD learners with or at risk for disability.

Chapter 7

Lwazi Sibanda, National University of Science and Technology, Zimbabwe

This chapter focuses on strategies for achieving equity-based education. The concept of equity-based education has been examined. Factors that influence equity in education which include funding, access to high-level curriculum, teacher quality and discipline have been discussed. The discussion revealed that funding is a distinct indicator of equity in education, hence, establishing sustainable partnerships between the government and other potential funders is advisable. The chapter also revealed numerous equity strategies such as free and compulsory primary and secondary education for children, providing access to excluded groups of learners, improving the quality of teaching, adopting various forms of assessment strategies, increasing resource allocation, creating equitable learning environments, and creating an equity framework. The chapter suggests solutions and recommendations, and provides future research directions. Finally, conclusion is drawn from the arguments posed by literature observations.

Chapter 8

Edson Nyasha Muresherwa, University of the Free State, South Africa
Loyiso C. Jita, University of the Free State, South Africa

This chapter explores the state of inclusive education in the secondary schools in Zimbabwe decades after independence and the Salamanca Declaration. The thrust of the chapter is very important at a time when inclusive education is increasingly being viewed as a critical element of basic education and a step towards social justice. The chapter shows that inclusive education has remained an illusion at a time when the inclusive framework is expected to have fully developed and to be bearing fruit. This paradox is explained in terms of the historical, cultural, and economic context prevailing in the country. This Zimbabwean context focuses public education on political and economic goals only, disregarding equity and social justice objectives. It is therefore recommended that the purpose of education be redefined to fully embrace the needs of 'all' and the social justice logics, bearing in mind the context of the local environment.

Section 3
Inclusive Education

This chapter looks at inclusive pedagogies and social justice for transforming teaching and learning in South African classrooms. Learners should not be marginalised or be made to feel that they do not belong. Therefore, teachers need to utilize inclusive pedagogies to ensure that learners' individual needs are met. The first section of this chapter defines the concepts of inclusive education and social justice, followed by the contextualisation of inclusive education in South Africa. The section that follows then engages the reader with issues of inclusive education globally. Finally, the chapter concludes with a discussion on instructional strategies that promote inclusive pedagogies and social justice.

Inclusive education, without excluding anyone regardless of his/her physical features, gender, or any other reasons, is considered a powerful instrument in achieving an inclusive society. The study aims to investigate the literature on inclusive education in K-12 classes in Turkey. In the study, document analysis method, one of the qualitative research designs, was adopted. The data were collected online via typing variations of the key words "problems, suggestions of inclusive education in Turkey" into several databases including Google Scholar, ProQuest, EBSCOhost, ERIC, and the search engine of the Higher Education Institution's thesis archive for the years of 2009-2022. The results have revealed that there are needs for a better inclusive education in Turkey, such as improving of educational facilities and reducing class sizes, developing inclusive education policies and approaches, increasing the quantity and quality of special education personnel, and more financial support.

Focusing on content, pedagogy, and dispositions, individually and collectively, with preservice teachers contributes to understanding the intersectionality of identities and structural inequities. In this chapter, the authors describe their backgrounds as an entry point to teaching about social justice and identity in their courses. They share guiding theoretical perspectives used to ground their practice and build classroom communities with preservice teachers. The authors emphasize content, applied assignments, and activities to build an understanding of social justice and equity and bring students closer to understanding their life experiences and their impact when working with students and families. This chapter offers a means to bring the margins to the forefront in preservice teacher education to affect lasting change in how preparation can better address educational inequities in schools and communities.

Section 4
Educator Training

Chapter 12
Derya Ası, University of Dundee, UK
Tracey Joyce, University of Dundee, UK

In early years settings and schools, the population of children from diverse ethnic backgrounds has been increasing all over the world. Along with this increase, there is growing interest and concern in meeting the needs of these children and their families throughout their early years and school experience. Within any mainstream culture it is assumed that an ethnically diverse population should be able to be successfully integrated; however, it is not always clear how this could be achieved. Adaptation and integration to a new culture or school environment may be best achieved via effective communication between students, parents, and professionals. In this chapter, teacher beliefs and attitudes and how these affect communication will be discussed. The power of teacher-child relationships will be highlighted and suggestions will be made about effective practices to promote communication and build relationships.

Chapter 13
Juland Dayo Salayo, University of Santo Tomas, Philippines
Merry Ruth M. Gutierrez, Philippine Normal University, Philippines

This qualitative research aims to determine how language teachers' ontological beliefs on critical pedagogy build teacher identity and language ideology. Participants included 18 public junior high school teachers. Results revealed that critical language pedagogy (CLP) constructed teacher identities against its trajectory. These identities include the lack of familiarity and misunderstanding of CLP, resistance to a critical teaching approach, dependency on the official textbook or learning modules, and confidence in their traditional practices. Similarly, distorted critical language ideologies were also determined, such as language as an apolitical entity, CLP as a threat to social and cultural harmony, L1 as a threat to L2 learning, and the perceived dominance of American English. Both identities and ideologies are attributed to social conflicts and sociopolitical activities that produce oppression and marginalization. Hence, it is recommended that the education sector provide an opportunity to fully understand the role of criticality through dialogue, reflection, and praxes.

Chapter 14

Lena Shulyakovskaya, University of Toronto, Canada
Arlo Kempf, University of Toronto, Canada

This chapter explores teachers' interpretations of racial justice-oriented professional development (PD). Findings emerge from surveys and interviews conducted with 74 teachers in Toronto, Canada. Data reveals that teachers' ideological positions have a direct relationship to their understanding of racial justice. Three patterns of thought emerged: 1) The majority of teachers interpreted racial justice to be a commodity that they expected be given to them. 2) Some teachers interpreted racial justice as a way to "save" racialized Others, and 3) a small number of teachers recognized racial justice to be an ongoing process of self-reflection. In this chapter, the authors argue white supremacist logics at the systemic level influence what racially just strategies and activities teachers imagine in terms of individual teachers' institutionalized ideological stances. Most importantly, the authors demonstrate how many teachers' uncritical interpretations of racial justice serve to reinforce white supremacy already present in the organizational norms of Canada's K-12 schooling.

Chapter 15

William Clark, University of Pittsburgh, Bradford, USA

When considering the many cases brought before the Supreme Court of the United States, one that had the greatest impact on the field of education when it came to diversity, equity, and inclusion was Brown v. Board of Education (1954). The outcome of Brown (1954) did bring changes in the operations of public schools with the concept of "separate but equal" no longer being the standard. The ruling, which was not always received with open arms, brought student diversity into schools across the country. This chapter will present the concept of hiring practices for teachers from underrepresented backgrounds by looking at several areas such as hiring for diversity, recruitment, interviews, and retention. Each of these areas must be considered if the current hiring practices for underrepresented populations are to be impacted. Scholars studying staffing in education consider human capital management to be strategic when it involves recruiting, developing, and retaining effective teachers who make a positive contribution to student learning.

Foreword

Social Justice and Culturally-Affirming Education in K-12 Settings is a compilation of deeply exploratory and investigatory chapters that affirm the importance of social justice as reality not rhetoric. The K-12 educational landscapes are increasingly diverse therefore social justice as integral and not as an "add-on" must be addressed fully and specifically in all corridors of K-12 education. What this text uncovers and expertly highlights is that social justice is not a new concept neatly placed in mission/vision statements and strategic plans of educational institutions.

What is especially affirming and important about *Social Justice and Culturally-Affirming Education in K-12 Settings* is its focus on the very foundation of "showing up in the world" – K-12 education. It is at the level of K-12 education that many foundational understandings about the values and possibilities of growth through education are formed and extended toward the next levels of individuals' personal and professional/work lives.

Dr. Jonathan Chitiyo and Dr. Zachary Pietrantoni have compiled a text of fifteen chapters which are holistic in their discussion of social justice yet delve into specificities that touch on areas of social justice that readers will find both expected topics of discourse as well as unexpected in the innovative and creative implementation perspectives. As I moved through reading the chapters– the words that continued to resonate with me were *magnanimous* and *courageous*. It is truly magnanimous and coura-geous to lift up social justice conversations within the K-12 realm at a time when the concept of social justice is still being grappled with as something novel and unknown in the twenty-first century. It is upliftingly magnanimous and boldly courageous to examine and expose the voids that have existed for far too long in the K-12 realm yet to do so with clarity and informed research surrounding competing ideologies and methodologies.

Social Justice and Culturally-Affirming Education in K-12 Settings has as its goal the creation of a community of social scientists, researchers, and other practitioners to engage in research, sharing, and the development of strategies to change the very uneven paradigms and voids that mimic social justice best practices in K-12 settings. Further, Chitiyo and Pietrantoni, along with the chapter authors, engage readers with the various challenges and potential pathways toward revisionary practices for enhanced and purposeful social justice practices and implementation in the K-12 realm.

Social Justice and Culturally-Affirming Education in K-12 Settings argues for the heightened and purposeful implementations of social justice in the K-12 realm for students who are identified as margin-alized and classified as minorities. It argues for both dramatic change as well as revisionist strategies in the areas of K-12 social justice, special education, educational inequities, educational reforms, inclusive education, school policies, culturally affirming education, critical race theory, community engagement, and intersections of these areas of inquiry. I return to one of the words that continues to resonate as I review this text and write this foreword – *courageous*. The editors of this text and the essay authors are courageous in their direct and unapologetic discussions and proposals for change and revisionist strategies to lift up and change the shape and tone of social justice in the K-12 realm.

It is no doubt that *Social Justice and Culturally-Affirming Education in K-12 Settings* is both an important and timely text for K-12 administrators, teaching faculty, staff, and community stakeholders. It also will arguably be a challenging text to some of these same key persons—administrators, teaching faculty, staff, and community stakeholders—who may be resistant to change and revisionist strategies. There is yet illuminating value in such resistance as *Social Justice and Culturally-Affirming Education in K-12 Settings* sparks the dialectic and resists shadow-boxing the importance of filling the voids too long existent in K-12 education.

Emily Williams
University of the West Indies, Mona, Jamaica

Emily Allen Williams *is Director of Educational Research Analysis and author of seven books and numerous scholarly essays on Caribbean Culture and Literature and Higher Education Best Practices. She is former Vice President of Academic Affairs and Tenured Full Professor (University of Pittsburgh), Vice Provost of Curriculum and Assessment (Ramapo College), Dean of Liberal Arts and Social Sciences (University of the Virgin Islands), Department Chair of English and Tenured Full Professor (Texas Southern University), and Tenured Associate Professor at Morehouse College. Williams holds a Ph.D./D.A. in Humanities from Clark Atlanta University (Atlanta, GA) and a Master of Arts in Linguistics and Literature from Virginia Commonwealth University/VCU (Richmond, VA). Williams is a Fulbright Scholar-in-Residence with her residency at the University of the West Indies, Mona Campus/JA (2000). Williams is a trainer and facilitator of DEI workshops and has presented several international conferences on social justice, race, equity, and diversity in the states of GA, MA, and PA. She serves as a Site Visit Chair, Peer Reviewer, and Committee Member with MSCHE and CHEA.*

Preface

The concept of social justice has existed for hundreds of years, but it has recently gained attention as a result of people standing up to unfair conditions, exploitation and other oppressive systems. Social justice emphasizes equal access to resources, dismantling hierarchies of power and the promotion of well-being of marginalized populations (Constantine, et al., 2007). The concept is built upon five important principles: (1) access, (2) equity, (3) participation, (4) diversity, and (5) human rights (Carlisle et al., 2006; Constantine, et al., 2007). Access as a principle of social justice ensures that all individuals, especially those coming from marginalized backgrounds, have access to resources and opportunities based on their needs. With respect to participation, social justice posits that all individuals have equitable opportunities to participate in activities and programs that may benefit their wellbeing. Equity deals with the promotion of policy, legislation and scholarly work that address the systemic barriers that hinder the access and participation of all individuals in different realms of society. Diversity as a principle of social justice looks into the importance of cultural differences. Finally, human rights as a principle of social justice purports that societies and institutions should honor, respect and appreciate the rights of all individuals regardless of race, gender, sexual orientation, or ethnic background.

While the concept of social justice is primarily centered on equitable distribution of wealth and property, it has been extended to other areas such as education and health care. In the field of education, social justice brings to light the plight that students who are marginalized (i.e., students with disabilities, students of color, English Language Learners, and other students from minority backgrounds face in their education (Carlisle et al., 2006). There is a large body of research that shows that there are systemic barriers against marginalized students that hinders their school outcomes as evidenced by standardized test scores, educational attainment, and course enrollment patterns (Arujo et al., 2018; Gandara & Contreras, 2009; Menken, 2013). Consequently, social justice scholarship has become a prominent topic in educational research.

As previously discussed, in the field of education, social justice brings to light the challenges that students from marginalized backgrounds face, culturally affirming education can be used to strategically promote safe spaces that support students' cultural identities and assets (Alim & Paris, 2017; Ferlazzo, 2017; Price-Dennis et al., 2017). Existing research shows that school districts can adopt culturally affirming practices as a change agent in their curricula to combat some of the microaggressions that students from marginalized backgrounds experience in their education (Allen, Scott, & Lewis, 2013). At the core, culturally affirming education requires educators to serve as culturally competent instructors who are sensitive to the cultural identities, values, and assets of students and their families while intentionally working to dismantle systems of oppression.

This book explores social justice and culturally affirming issues in K-12 settings from different perspectives. The text is comprised of chapters that deal with marginalized and vulnerable student populations, equity-based education, inclusive education, and educator training.

Chapter 1 explores the intersection of race, culture, and language, so teachers can provide racially, linguistically, and culturally responsive teaching for diverse learners because classrooms around the world are increasingly diverse. There has been an urgent call for teacher training to move beyond color-blindness to serve racially, linguistically, and culturally diverse learners in an equitable, antiracist and socially-just climate.

Chapter 2 examines how transgender and gender diverse educators have to be supported in education. The chapter discusses that educators and students who are transgender and gender diverse face intolerable conditions even in states with long-standing anti-discrimination policies in place. The author recommends that the culture surrounding these issues needs to change to help gender diverse educators and students.

Chapter 3 is focused on multilingual learners who are identified as gifted. Specifically, the chapter critically examines the barriers that gifted multilanguage learners (ML) face that can hinder or prevent their access to gifted and talented programs to identify promising solutions and actionable change.

Chapter 4 is focused on students who have refugee experiences. The chapter maps relationships during a year-long identity text project with Grade 6 students in an ESL/ELD classroom by two educator researchers. Using an intersectional lens, the authors identify gaps and highlight promising pathways and practices for the integration of students with refugee backgrounds.

Chapter 5 investigates the problems children who enter the child protection system face in their schooling and the role of the school. Due to their traumatic past experiences, these children's academic and social-emotional skills lag behind their peers. This situation can result in social exclusion, academic failure, absenteeism, and drop-out of school. This chapter explores the role of the school in providing an environment that is protective.

Chapter 6 provides an overview of a framework for equity-based multi-tiered systems of support (MTSS), practical strategies for its implementation, and resources to be used by stakeholders when implementing these supports. Through a social justice and culturally responsive lens, this chapter provides an in-depth analysis of existing MTSS systems and ways that inequities in schools can be mediated.

Chapter 7 focuses on strategies for achieving equity-based education. Factors that influence equity in education include funding, access to high-level curriculum, teacher quality and discipline. The chapter also reveals numerous equity strategies such as free and compulsory primary and secondary education for children, providing access to excluded groups of learners, improving the quality of teaching, adopting various forms of assessment strategies, increased resource allocation, creating equitable learning environments and creating an equity framework.

Chapter 8 explores teachers' interpretations of racial justice-oriented professional development (PD) in Canada. Results show that teachers' ideological positions have a direct relationship to their understanding of racial justice. Most importantly, the authors demonstrate how many teachers' uncritical interpretations of racial justice serve to reinforce white supremacy already present in the organizational norms of Canada's K-12 schooling.

Chapter 9 explores the state of inclusive education in the secondary schools in Zimbabwe decades after independence and the Salamanca Declaration. The chapter shows that although other countries have made significant strides in making inclusive education a reality, it remains an illusion at a time when the inclusive framework is expected to have fully developed and to be bearing fruits. The chapter recommends that the purpose of education needs to be redefined to fully embrace the needs of 'all' and the social justice logics, bearing in mind the context of the local environment.

Chapter 10 examines inclusive pedagogies and social justice for transforming teaching and learning in South African classrooms. The chapter defines the concepts of inclusive education and social justice, followed by the contextualisation of inclusive education in South Africa. The chapter also provides a discussion of the instructional strategies that promote inclusive pedagogies and social justice in South African schools.

Chapter 11 examines the state of inclusive education in Turkey. Using a document analysis method, results the authors report that there are needs for a better inclusive education in Turkey, such as improving of educational facilities and reducing class sizes, developing inclusive education policies and approaches, increasing the quantity and quality of special education personnel, and more financial support.

Chapter 12 examines how the authors' background as teacher educators gives them a unique perspective to teach about social justice and identity in their courses. The authors share guiding theoretical perspectives used to ground their practice and build classroom communities with preservice teachers. The authors emphasize content, applied assignments and activities to build an understanding of social justice and equity and bring students closer to understanding their life experiences and their impact when working with students and families.

Chapter 13 focuses on the power and potency of teacher-child relationships as a means to promote communication and build relationships. The chapter shows that the population of children from diverse ethnic backgrounds has been increasing all over the world. Asa result of this increase, there is growing interest and concern in meeting the needs of these children and their families throughout their early years and school experience. The first step in meeting the needs of the students and their parents is through communication.

Chapter 14 examines how language teachers' ontological beliefs on critical pedagogy build teacher identity and language ideology in the Philippines. The participants included 18 English public junior high school teachers. The authors report that critical language pedagogy (CLP) constructed teacher identities against its trajectory. These identities include the lack of familiarity and misunderstanding of CLP, resistance to a critical teaching approach, dependency on the official textbook or learning modules, and confidence in their traditional practices.

Chapter 15 presents the concept of hiring practices of teachers from underrepresented backgrounds by looking at several areas such as hiring for diversity, recruitment, interviews, and retention. The authors stress that each of these areas must be considered if the current hiring practices for underrepresented populations are to be impacted.

Jonathan Chitiyo
University of Pittsburgh, Bradford, USA

Zachary Pietrantoni
Florida International University, USA

REFERENCES

Alim, H. S., & Paris, D. (Eds.). (2017). *Culturally sustaining pedagogies: Teaching and learning for justice in a changing world*. Teachers College Press.

Allen, A., Scott, L. M., & Lewis, C. W. (2013). Racial microaggressions and African American and Hispanic students in urban schools: A call for culturally affirming education. *Interdisciplinary Journal of Teaching and Learning, 3*(2), 117–129.

Carlisle, L. R., Jackson, B. W., & George, A. (2006). Principles of social justice education: The social justice education in schools project. *Equity & Excellence in Education, 39*(1), 55–64. doi:10.1080/10665680500478809

Constantine, M. G., Hage, S. M., Kindaichi, M. M., & Bryant, R. M. (2007). Social justice and multicultural issues: Implications for the practice and training of counselors and counseling psychologists. *Journal of Counseling and Development, 85*(1), 24–29. doi:10.1002/j.1556-6678.2007.tb00440.x

Ferlazzo, L. (2017, July 6). Culturally sustaining pedagogies. *Education Week*. https://www.edweek.org/teaching-learning/opinion-author-inte rview-culturally-sustaining-pedagogies/2017/07

Price-Dennis, D., Muhammad, G. E., Womack, E., McArthur, S. A., & Haddix, M. (2017). The multiple identities and literacies of Black girlhood: A conversation about creating spaces for Black girl voices. *Journal of Language & Literacy Education, 13*(2), 1–18.

Section 1
Marginalized and Vulnerable Students

Chapter 1
Educating Racially, Culturally, and Linguistically Diverse Children in a Global Era:
The World at Home and at Home in the World

Kim H. Song
University of Missouri-St. Louis, USA

Shea N. Kerkhoff
iD https://orcid.org/0000-0003-0052-4923
University of Missouri-St. Louis, USA

Alina Slapac
iD https://orcid.org/0000-0002-2210-1959
University of Missouri-St. Louis, USA

ABSTRACT

This chapter explores the intersection of race, culture, and language, so teachers can provide racially, linguistically, and culturally responsive teaching for diverse learners, as classrooms around the world are increasingly diverse. There has been an urgent call for teacher training to move beyond colorblindness to serve racially, linguistically, and culturally diverse learners in an equitable, antiracist, and socially-just climate. The purpose of this chapter is to present teaching materials framed by a cosmopolitan lens that help teachers examine who they are as a racial, linguistic, and cultural being to help super diverse learners in this global era.

DOI: 10.4018/978-1-6684-6386-4.ch001

INTRODUCTION

What Does It Mean to Be at Home in the World?

To be "at home in the world" may seem like an oxymoron or even paradoxical. How can one be "at home" and "in the world" at the same time? Home is a place where one feels comfortable, feels a sense of belonging, and feels safe. "In the world" means new or other places, places that by definition are outside of one's home. So how does that work? Being "at home in the world" means being okay with paradox, being comfortable with being uncomfortable. In other words, it means navigating places and spaces that are different from one's home, and doing so without fear or judgment, but with a sense of open mindedness and equality. Educators of racially, culturally, and linguistically (RCL) diverse learners need to explore their "home" or local mindset toward their learners and develop their "world" or global mindset to connect to learners from around the world and learners to the world, so learners can be citizens of "home" and "world."

Being at home in the world is called *cosmopolitan* or *global citizen* in education theory. Cosmopolitan is an ancient Greek word that roughly translates to citizen of the world. A cosmopolitan person has a global mindset and is open-minded. A cosmopolitan is open to new people, experiences, and ideas, both by being hospitable to new people and ideas in one's home spaces and experiencing other cultures by journeying across borders. Borders can be political, like the lines that create counties, states, and nations. Borders can also be metaphorical, like differences in religion, race, or language. A cosmopolitan goes beyond their comfort zone and crosses borders to learn about different perspectives. A cosmopolitan person does not replace their local identity or national citizenship with global citizenship (e.g., inner circle), but rather adds a global identity to their sense of self (e.g., outer circle). They see themselves as a part of a global community in addition to their local and national affiliations (Kerkhoff, 2022; Kerkhoff & Cloud, 2020; Kerkhoff & Ming, 2022; Slapac, 2021).

Why Is It Important to Be Cosmopolitan in English Language Education?

Cosmopolitan may sound like an elitist word. However, in education, cosmopolitanism is open to all people from all walks of life. Teachers, students, principals, family members, and anyone else can be cosmopolitan if they care about other people regardless of whether they are local or global. This means that people care about others across political and metaphorical borders, such as cultural, racial, and linguistic. From a cosmopolitan worldview, diversity is valued, and diversity of race, culture, and language is seen as an asset to our world. A cosmopolitan view extends social justice in education from a concern of local issues to a global worldview (Kerkhoff et al., 2021).

Caring about people like oneself is much easier than relating across differences. Psychologists call the propensity to associate with people who are like oneself "affinity bias." Affinity bias refers to the unconscious propensity to relate to someone with similar characteristics or resembles oneself. For example, suppose one walked into a cafeteria full of people one did not know. In that case, one may gravitate towards a table of people of the same gender, ethnicity, age, or other similar characteristics. Affinity bias can lead to implicit bias, which is also unconscious and refers to acting on one's assumptions about people based on their visible characteristics, such as sociocultural, linguistic, or racial backgrounds. Being aware of biases can help a person relate to others with more hospitality and empathy, rather than assumptions and generalizations (Song et al., 2021).

Imagine how different the world would be if people cared not only about people similar to them but also those different from them. Part of being able to empathize is imagining what other people are thinking and feeling. Imagination is actually an important part of being at home in the world. In order to put oneself in someone else's shoes, one has to imagine the similarities shared with the person one is attempting to relate to feeling comfortable across differences.

The authors incorporate cosmopolitanism into education with the goal of all teachers becoming racially, linguistically, and culturally competent, so that they can teach in a way that is racially, linguistically, and culturally responsive and meet all learners' needs. Education research has analyzed issues of culturally responsive (Gay, 2010) and relevant teaching (Ladson-Billings, 2014) as well as racially responsive by bringing critical race theory into education (Ladson-Billings & Tate, 1995). However, research has not analyzed the intersection of race, culture, and language, which is at the center of discrimination or raciolinguistic profiling (Flores & Rosa, 2015) for many people who speak English different from the so-called 'standard English' (Viesca, 2013). Informed by situated experiences and/or identities as socioculturally and globally constructed (Kumaravadivelu, 2012), we argue that building racial, linguistic, and cultural backgrounds is foundational and critical to serving RLC diverse learners (Kubota & Lin, 2006; Slapac et al., 2019; Kim & Slapac, 2015).

According to the Center for Immigration Studies, children who speak languages other than English at home are the fastest-growing group of students in the U.S. (Camarota et al., 2017). Meeting their needs requires teachers to develop a cosmopolitan worldview or mindset since teaching diverse learners moves beyond the normative culture-only or US-centric culture approach. We define racially, linguistically and culturally responsive/sustaining teachers as those who (a) demonstrate content knowledge with differentiated instruction and differentiated discourse or language use (Slapac, 2013; Villegas et al., 2018), (b) value and sustain students' diverse backgrounds and languages from home to world (Feiman-Nemser, 2001; Moll, 2015; Slapac & Kim, 2020), (c) attend to RLC diverse learners' situated sociocultural and political identities (Villegas et al., 2018), (d) reflect on their teaching beliefs, biases, and vision for a better world (Kim & Slapac, 2015; Slapac et al., 2019; Slapac, 2021) and (e) connect the content curriculum to students' lived experiences and identities (Feiman-Nemser, 2001; Kim & Slapac, 2015; Paris & Alim, 2014; Slapac & Kim, 2020; Villegas et al, 2018). The RLC responsive teaching framework, thus, embraces teachers' content-related and meta-content competency development for diverse learners and their families (Song et al., 2021; Yoon, 2016), socially and politically just beliefs (Villegas et al., 2018), culturally and linguistically inclusive environments (Feiman-Nemsee, 2001), translanguaging (Garcia & Wei, 2014) and raciolinguistic ideology (Flores & Rosa, 2015) as essential features.

The Intersection of Culture, Race, and Language

Current conversations about teaching emerging bilinguals focus on being culturally and linguistically responsive; however, students from racialized international communities experience injustices that are qualitatively different than students from other communities. Addressing these injustices is a matter of social justice in education. Culture, race, and language are entwined into everything a person does and believes. Because of being entwined, it can be hard to see what makes up our idiosyncrasies; what is influenced by our culture, race, and language; and what is part of being human for everybody. Some people, families, or communities spend a great deal of time discussing culture, race, and language and have a strong sense of identity around these features. Others may never have considered how these features are reflected in their values, beliefs, and behaviors. Whether one understands one's cultural, racial, and linguistic identities or not, because identity develops over a lifetime, it is always worthwhile to spend time in reflection and to consider how, as teachers, one's values, beliefs, and behaviors may impact their students.

Although culture, race, and language are different concepts, they are interdependent. Therefore, it is difficult to separate them when thinking about our own identities. This chapter starts by examining culture and how it intersects with language and race. We begin with culture because good teaching builds upon the cultural assets the learners bring into the classrooms. Most universities in the U.S., where the authors are teacher educators, require at least one course with an explicit focus on culture. For example, a large university in the Midwest U.S. asserts that the goal of general education requirements is "breadth of knowledge and cultural appreciation." Culture is explicitly stated in the goal, but language and race are not. In fact, studying languages other than English is declining in K-12 schools in the U.S. (AAA&S, 2016) and universities (Looney & Lusin, 2018). Therefore, the authors begin with the assumption that many of our readers may have more prior knowledge of culture than language or race. For those readers who are multilingual, culturally competent, and hold robust racial identities, the authors believe that this chapter will also serve the readers by providing research-based theories, clear articulations, and fully formulated arguments for why cultural, racial, and linguistic identity development is important and how they relate to education.

For the past several decades, education research has focused on multicultural education (Banks, 2004; 2019), culturally responsive teaching (Gay, 2010), culturally relevant pedagogy (Ladson-Billing, 2014), and culturally sustaining pedagogy (Paris & Alim, 2014). These educational theories consider culture an asset and advocate for equity and inclusion for students from diverse cultural backgrounds, each moving the field forward in specific ways. Ladson-Billings' work added a specific emphasis on race, and Paris and Alim added linguistic diversity to the conversation on culture. See Table 1 for nuanced definitions of these four theories. While the theories are nuanced, the dimensions can be intertwined and difficult to distinguish between in practice. Classroom examples of these theories in practice include reading diverse books, learning about historical resistance movements, and showcasing scientists from diverse cultural backgrounds.

The field has continued to build on these foundational concepts, adding an emphasis on global identities more recently. Ladson-Billings (2014) was intentional in her work to racialize global identity in a way that connects culture and race in a global context. In Banks' later work (2019), he connects culture, language, and identity to local, national and global contexts. Connecting race, culture, language and identity to education is important because our students do not drop their multiple identities when they walk through the school doors. The rest of the chapter is organized in four main sections: Culture, Language, Race, and then Putting It All Together. This chapter moves the field forward by explaining how teachers can develop robust cultural, racial, and linguistic identities to enhance students' content learning and help them become global citizens.

CULTURE, CULTURAL IDENTITY, AND CULTURAL COMPETENCE

Definition of Culture

Culture is an abstract and complex concept that surrounds us every day. There is an analogy that culture is the water and we are fish. A fish does not notice the water until it is out of the water. Likewise, one

Table 1. Definitions and Dimensions of Multicultural Education Theories

Theory	Multicultural Education	Culturally Responsive Teaching	Culturally Relevant Pedagogy	Culturally Sustaining Pedagogy
Foundational Author	James Banks	Geneva Gay	Gloria Ladson-Billings	Django Paris and Samy Alim
Definition	"Multicultural education is an approach to school reform designed to actualize educational equality for students from diverse racial, ethnic, cultural, social class, and linguistic groups" (2019, p. 13)	"Culturally responsive teaching is defined as using the cultural characteristics, experiences, and perspectives of ethnically diverse students as conduits for teaching them more effectively" (2002, p. 106)	"I have defined culturally relevant teaching as a pedagogy of opposition (1992c) not unlike critical pedagogy but specifically committed to collective, not merely individual, empowerment" (1995, p. 160)	Culturally sustaining pedagogy "seeks to perpetuate and foster—to sustain—linguistic, literate, and cultural pluralism as part of the democratic project of schooling and as a needed response to demographic and social change" (2014, p. 88)
Dimensions	a) Content integration, b) Knowledge construction, c) Prejudice reduction, d) Equity pedagogy, and e) Empowering school culture and structure	(a) Developing a knowledge base about cultural diversity, (b) Including ethnic and cultural diversity content in the curriculum, (c) Demonstrating caring and building learning communities, (d) Communicating with ethnically diverse students, and (e) Responding to ethnic diversity in the delivery of instruction.	(a) Students must experience academic success, (b) Students must develop and/or maintain cultural competence, and (c) Students must develop a critical consciousness through which they challenge the status quo of the current social order	(a) Valuing community languages, practices, and ways of being, (b) Schools are accountable to the community, (c) Curriculum that connects to cultural and linguistic histories, and (d) Sustaining cultural and linguistic practices, while providing access to the dominant culture

may not notice one's culture unless one happens to be outside of one's culture and notices that the routines and assumptions of how the world works may differ from the people around us. This is one reason Mark Twain said that travel is the best teacher. When one travels outside of their home country, they may experience what is called cognitive dissonance (Festinger, 1957). 'Cognitive' refers to thinking, and 'dissonance' means disagreement. Put together, cognitive dissonance refers to the state where what one is experiencing is in disagreement with what one expected or previously thought.

For example, if Maya grew up always putting hot sauce on rice and everyone in Maya's family and social circle always put hot sauce on their rice, then Maya might assume that everyone puts hot sauce on their rice. If she went to a house that did not serve hot sauce, then this new experience would disagree with Maya's thinking that everyone puts hot sauce on rice. The disagreement would cause cognitive dissonance and perhaps cause her to ask questions about other ways of eating rice. Receiving new information can cause a person's thinking to include the new information. Let's take this example a little further. If Maya traveled to other countries, and asked her hosts for hot sauce, she might be served tabasco, Kochujang, or another spicy condiment. After the first couple of experiences, Maya might continue to experience cognitive dissonance, and her thinking would have to expand to include the new information. After a few dissonant experiences, her thinking might adapt to understanding that different cultures eat rice differently and use different ingredients to create hot sauce. Then, when Maya experiences a new hot sauce, it would still add new information to her brain, and tasting it would be a novel experience.

However, she would not be in cognitive dissonance because the new information confirms what she already understood to be true. Food is a universal part of people's cultures, but food is only the tip of the iceberg when examining one's identity. Therefore, we may need to look deeper at what constitutes cultural identities.

According to the Center for Advanced Research on Language Acquisition (2022), culture is the shared symbols, understandings, and patterns of behaviors that are learned through socialization. Everyone is influenced by 'their' social norms and expectations. To provide equitable but tangible teaching practices, teachers must identify and assess their values, behaviors, and beliefs and learn to manage the dynamics of differences.

American Council on the Teaching of Foreign Languages (2015) suggests that culture comprises three dimensions: products, practices, and perspectives. Practices are behaviors that are considered appropriate for certain social interactions. They are the cultural norms (Browaeys & Price, 2015). Examples of practices include table manners, customary greetings, and turn-taking in conversations. Practices sometimes require the use of products. Products are the tangible--such as sculptures, literature, and gardens--or intangible--such as laws, education systems, and rituals--creations of culture. Lastly, perspectives are the basic assumptions that influence the practices and products of a culture. Perspectives include attitudes, identities, values, and beliefs.

Cultural Identity. Why is culture an important consideration in teaching and learning from a social justice lens? People do not leave their culture at the door when they enter the school building. Knowledge of one's own cultural identity and students' cultural identities is the first step in becoming culturally competent. Culturally competent teachers communicate in ways that are culturally sensitive and teach in ways that are culturally responsive.

When considering one's own or others' cultural identities, it is important to note that according to sociocultural theories, identity is not fixed but is constantly shifting and shaping as one experiences the world and interacts with other people. Relatedly, identity is contextual and changes depending on the context one is interacting within. James Banks, a foundational scholar of multicultural education, created a series of stages of cultural identity formation (2019). These phases are not steps that all people move through at the same age or in the same order. Instead, they are phases that are helpful as one reflects on one's own cultural identity.

One might have a strong identification with a culture or a few different cultures already.. Regardless of one's self-awareness level, there are parts of culture that will continue to become more clear and parts of culture that one will identify with more and less over time. Earlier, we mentioned that one might identify with a few different cultures. This is because culture is created by groups, and therefore our culture is dependent upon membership with a group. One might be a member of several groups or subgroups that have different cultures. One might relate as both cultures, or one might create your own hybrid culture by fusing the two groups. For example, if a person's mother is German and father is Chinese American and grew up in Canada, the person might identify as Chinese, American, German, and Canadian. And while those are national identities, they carry with them some cultural ways of being and belief systems as well.

Some of the practices and products that relate to culture consist of things one can see, like special food dishes, traditional clothing, and prized sporting events. Nevertheless, there is much more to culture than what one can see. In fact, what one can see may only be the superficial parts of a whole-being. This is why theorists talk about the iceberg model of identities. The tip of the iceberg is what one can see, and consists of food, fashion, festivals, skin colors, and flags, among other things. Below the surface

Figure 1. Iceberg Model of Culture

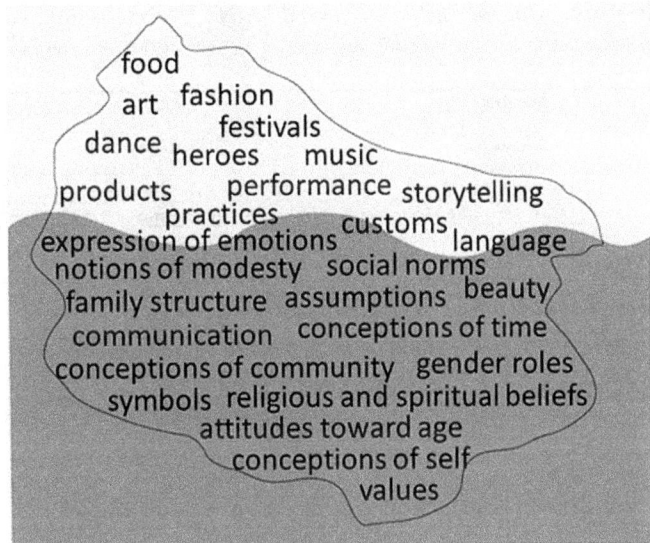

are the perspectives, religious beliefs, and others that make people who they are. View Figure 1 to see what else lies beneath the surface regarding identities.

Cultural Competence

Understanding what culture is, how one identifies culturally, and how one's worldview is impacted by culture is called cultural competence. Cultural competence is important for all people, teachers and students alike. Cultural competence enables one to engage in actions or create conditions that maximize intergroup communication and understanding (Sue, 2001). Cultural competence is multifaceted and includes understanding how language and race intersect with culture to position some groups as having power and others as oppressed or marginalized (Kim & Slapac, 2015; Warren & Moghaddam, 2018).

The Cultural Proficiency Continuum is a conceptual framework that can be used to assess personal and organizational identity progress and provide a common language to describe healthy and dysfunctional events and policies. The points along the continuum can identify the current state of a situation or practice, project a future state of development, or gauge the distance between the current and future states. The six levels of cultural competence are: 1) Cultural Destructiveness, 2) Cultural Incapacity, 3) Cultural Blindness, 4) Cultural Pre-Competence, 5) Cultural Competence, and 6) Cultural Proficiency (Nuri-Robins et al., 2019).

Consider the examples below in Table 2 to reflect on cultural competency and the steps that move toward higher proficiency levels.

Figure 2. From Reactive to Proactive Cultural Competence
Note. This figure illustrates the characteristics of the six cultural competencies. The left column starts with culturally incompetent behaviors and practices that are reactive. The right column describes proactive activities and attitudes that proactively seek personal transformation to support a goal of educational equity (Nuri-Robins et al., 2019).

Reactive: Tolerance for Mandated Equality	Proactive: Transformation for Desired Equity
Destructiveness ⇨ Incapacity ⇨ Blindness ⇨	*Pre-competence ⇨ Competence ⇨ Proficiency ⇨*
• Focuses on "them" being problems • Tolerates, excludes, separates • Diversity is a problem to be solved • Prevent, mitigate, avoid cultural dissonance and conflict • Stakeholders expect or help others assimilate • Information added to existing policies and procedures	• Focuses on "us" and "our practices" • Esteems, respects, includes • Diversity and inclusion are goals to be attained • Manage, leverage, facilitate conflict • Stakeholders adapt to meet needs of others • Existing policies, procedures, practices examined and adapted to changing environment

RACE AND RACIAL IDENTITY

Definition of Race

Race refers to groupings of people based on physical and social characteristics (Kubota & Lin, 2006). The groups of people are classified as White, Black, Asian, and other races have changed over time. As such, race is socially not biologically determined. In other words, race is a social construct. It is not biological and not coded in our DNA (Kolbert, 2018). For example, in the 1800s in the U.S., immigrants from Ireland and Italy were not considered White. According to the US Census, people from the Middle East and North Africa (MENA) could select the White racial category. However, groups such as the Arab American Institute Foundation have lobbied for a separate MENA race category.

Sociologists have come to consensus that different races are not discrete categories. This means that race can overlap and that the boundaries between categories are sometimes unclear. As there are not biological or genetic markers of race, people make decisions based on what they consider to be the essential physical characteristics of a person, such as their skin color, hair texture, or eye shape. However, a person who identifies as Black, may have lighter color of skin than a person who identifies as Asian. A different person who identifies as Asian might have a lighter skin color than someone who identifies as White. Skin color, hair texture, and eye shape are separately inherited genes and there are as many variations within a race as there are between races. According to this same PBS website, "Of the small amount of total human variation, 85% exists within any local population, be the Italians, Kurds, Koreans or Cherokees. About 94% can be found within any continent. That means two random Koreans may be as genetically different as a Korean and an Italian." If people from different races are not genetically or biologically different, why does race continue to be an identity marker?

Originally, White people perpetuated the idea of race because it served to justify the poor treatment of other groups of people. Now, race is institutionalized within government processes, such as the US Census, and within educational policy, such as desegregation, in such a way that it would be very difficult to untangle race from society. While race is not real, institutional racism is real.

Table 2. Cultural Proficiency Continuum

Phase	Cultural Destructiveness	Cultural Incapacity	Cultural Blindness	Pre-competence	Cultural Competence	Cultural Proficiency
Definition	**Cultural Destructiveness** refers to educators seeking to **eliminate** the cultures of others in all aspects of the school and in relationship to the community served.	**Cultural Incapacity** refers to educators trivializing and **stereotyping** other languages and cultures and seeking to make the 'other' races, languages and cultures appear to be wrong or inferior to the dominant language and culture.	**Cultural Blindness** posits educators **not noticing** or acknowledging other races/ languages/ cultures within the school community and treating everyone in the educational system without recognizing the diverse needs that require differentiated communication and interaction.	**Cultural PreCompetence** shows educators' **increasing awareness** of what you and the school don't know about working in diverse settings, and at this level of development, educators and the school are ready to move in a positive, constructive direction. Or you can falter, stop, and possibly regress settings and to move in a positive, constructive direction, or you can falter, stop, and possibly regress.	**Cultural Competence** level shows educators **aligning** their personal values and behaviors, with the school policies and practices, in a manner that is inclusive of races/ languages/ cultures that enables healthy and productive interactions.	**Cultural Proficiency** refers to educators **holding the vision** that educators and the school are instruments for creating a socially just democracy. Cultural proficiency level means interacting with your colleagues, students, families, and the community as an advocate for life-long learning to serve equitably and effectively the educational needs of all racial/linguistic/cultural groups.
Narrative	"In this class, we speak English-Only, and follow the predetermined classroom policies."	"You know that those parents never show up to school functions. They may not be able to understand what we are discussing anyway."	"I do not see colors. I only see children."	"We valued all cultures. We have a night where parents bring food representing their countries."	"The co-teaching model with the push-in English language learning or special education teacher is allowing us to have honest conversations about differentiation of our teaching."	"Our school's Social Justice and Equity team are doing a great job of embedding culturally responsive lesson activities and assessments to our curriculum."
Action Steps	Keep a journal of every time you feel uncomfortable around another person. What patterns do you notice across these experiences?	Reflect on the stereotypes other people have about a social group you identify with (maybe your gender, religious affiliation, or hometown). To what extent do the stereotypes describe you? Watch this TED talk called The Danger of a Single Story.	View a TV show, movie, artistic performance, or play from a different culture. Reflect on new understandings you gained. Inquire about things you did not understand..	Immerse yourself in a place where you are the minority, perhaps a church service, concert, or festival. Reflect on new understandings you gained. Inquire about things you did not understand.	Engage in professional learning on how to differentiate instruction to meet the needs of diverse learners. Check out colorincolorado.org	Engage in professional learning on how to teach for antiracism, anti-xenophobia, and social justice. Check out tolerance.org/

Among institutional racism discourses, colorblindness has been an expression among the US people. Colorblindness refers to minimizing or refusing to acknowledge different people including people of colors, which is almost like a 'melting pot' concept. By refusing to see or discuss race, colorblindness can unintentionally reinforce the concept that we are not responsible for inequalities in education outcomes. 'Race' discourse in which educators have avoided discussing such as discrimination against and inequity towards people of colors, contributes to the masking of implicit bias among teachers towards learners from a different race. Bonilla-Silva (2003) has termed *colorblind racism* as a refusal to talk about race because the act of mentioning "race" itself is perceived as racism (Kubota & Lin, 2006). Colorblindness perpetuates institutionalized racism without explicitly devaluing certain culture. Colorblindness can be "a mode of thinking about race organized around an effort not to see or at any rate not to acknowledge race differences" (Frankenberg, 1993, p. 142).

The real harm of a colorblind stance is when it denies how race constitutes the division and inequality across social lines, and these are the same lines which colorblindness aims to overcome (Markus et al., 2000). The attitude of essentializing and othering of cultures is often called *cultural racism* (Bonilla-Silva, 2003) through which teachers overgeneralize or binarize different cultures and reify their stereotypes (Kreamelmeyer et al., 2016). Cultural racism may support colorblind rhetoric, which may lead to the fallacy and violence of White colorblind rhetoric that encourages a White cultural and language space, thus symbolically and politically erasing histories and peoples that use the diverse racial rhetoric (Ramasubramanian & Miles, 2018; San Pedro, 2018).

Teachers need to notice that the impact of colorblind rhetoric is not benign because it may let them overgeneralize and/or stereotype the utterances, and it also serves to produce and maintain inequitable educational outcomes (Markus et al., 2000; McCarty & Lee, 2018). Teachers cannot be neutral bystanders because they are "either part of the problem or part of the solution" (Derman-Sparks & Phillips, 1997, p. 24). Teachers need to explore and understand, not ignore, how race impacts teaching and learning. One way to begin is by exploring racial identity.

Racial Identity

The three identity features, i.e., racial, linguistic, and cultural identities, are not independent; rather, they are interdependent. For example, culture determines how we conceptualize ourselves as a racial being and how we express our racial identity. We will now turn our attention to racial identity. Racial identity, as is the case with cultural identity, is perceived and communicated. People perceive other people as belonging to a certain racial group. Also, people display and communicate a racial identity in order to be perceived by others as belonging to a certain racial group. To understand more about perceiving and performing identities and how that intersects with race, consider this example. When Tara is at work, she dresses a certain way or a US-centric way to send a message of professionalism because she wants to be perceived as competent, something she values in the workplace. When Tara is with her family, she dresses in a way that allows her to be physically active or culturally comfortable, another value that is important to her.

Pennycook (1999), however, criticizes the problematic ways that contemporary White culture positions people from other racial identities, creating *Self* and *Other* categories and creating a sense of *Us* versus *Them*. The *Us* in a privileged position of power creates the norms of language, culture, and behavior, whereas the *Them*, recipients of these norms, may speak and act differently, and so feel degraded. Privilege in respect to racial identity is referred to as White privilege. White privilege includes the convenience of finding a suitable make-up color, the benefit of seeing positive portrayals of people who are of the same race, and the assumption of being honest. This invisibility of White privilege can prevent White people from seeing racial differences and inequality (DiAngelo, 2018). Even if White people are cognizant of or against their unearned privileges, they certainly benefit from them. Read through the statements in *The Anti Racist Educator* (2020) to learn more about invisible privilege.

DiAngelo (2018) explains White people's discomfort about talking about race and denial of White privilege as White fragility. She defines White fragility as such,

Socialized into a deeply internalized sense of superiority that we either are unaware of or can never admit to ourselves, we become highly fragile in conversations about race. We consider a challenge to our racial worldviews as a challenge to our very identities as good, moral people. Thus, we perceive any attempt to connect us to the system of racism as an unsettling and unfair moral offense. The smallest amount of racial stress is intolerable--the mere suggestion that being White has meaning often triggers a range of defensive responses. These include emotions such as anger, fear and guilt, and behaviors such as argumentation, silence and withdrawal from the stress-inducing situation. These responses work to reinstate White racial equilibrium. (p. 3)

White fragility often leads to White silence on issues of racism, and silence keeps the status quo, systematic racism. Constructing a racial identity, for White people and people of color, is an important foundation for anti-racist work. We must acknowledge that in a racist world, we move through that world as racialized beings (San Pedro, 2018). Connecting to a racial identity helps to see how one's lived experience is different from people's experiences who have a different racial identity.

Racial identity discourse is closely connected to linguistic identity, which is a result of viewing their first- and second-language ability and viewing non-dominant racial groups' discourse with negative mindsets (Rosa, 2016). Dominant White discursive processes draw on monolingual ideologies to construct the White mainstream American English language as normal, and consequently position other accents or grammar as deficient or inferior (Shuck, 2006).

LANGUAGE AND LINGUISTIC IDENTITY

Definition of Language

The definition of language is simple, a system of communication that consists of a set of sounds or written symbols. However, language is complex and multidimensional. Language is used differently by people of a particular region for speaking or writing. In addition to speaking and writing, language includes reading, listening, and visually representing. Language requires physical, cognitive, and affective dimensions of learning. Language requires the ability to physically receive communication--through hearing, seeing, or feeling--and physically create symbols--through speech or writing. Different languages require different physical elements, such as the rhythm of signing or rolling the letter *R*. From a linguistic perspective, language involves the cognitive processes of producing and understanding phonics, morphemes, syntax, grammar, and semantics. From a sociolinguistics perspective, any form of communication that has rules and is used and understood by a group is a language. No language is better than any other language.

Teachers might have good intentions about applying culturally relevant teaching when they prepare content curriculum for RLC diverse learners, but culturally relevant pedagogy does not always embrace the needs of linguistically diverse students (Kubota, 2002). Instead of approaching a language as a tool to teach culture or race, we have to break apart the view that language and culture are interdependent but independent at the same time, so we can rebuild a new view. We also need to think about language as a fluid system, not a fixed one. For example, there are many languages, and many Englishes even in the U.S. as well as in the world, such as New York English, Southern English, and Midwestern English in the US; Indian English, British English, and Australian English in the world. Then, instead of thinking about which English is the 'better' or 'standardized' one, we may embrace diversity and try to develop

Table 3. Syntactic and Phonemic Variation Examples of World Languages

Linguistic Element	Subject Verb Object (SVO) Order	SOV Order	VSO Order	Noun Adjective	Adjective Noun	No /th/ sound: [θ] and /ð/
Example Languages	Italian	Turkish	Welsh	Italian	German	Turkish
	Vietnamese	Japanese	Arabic	Spanish	English	Korean
	English	Korean		Romanian	French	Japanese
Example structure	The girl reads a book.	The girl the book reads	Read the girl the book	Tree Green	Green Tree	[sɪn] for[θɪn] and [dɪs] for [θɪs])

an inclusive attitude towards language difference rather than judging any language according to fixed standards.

Although many institutions in society are built on racially and linguistically biased language ideology (Cho, 2017; Omi & Winant, 1994), White monolingual teachers are often unaware of this, and maintain idealizing Standard American (White upper and middle-class) English (Motha, 2014). However, according to race, language, and linguistic experts, Standard English is a myth (Baker-Bell, 2020). Raciolinguistic perspectives (Flores & Rosa, 2015) may shift the focus from utilizing the idealized standard language to locating the speaker as either a member or a dissident of a certain racial group (Rosa, 2016). The belief that non-standardized language use conveys stereotypical negative information about the speaker or the racial group to which the speaker belongs is what Rosa (2016) refers to as raciolinguistic ideologies or profiling.

When discussing languages, educators need to be aware of their assumptions around certain language use that may relate to negative stereotypes and work to dismantle these stereotypes. One way to break down stereotypes is to gain knowledge about the similarities and differences in structures of different languages, i.e., syntactic, phonological, and morphological rules. Table 3 illustrates language norms for ordering subject (S), object (O), and verb (V) as well as those of noun (N) and adjective (A) in different languages. This knowledge of linguistics (language structures) helps language educators understand why RLC diverse learners have difficulties when learning the target language, e.g., English in the U.S.

African American Vernacular English (AAVE) is another language or dialect that has its own syntactic and phonemic rules. Some aspects of AAVE stem from West African languages. For example, in addition to the languages cited in Table 3, many West African languages do not have a /th/ sound (Smitheran, 2000), and /f/ is often used for /th/ sound, e.g., /f/ank for /th/ank. Language educators need to understand the AAVE linguistics that have distinctive meaning rather than devaluing the language. For the syntactic rule, *in AAVE,* auxiliary verbs such as *been* and *done* must occur as the first auxiliary; when they occur as the second, they carry additional aspects:

He been done work means he finished work a long time ago.
He done been working means until recently, he worked over a long period of time.

The latter example shows one of the most distinctive features of AAVE: the use of *be* to indicate that performance of the verb is of a habitual nature. In most other American English dialects, this can only be expressed unambiguously by using adverbs such as *usually.*

The aspect in AAVE has been given several names, including *perfect phase*, *remote past*, and *remote phase*. As shown above, *been* places action in the distant past. However, when *been* is used with stative verbs or gerund forms, *been* shows that the action began in the distant past and that it is continuing now. Rickford (1999) suggests that a better translation when *been* is used with stative verbs is 'for a long time'. For instance, in response to "I like your new dress", one might hear *Oh, I been had this dress*, meaning that the speaker has had the dress for a long time and that it isn't new.

To see the difference between the simple past and the gerund when used with *been*, consider the following expressions:

I been bought her clothes means I bought her clothes a long time ago.
I been buying her clothes means I've been buying her clothes for a long time.

Linguistic Identity

Linguistic identity, like racial and cultural identity, is socially constructed, and identities are: multiple, dynamic, dialogic, and situated rather than unitary and fixed. Linguistic identities are negotiated and co-constructed in specific social contexts. Therefore, in order to view linguistic identities, it is important "to examine the racial, social, cultural, and political contexts in which they are co-constructed" (Faez, 2012, p.128).

The dominant assumption that underlies linguistic identity suggests that dominant White people are native speakers and as such, are better qualified than teachers of color (Curtis & Romney, 2006; Flores & Rosa, 2015). We cannot discuss linguistic identity without discussion about race (Kubota & Lin, 2006). Other studies reveal that factors such as speakers' accents and race affect how learners comprehend and evaluate their instructors regardless of their English proficiency (Lindemann, 2002). Therefore, teachers in the highest demand are White native speakers even though there is the invaluable contribution of multilingual and non-White teachers in relating to the RLC diverse learners through similar experiences in learning a second language and in dealing with discrimination, question (Auerbach, 2016; Phillipson, 1999). Thus, when educators are identifying 'who they are', they need to consider the co-constructed characteristics of the linguistic identity with racial, cultural, and political contexts (Bacon, 2020; Flores & Rosa, 2015). So teachers have to consider White privilege, which prevails as an invisible norm for which diverse groups are 'othered' and racially biased even when defining their linguistic identity (Marx, 2004; McIntosh, 2015).

Positioning theory provides another paradigm for examining the diverse categories people use when defining who they are (Harré & van Langenhove, 1999; Warren & Moghaddam, 2018). The positions that educators occupy in diverse criteria (e.g., race/ethnicity, the first and second languages, developmental and emotional disabilities, gender, socioeconomic status), depend on the educators' perception of their rights, duties, and the place they hold in the sociocultural context in which they engage. In this framework, the distribution of power is closely linked to the designation of rights and duties. Therefore, if one member is positioned as an incompetent member, he or she may not be granted the right to engage in conversation with that group. It is important to acknowledge that these positions are dynamic rather than fixed, and they are socially constructed. Positioning theory is, therefore, a powerful method to examine how people of White and of color position themselves and are positioned in educational contexts. According to Moghaddam and Harré (2010), this theory is about:

How people use words (and discourse of all types) to locate themselves and others. It is with words that we ascribe rights and claim them for ourselves and place duties on others. Positioning has direct moral implications, such as some person or group being located as 'trusted' or 'distrusted', 'with us' or 'against us', 'to be saved' or 'to be wiped out.' (pp. 2-3)

Among many sociocultural identities such as culture, language, gender, sexuality, age, and social class that contribute to educational inequality, racial identity is another important feature when educators position their identities.

Faez's (2012) studied linguistic identity in relation to racial identities of White and Chinese 1.5 generation teachers, meaning teachers who came to the US after they acquired their native languages. These White and Chinese 1.5 generation teachers in Faez's study had native-like English proficiency. However, unlike White European 1.5 generation teachers, Chinese 1.5 generation teachers, due to their racial backgrounds (nonwhite), believed that their English would not be verified as native-like by the school community (Faez, 2012). Chinese teachers were concerned that their professional identity as teachers were questioned by students who came to the classroom space with raciolinguistic bias. Whereas discourses of White 1.5 generation educators revealed privilege and acceptance, discourses of non-White 1.5 generation were associated with marginalization, discrimination, and racism. Postcolonial racism is a term used to refer to experiences of marginalization and discrimination of non-White 1.5 generation educators where instances of racism were subtle, not overt or blatant, and similar to those of the colonial era (Faez, 2012).

PUTTING THEM ALL TOGETHER

In addition to culture, race, and language, there are other sociocultural identity features that may be a part of a person's identity. Speaking generally, some different sociocultural identity features might include ethnicity, gender, sex, sexual orientation, cis-gender, religious affiliation and spirituality, socioeconomic status, age, emotional and developmental disabilities, physical disabilities, body size, health, education level, national origin, marital status, and occupation. They are sometimes obvious and clear, sometimes not, often self-claimed and frequently ascribed by others. For example, racial groupings are often ascribed as well as self-claimed. Government, schools, and employers often ask an individual to claim a racial identity group or simply ascribe one to an individual based on visual perception. Other identities are personally claimed but not often announced or easily visually ascribed such as sexual orientation, religion, or disability status. Exploring these multiple identity features may help teachers and learners to engage across differences locally and globally with empathy and open-mindedness, ultimately in service of building a community of learners at home (within classrooms, schools, and local communities) to support education presently and prepare students for an increasingly global future with a cosmopolitan mindset.

For the purpose of teachers' self-examination of their identities, Table 4 shows examples of the generalized identity memberships that one may perceive are part of one's identity or features that others ascribe to one. Since issues of identity groupings often are the basis of racial, linguistic and cultural conflicts and/or biases, it is reasonable to expect that even the terms one uses to describe oneself may cause surprise or disagreement.

The *Who Am I? Wheel* shows 12 identity features, some of which were explained in Table 4.

Figures 3 and 4 illustrate the sample "Who Am I?" wheels that serve as examples.

Table 4. Sociocultural Features of Intergroup Membership

Identity Features	Examples
Ethnicity	American, Irish, Chinese, Puerto Rican, Italian, Mohawk, Jewish, Guatemalan, Lebanese, European-American
Gender	Woman, Man, Transgender, Post-Gender
Sex	Female, Male, Intersex
Sexual orientation	Lesbian, Gay, Bisexual, Pan-Attractional, Heterosexual, Queer, Attractional, Questioning
Religion and Spirituality	Hindu, Muslim, Buddhist, Jewish, Christian, Pagan, Agnostic, Faith/Meaning, Atheist, Secular Humanist
Socioeconomic Class	Poor, Working Class, Lower-Middle Class, Upper-Middle Class, Owning Class, Ruling Class
(Dis)Abilities	People with disabilities (cognitive, physical, emotional, etc.), Temporarily able-bodied, Temporarily disabled
Body Size/Type & Health	Fit, Fat, Person of Size, Thin, Skinny
Education Level/Degree	GED., High School Diploma, Bachelor's Degree, Master's Degree, Doctoral Degree
Nations of Origin	United States, Nigeria, Korea, Turkey, Argentina, Egypt, Romania
Age	Child, Young Adult, Middle-Age Adult, Elderly

Examining one's identity can help one understand how multiple features of one's identity can impact one's life experiences (Kerkhoff et al., 2021). For example, in George's wheel analysis, he was able to see that while race was not something he typically thought about, it was something that impacted how others saw him. It is also important to learn about how others in our home communities view themselves as this impacts how they view the world. In Kyesoo's wheel, as a person of color whose first language is Korean, she says that she thinks about race, ethnicity, and language a lot. In a classroom setting, this can be a point of conversation where deeper understanding about different identity features is reached. In this way, examining one's own identity is a bridge to exploring differing identities and perspectives within and across features (Kerkhoff, 2022; Kerkhoff et al., 2021).

This knowledge can help educators understand that students who belong to the same racial category may have very different linguistic and cultural identities and experiences. At the same time, they may encounter similar patterns of discrimination. This knowledge may also help educators to understand that children from communities who have been historically marginalized on multiple fronts are positioned by the world in qualitatively different ways (Crenshaw, 2017). As a person of color whose first language is not English, Kyesoo experienced discrimination based on her Korean accent. While everyone has an accent, accents that are typically associated with marginalization on local and global levels, such as societies who experience poverty or BIPOC, are typically seen as a deficit, whereas accents that are associated with power, such as European, are typically seen as an asset. In our globally connected world, speaking multiple languages is desired, and all children deserve to have their multilingualism counted as an asset. Likewise, all children deserve an education that helps them become global citizens, not just the elite. In this way, our globally diverse local community provides a rich home for all of our students to learn about the world through personal and relational connections.

Figure 3. Example of Who Am I? Wheel by George
Note. This figure is by George, a young White male English native speaking teacher.

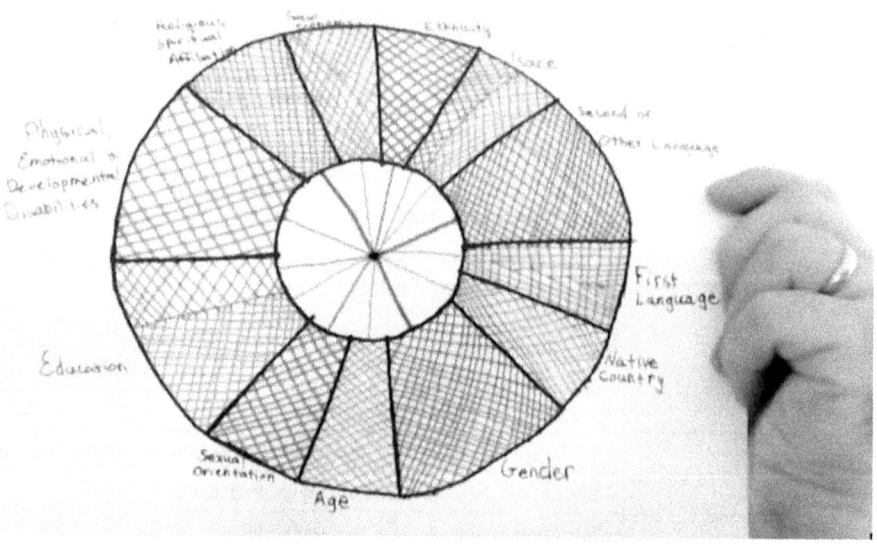

- ❏ The three categories that I think of most often are Religious and Spiritual Affiliation, Second or Other Language, and Gender. These three categories relate directly to my personal and professional identities (father, teacher, Christian).
- ❏ The identities I think least about are Physical Emotional & Developmental Disabilities, Ethnicity, and Sexual orientation. At times these categories are important to me, but unless there is something that calls my attention to them, they are not usually on the forefront of my mind.
- ❏ The three characteristics that I would like to learn more about are my Native Country, First Language and Age. I am more interested in the impact these have on who I am; the more I work with linguistically and culturally diverse individuals the more I realize that I had blinders on regarding the privileges I have been granted because of these features.
- ❏ The three identity features that have the strongest effect on who I am are Socio-economy, Race, and Education. I frequently find myself thinking about my financial situation and trying to better myself so that I can provide more for my family (my desire to buy a home drives a lot of what I do). I frequently find myself contemplating my life situations, and I cannot help but include my race and education in how I perceive my current and potential socio-economic situations.
- ❏ There were two characteristics that I believe impact how others perceive me. Those are my education and race; when I graduated with a Ph.D. I did not feel different, but I have been treated differently as a Ph.D. than I was prior. I have also had several experience with RCLD learners when they tell me that I am white and so it is not the same or that I will not understand; while frustrating to me that a conversation would end based on my race, I have come to see how important that category is even if I do not always acknowledge it.

CONCLUSION

The purpose of the chapter was to examine racial, linguistic, and cultural identity as a teacher of RLC diverse learners. In order to help young students reflect on their cultural, linguistic, and racial identities, first teachers have to establish an understanding of who they are. Understanding who one is and how

Figure 4. Example of Who Am I? Wheel by Kyesoo
Note. This figure is by Kyesoo, a mature non-White female emerging bilingual teacher.

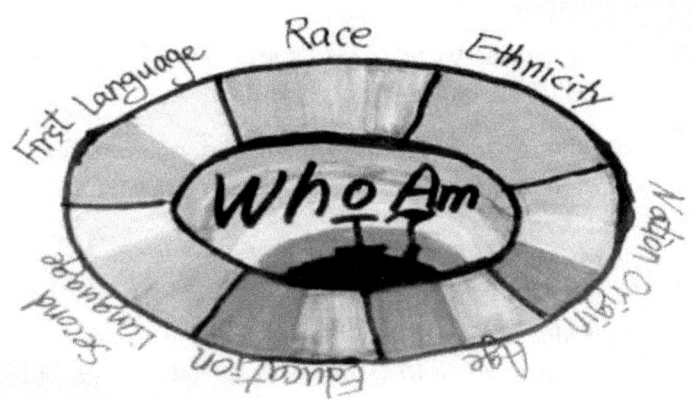

I have chosen seven of twelve identity features; Race, Ethnicity, First Language, Second Language, Age, Education, and National Origin. Among them, Race, Second Language, and National Origin had the three of five colors; Age, First Language and Education had two of five colors, and Ethnicity had only one color. The five identity features I have not identified in a "Who Am I" wheel were; Gender, Sexual Orientation, Physical, Emotional and Developmental Disabilities, Religion, and Socioeconomic Status. I might have chosen these when I was younger, but I guess these seven identity features what I am more interested in. The details include:

- ❑ Race, Ethnicity, First Language, and Second Language are the four identity features I have chosen as I most often think about.
- ❑ I have also chosen three of five (Race, First Language and Second Language) as the strongest identity features as I perceive myself (cf. raciolinguistic ideologies)
- ❑ Education, National Origin, and Age are the three features I have chosen as I think least often;
- ❑ Education, National Origin, and Age are identities that have the greatest effect on how others perceive me; and
- ❑ Race, Second Language, and National Origin are the features I want to learn more about.

one's values and experiences shape one's worldview can also contribute to understanding RLC diverse learners and their families, and help teachers celebrate the diverse values, experiences, and worldviews that they bring to our classrooms as assets.

REFERENCES

AAA&S. (2016, December). *The state of languages in the U.S: A statistical portrait.* American Academy of Arts and Sciences. https://www.amacad.org/publication/state-languages-us-statistical-portrait

American Council on the Teaching of Foreign Languages. (2015). *World-readiness standards for learning languages.* ACTFL. https://www.actfl.org/sites/default/files/publications/standards/World-ReadinessStandardsforLearningLanguages.pdf

Auerbach, E. R. (2016). Reflections on Auerbach (1993), 'Reexamining English only in the ESL Classroom'. *TESOL Quarterly, 50*(4), 936–939. https://doi.org/10.1002/tesq.310

Bacon, C. K. (2020). "It's not really my job": A mixed methods framework for language ideologies, monolingualism, and teaching emergent bilingual learners. *Journal of Teacher Education, 71*(2), 172–187. https://doi.org/10.1177/0022487118783188

Baker-Bell, A. (2020). *Linguistic justice: Black language, literacy, identity, and pedagogy.* Routledge.

Banks, J. A. (2004). Multicultural education: Historical development, dimensions, and practice. In J. A. Banks, & C. A. M. Banks (Eds.), Handbook of Research on Multicultural Education (2 ed., pp. 3-29). Jossey Bass.

Banks, J. A. (2019). Civic education for non-citizen and citizen students. In J. A. Banks & C. M. Banks (Eds.), *Multicultural Education: Issues and Perspectives* (pp. 198–214). Wiley.

Bonilla-Silva, E. (2003). *Racism without racists: Color-blind racism and the persistence of racial inequality in the United States.* Rowman & Littlefield.

Browaeys, M. J., & Price, R. (2015). *Understanding cross-cultural management* (3rd ed.). Pearson.

Camarota, S. A., Griffith, B., & Zeigler, K. (2017). Mapping immigration's impact on public schools. *Center for Immigration Studies.* https://cis.org/sites/cis.org/files/camarota-pumas_2.pdf

Center for Advanced Research on Language Acquisition. (2022). What is Culture? *CARLA.* https://carla.umn.edu/culture/definitions.html

Cho, H. (2017). Racism and linguicism: Engaging language minority preservice teachers in counter-storytelling. *Race, Ethnicity and Education, 20*(5), 666–680. https://doi.org/10.1080/13613324.2016.1150827

Crenshaw, K. W. (2017). *On intersectionality: Essential writings.* The New Press.

Derman-Sparks, L., & Phillips, C. B. (1997). *Teaching/learning anti-racism: A developmental approach.* Teachers College Press.

DiAngelo, R. J. (2018). *White fragility.*

Faez, F. (2012). Linguistic identities and experiences of Generation 1.5 teacher candidates: Race matters. *TESOL Canada Journal, 29*(6), 124-141. doi:10.18806/tesl.v29i0.1113

Feiman-Nemser, S. (2001). From Preparation to practice: Designing a continuum to strengthen and sustain teaching. *Teachers College Record, 103*(6), 1013–1055. https://doi.org/10.1111/0161-4681.00141

Festinger, L. (1957). *A theory of cognitive dissonance.* Stanford University Press.

Flores, N., & Rosa, J. (2015). Undoing appropriateness: Raciolinguistic ideologies and language diversity in education. Harvard Educational Review, 85(2), 149–171

Garcia, O., & Wei, L. (2014). *Translanguaging: Language, bilingualism, and education*. Palgrave.

Gay, G. (2010). Culturally responsive teaching: Theory, research, and practice (2nd ed.) Teachers College Press.

Harré, R., & van Langenhove, L. (1999). *Positioning theory*. Blackwell.

Kerkhoff, S. N. (2022). A pedagogical framework for critical cosmopolitan literacies. *Changing English, 29*(3), 1–23. https://doi.org/10.1080/1358684X.2022.2042673

Kerkhoff, S. N., & Cloud, M. E. (2020). Equipping teachers with globally competent practices: A mixed methods study on integrating global competence and teacher education. *International Journal of Educational Research, 103*. doi:10.1016/j.ijer.2020.101629

Kerkhoff, S. N., Mardi, F., & Rong, H. (2021). An action research study on globally competent teaching in online spaces. In A. Slapac, P. Balcerzak, & K. O'Brien (Eds.), *Handbook of research on the global empowerment of educators and student learning through action research* (pp. 264–288). IGI Global.

Kerkhoff, S. N., & Yi, M. (2022). Cosmopolitanism to frame teaching global literacies. In L. Assaf, P. Sowa, & K. Zammit (Eds.), *Global meaning making: Disrupting and interrogating international language and literacy research and teaching* (pp. 179–201). Emerald.

Kim, S., & Slapac, A. (2015). Culturally responsive, transformative pedagogy in the transnational era: Critical perspectives. *Educational Studies, 51*(1), 17–27. doi:10.1080/00131946.2014.983639

Kolbert, E. (2018). There's no scientific basis for race-It's a made-up label. *National Geographic*. https://www.nationalgeographic.com/magazine/2018/04/race-genetics-science-africa/

Kreamelmeyer, K., Kline, A., Zygmunt, E., & Clark, P. (2016). To see or not to see: Preservice teacher attitudes toward color blindness. *Teacher Educator, 51*(2), 136–152. doi:10.1080/08878730.2016.1152841

Kubota, R. (2002). The Impact of globalisation on language teaching in Japan. In D. Block & D. Cameron (Eds.), *Globalization and language teaching* (pp. 13–28). Routledge.

Kubota, R., & Lin, A. (2006). Race and TESOL: Introduction to concepts and theories. *TESOL Quarterly, 40*(3), 471–493. https://doi.org/10.2307/40264540

Kumaravadivelu, B. (2012). Individual identity, cultural globalization and teaching English as an international language: The case for an epistemic break. In L. Alsagoff, W. Renandya, G. Hu, & S. L. Mckay (Eds.), Teaching English as an international language: Principles and practices (pp. 9-27). Routledge.

Ladson-Billings, G. (2014). Culturally relevant pedagogy 2.0: Aka the remix. *Harvard Educational Review, 84*(1), 74–84. https://doi.org/10.17763/haer.84.1.p2rj131485484751

Ladson-Billings, G., & Tate, W. F. (1995). Toward a critical race theory of education. Teachers. College Record, 97, 47–68.

Lindemann, S. (2002). Listening with an attitude: A model of native-speaker comprehension of non-native speakers in the United States. *Language in Society, 31*(3), 419–441. https://doi.org/10.1017/S0047404502020286

Looney, D., & Lusin, N. (2018). *Enrollments in languages other than English in United States institutions of higher education: Preliminary report.* MLA. https://www.mla.org/content/download/83540/2197676/2016-Enrollments-Short-Report.pdf

Markus, H. R., Steele, C. M., & Steele, D. M. (2000). Colorblindness as a barrier to inclusion: Assimilation and nonimmigrant minorities. Daedalus, 129(4), 233–259

Marx, S. (2004). Regarding whiteness: Exploring and intervening in the effects of white racism in teacher education. *Equity & Excellence in Education, 37*(1), 31-43. doi:10.1080/10665680490422089

McCarty, T., & Lee, T. (2018). Critical culturally sustaining/revitalizing pedagogy and indigenous education sovereignty. *Harvard Educational Review*, *84*(1), 101–124.

McIntosh, P. (2015). Extending the knapsack: Using the white privilege analysis to examine conferred advantage and disadvantage. *Women & Therapy*, *38*(3-4), 232–245. https://doi.org/10.1080/02703149.2015.1059195

Moghaddam, F., & Harré, R. (2010). Words, conflicts and political processes. In F. Moghaddam & R. Harré (Eds.), *Words of conflict, words of war: How the language we use in political processes sparks fighting* (pp. 1–28). Praeger.

Moll, L. (2015). Tapping into the "hidden" home and community resources of students. Kappa Delta Pi Record, 51(3), 114–117. .

Motha, S. (2014). *Race, empire and English language teaching: Creating responsible and ethical anti-racist practice.* Teachers College Press.

Nuri-Robins, K., Lindsey, D., Terrell, R., & Lindsey, R. (2019). *Cultural proficiency: Tools for school leaders.* AESA. https://www.aesa.us/about/Resources/CulturalProficiencyforLeaders.pdf

Omi, M., & Winant, H. (1994). *Racial formation in the United States* (3rd ed.). Routledge.

Paris, D., & Alim, H. S. (2014). What are we seeking to sustain through culturally sustaining pedagogy? A loving critique forward. *Harvard Educational Review*, *84*(1), 85–100.

Pennycook, A. (1999). Introduction: Critical approaches to TESOL. *TESOL Quarterly*, *33*(3), 329–348. https://doi.org/10.2307/3587668

Phillipson, R. (1999). International languages and international human rights. In M. Kontra (Ed.), *Language: A right and a resource* (pp. 25–46). Central European University Press.

Ramasubramanian, S., & Miles, C. (2018). Framing the Syrian refugee crisis: A comparative analysis of Arabic and English news sources. *International Journal of Communication*, *12*, 4488–4506.

Rickford, J. (1999). *African American vernacular English.* Blackwell.

Romney, M. (2006). The colour of English. In A. Mahboob (Ed.), The NNEST lens: Nonnative English speakers in TESOL (pp. 18-34). Cambridge Scholars.

Rosa, J. D. (2016). Standardization, racialization, languagelessness: Raciolinguistic ideologies across communicative contexts. *Journal of Linguistic Anthropology*, 26(2), 162–183. https://doi.org/10.1111/jola.12116

San Pedro, T. (2018). Abby as ally: An argument for culturally disruptive pedagogy. *American Educational Research Journal*, 55(6), 1193–1232. https://doi.org/10.3102/0002831218773488

Shuck, G. (2006). Racializing the nonnative English speaker. *Journal of Language. Identity* Education, 5, 259-276. . doi:10.120715327701jlie0504_1

Slapac, A. (2013). A conceptualization of diversity from three teacher educators' perspectives: Teaching about social justice and equity. *Scholar-Practitioner Quarterly: A Journal for the Scholar-Practitioner Leader, 7*(1), 24-45.

Slapac, A. (2021). Advancing students' global competency through English language learning in Romania: An exploratory qualitative case study of four English language teachers. *Journal of Research on Childhood Education: Preparing Teachers to Serve in the Global Landscape.* (Special Issue on Global Education), *35*(2), 1-17. doi:10.1080/02568543.2021.1880993

Slapac, A., & Kim, S. (2020). Negotiating teaching cultures and developing cultural competency towards classroom communities in early childhood (K-2) language immersion schools. In M. E., Gómez Parra, & C. Aránzazu Huertas Abril (Eds.), International Perspectives on Modern Developments in Early Childhood Education (pp. 77-93). IGI Global.

Slapac, A., Kim, S., & Coppersmith, S. A. (2019). Preparing and enriching linguistically and culturally responsive educators through professional development. In A. Slapac & S. Coppersmith (Eds.), *Beyond language learning instruction: Transformative supports for emergent bilinguals and educators* (pp. 282–304). IGI Global.

Song, K., Kim, S., & Preston, L. (2021). "No difference between African American, immigrant, and White children! They are all the same." Working toward developing teachers' raciolinguistic attitudes towards ELs. *International Journal of Multicultural Education, 23*(1), 47–66. https://dx.doi.org/10.18251/ijme.v23i1.1995

Sue, D. W. (2001). Multidimensional facets of cultural competence. *The Counseling Psychologist, 29*(6), 790–821.

Viesca, K. (2013). Race, difference, meritocracy, and English: Majoritarian stories in the education of secondary multilingual learners. *Race, Ethnicity and Education, 16*(3), 339–364. https://doi.org/10.1080/13613324.2011.645569

Villegas, A. M. SaizdeLaMora, K., Martin, A. D., & Mills, T. (2018). Preparing future mainstream teachers to teach English language learners: A review of the empirical literature, *The Educational Forum, 82*(2), 138-155. doi:10.1080/00131725.2018.1420850

Warren, Z., & Moghaddam, F. M. (2018). Positioning theory and social justice. In P. Hammock (Ed.), *The Oxford handbook of social psychology and social justice* (pp. 319–331). Oxford University Press.

Yoon, B. (2016). *Critical literacies: Global and multicultural perspectives*. Springer.

KEY TERMS AND DEFINITIONS

Colorblind: A perspective that race should not be seen, acknowledged, discussed, or considered.

Culture: Values, beliefs, social norms, customs, and material traits of a group of people.

1.5 Generation: Students who are US residents or citizens but whose first or home language was not English, and who were not born in the U.S., although for some of these students, English does, in fact, function as the primary language.

Cultural Competence: Understanding of one's own culture and valuing of diverse cultures.

Intercultural Competence: Cultural competence, perspective-taking, and interpersonal skills across cultures.

Language: System of communication including reading, writing, speaking, and listening.

Race: Grouping of people based on physical and social characteristics, which groups of people are classified as which race has changed over time and is socially not biologically determined.

Raciolinguistic Ideologies: Belief either that non-standardized language use conveys or does not convey stereotypical negative information about the speaker or the racial group to which the speaker belongs.

Sociocultural Theories of Identity: The idea that identity is not inherent with a person but that it is shaped through relationship to other people.

Sociolinguistics: Study of language and social dimensions, such as gender, race, geographic region, and socioeconomic status.

Social Justice: Equality of treatment and equity of distribution of resources so that everyone in society is treated with fairness, humanity, and justice.

Chapter 2
Moving Towards Equity:
Supporting Transgender and Gender–Diverse People in Education

Matthew D. Rice

https://orcid.org/0000-0002-7542-8736

Baylor University, USA

ABSTRACT

Two Spirit, transgender, intersex, non-binary, and gender non-conforming (2STING) teachers face significant additional stress in their careers. Research shows intolerable conditions for many teachers, even those in states with long-standing anti-discrimination policies in place. Educators reported experiencing harassment at work, hostile colleagues, hostile families, and doxing and social media bullying. Twenty-five percent of participants interviewed for a recent study had left their careers in education within a month of the study completion. Transgender and gender-diverse educators reported shocking rates of non-suicidal self-injury, suicidal ideation, and suicide attempts. All learning communities must change the culture surrounding these issues to help keep our LGB and 2STING educators and students alive.

INTRODUCTION

Two Spirit, transgender, intersex, non-binary, and gender non-conforming (2STING) people and other gender-diverse people in education face daunting circumstances, especially in educational spaces. This chapter will use the umbrella term gender-diverse because it is not just those with named identities like those encapsulated in the 2STING acronym who suffer in a pejorative cisgender heteronormative system. Gender-diverse students and educators alike in PreK–12 education are subjected to marginalization, exclusion, and even violence in spaces that are supposed to be safe and welcome to all (Blair & Deckman, 2019; Clark et al., 2014; Goguen, 2017; Kosciw et al., 2020). Learning community norms have traditionally supported cisgender heterosexuality as normal and all else as deviant (Donelson & Rogers, 2004). Schools often include racial, religious, ability, language diversity, immigration status, and other intersectional issues in justice but purposely exclude sexual orientation and gender identity (DePalma

DOI: 10.4018/978-1-6684-6386-4.ch002

& Atkinson, 2010). Cisnormativity and heteronormativity are individual and systemic (Chesir-Teran, 2003; Whittle, 2006).

Regardless of how they are trans or gender non-conforming, each person embodies their true self in unique and beautiful ways that are sometimes outside the comfort zone of traditional heteronormativity. When our identities or gender presentations flow outside conventional boundaries, one thing is evident: we face stigma, discrimination, othering, and abuse. Those negative consequences escalate when those transcending are Black, Indigenous, or People of Color (BIPOC) (Kumashiro, 2004).

People are also actively trying to harm teachers who identify as lesbian, gay, bisexual, transgender, queer, intersex, asexual, and other non-cisgender and non-heterosexual identities (LGBTQIA+). As the visibility of LGBTQIA+ people in education increases, the rhetoric of opposition and its consequences have become increasingly toxic. Doxing educators, including publishing their home addresses with calls for assassination and letter-writing campaigns to their principals and school boards to have them removed from their jobs, is all too real (Gilbert, 2022; Suen & Drennen, 2022; Wakefield, 2022). Attacks by Twitter accounts like *Libs of TikTok* have called for the execution of school superintendents. They have published their home addresses and aggressively promoted the "groomer" discourse that has led to death threats and job loss for LGBTQIA+ educators (Lorenz, 2022).

The increasingly polarized conditions faced by LGBTQIA+ and especially gender-diverse students and teachers in schools put LGBTQIA+ students and teachers, especially gender-diverse ones, at greater risk of poor mental and physical health outcomes (Kennedy et al., 2021; The Trevor Project, 2021). The future for LGBTQIA+ people in schools will depend on local attitudes, and in some places, entrenched homophobia and transphobia in educational leadership will continue to place LGBTQIA+ people at risk. The United Nations frames conversations about gender identity as fundamental human rights. A UN independent expert, after a 2022 visit to the United States, wrote, "I am deeply alarmed by a widespread, profoundly negative riptide created by deliberate actions to roll back the human rights of LGBT people at the state level" (United Nations Office of the High Commissioner on Human Rights, 2022). Until the discourse in the United States models the UN framing and addresses the misinformation rampant in the social media assault on LGBTQIA+ people that seeks to restigmatize LGB and particularly transgender and gender-diverse identities, many people in the United States who are unsupported in their families and schools will continue to suffer (Ivan Simonović, 2011; Suen & Drennen, 2022).

About 1-2% of Americans identify as transgender or non-binary. More people under age 30 identify as transgender and non-binary than ever, 5.1% (A. Brown, 2022; Ghorayshi, 2022). Increasing numbers of trans and non-binary people are entering educational careers, many warmly embraced by their learning communities. Many may experience treatment so harsh they cannot safely remain in education (Hart & Hart, 2018). Learning communities must systematically examine their relationship to intersectional social justice issues, including gender identity, sexual orientation, race, ability, language diversity, and economic disparity, in a way that facilitates changes that can allow all people in their community to feel explicitly welcome. This chapter reviews the realities faced by gender-diverse people in schools and recommends changes in educational leadership, teacher education, and professional learning for in-service educators.

BACKGROUND

Systemic Bias in Education and Community

School systems and the surrounding communities can mold and shape students' daily lives, futures, and even perceptions of their past. American schools are founded on the systems of inequity that built this nation (Kumashiro, 2004; Spade, 2015). There is no real meritocracy. Not everyone has an equal chance at the American dream. Students born into poverty today are more likely to remain in poverty (Semuels, 2017). Schools today can create a more equitable future, but only if educational leaders critically examine students' historic and continuing oppression and end practices that preserve the status quo that has benefitted some and marginalized others (Brown, 2006).

Schools must pursue academic excellence and social justice for their students, teachers, and communities (Kumashiro, 2002). Many school systems are still rooted in a factory model of processing students in age-based batches with curricula that no longer match the current skills needed for their careers and have been for far too long (Hargreaves, 1994). Transforming the vision of what schools can be will allow visionary educational leaders and teachers to create the learning communities all students deserve. Paulo Freire posed that public education's work is to end the oppression of these students (Freire, 1970).

Critical theory can frame this work. Through its lens, educational leaders can structure curricula, train staff, and build schools that deliver a more equitable future for all students. Critical theory in the pedagogical context provides an alternative model of teachers and students working together. Through redistribution of classroom power, a collaborative reflection on systems of power in their world allows students and teachers to work together as colleagues to address the systemic problems they identify (De-Jean & Sapp, 2017). When students observe and reflect, they can build critical consciousness to critique inequity and establish a dialogue about ways to change it, especially around race and gender diversity.

Instead of including the myriad of ways people do gender and sexuality as a natural and normal part of life, educators more often exclude and fail to protect gender-diverse people. Teachers often fail to disrupt everyday gendering and misgendering in systematic processes that stigmatize students who do gender differently. Professional learning for all needs to go beyond framing "trans" issues as identity problems of a few students to consider how 2STING discrimination fits into an intersectional, dynamic understanding of oppression (Blair & Deckman, 2019).

When teachers or students have 2STING or LGBTQIA+ identities, they may experience pressure to conform to stereotypes, bullying, harassment, violence, and abuse (Mayo & Blackburn, 2019). These experiences also include people who do not fit heterosexist binary gender assumptions even if they do not identify as trans or gender-diverse (Sears et al., 2021).

The National Transgender Discrimination study revealed that 78 percent of trans and gender-diverse people surveyed experienced harassment in the K-12 setting (Grant et al., 2011). The national survey of more than 6,000 trans and gender-diverse people showed that 90 percent reported harassment, mistreatment, or discrimination at work, 57 percent experienced significant family rejection, and 41 percent had attempted suicide. The suicide attempt rate in the general population is 1.6 percent. The suicide attempt rate increased to over 60 percent of the gender-diverse person was a survivor of physical or sexual assault. More than a quarter of trans and gender-diverse people reported losing a job because they were trans or gender-diverse. Those who lost a job had four times greater homelessness rate. Seventy percent coped with more drinking and substance use and had an 85 percent greater incarceration rate. Nineteen percent reported having experienced homelessness, and two percent reported being homeless. Fifty-five percent of trans and gender-diverse people who tried to access a homeless shelter suffered harassment from staff or residents. Shelters denied access to 29 percent of trans and gender-diverse people surveyed altogether. Twenty-two percent were sexually assaulted by staff or residents at the shelter (Grant et al., 2011).

The GLSEN School Climate Survey gathered data from more than 16,000 students aged 12–21 and showed similarly devastating experiences from students in schools in the United States (Kosciw et al., 2020). The Williams Institute shows a pattern of exclusion, marginalization, and discrimination that follows students into the workplace (Sears et al., 2021). As a result of their exclusion and marginalization, transgender, non-binary, and gender-diverse people face stigma, mistreatment, exclusion, and even violence in schools (Bradbury-Jones et al., 2020; Greytak et al., 2017). Regardless of the metric, the devastating effects disproportionately impact trans and non-binary Black, Indigenous, and People of Color (BIPOC) people (Balsam et al., 2011; Kosciw et al., 2020; Sears et al., 2021). Marginalization and discrimination against gender-diverse students and teachers contribute to lasting harmful physical & mental health disparities (Bariola et al., 2016; Bockting et al., 2013; The Trevor Project, 2021).

Prejudice and stigma against lesbian, gay, bisexual, transgender, queer, intersex, asexual, and other sexual-minority and gender-diverse (LGBTQIA+), especially regarding gender-diverse people, abets discrimination, marginalization, and violence directed at LGBTQIA+ and gender-diverse people. The historic and continuing cultural stigma is associated with gender-diverse identities and gender-diverse presentations. Legislative protections against discrimination have been absent or patchwork (Attia, 2016). Beginning with the *Price Waterhouse v. Hopkins* decision in 1989, through Bostock v. Clayton County, 2020, the development of protections for trans and gender-diverse people in the United States is ever-evolving. People in the United States need state and federal protections that ban discrimination against trans and gender-diverse people just as other protected classes. Legislated protection decreases suicide attempts and other adverse outcomes for LGBTQIA+ and gender-diverse people (Attia, 2016; Kennedy et al., 2021).

The current legal trend is a backlash against the increased visibility of transgender people (Fischer, 2019). State legislatures have passed more than 300 anti- LGBTQIA+ bills in 2022 alone (Jones & Navarro, 2022). Many of these bills have been targeted explicitly at LGBTQIA+ youth in schools and health care for trans and non-binary youth (Sawchuk, 2022). This legislation prevents students from accessing many things known to decrease the risk of suicide: seeing yourself represented in the classroom, being accepted by your parents, the ability to participate in team sports, and access to gender-affirming health care (GLSEN, 2020; Harris Interactive & GLSEN, 2005; The Trevor Project, 2021). This legislative backlash impacts more than just students.

There is also a backlash against LGBTQIA+ people working honestly and openly with students by restricting LGBTQIA+ representation in the curriculum, which school clubs are permissible, and even which pronouns students and teachers can use (Sawchuk, 2022). Accusations of pedophilia, indoctrination, and grooming, the act of befriending a child to molest them, are rampant in public discourse (Block, 2022; Gilbert, 2022; Lorenz, 2022; Suen & Drennen, 2022; Wakefield, 2022). Though not new, these accusations are harmful and dangerous to LGBTQIA+ educators and students (Block, 2022; Gilbert, 2022; Suen & Drennen, 2022; Wakefield, 2022). These far-right followers target LGBTQIA+ educators with these accusations and have led to educators receiving threats of rape, assassination, and loss of their careers. Educators have had their residential addresses, and contact information made public to increase pressure through the threats and harassment from social media accounts like the "Libs of Tiktok" (Gilbert, 2022; Suen & Drennen, 2022; Wakefield, 2022). This escalation in ultra-violent rhetoric and promotion by public figures like Rep. Marjorie Taylor Greene, podcaster Joe Rogan, and Fox News's

Tucker Carlson have given rise to genuine fears of real-life violence against advocates for LGBTQIA[+] people, especially young people.

One of the strengths gender-diverse teachers bring to the classroom is the advocacy and ability to create safe classroom spaces for all students. By interrupting bias and disrupting cisgenderism and heteronormativity, gender-diverse teachers and allies make schools safer for all students beyond just a sticker on their classroom door (DeJean & Sapp, 2017). Gender-diverse teachers and other LGBTQIA[+] teachers who return to spaces that were historical sites of trauma for themselves to prevent that trauma from reoccurring for their students are a special kind of brave. Gender-diverse teachers are the antidote to gender-diverse student despair.

Gender-Diverse Students

The U.S. Department of Education clarified in 2021 that Title IX did protect students based on sexual orientation and gender identity (Rogers, 2021). Again, in June of 2022, the Biden administration, through Department of Education Secretary Miguel Cardona, proposed changes to Title IX to clarify LGBTQIA+ students' protections further. Clarifying the intent for future interpretation of the federal civil rights legislation does not instantaneously create a change in culture in all educational institutions nationwide. The increased anti-trans legislation in many states targeting LGBTQIA[+]-supportive educators has created a hostile atmosphere nationwide.

There has been decades-long resistance in education to changing the entrenched, systematic promotion of cisgender heterosexuality as the only healthy, moral option presented or endorsed with students (Kim et al., 2009). By being cast as outsiders, gender-diverse educators and students face stigma, marginalization, and the stress of feeling unsafe and unwelcome (Ferfolja, 2009; Ferfolja & Hopkins, 2013; Kumashiro, 2002a; Rofes, 2005). Feelings of isolation, lack of safety, and lack of belonging are common (Kim et al., 2009; Sears et al., 2021).

The GLSEN School Climate Survey surveyed more than 16,000 students in grades 6-12 in 2019 (Kosciw et al., 2020). Over 40% of students felt unsafe at school because of their gender expression, and 37.4% because of their gender. Nearly half, 45.2%, avoided bathrooms, and 43.7% avoided locker rooms because they felt unsafe. More than three-quarters of students (77.6%) avoided school functions, and nearly three-quarters (72%) avoided extracurricular activities because they felt unsafe. Nearly one in five (17.1%) felt so unsafe they changed schools.

Many students hear toxic language and anti-LGBTQIA[+] rhetoric daily in schools. Hearing negative comments about people's gender expression was a fairly universal experience (91.8%). More than half of students frequently heard these negatively biased comments, and 87.4% heard negative comments specifically about transgender people. This toxic and damaging language was reported coming from teachers and other school staff by 66.7% of students surveyed. Much of that hate speech is directed at students. More than half, 56.9% of students, reported experiencing verbal attacks based on their gender expression, and 53.7% about their gender.

The harmful speech about trans and gender-diverse people mostly goes unaddressed by teachers and staff. Only 9% of students reported that adults in school intervened most of the time when they overheard negative remarks about gender-diverse people. Physical harassment was reported by 22.2% of students based on their gender, and 21.8% of students based on their gender expression. Nearly one in ten students (9.5%) reported physical assault based on gender expression, and 9.3% reported physical assault based on gender. More than half of students who were physically harassed or assaulted in school did not report it to staff because they doubted reporting it would make any difference or make the situation worse. More than 60% of students who did report an incident said that school staff did nothing or told the student to ignore it.

Gender-Diverse Teachers

Two Spirit, transgender, intersex, non-binary, and gender non-conforming teachers face marginalization, isolation, and significant social stress in their careers relating to their gender identities and gender expressions (e.g., (Dow, 2020)). Teachers must rigidly conform to very gendered expectations, and deviations can be subject to disciplinary action ranging from reprimands to loss of employment (Kahn & Gorski, 2016). The pressures created by those expectations lead to stressful and hostile working conditions, which are exacerbated when people have additional minoritized identities, such as race, class, and ability, increasing their stress (e.g.(Dow, 2020)). Therefore, little research exists about gender-diverse adults in schools and their experiences with discrimination.

In the author's recent mixed methods study of trans and non-binary educators in the United States, educators have reported social isolation, deliberate misgendering, being evaluated more harshly after their trans identity became known, and being fired from their jobs (Rice, 2022). Participants have also reported experiences with harassment through social media, attempts by people who have learned of their gender-diverse identity to remove students from their classes, attempts to get them fired directly or by sending anonymous letters to their principals and school boards, child protective services, and doxxing and harassment outside of the workplace including on social media.

The study used the Gender Minority Stress and Resilience Measure (GMSR) to evaluate external stress, internal stress, and resilience. Gender Minority Stress Theory (GMST) is an adaptation of Minority Stress Theory (MST) that acknowledges that non-cisgender people have unique experiences and needs that necessitate culturally specific adaptations to measure the stress that is unique to those experiences (Scandurra et al., 2020; Testa et al., 2015). Initially developed with cisgender sexual minority populations, MST explores how experiencing stigma contributes to adverse outcomes for people with non-heterosexual identities and non-cisgender identities or histories (Bockting et al., 2013; Clements-Nolle et al., 2006; Scandurra et al., 2018; Westbrook, 2021; Williams & Mann, 2017). Both MST and GMST identify mitigating factors, referred to as resilience, including social support and affirmation that reduce some of the adverse effects associated with the stress of living with stigmatized identities (Testa et al., 2015). GMST suggests that Proximal Stress (internal stress) mediates the relationship between Distal Stress (external stress) and health. GMST also suggests that Resilience, the protective factor, moderates the relationship between both types of stress and health (Scandurra et al., 2020, p. 210). The GMSR can quantify aspects of that stress and resilience (Testa et al., 2015).

The disharmony between gender-diverse educators' identities and the systems of power in their workplaces places them at risk of marginalization, violence, and additional stress (Dow, 2020). Stigma is stressful (Hatzenbuehler, 2009; Meyer, 2003; Meyer et al., 2011). Gender-diverse people are particularly vulnerable to mental and physical health disparities, and the stress of living with stigma contributes to these disparities (Budge et al., 2013; Meyer et al., 2011; Nuttbrock et al., 2010). The concept of minority stress argues, "when an individual is a member of a stigmatized minority group, the disharmony between her or him and the hegemonic culture in which she or he lives can be oppressive and the consequent stress significant" (Meyer et al., 2011, p. 2). To measure gender-related workplace stress and evaluate its impact on educators' lives, this study centered the framework of minority stress, particularly GMST, which has a psychometrically sound measure for assessment, the GMSR (Scandurra et al., 2020; Testa et al., 2015).

The GMSR is a 58-item scale to assess minority stress and resilience in transgender and other gender-diverse people (Testa et al., 2015). The GMSR is an extension of GMST, which states that people with sexual and gender-diverse identities experience adverse physical and mental health outcomes because of stress caused by persistent social stigmatization (Scandurra et al., 2020; Testa et al., 2015). An essential aspect of GMST is that it locates the experience of social stigma as the cause of the health disparities instead of blaming or pathologizing gender-diverse people (Scandurra et al., 2017).

Research illustrates that people who are not cisgender and heterosexual have stress that impacts their mental and physical health (Bockting et al., 2013; Bradford et al., 2013; Hatzenbuehler, 2009; Institute of Medicine et al., 2011; Meyer, 2003; Scandurra et al., 2020; Testa et al., 2017). These disparities for gender-diverse people continue throughout the lifespan but begin in education (Baldwin et al., 2018; Bariola et al., 2016; Breslow et al., 2015; Brewster et al., 2014; Clark et al., 2014; Clements-Nolle et al., 2006; Goguen, 2017; Gonzales & Henning-Smith, 2017; Grossman et al., 2005; Hatzenbuehler, 2009; Higa et al., 2014; Wesp et al., 2019). Since 1999, GLSEN has well-developed empirical research about the experiences of gender-diverse students in schools, but less is known about gender-diverse educators and their experiences (Ashton, 2009; Cianciotto & Cahill, 2012; Clark et al., 2014; Goguen, 2017; Kosciw et al., 2020; Martino et al., 2020; Mayo, 2014; McGuire et al., 2010; Toomey et al., 2010; Weinhardt et al., 2017). Awareness of the experiences with stress and resilience may help identify specific interventions in mitigating stress and supporting resilience in gender-diverse educators (Bockting et al., 2013; Hatzenbuehler, 2009).

GMST divides stress into two categories: Distal (external) Stress and Proximal (internal) Stress (Testa et al., 2015). Distal Stress or external stress involves direct experience with discrimination, rejection, non-affirmation, or violence related to one's gender identity, presentation, or history (Testa et al., 2015). Proximal Stress, or internal stresses, include fear of future victimization or discrimination, internalized transphobia, mistrust of others, and the stress of concealing one's gender identity or history (Testa et al., 2015). These negative experiences increase stress and negatively impact mental well-being (Bockting et al., 2013; Scandurra et al., 2020; Testa et al., 2015). The model also includes Resilience, community support, personal connection, and affirmation that can bolster one's sense of self and contribute positively to mental health (Bockting et al., 2013; Hatzenbuehler, 2009; Testa et al., 2015).

Distal Stress includes challenges faced by gender-diverse people, including the stress of receiving quality, compassionate medical care and mental health treatment given one's gender identity or gender history (Testa et al., 2015). Also included in Distal Stress is the stress associated with finding a safe public restroom to use, the stress associated with managing identity documents, the stress of finding and keeping housing and employment, and being denied promotion or advancement at work because of one's gender identity or gender history (Testa et al., 2015).

Distal Stress is important in K–12 education (Dow, 2020). Gender-diverse educators are particularly stigmatized in educational workspaces (Ashton, 2009). Trans and other gender-diverse educators experience major traumatic events in the workplace, including violence and loss of employment, and minor stressors, including disrespect and harassment, that constantly remind them of their stigmatized identity (Meyer et al., 2011). These external stressors begin a chain of events that leads to increased mental and physical health challenges in gender-diverse people (Breslow et al., 2015). Non-events, such as not receiving a promotion, can serve as reminders of a gender-diverse educator's excluded status (Meyer et al., 2011).

Table 1. Distal Stress Significance by Gender Identity

Gender Identity		Distal Stress Mean (M, *SD*)
Trans women	Highest	M = 24.4, *SD* = 8.3
Trans men	Middle	*M* = 22.1, *SD* = 10.8
Non-binary	Lowest	*M* = 21.1, *SD* = 10.8

The GMST model also includes Resilience, which moderates the effects of Proximal Stress and Distal Stress (Testa et al., 2015). Resilience describes protective factors that mitigate adverse physical and mental health outcomes of Distal Stress and Proximal Stress factors (Testa et al., 2015).

For this study, Resilience may relate to support from colleagues, friends, and families, even support from students. Resilience may also include how teachers create safe spaces for students in schools and how students create safe spaces for each other and their teachers. The GMSR was a valid, reliable measure piloted in the United States and validated for other cultural contexts like Italy and Switzerland. It was specific to the stress experienced by gender-diverse people beyond everyday life stress, so it was a good choice for this study (Bockting et al., 2013; Scandurra et al., 2020; Testa et al., 2015).

The methodological choice of transformative mixed methods allowed the integration of the qualitative data on K–12 educator experience and the quantitative data on stress and resilience to yield a more impactful synthesis than either dataset alone (Tashakkori et al., 2020). The initial quantitative phase administered an online survey including demographics, questions about non-suicidal self-injury, suicidal ideation, and suicide attempts, and the GMSR. The inclusion of quantitative data allowed insight into the impact of experiences with marginalization and stigmatization of gender-diverse people in the educational workspace on internal stress, external stress, and support of gender-diverse educators (Creswell & Creswell, 2018).

The working conditions described by trans and non-binary participants identified levels of Distal Stress and Proximal Stress, which are intolerable. The Resilience described by participants varied from absent to significant. Teachers both received support from colleagues and students and provided support to colleagues and students. The impact on many teachers' lives and well-being is profound and, in some cases, devastating. Analysis was completed of 134 participants from 35 states plus D.C. and Puerto Rico. The study used the GMSR to evaluate distal stress (external stress), proximal stress (internal stress), and resilience. Trans women had the highest mean overall distal stress, proximal stress, and resilience of the three identity groups evaluated. A one-way or Welch ANOVA evaluated if distal stress, proximal stress, and resilience differed for groups with different gender identities. The author grouped participants into three categories based on their self-identification: trans women ($n = 24$), trans men ($n = 49$), and non-binary individuals ($n = 61$).

Distal or external stress describes experiences of stigma and discrimination unique to gender-diverse people. The Distal stress factor contained 23 items divided into four constructs: gender-related discrimination, gender-related rejection, gender-related victimization, and non-affirmation of gender identity. For Distal Stress, the mean score was highest for trans women ($M = 24.4$, $SD = 8.3$), lower for trans men ($M = 22.1$, $SD = 8.3$), and lowest for non-binary individuals ($M = 21.1$, $SD = 10.8$). No statistically significant difference between these groups was found F(2,66) = 1.155, p = .321.

Overall, Proximal Stress contained three constructs, Internalized Transphobia (eight items), Negative Expectations of Future Events (nine items), and Non-Disclosure of Gender Identity (five items).

Table 2. Proximal Stress Significance by Gender Identity

Gender Identity		Proximal Stress Mean (M, *SD*)
Trans women	Highest	*M* = 46.3, *SD* = 17.1
Trans men	Middle	*M* = 42.2, *SD* = 16.8
Non-binary	Lowest	*M* = 32.3, *SD* = 20.0
Welch ANOVA	Significant	*F*(2, 64.800) = 6.437, p = .003
Games-Howell	Non-binary significantly lower than trans women, *p* = .006	
	Non-binary significantly lower than trans men, *p* = .016	

Proximal Stress was highest in trans women with a range of values from 16 – 76 (*M* = 46.3, *SD* = 17.1), lower in trans men with a range of values from 3 – 86 (*M* = 42.2, *SD* = 16.8), and lowest in non-binary individuals with a range of values from 4 – 79 (*M* = 32.3, *SD* = 20.0). The sample did not show homogeneity of variance, as assessed by Levene's statistic (*p* = .046), and ANOVA analysis showed a significant difference between the groups, *F*(2, 64.800) = 6.437, p = .003. Games-Howell post hoc testing showed the increase from trans men to trans women, a mean difference of 4.1, 95% CI [-6.1, 14.4], was not statistically significantly different (*p* = .596). The increase from non-binary individuals to trans women, a mean increase of 14.0, 95% CI [3.6, 24.5], was statistically significantly different (*p* = .006). The increase from non-binary individuals to trans men, a mean increase of 9.9, 95% CI [1.6, 18.3], was statistically significantly different (*p* = .016).

Proximal Stress was also evaluated for significance between the groups for race and ethnicity. Proximal Stress scores ranged from 3 – 86. Proximal Stress was highest in White individuals, lower in Asian, Multiracial, Indigenous, and Black individuals, and lowest in Latinx individuals. The sample showed homogeneity of variance as assessed by Levene's statistic (*p* = .408), so ANOVA was used to evaluate group differences. ANOVA showed significant differences between the groups *F*(5, 128) = 4.187, p < .001. Tukey's post hoc testing evaluated the differences between the groups and found significant differences only between the Latinx group lower than the White groups, a mean difference of 17.0, 95% CI [6.9, 27.1], *p* < .001.

Table 3. Resilience Significance by Gender Identity

Gender Identity		Resilience Mean (M, *SD*)
Trans women	Highest	*M* = 36.4, *SD* = 6.6
Trans men	Middle	*M* = 33.2, *SD* = 7.8
Non-binary	Lowest	*M* = 32.7, *SD* = 12.0
Welch ANOVA	Not Significant	*F*(2, 72.892) = 2.124, p = .127

Impact of Systemic Bias

The bias experienced by students and teachers profoundly impacts their lives, future schooling, and careers. Students who experience victimization for gender expression were more likely to have missed

Table 4. Percentage and number of individuals that reported Non-suicidal Self Injury (NSSI), Suicidal Ideation (S.I.), or Suicide Attempt (S.A.)

Gender Identity	NSSI Percentage (n)	S.I. Percentage (n)	S.A. Percentage (n)	Total in Sample
Trans Women	50% (12)	58% (14)	33% (8)	24
Trans Men	61% (30)	71% (35)	31% (15)	49
Non-Binary	46% (28)	61% (37)	26% (16)	61
Expected Percentage	4%	9%	3%	

school, more likely to have reported having been disciplined at school, have lower GPAs, lower self-esteem, and were less likely to have post-secondary education plans (Kosciw et al., 2020).

The impact of systemic bias on gender-diverse teachers is also profound. The study began in January 2022, and interviews were completed by June 2022. One in four interviewed participants had left their education careers by July 2022. A White trans woman from North Carolina went back to engineering. A White non-binary person in Washington took a job closer to their support network. A White non-binary person in New Jersey took a job at a software company. A Black trans woman left her job in Virginia but had not yet found another.

Participants reported significantly increased rates of non-suicidal self-injury, suicidal ideation, and suicide attempt than the general U.S. population, as shown in Table 4 (Cipriano et al., 2017).

Of the 2STING teachers surveyed, 49.6% (n = 70) reported non-suicidal self-injury in their lifetime, compared to a general population incidence of 4% (Cipriano et al., 2017). Sixty-one percent (n = 86) of participants reported suicidal ideation in their lifetime, compared to 9% globally (Nock et al., 2008). More than a quarter, 27% (n = 38), of participants reported suicide attempts compared to 3% of people globally (Nock et al., 2008). Four participants (2.8%) reported a suicide attempt in the past year.

Chi-square analysis of the observed and expected values for non-suicidal self-injury showed a significant difference between the categories of trans women, trans men, and non-binary individuals. The expected value for non-suicidal self-injury is 4% (Cipriano et al., 2017). Observed values for trans women (50%), trans men (61%), and non-binary individuals (46%) were significantly different than the general population, $x^2(2) = 786$, $p < .001$. Observed values for race and ethnicity categories significantly differed from the expected value, $x^2(5) = 48.16$, $p < .001$.

A Chi-square analysis of the observed and expected values for suicidal ideation showed a significant difference between trans women, trans men, and non-binary individuals. The expected value for non-suicidal self-injury is 4% (Cipriano et al., 2017). Observed values for trans women (58%), trans men (71%), and non-binary individuals (61%) were significantly different than the general population, $x^2(2) = 672$, $p < .001$. Observed values for race and ethnicity categories significantly differed from the expected value, $x^2(5) = 48.16$, $p < .001$.

A Chi-square analysis of the observed and expected values for suicidal attempts showed no significant difference between trans women, trans men, and non-binary individuals. The expected value for non-suicidal self-injury is 4% (Cipriano et al., 2017). Observed values for trans women (58%), trans men (71%), and non-binary individuals (61%) were significantly different than the expected value, $x^2(2) = 672$, $p < .001$.

MOVING TOWARD EQUITY IN EDUCATION

Leadership and Vision

A significant shift has occurred in legislative protections for lesbian, gay, bisexual, and transgender (LGBT) people in the United States. Marriage, including same-sex marriage, is now legal in all fifty states, and LGBT people are protected by Title IX and Title VII (*Bostock v. Clayton County*, 2020; Payne & Smith, 2018; U.S. Department of Education, 2021). These protections, however, have not erased the stigma, marginalization, and discrimination faced by LGBT people in educational careers (Anya Kamenetz, 2018; Dow, 2020).

There is a critical need for anti-sexist, anti-homophobic educational leaders (Payne & Smith, 2018). Leaders in schools are drivers essential to changes for equity (Payne & Smith, 2018). Most school leaders are male, married, and "fiercely homophobic" (Lugg, 2003, p. 76). Most school leaders are reluctant to address issues of sexual orientation or gender identity outside of a bullying program, yet are key drivers of successful cultural shifts needed to support the diverse students they serve (K. Brown M., 2006).

The future-directed vision of leaders, including school leaders, about the future of their organization is an essential part of creating a culture successful in ameliorating endemic inequity and rising inequality and helping identify potential opportunities and threats (Anand, 2022; Hargreaves & Shirley, 2021). This vision can allow them to structure the organization to deliver equitable solutions for all stakeholders. Still, these changes are likely to be stifled until there is greater inclusion of women, LGBT people, and Black, Indigenous, and people of color (BIPOC) integrated into the leadership ranks (Payne & Smith, 2018)

Leadership through organizational change always balances opposing choices by making the best decision you can with the data you can gather. The stories can help create the necessary sense of urgency described in Kotter's organizational change model (Kotter & Rathgeber, 2005). Stories alone are not enough to bring about lasting organizational change. For the change to become embedded in the organization's culture takes commitment at all levels and systematic implementation. The work after the introductory story includes considering the compelling reasons for change which can consist of business interests, legal requirements, and fairness and equality (Anand, 2022).

The communication plan must keep stakeholders aware of progress by celebrating small wins to cement that shared vision. As Fullan reminds us, a common vision is more a quality process outcome than a precondition (Fullan, 2008). By keeping the initiative in the communication channel for all to see, both in the initial roll-out and by celebrating successes, the guiding coalition continues to garner support and enthusiasm. By connecting the wins to collective success, the team can create momentum to celebrate the new behaviors linked to the collective mission. This celebration and connection can cement the new paradigm into the organization's culture.

The learning community communication plan should include messaging about inclusivity as part of the learning community's brand. Leaders must clearly articulate formal intersectionally-inclusive expectations. To ensure the success of meeting those expectations, leaders can quantify those expectations and tie them to how learning community leaders are evaluated.

Many businesses have moved on from a place of deliberate exclusion to deliberate inclusion of diversity and, in doing so, have tightly aligned plans for diversity, equity, and inclusion (DEI) with the core business values tailored to each country in which the corporation does business (Anand, 2022). This specificity is exceptionally relevant to educational change. Even in the same school district, two schools can have vastly different cultures, so the team leading the change at each school will have to ensure their solution is specifically relevant to their local school culture.

When an anti-discrimination policy is in place, but evaluation shows it is not in practice, leaders must change organizational culture. Leaders can push to include anti-trans bias in annual Title IX training requirements. When leaders face pushback from stakeholders, a strategy that may be effective is framing obligations to eliminate anti-trans bias as legal obligations under Title IX. When addressing anti-trans rhetoric, stick to the facts that support keeping kids alive. When the anti-trans bias is repeated and deliberate, explicitly name the social violence enacted when people continually misgender others and share how that is not in line with shared values.

Educational leaders must begin by sharing their compelling vision for change because this work requires inspired commitment, not compliance. Special guests are not enough; trans and gender-diverse people must be included at all levels in learning communities (Malatino, 2015). Some foundational expectations can include reframing gender diversity from an illness or a liability to a natural part of human diversity. Reframing can also include gender diversity not as a problem that impacts a small number of people, but as a valuable asset for all people. This perspective should include the belief that special guests who are trans and non-binary are not enough. The organization should prioritize hiring gender-diverse people, especially gender-diverse people who are Black, Indigenous, and People of Color (BIPOC) across the organization at every level. Gender diversity should be included in all system-wide sexual harassment and anti-bullying initiatives at every level.

School policies can discourage or facilitate discrimination. Many school policies leave students unable to use bathrooms and locker rooms aligned with their gender identity, prevent students from using their affirmed names and pronouns, restrict students in the clothing choices they can make based on gender, and even prevent students from participating in school sports if they are trans (Kosciw et al., 2020). Even when supportive policies are in place, if they are not comprehensive and reinforced, students are more likely to experience discrimination. When comprehensive policies are in place and enforced, gender-diverse students experience less discrimination and violence, are less likely to miss school, and feel greater belonging (Kosciw et al., 2020).

It is vital to develop a learning community culture that values each individual's duty to interrupt bias every time it happens. Microaggressions are not named with a micro prefix because they are small and meaningless but because they are reproductions of systematic bias delivered at the micro level from one person to another (Alexandra Beauregard et al., 2018; Balsam et al., 2011; Nordmarken, 2014). The impact of microaggressions is profound, and by modeling inclusive language and interrupting bias, learning community leaders can begin to transform organizational culture (E. R. Green et al., 2017).

Structured evaluation of organizational culture can begin to identify strategies to end bullying and stigma associated with gender diversity at all levels. Information technology audits across the organization should ensure that every instance of inquiry about gender or sex is needed and have options that explicitly include gender-diverse people.

Organizations must ensure that best practices for human resources management and administrative support of public-facing digital information are protective of and honor employee identity. Employee data management must include efficient processing of employee name changes and administrative support for employees navigating civil processes to codify those changes. Organizations should also ensure access to gender-diverse people's healthcare needs, including transition-related care in the health plans available to employees. Any medical procedures available to cisgender people should be available to trans and non-binary people if their physician prescribes them. Leaders should be accountable for effectively implementing these recommendations and how inclusive their learning communities are, from curriculum frameworks to hallway posters.

Supportive Educators

All teachers today face a litany of unreasonable expectations. Expectations hold teachers and students to higher standards than ever before. (Darling-Hammond, 2006) Teachers must seamlessly and simultaneously manage classroom activities while conducting the business of education. Teachers must communicate efficiently and effectively with students, families, the community, and colleagues. Teachers must learn and creatively implement ever-changing technology. Teachers must do all of those things while creating, delivering, and supporting learning that contains valuable information for more diverse students. Teachers must provide this information in engaging, exciting ways and help students build the skills they will need for their careers and lives. And while teachers do all that, they must reach across race and religion, culture and gender, class, and ability to understand each child's person and spirit and find a way to warmly nurture that spirit (Darling-Hammond, 2006). Teachers must deeply understand the psychology of learning and learning differences to be effective. Teachers must reflect on their practice and continually improve their students' performance (Darling-Hammond, 2006).

Teachers' personal beliefs influence their teaching and their perceptions and judgments of others. These beliefs are hardy and resistant to change (Pajares, 1992). Though it is undoubtedly an aspirational goal, all teachers and teacher leaders must be equity activists. Teachers and teacher leaders must be willing to explore their relationship to their own culture and the cultural context of their students and critically examine those relationships. Critical evaluation can identify the destructive effects of race, class, gender, language diversity, and ability on their learning communities so teachers and leaders can work together to decrease those effects.

Support for teachers in the classroom should include scaffolding the ability to empathize across social identities deeply and cope with feelings of distress, uncertainty, trauma, and fear that genuine care for marginalized students can invoke (Blair & Deckman, 2019). Teachers and teacher leaders must explore the complicated role of cultural dialogue and everyday schooling practices that reproduce systematic oppression (Kumashiro, 2004; Blair & Deckman, 2019). This evaluation can be extended to explore the traditional expectations for students in the hegemonic systems embedded in schools and the curricula used to teach them.

For a more equitable future that allows all students to engage in learning at high academic levels, learning communities need to be committed to collective empowerment. (Ladson-Billings, 1995). Empowered and included students can learn. This work must be fluid and crafted for each learning community (Kumashiro, 2000). Identities of all people change with context and include many facets, including race, gender, ability, language, ethnicity, religion, and class. Equity initiatives in schooling systems cannot revolve around only one identity or form of oppression. There is no one size fits all solution to such complicated problems. The voices of those who may not express their needs first or loudest are still worth hearing. Teachers must look beyond their own experiences and stories for perspectives their position might obscure (Kumashiro, 2004).

A better understanding of the experiences of trans and non-binary people can foster changes and help create full equitable inclusion for trans and non-binary people in educational settings. Culturally competent educators do not miraculously appear after a one-hour training to teach them some new vocabulary about gender diversity (Green, 2014). This understanding can be fostered by improvements in best practices in teacher education and professional learning for in-service teachers (Brant & Willox, 2019; Gorski et al., 2013; Kumashiro, 2004; Martin & Strom, 2019; Robinson & Ferfolja, 2008).

Teacher Education

Teacher education programs must interrogate how they help pre-service teachers examine cultural myths about what schools should be and how silence and inaction are as significant in learning as the intended curriculum (Kumashiro, 2002). Most multicultural education texts lack the necessary LGBTQ+ inclusive content, so supplemental materials should be included (Jennings & Macgillivray, 2011; Szelei et al., 2020).

Teacher education programs do not adequately prepare cisgender and heterosexual pre-service teachers to interrupt bias and act as effective advocates for their LGBTQIA⁺ colleagues and students (Blair & Deckman, 2019; Brant, 2014; Brant & Willox, 2019; Jenlink, 2020; Kumashiro, 2004). Teacher education programs often fail to adequately support their LGB, trans, and non-binary student teachers (Diversity in Education, 2020; Lee & Carpenter, 2015). The supportive textbooks for diversity courses in teacher education do not adequately cover LGBTQIA⁺ issues (Jennings & Macgillivray, 2011).

Teacher education programs generally include one course that addresses diversity in education (Gorski et al., 2013). One diversity course should not be the only encounter pre-service teachers have with strategies for disrupting bias and engaging with gender diversity in the classroom. (Martin & Strom, 2019). Often, diversity course fails to address LGBT concerns adequately, and when they do, they do so in a way that precludes any critique of heteronormativity (Kahn & Gorski, 2016). Often heteronormativity is not critiqued due to discomfort and resistance to admitting heteronormative privilege is unearned and damaging to those who do not share it (DePalma & Atkinson, 2009; Kumashiro, 2002b).

In most places, teacher education steadfastly maintains heteronormativity, even when there is occasional inclusion of isolated LGBT-inclusive content (Martin & Strom, 2019). The rare inclusion of LGBT topics is often only sparing and often only in the context of bullying or, even less often, sexual health (Brant & Willox, 2019). "By most counts, U.S. teachers in K–12 settings are woefully ill-prepared to teach LGBTQ and non-gender conforming youth and to work against heterosexism and homophobia in schools." (Clark, 2010, p.711). Teacher education programs must examine how they help pre-service teachers examine cultural myths about what schools should be and how silence and inaction are as significant in learning as the intended curriculum (Kumashiro, 2002b).

Teacher education should provide reflective, collaborative, intersectional guidance that expands pre-service teachers' ability to serve the students ethically, culturally, and as their complete best self, especially when part of that self is LGBT (Brown, 2006; Kumashiro, 2004; Lee & Carpenter, 2015). Pre-service and in-service teachers need time to reflect and collaborate (Brown, 2006; Greytak et al., 2013a). Pre-service and in-service teachers need to learn perspective-taking with and from people who have lives like, look like, and sound like the students they teach (McDermott et al., 2018). Pre-service and in-service teachers need support to build empathy for their students who are different, including sexual and gender-diverse students (Robinson & Ferfolja, 2008). If we can invest the time and energy into those who will teach our students, allow them to reflect, and build self-efficacy in disrupting bias when they see it, we can begin to put a stop to the overwhelming discrimination experienced by LGB and 2STING people (Brant & Willox, 2019; Brown, 2006; McDermott et al., 2018; Robinson & Ferfolja, 2008).

There has been decades-long resistance in education to changing the entrenched, systematic promotion of cisgender heterosexuality as the only healthy, moral option presented or endorsed (Kim et al., 2009). By being cast as outsiders, educators and students who are not cisgender and heterosexual face stigma, marginalization, and the stress of feeling unsafe and unwelcome (Ferfolja, 2009; Ferfolja & Hopkins, 2013; Kumashiro, 2002a; Rofes, 2005). Feelings of isolation, lack of safety, and lack of belonging are common (Kim et al., 2009; Sears et al., 2021).

People can be moved to the outgroup "other" by their lack of heterosexuality, their gender presentation, their gender history, or even their gender performance's alignment with someone else's assumptions about what their biological sex might be (Blair & Deckman, 2019; Carpenter, 2018; Kumashiro, 2002a). Othering people in this way happens all the time and is essential to upholding normative sexual orientations and gender identities and policing those who transgress those expectations of normative sexual orientations and gender identities in conflict with heteronormativity and cissexism (Dow, 2020; Green et al., 2020; Mayo & Blackburn, 2019). As Lee and Carpenter clarify, othering does not have to be a conscious act, but its effects still silence sexual and gender-diverse voices (Lee & Carpenter, 2015).

Professional Learning

The solution continues with Professional Learning for all stakeholders (Bradbury-Jones et al., 2020). Work must be aligned with standards for professional conduct in each area (Kim & Greene, 2011). Learning communities must dig deep into issues of their culture in the classrooms and the workplace and address issues of mistrust, interpersonal tensions, doubts, and fears. There are several choices educational leaders face, including continuing denial that systemic barriers exist. Leaders may also choose to work to identify and eliminate those barriers. Leaders may continue to pretend that cisgenderism and heteronormativity harm only a small subset of people and are therefore not worth challenging the status quo or admit they harm everyone. Leaders may continue to allow the status quo to continue harming people, especially when this is sometimes to their direct benefit. Leaders may remain mired in guilt, doubt, or fear or lean into the teachable moment even if it is uncomfortable. Leaders may continue to see diverse talent, including trans and non-binary educators, as a risk or embrace the best talent as their greatest treasure regardless of gender history or gender presentation. Those who welcome trans and non-binary people not as liabilities but as assets can share their successes beyond their schools, school districts, and even beyond state-wide connections they may have.

Transformational learning is an adult learning helpful strategy in such organizational change. Transformational learning begins with a disorienting dilemma, in this case, identifying that people are being marginalized and suffer grave consequences because of their treatment in educational systems (Merriam & Bierema, 2014). Learning about the dilemma will be disruptive for many, and stories can help the transformational learning experiences stick. The stories can give leaders the courage to work through that shift internally and with their organization. When combined with reflective discourse, exploring personal beliefs can yield new understandings that increase inclusivity (K. Brown M., 2006).

CONCLUSION

The status quo policies and practices and the ideologies that underlie them that are common in educational workspaces serve to marginalize and stigmatize LGB and gender-diverse people, especially LGB and gender-diverse BIPOC people. Recruitment, hiring, assignment of job responsibilities, performance appraisal, and informal interactions all reinforce these inequality regimes (Kelly et al., 2021, p. 1079).

Encouraging others to engage in the brave work of examining how the status quo puts gender-diverse students and colleagues at risk must be a priority for all who are committed to equity in education.

The impact of bias is shockingly clear when examining the increased rates of non-suicidal self-injury, suicidal ideation, and suicide attempt in transgender and non-binary professional educators. The increased rates show that the adverse outcomes described by GMST are impacting educators. Educators continue to place themselves in increasingly hostile work environments to help create safe spaces for students to learn and grow. The anti-trans and anti-gender diversity bias that drives these adverse outcomes must not continue.

Comprehensive policies, including leadership changes, teacher education, and professional learning, can help ameliorate the impact of bias by creating a culture supportive of all educational professionals and leaders. Inclusive curricula can begin to help students develop the critical consciousness and skills to continue to change the world they will inherit to serve them better. However, the divisive nature of the debates surrounding trans and gender-diverse people in current social discourse will continue to make it impossible for trans and non-binary adults and children to be even marginally safe in some places. Those who can advocate for them must continue to carve out safe spaces, however small and fleeting (Freedom for All Americans, 2022). A student with at least one supportive adult is 40% less likely to have attempted suicide in the past year (The Trevor Project, 2021). My most fervent wish for anyone reading this: be that adult.

REFERENCES

Alexandra Beauregard, T., Arevshatian, L., Booth, J. E., & Whittle, S. (2018). Listen carefully: Transgender voices in the workplace. *International Journal of Human Resource Management, 29*(5), 857–884. doi:10.1080/09585192.2016.1234503

Anand, R. (2022). *Leading global diversity, equity, and inclusion: A guide to systemic change in multinational organizations* (1st ed.). Berrett-Koehler.

Ashton, S. (2009). *Transgender teachers as role models for a tolerant society: The impact of societal views and their influence on employment anti-discrimination laws*. Chicago-Kent College of Law. https://scholarship.kentlaw.iit.edu/louis_jackson/18/

Attia, A. (2016). Explicit Equality: The Need for Statutory Protection against Anti-Transgender Employment Discrimination Notes. *Southern California Interdisciplinary Law Journal, 25*(1), 151–178.

Baldwin, A., Dodge, B., Schick, V. R., Light, B., Scharrs, P. W., Herbenick, D., & Fortenberry, J. D. (2018). Transgender and genderqueer individuals' experiences with health care providers: What's working, what's not, and where do we go from here? *Journal of Health Care for the Poor and Underserved, 29*(4), 1300–1318. doi:10.1353/hpu.2018.0097 PMID:30449748

Balsam, K. F., Molina, Y., Beadnell, B., Simoni, J., & Walters, K. (2011). Measuring multiple minority stress: The LGBT People of color microaggressions scale. *Cultural Diversity & Ethnic Minority Psychology, 17*(2), 163–174. doi:10.1037/a0023244 PMID:21604840

Bariola, E., Lyons, A., & Leonard, W. (2016). Gender-specific health implications of minority stress among lesbians and gay men. *Australian and New Zealand Journal of Public Health*, *40*(6), 506–512. doi:10.1111/1753-6405.12539 PMID:27372452

Blair, E. E., & Deckman, S. L. (2019). "We cannot imagine": U.S. pre-service teachers' othering of trans and gender creative student experiences. *Teaching and Teacher Education*, *86*, 102915. doi:10.1016/j. tate.2019.102915

Block, M. (2022, May 11). Accusations of "grooming" are the latest political attack—With homophobic origins. *NPR*. https://www.npr.org/2022/05/11/1096623939/accusations-grooming-political-attack-homophobic-origins

Bockting, W. O., Miner, M. H., Romine, R. E. S., Hamilton, A., & Coleman, E. (2013). Stigma, mental health, and resilience in an online sample of the U.S. transgender population. *American Journal of Public Health*, *103*(5), 943–951. doi:10.2105/AJPH.2013.301241 PMID:23488522

Bostock v. Clayton County. 17-1618 U.S. 964 (2020). https://www.law.cornell.edu/supremecourt/text/17-1618

Bradbury-Jones, C., Molloy, E., Clark, M., & Ward, N. (2020). Gender, sexual diversity and professional practice learning: Findings from a systematic search and review. *Studies in Higher Education*, *45*(8), 1618–1636. doi:10.1080/03075079.2018.1564264

Bradford, J., Reisner, S. L., Honnold, J. A., & Xavier, J. (2013). Experiences of transgender-related discrimination and implications for health: Results from the Virginia transgender health initiative study. *American Journal of Public Health*, *103*(10), 1820–1829. doi:10.2105/AJPH.2012.300796 PMID:23153142

Brant, C. (2014). *Pre-service teachers' perspectives on methods, pedagogy and self-efficacy related to gender and sexuality as a part of their multicultural teacher education.* The Ohio State University. https://etd.ohiolink.edu/apexprod/rws_olink/r/1501/10?clear=10&p10_accession_num=osu1393177002

Brant, C., & Willox, L. (Eds.). (2019). *Teaching the teacher: LGBTQ issues in teacher education.* Information Age Publishing, inc.

Breslow, A. S., Brewster, M. E., Velez, B. L., Wong, S., Geiger, E., & Soderstrom, B. (2015). Resilience and collective action: Exploring buffers against minority stress for transgender individuals. *Psychology of Sexual Orientation and Gender Diversity*, *2*(3), 253–265. doi:10.1037gd0000117

Brewster, M. E., Velez, B. L., Mennicke, A., & Tebbe, E. (2014). Voices from beyond: A thematic content analysis of transgender employees' workplace experiences. *Psychology of Sexual Orientation and Gender Diversity*, *1*(2), 159–169. doi:10.1037gd0000030

Brown, A. (2022). About 5% of young adults in the U.S. say their gender is different from their sex assigned at birth. *Pew Research Center*. https://www.pewresearch.org/fact-tank/2022/06/07/about-5-of-young-adults-in-the-u-s-say-their-gender-is-different-from-their-sex-assigned-at-birth/

Brown, K. M. (2006). Leadership for social justice and equity: Evaluating a transformative framework and andragogy. *Educational Administration Quarterly*, *42*(5), 700–745. doi:10.1177/0013161X06290650

Budge, S. L., Adelson, J. L., & Howard, K. A. S. (2013). Anxiety and depression in transgender individuals: The roles of transition status, loss, social support, and coping. *Journal of Consulting and Clinical Psychology*, *81*(3), 545–557. doi:10.1037/a0031774 PMID:23398495

Chesir-Teran, D. (2003). Conceptualizing and Assessing Heterosexism in High Schools: A Setting-Level Approach. *American Journal of Community Psychology*, *31*(3–4), 267–279. doi:10.1023/A:1023910820994 PMID:12866684

Cho, S., Crenshaw, K. W., & McCall, L. (2013). Toward a field of intersectionality studies: Theory, applications, and praxis. *Signs (Chicago, Ill.)*, *38*(4), 785–810. doi:10.1086/669608

Cianciotto, J., & Cahill, S. (2012). *LGBT youth in America's schools*. University of Michigan. doi:10.3998/mpub.4656286

Cipriano, A., Cella, S., & Cotrufo, P. (2017). Non-suicidal self-injury: A systematic review. *Frontiers in Psychology*, *8*, 1946. doi:10.3389/fpsyg.2017.01946 PMID:29167651

Clark, T. C., Lucassen, M. F. G., Bullen, P., Denny, S. J., Fleming, T. M., Robinson, E. M., & Rossen, F. V. (2014). The health and well-being of transgender high school students: Results from the New Zealand adolescent health survey (youth'12). *The Journal of Adolescent Health*, *55*(1), 93–99. doi:10.1016/j.jadohealth.2013.11.008 PMID:24438852

Clements-Nolle, K., Marx, R., & Katz, M. (2006). Attempted suicide among transgender persons. *Journal of Homosexuality*, *51*(3), 53–69. doi:10.1300/J082v51n03_04 PMID:17135115

Creswell, J. W., & Creswell, J. D. (2018). *Research design: Qualitative, quantitative, and mixed methods approaches* (5th ed.). SAGE.

DeJean, W., & Sapp, J. L. (Eds.). (2017). Dear gay, lesbian, bisexual, and transgender teacher: Letters of advice to help you find your way. IAP, Information Age Publishing, Inc.

DePalma, R., & Atkinson, E. (2010). The nature of institutional heteronormativity in primary schools and practice-based responses. *Teaching and Teacher Education*, *26*(8), 1669–1676. doi:10.1016/j.tate.2010.06.018

Diversity in Education. (2020, September 16). Hiring (and Protecting) LGBTQ Teachers Can Create Better School Climates for Students, Too. *DIVERSITY in Ed*. https://www.diversityined.com/blog/2020/09/hiring-and-protecting-lgbtq-teachers-can-create-better-school-climates-for-students-too/

Donelson, R., & Rogers, T. (2004). Negotiating a research protocol for studying school-based gay and lesbian issues. *Theory into Practice*, *43*(2), 128–135. doi:10.120715430421tip4302_6

Dow, M. (2020). *Transgender educators: Understanding marginalization through an intersectional lens*. Lexington Books.

Fertig, R. (Director). (2007). *Two Spirits*. https://video.alexanderstreet.com/watch/two-spirits

Fischer, M. (2019). Introduction: A transgender tipping point? In Terrorizing Gender (pp. 1–28). University of Nebraska Press. doi:10.2307/j.ctvpwhf5f.5

Freedom for All Americans. (2022). Legislative Tracker: Anti-Transgender Legislation Filed for the 2022 Legislative Session. *Freedom for All Americans*. https://freedomforallamericans.org/legislative-tracker/anti-transgender-legislation/

Fullan, M. (2008). *The six secrets of change: What the best leaders do to help their organizations survive and thrive* (1st ed.). Jossey-Bass.

Ghorayshi, A. (2022, June 10). Report reveals sharp rise in transgender young people in the U.S. *The New York Times*. https://www.nytimes.com/2022/06/10/science/transgender-teenagers-national-survey.html

Gilbert, D. (2022, April 13). 'She needs to be executed': The far-right is doxxing school officials they think are 'groomers.' *Vice*. https://www.vice.com/en/article/jgm3xx/far-right-groomers-doxxing-school-officials

GLSEN. (2020). *GLSEN's four supports*. GLSEN. https://www.glsen.org/sites/default/files/2020-01/GLSEN_Four_Supports_Resource_2020.pdf

Goguen, Y. (2017). Pour l'amour de nos jeunes: Le droit d'être libre de discrimination et de violence à caractère homophobe et transphobe à l'école. *Revue de l'Université de Moncton*, *46*(1–2), 201–228. doi:10.7202/1039037ar

Gonzales, G., & Henning-Smith, C. (2017). Barriers to care among transgender and gender non-conforming adults: Barriers to care among transgender and GNC adults. *The Milbank Quarterly*, *95*(4), 726–748. doi:10.1111/1468-0009.12297 PMID:29226450

Grant, J., Keisling, M., Harrison, J., Mottet, L., Herman, J. L., & Tanis, J. (2011). *Injustice at every turn: A report of the national transgender discrimination survey*. National Center for Transgender Equality. https://www.transequality.org/sites/default/files/docs/resources/NTDS_Report.pdf

Green, E. R., Maurer, L., & Planned Parenthood of the Southern Finger Lakes. (2017). *The teaching transgender toolkit: A facilitator's guide to increasing knowledge, decreasing prejudice & building skills*. Planned Parenthood.

Green, E. R. (2014). *Does teaching transgender content effectively reduce anti-transgender prejudice? The findings from a national study*. [Thesis, Widener University, PA, USA, Proquest Dissertations and Theses Global].

Green, J., Hoskin, R. A., Mayo, C., & Miller, S. I. (2020). *Navigating trans*+ and complex gender identities*. https://search.ebscohost.com/login.aspx?direct=true&scope=site&db=nlebk&db=nlabk&AN=2250837

Mayo, C. (2014). *LGBTQ youth and education: Policies and practices.* Teachers College Press, Columbia University.

Mayo, C., & Blackburn, M. V. (Eds.). (2019). *Queer, trans, and intersectional theory in educational practice: Student, teacher, and community experiences* (1st ed.). Routledge. doi:10.4324/9780367816469

McGuire, J. K., Anderson, C. R., Toomey, R. B., & Russell, S. T. (2010). School climate for transgender youth: A mixed method investigation of student experiences and school responses. *Journal of Youth and Adolescence, 39*(10), 1175–1188. doi:10.100710964-010-9540-7 PMID:20428933

Merriam, S., & Bierema, L. (2014). *Adult learning.* Jossey Bass.

Meyer, I. H. (2003). Prejudice, social stress, and mental health in lesbian, gay, and bisexual populations: Conceptual issues and research evidence. *Psychological Bulletin, 129*(5), 674–697. doi:10.1037/0033-2909.129.5.674 PMID:12956539

Meyer, I. H., Ouellette, S. C., Haile, R., & McFarlane, T. A. (2011). "We'd be free": Narratives of life without homophobia, racism, or sexism. *Sexuality Research & Social Policy, 8*(3), 204–214. doi:10.100713178-011-0063-0 PMID:24009487

Nock, M. K., Borges, G., Bromet, E. J., Alonso, J., Angermeyer, M., Beautrais, A., Bruffaerts, R., Chiu, W. T., de Girolamo, G., Gluzman, S., de Graaf, R., Gureje, O., Haro, J. M., Huang, Y., Karam, E., Kessler, R. C., Lepine, J. P., Levinson, D., Medina-Mora, M. E., & Williams, D. R. (2008). Cross-National Prevalence and Risk Factors for Suicidal Ideation, Plans, and Attempts. *The British Journal of Psychiatry, 192*(2), 98–105. doi:10.1192/bjp.bp.107.040113 PMID:18245022

Nordmarken, S. (2014). Microaggressions. *Transgender Studies Quarterly, 1*(1–2), 129–134. doi:10.1215/23289252-2399812

Nuttbrock, L., Hwahng, S., Bockting, W., Rosenblum, A., Mason, M., Macri, M., & Becker, J. (2010). Psychiatric impact of gender-related abuse across the life course of male-to-female transgender persons. *Journal of Sex Research, 47*(1), 12–23. doi:10.1080/00224490903062258 PMID:19568976

Payne, E. C., & Smith, M. J. (2018). Refusing Relevance: School Administrator Resistance to Offering Professional Development Addressing LGBTQ Issues in Schools. *Educational Administration Quarterly, 54*(2), 183–215. doi:10.1177/0013161X17723426

Rogers, K. (2021, June 16). Title IX protections extend to transgender students, Education Dept. Says. *The New York Times.* https://www.nytimes.com/2021/06/16/us/politics/title-ix-transgender-students.html

Sawchuk, S. (2022, April 19). What's Driving the Push to Restrict Schools on LGBTQ Issues? *Education Week.* https://www.edweek.org/leadership/whats-driving-the-push-to-restrict-schools-on-lgbtq-issues/2022/04

Scandurra, C., Bochicchio, V., Dolce, P., Caravà, C., Vitelli, R., Testa, R. J., & Balsam, K. F. (2020). The Italian validation of the gender minority stress and resilience measure. *Psychology of Sexual Orientation and Gender Diversity, 7*(2), 208–221. doi:10.1037gd0000366

Sears, B., Mallory, C., Flores, A., & Conron, K. (2021). *LGBT people's experiences of workplace discrimination and harassment*. UCLA School of Law, Williams Institute. https://williamsinstitute.law.ucla.edu/publications/lgbt-workplace-discrimination/

Semuels, A. (2017, April 4). Why It's So Hard to Get Ahead in the South. *The Atlantic*. https://www.theatlantic.com/business/archive/2017/04/south-mobility-charlotte/521763/

Simonović, I. (2011, December 8). *Message to event on ending violence and discrimination based on sexual orientation and gender identity*. United Nations Secretary-General. https://www.un.org/sg/en/content/sg/statement/2011-12-08/message-event-ending-violence-and-discrimination-based-sexual

Spade, D. (2015). Normal life: Administrative violence, critical trans politics, and the limits of law (Revised and expanded edition). Duke University Press.

Stryker, S. (1994). My words to Victor Frankenstein above the village of Chamounix. *GLQ: A Journal of Lesbian and Gay Studies, 1*, 237–254.

Stryker, S., & Whittle, S. (Eds.). (2006). *The transgender studies reader*. Routledge.

Suen, B., & Drennen, A. (2022, April 19). The real victims in the "Libs of TikTok" discourse are the teachers and LGBTQ people harassed because of the account. *Media Matters for America*. https://www.mediamatters.org/twitter/real-victims-libs-tiktok-discourse-are-teachers-and-lgbtq-people-harassed-because-account

Szelei, N., Tinoca, L., & Pinho, A. S. (2020). Professional development for cultural diversity: The challenges of teacher learning in context. *Professional Development in Education, 46*(5), 780–796. doi:10.1080/19415257.2019.1642233

Tashakkori, A., Johnson, B., & Teddlie, C. (2020). *Foundations of mixed methods research: Integrating quantitative and qualitative approaches in the social and behavioral sciences* (2nd ed.). SAGE Publications, Inc.

Testa, R. J., Habarth, J., Peta, J., Balsam, K., & Bockting, W. (2015). Development of the gender minority stress and resilience measure. *Psychology of Sexual Orientation and Gender Diversity, 2*(1), 65–77. doi:10.1037gd0000081

Testa, R. J., Michaels, M. S., Bliss, W., Rogers, M. L., Balsam, K. F., & Joiner, T. (2017). Suicidal ideation in transgender people: Gender minority stress and interpersonal theory factors. *Journal of Abnormal Psychology, 126*(1), 125–136. doi:10.1037/abn0000234 PMID:27831708

The Trevor Project. (2021). *National survey on LGBTQ youth mental health*. The Trevor Project. https://www.thetrevorproject.org/wp-content/uploads/2021/05/The-Trevor-Project-National-Survey-Results-2021.pdf

Toomey, R. B., Ryan, C., Diaz, R. M., Card, N. A., & Russell, S. T. (2010). Gender-nonconforming lesbian, gay, bisexual, and transgender youth: School victimization and young adult psychosocial adjustment. *Developmental Psychology*, *46*(6), 1580–1589. doi:10.1037/a0020705 PMID:20822214

Twist, J., Vincent, B., Barker, M.-J., & Gupta, K. (Eds.). (2020). *Non-binary lives: An anthology of intersecting identities*. Jessica Kingsley Publishers.

United Nations Office of the High Commissioner on Human Rights. (2022, August 30). *United States: U.N. expert warns LGBT rights being eroded, urges stronger safeguards*. OHCHR. https://www.ohchr.org/en/press-releases/2022/08/united-states-un-expert-warns-lgbt-rights-being-eroded-urges-stronger

U.S. Department of Education. (2021, June 16). *U.S. Department of Education confirms Title IX protects students from discrimination based on sexual orientation and gender identity*. USDE. https://www.ed.gov/news/press-releases/us-department-education-confirms-title-ix-protects-students-discrimination-based-sexual-orientation-and-gender-identity

VandenBos, G. R., & American Psychological Association (Eds.). (2015). *APA dictionary of psychology* (Second Edition). American Psychological Association.

Wakefield, L. (2022, April 20). Teacher targeted by Libs of TikTok sent death threats and lost his job. *PinkNews*. https://www.pinknews.co.uk/2022/04/20/libs-of-tiktok-teacher-lgbt-death-threats-job-doxxing/

Weinhardt, L. S., Stevens, P., Xie, H., Wesp, L. M., John, S. A., Apchemengich, I., Kioko, D., Chavez-Korell, S., Cochran, K. M., Watjen, J. M., & Lambrou, N. H. (2017). Transgender and gender non-conforming youths' public facilities use and psychological well-being: A mixed-method study. *Transgender Health*, *2*(1), 140–150. doi:10.1089/trgh.2017.0020 PMID:29159308

Wesp, L. M., Malcoe, L. H., Elliott, A., & Poteat, T. (2019). Intersectionality research for transgender health justice: A theory-driven conceptual framework for structural analysis of transgender health inequities. *Transgender Health*, *4*(1), 287–296. doi:10.1089/trgh.2019.0039 PMID:31663035

Williams, C. (2014). Transgender. *Transgender Studies Quarterly*, *1*(1–2), 232–234. doi:10.1215/23289252-2400136 PMID:25341321

KEY TERMS AND DEFINITIONS

Cisgender: The person identifies with a gender congruent to the sex they were assigned at birth (Lennon & Mistler, 2014; VandenBos & American Psychological Association, 2015).

Gender diverse: The category of people who are not cisgender, also gender minority (Testa et al., 2015).

Heteronormativity: The idea that heterosexuality is the only normal option and that "male and female differences and gender roles are the natural and immutable essentials in normal human relations," and all else is disordered and disadvantaged (VandenBos & American Psychological Association, 2015, p. 492).

Intersectionality: The interaction of many types of oppression in social systems (Cho et al., 2013).

LGBTQIA[+]: Includes the terms Lesbian, Gay, Bisexual, Transgender, Queer, Intersex, Asexual, and the "+" represents the others not specifically named in the LGBTQ identities who are part of the broader community of sexual minority and gender-diverse people.

Non-binary: Not limited to a binary choice between male or female, masculine or feminine (Twist et al., 2020).

Trans: An umbrella term that can refer to transgender, transsexual, and people who transgress the gender binary, also written as trans* or trans*[+] to be more inclusive of non-cisgender identities that are not specifically trans (J. Green et al., 2020).

Transsexual: An outdated medical term that was used to describe people who had a cross-gendered identity to their sex assigned at birth who desired medical transition (J. Green et al., 2020; Lombardi, 2009).

Transgender: The umbrella term that can be used to refer to transgender, transsexual, and people who transgress the gender binary (Stryker, 1994; Williams, 2014).

Two Spirit: The umbrella term for a pan-Indigenous and Native American gender-variant spiritual, ceremonial, and cultural role (Fertig, 2007).

Chapter 3
Improving Access and Advancing Equity:
A Reconsideration of Barriers and Solutions to Multilingual Learner Access to Gifted Programs

Lori Leibowitz
Baylor University, USA

Leanne Howell
Baylor University, USA

Nicholas R. Werse
Baylor University, USA

ABSTRACT

The underrepresentation of linguistically diverse gifted learners continues to be a pervasive issue in schools across the United States. Many leaders in the field recognize the problem of this inequitable access to gifted education programs. In light of this persistent challenge, the present chapter critically examines the barriers that gifted multilanguage learners (ML) face that can hinder or prevent their access to gifted and talented programs to identify promising solutions and actionable changes. To achieve these ends, the following chapter unfolds in two parts. First, the authors examine four avenues through which gifted ML students may be identified and referred to gifted and talented programs to critically consider potential obstacles they face and solutions to those obstacles. Second, the authors then present the "talent development" model, combined with insights from Culturally Relevant Teaching, as a way to construct classroom environments that make the identification of gifted ML students more likely.

DOI: 10.4018/978-1-6684-6386-4.ch003

INTRODUCTION: THE PROBLEM OF ACCESS

The underrepresentation of ethnically and linguistically diverse gifted learners and gifted students from lower socio-economic groups continues to be a pervasive issue in schools across the United States (Esquierdo & Arreguín-Anderson, 2012; Yoon & Gentry, 2009; Ford, 2013). Disproportionality in gifted education is not a new phenomenon. Despite addressing the needs and readiness of gifted learners, VanTassel-Baska (2021) claims that gifted programming has been met with "hostility and suspicion" (p. 44) when it comes to meeting the needs of underrepresented students. According to Ford (2010), the roadblocks to increasing participation of students from underserved populations, such as Hispanic and Black students, have not changed dramatically in the past 20 years:

The most recent findings from the Office of Civil Rights (U.S. DOE, Office for Civil Rights, 2016) show that of students enrolled at "schools offering gifted and talented programs (GATE)" (p. 6), Black and Latinx children are 42% of the student population and White children are 49% of the student population. However, the student population actually in the GATE programs in these schools is only 28% Black and Latinx but 57% White, clear evidence of unequal representation in GATE programs. (Hurt, 2018, p.123, italics original)

Although the English Language Learner (ELL) school population continues increasing nationwide, these students remain underrepresented gifted programs across the country (Pereira & de Oliveira, 2015; Coronado & Lewis, 2017).

A major reason underrepresentation continues to plague gifted programs is the idea of deficit thinking (Ford, 2010; Harris et al, 2009; Ford & Grantham, 2003; Allen 2017; Wright et al., 2017). Wright et al. (2017) argue, "Historically, advocates for greater numbers of Black and Brown faces in gifted and advanced programs have been confronted by White power brokers or establishments that view difference as a deficit" (p. 48). Deficit thinking encompasses the "belief that culturally different students are genetically and culturally inferior to White students" (Ford, 2010, p. 32). Payne (2011) agrees that deficit thinking continues to be a barrier to identification.

Many leaders in the field of gifted education recognize the problem of this inequitable access to gifted education programs (Esquierdo & Arreguín-Anderson, 2012; Yoon & Gentry, 2009; Ford, 2013). Over a decade ago, the National Association of Gifted Children recognized this need, writing in a position statement,

Identifying and serving culturally and linguistically diverse students (CLD) enriches the fabric of gifted education and cultivates what is still an untapped national resource. To promote equitable access and school success for CLD students, schools and supportive organizations need to be strategic, purposeful, and committed to altering common identification and programming practices. Current policies, procedures, procedures, and practices need to be thoroughly examined and defensible identification protocols developed and implemented. Effective teaching and learning models and school support services should also be intentionally designed to address the specific needs of CLD students. (NAGC, 2011)

While the problem of inequitable access remains a recognized reality, the challenge educators and educational leaders face is identifying practical and effective solutions.

In light of this persistent challenge in gifted and talented research, we offer in the present chapter a critical assessment of the state of scholarship on the systemic and institutional barriers that gifted multilanguage learners (ML) face, which can hinder or prevent their access to gifted and talented programs to identify promising solutions and actionable changes. To achieve these ends, this chapter unfolds in two parts, focusing first on the known barriers and second on potential solutions. First, we examine four avenues through which gifted ML students may be identified and referred to gifted and talented programs to critically consider potential obstacles they face and solutions to those obstacles. Second, we then present the "talent development" model, combined with insights from Culturally Relevant Teaching, as a way to construct classroom environments that make the identification of gifted ML students more equitable.

AVENUES OF ACCESS: A CRITICAL ASSESSMENT

While school districts attempt to combat this underrepresentation in gifted programs, the problem for MLs is compounded by the language issue or lack of teacher training present in schools. Coronado and Lewis (2017) explain that schools are not necessarily able to meet the needs of MLs because of this lack of training and established support systems. Although their study addressed this issue only in Texas, they argue that the problem is pervasive across the United States. McBee (2010) finds that Hispanic students were the group "with the lowest probability of identification" (p. 294). Ford (2010) notes that the underrepresented students suffer from not having access to gifted programs, but their families and communities also suffer. Allen (2017) states that gifted MLs are the most "at-risk due to a lack of sufficient and appropriate educational services" (p.78). Allen cites the impact of the language barrier, overemphasis on testing, lack of collaboration, and professional development as barriers to alleviating the underrepresentation issue for ML students in gifted programs.

Allen (2017) also argues that building relationships with ML students is key to exploring their strengths and circumventing obstacles that could emerge as a result of language differences. Wright et al. (2017) cite "ignorance and indifference" as well as the prejudice, stereotypes, and deficit-based thinking as reasons gifted programs continue to be plagued with underrepresentation of Black and Hispanic students (p. 55). Esquierdo and Arreguín-Anderson (2012) expand this to include the definition of giftedness and lack of teacher preparation to work with ELLs as other barriers to alleviating this issue. It is clear that these obstacles are not going away and that they have a lasting effect on the identification of underserved populations for gifted programs.

While there have been many ideas presented to increase the participation of underserved populations throughout the literature pertaining to identification, the fact remains that these students continue to be disproportionately underrepresented in gifted programs nationwide (Ford, 2010, Ford 2013). ML students can often remain unseen by educators as gifted because they are not proficient in the English language. In the following critical assessment, we identify four commonly used measures and discuss their potential benefits and limitations for identifying gifted ML students. While no single screener offers a perfect solution in isolation, we argue that the use of multiple screeners in collaboration can increase the identification of gifted ML students. Four of these measures, in particular, can be leveraged and reexamined to make access to gifted programming more equitable for MLLs: non-verbal assessments, universal screeners, teacher referrals, and parent referrals.

The Benefits and Limitations of Non-Verbal Ability Assessments

Non-verbal assessments are often used to identify ML students, as they are known to circumvent un-intentional linguistic bias (Giessman et al., 2013). The problem, however, is that this practice may not be effective at increasing the participation of racial and ethnic minority students (Plucker & Callahan, 2014; Giessman et al. 2013; Payne 2011). According to Lohman and Gambrell (2012), "Single-format figural reasoning tests can be useful but have significant limitations for talent identification" (p. 17). A closer examination of the literature reveals that these non-verbal tests may not be "culture neutral" as claimed by the NNAT-2 (Naglieri, 2008), a common non-verbal screener in gifted identification, as they advertise (Hughes et al., 2006).

Plucker and Callahan (2014) argue that more research is needed to see if these assessments really yield the outcomes they intend or if they possibly worsen the disproportionality issue. These non-verbal assessments do not account for acculturation or school experience in the United States (Lohman & Gambrell, 2012). When lower SES status (as indicated by free and reduced lunch) is considered, performance on non-verbal assessments is often impacted. The authors argue, "Even after controlling for ethnicity and ELL status, students eligible for free/reduced-price lunch still scored approximately 6 IQ-like points lower than children who were not eligible for free/reduced-price lunch" (p. 31). Payne's (2011) analysis of non-verbal assessments furthered the argument that these assessments are not the only solution. She argues that these non-verbal assessments cannot alleviate the lack of command of English and cultural differences that make it difficult for these students to be identified as gifted through the identification process. Warne (2009) also points out that using a non-verbal ability test to identify diverse students for gifted programs that are "highly verbal" is an issue. "Furthermore, relying exclusively on nonverbal tests of ability provides a very limited view of a child's intellectual ability" (p. 51). While there is no perfect assessment that can level the playing field for underserved populations, non-verbal assessments are helpful in the more extensive identification process when used as one tool (Giessman et al., 2013). Therefore, it is essential to look at non-verbal assessments as a more extensive identification system for increasing the representation of underserved populations.

Even though the gifted field highly regards non-verbal assessments, Bartsch et al. (2020) confirmed that non-verbal assessments alone cannot solve the problem of underrepresentation as they are not singularly addressing this issue. While non-verbal assessments can open the door for many underrepresented students, they cannot stand alone as the only measure used. However, when coupled with other measures such as student work samples, growth scores, and gifted behavior rating scales, non-verbal assessments can provide teachers with essential data to aid in the identification process.

Universal Screening as a Strategy to Increase Participation

When school districts use non-verbal assessments as a universal screener, it often increases the identification of underserved populations in gifted programs, however, this cannot be the only mode of assessment. Card and Giuliani (2016) explain, "With no change in the minimum standards for gifted status the screening program led to a 180% increase in the gifted rate among all disadvantaged students, with a 130% increase for Hispanic students and an 80% increase for black students" (p. 22). A universal screening process can increase representation for underrepresented students dramatically even when done in isolation. According to Lakin (2016), "The advantage to universal screening is that it allows all students to have an equal (or closer to equal) chance of being identified and offered special services tailored to their instructional needs" (p. 140). Universal screeners can help widen the net cast to identify more students from underserved backgrounds.

However, Lakin points out that there are disadvantages to universal screeners, which include time and costs associated with this process. Lohman and Gambrell (2012) note that schools often base these identification decisions on assessments that are unreliable and only consider limited amounts of information. When universal screeners are the only method used to identify candidates for gifted programs, many students, especially those from underserved populations, are overlooked. Another issue with universal screeners is that they often do not match the programming offered in current gifted programming. Peters and Engerrand (2016) point out that even if administered tests are free from bias, they often do not align with current offerings. They explain that the most important aspect of identification for gifted programs is that the assessments used to identify students are closely aligned to the intervention that is utilized (p. 162). Universal screening opens doors for underrepresented students when the assessments minimize linguistic bias.

When a universal screen is offered, MLL students are automatically included in the identification process. This practice ensures that all students have an opportunity to be considered gifted even if other more traditional methods do not indicate there is a need to look further. By providing a universal screener, school districts can combat the bias in the identification process and make sure that gifted MLLs dot go undetected.

The Benefits and Limitations of Teacher Referrals

A referral to a gifted and talented program is another way districts attempt to increase underserved populations in gifted and talented programs; however, many teachers are not trained to identify talent or high potential in students. Many studies have referred to the role of teachers as "gatekeepers" of gifted and talented programming, meaning that they hold the key as to whether a student goes through more identification measures or is simply identified as gifted (McBee, 2006; Moon & Brighton, 2008; Szymanski & Lynch, 2020). Szymanski et al. (2018) argue further, "Teachers are especially important in the lives of gifted students as they are often the initial recommenders of students for gifted services" (p. 30). While this can be positive for some students, it can also be a negative aspect of the referral process. One issue is that some teachers bring their own linguistic biases to the identification table. "When teachers do not have awareness of how giftedness can occur in all students, identification suffers, and the initial door into gifted programming opportunities closes" (Szymanski & Lynch, 2020, p. 436). McBee (2006) agreed that biases could cloud the referral process. In McBee's study, he observed that teacher nominations rated Asian, White, and Native Americans higher in academic performance that Hispanic and Black students (p. 107). This bias often has significant implications on the identification of underserved populations for gifted programs.

Another reason that some teachers do not identify ML students for gifted programs is because of a common belief that students must master English before entering (Plucker et al., 2009). Callahan (2005) agreed with this viewpoint that limited English was a barrier to gifted referral, as well as a ticket into lower tracked classes, citing that teachers and school administrators often prohibit ML students from taking more advanced classes due to their limited knowledge of English (p. 310). This misinterpretation is also compounded by classroom teachers' lack of training to recognize giftedness, especially in underserved populations. Pereira (2021) found that classroom teachers rated ML students lower on teacher rating scales than they did for students who were proficient in English (p. 163). Hughes et al.

(2006) agree that many monolingual teachers are not aware of the nuances of bilingual students in terms of "code-switching," noting that when bilingual students can "alternate between their two languages with ease and can maintain the grammaticality of both languages, then this appears to be evidence of advanced language and higher-order thinking skills" (p. 21). This example illustrates why professional development is vital in gifted identification, especially as giftedness can look different across cultures.

Foreman and Gubbins (2015) assert that not enough research has occurred to examine the effectiveness of teacher referrals. They explain that while teacher influence in the nomination process is important, it is also essential to understand if these nominations have a role in determining future success in gifted programs (p. 8). So, the question remains about how effective gifted referral processes are in identifying underserved populations. Scholars are left wondering how well these referrals correlate with success for these students in gifted programming once they are placed.

The Benefits and Limitations of Parent Referrals

While there are plenty of studies on teachers' roles in the identification process, there is little information regarding the effectiveness of parent nominations (Bianco et al, 2011; Szymanski & Lynch, 2020; Pereira, 2021). While the idea of parental nominations sounds promising in theory, it raises the question of parental access and the opportunity to advocate and navigate the referral process (Lakin, 2016). Harris et al. (2009) noted the importance of having all the information about gifted programming and identification procedures translated into the native languages of the students present. Communication with these families is key to ensure a fair identification process. Questions also come into play about the validity of parent nominations. According to Rothenbusch et al. (2018), "Overall, teachers appear to be similarly or more accurate than parents in rating students' cognitive abilities, more accurate in rating creativity, and similarly or less accurate in rating motivation" (p. 232). This evidence fuels the argument that parent and teacher referrals cannot be the only measure that exists in this identification process and that there is a need for multiple measures.

Scholars agree that multiple measures are needed when it comes to identification, especially of underrepresented populations (Allen, 2017; Wiggin, 2017; Pereira, 2021). Payne (2011) takes this argument a step further and explains that multiple measures can even diminish teachers' bias in this process. Using multiple methods to identify gifted and high-potential learners, a wider net is cast in terms of identification. The doors to gifted programming can be opened even further than when a non-verbal assessment or universal screener is used alone.

Summary and Assessment

In summary, while many obstacles exist for gifted ML students, existing scholarship suggests that using multiple measures, including a universal screener, can help identify these students in greater numbers than single measures or test scores in isolation. However, more identification of underserved populations is not enough to break down the aforementioned barriers. A shift in thinking about giftedness as talent that can be developed is necessary to make changes in the status quo. There are various ways that districts have attempted to reduce disproportionality in gifted education, including a shift towards talent development with the Schoolwide Enrichment Model (Renzulli, 1978). The next section discusses these initiatives and their impacts on gifted programming.

THE SHIFT TOWARDS TALENT DEVELOPMENT AND THE QUEST FOR MORE EQUITABLE ACCESS

As identification has shifted to focus on gifted potential instead of just innate academic and intellectual ability, a movement towards talent development has ensued. Talent development, as defined in the 1993 federal report explains:

Youth with outstanding talent perform or show potential for performing at remarkably high levels of accomplishment with compared with others of their age, experience, or environment. These children and youth exhibit high performance capability in intellectual, creative, and/or artistic areas, possess an unusual leadership capacity, or excel in specific academic fields. (U.S. Department of Education, 1993, p. 3)

Many well-known gifted scholars wrote about talent development as a framework for giftedness, which included a much "broader conception of intelligence and ability, beyond IQ; a recognition of the role of noncognitive traits in gifted achievement; and a focus on serving a broader range of gifted students…" (Olszewski-Kubilius & Thomson, 2015, p. 49). In fact, according to Hernández-Torrano and Saranli (2015), all people have the right to talent development (p. 258). This shift in mindset about giftedness has significant implications for serving students from diverse backgrounds. This framework was vital in opening the door to students from diverse cultural backgrounds and various income levels, as the demographics in United States' schools and the excellence gap started widening.

Hertzog (2018) argues that classrooms need to be designed with talent development in mind, from the physical classroom environment to the critical thinking activities they use. He explains, "Schools must be inviting safe zones for exploration, collaboration, and high-achievement in all domains" (p. 225). Gentry (2009) agreed that opportunities must exist in schools for students to explore their talents and gifts along a continuum of services that nurture these gifts. Furthermore, Olszewski-Kubilius and Thomson (2015) believe that a talent development framework is essential for creating an organizational system to foster this talent that has implications for programming, assessment, and social-emotional development.

The Schoolwide Enrichment Model

One widely known and respected talent development model used worldwide in gifted education is the Schoolwide Enrichment Model (Renzulli, 1978). A talent development approach requires flexibility and a continuum of services designed to meet the needs of identified students and students who are showing potential (Gentry, 2009). This continuum became popular and widely used in gifted education as Dr. Joseph Renzulli coined the Schoolwide Enrichment Model (SEM) in the 1970s (Sternberg, 1999). Renzulli's Three-Ring Conception of Giftedness examines the intersection of three gifted characteristics (creativity, above-average ability, and task commitment) (Renzulli, 1978, 1986). Hernández-Torrano and Saranli (2015) explain, "The SEM is an organizational plan for talent development that aims to develop creative productivity by exposing students to a variety of challenging learning experiences based on their abilities, interests, learning styles, and preferred modes of expression" (p. 259). In this model, giftedness is not a fixed trait. Renzulli and Reis (2012) explains that gifted traits are not fixed and can be developed by exposing students to problem-solving opportunities.

As school stakeholders attempt to diversify their gifted programs to become more representative of their student populations, SEM opens the doors for whole-school enrichment. Hernández-Torrano and Saranli explain that SEM allows educators to infuse enrichment in the regular curriculum, enhancing programming, not replacing it (p. 262). In this manner, enrichment is infused across the curriculum and not offered in isolation. In addition, SEM casts a wider identification net, focusing on above-average ability and not just IQ scores in the 95th percentile or above. Students are identified for the talent pool using multiple identification measures that examine the areas of above-average ability, task-commitment, and creativity. These areas are known as Renzulli's three rings of giftedness (Renzulli & Reis, 2012). Educators look for the intersection of these three rings to identify gifted potential. By using the SEM talent development model, teachers can nourish the gifted potential of ML students through a strength-based approach that focuses on students' interests. Furthermore, SEM provides opportunities for all students and works toward developing talent and identifying students from underserved groups to create the "talent pool." This model does not just focus on identifying gifted students; it focuses on the entire school population, allowing students' diverse talents and needs to be met (Gentry, 2009; Reis & Peters 2021). Through SEM, a talent pool, accompanied by a wider range of services, allows a true talent development model to exist and more students to receive enrichment and accelerated learning experiences.

A SEM model not only casts a wider net, it also creates more enrichment opportunities for all students, especially for students who were not previously included in enrichment activities. These enrichment opportunities are an essential component to talent development. Through talent development, gifted behaviors can be observed, and students can be identified for gifted services.

Strength-based Response to Intervention (RTI) as a Talent Development Strategy for MLs

The idea of using Response to Intervention (RTI) in developing giftedness in students is a more recent idea that stemmed from interventions for students who were over-referred to special education, namely English Language Learners (Bianco & Harris, 2014). They argue that RTI can be used to develop gifted potential in ELLs when a strength-based model is used "with an intentional focus on student's culture, linguistic abilities, interests, needs, and strengths" (p. 169). Ford and Trotman Scott (2013) agree that the RTI model can be promising when nurturing students from various cultural backgrounds. However, teachers must possess the knowledge and skills necessary to make this a successful undertaking. The idea of moving from a deficit-focused RTI model to a strengths-based model is vital to create significant change for underrepresented gifted populations (Ford & Russo 2014). Collaboration between gifted specialists, ML specialists, and classroom teachers is also crucial in employing this strengths-based RTI model as a mode to develop and nurture giftedness in ML students (Bianco & Harris, 2014). Other scholars refer to this intervention as "front-loading." Warne (2009) explains this process as identifying underserved students who have "fallen short" of the identification for gifted programs. He explains that "Those children are then funneled into intensive programs that build up their study skills, verbal ability, factual knowledge, and academic performance until the students do qualify…" (p. 51). When a strength-based approach to interventions exists, high expectations of learners can be set, and talent can be nurtured in students showing high potential.

Culturally Affirming Strategies to Engage With Gifted MLs

Throughout this process, the use of culturally affirming pedagogy holds immense promise for improving equitable access to gifted and talented programs for high-potential ML students. Many scholars suggest using Culturally Responsive Teaching (CRT) to help further develop these learners' critical thinking and retain them in gifted programs (Ford, Moore & Harmon, 2005; Ecker-Lyster & Niieksela, 2017; Banks, 1993). While the literature on CRT in schools is extensive, it is less studied in the gifted realm (Ecker-Lyster & Niieksela, 2017). To accomplish diversifying gifted programs, they suggest a shift in thinking about equitable educational services to using "culturally sensitive identification methods" as well as strategies that embrace student strengths and not highlight their deficits (p. 90). This shift includes having diverse classroom libraries and texts where students can see themselves and their experiences in the literature (Ford & Grantham, 2003). Ford (2010) argues that when a curriculum is both rigorous and multicultural, underrepresented students will thrive as they are more motivated and achieve at higher levels.

Of course, engaging students with culturally affirming pedagogies requires humility and care from educators. Sleeter (2012) notes that it is easy for multicultural education to become too trivial or straightforward, citing the idea of using holiday celebrations to teach multicultural education. She explains that this idea of multiculturalism can backfire and argues, "Oversimplified and distorted conceptions of culturally responsive pedagogy, which do not necessarily improve student learning, lend themselves to dismissal of the entire concept" (p. 572). Wenger-Traynor and Wenger-Traynor (2020) explain, "Imagination is needed to reflect, see oneself in a broader context, or envision a different future" (p. 22). This type of imagination is necessary for creating a classroom environment built on critical reflection and fosters critical action. Merriam and Bierema (2014) suggest engaging students in change projects that interest them or creating service-learning projects. They write, "Critical thinking causes learners to begin questioning their assumptions, which allows them to see the injustice in the world" (p. 233). A culturally affirming curriculum provides opportunities for educators and students critically and compassionately consider the present, imagine potential futures, and create plans for meaningful change (Freire; 1970).

Establishing and then keeping expectations high, as well as ensuring a rigorous curriculum, are vital contexts of CRT (Rojas & Liou; 2017). Swanson (2016) investigated known curriculums for gifted MLs, such as Project Athena from the College of William and Mary, Project Clarion, Mentoring Mathematical Minds (M3), U Stars Plus, and Schoolwide Enrichment Model-Reading (SEM-R). All projects received Javits grants, and these projects worked with high-potential students from underrepresented populations. Swanson examined their commonalities and their effectiveness. She found that all projects had "powerful engagement of students previously unengaged and unmotivated" (p. 183). While motivation is indeed the catalyst for learning, there need to be rigorous activities to sustain this motivation over time and connection to real-world issues that engage students in critical thinking skills to bring their understanding to higher levels where they can synthesize and evaluate information.

Another strategy to employ with gifted MLs is Linguistically Responsive Teaching (LRT). Pereira and de Oliviera (2015) explain that LRT respects the linguistic diversity of students while understanding second-language acquisition and the demands of classroom discourse. "High-potential ELLs often have the ability to learn a second language at a faster pace but need teachers who will challenge them and provide structured opportunities to develop academic language proficiency" (p. 211). Thus, teachers can have an integral role in helping MLs be successful. Villegas and Lucas (2002) put teachers at the center of this work to create positive classroom environments that encourage MLs to take risks and construct their meaning through inquiry.

Merriam and Bierema (2014) suggest engaging students in change projects that interest them or creating service-learning projects. They write, "Critical thinking causes learners to begin questioning their assumptions, which allows them to see the injustice in the world" (p. 233). A culturally affirming pedagogy provides opportunities for educators and students critically and compassionately consider the present, imagine potential futures, and create plans for meaningful change.

Culturally affirming strategies are not only engaging for gifted ML students, they can aid in breaking down systemic barriers that MLs face. When teachers keep the level of rigor high and engage ML students in critical thinking, these students begin to be part of the solution. Gifted ML students need opportunities to develop academically and emotionally as they discover their identities, strengths, and even challenges. Culturally affirming pedagogy is essential in providing ML students opportunities to find their voices and enact change.

CONCLUSION: IMPROVING ACCESS AND ADVANCING EQUITY

While questions still remain about how best to support this student population, available information suggests that school districts can make data-informed changes to increase ML student access to gifted and talented programs. Providing many avenues for access increases the chances of identifying gifted ML students for placement in gifted and talented education programs. While no single avenue functions as a flawless entry point for all gifted ML students, utilizing a combination of non-verbal ability assessments, universal screening, teacher referrals, and parent referrals increases the opportunities for school districts to identify gift ML students and connect them with appropriate educational opportunities. Furthermore, in keeping with broader trends in gifted and talented research, investing in talent development programs with ML students in mind will open additional opportunities for this student population.

While disproportionality is still present across the country, removing the barriers to identification and utilizing a talent-development model can put school districts on the right path to improving access to gifted and talented programs. Advancing equity takes an immense focus on resources and human capital, a growth mindset, and a willingness to imagine systemic change. Once the barriers to identification are removed, it is time to focus on choosing the proper programming to meet the needs of diverse gifted students. At the very least, this programming should consider culturally affirming pedagogy that keeps rigor high and fosters critical thinking skills. This is not a one-size-fits-all approach, and scholars do not agree on how to best service multilingual gifted students. It is clear that MLs should not be held back from rigor because they have not yet mastered English. Using a strength-based approach, keeping expectations high, and engaging MLs in real-world issues can open doors of opportunity while creating agents of change.

REFERENCES

Allee-Herndon, K. A., Kaczmarczyk, A. B., & Buchanan, R. (2021). Is it "just" planning? Exploring the integration of social justice education in an elementary language arts methods course thematic unit. *Journal for Multicultural Education*, *15*(1), 103–116. doi:10.1108/JME-07-2020-0071

Allen, J. K. (2017). Exploring the role teacher perceptions play in the underrepresentation of culturally and linguistically diverse students in gifted programming. *Gifted Child Today*, *40*(2), 77–86. doi:10.1177/1076217517690188

Banks, C. A. M., & Banks, J. A. (1995). Equity pedagogy: An essential component of multicultural education. *Theory into Practice*, *34*(3), 152–158. doi:10.1080/00405849509543674

Banks, J. A. (1993). Approaches to multicultural curricular reform. In J. A. Banks & C. A. M. Banks (Eds.), *Multicultural education: Issues and perspectives* (2nd ed., pp. 355–365). Allyn & Bacon.

Bernal, E. M. (2001). Three ways to achieve a more equitable representation of culturally and linguistically different students in GT programs. *Roeper Review*, *24*(2), 82–88. doi:10.1080/02783190209554134

Bianco, M., & Harris, B. (2014). Strength-based RTI: Developing gifted potential in Spanish-speaking English language learners. *Gifted Child Today*, *37*(3), 169–176. doi:10.1177/1076217514530115

Bianco, M., Harris, B., Garrison-Wade, D., & Leech, N. (2011). Gifted girls: Gender bias in gifted referrals. *Roeper Review*, *33*(3), 170–181. doi:10.1080/02783193.2011.580500

Callahan, C. M., Moon, T. R., Oh, S., Azano, A. P., & Hailey, E. P. (2015). What works in gifted education: Documenting the effects of an integrated curricular/instructional model for gifted students. *American Educational Research Journal*, *52*(1), 137–167. doi:10.3102/0002831214549448

Callahan, R. M. (2005). Tracking and high school English learners: Limiting opportunity to learn. *American Educational Research Journal*, *42*(2), 305–328. doi:10.3102/00028312042002305

Cammarota, J. (2007). A social justice approach to achievement: Guiding Latina/o students toward educational attainment with a challenging, socially relevant curriculum. *Equity & Excellence in Education*, *40*(1), 87–96. doi:10.1080/10665680601015153

Cammarota, J. (2011). The value of a multicultural and critical pedagogy: Learning democracy through diversity and dissent. *Multicultural Perspectives*, *13*(2), 62–69. doi:10.1080/15210960.2011.571546

Card, D., & Giuliano, L. (2015). *Can universal screening increase the representation of low income and minority students in gifted education?* National Bureau of Economic Research. doi:10.3386/w21519

Coffey, H., & Fulton, S. (2018). The responsible change project: Building a justice-oriented middle school curriculum through critical service-learning. *Middle School Journal*, *49*(5), 16–25. doi:10.1080/00940771.2018.1509560

Coronado, J. M., & Lewis, K. D. (2017). The disproportional representation of English language learners in gifted and talented programs in Texas. *Gifted Child Today*, *40*(4), 238–244. doi:10.1177/1076217517722181

Crocco, M. S., & Costigan, A. T. (2007). The narrowing of curriculum and pedagogy in the age of accountability urban educators speak out. *Urban Education*, *42*(6), 512–535. doi:10.1177/0042085907304964

Daggett, W. R. (2000). Moving from standards to instructional practice. *NASSP Bulletin*, *84*(620), 66–72. doi:10.1177/019263650008462008

Ecker-Lyster, M., & Niileksela, C. (2017). Enhancing gifted education for underrepresented students: Promising recruitment and programming strategies. *Journal for the Education of the Gifted, 40*(1), 79–95. doi:10.1177/0162353216686216

Esquierdo, J. J., & Arreguín-Anderson, M. (2012). The "invisible" gifted and talented bilingual students: A current report on enrollment in GT programs. *Journal for the Education of the Gifted, 35*(1), 35–47. doi:10.1177/0162353211432041

Ezzani, M. D., Mun, R. U., & Lee, L. E. (2021). District leaders focused on systemic equity in identification and services for gifted education: From policy to practice. *Roeper Review, 43*(2), 112–127. doi:10.1080/02783193.2021.1881853

Ford, D. Y. (2010). Multicultural issues: Underrepresentation of culturally different students in gifted education: reflections about current problems and recommendations for the future. *Gifted Child Today, 33*(3), 31–35. doi:10.1177/107621751003300308

Ford, D. Y. (2013). Multicultural issues: Gifted underrepresentation and prejudice—learning from Allport and Merton. *Gifted Child Today, 36*(1), 62–67. doi:10.1177/1076217512465285

Ford, D. Y. (2014). Why education must be multicultural: Addressing a few misperceptions with counterarguments. *Gifted Child Today, 37*(1), 59–62. doi:10.1177/1076217513512304

Ford, D. Y., & Grantham, T. C. (2003). Providing access for culturally diverse gifted students: From deficit to dynamic thinking. *Theory into Practice, 42*(3), 217–225. doi:10.120715430421tip4203_8

Ford, D. Y., Moore, J. L., & Harmon, D. A. (2005). Integrating multicultural and gifted education: A curricular framework. *Theory into Practice, 44*(2), 125–137. doi:10.120715430421tip4402_7

Ford, D. Y., & Russo, C. J. (2014). No Child Left Behind … unless a student is gifted and of color: Reflections on the need to meet the educational needs of the gifted. *Journal of Law and Society, 15*(2), 213–241.

Ford, D. Y., & Trotman Scott, M. (2013). Culturally responsive response to intervention: Meeting the needs of students who are gifted and culturally different. In M. R. Coleman & S. K. Johnsen (Eds.), *Implementing RTI with gifted students: Service models, trends and issues* (pp. 209–228). Proofrock Press.

Foreman, J. L., & Gubbins, E. J. (2015). Teachers see what ability scores cannot: Predicting student performance with challenging mathematics. *Journal of Advanced Academics, 26*(1), 5–23. doi:10.1177/1932202X14552279

Freire, P. (1970). *Pedagogy of the oppressed*. Bloomsbury Academic.

Giessman, J. A., Gambrell, J. L., & Stebbins, M. S. (2013). Minority performance on the Naglieri Nonverbal Ability Test, Second Edition, versus the Cognitive Abilities Test, Form 6: One gifted program's experience. Gifted Child Quarterly, 57(2), 101–109. doi:10.1177/0016986213477190

Harris, B., Plucker, J. A., Rapp, K. E., & Martínez, R. S. (2009). Identifying gifted and talented English language learners: A case study. *Journal for the Education of the Gifted, 32*(3), 368–393. doi:10.4219/jeg-2009-858

Haydan, H. (2008). "Who's got the chalk?": Beginning mathematics teachers and educational policies in New York City. *Forum on Public Policy: A Journal of the Oxford Round Table.* https://link.gale.com/apps/doc/A218606498/AONE?u=txshracd2488&sid=bookmark-AONE&xid=a882e526

Hernández-Torrano, D., & Saranli, A. G. (2015). A cross-cultural perspective about the implementation and adaptation process of the schoolwide enrichment model: The importance of talent development in a global world. *Gifted Education International, 31*(3), 257–270. doi:10.1177/0261429414526335

Hughes, C. E., Shaunessy, E. S., Brice, A. R., Ratliff, M. A., & McHatton, P. A. (2006). Code switching among bilingual and limited English proficient students: Possible indicators of giftedness. *Journal for the Education of the Gifted, 30*(1), 7–28. doi:10.1177/016235320603000102

Hurt, J. W. (2018). "Why are the gifted classes so white?" Making space for gifted Latino students. *Journal of Cases in Educational Leadership, 21*(4), 112–130. doi:10.1177/1555458918769115

Kavanagh, K. M., & Fisher-Ari, T. R. (2020). Curricular and pedagogical oppression: Contradictions within the juggernaut accountability trap. *Educational Policy, 34*(2), 283–311. doi:10.1177/0895904818755471

Kirshner, B. (2007). Introduction: Youth activism as a context for learning and development. *The American Behavioral Scientist, 51*(3), 367–379. doi:10.1177/0002764207306065

Kraft, M. (2007). Toward a school-wide model of teaching for social justice: An examination of the best practices of two small public schools. *Equity & Excellence in Education, 40*(1), 77–86. doi:10.1080/10665680601076601

Lakin, J. M. (2016). Universal screening and the representation of historically underrepresented minority students in gifted education: Minding the gaps in Card and Guliano's research. *Journal of Advanced Academics, 27*(2), 139–149. doi:10.1177/1932202X16630348

Lohman, D. F., & Gambrell, J. L. (2012). Using nonverbal tests to help identify academically talented children. *Journal of Psychoeducational Assessment, 30*(1), 25–44. doi:10.1177/0734282911428194

McBee, M. (2010). Examining the probability of identification for gifted programs for students in Georgia elementary schools: A multilevel path analysis study. *Gifted Child Quarterly, 54*(4), 283–297. doi:10.1177/0016986210377927

McBee, M. T. (2006). A descriptive analysis of referral sources for gifted identification screening by race and socioeconomic status. *Journal of Secondary Gifted Education, 17*(2), 103–111. doi:10.4219/jsge-2006-686

McBee, M. T. (2016). A descriptive analysis of referral sources for gifted identification screening by race and socioeconomic status. *Journal of Secondary Gifted Education, 17*(2), 103–111. https://journals.sagepub.com/doi/abs/10.4219/jsge-2006-686. doi:10.4219/jsge-2006-686

Merriam, S., & Bierema, L. (2014). *Adult learning: Linking theory and practice.* John Wiley & Sons.

Mun, R. U., Ezzani, M. D., Lee, L. E., & Ottwein, J. K. (2021). Building systemic capacity to improve identification and services in gifted education: A case study of one district. *Gifted Child Quarterly, 65*(2), 132–152. doi:10.1177/0016986220967376

Mun, R. U., Hemmler, V., Langley, S. D., Ware, S., Gubbins, E. J., Callahan, C. M., McCoach, D. B., & Siegle, D. (2020). Identifying and serving English learners in gifted education: Looking back and moving forward. *Journal for the Education of the Gifted*, *43*(4), 297–335. doi:10.1177/0162353220955230

NAGC. (2011). *Identifying and serving culturally and linguistically diverse gifted students*. NAGC. http://www.nagc.org/sites/default/files/Position%20Statement/Identifying%20and%20Serving%20Culturally%20and%20Linguistic
ally.pdf

NAGC. (n.d.) *Gifted Education in the U.S. National Association for Gifted Children*. NAGC. https://www.nagc.org/resources-publications/resources/gifted-education-us

Naglieri, J. A. (2008) *Naglieri nonverbal ability test* (2nd ed.) Pearson National Association for Gifted Children.

Olszewski-Kubilius, P., & Thomson, D. (2015). Talent development as a framework for gifted education. *Gifted Child Today*, *38*(1), 49–59. doi:10.1177/1076217514556531

Payne, A. (2011). *Equitable access for underrepresented students in gifted education*. George Washington University Center for Equity and Excellence in Education. https://eric.ed.gov/?id=ED539772

Pereira, N. (2021). Finding talent among elementary English learners: A validity study of the hope teacher rating scale. *Gifted Child Quarterly*, *65*(2), 153–166. doi:10.1177/0016986220985942

Pereira, N., & de Oliveira, L. C. (2015). Meeting the linguistic needs of high-potential English language learners: What teachers need to know. *Teaching Exceptional Children*, *47*(4), 208–215. doi:10.1177/0040059915569362

Peters, S. J., & Engerrand, K. G. (2016). Equity and excellence: Proactive efforts in the identification of underrepresented students for gifted and talented services. *Gifted Child Quarterly*, *60*(3), 159–171. doi:10.1177/0016986216643165

Peters, S. J., & Gentry, M. (2012). Group-specific norms and teacher-rating scales: Implications for underrepresentation. *Journal of Advanced Academics*, *23*(2), 125–144. doi:10.1177/1932202X12438717

Picower, B. (2012). Using their words: Six elements of social justice curriculum design for the elementary classroom. *International Journal of Multicultural Education*, *14*(1). https://go.gale.com/ps/i.do?p=AONE&sw=w&issn=19345267&v=2.1&it=r&id=GALE%7CA420198248&sid=googleScholar&linkaccess=abs. doi:10.18251/ijme.v14i1.484

Plucker, J. A., & Callahan, C. M. (2014). Research on giftedness and gifted education: Status of the field and considerations for the future. *Exceptional Children*, *80*(4), 390–406. doi:10.1177/0014402914527244

Pratt, S. (2008). Complex constructivism: Rethinking the power dynamics of "understanding." *Journal of the Canadian Association for Curriculum Studies*, *6*(1), 113–132.

Reis, S. M., & Peters, P. M. (2021). Research on the schoolwide enrichment model: Four decades of insights, innovation, and evolution. *Gifted Education International*, *37*(2), 109–141. doi:10.1177/0261429420963987

Renzulli, J. S. (1978). What makes giftedness? Reexamining a definition. *Phi Delta Kappan*, *60*(3), 180–261.

Renzulli, J. S. (1986). The three-ring conception of giftedness: A development model for creative productivity. In R. J. Sternberg and J. Davidson (Eds) Conceptions of Giftedness (pp.332–357). Cambridge University Press.

Renzulli, J. S., & Reis, S. M. (2012). A virtual learning application of the schoolwide enrichment model and high-end learning theory. *Gifted Education International*, *28*(1), 1. doi:10.1177/0261429411424382

Rojas, L., & Liou, D. D. (2017). Social justice teaching through the sympathetic touch of caring and high expectations for students of color. *Journal of Teacher Education*, *68*(1), 28–41. doi:10.1177/0022487116676314

Rothenbusch, S., Voss, T., Golle, J., & Zettler, I. (2018). Linking teacher and parent ratings of teacher-nominated gifted elementary school students to each other and to school grades. *Gifted Child Quarterly*, *62*(2), 230–250. doi:10.1177/0016986217752100

Sleeter, C. E., & Grant, C. A. (2007). *Making choices for multicultural education: five approaches to race, class, and gender* (5th ed.). John Wiley & Sons.

Sternberg, R. J. (1999). Rising tides and racing torpedoes: Triumphs and tribulations of the adult gifted as illustrated by the career of Joseph Renzulli. *Journal for the Education of the Gifted*, *23*(1), 67–74. doi:10.1177/016235329902300104

Szymanski, A., & Lynch, M. (2020). Educator perceptions of English language learners. *Journal of Advanced Academics*, *31*(4), 436–450. doi:10.1177/1932202X20917141

Torres-Harding, S., Baber, A., Hilvers, J., Hobbs, N., & Maly, M. (2018). Children as agents of social and community change: Enhancing youth empowerment through participation in a school-based social activism project. *Education, Citizenship and Social Justice*, *13*(1), 3–18. doi:10.1177/1746197916684643

VanTassel-Baska, J. (2021). Curriculum in gifted education: The core of the enterprise. *Gifted Child Today*, *44*(1), 44–47. doi:10.1177/1076217520940747

Wade, R. C. (2007). Service-learning for social justice in the elementary classroom: Can we get there from here? *Equity & Excellence in Education*, *40*(2), 156–165. doi:10.1080/10665680701221313

Warne, R. T. (2009). Comparing tests used to identify ethnically diverse gifted children: A critical response to Lewis, Decamp-Fritson, Ramage, McFarland, & Archwamety. *Multicultural Education*, *17*(1), 48–48.

Wenger-Trayner, E., & Wenger-Trayner, B. (2014). Learning in a landscape of practice: A framework. In E. Wenger-Trayner, M. Fenton-O'Creevy, S. Hutchinson, C. Kubiak, & B. Wenger-Trayner (Eds.), *Learning in landscapes of practice: Boundaries, identity, and knowledgeability in practice-based learning* (pp. 13–30). Routledge. doi:10.4324/9781315777122-3

Wiggin, L. P. (2017). Demography in America: Gifted education for a growing population of English language learners. *Indiana Journal of Law and Social Equality*, *5*(2), 1–13.

Wright, B. L., Ford, D. Y., & Young, J. L. (2017). Ignorance or indifference? Seeking excellence and equity for under-represented students of color in gifted education. *Global Education Review*, *4*(1). https://link.gale.com/apps/doc/A544247889/AONE?u=txshracd2488&sid=AONE&xid=6fa3f2c4

Wright, W. E. (2002). The effects of high stakes testing in an inner-city elementary school: The curriculum, the teachers, and the English language learners. *The Curriculum*, *5*(5), 1–23.

Zimmerman, B. J., & Dibenedetto, M. K. (2008). Mastery learning and assessment: Implications for students and teachers in an era of high-stakes testing. *Psychology in the Schools*, *45*(3), 206–216. doi:10.1002/pits.20291

Chapter 4
Duoethnographic Perspective on Supporting Students of Refugee Background in Middle School

Antoinette Gagné

https://orcid.org/0000-0002-6179-177X
OISE, University of Toronto, Canada

Thursica Kovinthan Levi

https://orcid.org/0000-0002-4491-9292
OISE, University of Toronto, Canada

ABSTRACT

Students with refugee experiences face several social and academic challenges in the Canadian school system. Supportive relationships and school spaces where educators, parents, and peers act as cultural brokers to help students navigate challenges can contribute to reducing experiences of educational inequality for children with refugee experiences. This duoethnography maps these relationships during a year-long identity text project with Grade 6 students in an ESL/ELD classroom by two educator researchers. Using an intersectional lens, the authors identify gaps and highlight promising pathways and practices for the integration of students with refugee backgrounds, including 1) working towards the greater interconnectedness of service and referrals between welcome centres, schools and service organizations; 2) knowledge exchange surrounding different education pathways and practices and the opportunities afforded by these for the integration of students with refugee experiences; 3) individually tailored educational support and services; and 4) translanguaging pedagogy.

INTRODUCTION

In this duoethnography, we describe and reflect on our experiences working with students of refugee

DOI: 10.4018/978-1-6684-6386-4.ch004

background within the context of a middle school program for students who have experienced significant interruptions in their education. We explore our contrasting and sometimes overlapping experiences as teachers, teacher educators and researchers supporting students of refugee background as well as promising pathways leading to positive school experiences for them in Ontario. The Bridging Multiple Worlds model (Cooper, 2014) and Intersectionality theory (Crenshaw, 1989 & 2017; Hankivsky, 2014) are central in our critical reflection. Through discussions about our experiences working with students on a yearlong 'me mapping' identity text project in a Grade 6 classroom dedicated to accelerated learning in math and language, we highlight promising practices for the successful inclusion of students with refugee experiences as well as their smooth transition between their various classrooms and other spaces in the school. As much of the literature focuses on one aspect of programming or pedagogical practice in support of refugee students, our chapter addresses the need for an integrated description of effective programming in middle school.

CONTEXT

Canada is a world leader in the resettlement of refugees welcoming over 1 088 015 refugees since 1980 (UNHCR, 2022). Many of these newcomers settle in urban centers where their children attend schools that sometimes provide specialized programs to support the specific needs of children who may have significant gaps in their education due to their pre-migration experiences as well as their migration experiences while fleeing their homeland. This chapter focuses on the Literacy Enrichment Academic Program (LEAP) in one Ontario school district which offers a specialized self-contained classroom program to support children and youth with significant educational gaps, often due to conflict and war. The program falls under the English Literacy Development (ELD) stream of programs offered by the Ontario Ministry of Education (OME, 2007) to support multilingual language learners in elementary schools from Grades 4 to 8. The OME (2016) also produced a resource guide for teachers focussed on working with students of refugee background. Students in the ELD program are usually two to four years behind in their education and have limited literacy skills in their first language and English. Class sizes are limited to approximately 14 students and are led by a teacher specialized in teaching English as an additional language (EAL). While students in the ELD program are kept together in this specialized class in the mornings, they are integrated into regular classrooms with similar-aged peers in the afternoon. During this time, students learn subjects such as Art, Science, History, Geography, Music, Health and Physical Education in an integrated classroom model. This inquiry's main objective is to understand better how students navigate these very different classroom experiences and how they move between them in the context of the school, home, and community. Our chapter provides front row seating in a middle school that welcomes students with refugee experience that allows for an immersive experience where the practices suggested in the literature come to life.

LITERATURE REVIEW

Our literature review includes four areas directly related to schools and classrooms that welcome students with refugee experiences.

The Challenges Faced by Canadian Education Systems in Effectively Meeting the Needs of Refugee Children and Youth

Schools have an essential role to play in the resettlement and integration of refugee students; however, several studies have noted the challenges faced by Canadian education systems in effectively meeting the needs of refugee children and youth (Dachyshyn & Kirova, 2011, 2011; Gagné et al., 2018; Kanu, 2008; Kovinthan Levi, 2019; Kovinthan, 2016; MacNevin, 2012; Stewart, 2017). Refugee children and youth must contend with complex issues that differentiate their experiences from other newcomer groups. A national study by Chuang et al. (2011) highlights challenges faced by refugee youth, including language acquisition, learning to fit in with peers, navigating the Canadian school system, accessing programs that support integration, adapting to Canadian norms and expectations, aggressive or delinquent behaviour, renegotiating parent-child relationships, poverty, mental health issues including post-traumatic stress, parent-child separation anxiety, strict parental discipline, racism and discrimination.

The Role of Supportive Relationships

In the face of these challenges, the role of supportive relationships (Gagné et al., 2018) and holistic or whole-school approaches that bridge home, school and community divides (Dachyshyn & Kirova, 2011; Nakeyar et al., 2018) have been identified as promising practices to create inclusive learning environments that support the wellbeing of students of refugee background and their adjustment to settling into their new home country (Nakeyar et al., 2018). In another study conducted in Canada, Barber (2021) reports that teachers working with students of refugee background recognize the central role played by listening and interaction. As such, these teachers report spending more time with refugee students, and, in many cases, with their families when they need help with processes that are new to them. Barber (2021) also explains that these teachers understand caring as their main emotional response to their refugee students and what motivates them to action. Their caring attitude sharpens teachers' ability to see what their students need, consider how best to meet these needs and then observe what is working to ensure the wellbeing of their refugee students in the classroom and school. Barber (2021) also speaks of the key role of holistic care that can be seen 'in the moment' in schools in response to trauma which refugee students may exhibit in various ways.

Promising Program Practices

Refugee students require specialised educational programs that address their unique and diverse needs; however, access to such programs is inconsistent across Canadian schools (Stewart, 2011, 2017). In their analysis of education policies related to refugee education in Canada's 13 provinces, Schutte et al. (2022) identified significant gaps and inconsistencies in five critical areas: (1) access to education, (2) accelerated education, (3) language education, (4) mental health and psychosocial support, and (5) special education. Schutte et al. (2022) recommend a bottom-up approach to improve policies for refugee education in Canada by extracting important lessons from school districts that effectively address these five components. One such program is the Calgary Board of Education's Literacy, English, and Academic Development Program (LEAD). The LEAD program serves students from grades 4-12 with limited prior schooling and literacy (Miles & Bailey-McKenna, 2016). Like its Ontario counterpart, LEAP, LEAD provides intensive English language development and math support to help children with educational gaps transition into the regular ESL program. LEAD teachers specialize in trauma-informed practices, cultural responsiveness, and instruction in English Language Development (ELD) (Miles & Bailey-McKenna, 2016). Programs like LEAP and LEAD, which provide intensive interventions at the start of a refugee student's education journey, have been effective at addressing educational gaps and fostering inclusion (Gagné et al., 2017; Miles & Bailey-McKenna, 2016; Stewart, 2017). Stewart (2011) provides student and teacher perspectives on the type of structures and programs required for the inclusion and success of refugee students at school where the need for multiple supports for the socio-emotional development of students is highlighted. Nakeyar *et al.,* (2018) echo these perspectives in their review article.

Promising Pedagogical Practices

A number of pedagogical practices have proven effective with multilingual newcomer students including translanguaging, arts-based activities, multimodal identity texts and projects that are cross-curricular and make connections to the lives of students.

The research on translanguaging pedagogy in various contexts suggest the power of viewing multilingual learners through an asset-based lens. Cenoz and Gorter (2020) explain that when teachers insist that multilingual students use only the language of the school, these students cannot easily demonstrate what they have previously acquired in other languages. They describe pedagogical translanguaging as the intentional use of instructional strategies that integrate two or more languages and aim at the development of a multilingual repertoire as well as metalinguistic and language awareness among multilingual learners. The Language Friendly School (https://languagefriendlyschool.org/) movement provides guidance and examples of how to recognize and embrace students' multilingualism and take action to give space to these languages within the school community.

Several studies (e.g., Stewart & Martin, 2018; Woodgate & Busolo, 2021) have highlighted the importance of recognizing refugee students' pre- and post-migration experiences as well as their multiple identities through an intersectional lens (Crenshaw, 2017). When teachers create opportunities for newcomer students to share their migration experiences and histories of living in other countries, it helps them adjust to their new life and contributes to their evolving sense of who they are (Feuerverger, 2011; Seidel & Rokne, 2011; Suzuki et al., 2015).

In a review of Canadian research, Ratković et al. (2017) highlight that art-based programs can foster harmony, open-mindedness and resilience while creating an atmosphere conducive to respectful negotiations between students where new relationships can grow. Stewart and Martin (2018) suggest that teachers listen to the stories of their refugee students with empathy and respect and encourage their students to tell their stories and express their emotions through dance, drama, painting and other visual arts.

Several studies with students of refugee background and their teachers in Canada (see for example, Cummins & Early, 2011; Barber & Ramsay, 2020; Gagné et al., 2021; Johnson & Kendrick, 2021; Kendrick et al., 2022) call for multimodal projects that allow for connections between curricular requirements and students' personal histories and multiple identities so as to truly reach the potential of culturally relevant pedagogy.

This chapter explores these relationships and promising pedagogical practices as well as how refugee children and youth navigate in and between their spaces of the school, home, and community.

CONCEPTUAL FRAMEWORKS

Two frameworks that guide the analysis of the primary data source, our discussions on working together with students in the ELD classroom, are the Bridging Multiple Worlds (BMW) Theory (Cooper, 2011, 2014) and Crenshaw's (2017) notion of Intersectionality. Cooper's (2011, 2014) BMW Theory maps how culturally diverse students navigate accessing resources and overcoming challenges across their worlds of family, peers, school, and community. Within these spheres, Cooper (2014) differentiates between 'cultural brokers' - individuals who provide support and resources to bridge cultural worlds and thereby reduce educational inequities - and 'gatekeepers,' who are individuals who create obstacles in newcomer children and youth's pathways to educational success. Educators, parents, peers, and community members who frequently interact with newcomer youth can be viewed as these mediators, who often fall somewhere on the spectrum between cultural brokers and gatekeepers (Cooper, 2014; Gagné et al., 2018). Cooper (2014) notes that youth's cultural brokers and gatekeepers evolve over time; thus, there is a need to map these relationships to understand better where gaps exist and ensure that newcomers have access to building relationships with cultural brokers during critical moments of academic and social challenges (Figure 1).

In researching challenges and resources and thinking about the multiple identities that immigrant youth are navigating, Cooper (2014) advocates for an intersecting (cultural, structural, social, and personal) approach to understanding the different degrees of success in newcomer youth's academic pathways to post-secondary education. For this, we draw on black feminist Kimberlé Crenshaw's (1989) work, highlighting how the various forms of inequality (race, gender, socioeconomic status, sexuality, immigrant status, etc.) experienced by an individual often operate together and magnify each other. Thus, when thinking about newcomer students, we focus on how their other identities intersect with their refugee experience or status and how this impacts their access to resources and ability to overcome challenges (Figure 2). We also consider how the multiple identities of the cultural brokers or gatekeepers in their midst might influence their experiences.

OUR METHODOLOGY - DUOETHNOGRAPHY

We use duoethnography to examine our shared experiences of working together on an identity text project with Grade 6 students in an ESL/ELD classroom for a year. First introduced by Norris and Sawyer in 2004, this dialogic research methodology allows two researchers to interrogate the cultural context of a shared experience to gain insights and new perspectives on a social issue (Breault, 2016; Sawyer & Norris, 2015). Norris and Sawyer (2004) build on Pinar's (1975) autobiographical method of 'currere,' the process of examining one's personal experience and history as curricula to uncover insights about a person's own null and hidden curriculum. The methodology aims to disrupt the single narrative point of view on any particular social issue through conversation, thereby inviting the reader to discern their own interpretation of what is taking place. In conducting our inquiry through duoethnography, we, the authors, become both the researcher and researched. Thus, we arrive at our research by understanding the limitations of our frames of reference and look to each other and the reader to help reconceptualize our interpretations. We provide some autobiographical information to highlight our convergences and divergences as duoethnographers (Figure 3).

Figure 1. Bridging Multiple Worlds Theory
Adapted from Cooper 2014

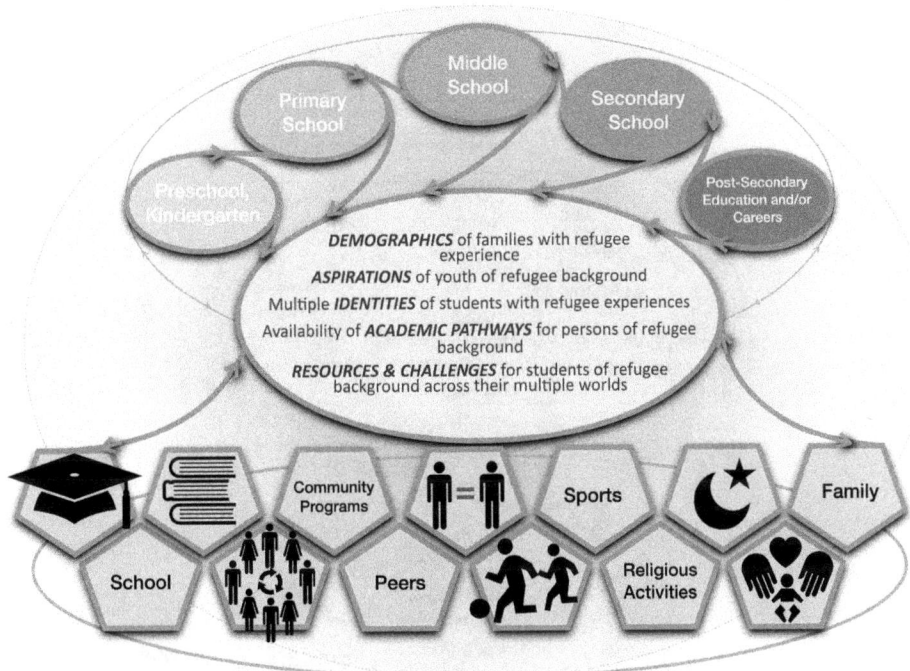

Our duoethnography was shaped by multiple conversations and opportunities for interaction since 2017 as teacher educators preparing mainstream K-12 teachers to support multilingual learners and as researchers collaborating on a study of the experiences of students of refugee backgrounds. We used Google Drive to store our videotaped conversations and to organize the background readings for this chapter. We created a folder with our drafts and wrote using different colours to highlight our contributions to each draft. By using a Google Doc draft we were able to asynchronously access our growing conversations and respond to each other.

PROCESS AND LEARNINGS

To illustrate both our process and our learnings, we offer three dialogues. The first is related to how, as educators, we can support students with refugee experiences to self-regulate, identify emotions and learn subject matter content in a safe space within the LEAP classroom. The second explores how we can create inclusive environments for students of refugee background in middle school in Canada with a particular focus on accommodating their needs and integrating them in mainstream classrooms. The final conversation explores facilitating the movement between the multiple worlds of the middle school. Each dialogue provides an opportunity to share our findings, connect to the relevant literature and weave in our conceptual frameworks.

Figure 2. Intersectionality wheel diagram
Adapted from CRIAW/ICREF Published in Everyone belongs: A toolkit for applying Intersectionality (Simpson, 2009, p.5)

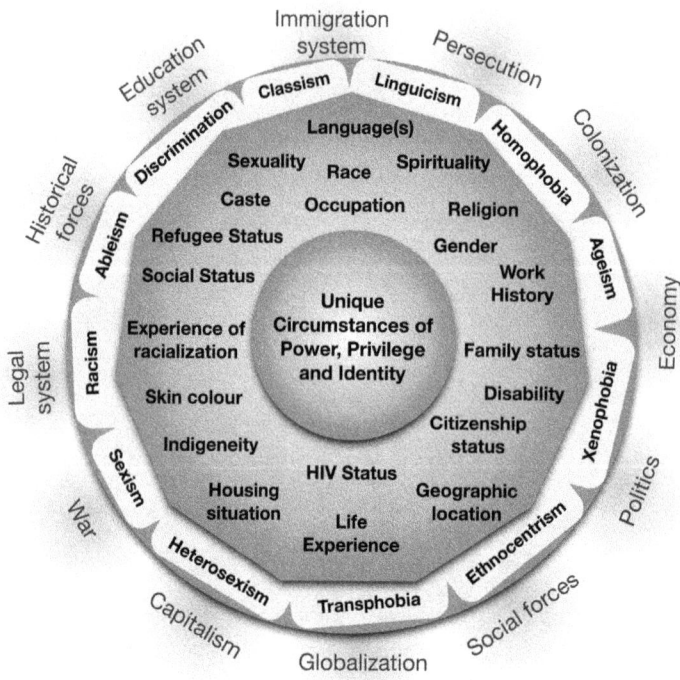

Conversation 1 - A Look Inside the Leap Classroom

Antoinette: *I was delighted when you welcomed me and my colleague Emmanuelle Le Pichon to your middle school classroom to conduct Me Mapping workshops. I really appreciated being able to visit you and your students multiple times during one school year.*

Figure 3. Our convergences and divergences as duoethnographers

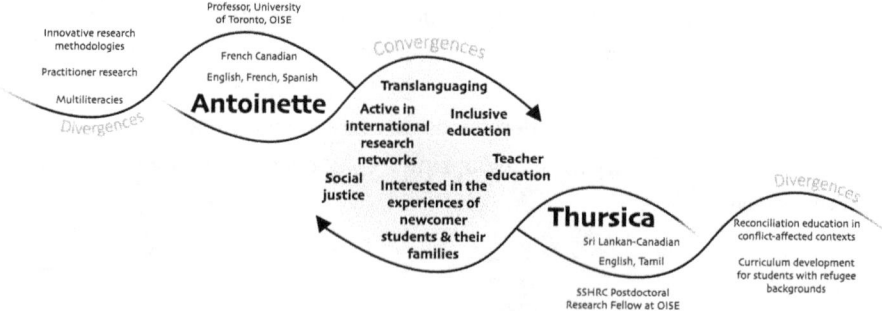

Thursica*: We appreciated having you in the class. The students enjoyed doing all the Me Mapping activities, particularly using the Flipgrid app to talk about their lives and experiences. I think they appreciated that their stories were worth telling and learning from (Kendrick et al., 2022).*

Antoinette*: I noticed how engaged and open your students are to share their stories, particularly their experiences coming to Canada and the challenges they face. It seems like they feel very safe in the classroom sharing these personal details (Stewart, 2011; Barber, 2021).*

Thursica*: Yes, many of the students are very open about their experiences while some are just beginning to tell their stories. I find that each student is on their own journey to feel safe enough to start talking about these experiences. Time plays a significant role in their level of trust with their LEAP teacher and peers (Stewart, 2011).*

Antoinette*: I recall how you and I would negotiate which topics to foreground in the identity-focussed activities we planned for our regular Me Mapping workshops with your students (Gagné et al., 2020). I would share the resources and topics available as shown in Figures 4 and 5. Then, we would plan so as to gently increase the cognitive and emotional complexity of the tasks while keeping in mind the need to gradually increase the trust level of students with each other and with us as well as the tasks.*

Figure 4. Me Mapping themes and topics

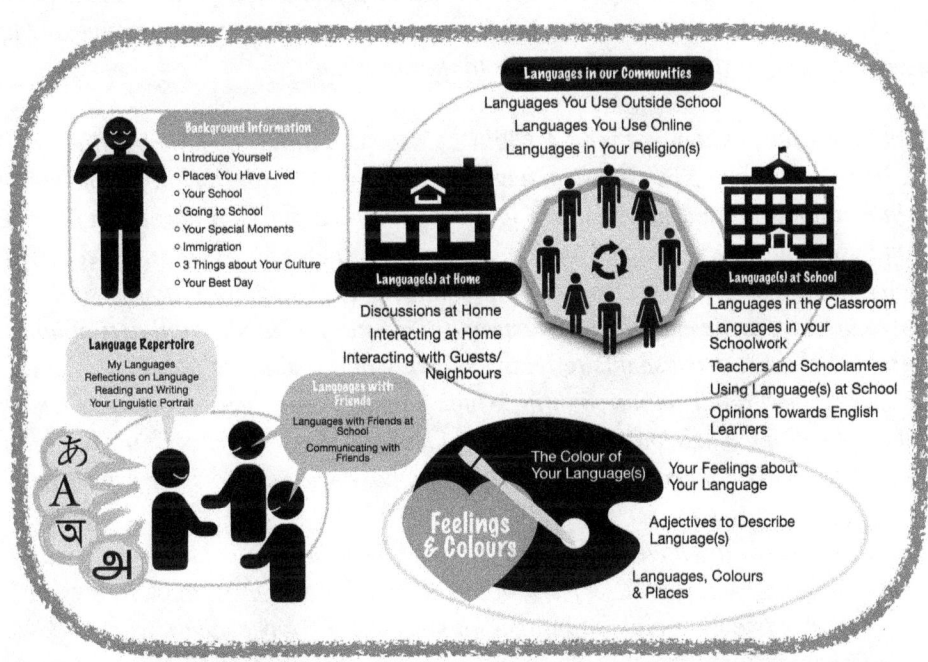

Figure 5. Two examples of prompts for Me Maps

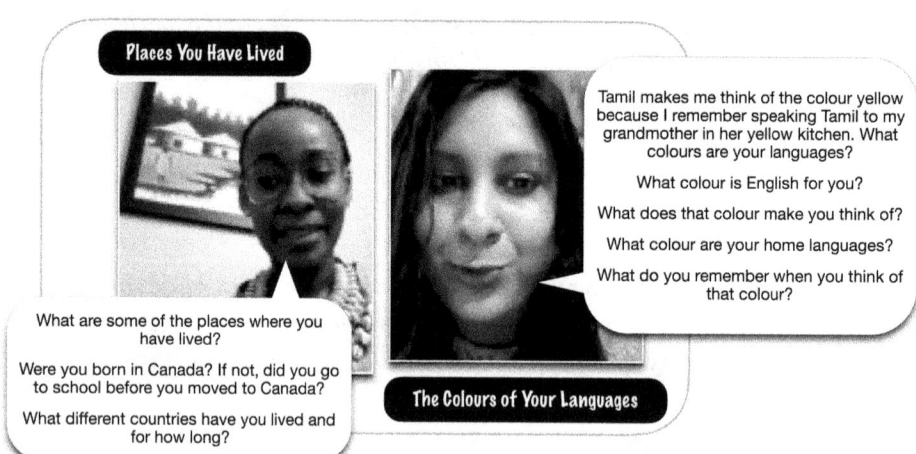

Thursica: *I typically start the school year by reading stories about newcomer journeys to normalize talking about these stories and experiences while modelling norms to help create a safe space (Stewart & Martin, 2018).*

Antoinette: *I recall your reading of a storybook during circle time one morning after which you invited the students to work in small groups to re-enact part of the story. Do you remember this book that included some illustrations of soldiers and camps? I was a bit worried about how your students might interpret part of the story as a roleplay. However, I recall that their interpretation was sensitive and appropriate with each group bringing a slightly different take to the situation.*

Thursica: *Yes I remember that day. I read A Child's Garden: A Story of Hope by Michael Foreman, a picture book. It is about a young boy living in a war-ravaged world, experiencing both war and poverty. His home is in ruin and rubble where nothing grows and barbed fences prevent him from returning to the streams and green hills he once used to visit. One day he comes across a tiny speck of green on his side of the fence that he nurtures to grow into a beautiful garden and even though soldiers eventually come and rip up his garden, he continues to nurture it. This story is about small acts of hope in the face of great adversity. I chose it because it is reflective of many of the students' experiences. Also, the book does not name or suggest a particular country, which is important when introducing a sensitive topic like this because it will not single out a particular student's experience before they are ready to tell it. Further, everyone can make connections to the story, even those who may not have experienced a conflict.*

Antoinette: *In fact, you always have a display of some of these books in your classroom. I have added some of these to the <u>Refugee Experience</u> page of <u>The Education of Students of Refugee Backgrounds</u> (https://sites.google.com/view/educationofrefugees/home) website for teachers who work with students with refugee experience. I wonder if you could suggest some other picture books that I might introduce to teachers working with newcomers.*

Thursica: *I'd be happy to as I have been growing a list of books about children and youth on the move from one country to another. One of my favourite books is When I Get Older: The Story Behind "Wavin' Flag" by Somali-Canadian artist K'naan. The book is based on Kanaan's life and his journey to Canada from Somalia. This book is more explicit on the challenges of war and migration journey. It also specifically speaks about the racism and discrimination experienced by immigrants of colour. I often read this book later in the year when I know my students better and can ensure they are ready for this content. They all experience overt racism in the school and openly naming and talking about this issue in the classroom validates their lived experiences and helps them develop strategies to confront and challenge these negative experiences (Suzuki et al., 2015).*

Antoinette: *One of your multiple identities is that you have a refugee background yourself. Do you draw on that when teaching?*

Thursica: *Yes, I came to Canada when I was six years old from war-ravaged Sri Lanka. I did not speak any English, my family was very poor, the war and sounds of bombs were fresh in my memory and I was very scared in school most of the time for those first few months. However, I had some amazing classroom and ESL teachers and even peers, who supported me through those difficult months when I first arrived. Today, whether I am teaching newcomer students in school or teaching about supporting newcomers in my work with teacher candidates, I frequently draw on and share my experience. It helps me talk about these challenging topics in a way that connects to learners (Barber, 2021).*

Antoinette: *How do your students respond to your openness?*

Thursica: *When my students see their stories mirrored in mine, it helps to normalize conversations about their journeys and trajectories as a part of their daily classroom experience. Some of the more outgoing students who have been in Canada longer start to connect with my story or the stories we have been reading, and they act as cultural brokers for their less talkative peers. They also start to share their thoughts and feelings about their journey to and in Canada. Having a peer share their story about coming to Canada in their first language is a scaffold for those who are not ready to share yet. It shows them that this is a safe space to be and share who they are and the languages they know (Cenoz & Gorter, 2020).*

Antoinette: *I notice that you use a circle for sharing time with your students and that some students seemed very familiar with the structure of how things worked, like taking turns and asking questions.*

Thursica: *Yes, this is a very intentional classroom management strategy on my part, and it takes various iterations to actualize (Stewart, 2011). When we first start sharing and talking in a large group, many students require significant support and scaffolding to actively listen to their peers speak and respond to or comment on what someone has said. As such, I begin class discussions with high structure, sitting in a circle, with my students facing each other, and using a talking stick so that everyone can take a turn to talk and be heard or pass if they are not ready to speak. It takes several months of practice for my students to be able to discuss a topic in-depth in our circle. The topics we explore include challenges in school or problems my students are having with peers inside and outside the classroom. The discussion circle is one of many examples of the highly structured aspect of the LEAP classroom (Miles & Bailey-McKenna, 2016).*

Antoinette: *It seems that many of the processes in your class include an element of learning to self-regulate. I can see how you encourage your students to monitor and manage their energy states, emotions, thoughts, and behaviors in ways that produce positive results such as well-being, loving relationships, and learning (Stewart, 2011).*

Thursica: *I do indeed guide my students in learning to deal with stressors by giving them opportunities to become more self-aware, aware of others' emotions, and filter sensory stimulation more effectively. Modelling how to deal with difficult emotions is something we work on in the classroom quite frequently. The classroom space is also set up in a way that students can get up and take a break when they need to. There is a quiet spot they can go to when they need to be alone and I encourage them to communicate if and when they are not feeling just right so that I can ensure the day's activities do not conflict with their emotional state. Facilitating this process of self-regulation really does set them up for success socially, emotionally, and academically (Nakeyar et al., 2018; Stewart, 2011; Stewart & Martin, 2018).*

Antoinette: *I think that the various visual supports in your classroom help your students in learning to self-regulate. As they are learning English, you have visuals with emotions and words so that they have easy access to the words necessary to describe their emotions. In addition, you have charts with the steps involved in various daily activities as reminders of what was expected of them. I took some photos of your LEAP classroom that I have assembled into a collage in Figure 6.*

Figure 6. Some of the wall charts in Thursica's class

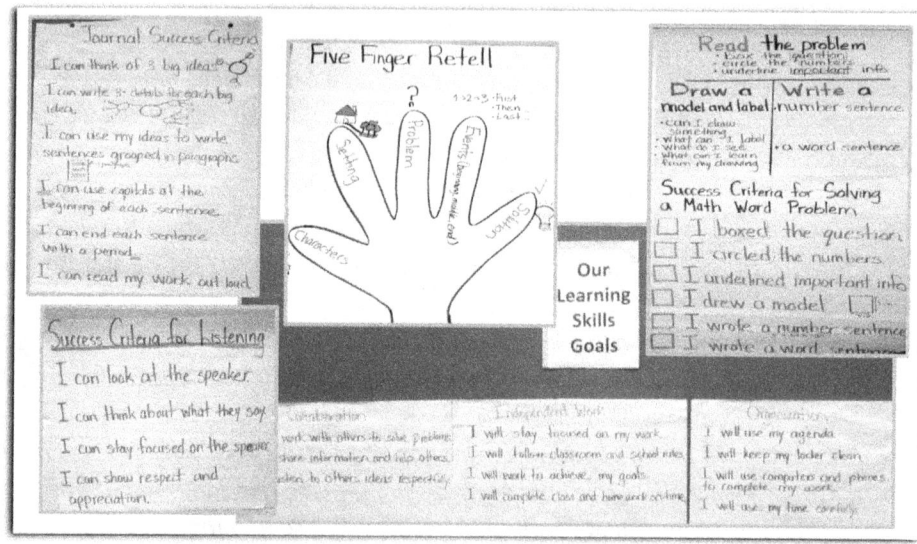

Thursica: *You are a good observer, Antoinette. My classroom is indeed a carefully designed high structure environment. If you look around, you will see a monthly and daily calendar using pictures for those learning to read and a learning outcome board for each subject that we review each day, so students understand why we are doing some of the activities we do in class. Our morning routine is the same, and*

although these are standard features of most classrooms, they are essential in the LEAP classroom. The high structure environment is to ensure that there is clarity and predictability in the students' day. They know what is coming next, giving them a sense of agency. Many students come from situations where they did not have the opportunity to attend a school or have significant breaks in their schooling. As a result, they are still learning the basic norms of schooling that teachers assume they understand, such as sitting at a desk for extended periods, going out for recess, opening and closing a locker, working in a group or with a partner, the rotary schedule, wearing a backpack, or doing homework.

Antoinette: *The half-day newcomer students spend with you is indeed very important for their wellbeing in terms of ensuring a smoother transition into the mainstream classes they take during the other half of the day.*

Thursica: *You're right. When students in the LEAP classroom see their peers in their mainstream classroom going about these new activities, many feel a sense of helplessness because they are not yet familiar with these routines, the school world feels unpredictable, and they are often in reactive mode. The purpose of the LEAP program and my role is to help them slowly transition out of this reactive mode. A balance must be struck between supporting students to self-regulate their own behaviour through these highly structured classroom routines and spaces, something they desperately need when they first arrive, while still honouring students' voices in the classroom. I have learned that student input is critical for developing the routines that are put into place, and they must be negotiated and constantly renegotiated democratically, as students' needs change over the school year. Student self-regulation is supported by giving up a certain level of control that teachers are used to. For example, my students will often have long conversations in their various home languages during learning tasks; I often have no idea what they are saying but they know that I know they are on task and that I trust them (Cenoz & Gorter, 2020). They have also learned to switch to English when they have to explain their thinking to a peer in the group who does not speak their first language. The peer in turn has developed the skill to be okay with someone in the group switching to a language they may not understand because they know it will be soon explained in English or their own first language (Cenoz & Gorter, 2020). This form of communication takes time and a great deal of scaffolding, on the part of the teacher, to develop in the classroom.*

Antoinette: *I think this is why your students are so responsive and open to creating 'me maps'. They are excited that we are genuinely interested in learning who they are. There are several research teams (e.g., Ratković et al., 2017; Woodgate & Busolo, 2021) who highlight the importance for teachers to learn more about their students' backgrounds and pre-migration and post-migration experiences as well as their multiple identities through an intersectional lens (Crenshaw, 2017). A number of research teams working with refugee students and their teachers, (e.g., Barber & Ramsay, 2020; Cummins & Early, 2011; Gagné et al. 2021; Johnson & Kendrick, 2021; Kendrick et al., 2022; Stewart & Martin, 2018) recommend multimodal projects where students can make connections between their histories and identities and particular aspects of the curriculum.*

Thursica: *I learned a lot about my students from their me maps. In fact, it gave me a much better sense of their migration trajectories and their experiences in their multiple worlds of home, school and community. I am also thrilled that some of my students' Me Maps are featured on the <u>Me Mapping with</u>*

Multilingual Learners (*https://sites.google.com/view/memapping/home*) website *so that preservice and inservice teachers can learn more about the multifaceted lives of newcomer students.*

Conversation 2 - Looking Beyond the Leap Classroom

Antoinette: *In your school district, the preferred program model for newcomer students with gaps in their schooling before their arrival in middle school is one that combines a half-day in a stand-alone class referred to as a LEAP class and a half-day in mainstream classes.*

Thursica: *That's right! The 'integration' component of this program is essential for newcomer students because it is where they get to interact with similar-aged peers and experience what a mainstream classroom is like. In the afternoon, my students experience a rotary system where they move to a different classroom for each subject including Science and Technology, French, Music, Health and Physical Education, and Art. In this model the subject teachers are to provide modifications and accommodations for each LEAP class student based on their individual needs so as to set them up for success.*

Antoinette: *I understand that one of the roles of mainstream teachers is to modify the curriculum and make accommodations for LEAP students as necessary (Ontario Ministry of Education, 2008, 2016). Can you tell me how this actually happens?*

Thursica: *Sure, I can. First, it is important to note that this model only works well under certain conditions. There is an assumption in the LEAP model that all mainstream classroom or subject teachers have the knowledge, resources, and time to put in place all the appropriate modifications and accommodations for each LEAP student, in addition to creating an inclusive classroom space for multilingual language learners (MLLs). However, we know that not all teachers have been given the opportunity and time to learn the knowledge needed to modify the curriculum and make appropriate accommodations (Kovinthan Levi, 2019).*

Antoinette: *I imagine that teachers who completed their teaching certification after 2015 when the Ontario Ministry of Education mandated that there be a module focussed on supporting K-12 MLLs and another to support students with special learning needs in teacher education programs, would be better prepared to include LEAP students in their mainstream classes (Ontario College of Teachers, 2017).*

Thursica: *It is quite a shift in thinking and practice for teachers who have not taken coursework focussed on including newcomers. Sometimes my students come to me in a state of panic or in tears because they cannot complete an assignment in one of their rotary subjects. When I try to assist them, I can see that the expectations of the assignment are far beyond what the student can do at their stage in language development and background knowledge in the particular subject. Usually, a quick conversation with the subject area teacher is all it takes for the teacher to modify the assignment to make it accessible and 'doable'.*

Antoinette: *It is great to hear that the rotary teachers are so open to making these adjustments in collaboration with you.*

Thursica*: Typically, after one or two conversations about how to modify assignments and activities, I see that the rotary teachers are automatically making appropriate modifications for other assignments.*

Antoinette: *My experience is that teachers want and are willing to learn and make changes if they are supported in doing so. Time, resources, and opportunities to learn about how to support MLLs, particularly students with gaps in their education, are needed to get all teachers on board in creating an inclusive learning environment for newcomers and LEAP students in particular. In fact, nearly every article on the education of students with refugee experiences call for specialized coursework, modules and workshops for all preservice and inservice teachers because of the increasing number of newcomer students in schools (see for example, Barber, 2021; Walker & Zuberi, 2020).*

Thursica*: I agree that these would be good steps in the right direction. The mechanical aspects of teaching, such as modifying an assignment or curriculum expectations, are undoubtedly essential, but there is much more to providing an inclusive and safe learning environment for newcomer students. It also depends on a teacher's openness to accepting and integrating new approaches to teaching and learning to make the ideological shift about how learning can happen in the classroom (MacNevin, 2012).*

Antoinette: *One of the most significant changes in recent years is a shift to translanguaging away from English-only policies in the classroom. Cenoz and Gorter (2020) suggest that teachers intentionally adopt instructional strategies that integrate or allow for the use of two or more languages to support the development of a multilingual repertoire and increased language awareness among multilingual learners. Cummins (2021) describes another potential benefit of translanguaging pedagogy as it can encourage students of refugee background to challenge societal power relations that position them as less powerful because their first language is not English. As you can imagine, it can be difficult for long-time teachers to move in new directions and embrace translanguaging pedagogy because they have become very adept at implementing English-only practices in their classrooms.*

Thursica: *In fact, translanguaging practices have been very slow to trickle down into middle school classrooms. For example, something as simple as allowing students to use their first language to learn and show their understanding is still a foreign concept to some teachers. More problematic, there is resistance to these types of approaches because they challenge the status quo of English dominance. I have been fortunate to work in schools, often urban and highly diverse, where multilingual and translanguaging practices are the norm and I think this has to do with strong leadership from administrators on this issue and colleagues who are open and ready to do what they can to support their students. However, I still hear, particularly from my teacher candidates working in less diverse schools, about teachers telling their students not to use their first language in class because they believe it will prevent them from learning English. This is very frustrating to hear given that the Ontario Ministry of Education (2007) and school boards policies have long acknowledged that English-only approaches can slow students' progress, are discriminatory and hurtful to students.*

Antoinette*: What kind of professional development (PD) is offered, if any, on how to work with MLLs?*

Thursica*: The teachers at my school and in schools with high numbers of MLLs get some training and support on promising practices to accommodate refugee students' learning needs, including guidelines* *to modify the curriculum. In fact, the school administrator is very supportive and takes an active role in ensuring that resources and training are provided. There are several full-time ESL teachers on staff, including one who is responsible for providing leadership and support for mainstream classroom teachers.*

Antoinette: *Does this PD help?*

Thursica: *Yes. I noticed that many mainstream/rotary teachers are starting to encourage students to write in their first language, provide shorter assignments, and collaborate with me as a LEAP teacher as well as with other ESL teachers to co-plan units. However, I think more time and resources are needed to standardize this practice for all teachers in the school as well as familiarize them with some of the challenges that students with refugee experiences have with day-to-day classroom norms. Not understanding these challenges has resulted in students coming to me saying that they were yelled at by a teacher because they were not able to remain seated for the entire class period or follow instructions. Classroom teachers also need support to become familiar with board policies around assessment, in some cases, they will fail a student not knowing that students on modified programs can not be failed.*

Antoinette*: I see how some teachers acted as cultural brokers who supported students with refugee backgrounds while others were gatekeepers who knowingly or unknowingly limited the success of these students (Cooper 2014). The role teachers adopt seems related to their knowledge of the refugee experience as well as their willingness to learn more about their students of refugee background and the strategies to support them.*

Thursica: *So, yes, time, resources, and PD make a difference, but other ideological factors also need to be addressed to ensure that all teachers can provide inclusive learning environments in the integrated model (Parhar & Sensoy, 2011).*

Conversation 3 - Facilitating the Movement of Leap Students Between the Multiples Worlds of the School

Thursica*: The school space is as important as the classroom space in creating an inclusive and welcoming learning environment for students with refugee experiences. My school has a variety of supports in place to support newcomer students and their families, and some of these supports are particularly helpful for LEAP students and their families (Stewart, 2011). Some examples include the free hot breakfast program, the availability of interpreters during interviews with families, a settlement worker who comes by the school frequently and daily announcements in different languages that reflect the students' home languages.*

Antoinette: *I can imagine how these programs, people and initiatives create a school space that is welcoming for students with refugee experience.*

Thursica: *Teachers also play an essential role in connecting students to the right resources and programs that can make a big difference in how integrated a new student feels. Many of the students in the LEAP program view the library as a safe space, primarily due to the amazing work of our librarian who welcomes students in LEAP to volunteer as library helpers to put away books after school or during lunch.*

Antoinette*: This sounds like a great initiative! Were your students excited about their work in the library?*

Thursica: *Many of my students are still learning to read in English while others are becoming familiar with the alphabet. The librarian works closely with the students throughout the year as they learn to check books in and out, put books away, and help with other tasks in the library. She makes them accountable and speaks to them about responsibility when they miss their shift. The experience gives students with a refugee background a sense of agency, ownership, and place in the school because they are seen as contributors by their teachers and peers.*

Antoinette*: What does your librarian do to support your students' movement out of the safety of the LEAP classroom and into a common school space like the library?*

Thursica*: I think our librarian sees my students as more than just the "ESL students" or "LEAP kids" or "the ones who cannot speak English or read." She sees them as capable individuals who can participate and contribute with a little extra support. Further, when other students and teachers come into the library, the students from the LEAP classroom assist them to check out books, which puts them in a position of providing rather than receiving help.*

Antoinette: *Teachers can facilitate the movement of students with refugee experiences in school and community spaces when they adopt an asset-based perspective and view these students as capable individuals who need a little extra support and guidance to participate and contribute to the life of the school (Stewart, 2011). What else do you see mainstream classroom teachers do to support students from the LEAP program?*

Thursica*: Sometimes this extra support is as simple as a teacher connecting a newly arrived student with a peer who speaks the same language. The students in the LEAP program who enjoy their afternoon classes are typically those who have a friend who speaks the same first language in their afternoon classes (Cenoz & Gorter, 2020); these peers act as important cultural brokers because they help students with refugee experiences navigate the complex social and academic terrain of the middle school environment (Cooper, 2014). Whether it be getting to their first-afternoon class from the lunch room or making sure they go to their locker and get the correct books, a reliable peer can really scaffold the complex transitions in a middle school environment.*

Antoinette*: It seems that when a newly arrived student in the LEAP program can establish strong friendships with peers who speak the same first language, their experience in school is significantly better.*

Thursica*: That's right. However, it can take time for these friendships to develop. Although my LEAP students typically look out for each other when they leave the LEAP classroom at the end of the morning, I find it difficult to see some of my most recently arrived students walk down the hallway to lunch as I know they do not know the school routines yet or feel safe.*

Antoinette*: Tell me more about what you worry about for your students when they leave the LEAP classroom?*

Thursica: *I think about whether her teachers and peers will see her, acknowledge her, and understand what she is going through. Some of this fear and worry is connected to my own experience as a refugee child in the public school system, not being seen or understood, having to hide who I was, what I saw or experienced. There is a sense of loneliness that comes with being a refugee because you often think you are the only one who has gone through what you have experienced (Kovinthan, 2016).*

Antoinette: *I guess that is why sharing stories about children and their journeys as refugees is so important (Kendrick et al., 2022).*

Thursica: *Exactly. I want my students to know these challenges are not unique to them and that the experiences are temporary. I also worry because I know that refugee students experience various forms of discrimination within the school and community from educators and peers.*

Antoinette: *This is too true. There are several studies that document the high number of refugees who experience discrimination because of their race, economic status, language skills, social status, ethnic affiliation, geographic location in the host country or level of acculturation (Mercier-Dalphond & Helly, 2021; Walker & Zuberi 2020). It would seem that every person's experiences discrimination differently.*

Thursisca: *Yes, for example, the only Black student in the class experienced higher levels of violence and social exclusion from the mainstream students, and sometimes from his LEAP peers, than the other students in the LEAP program. To mitigate this as much as possible, I often make sure I stand in the hallway during transitions and locker times to ensure that this student is safe and gets to his next class. We also had discussions about anti-black racism in the class after a race related conflict in school.*

Antoinette: *I also wonder about the nature of the connection between the families of your students of refugee background and the school. Are there any initiatives to facilitate this?*

Thursica: *When a new student arrives in the LEAP program, we often get a chance to meet the parents/ families when they first visit the school and the LEAP class. The school has a great welcoming program for newcomers that brings together the lead ESL teacher, the settlement worker, and translators and even sometimes the Canadian sponsors of the refugee families. A collaborative approach to welcoming families to the school sets the stage for positive and trusting relationships with parents. The parents/ families and students see the classroom and meet their peers and me. When I meet the parents, I often see in their eyes both a sense of fear for their child entering a new school and relief that their child will be getting some extra support and be placed in a smaller classroom. That look is very familiar to me because I saw it in my mother's tearful eyes the first few times she dropped me off at my new Canadian school in Grade 1.*

Antoinette: *It is generally agreed that communication with parents throughout the year is crucial for setting up students to succeed (Gagné, 2007).*

Thursica: *Yes, you're right. The more I can learn about a student, socially and academically, the better I can support them in the classroom, which requires ongoing conversations with parents (Nakeyar et al., 2018). Also, once a learning plan is in place, having the parents support the development of basic* routines such as reading at home a few minutes every day or getting used to signing their child's agenda, can go a long way in supporting the integration process. Moreover, in Ontario, we have an excellent phone communication tool that offers translation services in almost any language during the day, so there is no language barrier when communicating with newcomer families.

Antoinette: It seems like you are coming at inclusion from various directions, colleagues, peers, parents etc...A lot of this work goes beyond the curriculum and classroom. What challenges do you face as a LEAP teacher in pulling together all these pieces in a typical day to ensure your students' success?

Thursica: Aside from feeling very busy, which I think most teachers experience, there is an emotional strain to doing this work well. Moreover, I can never do it as well as I want to because the needs of the students are high and constantly changing. A LEAP teacher has to teach the curriculum but also be mindful of the complex experiences of the students in the classroom.

Antoinette: Aside from the typical social and emotional challenges in the middle school years, many of the students of the LEAP classroom and their families have undergone traumatic experiences and continue to live in very precarious situations at home, be it related to immigration status, finance, housing, family members who are still back home in conflict zones and so on (Dachyshyn & Kirova, 2011; Kanu, 2008; Nakeyar et al., 2018; Stewart, 2011; Woodgate & Busolo, 2021).

Thursica: These issues impact my students who come to school with 'big' feelings which sometimes manifest in challenging ways, be it misbehaviour or long periods of silence and withdrawal. However, one of the most prominent emotional strains of being a LEAP teacher is not related to all the things that I have to do or deal with to support my students, rather it is how I feel about what I cannot do - I am not an immigration officer or the housing authority. There are some issues that I cannot fix, but I can support my students in learning to cope with these challenges.

Antoinette: You embody the 'caring' teacher that Barber (2021) describes in her recent study. Barber found that educators working with students of refugee background understood caring as their central emotional response towards their students which enabled them to meet their complex needs and work to ensure their wellbeing. Barber (2021) also describes the importance of holistic care in schools where it is often necessary to respond 'in the moment' to trauma which students of refugee background may experience in various ways.

CONCLUSION

We conclude by revisiting our conceptual lenses and describing the implications for teachers who work with children and youth of refugee backgrounds. We have also reimagined our two original lenses as one integrated lens (see Figure 6) to understand how students with refugee experiences can navigate the multiple spaces of the school with the assistance of multiple cultural brokers.

Figure 7. Our integrated lens

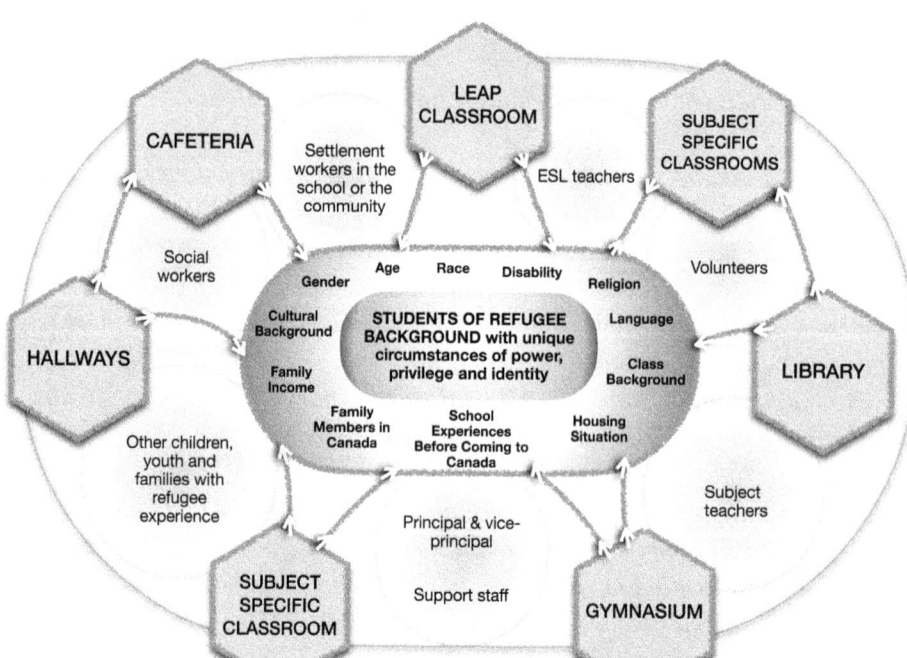

Teachers are critical catalysts and need to become cultural brokers (Cooper, 2014) in the integration of students with refugee backgrounds at school. Most of their responsibilities should cluster around 1) pooling together resources to support refugee students and their families, 2) adapting curriculum resources to help students reach learning goals, 3) helping their students learn to self-regulate and get involved in shaping their learning journey, 4) creating an inclusive classroom and school culture by working with other teachers, 5) building bridges between home and school cultures, and 6) supporting students in learning about life in Canada.

Promising pathways and practices for the integration of student with refugee backgrounds include 1) working towards the greater interconnectedness of service and referrals between welcome centres, schools and service organizations, 2) knowledge exchange surrounding different education pathways and practices and the opportunities afforded by these for the integration of students with refugee experiences, 3) individually tailored educational support and services, and 4) translanguaging pedagogy.

It is important to keep in mind the various aspects of the multiple identities of educators and students of refugee background. Identity markers such as language, schooling background, SES, cultural background, refugee status, age, religion, gender, and the myriad other identitary features should be carefully considered by educators and settlement workers when providing assistance or interventions with children and youth of refugee background. The multiple identities of the professionals providing support to refugees also need to be considered in understanding why some pathways and practices are more promising than others.

Subject teachers, ESL teachers, settlement workers in schools and the community, social workers, support staff, volunteers as well as other children, youth and families with refugee experience can become cultural brokers to facilitate the transition of LEAP students through the multiple school 'worlds' they inhabit. Together with the necessary material resources such as funding, space, teaching resources, the potential cultural brokers can create a truly welcoming and inclusive school where students with refugee backgrounds can thrive.

REFERENCES

Barber, S. (2021). Achieving holistic care for refugees: The experiences of educators and other stakeholders in Surrey and Greater Vancouver, Canada. *British Educational Research Journal, 47*(4), 959–983. doi:10.1002/berj.3730

Barber, S., & Ramsay, L. (2020), Literally speechless? Refugees to Canada overcome preliteracy and trauma through a literacy of the heart. *English 4-11 online article.* https://englishassociation.ac.uk/wp-content/uploads/2019/07/Barber-and-Ramsay-Sept-2020-1.pdf

Breault, R. A. (2016). Emerging issues in duoethnography. *International Journal of Qualitative Studies in Education: QSE, 29*(6), 777–794. doi:10.1080/09518398.2016.1162866

Cenoz, J., & Gorter, D. (2020). Teaching English through pedagogical translanguaging. *Special Issue: World Englishes and Translanguaging, 39*(2), 300–311.

Chuang, S., Rasmi, S., & Friesen, C. (2011). Service Providers' Perspectives on the Pathways of Adjustment for Newcomer Children and Youth in Canada. In S. S. Chuang & R. P. Moreno (Eds.), *Immigrant children: Change, adaptation, and cultural transformation* (pp. 149–170). Lexington Books.

Cooper, C. R. (2011). *Bridging multiple worlds: Cultures, identities, and pathways to college.* Oxford University Press. doi:10.1093/acprof:oso/9780195080209.001.0001

Cooper, C. R. (2014). Cultural brokers: How immigrant youth in multicultural societies navigate and negotiate their pathways to college identities. *Learning, Culture and Social Interaction, 3*(2), 170–176. doi:10.1016/j.lcsi.2013.12.005

Crenshaw, K. (1989). Demarginalizing the intersection of race and sex: A Black feminist critique of antidiscrimination doctrine, feminist theory and antiracist politics. *University of Chicago Legal Forum, 1989*(1). https://chicagounbound.uchicago.edu/uclf/vol1989/iss1/8

Crenshaw, K. (2017). *On intersectionality: Essential writings.* The New Press.

Cummins, J. (2021). *Rethinking the education of multilingual learners: A critical analysis of theoretical concepts.* Bristol, Blue Ridge Summit: Multilingual Matters. https://doi-org.myaccess.library.utoronto.ca/10.21832/9781800413597

Cummins, J., & Early, M. (2011). *Identity texts: The collaborative creation of power in multilingual schools.* Trentham Books.

Dachyshyn, D., & Kirova, A. (2011). Classroom challenges in developing an intercultural early learning program for refugee children. *The Alberta Journal of Educational Research, 57*(2), 220–233.

Feuerverger, G. (2011). Re-Bordering spaces of trauma: Auto-ethnographic reflections on the immigrant and refugee experience in an inner-city high school in Toronto. *International Review of Education*, *57*(3-4), 357–375. http://dx.doi.org.proxy.bib.uottawa.ca/10.1007/s11159-011-9207-y. doi:10.100711159-011-9207-y

Foreman, M. (2009). *A child's garden: A story of hope*. Candlewick Press.

Gagné, A. (Ed.). (2007). *Growing new roots: The voices of immigrant families and the teachers of their children. Resource book for educators and immigrant families*. OISE/UT., https://wordpress.oise.utoronto.ca/diversityinteaching/wp-content/uploads/sites/24/2012/11/VIF_ResBook.pdf

Gagné, A., Al-Hashimi, N., Little, M., Lowen, M., & Sidhu, A. (2018). Educator perspectives on the social and academic integration of Syrian refugees in Canada. *Journal of Family Diversity in Education*, *3*(1), 48–76. doi:10.53956/jfde.2018.124

Gagné, A., Schmidt, C., & Markus, P. (2017). Teaching about refugees: Developing culturally responsive educators in contexts of politicised transnationalism. *Intercultural Education*, *28*(5), 429–446. doi:10.1080/14675986.2017.1336409

Gagné, A., Wattar, D., & Rajendram, S. (2020), *Me Mapping activities: A guide for teachers*. Supporting English Learners (SEL) & Supporting the Academic and Social Integration of Children and Youth of Refugee Backgrounds (SAIRCY) Projects, Ontario Institute for Studies in Education, University of Toronto, Canada. https://sites.google.com/view/memapping/guides-for-teachers/full-activity-guides

Hankivsky, O. (2014). Rethinking care ethics: On the promise and potential of an intersectional analysis. *The American Political Science Review*, *108*(2), 252–264. doi:10.1017/S0003055414000094

Johnson, L., & Kendrick, M. (2021). Digital storytelling: Opportunities for identity investment for youth from refugee backgrounds. In L. Green, D. Holloway, K. Stevenson, T. Leaver, & L. Haddon (Eds.), *Routledge Companion to Digital Media and Children* (pp. 469–479). Routledge.

K'naan & Guy. S. (2012). When I get older: The story behind "Wavin' Flag." Tundra Books.

Kanu, Y. (2008). Educational needs and barriers for African refugee students in Manitoba. *Canadian Journal of Education*, *31*(4), 915–940.

Kendrick, M., Early, M., Michalovich, A., & Mangat, M. (2022). Digital storytelling with refugee background youth: Possibilities for language and digital literacies learning. *TESOL Quarterly*, *56*(3), 961–984. doi:10.1002/tesq.3146

Kovinthan, T. (2016). Learning and teaching with loss: Meeting the needs of refugee children through narrative inquiry. *Diaspora, Indigenous, and Minority Education*, *10*(3), 141–155. http://dx.doi.org.proxy.bib.uottawa.ca/10.1080/15595692.2015.1137282. doi:10.1080/15595692.2015.1137282

Kovinthan Levi, T. (2019). Preparing pre-service teachers to support children with refugee experiences. *The Alberta Journal of Educational Research*, *65*(4), 285–304.

MacNevin, J. (2012). Learning the way: Teaching and learning with and for youth from refugee backgrounds on Prince Edward Island. *Canadian Journal of Education, 35*(3), 48–63.

Me Mapping with Multilingual Learners. (n.d.) https://sites.google.com/view/memapping

Mercier-Dalphond, G., & Helly, D. (2021). Anti-Muslim violence, hate crime, and victimization in Canada: A study of five Canadian cities. *Canadian Ethnic Studies, 53*(1), 1–22. doi:10.1353/ces.2021.0000

Miles, J., & Bailey-McKenna, M.-C. (2016). Giving refugee students a strong head start: The LEAD program. *TESL Canada Journal, 33*, 109–128.

Nakeyar, C., Esses, V., & Reid, G. J. (2018). The psychosocial needs of refugee children and youth and best practices for filling these needs: A systematic review. *Clinical Child Psychology and Psychiatry, 23*(2), 186–208. doi:10.1177/1359104517742188 PMID:29207880

Norris, J., & Sawyer, R. (2004). Null and hidden curricula of sexual orientation: A dialogue on the curreres of the absent presence and the present absence. In L. Coia, M. Birch, N. J. Brooks, E. Heilman, S. Mayer, A. Mountain, & P. Pritchard (Eds.), *Democratic responses in an era of standardization* (pp. 139–159). Educator's International Press, Inc.

Ontario College of Teachers. (2017). *Accreditation resource guide*. OCT. https://www.oct.ca/-/media/PDF/Accreditation%20Resource%20Gu ide/Accreditation_Resource_Guide_EN_WEB.pdf

Ontario Ministry of Education. (2007). *English language learners - ESL and ELD programs and services - Policies and procedures for Ontario elementary and secondary schools, Kindergarten to Grade 12*. OME. https://www.edu.gov.on.ca/eng/document/esleldprograms/esleldprograms.pdf

Ontario Ministry of Education. (2008). *Supporting English language learners with limited prior schooling: A practical guide for Ontario educators - Grades 3 to 12*. OME. https://www.edu.gov.on.ca/eng/ document/manyroots/ELL_LPS.pdf

Ontario Ministry of Education. (2016). Supporting students with refugee backgrounds: A framework for responsive practice. *Capacity Building Series, Special Edition #45*. https://drive.google.com/file/d/1HBR_60cUuTX1sWZN-qhMMPF8MP8 i_zmF/view

Parhar, N., & Sensoy, Ö. (2011). Culturally relevant pedagogy redux: Canadian teachers' conceptions of their work and its challenges. *Canadian Journal of Education / Revue Canadienne de l'éducation, 34*(2), 189-218.

Pinar, W. F. (1975). *Curriculum theorizing: The reconceptualists*. McCutchan Pub. Corp.

Ratković, S., Kovačević, D., Brewer, C., Ellis, C., Ahmed, N., & Baptiste-Brady, J. (2017), *Supporting refugee students in Canada: Building on what we have learned in the past 20 Years*. https://torontolip.com/wp-content/uploads/2021/03/Supporting -Refugee-Students-in-Canada-Report.pdf

Sawyer, R., & Norris, J. (2015). Duoethnography: A retrospective 10 years after. *International Review of Qualitative Research, 8*(1), 1–4. https://doi-org.myaccess.library.utoronto.ca/10.1525/irqr.2015.8.1.1. doi:10.1525/irqr.2015.8.1.1

Schutte, V., Milley, P., & Dulude, E. (2022). The (in)coherence of Canadian refugee education policy with the United Nations'. *Education Policy Analysis Archives, 30*(39–41), 1–59. doi:10.14507/epaa.30.6887

Seidel, J., & Rokne, A. (2011). Picture books for engaging peace and social justice with children. *Diaspora, Indigenous, and Minority Education, 5*(4), 245–259. doi:10.1080/15595692.2011.606007

Simpson, J. (2009). *Everyone belongs: A toolkit for applying intersectionality.* Canadian Research Institute for the Advancement of Women (CRIAW). https://also-chicago.org/also_site/wp-content/uploads/2017/03/Everyone_Belongs-A-toolkit-for-applying-intersectionality.pdf

Stewart, J. (2011). *Supporting refugee children: Strategies for educators.* University of Toronto Press.

Stewart, J. (2017). A culture of care and compassion for refugee students. *Ed-Can Network.* https://www.edcan.ca/articles/a-culture-of-care-and-compassion-for-refugee-students/

Stewart, J., & Martin, L. (2018), *Bridging two worlds: Supporting newcomer and refugee youth. A guide to curriculum implementation and integration.* Toronto: CERIC. Canadian Education and Research Institute for Counselling (CERIC). https://ceric.ca/resource/bridging-two-worlds-supporting-newcomer-refugee-youth/

Suzuki, T., Huss, J., Fiehn, B., & Spencer, R. M. (2015). Realities of war: Using picture books to teach the social effects of armed conflicts. *Multicultural Education, 22*, 54–58.

The Education of Students with Refugee Backgrounds. (n.d). https://sites.google.com/view/educationofrefugees/home

The Refugee Experience. (n.d.) https://sites.google.com/view/educationofrefugees/refugee-experience

Walker, J., & Zuberi, D. (2020). School-aged Syrian refugees resettling in Canada: Mitigating the effect of pre-migration trauma and post-migration discrimination on academic achievement and psychological well-being. *Journal of International Migration and Integration, 21*(2), 397–411. doi:10.100712134-019-00665-0

Woodgate, R., & Busolo, D. S. (2021). African refugee youth's experiences of navigating different cultures in Canada: A "push and pull" experience. *International Journal of Environmental Research and Public Health, 18*(4), 2063. doi:10.3390/ijerph18042063 PMID:33672518

Chapter 5
The Social Exclusion Problems of Children Under Protection in School Life

Selvinaz Saçan

https://orcid.org/0000-0002-6894-4118

Aydın Adnan Menderes University, Turkey

Serap Öztürk

Ministry of Family and Social Policies, Turkey

ABSTRACT

Children enter the child protection system as a result of neglect or abuse. Due to their past experiences, these children's academic and social-emotional skills lag behind their peers. This situation can result in social exclusion, academic failure, absenteeism, and dropping out of school. The school stands out with its supportive value for children in the child protection system. However, in cases where school personnel do not have sufficient information about the child protection system, policies, and the characteristics of these children, the school cannot fulfill its protective-preventive and supportive role. However, a positive school experience has a protective, preventive, developing, and curative potential, especially for at-risk children.

INTRODUCTION

Children may be deprived of family care and are in the child protection system for many reasons such as migration, poverty, family conflicts, death of parents, parents' mental and psychological problems, neglect, and child abuse. Children who benefit from child protection system support and services encounter two forms of labeling and exclusion. The first of these is the social and emotional problems experienced by children due to neglect and abuse, and the other is society's dogmatic approach to this topic. Both society and the children approach each other with mutual feelings of distrust. Society is reluctant to open its

DOI: 10.4018/978-1-6684-6386-4.ch005

arms to these children, who are similarly reluctant and distrustful when it comes to participating in and adapting to society because they could not undergo an adequate process of socialization (Kalaycı, 2007).

Children in the child protection system are excluded from many social areas and may try to hide themselves based on their previous experiences. For example, some children avoid telling their school friends or teachers that they are in the child protection system. However, it is hard to keep this a secret. They need institutional permission for specific events such as visiting a friend's house, inviting a friend home, contributing to the school website, etc. Children in the child protection system have to cope with social value judgments on their own, and they also experience individual difficulties due to their current situation (Erol, 2004; Montserrat, 2014). The media also plays an essential role in forming these value judgments. The way these children's experiences are reported in the media may contain labeling and unethical elements. The media's insensitivity makes it inevitable that these children are going to face discrimination and exclusion.

Publications about children in need of protection provide a wide range of information about the general characteristics of these children, the reasons for protecting them, the problems they face, child protection systems, and care practices. However, the school life of these children, particularly the social exclusion problems they experience at school, is not given the same amount of coverage. Upon review of the literature on social exclusion problems at school, it was seen that the exclusion problems faced by children with special needs and poor family children were emphasized, though the social exclusion problems experienced by children under protection at school are again not covered to the same extent. This section aims to explain

- the general characteristics of children under protection,
- the reasons for their protection,
- the current situation regarding this topic,
- social exclusion from a developmental perspective, and
- social exclusion at school.

BACKGROUND

It is known that children who need child protection services and support mostly come from the disadvantaged or marginalized regions of the country or territory where they live (Waldock, 2019), and children who have been neglected and abused have lower cognitive, language, social, literacy, and mathematical skills than their peers. This can cause problems in terms of school attendance and academic achievement, and can sometimes lead to truancy, dropping out, and delinquency.

School is one of the most critical social institutions after the family. Considering that children spend a significant part of their time at school, the importance of school and teachers cannot be overstated. For children who cannot find enough attention and support in their families, the school takes on the role of "listener" and "valuer." Schools not only support children's academic skills but also their social development and their acquisition of prosocial attitudes and behaviors. through trusted teachers who are positive role models, while helping them discover themselves and the world. Schools are a natural environment in which to monitor students' daily behavior and detect potential risks early. The positive effect of education is that it protects young people against threats by providing a sense of social belonging and leisure activities. It also has the role of providing resources to disadvantaged neighborhoods that lack resources. In short, a positive school experience has the potential to protect, prevent, and improve, and this is particularly valid for risk group children (Gilligan, 1998).

The literature contains conflicting results regarding not only what teachers know about child protection policies but also the implementation of practices in line with child protection policies in schools (Asio et al., 2020). Some studies have found that school staff does not know enough about child protection policy and procedures (Cossar et al., 2014), they have different attitudes toward adopting the child protection policy (Al-Qaysi, 2018), and they do not know enough about domestic violence (Münger & Markström, 2019). Other studies conducted in Turkey reported that teachers know very little about recognizing child abuse (Dilsiz & Mağden, 2015; Him, 2017; Bağla et al., 2017; Yıldız et al., 2017; Bayındır, 2021). In contrast to these studies, Bayuca (2020) said that most teachers knew about the child protection policy. However, the teachers applied only some items in the child protection policy and did not apply others sufficiently. From another perspective, teachers may have low expectations of academic success from these children (Montserrat, 2014). While a significant part of the teachers know about the approach to children in the child protection system and are mindful of it, some teachers still exclude the child, leave him alone, and cause him to feel outcast for reasons such as *"I can't stand this child anymore"* or *"This child won't amount to anything"* (Erol, 2008).

CHILD PROTECTION AND SOCIAL EXCLUSION

Child in Need of Protection and Child Protection System

The family is the most natural environment for a child's healthy growth and development in terms of the child's physical, social, emotional, and cognitive needs. However, children may be deprived of family care for many reasons such as war, migration, poverty, family conflicts, death of parents, mental and psychological problems, neglect, and child abuse. Such children are afforded the protection of the law.

The concept of a child in need of protection is universal. Throughout history, all states have produced various services and created child protection systems by taking measures regarding children who need protection. Children in need of protection are, therefore, considered children whom the state must protect by following legal regulations. Significant changes in child welfare policies, relevant legislation, and organization have been observed throughout history in parallel with countries' development levels. Positive developments in society's perception of children and child welfare policies laid the foundation for the emergence of the child protection system. "The Convention on the Rights of the Child" constitutes the most critical and fundamental international legal basis of childcare practices, including the child protection system. The United Nations Convention on the Rights of the Child was adopted on 20 November 1989, and the state parties signed the Convention. The Convention determines not only the responsibilities of the child's family to the child but also the responsibilities of the state to the child. Turkey signed the Convention on 14 September 1990 and ratified it in 1995 (Erbay, 2019). The Convention has four basic principles such as non-discrimination (Article 2), the best interests of the child (Article 3), the right to survival and development (Article 6), and participation (Article 12). Article 9 assures that the child will not be separated from his parents against his will unless there is a situation contrary to the best interests of the child (Unicef, 2022).

The child protection system provides services to prevent the neglect and abuse of children and meet their needs in the face of risk factors that threaten their well-being, such as social problems, migration, refugee problems, unemployment, and poverty in countries and has an important place in social welfare systems (Yolcuoğlu, 2009). It is seen that volunteers first provided the services offered to children in need of protection in the world in the early days. The services started to be institutionalized with the need for professional care in the process, and institutional care turned into a general service over time (Koşar, 1992).

The best-known service in the field of child protection is institutional care (Küsmez, 2020). In 1945, Spitz was the first to state that the lack of a one-to-one relationship in institutional care negatively affected children's physical, mental, and cognitive development. Later studies emphasized that the adverse effects of institutional care should be avoided as much as possible. Foster family programs were supported and expanded worldwide, particularly after the 1950s (Spitz, 1951; Bowlby, 1952; Beckett et al., 2002; Maclean, 2003). Studies found that the children who grew up in institutions were much further behind in terms of development than the children who grew up with their families and that the developmental gaps of the children who were placed in foster care closed rapidly and they could partially catch up with their peers who grew up in the family. Studies also reported that the earlier the child was placed in foster care, the better this gap was closed (Nelson et al., 2014; Schoemaker et al., 2020). Moreover, institutional care is an expensive service, and the cost of institutional care is three-four times more than it is for a child growing up with a family (Grigore, 2014).

While child protection in Turkey commonly takes the form of institutional care, the current family-oriented approaches started to gain traction with the Ministry of Family and Social Policies in 201 (İzci et al., 2021). In Turkey, care services for children are carried out in the Children's Homes model. According to figures for the end of 2021, the number of children staying in children's homes (children's homes, children's home sites, child support centers) was 13,302. The number of children in foster care was 8,459, and the number of children cared for in families with socioeconomic assistance was 137,863 (Turkish Ministry of Family and Social Services, 2022).

Family care positively affects the child's mental health by establishing a trust-based, healthy, and loving relationship between the child and the caregiver. However, it is essential to choose the right family and match the family to the child, organize training to strengthen prospective foster families' caregiving capacity, and follow up and support families in the process. Otherwise, the child is bound to go back.

Reasons for Protection and Characteristics of Children in Need of Protection

The reasons for taking children under protection vary from country to country. On examining the reasons why children under the age of 3 are taken into institutional care in European Union (EU) member states, it was seen that child abuse and neglect (69%) takes first place, followed by special needs (4%), and parental abandonment (4%). In non-EU countries, parental abandonment (32%) takes first place, followed by special needs (23%) then neglect and abuse (14%) (Browne, 2008).

Although the reasons vary from case to case, generally, domestic violence, neglect, abuse, parental abandonment, being an unaccompanied child, and being dragged into crime are among the main reasons children need protection status (UK Department of Education, 2018).

Examining the reasons for being taken under protection in Turkey, the authors found that domestic violence, loss of parents, divorce (Lök et al., 2016; Varol, 2017; Afyonoğlu et al., 2021), economic hardships (Çayır, 2019), neglect and abuse, child labor, substance use, delinquency and child marriages (Barış & Taylan, 2020), and criminal behavior in the family (Afyonoğlu et al., 2021) stand out.

As can be understood from the reasons for being placed under protection, children in need of protection are exposed to various difficult experiences and develop specific characteristics. These children can be quick to anger and overreact to the slightest change. Often, they cannot consider the potential consequences of their behavior before acting because of the physical stimulation in their brains. These children must feel safe and loved first (Perry & Slazavitz, 2018).

As mentioned above, these children experience trauma for various reasons. Traumatized children have learned from experience that non-verbal information is more important than verbal information.

These children feel anxiety and fear. Therefore, for these children, the tone of voice, facial expressions, and gestures of their parents, friends, teachers, and other adults are more important than their words. They may perceive long-standing eye contact as a threat. When people feel fear, the major networks in the cortex (areas related to logic, planning, and other complex thinking functions) are shut down. A child in a state of fear will have difficulty learning something, including physical activities such as sports. When they are scared, they are ready to fight, flee, or freeze (Perry & Slazavitz, 2018).

In addition, children in need of protection usually have problems with their self-regulation skills and executive functions due to the traumas they experience. Self-regulation skills and executive functions are critical to the child's learning as well as development. Self-regulation skills are the individual's control over one's feelings, thoughts, and behaviors. From the child's birth, he learns to regulate his emotions with his caregiver's warm, sensitive, and responsive care. Two years old is specifically critical for the development of impulse control. This is why the adults who are responsible for the child's care have to be sensitive to the needs and individual characteristics of the children and organize the child's environment accordingly (Ertürk-Kara et al., 2018). Unfortunately, self-regulation skills cannot develop healthily in children who cannot grow up in healthy environments during infancy, such as children in need of protection. This situation affects their ability to control their emotions, thoughts, and behaviors and inhibits their social and emotional development.

Humans are social beings by nature. The most vital rewards they can obtain are the love, care, and approval of loved and respected people. The most traumatic elements are associated with the breakdown of human bonds, especially for children. Likewise, overcoming trauma is all about relationships, such as building trust and bonding with love. What abused children need most is the existence of a healthy community that relieves their pain and improves their connections and quality of relationships. Traumatized children experience pain that makes them irritable, anxious, and aggressive. Consistent care, given with patience and love, will ease their pain (Perry & Slazavitz, 2018). For this reason, adults working with such children need to pay attention to the teacher's tone of voice, mimics, and gestures and understand the reason for the child's sudden emotional changes.

Children in need of protection often face the problem of social exclusion due to the above-mentioned characteristics.

Social Exclusion

French political consultant René Lenoir first used the term social exclusion in the early 1970s to refer to individuals excluded from the economic resources, social security, and social protection system based on the French societal structure. It later spread to other European countries and continues to be used as a tool to analyze and monitor disadvantage and inequality with its opposite, social inclusion (Redmond et al., 2022).

Social exclusion is difficult and complex to define because it is a multifaceted concept. Although there is not much agreement on precise definitions in the literature, a consensus has been achieved on three main points. These are:

- Being multidimensional,
- Relativity (such as degree of exclusion), and
- Being a process (having an intergenerational character) (Redmond et al., 2022).

The multidimensionality side of it can be explained as exclusion taking place for many reasons and manifesting itself in many different fields, such as individual, political, economic, social, etc. The relativity aspect can be explained by the fact that since the earlier ages of history, cultures, values, policies, and financial structures of societies differed from each other, thus is a reason for exclusion in one culture may not be a reason for exclusion in another culture. Finally, social exclusion is a process that refers to the individual both affecting and being affected by his current situation and circumstances and those in his past and future (Redmond et al., 2022).

Just as the causes of social exclusion are diverse, the views explaining these causes are also diverse. Economic, political, social, and personal causes of social exclusion can be mentioned. Personal reasons include gender, age, marital status, special needs status, health status, having a child, and educational status. Social causes consist of the nature of family and friend relationships, social support systems, social status, and participation in social activities. Economic reasons include unemployment, poverty, and changes in the quality of work. Political causes, on the other hand, are the exclusion of certain people and groups from the social sphere due to the policies implemented (Şahin, 2009).

Dimensions of Social Exclusion

Levitas addressed social exclusion in three dimensions: resources, participation, and quality of life. In terms of resources, economic and material resources, access to public services, and social resources are under the lens. Within the dimension of participation, economic participation, social participation and culture, education and skills, and political and civic participation are the relevant concepts. Finally, the dimension of quality of life includes health and well-being, living environment, crime, harm, and criminalization (Levitas et al., 2007).

Examining Levitas's dimensions, the authors found that the groups with a high risk of social exclusion are long-term unemployed, homeless, children from low-income families, families with multiple people with special needs, immigrants, broken families, refugees, ethnic groups, those living in care institutions, those living on welfare, the elderly, temporary agricultural workers and their children, gender-based discrimination. They saw also that women and girls are vulnerable.

It should be noted that social exclusion in risky groups is a two-way street. On the one hand, these groups see themselves as inadequate to integrate with society. On the other, society is reluctant to include these groups.

Social Exclusion From a Developmental Perspective

This section discusses social-emotional development, moral development, and friendship relations.

Figure 1. Social exclusion dimensions
(Levitas et al., 2007).

Resources	Participation	Quality of Life
• **Material/economic resources** (income, home ownership, Other assets and savings) • **Access to public and private services** (Public services, transport, utilities, private services, access to financial services) • **Social resources** (Institutionalisation/separation from family, Social support, Frequency and quality of contact with family members/friends/co-workers)	• **Economic participation** (Paid work, providing unpaid care, nature of working life, quality of working life) • **Social participation** (Participation in common social activities, social roles) • **Culture, education and skills** (Basic skills (literacy, numeracy), educational attainment, access to education, cultural leisure activities) • **Political and civic participation** (Citizenship status, enfranchisement, civic efficacy, political participation)	• **Health and well-being** (Physical health and exercise, mental health, life satisfaction, disability, Self-esteem/ personal efficacy, personel development, vulnerability to stigma, Self-harm and substance misuse) • **Living environment** (Housing quality, homelessness, neighbourhood safety, neighbourhood satisfaction, access to open space) • **Crime, harm and criminalisation** (Objective safety/victimisation, subjective safety, exposure to bullying and harassment, discrimination, criminal record, imprisonment)

Social-Emotional Development

As a social being, a human is born in relationships and continues his life in these relationships. The baby begins to recognize and adapt to the world within the framework of the caregiving capacity, parenting skills, relationships, values, attitudes and behaviors, resources, social status, and rules of the family in which he was born. During infancy, the child's social environment usually consists of family members, relatives, neighbors, and parents' close friends. Through the development of shared attention and gaze following, infants begin to understand other people's intentions at 7-8 months. These skills increase at 10-11 months. At an average age of 1 year old, the ability to read other people's emotions develops. To determine how to behave in uncertain situations, they gain social reference skills that enable them to understand their mothers' emotional expressions. At the age of 2, they become better at taking social cues and checking their mothers before taking action (Santrock, 2021). The baby's values are thus shaped by the mother, other family members, relatives, close neighbors, and parents' friends.

Between the ages of 2 and 4, they learn the causes and consequences of emotions, and the number of words they can express their feelings with increases considerably. They also observe the relationships of their parents in the social environment. When my son was 3-3.5 years old, during a family visit, when he realized that his father was not involved in the conversations going on, he asked, *"Dad, are you a statue?"* Other families visited the patient, and they were the patient's colleagues. When the topic of conversation was business, his father could not be involved in the conversation for a while because he was out of the loop.

From 4 to 5, they begin to understand that the same event can cause different emotions and that people can make false statements to get what they want or avoid the problem. Around the age of 5, they begin to help their peers in distress, calm them down, and share their pain (Santrock, 2021).

Early childhood is also when children discover what kind of person they will become. They define themselves according to bodily features, physical activities (play activities), and material possessions (Santrock, 2015). Here, in all these identification processes and self-development, the adults around them communicate with them, and their descriptions (you are beautiful, intelligent, lazy, naughty, etc.) and conversations with their friends about their children (He is so intelligent that he tries every way to get his job done and gets what he wants; our boy is very kind, kind to his friends, respectful, always waits his turn, etc.) are crucial. Not only verbal communication but also nonverbal communication elements are essential. A positive relationship is said to exist between parental attitudes and children's social skill levels (Özyürek, 2015), and a negative one between parental attitudes and children's behavioral problems (Gözübüyük, 2015; Çiftçi-Topaloğlu, 2013) because children pay more attention to gestures, facial expressions, and tone of voice, which are the elements of nonverbal communication, rather than what adults say. Furthermore, a significant relationship is said to exist between the psychological well-being of the parents and the social behavior and competence of the children (Kındıroğlu & Yaşar-Ekici, 2019).

With school, significant changes occur in the child's social environment, and friendship and peer relations begin to gain importance. During this period, close friendships start taking shape. This is when children determine who their closest friends are. Children make this determination according to specific criteria. In the first stage, these criteria are material possessions (possessing a nice bag or pen) or achievement (sports or academic achievement). At the same time, the feature of being someone to be trusted comes to the fore in later periods with the characteristics of sharing the same thoughts and feelings (Santrock, 2021).

From 8 to 11, children define themselves primarily according to their psychological characteristics and qualities, such as "helpful, nice, naughty, lazy, and smart." They include their social aspects in their self-descriptions concerning social groups. Like "Volleyball girl," "Ali's close friend." They give more space for social comparisons. They think about what they can do compared with others. E.g., "I'm the hardest worker in the class." Their ability to grasp the perspective of others, to understand their feelings and thoughts, i.e., to gain perspective increases. Gaining perspective is **critical** in children's development of prosocial or antisocial behaviors (Santrock, 2021).

During adolescence, young people's need for close relationships increases and they tend to have this need satisfied by their friends rather than their parents, and they seek close friends. They turn to peer groups that listen to them, understand them, and respect their opinions. They adhere to group standards. Peer compatibility reaches its peak in the 8-9th grades. The reward-punishment system within the group directly affects adolescents (Santrock, 2015).

Moral Development

According to Piaget, children's moral judgments are externally dependent until age 10-11. The rules determined by (adult) people who are accepted as authority are accepted by children without question (Bencik-Kangal, 2017). They see customs and rules as unchangeable features of the world. They believe that if the rules are violated, punishment will be immediate. Therefore, when they do something wrong, they look around with anxiety in anticipation of punishment (Santrock, 2021). Gaining relativity after the age of 10-11, children start taking into account not only the results of the behaviors but also the conditions in which they occur and the person's intentions (Arı, 2018). Even though Piaget says that children do not take into account the intention of the person until the age of 10-11, it has been reported that children take into account the intention of individuals at an earlier age, although young children's moral progress is said to be inconsistent due to limitations in self-control, cognitive flexibility, and social understanding skills (Santrock, 2021).

Kohlberg states that between the ages of 5 and 9, the child behaves according to the good and bad criteria accepted by the culture and that while physical appearance in events, the scale of the damage, and the outcome are the criteria, the reasons behind the events are not considered. He states that in the 10-15 age group, the expectations of families and groups gain importance, these expectations are valuable, and they are accepted without considering the consequences. At the age of 15 and beyond, universal values and principles such as justice, equality, and rights come to the fore. Kohlberg emphasizes the importance of peer interactions in children's moral reasoning. He states that while adults try to teach children about rules and regulations, peer-to-peer interactions contribute to moral reasoning by looking at children from the perspective of others and acting more democratically about rules (Santrock, 2021). In short, it is stated that the basic components of morality emerge in the first four years of life, and transitions in early moral development include genetic, environmental, and social-cognitive factors (Dahl & Killen, 2018).

Friendships and Social Exclusion

Friendship, as a voluntary, mutual, and particular type of relationship is a critical phenomenon that occupies an important place in the development process of the individual and affects the development and harmony of the individual. Children gain essential social skills such as initiating and maintaining social relationships, showing kindness, reconciliation, and solving social problems in peer relationships. Every child's friendship is different. While some children gain trust, commitment, and satisfaction from friendships, others may experience issues such as exclusion, being ignored or neglected, conflict and violence. Even some popular kids who have many friends can feel lonely and unhappy (Santrock, 2021).

Social behavior, similarity/dissimilarity, family problems, and the reputation of the family in society, i.e., social status, are factors in the problems that children experience in peer relationships. *Social behavior* includes the inability of a shy child to be involved in peer relations, the rejection of a child with aggressive and destructive behaviors by his peers, his lack of acceptance among his peers due to skill deficiencies such as lack of social skills, or low academic achievement. *(Dis)similarity* means that children with similar characteristics (such as family structure, personal characteristics, hobbies, academic success, etc.) are more readily accepted by their peers and that children who are perceived as different by their peers have a higher rate of encountering social exclusion. *Family problems* (including divorce, alcohol, drug use in family members, domestic violence, etc.) affect how the child reflects his anger on his school and friends, and his reluctance to invite friends home. *The family's reputation* includes what other children's families and other individuals in society say about the social status of the child's family. Although children individually try to overcome the problem they experience in peer relationships, it is very hard to change a social outcast's reputation (Burton, 1986).

As children grow, the norms of their peer group become a source of information on how other peer groups are evaluated and how they should be interacted with. School standards are also another factor that determines the relationships within and between groups (Nipedal et al, 2010). Another study found that peer norms predicted students' comfort, interest, communication quality, and inter-ethnic friendships.

By contrast, school norms more strongly predicted the number of friendships among ethnic minority students (Tropp et al., 2016).

Children with special needs and students with social-emotional problems and behavioral difficulties experience more social exclusion. Studies indicate that peers and teachers generally have negative attitudes toward children with social and emotional issues and behavioral problems, and these attitudes negatively affect the social acceptance of these children (De Boer et al., 2013).

Primary school children in one study reported that their experiences of exclusion mainly occurred outside the classroom and in the playground during recess. Some special needs students stated that they prefer to receive social support from their teachers to solve social problems, but they cannot get the help they want because they do not trust their teachers' skills or they believe that the teachers will punish them if they ask for assistance (De Leeuw et al., 2018).

Children form in-group and out-of-group categories from an early age, and these categories begin to guide their friend preferences and decisions about who to include and who to exclude. Although the messages received from peers, adults, school, and society for characteristics that are prominent in the culture such as gender, race, language, religion, ethnicity, and social status contribute to the categories created by the children, the social-cognitive development levels and individual characteristics of the children significantly guide these decisions. (Killen et al., 2013). Mulvey (2016) stated that four factors play a role in the reasoning and evaluations of children and adolescents regarding group-based exclusion. These are:

- Social-cognitive skill level,
- Social-contextual factors,
- Emotional assessments and
- Competition between moral and group-based norms.

Social exclusion involves balancing moral principles with the child's commitment and loyalty to the group. For example, while children sometimes accept that exclusion is wrong because of the psychological difficulty it causes, they may also argue that exclusion is appropriate due to the nature of group norms. Children assess the events or situations according to their knowledge levels and social cognitive skills by weighing the social contextual factors related to the event and taking into account the feelings of the excluded people (Mulvey, 2016).

With the increase in social-cognitive competencies, children accept that social exclusion may not always be wrong, and they begin to make complex decisions about when exclusion is justified. With age, children understand that exclusion is a multifaceted issue involving morality and group cohesion. They become more attracted to group cohesion and perceive exclusion as appropriate for maintaining it. For example, a child who does not play basketball will not join a social group whose members are members of a basketball group. Sometimes, they may not include their friends in the group to protect them from embarrassment. An adult equivalent of this behavior would be not inviting a friend with financial difficulties to an expensive auction banquet. As social-cognitive skills improve, children are less likely to reject indiscriminate exclusion and more likely to consider many factors and perspectives (Mulvey, 2016). One study determined that young people who think they have gained a privileged status due to relational aggression in their peer group treat these behaviors of theirs positively (Werner & Hill, 2010).

The Social Information Processing Model, proposed by Dodge (1986) and revised by Crick and Dodge (1994), describes the social cognitive processes underlying children's behavioral responses to

Figure 2. Social Information Processing Process
(Dodge 1986; Crick & Dodge, 1994).

Paying attention to rejection cues

Interpreting clues about rejection

Generating reactions to the event

Imagining the potential consequences of one's own behavioral
responses in order to decide on an action

Performing the selected response

Evaluation

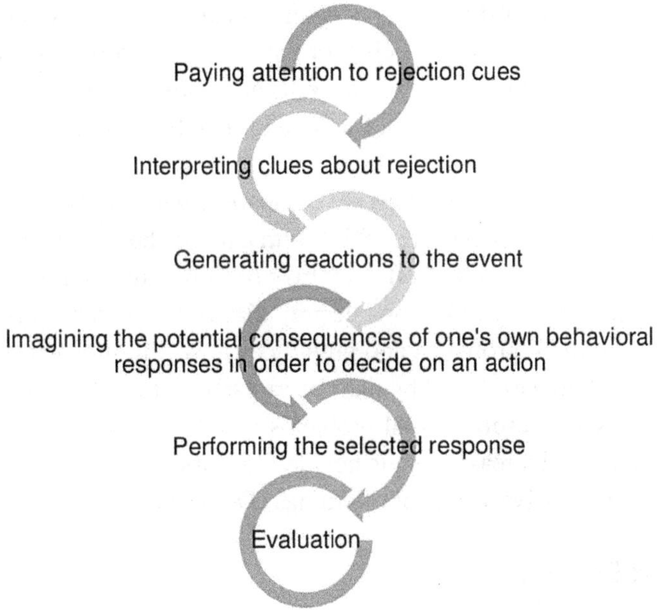

social situations. According to the model, individuals and children respond to social conditions accord-ing to their characteristics (abilities, capacities) and the knowledge stored in long-term memory due to past experiences. At the same time, the reactions they receive from their social environment in response to their behaviors are also processed into the information stored in this memory and this information may have the power to change that child's behavior in the future. It is emphasized that when processing social information, what matters in the child's reaction to other individuals and children is the way he thinks about the world and how he perceives other individuals and children.

Repeated rejection plays a vital role in the formation of later behavioral problems. Children, during peer relationships, develop the skills of regulating their emotions, recognizing and interpreting social cues, resolving social issues, and considering the social environment they are in while expressing their feelings and thoughts. However, children who experience social exclusion may not develop these skills sufficiently because they are unable to develop good peer relations (Dodge et al., 2003). Children's behaviors alone do not cause psychological adjustment problems, but peer rejection behaviors such as exclusion, being ignored, and ill-treatment are permanent risk factors throughout childhood; furthermore, they cause children to seek revenge out of anger and display antisocial behaviors (Ladd, 2006). Intense experiences of peer rejection in childhood have also been associated with depression, withdrawal, and low academic achievement (Killen et al., 2013).

The social information processing model states that the child's reaction to a social situation, such as peer rejection and exclusion, occurs in six steps (Dodge 1986; Crick & Dodge, 1994). These steps are given in Figure 2.

Individuals assess the social situations that they are in according to their past knowledge and experi-ences, create some clues and determine how they will assess these clues with their past knowledge and experiences. In the first two steps, past knowledge and experiences guide the individual. In the third step, in addition to past knowledge and experience, the conditions of the social setting are also taken into account. In the fourth step, an effort is made to reach the appropriate behavioral response from long-term memory. In the fifth and sixth steps, the decision is made according to behavior in line with the individual's moral value judgments, and the behavior that is put into action is evaluated by considering peer assessment and reaction. Children with social skills and competence can correctly interpret social cues and clues and respond to the message in a way that is socially appropriate (Dodge, 1986; Crick & Dodge, 1994).

It is stated in the literature that these six steps are compatible with two types of reactions to rejection. First, repetitive social rejection may prevent the child from gaining the ability to read social cues; he may develop low self-efficacy, and this low self-efficacy may prevent him from practicing this subject. The other is that it may cause the child to establish hostile prejudices toward peer motives (Dodge et al., 2003).

Studies have shown that initial problems and prejudices in social information processing cause behaviors that lead to children being excluded by their peers early on in primary school, changing the way children process social cues and resolve social problems by altering the way they process information during future peer interactions, increasing their hostile attribution biases, their sensitivity to cue, and their tendency to respond aggressively to peer dilemmas (Dodge et al., 2003).

Social Exclusion at School

School is a key environment where children learn and shape the inclusive behaviors necessary to promote global inclusion in adulthood (Mulvey et al., 2021). Although the families of children under protection experience social exclusion, school is still an important place for them to break this exclusion and make a new start in life. Just like children with special needs, the key barriers that prevent children under protection from reaching their potential are stereotypes, prejudices, and low academic expectations (Almomani, 2022).

Social exclusion is a common phenomenon at school and can have serious consequences for both the healthy development and academic achievement of students (Beißert et al., 2022). While the school provides an important setting for students' sense of belonging, academic achievement, and mental and physical health, social exclusion at school negatively affects students' well-being and academic performance (Raufelder et al., 2021). In the Council of Europe Strategy for the Rights of the Child (2022-2027), it is emphasized that schools have an important role in protecting children (Council of Europe, 2022).

A study conducted with 12-year-old children in Israel by Gross-Manos investigated the relationship between the poverty experienced by children and youth growing up in poor families and exclusion in the community and school settings. Gross-Manos stated that children who are materially deprived are not necessarily socially excluded, and vice versa. It has been found that children who are both financially deprived and socially excluded are less satisfied with their health, more anxious, exposed to more bullying at school, and less satisfied with their family relationships than children who are only financially deprived or just excluded (Gross-Manos, 2015).

When it comes to the teacher, staff, other children, and their families developing a positive approach toward the child in need of protection, the training and attitude of the principal and teacher are crucial. Principals and teachers should first get rid of their own negative thoughts and prejudices and guide the other children and their families. Everyone involved in the process should strive to contribute to the well-being of children in need of protection or stop themselves from adopting a destructive and rejecting attitude toward the child. Teachers' behaviors in the classroom can have a strong effect on students' attitudes toward exclusion (Beißert et al., 2022). Mulvey et al. (2021), emphasized the complex interaction of the school social environment and teacher factors in shaping the onlooker reactions of adolescents to social exclusion. They found that students who perceive the relations between students and teachers as good are more likely to consider the exclusion behavior as wrong and that students who are worried about being rejected by their teachers and who report that their teacher discriminates are less likely to consider the exclusion behavior as wrong.

One study reported that the attitudes and behaviors of school administrators and teachers towards protected children vary and that positive interactions create a sense of belonging in children, which in turn affects both behavior and academic achievement positively, while negative interactions negatively affect especially academic achievement. It also reported that school administrators and teachers did not receive any training in terms of approaching children under protection in their education and working life and supporting their academic achievement (Kabakulak, 2019).

School experiences of protected children vary. While some children are satisfied with the time they spend at school, their schoolmates, and teachers, some are not. Some children state that they are ostracized by their friends when they say that they are staying at the children's home because they are under protection and that this is why they pay great attention to their behavior and usually hide the fact that they stay in institutional care from everyone to avoid exclusion.

"I get on well with my friends, I'm trying not to ruin that friendship. Even if it is ruined, no one can say anything because no one knows that I am staying here (children's home)." 12-year-old girl.

"When I was in the class, I had a friend named S. We used to walk around and chat together during recess. We used to play games together in physical education classes. After I told my friend that I was staying in the children's home, she started excluding me. She didn't speak and she ignored me. Then all of a sudden, our friendship ended. I only said I was staying in the children's home." 13-year-old girl.

"I am currently in the 5th grade. I never experienced exclusion before or after the 5th grade because I was very careful with my behavior and speech. My teachers have always treated me well." 11-year-old girl.

"I get along well with my friends and teachers at school. I don't meet with my teachers outside of school. My studies are much better than before." 10-year-old boy.

Even if these children do not have any behavioral problems, they can be excluded because they are under protection. The reasons for being taken under protection are not the children themselves. Their parents cannot continue caring for them for various reasons. As stated in Articles 2 and 6 of the "Convention on the Rights of the Child," these children, like all other children, have the right to live, be protected, develop, and participate in dignity, and all states that have signed the convention have a responsibility to protect the rights of children. Within the framework of these provisions, the right to life and development of all children is protected, no matter where they live, and all institutions and organizations providing services for children have a responsibility to act under these provisions.

Professional staff working in the field of child protection state that one of the most important problems they have with the school is that they do not want children to be enrolled in school by the school administrator during school enrollment. It is understood that some school administrators are not aware of the importance of consistency and stability for the child and that they say, *"These children must change schools every year so that all schools take responsibility,"* and they see these children as a burden. In addition to these, it is remarkable that they behave with the prejudice that the children will have behavioral problems and fail academically. The fact that administrators and teachers compare their performance based on the academic achievement of the students in the schools and classrooms, plus the fact that parents select schools and teachers based on this are thought to be contributing factors.

When the problems experienced in school by children who receive support and service from the child protection system are examined in general, is it seen that:

- If there is a problem in the classroom or school, these children are blamed first,
- There is prejudice against children's achievements, low expectations of success,
- Staff behave subjectively when assessing children's performance,
- The school administration is sometimes unwilling to enroll children under protection in their schools due to the prejudice and concern that it will reduce their school achievement and show problem behavior at school.

When looking at the attitudes of classmates and families toward these children at school, observe instances of:

- Not wanting the child to be in their child's class
- Not wanting their children to make friends with these children
- Showing these children as troublemakers when problems arise.
- Classmates not lending the necessary support (Ataman, 2008).

The cultural environment and values shape children's social and emotional development. The culture, the values of the society in which one lives, and the values that are possessed by the person determine these behaviors (Cüceloğlu, 2002). The concept of value directs relationships in every environment where human relations exist and affect our daily lives in a wide range of areas from communication methods to business ethics, from teaching children how to behave toward others. Values are so effective in our lives that they determine and guide relationships and ensure that humans maintain a healthy social life. This transfer takes place mainly through communication. Children learn values by living in the family, in their social environment, and in school. Thus, the school climate and values are critical. Today, individuals spend much of their time on social media. One of the most vital features of social media is its power to create public opinion and change public perception. Social media posts, which have recently been called the "duck syndrome," only emphasize the best, the most beautiful, and the strongest, pushing individuals to question themselves and their values. Values such as tolerance, hard work, and honesty can be described as naivety and foolishness. However, fundamental human values such as love, respect, equality, honesty, benevolence, justice, compassion, tolerance, generosity, and responsibility must be preserved to ensure social and global peace, tranquility, and integrity.

Rejection, exclusion, stigmatization, and low academic achievement of the child at school lead to him being pushed out of education life. Children who are excluded from education have different orientations. It is known that truancy and unexcused absences are often significantly related to committing crimes (Aydın, 2003). When the authors look at the results of exclusion in school and social life in general, the authors see:

- The individual's loss of self-esteem and self-confidence,
- The individual's feeling of helplessness,
- Early school leavers,
- Alienation of the individual from society
- Development of mental health problems,
- Development of various addictions such as substance abuse,
- Worsening poverty and
- An increase in criminal tendencies.

School is one of the most important institutions where risk group children can be identified early, and necessary interventions can be made. In this sense, early detection of children with family problems and making necessary interventions will prevent children from entering the protection system. School administrators and teachers should know children's rights and the child protection system, not because such knowledge is part of the general culture but because it is their responsibility to know this.

Schools' success and performance are evaluated based on their academic, sportive, and artistic achievements. This is why school administrators and teachers focus on efforts to increase their success and performance and prefer to avoid children and family groups that they think will adversely affect this success and performance. If the social-emotional development of children as well as services and improvements for risk group children are included among the criteria for measuring schools' success and performance along with the ratio of risk group children to non-risk group children, this will go a long way to preventing these problems.

SOLUTIONS AND RECOMMENDATIONS

A child's brain needs love, companionship, and freedom to play and dream. Brain development depends on use. Used areas develop, but unused regions cannot. This is why children must be taught how to connect with others, deal with problems, and participate in social settings. Otherwise, those areas of their brains will remain underdeveloped, and they will not be able to develop social skills and empathy (Perry & Slazavitz, 2018). Children under protection and care are seen to have very negative experiences and these experiences occur during the period when development is the fastest.

Stating: "*In an increasingly competitive environment, middle-class or upper-class parents have begun to act more and more extreme to offer their children more and more of what they consider to be an 'advantage.' This constant emphasis on competition blunts the lessons of cooperation, empathy, and self-sacrifice necessary for people's mental health and social connectedness.*" Perry & Slazavitz (2018) expressed the negative consequences of being constantly at the forefront of competition. For this reason, it would be beneficial to prefer play and activities that encourage cooperation at all educational levels, starting from the pre-school period, instead of play and activities that involve competition in schools. In cooperative play where no one is eliminated or left behind, the players have to work together and cooperate to win. However, one has to lose in competitive play while the other wins. In competitive play, insecurity can lead to unhealthy group dynamics that start with anxiety and anger and can lead to outright aggression. Cooperative play has four key characteristics, namely, cooperation, inclusion, positive emotions such as acceptance and respect, and fun (Lyons, 2022).

As important as academic achievement is in school, for children to take their place in society as virtuous people, studies aimed at fostering such values as honesty, equality, fairness, benevolence, respect, love, tolerance, and justice need to be carried out (Yörükoğlu, 2002). The behavior of administrators and teachers as role models for children congruent with these values will positively affect not only the school climate but also the mental health of the students and the teachers who teach at the school.

As school is where children and adolescents spend much of their lives, it is a key institution for social inclusion, equality, tolerance, and cultural sensitivity. Considering the strong impact of social exclusion on both the health and academic achievement of the individual, schools should work on encouraging friendship among students, increasing cooperation, and preventing exclusion. A road map should be created so that children who need protection can be accepted and successful in the education system. When creating the roadmap variables other than the elements related to the school environment that affect the school's perception of the children under protection must be considered, too. Only then will it be possible to support the academic skills of children in need of protection and to develop solutions by identifying the factors that can contribute to them adapting to school. School administrators and teachers have an important role to play in this regard. It would be beneficial for administrators and teachers to receive in-service training on the characteristics of children under protection, their rights, and how to approach and support them.

Furthermore, countries must focus on family-oriented services by considering the disadvantages that children experience in institutional care when formulating their policies for child protection and should not prefer institutional care services except when necessary. Family-oriented services contribute significantly to the child's life. Children under the protection provided with family care can invite their schoolmates to their homes and are less exposed to situations such as stigmatization and exclusion. Their social acceptance increases as they will have healthier behaviors compared with institutional care. Similarly, having families who care for them and are in contact with them is highly effective in preventing social exclusion. To illustrate, a shy and quiet boy who attended the second grade of primary school and lived in the children's home was harmed both physically and emotionally by some of his classmates. At this time, the child was placed with a foster family. The child, whose relationship with his foster family grew stronger in about six months, started to stand up against his peers who hurt him and protect himself. When the school administrator questioned the subject after his peers complained, the child said, "*Now I have parents too. They can't hurt me.*" As can be understood from the example, children who need protection must be cared for by well-selected families who are trained on this subject and monitored.

FUTURE RESEARCH DIRECTIONS

The authors recommend that the topic be evaluated from the broadest perspective taking into account how everyone involved in the education system – students, families, teachers, administrators, etc. – regard and approach children in need of protection, how these children perceive school, and what professionals who work in the child protection system expect of education. Future studies could benefit from using both quantitative and qualitative research methods.

CONCLUSION

For children who spend a significant part of their time at school, school has protective, preventive, developmental, and curative potential. When it comes to protecting children from all possible risks, the protective and preventative role played by schools should be emphasized and the reasons for failure in school should be highlighted in the context of friendships, academic achievement, and social cohesion. Due to the nature of protective, preventive studies, detecting negative behavior before it occurs, preparing an intervention plan by taking the necessary precautions, developing alternative models, and highlighting the positive characteristics of children in different areas will contribute significantly to the school's functioning.

REFERENCES

Al-Qaysi, N. (2018). The Impact of Child Protection Policy on Omani Classrooms. *International Journal of Information Technology and Language Studies*, 2(1), 1–11.

Almomani, S. (2022). Only Half the Story: How Stigma and Discrimination Shape the Lives of Children with Disabilities. *World Forgotten Children Foundation.* https://www.worldforgottenchildren.org/blog/only-half-the-story-how-stigma-and-discrimination-shape-the-lives-of-children-with-disabilities/147?utm_source=IGI+Global+Products+and+Publishing+Opportunities&utm_campaign=edc41ebff8-EMAIL_CAMPAIGN_2018_04_30_COPY_01&utm_medium=email&utm_term=0_bcbd627034-edc41ebff8-50311603

Arı, R. (2018). Eğitim Psikolojisi. Nobel Yayıncılık. [Education psychology. Nobel Publishing].

Asio, J. M. R., Bayucca, S. A., & Jimeniez, E. C. (2020). Child Protection Policy Awareness of Teachers and Responsiveness of the School: Their Relationship and Implications. *Shanlax International Journal of Education*, 9(1), 1–10. doi:10.34293/education.v9i1.3384

Ataman, A. (2008). Okullar, Öğretmenler, Öğrenciler ve Özel Eğitim. N. Erol, (Ed.), Koruyucu Aile, Evlat Edinme Hizmetleri ve Ruh Sağlığı içinde (pp.227-231). Ankara Üniversitesi Çocuk/Ergen Ruh Sağlığı ve Hastalıkları Anabilim Dalı Yayınları, 6. [Schools, Teachers, Students and Special Education. N. Erol, (Ed.), In Foster Family, Adoption Services and Mental Health (pp.227-231). Ankara University Child/Adolescent Psychiatry Department Publications, 6.].

Aydın, İ. (2003). Risk Altındaki Çocukların Eğitimde Alternatif Okullar: ABD Örneği. *Kriminoloji.* [Alternative Schools in the Education of Children at Risk: The Case of the USA. *Criminology.*] https://www.kriminoloji.com/Risk_Altindaki_Cocuklarin_Egitimi-Inayet_Aydin.htm

Bağla, A. G., Arıkan, M., Kılıç, R. Ö., Orulluoğlu, F., Kuyucu, İ., Özğan, M., Öngü, B., Özdemir, T., Gerger, A. S., Baykan, A. Y., Tutar, E. F., Korkmaz, D., Ursavaş, S., Sümbüloğlu, V., & Soran, Ö. (2017). Sağlık Çalışanları, Öğretmenler Ve Üniversite 1. Sınıf Öğrencilerinin Çocuk İstismarı Ve İhmali İle İlgili Bilgi Düzeylerinin Değerlendirilmesi. *Balıkesir Sağlık Bilimleri Dergisi*, 6(1):1-10. (Evaluation of Knowledge Levels of Healthcare Professionals, Teachers and First Year University Students about Child Abuse and Neglect. *Balıkesir Journal of Health Sciences*, 6(1), 1–10.

Bayındır, N. (2021). Risk Altındaki Çocukların Tespiti Ve Korunmasına Yönelik Öğretmen Adaylarının Görüşleri. *21. Yüzyılda Eğitim ve Toplum, 10* (28): 167-182. [Opinions of Pre-service Teachers on the Identification and Protection of Children at Risk. *Education and Society in the 21st Century, 10* (28): 167-182].

Bayuca, S. A. (2020). Teachers' Awareness and School's Responsiveness to the Child Protection Policy: Basis for a Development Plan. [IJAMR]. *International Journal of Academic Multidisciplinary Research*, 4(6), 59–65. doi:10.2139srn.3640895

Beckett, C., Bredenkamp, D., Castle, J., Groothues, C., O'Connor, T. G., & Rutter, M. (2002). Behavior patterns associated with institutional deprivation: A study of children adopted from Romania. *Journal of Developmental and Behavioral Pediatrics, 23*(5), 297–303. doi:10.1097/00004703-200210000-00001 PMID:12394517

Beißert, H., Staat, M., & Bonefeld, M. (2022). The Role of Gender for Teachers' Reactions to Social Exclusion Among Students. *Front. Educ., 7*, 819922. doi:10.3389/feduc.2022.819922

Bencik-Kangal, S. (2017). Ahlak Gelişimi. Nilgün Baysal Metin (Ed.), Doğum Öncesinden Ergenliğe Çocuk Gelişimi içinde (pp. 197-226). 2. Baskı. Ankara: Pegem Akademi. [Moral Development. Nilgün Baysal Metin (Ed.), In Child Development from Prenatal to Adolescence (pp. 197-226). 2nd Edition. Ankara: Pegem Academy].

Bowlby, J. (1952). *Maternal care and mental health* (2nd ed.). World Health Organization., https://darkwing.uoregon.edu/~eherman/teaching/texts/Bowlby%20Maternal%20Care%20and%20Mental%20Health.pdf

Browne, K. (2008). Çocuk İstismarı ve İhmalini Önleme Konusunda Dünya Sağlık Örgütü Tarafından Yürütülen Bilgilendirme ve Eğitim Paketi, (İ. Altınoğlu-Dikmeer, Trans.). *Koruyucu Aile, Evlat Edinme Hizmetleri ve Ruh Sağlığı, Prof. Dr. Mualla Öztürk Anısına XX. Sempozyum Sunumları* içinde (pp.251-257). Üniversitesi Tıp Fakültesi Yayınları. [Information and Education Package Conducted by the World Health Organization on the Prevention of Child Abuse and Neglect, (İ. Altınoğlu-Dikmeer, Trans.). *In Foster Family, Adoption Services and Mental Health, Prof. Dr. In Memory of Mualla Öztürk XX. Symposium Presentations* (pp.251-257). University Faculty of Medicine Publications].

Burton, C. B. (1986). Children's Peer Relationships. *ERIC Publications*. https://files.eric.ed.gov/fulltext/ED265936.pdf

Çiftçi-Topaloğlu, Z. (2013). *4-5 yaş çocuklarının sosyal yetkinlik, saldırganlık, kaygı düzeyleri ile anne-babalarının ebeveyn özyeterliği algısı arasındaki ilişkilerin incelenmesi.* [Yayınlanmamış yüksek lisans tezi. Pamukkale Üniversitesi,Türkiye]. [*Investigation of the relationships between the social competence, aggression and anxiety levels of 4-5 year old children and their parents' perception of parental self-efficacy.* [Unpublished master's thesis. Pamukkale University, Turkey].]

Cossar, J., Brandon, M., & Jordan, P. (2014). "You've got to trust her and she's got to trust you": Children's views on participation in the child protection system. *Child & Family Social Work, 21*(1), 103–112. doi:10.1111/cfs.12115

Council of Europe. (2022). *Report on child consultations informing the elaboration of the Council of Europe Strategy for the Rights of the Child 2022-2027.* COE. https://rm.coe.int/council-of-europe-child-consultations-to-inform-the-elaboration-of-the/1680a697d5

Crick, N. R., & Dodge, K. A. (1994). A review and reformulation of social information-processing mechanisms in children's social adjustment. *Psychological Bulletin, 115*(1), 74–101. doi:10.1037/0033-2909.115.1.74

Cüceloğlu, D. (2002). İletişim Donanımları. 'Keşke'siz Bir Yaşam İçin İletişim. 46. Baskı. Remzi Kitabevi. [Communication Skills. Communication for a Life Without 'I Wish'. 46th Edition. Remzi Bookstore].

Dahl, A., & Killen, M. (2018). A Developmental Perspective on the Origins of Morality in Infancy and Early Childhood. *Frontiers in Psychology, 9*, 1736. doi:10.3389/fpsyg.2018.01736 PMID:30294291

De Boer, A., Pijl, S. J., Post, W., & Minnaert, A. (2013). Peer Acceptance and Friendship of Students with Disabilities in Regular Education: The Role of Child, Peer, and Classroom Variables. *Social Development, 22*(4), 831–844. doi:10.1111/j.1467-9507.2012.00670.x

De Leeuw, R. R., De Boer, A. A., & Minnaert, A. E. M. G. (2018). Student voices on social exclusion in general primary schools. *European Journal of Special Needs Education, 33*(2), 166–186. doi:10.1080/08856257.2018.1424783

Dilsiz, H. ve Mağden, D. (2015). Öğretmenlerin Çocuk İstismar Ve İhmali Konusunda Bilgi Ve Risk Tanıma Düzeylerinin Tespit Edilmesi [Determination of Teachers' Knowledge and Risk Recognition Levels on Child Abuse and Neglect]. *Hacettepe University Faculty Of Health Sciences Journal, 1*(2), 678–694.

Dodge, K. A. (1986). *A social information processing model of social competence in children.* Lawrence Erlbaum.

Dodge, K. A., Lansford, J. E., Burks, V. S., Bates, J. E., Pettit, G. S., Fontaine, R., & Price, J. M. (2003). Peer Rejection and Social Information-Processing Factors in the Development of Aggressive Behavior Problems in Children. *Child Development, 74*(2), 374–393. doi:10.1111/1467-8624.7402004 PMID:12705561

Ekinci, C., & Ve Tösten, R. (2018). Koruma Altında Bulunan 13-18 Yaş Arası Çocukların Okul Algısı. *Sosyal Bilimler Enstitüsü Dergisi,* 12: 360 – 378. (School Perception of Protected Children aged 13-18. *Journal of Social Sciences Institute,* 12: 360 – 378). ISSN: 2147-8406.

Erbay, E. (2019). Çocuk Hakları. 2. Basım. Yeni İnsan Yayınevi. [Children's Rights. 2nd Edition. Yeni İnsan Publisher].

Erol, N. (2004). Yuva ve Yetiştirme Yurtları Sorunun mu Yoksa Çözümün mü Parçası? Uslu, R. (Ed.). Koruma Altındaki Çocuklar içinde (pp:133-140). Ankara Üniversitesi Tıp Fakültesi Çocuk Ruh Sağlığı ve Hastalıkları Anabilim Dalı Yayını. No:IX. [Are Kindergartens and Orphanages Part of the Problem or the Solution? Uslu, R. (Ed.). In Protected Children (pp:133-140). Ankara University Faculty of Medicine, Department of Child Psychiatry and Diseases Publication. No: IX].

Erol, N. (2008). Evlat Edinme ve Okul Sorunları. N. Erol (Ed.). Koruyucu Aile, Evlat Edinme Hizmetleri ve Ruh Sağlığı içinde (pp.219-225). Ankara Üniversitesi Çocuk/Ergen Ruh Sağlığı ve Hastalıkları Anabilim Dalı Yayınları. No: 6 [Adoption and School Problems. N. Erol (Ed.). In Foster Family, Adoption Services and Mental Health (pp.219-225). Ankara University Child/Adolescent Psychiatry Department Publications. No: 6].

Ertürk-Kara, H. G., & Yıldız, T. G. ve Fındık, E. (2018). Erken Çocukluk Döneminde Öz Düzenleme İzleme, Değerlendirme ve Destekleme Yöntemleri. Anı Yayıncılık. [Self-Regulation Monitoring, Evaluation and Support Methods in Early Childhood. Anı Publishing].

Gilligan, R. (1998). The importance of schools and teachers in child welfare. *Child & Family Social Work, 3*(1), 13–25. doi:10.1046/j.1365-2206.1998.00068.x

Gözübüyük, N. (2015). *Okul öncesi dönem çocuklarında davranış sorunlarının anne-baba tutumu ve öz-kontrol ile ilişkisinin incelenmesi.* [Yayınlanmamış yüksek lisans tezi, Adnan Menderes Üniversitesi, Türkiye]. (*Examination of the relationship between behavioral problems in preschool children and parental attitudes and self-control.* [Unpublished master's thesis, Adnan Menderes University, Turkey].]

Grigore, M.G. (2014). Psycho-Socio-Professional Aspects of Foster Care in Romania. *Journal of Experiential Psychotherapy, 17*(4) (68); 30-46.

Gross-Manos, D. (2015). Material deprivation and social exclusion of children: Lessons from measurement attempts among children in Israel. *Jnl Soc. Pol., 44*(1), 105–125. doi:10.1017/S0047279414000646

Him, T. (2017). Öğretmen Adaylarının Çocuk İstismarı Ve İhmaline Yönelik Farkındalık Düzeyleri. (Awareness Levels of Pre-service Teachers about Child Abuse and Neglect). *Journal of International Social Research, 10*(50), 541–546. doi:10.17719/jisr.2017.1687

İzci, L., Sarı, K. S., & Uyanık, M. N. (2021). Aile Odaklı Hizmet Modeli Olarak Koruyucu Aile Uygulaması. *T.C. Aile ve Sosyal Hizmetler Bakanlığı Çocuk Politikaları Serisi*, 1(3):1-44. (Foster Family Practice as a Family Oriented Service Model. *TR Ministry of Family and Social Services Child Policy Series, 1*(3), 1–44.

Kabakulak, K. (2019). *Çocuk Evleri Hizmet Modeli Kapsamında Olan Lise Öğrencisi Çocukların Akademik Başarı Bileşenlerinin Keşfedilmesi.* [Yayınlanmamış yüksek lisans tezi, Selçuk Üniversitesi, Türkiye]. [*Exploring the Academic Achievement Components of High School Students in the Children's Houses Service Model.* [Unpublished master's thesis, Selcuk University, Turkey].].

Kalaycı, H. (2007). *Yetiştirme Yurdundaki Çocuklarda Sosyal Dışlanma Riski (Tokat ve Turhal Örneği).* [Yayınlanmamış doktora tezi, Sakarya Üniversitesi, Türkiye]. (*The Risk of Social Exclusion in Children in Orphanage* (The Case of Tokat and Turhal). [Unpublished doctoral dissertation, Sakarya University, Turkey].].

Killen, M., Mulvey, K. L., & Hitti, A. (2013). Social Exclusion in Childhood: A Developmental Intergroup Perspective. *Child Development, 84*(3), 772–790. doi:10.1111/cdev.12012 PMID:23170901

Kındıroğlu, Z., & Ve Yaşar-Ekici, F. (2019). The Relationship between Psychological Well-Being and Psychological Resilience Levels of Parents and Social Competence and Behaviors of Children. *Adıyaman University Journal of Educational Sciences, 9*(1), 138–157. doi:10.17984/adyuebd.458224

Koşar, N. (1992). Sosyal Hizmetlerde Koruyucu Aile Hizmeti, Aile ve Çocuk Refahı Alanı. Hacettepe Üniversitesi Yayını. [Foster Family Service in Social Services, Family and Child Welfare Field. Hacettepe University Press].

Küsmez, B. (2020). Korunma İhtiyacı Olan Çocuklar İçin Kurumsal Ve Alternatif Hizmet Modelleri: Bir Değerlendirme. (Institutional and Alternative Service Models for Children in Need of Protection: An Evaluation). [IJSHS]. *International Journal of Social and Humanities Sciences, 4*(3), 201–225.

Ladd, G. W. (2006). Peer Rejection, Aggressive or Withdrawn Behavior, and Psychological Maladjustment from Ages 5 to 12: An Examination of Four Predictive Models. *Child Development, 77*(4), 822–846. doi:10.1111/j.1467-8624.2006.00905.x PMID:16942492

Levitas, R., Pantazis, C., Fahmy, E., Gordon, D., Lloyd, E., & Patsios, D. (2007). The Multi-Dimensional Analysis Of Social Exclusion (pp:86-95). https://dera.ioe.ac.uk/6853/1/multidimensional.pdf

Lyons, S. (2022). Let's Play! Cooperative Games In Early Childhood Programs. *Early Childhood Webinars.* https://www.earlychildhoodwebinars.com/wp-content/uploads/2022/05/Slides_Cooperative-Games-in-Early-Childhood-Programs_05_19_2022.pdf

MacLean, K. (2003). The impact of institutionalization on child development. *Development and Psychopathology, 15*(4), 853–884. doi:10.1017/S0954579403000415 PMID:14984130

Montserrat, C. (2014). The Child Protection System from the Perspective of Young People: Messages from 3 Studies. *Soc. Sci., 3*(4), 687–704. doi:10.3390ocsci3040687

Mulvey, K. L. (2016). Children's reasoning about social exclusion: Balancing many factors. *Child Development Perspectives, 10*(1), 22–27. doi:10.1111/cdep.12157

Mulvey, K. L., Gönültaş, S., Irdam, G., Carlson, R. G., DiStefano, C., & Irvin, M. J. (2021). School and Teacher Factors That Promote Adolescents' Bystander Responses to Social Exclusion. *Frontiers in Psychology, 11*, 581089. doi:10.3389/fpsyg.2020.581089 PMID:33505333

Münger, A. C., & Markström, A. M. (2019). School and Child Protection Services Professionals' Views on the School's Mission and Responsibilities for Children Living with Domestic Violence - Tensions and Gaps. *Journal of Family Violence, 34*(5), 385–398. doi:10.100710896-019-00035-5

Nelson, C. A., Fox, N. A., & Zeanah, C. H. (2014). *Romania's Abandoned Children.* Harvard University Press. doi:10.4159/harvard.9780674726079

Nipedal, C., Nesdale, D., & Killen, M. (2010). Social group norms, school norms, and children's aggressive intentions. *Aggressive Behavior, 36*, 195–204. doi:10.1002/ab.20342 PMID:20301137

Özyürek, A. (2015). Okul öncesi çocukların sosyal beceri düzeyleri ile anne tutumları arasındaki ilişkinin incelenmesi. *Milli Eğitim Dergisi, 206*, 106-120. (Examination of the relationship between the social skill levels of preschool children and their mother attitudes. *Journal of National Education, 206*, 106–120.

Perry, B. D., & Slazavitz, M. (2018). Köpek Gibi Büyütülmüş Çocuk. (B.S. Haktanır, Trans.). Koridor Yayıncılık. [The Child Raised Like a Dog. (B.S. Haktanir, Trans.). Koridor Publishing].

Raufelder, D., Neumann, N., Domin, M., Lorenz, R. C., Gleich, T., Golde, S., Romund, L., Beck, A., & Hoferichter, F. (2021). Do Belonging and Social Exclusion at School Affect Structural Brain Development During Adolescence? *Child Development, 92*(6), 2213–2223. doi:10.1111/cdev.13613 PMID:34156088

Redmond, G., Main, G., O'Donnell, A.W., Skattebol, J., Woodman, R., Mooney, A., Wang, J., Turkmanı, S., Thomson, C. & Brooks, F. (2022). Who excludes? Young People's Experience of Social Exclusion. *Jnl. Soc. Pol.,* 1–24. . doi:10.1017/S0047279422000046

Şahin, T. (2009). *Sosyal Dışlanma ve Yoksulluk İlişkisi.* [Yayınlanmamış sosyal yardım uzmanlık tezi. T.C.Başbakanlık Sosyal Yardımlaşma Ve Dayanışma Genel Müdürlüğü, Türkiye]. (*Relationship between Social Exclusion and Poverty.* [Unpublished social assistance dissertation, T.R. Prime Ministry General Directorate of Social Assistance and Solidarity, Turkey].].

Santrock, J. W. (2015). İlk Çocuklukta Sosyoduygusal Gelişim. (A. Aslan, Trans.). Ergenlikte Sosyoduygusal Gelişim. (G. Yüksel, Trans). G. Yüksel (Trans Ed.). Yaşam Boyu Gelişim içinde (pp. 241-247; 382-396). Nobel Yayıncılık. [Socioemotional Development in Early Childhood. (A. Aslan, Trans.). Socioemotional Development in Adolescence. (G. Yuksel, Trans). G. Yuksel (Trans Ed.). In Lifetime Development (pp. 241-247; 382-396). Nobel Publishing].

Santrock, J. W. (2021). Sosyal duygusal Gelişim. A. Güre (Trans Ed.). (D.S. Atalar & Z. Çakmak, Trans). Çocuk Gelişimi içinde(pp. 278-383) Nobel Yayıncılık. [Social Emotional Development. A. Gure (Trans Ed.). (D.S. Atalar & Z. Cakmak, Trans). In Child Development. (pp. 278-383) Nobel Publishing].

Schoemaker, N. K., Wentholt, W. G. M., Goemans, A., Vermeer, H. J., Juffer, F., & Alink, L. R. A. (2020). A meta-analytic review of parenting interventions in foster care and adoption. *Development and Psychopathology, 32*(3), 1149–1172. doi:10.1017/S0954579419000798 PMID:31366418

Spitz, R. A. (1951). The Psychogenic Diseases in Infancy. *The Psychoanalytic Study of the Child, 6*(1), 255–275. doi:10.1080/00797308.1952.11822915

Tropp, L. R., O'Brien, T. C., Gutierrez, R. G., Valdenegro, D., Migacheva, K., de Tezanos-Pinto, P., Berger, C., & Cayul, O. (2016). How School Norms, Peer Norms, and Discrimination Predict Interethnic Experiences Among Ethnic Minority and Majority Youth. *Child Development, 87*(5), 1436–1451. doi:10.1111/cdev.12608 PMID:27684397

Turkish Ministry of Family and Social Services. (2022). *Services for Children.* AILE. https://www.aile.gov.tr/media/108736/kurumsal-istatistikler.pdf

UK Department of Education. (2018). Children in Need of Help and Protection. *Assets.* https://assets. publishing.service.gov.uk/government/uploads/system/uploads/attachment_data/file/690999/Children_ in_Need_of_help_and_protection_Data_and_analysis.pdf

Unicef (2022). *Convention on the Rights of the Child.* UNICEF. https://www.unicef.org/ turkiye/%C3%A7ocuk-haklar%C4%B1na-dair-s%C3%B6zle%C5%9Fme

Waldock, T. (2019). Marginalized Children and Discrimination: A Focus on Child Welfare, Race, and Culture. *Carleton University.* https://ojs.library.carleton.ca/index.php/pcran/article/view /2371

Werner, N. E., & Hill, L. G. (2010). Individual and Peer Group Normative Beliefs About Relational Aggression. *Child Development, 81*(3), 826–836. doi:10.1111/j.1467-8624.2010.01436.x PMID:20573107

Yıldız, Y., Kaçar, M., Albayrak, E., Çalaboğlu, T., Çakmak, S., & Bayraktar, T. (2017). Çocuk İhmali Ve İstismarı Hakkında İlköğretim Öğretmenlerinin Bilgi Düzeylerinin Değerlendirilmesi. *Van Tıp Dergisi,* 24(4):303-309. (Evaluation of Primary Education Teachers' Knowledge Levels about Child Neglect and Abuse. *Van Medical Journal, 24*(4), 303–309. doi:10.5505/vtd.2017.99609

Yolcuoğlu, İ. (2009). Türkiye'de Çocuk Koruma Sisteminin Genel Olarak Değerlendirilmesi. *Aile ve Toplum, 5*(18): 43-57. [General Evaluation of Child Protection System in Turkey. *Family and Society,* 5(18): 43-57].

Yörükoğlu, A. (2002). Çocuk Ruh Sağlığı. (25. Basım). Özgür Yayınları. [Child Mental Health. (25th Edition). Özgür Publications].

Section 2
Equity-Based Education

Chapter 6
Enhancing Social Justice via Equity-Based Multi-Tiered Systems of Support

Elizabeth D. Cramer

https://orcid.org/0000-0002-8874-114X

Florida International University, USA

Sharde Theodore

Florida International University, USA

Aniva Lumpkins

Florida International University, USA

Chauntea S. Cummings

Florida International University, USA

Helen Rose Flores

Florida International University, USA

ABSTRACT

The purpose of this chapter is to provide an overview of a framework for equity-based multi-tiered systems of support (MTSS), practical strategies for its implementation, and resources to be used by stakeholders when implementing these supports. Special education referral and placement have historically been contingent upon subjective decisions fraught with discriminatory practices that affect racially, ethnically, and linguistically diverse (RELD) students. Through a social justice and culturally responsive lens, this chapter provides an in-depth analysis of existing MTSS systems and ways that inequities in schools can be mediated. Equitable practices are then described across academic and socioemotional supports. The chapter includes: (1) focus on an equity-based MTSS framework for RELD students; (2) implementation of equity-based approaches across three tiers; (3) equity-based assessment and progress monitoring; (4) recommendations for implementation; and (5) future research directions to ensure equity-based supports for RELD learners with or at risk for disability.

DOI: 10.4018/978-1-6684-6386-4.ch006

INTRODUCTION

The United States (US) educational system has a long and deep-rooted history of inequitable policies and procedures fueled by racialized oppression and discrimination affecting racially, ethnically, and linguistically diverse (RELD) students (Artiles et al., 2013; Avant, 2016). RELD learners consistently realize the gravest academic, psychosocial, and behavioral outcomes (Office of Special Education Programs, 2021). Moreover, RELD youth from low-income families often face the poorest outcomes in school that have long-lasting effects, including higher rates of suspensions, expulsions, and school dropout; higher incarceration rates; and lower rates of employment (Anyon et al., 2014; Avant, 2016; Sullivan & Proctor, 2016).

Educators must promote safe and affirming spaces where students are provided the necessary support to successfully navigate life's challenges, including the systemic injustices that have plagued public education. Data-driven and evidence-based practices (EBPs) created to negate levels of subjectivity, such as the response to intervention/multi-tiered systems of support (RTI/MTSS) framework, emerged with promise (Avant 2016; Sullivan & Proctor, 2016). The US Department of Education (DOE)'s Institute for Educational Sciences (IES) established the What Works Clearinghouse in 2002 to review research and determine what practices show evidence of effectiveness as recommended interventions. However, these frameworks and interventions have failed to promote cultural responsivity and equitable approaches necessary to support RELD students (Bal & Trainor, 2016), calling into question the scientific processes used in education to determine "what works" and for whom.

Standardized models and curricula intended to be a panacea for disparities have instead served to shift away from the flexibility encompassed in culturally responsive practices (Cramer et al., 2018). A recent consensus report of the National Academies of Sciences, Engineering, and Medicine (2022) calls for the advancement of "equity-oriented science" in education research. The recommendations of the report suggest that IES must reframe research and funding models to better account for educational complexities associated with equity in education. Further, focus and funds must be shifted toward underserved communities.

Thus, equity-based approaches are needed to support students beyond current practices that have not adequately served them. This chapter provides a framework for equity-based MTSS, practical strategies for its implementation, and resources to be used by stakeholders when implementing these supports. Our examination of the intersectionality of race, disability, inequities, bias, and failed attempts of inclusivity in education is grounded in a Dis/ability Studies and Critical Race Theory (DisCrit) framework (Annamma et al., 2013). DisCrit highlights the social construction of disability and helps unpack systems of oppression and the mechanisms by which they operate (Annamma et al., 2013). Its seven tenets can be applied to guide ethical solutions central to equity-focused MTSS (Annamma et al., 2013; Rausch et al., 2019). Without such consideration, RELD students with disabilities continue to be perceived as problematic (Eilers, 2021), rather than acknowledging systemic issues that have perpetuated widening gaps in education, as well as the stakeholders contributing to such inequities (i.e., teachers, administrators, researchers, politicians, and others influencing education policy and practice).

Through this social justice lens, the chapter provides an in-depth analysis of existing MTSS that have left RELD students behind and examines ways that pervasive inequities in schools can be mediated via an equity-based MTSS framework. It begins with an overview of the background of systemic inequities in the US educational system that have led to disparate results for RELD learners. The chapter continues with a critical examination of existing MTSS systems' role in instruction within a socio-historical context of race and inequity. Equitable practices are then explored, including a detailed framework for implementing equity-based MTSS and supplemental resources for educators. These provide practices that can be infused into existing MTSS frameworks to ensure that RELD students are appropriately supported. Given the complex and diverse learning, social, emotional, and behavioral needs of RELD students, this chapter also highlights trauma-informed practices that can be implemented within the framework.

BACKGROUND

Educational decision-making, including special education referral and placement, has historically been contingent upon subjective decisions. Discriminatory practices affecting school systems and policies result in the overrepresentation of RELD students in special education and exclusionary discipline practices (Bal et al., 2018). Some researchers posit that implicit biases due to unconscious, stereotyped perceptions of ability may explain disparate practices and issues of overrepresentation of RELD students in special education programs (Girvan et al., 2017; Zakszeski et al., 2021). Others (e.g. Paris, 2021) argue that racism and ableism tied to Whiteness and settler logic in institutional, governmental, and agencies that create educational policies reinforce "false and damaging beliefs in superiority in extraction, in dispossession" (p.369) that continue to oppress students based on race, ethnicity, language, gender, sexuality, migration status, social class, disability, and other identity markers.

The traditional medical model approach to special education and the notion that subpar achievement and low performance are a direct function of genetics, cultural influences, or poor effort has further sustained false beliefs, creating a hostile school climate (Connor et al., 2019). Such assumptions fail to account for the inequitable access to critical educational resources (e.g., skilled teachers and quality instruction/content) and ignore how such disparities are a function of race. Furthermore, an exploration of the complex history of education is incomplete without acknowledgment of events such as segregation and institutionalization (US Department of Health and Human Services & USDOE, 2015) affecting RELD students, especially those with disabilities. Such students routinely receive dramatically different learning opportunities and expectations.

Zakszeski et al. (2021) shed light on the disparities in suspension rates of RELD students by looking at the implementation of Tier I interventions across 27 urban schools. The researchers found that male Black and Latinx high school students were more likely to receive office discipline referrals than their White peers. Research has also demonstrated how inequitable disciplinary practices, including zero-tolerance policies, impact marginalized groups in substantially disproportionate ways (Girvan et al., 2017; Payne & Welch, 2015). For example, Okilwa and Robert (2017) found that Black male students face inordinate rates of behavioral consequences for minor infractions, such as dress code violations.

Moreover, Rueda (2015) investigated longitudinal trends of disproportionate behavioral practices among diverse student populations. Data revealed discrepancies in behavioral practices for students based on race. Latinx students were underrepresented in the number of disciplinary referrals during kindergarten through fifth grades but were overrepresented in seventh to ninth grades compared to their White counterparts. Black students, however, were overrepresented in receiving disciplinary referrals across all grades (Rueda, 2015). Significant disproportionalities place RELD students at higher risk of being identified for special education services and facing inappropriate placement in restrictive environments (National Center for Learning Disabilities, 2020). These examples highlight the intersectionality of race, special education, and exclusionary practices and provide startling evidence of how students of color, English learners, youth living in poverty, and students with disabilities face disparate and restrictive practices that deny them access to an appropriate education (Connor et al., 2019). The delivery of necessary supports for emerging bilingual students, students with challenging behaviors, and students identified with disabilities within inclusive settings poses challenges for many schools, demonstrating inequities in education.

MTSS AS AN APPROACH TO EQUITABLE EDUCATION

In efforts to address such disparities, multiple federal regulations have been mandated over the last 25 years including identification of significant disproportionality, allocating special education funds for coordinated early intervening services if significant disproportionality is identified (Sullivan et al., 2018), and the use of systematic procedures for screening, intervening, and monitoring students who are demonstrating deficits before making evaluation decisions for disability placement (National Center for Learning Disabilities, 2011). In response, evidence-based MTSS frameworks, such as RTI for addressing academic achievement and positive behavior interventions and supports (PBIS) to promote socio-emotional success, have been widely adopted in schools to meet these mandates and attempt to reduce inappropriate disability diagnosis.

In theory, MTSS would remove subjectivity and potential biases and ensure all students are receiving a quality and evidence-based education. The key component of MTSS is progress monitoring using formative assessments and problem-solving using data-based decisions. However, disproportionality in special education persists, and questions remain about the equity and fidelity of MTSS implementation. Recent studies demonstrate that many school professionals feel unprepared to implement MTSS approaches with fidelity and lean on their cultural values, oftentimes leading to misinterpretations of RELD students' behaviors (Avant, 2016; Sabnis et al., 2020). Additionally, Cramer (2015) points out that MTSS is used inconsistently across states, districts, and schools, making it difficult to pinpoint effective MTSS approaches for RELD students. Thus, a systematic equity-based approach to MTSS is crucial for the success of minoritized students at risk for disabilities.

Defining Equity-Based MTSS

As defined by McCart and Miller (2020), equity-based MTSS considers opportunity, access, resources allocated, and student backgrounds in a school. These backgrounds go beyond race, ethnicity, language, and disability status. Equity-minded schools also consider housing status, a child's role in a family (e.g., an older child may be a wage earner for a family), foster care placement, sexuality, gender expression, migration status, rural or urban settings of communities, mental and physical health challenges, situations occurring in a child's home, and anything else that may be salient to a school or community (McCart & Miller, 2020). Each classroom and school must be reflective, as this definition is not inclusive of all potential identities and markers of difference. Whereas traditional MTSS is a tiered system of academic and behavioral supports, equity-based MTSS is a schoolwide, structural framework that uses data-driven decisions to ensure that all students receive academic, behavioral, and social supports (McCart & Miller, 2020) that are both culturally relevant and sustaining (Ladson-Billings, 2014; Paris & Alim, 2017). This means that marginalized students are subjects (rather than objects) in the instructional process, and educators can learn from their students rather than simply about their students. Keeping students'

Figure 1. Integrated Framework for Equity-Based Multi-Tiered Systems of Support
Note. Adapted from Theodore et al., 2022 and Thurlow et al., 2020.

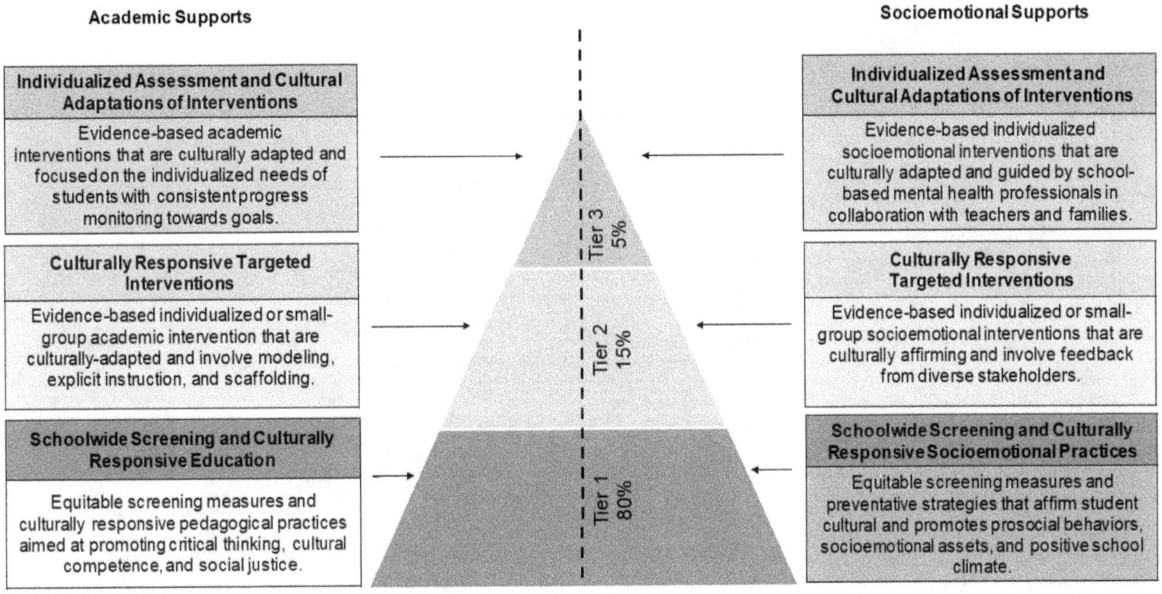

Academic Supports

Individualized Assessment and Cultural Adaptations of Interventions

Evidence-based academic interventions that are culturally adapted and focused on the individualized needs of students with consistent progress monitoring towards goals.

Culturally Responsive Targeted Interventions

Evidence-based individualized or small-group academic intervention that are culturally-adapted and involve modeling, explicit instruction, and scaffolding.

Schoolwide Screening and Culturally Responsive Education

Equitable screening measures and culturally responsive pedagogical practices aimed at promoting critical thinking, cultural competence, and social justice.

Socioemotional Supports

Individualized Assessment and Cultural Adaptations of Interventions

Evidence-based individualized socioemotional interventions that are culturally adapted and guided by school-based mental health professionals in collaboration with teachers and families.

Culturally Responsive Targeted Interventions

Evidence-based individualized or small-group socioemotional interventions that are culturally affirming and involve feedback from diverse stakeholders.

Schoolwide Screening and Culturally Responsive Socioemotional Practices

Equitable screening measures and preventative strategies that affirm student cultural and promotes prosocial behaviors, socioemotional assets, and positive school climate.

Tier 3 5%

Tier 2 15%

Tier 1 80%

various and complex intersecting identities in mind, equity-based MTSS can be a tool to increase academic and behavioral outcomes of students from RELD backgrounds, including those with disabilities, and address and mitigate educational discrepancies uncovered by the COVID-19 pandemic (Choi et al., 2020; Sullivan et al., 2020).

SOLUTIONS AND RECOMMENDATIONS

A Framework for Equity-Based MTSS

The following section provides a framework that describes culturally sustaining procedures and examples of EBPs that align with equity-based MTSS. A visual depiction of this framework for implementing equity-based academic and socioemotional support within schools is provided in Figure 1. This modification of traditional models of tiered instruction depicts culturally affirming suggestions across each tier.

As displayed in Figure 1, Tier 1 programs emphasize preventative and schoolwide skill development through culturally responsive academic and psychoeducational approaches with valuable opportunities to practice skills learned and gain feedback. Additionally, school personnel utilize equitable assessments to administer universal screeners and plan for further intervention at Tier 2. Tier 2 provides extra support based on universal screening data (Bacete et al., 2019). At this level, students should receive supplemental, culturally adapted, and culturally affirming evidence-based interventions in small groups using targeted supports and inclusive practices (Malone et al., 2021). Tier 3 includes intensive, targeted approaches (e.g., individualized interventions) and assessments focused on specific academic or socioemotional needs of students and their families. Recommendations for implementing equity-based MTSS across socioemotional and academic domains for each tier are featured in Table 1. Examples of these and another highlighted approaches throughout the chapter are in Table 2 in the Appendix.

Table 1. Recommendations for Equity-Based Academic and Socioemotional MTSS

Academic	Socioemotional
Tier 1: Screening and Culturally Responsive School-Wide Approaches	
· Utilize equitable screeners and disaggregated data · Embed culturally responsive educational practices · Consider daily linguistic accommodations (e.g., language support in English and native language whenever possible)	· Use microaffirmations to create a culturally affirming and positive school climate · Engage in equity-focused SEL programming based on the model of transformative SEL · Develop family-school partnerships
Tier 2: Culturally Responsive Targeted Interventions	
· Choose critical literacy with a social justice lens, multicultural literature, and print-rich environments that are culturally representative · Utilize problem structure instruction (math) · Provide instruction in phonological awareness, phonics, and vocabulary · Incorporate teaching strategies of modeling, explicit instruction, and scaffolding · Instruct in small groups of 3-5	· Embed culturally relevant pedagogy to help foster and affirm positive racial identity · Utilize trauma-sensitive programs · Adapt Tier 2 interventions to include students' backgrounds and interests · Engage community stakeholders who reflect the values and cultures of those who will participate in the intervention
Tier 3: Individualized Assessment and Cultural Adaptations of Interventions	
· Employ an ecological approach when evaluating possible learning difficulties · Assess students' cultural and linguistic proficiency to determine the source of the difficulty and rule out environmental factors · Create specially designed instruction that affirms the culture of the student	· Utilize data from functional behavioral assessment to advise services through a culturally responsive lens · Incorporate culturally responsive and affirming practices into student plan of care throughout counseling sessions (e.g., reference DSM-5 cultural formulation interview to guide therapeutic interventions)

Note: Adapted from Malone et al., 2021

Tier 1: Equity-Based Universal Screening and Culturally Responsive Schoolwide Approaches

In an MTSS/RTI framework, universal screeners and progress monitoring assessments must be conducted by a child study team (CST), which includes trained and knowledgeable personnel who collect data from multiple sources to identify learning difficulties across contexts, including home and school. When monitoring student progress, the CST should use evidence-based assessment instruments that are reliable and include diverse forms for monitoring student progress; avoid discriminatory practices against RELD students when administering assessments; and provide assessments in the student's native language (Linan-Thompson et al., 2022). For example, when benchmark assessments do not provide norms for emerging bilingual students, state or district policies should provide explicit criteria for identifying emergent bilingual students who are not meeting grade-level expectations and providing appropriate supplemental interventions. Thus, CSTs should include members with expertise in areas such as bilingualism and biliteracy (Linan-Thompson et al., 2022).

Examples of non-biased assessments include self-reports of behavior (Raines et al., 2012), holistic assessments (Yee & Butler, 2020), and gated assessments (Klingbeil et al., 2019; Van Norman et al., 2017).

Self-reports of behavior are more accurate than teacher or parent reports alone and can mitigate risks associated with bias and overrepresentation (Raines et al., 2012). Holistic assessments consider student culture and the culture of a classroom that may be contributing to learning or behavioral challenges, as opposed to simply looking at test scores (Yee & Butler, 2020). Although more time-consuming than self-reports, they provide additional information as multiple test scores are combined instead of looking at multiple academic scores in isolation. Gated approaches are sensitive ways of identifying students who truly need help by looking at multiple tests across several time points. Although requiring a certain degree of statistical understanding, they are effective in elementary and secondary settings (Klingbeil et al., 2019; Van Norman et al., 2017). Appropriate assessments ensure that tiers are not being used to label students but rather to distribute necessary resources in timely and effective ways. Once universal screening measures are administered, data should be disaggregated to ensure that gaps shown demonstrate the needs of individual students and not systemic problems within the school's Tier 1 practices (Hernández Finch, 2012). Child study teams should disaggregate data to determine if outcomes are based on student groupings (e.g., ethnicity, language acquisition, social class). Schools should use disaggregated data to determine whether interventions benefit all student populations through a standard treatment protocol, a problem-solving model, or a combination of both (Hernández Finch, 2012). At the Tier 1 level, CSTs are responsible for utilizing a problem-solving approach to identify students who need more targeted support. The problem-solving approach involves:

1. Identification of the problem and determination of causation
2. Development of an action plan to address the problem
3. Implementation of the plan (i.e., the intervention)
4. Evaluation of the effectiveness of the plan (Hernández Finch, 2012).

Although standard treatment protocols are strongly supported by research, they are problematic because they consistently use a one-size fits all approach. When students demonstrate similar academic challenges, they are presented with one standard, research-based intervention, which is a major disadvantage in addressing skill deficits for diverse struggling learners. The hybrid approach, comprised of problem-solving and standard treatment protocol approaches is more accommodating because academic plans are customized to meet their unique needs, thus ensuring that appropriate and valid research-based interventions are selected.

Similar methods should be applied to addressing socioemotional and behavioral needs. For example, schools could use a dual-continua approach to guide the selection of mental health screeners (Malone et al., 2021). Within the dual-continua approach, one continuum indicates the presence or absence of positive mental health, and the other indicates the presence and absence of mental illness symptoms. Schools can also use the School Health Assessment and Performance Evaluation. This free online platform provides access to free and low-cost screening and assessment tools (National Center for Mental Health, 2020). RELD students needing additional supports based on screenings may complete follow-up measures that ask about racial-ethnic risk factors like microaggressions, racial stress and trauma, and acculturative stress, and protective factors like racial/ethnic identity. This additional information allows school-based mental health professionals (SBMHPs), such as school counselors, psychologists, and social workers, to assess the extent to which microaggressions and racial discrimination are contributing to students' social and emotional concerns or impacting their overall well-being, and plan for more targeted intervention in Tier 2. Schools may also use existing assessments to identify subgroups of students who report more negative perceptions of school climate. These include the School Climate Measure, which assesses adolescents' perception of teacher-student relationships, school connectedness, academic support, order and discipline, physical environment, social environment, perceived exclusion, academic satisfaction, parental involvement, and opportunities for student engagement (Zullig et al., 2015). This measure is valid for diverse populations.

The true goal of monitoring students within MTSS frameworks is to make interventions more intensive as necessary by adjusting instruction based on ongoing data collection (Choi et al., 2020; Vaughn, 2015). Data-Based Individualization (DBI) is a hallmark of effective educational practices for all students (Jung et al., 2018) with its ongoing data collection and analysis to adapt and adjust the intensity of instruction and support. This is an essential skill for culturally sustaining educators to possess. An in-depth understanding of ongoing feedback will provide practitioners with information to adjust students' instruction (Jung et al., 2018). The assessment of RELD students with disabilities must be comprehensive and detailed to differentiate between students whose difficulties are related to academic learning and behavioral/social skills from students who may be, for example, acquiring English. Issues in the assessment of language learning and behavior difficulties of RELD students (e.g., students from non-English speaking backgrounds), particularly those with or at risk for disabilities, must be handled with great care considering the previously reported suspension and achievement data.

Tier 1 Academic Supports

Tier 1 academic supports include the core curriculum, which applies to all students. Tier 1 academic practices are meant to help students master benchmark academic skills (e.g., literacy, mathematical computation). To provide equity-based MTSS, schools must first ensure that RELD students receive evidence-based, culturally sustaining supports aimed at building their critical thinking skills while promoting cultural competence. Therefore, school leaders should ensure that the curriculum is chosen appropriately based on students' backgrounds and required district mandates (e.g., curricular programs). Schools should consider comprehensive and contextual approaches that move away from a deficit model of understanding diverse learners.

Additionally, when planning instruction, teachers should consider ways to affirm the sociocultural backgrounds (e.g., language use and communication style) of RELD students (Montalvo et al., 2014). Teachers' awareness of students' cultural identity helps scaffold instruction to appropriate levels and enhances teacher-student relationships (Montalvo et al., 2014). Prioritizing the sociocultural experiences of RELD students can assist in developing and implementing more balanced, culturally sustaining pedagogies to prevent students from being inappropriately referred for special education services. Thus, teachers should use culturally responsive teaching (CRT; Aronson & Laughter, 2016; Gay, 2018; Ladson-Billings, 2014) to instruct RELD students at Tier 1.

Culturally responsive EBPs (Aronson & Laughter, 2016) are critical to the success of equity-based intervention at Tier 1. Culturally responsive teachers view students' cultural identity (e.g., language use, communication style) and contextual experiences as valuable resources for learning. These teachers value students' cultural capital (Bourdieu,1986) and use it to scaffold instruction. Moreover, teachers who use CRT apply interactive, collaborative teaching methods of interaction that support RELD students' cultural, linguistic, and racial experiences (Ladson-Billings, 2014) and integrate the methods with EBPs. These EBPs consist of approaches including collaborative teaching, responsive feedback, and child-centered instruction (Aceves & Orosco, 2014). For example, teachers who utilize child-centered instruction prioritize student choice and participation as integral components of their lessons. Teachers provide opportunities for choice in classroom activities, encourage child-directed learning, and assist students as they engage in these activities. Additionally, equity-focused teachers create opportunities for students to demonstrate leadership and autonomy over their learning. For example, Saunders and Goldenberg (2007) found that Instructional Conversation, a literacy strategy for students to use linguistic skills to engage in conceptually rich dialogue, demonstrated positive effects on the academic performance of emerging bilingual students.

Once a strong foundation is established, reorganization should start by ensuring that appropriate Tier 1 supports are being implemented with fidelity. Instructional fidelity is critical to ensure that learning difficulties are not due to poor instruction. Effective instruction should be integrated, evidence-based, and administered by all staff within the school. Successful implementation and sustainability of an equitable Tier 1 system depend on consistent training and evaluations for instructional staff (e.g., teachers; Eagle et al., 2015). An integrated approach means that academic, behavioral, and social supports are occurring simultaneously, addressing the whole child. Interconnected approaches include strategies such as explicit instruction, feedback, and opportunities to respond.

Tier 1 Socioemotional Supports

Tier 1 socioemotional practices should include proactive strategies that promote students' prosocial behaviors and mental health development embedded within school and classroom systems. To enhance their effectiveness for RELD students, SBMHPs can encourage school personnel to use culturally responsive evidence-based schoolwide practices (Dong et al., 2020). Tier 1 services and supports include activities to promote a positive school climate, positive prosocial behaviors, social-emotional competence, and mental health literacy. Emphasis on mental health promotion can increase students' well-being and reduce the need for costly and time-intensive interventions. School climate is addressed at Tier 1 because of its relationship with student outcomes. A positive school climate is associated with several adaptive outcomes, including improved academic outcomes, reduced school dropout, improved attendance, and better student-teacher relationships (Huang & Cornell, 2018).

Social-emotional learning (SEL) should also be embedded at Tier 1(Malone et al., 2021). Social-emotional competencies, including self-management and emotional regulation, are necessary to establish and maintain a positive identity, achieve personal goals, and cultivate caring relationships with others (CASEL, 2020). These skills lay the foundation for school and life-long success. For example, social-emotional competencies support students in being able to form positive relationships with others and use deductive reasoning to make responsible decisions (CASEL, 2020) which are skills necessary for academic and professional success. Notably, when students are educated in adverse situations or experience pervasive stress (e.g., living in poverty), it affects their socioemotional skills (Blitz et al., 2020), cognitive functioning (e.g., working memory), academic performance, and overall school success (e.g., social engagement, work ethic). This also compounds existing social-emotional difficulties in at-risk students (Chafouleas et al., 2021).

With the prevalence of Adverse Childhood Experiences (ACEs) and trauma among school-age children, schools should improve outcomes through equitable intervention (Blitz et al., 2020). Research has demonstrated that trauma-informed approaches within MTSS can increase resilience in RELD students exposed to trauma beginning with Tier 1 strategies (Chafouleas et al., 2016; Fondren et al., 2020). Crosby et al. (2020) define trauma-informed practices as a set of trauma-sensitive practices to address student needs, using flexible instructional delivery and behavioral management that promotes prosocial behaviors. The Substance Abuse and Mental Health Services Administration (SAMHSA; 2022) reports that two-thirds of children have experienced at least one traumatic event by age 16 and repeated exposure to traumatic stress in children without treatment can impact brain functioning and lead to increased risk of mental health diagnoses and behavioral challenges. RELD children living in poverty are at increased risk for exposure to traumatic events such as abuse, neglect, and family dysfunction (Blitz et al., 2020). Such ACEs have been shown to significantly impact individuals' physical and emotional health into adulthood (Boullier & Blair, 2018). Consequently, the need for prevention is as critical as intervention.

When addressing trauma, intervention goals include: realize, recognize, respond, and resist re-traumatization (SAMHSA, 2014). Further, SAMHSA outlines the six principles of a trauma-informed approach that sustains culture:

- Safety
- Trustworthiness and transparency
- Peer support
- Collaboration and mutuality
- Empowerment, voice, and choice
- Historical, cultural, and gender issues

Trauma-informed approaches are included in Tier 1 recommendations, as schoolwide practices can build awareness of the significant impact of trauma that may interfere with learning. Blitz et al. (2020) emphasize the recognition of trauma symptoms in children and their impact on school functioning within the context of marginalization and oppression. A culturally responsive, trauma-informed school incorporates the values of the community and builds relationships with children and families.

Fondren et al. (2020) and Chafouleas et al. (2016) discuss trauma-informed MTSS models that address all levels of intervention. At Tier 1, universal supports may be addressed through a positive school climate, teaching problem-solving, coping skills, and resiliency. Tier 1 focuses on building social-emotional competencies through curricula that embrace cultural diversity. An effective, whole-school trauma-informed approach requires collaboration between schools, families, and the community. Sustainability of progress requires professional development of teachers and school staff and the education of families to avoid re-traumatization and promote social-emotional skill building (SAMHSA, 2014). To be culturally responsive, schools may use restorative practices that consider community and cultural values. Restorative practices provide a critical opportunity for students who are often seen as offenders to learn effective ways to reconcile conflict with the support of the class community. Moreover, all students build compassion, empathy, forgiveness, and acceptance through this rehabilitative practice. Restorative disciplinary approaches mitigate exclusionary practices (Caldera et al., 2019; Payne & Welch, 2015).

Tier 2: Culturally Responsive Progress Monitoring and Targeted Interventions

Students who are not meeting their goals at Tier 1 receive additional targeted supports at Tier 2, often in small groups. Culturally responsive progress monitoring continues with culturally affirming feedback.

Tier 2 Academic Supports

Academic supports become more targeted to students' areas of need at Tier 2. Meta-analyses and systematic reviews of Tier 2 math interventions (Jitendra et al., 2021) and reading interventions (Goldfeld et al., 2022) describe effective EBPs. Notably, a meta-analysis by Jitendra et al. (2021) looked at interventions for students in grades K-12 with math difficulties, and 70% of participants were identified as English learners. Problem-structure instruction (e.g., visual representation of problems) was the only type of intervention that significantly improved math scores for students. Group sizes of two to three were found more effective than one-on-one or larger group sizes, as students could consistently interact with both the teacher and their peers. Jitendra and colleagues found that treatment was equally effective whether administered by school personnel or researchers.

Goldfeld et al. (2022) completed a systematic review of reading interventions for students in preschool to second grade with reading difficulties. The review found that six interventions met the National Health and Medical Research Council's evidence matrix for very strong evidence and above. These interventions were provided in groups of 3-5, four times a week for 3-6 months, and a duration of 30 minutes per session and included phonological awareness, phonics, vocabulary, modeling, explicit instruction, and scaffolding (Goldfeld et al., 2022). However, these studies did not address nor disaggregate results by race, ethnicity, or any other identities.

Both reviews offer pertinent information and guidance to help stakeholders choose and implement Tier 2 academic supports. However, using data-driven intensive intervention and instruction through the implementation of culturally sustaining EBPs and monitoring must be a priority among educators (McLeskey et al., 2019). Many interventions have proven effective for developing skills among learners responding to Tier 2 instruction. Nevertheless, research is limited on additional supports for non-responders to MTSS (Braun et al., 2020) and those from RELD backgrounds (Goldfeld et al., 2022; Jitendra et al., 2021).

This need for supports extends beyond the student. Educators must understand the role culture and language play in how families perceive and cope with supporting a child with a disability. It has been extensively documented that culture, which mediates thought and language production, has a significant impact on how families accept, address, and advocate when a disability is identified (Brandon et al., 2021; Harry & Ocasio-Stoutenburg, 2020). Successfully addressing the omnipresent nature of culture can lead to better outcomes within the context of MTSS (Kramarczuk-Voulgarides et al., 2021). Pedagogy that facilitates cultural awareness and is responsive to differentiation of content increases learning outcomes for students with or at risk for disabilities in urban settings (Gunawardena et al., 2019). Examples of this include critical literacy with a social justice lens, multicultural literature, and print-rich environments that are culturally representative (Bennett et al., 2018).

Tier 2 Socioemotional Supports

To support RELD students, SBMHPs can adapt existing interventions and procedures to increase their cultural relevance and increase generalizability to students' school, home, and community lives. Intervention adaptations ensure that the language, metaphors, content, concepts, and goals are culturally appropriate for the target population (Malone et al., 2021). Additionally, procedural adaptations consider local contexts and address changes to program delivery to make interventions more culturally congruent. SBMHPs interested in delivering culturally adapted interventions are encouraged to collect data on students' backgrounds and interests, engage community stakeholders who reflect the values and cultures of those who will participate in the intervention, operationalize the selected adaptations, and document the change. Substantial research (e.g., Graves et al., 2017; Malone et al., 2021) has demonstrated that cultural adaptations of existing Tier 2 programs have been effective for RELD students at risk for mental health problems. For example, Graves and colleagues (2017) examine the effectiveness of a culturally adapted SEL intervention for Black male students at risk for emotional and behavioral disorders in an urban elementary school. Results of the study indicated positive outcomes on students' social-emotional knowledge, particularly in the areas of self-regulation and self-competence. For children displaying risk factors or those with known trauma exposure, SBMHPs can utilize more targeted trauma-sensitive Tier 2 interventions delivered in smaller groups (e.g., Cognitive Behavioral Intervention for Trauma in Schools; Allison & Ferreria, 2017).

Tier 3: Individualized Assessment and Cultural Adaptation of Interventions

Students who still do not respond to targeted Tier 2 supports require intensive, often individualized supports at Tier 3. Notably, Tier 3 is often where CSTs decide to initiate a referral for evaluation to determine potential need for special education services (Rodgers et al., 2021). For RELD students receiving Tier 3 interventions, it is critical to ensure that students' cultural and linguistic influences are examined before special education referral is considered (Montalvo et al., 2014). A mismatch between teachers and students in areas such as language, migration status, economic status, and prior life experiences can lead to inappropriate referrals.

Tier 3 Academic Supports

To address inappropriate special education referrals, Garcia and Ortiz (1988) developed a flowchart with questions intended to minimize teacher misinterpretations of RELD students who are struggling academically and assist with the decision-making process. Such questions include: Is the student experiencing academic difficulties, and, is there evidence of systematic efforts to identify the source of difficulty and take corrective action? Answers to these questions guide teachers in a self-assessment of their knowledge of students' cultural and linguistic proficiency, preferred teaching and learning styles, and motivational influences, compared to the needs of their RELD students.

All students can benefit from targeted support, regardless of identified disability. Specially designed instruction (SDI) refers to adaptations to the content, methodology, or delivery of instruction that addresses the unique needs of a child. SDI must be provided in the least restrictive setting which arguably could and should always be a general education classroom, regardless of potential disability. When SDI is applied at Tier 3, students typically demonstrate a need for sustained intensive interventions to maintain adequate rates of progress over time (Rodgers et al., 2021).

Tier 3 Socioemotional Supports

At Tier 3, socioemotional supports are often provided by trained SBMHPs (Chafouleas, 2016). Culturally responsive SBMHPs are aware of and sensitive to their cultural heritage and are comfortable with cultural differences between themselves and their students. Culturally responsive SBMHPs also demonstrate cultural humility by decentering their own identity and conveying openness to learning about the cultural identity that is most important to their students (Malone et al., 2021).

Such SBMPHs can assist with program reform because they understand the relationship between behavior and academics. Furthermore, they can act as change agents, assisting with communications with and training of staff (Avant, 2016), or delivering intensive interventions to meet socioemotional and behavioral needs through counseling and therapeutic interventions (Berger, 2019; Malone et al., 2021). Culturally responsive SBMHPs are cognizant of the relationship between racism and mental health and convey openness to discussing equity issues. They can use clinical intervention tools such as the Jones Intentional Multicultural Interview Schedule (Jones, 2009) or the Diagnostic and Statistical Manual of Mental Disorders, Fifth Edition (DSM-5) cultural formulation interview (American Psychiatric Association, 2013) to communicate about cultural factors and the extent to which they impact students' mental health functioning (Jones et al., 2015). In the ADDRESSING model (Hays, 2008) clinicians are trained to understand the cultural influences that shape students' experiences in the complexity of their identities. The model, comprised of nine cultural dimensions (i.e., age, developmental or other identi-fied disabilities, religion, ethnic/racial identity, socioeconomic status, sexual orientation, Indigenous group membership, nationality, and gender identity), is used to consider if students hold dominant or non-dominant status in a dimension to better understand their beliefs, behaviors, and experiences of privilege and marginalization. This model can also guide SBMHPs toward culture-specific information to better understand students and avoid biased generalizations.

For the most intensive Tier 3 needs, community agencies can partner with schools to deliver services during the school day, particularly in districts with limited SMBMPH. These services might include Trauma-Focused Cognitive Behavioral Therapy, often used as a means of intervention to build an awareness of the interaction between thoughts, feelings, and actions to increase coping and problem-solving skills and reduce symptoms of mental health conditions (e.g., anxiety, depression). At this level of intervention, consideration of family needs is important and may be addressed through wraparound services in the community (SAMHSA, 2014).

Implementing Equitable MTSS

Schools and communities already have strengths and capital that can aid in developing sustainable, equity-based MTSS. Critical educators can simultaneously acknowledge and fight for educational equality while also working with existing resources in their communities. To begin, schools should reflect on community supports or organizations that may be able to assist (McCart & Miller, 2020). Many necessary changes can be made through the restructuring of present practices and by identifying the most urgent needs of a community (Sullivan et al., 2018; Sullivan et al., 2020). On a deeper level, implementation of equitable MTSS practices in schools requires systemic and ideological changes which require the contribution and collaboration of several stakeholders. District and school-based administrators must place priority and value on equitable approaches to academic and behavioral interventions and communicate this commitment to change to staff. Leaders must be prepared to provide training and ongoing support to all school staff to equip them with the skills required to deliver a culturally responsive curriculum through a strengths-based approach (Khalifa et al., 2016). School personnel must examine their views and practices around issues of social justice, bias, and equity. Such an examination of social justice in educational practice cannot be used as an add-on. It sets the foundation of schoolwide practices. Schools should maintain an overt commitment to addressing school-wide diversity at Tier 1. All personnel, particularly SBMHPs, should receive cultural competency training to learn how to recognize microaggressions and other forms of racism so when these instances occur, they can interrupt accordingly. Engaging in the personal work of introspection and self-exploration and the interpersonal work of learning from and with other cultures helps educators feel more comfortable having critical conversations in the classroom and decreases the likelihood that they will engage in microaggressions toward students (Malone et al., 2021). Parents and families must be included as critical and valued members of this evaluative process.

FUTURE RESEARCH DIRECTIONS

Much of the focus of MTSS research to date has included standardized frameworks and implementation strategies. Future research should examine equity-based frameworks. Educators must consider the way diversity is being prioritized in teaching and learning and the impact on school practices overall. Given the urgency of promoting social justice, a closer look is needed at educator preparedness to: deliver culturally sustaining curricula, acknowledge social injustices affecting the students they serve, and advocate for marginalized populations (Avant, 2016). Future research should measure the impact of educator professional development on student academic and behavioral outcomes (Eagle et al., 2015).

Given the team-based approach to MTSS, both the leadership and dynamics among team members are worthy of study. Consideration should be given to the buy-in of team members, consistency of participation, efficient use of time and resources, and the components of effective leadership that result in a productive team. Schools also need specific roadmaps for adopting a whole-school approach to equity and ensuring buy-in from staff (Scott et al., 2019). Finally, more scholarship on equity-based MTSS's impact on exclusionary discipline practices and educational outcomes is warranted (Anyon et al., 2014). It is essential to mitigate the negative impacts of disproportionality on RELD students and ensure fidelity of equitable implementation (Eagle et al., 2015; Scott et al., 2019).

CONCLUSION

Educational inequities have a long and deeply-rooted history in US schools, particularly for RELD learners who are at risk for or diagnosed with a disability. Lack of understanding of the complex nuances associated with markers of difference such as race, language, social class, migration status, sexuality, and disability has exacerbated inequities and led to ineffective educational opportunities. Through a critical lens, schools can begin to remedy this via schoolwide, equity-based MTSS using culturally affirming, data-driven decisions to ensure that all students receive appropriate academic, behavioral, and social supports and services. By forming collaborative partnerships among diverse and interdisciplinary stakeholders, including families, essential relationships and commitments can guide best practices for all learners. By considering the complex needs of RELD students, including traumas related to racial oppression, instruction can be designed to meet the needs of the whole child and ensure every opportunity for student success. Standardized and evidence-based procedures such as MTSS sometimes feel contradictory to culturally responsive approaches. "If educators working for social justice wish to have an impact, they must creatively play by the rules while still seeking change in the everyday life of the classroom." (Aronson & Laughter, 2016, p. 199). This framework and the accompanying resources may serve as an initial start for schools aiming to do such.

REFERENCES

Aceves, T. C., & Orosco, M. J. (2014). *Culturally responsive teaching* (Document No. IC-2). University of Florida. https://ceedar.education.ufl.edu/tools/innovation-configurations/

Allison, A. C., & Ferreira, R. J. (2017). Implementing cognitive behavioral intervention for trauma in schools (CBITS) with Latino youth. *Child & Adolescent Social Work Journal, 34*(2), 181–189. doi:10.100710560-016-0486-9

American Psychiatric Association. (2013). *Diagnostic and statistical manual of mental disorders* (5th ed.)., doi:10.1176/appi.books.9780890425596

Annamma, S. A., Connor, D., & Ferri, B. (2013). Dis/ability critical race studies (DisCrit): Theorizing at the intersections of race and dis/ability. *Race, Ethnicity and Education, 16*(1), 1–31. doi:10.1080/13613324.2012.730511

Anyon, Y., Jenson, J. M., Altschul, I., Farrar, J., McQueen, J., Greer, E., Downing, B., & Simmons, J. (2014). The persistent effect of race and the promise of alternatives to suspension in school discipline outcomes. *Children and Youth Services Review, 44*, 379–386. doi:10.1016/j.childyouth.2014.06.025

Aronson, B., & Laughter, J. (2016). The theory and practice of culturally relevant education: A synthesis of research across content areas. *Review of Educational Research, 86*(1), 163–206. doi:10.3102/0034654315582066

Artiles, A. J. (2013). Untangling the racialization of disabilities: An intersectionality critique across disability models. *Du Bois Review, 10*(2), 329–347. doi:10.1017/S1742058X13000271

Avant, D. W. (2016). Using response to intervention/multi-tiered systems of supports to promote social justice in schools. *Journal for Multicultural Education, 10*(4), 507–520. doi:10.1108/JME-06-2015-0019

Bacete, F. J. G., Marande, G., & Mikami, A. Y. (2019). Evaluation of a multi-component and multi-agent intervention to improve classroom social relationships among early elementary school-age children. *Journal of School Psychology, 77*, 124–138. doi:10.1016/j.jsp.2019.09.001 PMID:31837721

Bal, A., Afacan, K., & Cakir, H. I. (2018). Culturally responsive school discipline: Implementing learning lab at a high school for systemic transformation. *American Educational Research Journal, 55*(5), 1007–1050. doi:10.3102/0002831218768796

Bal, A., & Trainor, A. A. (2016). Culturally responsive experimental intervention studies: The development of a rubric for paradigm expansion. *World Yearbook of Education, 2017*(2), 237–277. doi:10.3102/0034654315585004

Bennett, S. V., Gunn, A. A., Gayle-Evans, G., Barrera, E. S. IV, & Leung, C. B. (2018). Culturally responsive literacy practices in an early childhood community. *Early Childhood Education Journal, 46*(2), 241–248. doi:10.100710643-017-0839-9

Berger, E. (2019). Multi-tiered approaches to trauma-informed care in schools: A systematic review. *School Mental Health, 11*(4), 650–664. doi:10.100712310-019-09326-0

Blitz, L. V., Yull, D., & Clauhs, M. (2020). Bringing sanctuary to school: Assessing school climate as a foundation for culturally responsive trauma-informed approaches for urban schools. *Urban Education, 55*(1), 95–124. doi:10.1177/0042085916651323

Boullier & Blair, M. (2018). Adverse childhood experiences. *Pediatrics and Child Health, 28*(3), 132–137. doi:10.1016/j.paed.2017.12.008

Bourdieu, P. (1986). *The forms of capital.* J. Handbook of Theory and Research for the Sociology of Education. Greenwood.

Brandon, R. R., Higgins, K., Jones, V. T., & Dobbins, N. (2021). African American parents with children with disabilities: Gathering home-school reflections. *Intervention in School and Clinic, 57*(2), 119–125. doi:10.1177/10534512211001837

Braun, G., Kumm, S., Brown, C., Walte, S., Hughes, M. T., & Maggin, D. M. (2020). Living in Tier 2: Educators' perceptions of MTSS in urban schools. *International Journal of Inclusive Education, 24*(10), 1114–1128. doi:10.1080/13603116.2018.1511758

Caldera, A., Whitaker, M. C., & Conrad Popova, D. A. (2019). Classroom management in urban schools: Proposing a course framework. *Teaching Education, 31*(3), 343–361. doi:10.1080/10476210.2018.1561663

CASEL. (2020). CASEL's SEL framework: What are the core competence areas and where are they promoted? *CASEL.* https://casel.org/casel-sel-framework-11-2020/

Chafouleas, S. M., Johnson, A. H., Overstreet, S., & Santos, N. M. (2016). Toward a blueprint for trauma-informed service delivery in schools. *School Mental Health, 8*(1), 144–162. doi:10.100712310-015-9166-8

Chafouleas, S. M., Pickens, I., & Gherardi, S. A. (2021). Adverse childhood experiences (ACEs): Translation into action in K12 education settings. *School Mental Health, 2*(2), 213–2214. doi:10.100712310-021-09427-9

Choi, J. H., McCart, A. B., & Sailor, W. (2020). Reshaping educational systems to realize the promise of inclusive education. *FIRE: Forum for International Research in Education, 6*(1). doi:10.32865/fire202061179

Connor, D., Cavendish, W., Gonzalez, T., & Jean-Pierre, P. (2019). Is a bridge even possible over troubled waters? The field of special education negates the overrepresentation of minority students: A DisCrit analysis. *Race, Ethnicity and Education, 22*(6), 723–745. doi:10.1080/13613324.2019.1599343

Cramer, E. D. (2015). Inequities of intervention among culturally and linguistically diverse students. *Perspectives on Urban Education Journal, 12*(1).

Cramer, E. D., Little, M., & Alvarez McHatton, P. (2018). Equity, equality, and standardization: Expanding the conversations. *Education and Urban Society, 50*(5), 483–501. doi:10.1177/0013124517713249

Crosby, L. M. S. W., Shantel, D., Penny, B., & Thomas, M. A. T. (2020). Teaching through collective trauma in the era of COVID-19: Trauma-informed practices for middle level learners. *Middle Grades Review, 6*(2), 5. https://scholarworks.uvm.edu/mgreview/vol6/iss2/5

Dong, Q., Garcia, B., Pham, A. V., & Cumming, M. (2020). Culturally responsive approaches for addressing ADHD within multi-tiered systems of support. *Current Psychiatry Reports*, *22*(6), 1–10. doi:10.100711920-020-01154-3 PMID:32378025

Eagle, J. W., Dowd-Eagle, S. E., Snyder, A., & Holtzman, E. G. (2015). Implementing a multi-tiered system of support (MTSS): Collaboration between school psychologists and administrators to promote systems-level change. *Journal of Educational and Psychological Consultation, 25*(2-3), 160-177. doi :10.1080/10474412.2014.929960

Eilers, N. (2021). Critical disability studies and 'Inclusive' early childhood education: The ongoing divide. *Journal of Disability Studies in Education, 1*(1-2), 64–89. doi:10.1163/25888803-00101004

Fondren, K., Lawson, M., Speidel, R., McDonnell, C. G., & Valentino, K. (2020). Buffering the effects of childhood trauma within the school setting: A systematic review of trauma-informed and trauma-responsive interventions among trauma-affected youth. *Children and Youth Services Review*, *109*, 104691. doi:10.1016/j.childyouth.2019.104691

Garcia, S. B., & Ortiz, A. A. (1988). Preventing inappropriate referrals of language minority students to special education: Occasional papers in bilingual education. *NCBE New Focus, 5*, 1-21. http://eric.ed.gov/?id=ED309591

Gay, G. (2018). *Culturally responsive teaching: Theory, research, and practice* (3rd ed.). Teachers College Press.

Girvan, E. J., Gion, C., McIntosh, K., & Smolkowski, K. (2017). The relative contribution of subjective office referrals to racial disproportionality in school discipline. *School Psychology Quarterly*, *32*(3), 392–404. doi:10.1037pq0000178 PMID:27736122

Goldfeld, S., Beatson, R., Watts, A., Snow, P., Gold, L., Le, H. N. D., Edwards, S., Connell, J., Stark, H., Shingles, B., Barnett, T., Quach, J., & Eadie, P. (2022). Tier 2 oral language and early reading interventions for preschool to grade 2 children: A restricted systematic review. *Australian Journal of Learning Difficulties*, *27*(1), 65–113. doi:10.1080/19404158.2021.2011754

Graves, S. L. Jr, Herndon-Sobalvarro, A., Nichols, K., Aston, C., Ryan, A., Blefari, A., Schutte, K., Schachner, A., Vicoria, L., & Prier, D. (2017). Examining the effectiveness of a culturally adapted social-emotional intervention for African American males in an urban setting. *School Psychology Quarterly*, *32*(1), 62–74. doi:10.1037pq0000145 PMID:27124505

Gunawardena, C., Frechette, C., & Layne, L. (2019). *Culturally inclusive instructional design: A framework and guide to building online wisdom communities*. Routledge.

Harry, B., & Ocasio-Stoutenburg, L. (2020). *Meeting families where they are: Building equity through advocacy with diverse schools and communities*. Disability, Culture, and Equity.

Hays, P. A. (2008). *Addressing cultural complexities in practice: Assessment, diagnosis, and therapy* (2nd ed.). American Psychological Association. doi:10.1037/11650-000

Hernández Finch, M. E. (2012). Special considerations with response to intervention and instruction for students with diverse backgrounds. *Psychology in the Schools*, *49*(3), 285–296. doi:10.1002/pits.21597

Huang, F. L., & Cornell, D. (2018). The relationship of school climate with out-of-school suspensions. *Children and Youth Services Review*, *94*, 378–389. doi:10.1016/j.childyouth.2018.08.013

Jitendra, A. K., Alghamdi, A., Edmunds, R., McKevett, N. M., Mouanoutoua, J., & Roesslein, R. (2021). The effects of tier 2 mathematics interventions for students with mathematics difficulties: A meta-analysis. *Exceptional Children*, *87*(3), 307–325. doi:10.1177/0014402920969187

Jones, J. M. (2009). Counseling with multicultural intentionality: the process of counseling and integrating client cultural variables. In J. M. Jones (Ed.), *The psychology of multiculturalism in the schools: a primer for practice, training, and research* (pp. 191–213). NASP Publications.

Jones, J. M., Begay, K. K., Nakagawa, Y., Cevasco, M., & Sit, J. (2015). Multicultural counseling competence training: Adding value with multicultural consultation. *Journal of Educational & Psychological Consultation*, *25*, 1–26. doi:10.1080/10474412.2015.1012671

Jung, P. G., McMaster, K. L., Kunkel, A. K., Shin, J., & Stecker, P. M. (2018). Effects of data- based individualization for students with intensive learning needs: A meta-analysis. *Learning Disabilities Research & Practice*, *33*(3), 144–155. doi:10.1111/ldrp.12172

Khalifa, M. A., Gooden, M. A., & Davis, J. E. (2016). Culturally responsive school leadership: A synthesis of the literature. *Review of Educational Research*, *86*(4), 1272–1311. doi:10.3102/0034654316630383

Klingbeil, D. A., Van Norman, E. R., Nelson, P. M., & Birr, C. (2019). Interval likelihood ratios: Applications for gated screening in schools. *Journal of School Psychology*, *76*, 107–123. doi:10.1016/j.jsp.2019.07.016 PMID:31759460

Kramarczuk Voulgarides, C., Aylward, A., Tefera, A., Artiles, A. J., Alvarado, S. L., & Noguera, P. (2021). Unpacking the logic of compliance in special education: Contextual influences on discipline racial disparities in suburban school. *Sociology of Education*, *94*(3), 208–226. doi:10.1177/00380407211013322

Ladson-Billings, G. (2014). Culturally relevant pedagogy 2.0: Aka the remix. *Harvard Educational Review*, *84*(1), 74–84. doi:10.17763/haer.84.1.p2rj131485484751

Linan-Thompson, S., Ortiz, A., & Cavazos, L. (2022). An examination of MTSS assessment and decision making practices for English learners. *School Psychology Review*, *51*(4), 484–497. doi:10.1080/2372966X.2021.2001690

Malone, C. M., Wycoff, K., & Turner, E. A. (2021). Applying a MTSS framework to address racism and promote mental health for racial/ethnic minoritized youth. *Psychology in the Schools*, 1–15. doi:10.1002/pits.22606

McCart, A., & Miller, D. (2020). Leading equity-based MTSS. In McLeskey, J., Billingsley, B., Brownell, M. T., Maheady, L., Lewis, T. J., Billingsley, B. S., & Maheady, L. J. (2019) What are high-leverage practices for special education teachers and why are they important? *Remedial & Special Education*, *40*(6), 331–337. doi:10.1177/0741932518773477

Montalvo, R., Combes, B. H., & Kea, C. D. (2014). Perspectives on culturally and linguistically responsive RtI pedagogics through a cultural and linguistic lens. *Interdisciplinary Journal of Teaching and Learning*, *4*(3), 203–219.

National Academies of Sciences, Engineering, and Medicine (2022). *The Future of Education Research at IES: Advancing an Equity-Oriented Science*. The National Academies Press. . doi:10.17226/26428

National Center for Learning Disabilities. (2011). *Multi-tier system of supports aka response to intervention (RTI)*. NCLD. https://www.ncld.org/wp-content/uploads/2011/05/MTSS-brief-in-LJ-template.pdf

National Center for Learning Disabilities. (2020). *Significant disproportionality in special education: Current trends and actions for impact*. NCLD. https://www.ncld.org/wp-content/uploads/2020/10/2020-NCLD-Disproportionality_Trends-and-Actions-for-Impact_FINAL-1.pdf

National Center for School Mental Health. (2020). *School mental health quality guide: Mental health promotion services & supports (tier 1)*. NCSMH, University of Maryland School of Medicine.

Office of Special Education Programs. (2021). Individuals with Disabilities Education Act (IDEA) database. US Department of Education. https://www2.ed.gov/programs/osepidea/618-data/state-level-datafiles/index.html#bcc

Okilwa, N. S., & Robert, C. (2017). School Discipline Disparity: Converging Efforts for Better Student Outcomes. *The Urban Review*, *49*(2), 239–262. doi:10.100711256-017-0399-8

Paris, D. (2021). Culturally sustaining pedagogies and our futures. [). Routledge.]. *The Educational Forum*, *85*(4), 364–376. doi:10.1080/00131725.2021.1957634

Paris, D., & Alim, H. S. (Eds.). (2017). *Culturally sustaining pedagogies: Teaching and learning for justice in a changing world*. Teachers College Press.

Payne, A. A., & Welch, K. (2015). Restorative justice in schools: The influence of race on restorative discipline. *Youth & Society*, *47*(4), 539–564. doi:10.1177/0044118X12473125

Raines, T. C., Dever, B. V., Kamphaus, R. W., & Roach, A. T.Tara C. Raines; Bridget V. Dever; Randy W. Kamphaus; Andrew T. Roach. (2012). Universal screening for behavioral and emotional risk: A promising method for reducing disproportionate placement in special education. *The Journal of Negro Education*, *81*(3), 283. doi:10.7709/jnegroeducation.81.3.0283

Rausch, A., Joseph, J., & Steed, E. (2019, December 21). *DIS/ability critical race studies (DisCrit) for inclusion in early childhood education: Ethical considerations of implicit and explicit bias*. ZERO TO THREE. https://www.zerotothree.org/resource/dis-ability-critical-race-studies-discrit-for-inclusion-in-early-childhood-education-ethical-considerations-of-implicit-and-explicit-bias/

Rodgers, W. J., Weiss, M. P., & Ismail, H. A. (2021). Defining specially designed instruction: A systematic literature review. *Learning Disabilities Research & Practice*, *36*(2), 96–109. doi:10.1111/ldrp.12247

Rueda, E. (2015). The benefits of being Latino: Differential interpretations of student behavior and the social construction of being well behaved. *Journal of Latinos & Education*, *14*(4), 275–290. doi:10.1080/15348431.2015.1025955

Sabnis, S., Castillo, J. M., & Wolgemuth, J. R. (2020). RTI, equity, and the return to the status quo: Implications for consultants. *Journal of Educational & Psychological Consultation*, *30*(3), 285–313. doi:10.1080/10474412.2019.1674152

SAMHSA. (2022, April 22). *Understanding child trauma.* SAMHSA - Substance Abuse and Mental Health Services Administration. https://www.samhsa.gov/child-trauma/understanding-child-trauma

Saunders, W. M., & Goldenberg, C. (2007). The effects of an instructional conversation on English language learners' concepts of friendship and story comprehension. In R. Horowitz (Ed.), *Talking texts: How speech and writing interact in school learning* (pp. 221–252). Erlbaum.

Scott, T. M., Gage, N. A., Hirn, R. G., Lingo, A. S., & Burt, J. L. (2019). An examination of the association between MTSS implementation fidelity measures and student outcomes. *Preventing School Failure, 63*(4), 308–316. doi:10.1080/1045988X.2019.1605971

Substance Abuse and Mental Health Services Administration. (2014). *SAMHSA's concept of trauma and guidance for a trauma-informed approach.* (HHS Publication No. 14-4884). https://ncsacw.acf.hhs.gov/userfiles/files/SAMHSA_Trauma.pdf

Sullivan, A., Weeks, M., Kulkarni, T., & Goerdt, A. (2018). *Preventing disproportionality through nondiscriminatory tiered Services.* Great Lakes Equity. https://greatlakesequity.org/sites/default/files/20182706619_brief.pdf

Sullivan, A. L., Miller, F. G., McKevett, N. M., Muldrew, A., Hansen-Burke, A., & Weeks, M. (2020). Leveraging MTSS to Advance, Not Suppress, COVID-Related Equity Issues. *Communique, 49*(1), 1–26.

Sullivan, A. L., & Proctor, S. (2016). The shield or the sword? Revisiting the debate on racial disproportionality in special education and implications for school psychologists. *School Psychology Forum, 10*(3), 278–288.

Theodore, S., Cummings, C., Silva, M. S., Flores, H., Urquiza, N., & Cramer, E. D. (2022). The healer: A model for culturally responsive trauma-informed practices in urban schools. In Hunter, W., Taylor, J., Scott, L., The mixtape volume 1: Culturally sustaining practices within MTSS featuring the everlasting mission of student engagement. Council for Exceptional Children.

Thurlow, M. L., Ghere, G., Lazarus, S. S., & Liu, K. K. (2020). *MTSS for all: Including students with the most significant cognitive disabilities.* National Center on Educational Outcomes/TIES Center. https://nceo.umn.edu/docs/OnlinePubs/NCEOBriefMTSS.pdf

US Department of Health and Human Services & US Department of Education. (2015). Policy statement on inclusion of children with disabilities in early childhood programs. USDE. https://www2.ed.gov/policy/speced/guid/earlylearning/joint-statement-full-text.pdf

Van Norman, E. R., Nelson, P. M., & Klingbeil, D. A. (2017). Single measure and gated screening approaches for identifying students at-risk for academic problems: Implications for sensitivity and specificity. *School Psychology Quarterly, 32*(3), 405–413. doi:10.1037pq0000177 PMID:27684539

Vaughn, S. (2015). Building on past successes: Designing, evaluating, and providing effective treatment for persons for whom typical instruction is not effective. *Remedial and Special Education, 36*(1), 5–8. doi:10.1177/0741932514543928 PMID:25745278

Yee, N., & Butler, D. (2020). Decolonizing possibilities in special education services. *Canadian Journal of Education*, *43*(4), 1071–1103.

Zakszeski, B., Rutherford, L., Heidelburg, K., & Thomas, L. (2021). In pursuit of equity: Discipline disproportionality and SWPBIS implementation in urban schools. *The School Psychologist*, *36*(2), 122–130. doi:10.1037pq0000428

Zullig, K. J., Collins, R., Ghani, N., Hunter, A. A., Patton, J. M., Huebner, E. S., & Zhang, J. (2015). Preliminary development of a revised version of the School Climate Measure. *Psychological Assessment*, *27*(3), 1072–1081. doi:10.1037/pas0000070 PMID:25642931

KEY TERMS AND DEFINITIONS

Cultural Responsiveness: The ability to learn from and relate respectfully with students from various racial, ethnic, linguistic, or cultural backgrounds.

Data-Based Individualization (DBI): A research-based process for individualizing and intensifying interventions through the systematic use of assessment data, validated interventions, and research-based adaptation strategies.

Gated Assessments: Assessments where multiple test scores across several time points are combined, instead of looking at many academic scores in isolation.

Holistic Assessments: Assessments that consider student culture and the culture of a classroom may be contributing to learning or behavioral challenges, as opposed to looking at test scores alone.

Microaffirmations: Subtle acknowledgments of minoritized individuals' values and accomplishments that can foster a school climate that affirms students' racial identities, validates their racialized experiences, and protects against racism.

Racially, Ethnically, and Linguistically Diverse (RELD): A broad term used to describe communities or individuals whose races, ethnic backgrounds, languages, and other cultural factors differ from the culture of power.

Social Emotional Learning (SEL): A process by which children learn and develop self-awareness, self-management, responsible decision-making, social awareness, and relationship skills.

Specially Designed Instruction (SDI): Instruction that is tailored to the specific needs of a child. This often refers to adaptations to the content, methodology, or delivery of instruction that addresses the unique needs of a child to ensure educational access.

Trauma-Informed: A compassionate approach to working with individuals with or at risk of trauma exposure that recognizes trauma symptoms and the role they play in an individual's life.

APPENDIX

Table 2. Evidence-Based Resources for Equity-Based MTSS

Practice/Organization	Description	Website/Data Source
CEEDAR Center	The Collaboration for Effective Educator Development, Accountability, and Reform (CEEDAR) Center works to build the capacity of state personnel preparation systems to prepare teachers and leaders to implement evidence-based practices within multi-tiered systems of support. Detailed professional development modules on MTSS are provided and include resources for educators.	https://ceedar.education.ufl.edu/
Center on MTSS at the AIR	The Center on MTSS strives to support educators in implementing MTSS that addresses students' academic, behavioral, social, and emotional needs. AIR has continued to provide high-quality training, embedded coaching, and formative and summative evaluation of systems, instruction, and student-level outcomes on RTI.	https://mtss4success.org/sites/default/files/2021-07/MTSS_Equity_Brief.pdf https://mtss4success.org/
Center for Student Achievement Solutions (CSAS)	The Center for Student Achievement Solutions delivers customizable, practical, and actionable solutions designed to improve student outcomes, increase teacher retention, and impact student achievement. This resource provides detailed action steps to implement MTSS and culturally responsive PBIS practices within schools.	https://www.studentachievementsolutions.com/how-to-implement-mtss-and-culturally-responsive-pbis-in-your-school-to-promote-equity-and-reduce-the-opportunity-gap/
Culturally and Linguistically Responsive Multi-Tiered Systems of Support for English Learners	This comprehensive PowerPoint details culturally and linguistically responsive MTSS for English learners and references Model Demonstration Research funded by the Office of Special Education Programs, USDOE.	https://ncela.ed.gov/files/uploads/2017/Culturally_and_Linguistically-Slide_View.pdf
Culturally Responsive Education Hub	CRE Hub provides the history, tools, and resources to contextualize and build the movement for culturally responsive education and ethnic studies.	https://crehub.org/
Culturally Responsive PBIS	Culturally Responsive Positive Behavior Interventions and Supports (CRPBIS) is an educational initiative grounded in local to global justice theory. Using Cultural-Historical Activity Theory (CHAT) and various types of data collection, local schools work with members of their communities to identify tensions within schools, pose new solutions, and test their effectiveness. Bal's inclusive problem-solving activity, Learning Lab, brings together diverse voices of educational professionals, families, students, and community members.	http://www.crpbis.org
Culturally Responsive Teaching Guide	This publication serves as a guide to implementing culturally responsive teaching practices. It offers research-based, high-quality strategies that highlight best practice skills for teaching all students equitably.	https://educationnorthwest.org/sites/default/files/resources/culturally-responsive-teaching-508.pdf
Data-Based Individualization (DBI)	These resources highlight DBI, a research-based process for individualizing and intensifying interventions through the systematic use of assessment data, validated interventions, and research-based adaptation strategies. Both resource links introduce and describe the DBI process and how it can be used to support students who require intensive intervention in academics and behavior.	https://intensiveintervention.org/resource/data-based-individualization-framework-intensive-intervention https://iris.peabody.vanderbilt.edu/module/dbi1/cresource/q1/p02/
Education Development Center	This tool helps education leaders take a deeper look at inequities in student achievement, education opportunities, social-emotional support, climate, and school culture to understand the complex systems that affect student performance.	https://www.edc.org/systemic-equity-review-framework-practical-approach-achieving-high-educational-outcomes-all-students
IRIS Center Module on Culturally and Linguistically Diverse Learners	This module examines the ways in which culture influences the daily interactions that occur across all classrooms and provides practice for enhancing culturally responsive teaching.	https://iris.peabody.vanderbilt.edu/module/clde/#content
Meeting the Needs of Linguistically Diverse Students in The Mainstream Classroom	This article includes approaches to incorporate in literacy instruction to support the needs of emergent bilingual students.	https://scholarworks.gvsu.edu/cgi/viewcontent.cgi?article=1067&context=mrj
Office of Elementary and Secondary Education	The USDOE: Office of Elementary and Secondary Education offers this resource on Selecting Evidence-Based Practices for Tiers 1, 2, and 3: Navigating Clearinghouses and Databases. The process for selecting EBPs is highlighted, as well as several other best practices in supporting RELD students.	https://oese.ed.gov/resources/oese-technical-assistance-centers/state-support-network/resources/selecting-evidence-based-practices-tiers-1-2-3-navigating-clearinghouses-databases/#:~:text=Tier%201%20(Strong%20Evidence)%20requires,the%20same%20interventions%20and%20outcomes
PBIS Cultural Responsiveness Field Guide	This field guide is part of a 5-point intervention approach for enhancing equity in student outcomes within a schoolwide positive behavioral interventions and supports (SWPBIS) approach by aligning culturally responsive practices to the core components of SWPBIS. The goal of using this guide is to make school systems more responsive to the cultures and communities that they serve.	https://www.pbis.org/resource/pbis-cultural-responsiveness-field-guide-resources-for-trainers-and-coaches
Responsive Classrooms	This evidence-based approach to teaching and discipline focuses on engaging academics, positive community, effective management, and developmental awareness. Professional development and resources help educators to create safe, joyful, and engaging classrooms and school communities where students develop strong social and academic skills and every student can thrive.	https://www.responsiveclassroom.org/
Root Cause Analysis	This resource is designed to provide states and districts with information on root cause analysis as part of school improvement, including both high-level guidance as well as detailed examples of what root cause analysis can look like at the school level.	https://oese.ed.gov/resources/oese-technical-assistance-centers/state-support-network/resources/using-root-cause-analysis-part-continuous-improvement-process-education/
RTI Action Network	The RTI Action Network is committed to helping students with learning differences succeed through whole-school transformation.	http://www.rtinetwork.org/
Specially designed instruction (SDI)	This resource provides a guide to and examples of SDI.	https://www.uft.org/teaching/students-disabilities/specially-designed-instruction
SWIFT Center	This guide helps to establish a strong foundation of equity-based MTSS at a school	https://guide.swiftschools.org/
Transformative Educational Leadership	This group is a community of racially and culturally diverse leaders dedicated to creating transformative change in the communities they serve.	https://www.teleadership.org/
Twelve Indicators of Restorative Practices Implementation: A Framework for Educational Leaders	The 12 indicators offer a novel, practice-based guide for system-level consultation with a comprehensive approach to schoolwide buy-in, staff training, discipline policy reform, and equity and social justice.	https://doi.org/10.1080/10474412.2020.1824788_
What Works Clearinghouse	This site includes a wide range of evidence-based academic and behavioral interventions.	https://ies.ed.gov/ncee/wwc/

Chapter 7
Strategies for Achieving Equity-Based Education:
Towards an Equitable Education System

Lwazi Sibanda

National University of Science and Technology, Zimbabwe

ABSTRACT

This chapter focuses on strategies for achieving equity-based education. The concept of equity-based education has been examined. Factors that influence equity in education which include funding, access to high-level curriculum, teacher quality and discipline have been discussed. The discussion revealed that funding is a distinct indicator of equity in education, hence, establishing sustainable partnerships between the government and other potential funders is advisable. The chapter also revealed numerous equity strategies such as free and compulsory primary and secondary education for children, providing access to excluded groups of learners, improving the quality of teaching, adopting various forms of assessment strategies, increasing resource allocation, creating equitable learning environments, and creating an equity framework. The chapter suggests solutions and recommendations, and provides future research directions. Finally, conclusion is drawn from the arguments posed by literature observations.

INTRODUCTION

Worldwide, the role of education cannot be overemphasised as it has proved to be the bedrock of democracy. Public schools have the mandate of providing equitable access to education and ensuring that all learners have appropriate knowledge, skills and attitudes to succeed as contributing members of a rapidly changing, global society, irrespective of factors such as race, gender, sexual orientation, ethnic background, language proficiency, immigration status, socioeconomic status, or disability (Barth, 2016). It has been observed that in an equitable school environment, learners of all backgrounds, for instance, race, nationality, gender and many others, have the same opportunities to learn and develop their knowledge and skills. In creating an equitable learning atmosphere in schools, it is important for educators to be culturally proficient and possess the ability to communicate and work effectually across cultural

DOI: 10.4018/978-1-6684-6386-4.ch007

lines (Hanover Research, 2017). Hence, equity in education is usually linked to equal access to formal education opportunities and resources.

According to UNESCO, (2014) the right of all children to education is proclaimed in several international treaties, and has been confirmed by both legally binding and non-binding instruments. States therefore have responsibility to respect, protect and fulfil the right of all learners to education (UNESCO, 2014). This, therefore, suggests that fairness, impartiality, and justice should prevail in schools to enhance equity in the education systems. Hence, schools should be concerned with fairness, such that the education of all learners is seen as being of equal importance. Thus, this chapter intends to establish strategies that enhance equity based education. The chapter looks at the background and concept of equity-based education, factors that influence equity in education, strategies for achieving equity based education, and challenges encountered in achieving equity based education. The chapter suggests solutions and recommendations, and provides future research directions. Finally, conclusion is drawn from the arguments posed by literature observations.

BACKGROUND

The field of education is making a shift from thinking about academic achievement based on academic deficits to one that holistically meets students where they are in terms of academic, social and emotional learning, and developmentally. (Sturgis, & Jones, 2017). According to UNESCO (2018) education has long been recognised as a basic human right and a critically-important requisite for the productivity and well-being of individuals and for the economic and social development of entire societies. Sturgis and Jones (2017) add that the role of public education is the bedrock of democracy. In this regard, the importance of equal access to education has been emphasised repeatedly in international conventions. It is further stated that access to education and learning outcomes should not be affected by circumstances outside of the control of individuals, such as gender, birthplace, ethnicity, religion, language, income, wealth or disability (UNESCO, 2018). However, the failure to provide an equitable public education that enables equal access to opportunity unravels the American dream. There is, therefore, need to focus on competency-based structures for education which are unique powerful models for fostering equity (Sturgis, & Jones, 2017).

Ainscow (2016) mentions that a recent Education for All Global Monitoring Report indicates that, despite improvements over the last 15 years, there are still 58 million children out of school globally and around 100 million children who do not complete primary education. Further literature observation reveals that whilst this situation is most critical in the developing world, there are similar concerns in many wealthier countries, where almost one of five students does not reach a basic minimum level of skills to function in today's societies. It is also noted that students from low socio-economic background are twice as likely to be low performers, implying that personal or social circumstances are obstacles to achieving their educational potential (Ainscow, 2016). Accordingly, Levin (2003) affirms that current data indicate that despite expansion in access to learning opportunities in most countries, educational equity has proved highly elusive. There is evidence that countries vary considerably in the proportion of young children who have access to good quality care, in the proportion of students completing secondary education, in participation in postsecondary education and in opportunities for adult education and workplace learning. Thus, inequity in various learning outcomes varies across countries (Levin, 2003).

Additionally, UNESCO (2017) underscores that Sustainable Development Goal (SDG) 4 on education calls for inclusive and equitable quality education and lifelong learning opportunities for all by 2030. The emphasis is on inclusion and equity as laying foundations for quality education and learning. SDG 4 also calls for building and upgrading education facilities that are child, disability, and gender-sensitive and for providing safe, non-violent, inclusive and effective learning environments for all. To achieve this ambitious goal, countries should ensure inclusion and equity in and through education systems and programmes. This includes taking steps to prevent and address all forms of exclusion and marginalization, disparity, vulnerability and inequality in educational access, participation, and completion as well as in learning processes and outcomes. It also requires understanding learners' diversities as opportunities in order to enhance and democratize learning for all learners (UNESCO, 2017) Consequently, such an educational system requires personalization, high quality, and strong equity strategies, that is, those strategies necessary to ensure that all learners, including those who have been historically underserved, fully benefit from the educational system (Sturgis, & Jones, 2017). Sturgis and Jones (2017) further affirms that in thinking about how inequity occurs, it is important to consider the three types of causes, namely: the beliefs and attitudes of adults; systemic issues that impact learners and communities; and availability of effective instructional strategies.

According to Posti-Ahokas and Janhonen-Abruquah (2021) the social justice outcomes of education are influenced by societal structures, access and academic achievement as well as structures within classrooms. Social justice can be approached from both its distributive and relational dimensions. However, positioning oneself with regards to these dimensions is a challenge for teachers. Studies on early-career teachers has revealed polarised positions of commitment and resistance to social justice. As for early-career teachers, the focus may often be on the micro level and on the ways in which their own classrooms are sites for enacting more socially just relationships and practices. The teachers' role in advancing social justice is emphasised in Finland (Posti-Ahokas & Janhonen-Abruquah, 2021). The high level of autonomy that teachers have (e.g. decisions on teaching methods and material) makes teachers' attitudes, behaviours and actions with regard to justice or injustice powerful (Layne & Dervin as cited in Posti-Ahokas & Janhonen-Abruquah, 2021).

As means of creating equity in the classroom, Hanover Research (2017) advises that there should be consideration of three distinct dimensions, and each of them plays a unique and valuable role in promoting learner equity. These dimensions are necessary in improving outcomes among diverse learners. The dimensions consist of institutional level, which embraces ensuring appropriate policies and values are advocated across the institutions; the personal level, which involves critically reflecting on one's attitudes and beliefs about oneself and others to uncover biases; and the instructional level, which encompasses having materials, activities, and teaching strategies that represent a variety of backgrounds and cultural experiences. Considering the revelation from cited literature, it is evident that inequity is manifested in schools worldwide, hence, the need to identify strategies that enhance equity in schools. The following section focuses on the concept of equity based education.

CONCEPTUALISING EQUITY BASED EDUCATION

The crux of this section is to unveil the concept of equity based education as articulated by various scholars. This will assist in acquiring a deeper understanding of what equity based education entails. According to Ismail (2015) the term equity, refers to fairness, impartiality, and justice and is related to equal opportunity. UNESCO (2018) further elaborates that equity considers the social justice ramifications of education in relation to the fairness, justness and impartiality of its distribution at all levels or educational sub-sectors. Equity means that a distribution is fair or justified and involves a normative judgement of a distribution, but how people make that judgement varies. Equity requires securing all children's rights to education, and their rights within and through education to realize their potential and aspirations. Equity also requires implementing and institutionalizing arrangements that help ensure all children can achieve these aims. Equity is achieved when all learners receive the resources they need so they graduate prepared for success after high school (Ismail, 2015; United Nations Girls' Education Initiative (UNGEI), 2010; Barth, 2016). Thus, equity refers to the strategies that need to be in place to serve diverse communities of learners and lead to learning at high levels of those common expectations. Schools should ensure that historically underserved learners are learning, progressing, and reaching proficiency (Sturgis & Jones, 2017).

Additionally, Sturgis and Jones (2017) assert that educational equity means that each child receives what he or she needs to develop to his or her full academic and social potential. Sturgis and Jones emphasise that working toward equity in schools involves:

- Ensuring equally high outcomes for all participants in the educational system; removing the predictability of success or failures that currently correlates with any social or cultural factor;
- Interrupting inequitable practices, examining biases, and creating inclusive multicultural school environments for adults and children; and
- Discovering and cultivating the unique gifts, talents and interests that every human possesses.

The presented views of cited authorities are in line with Barth's (2016) observation that public schools should provide equitable access and ensure that all learners have the knowledge and skills to succeed as contributing members of a rapidly changing, global society, regardless of factors such as race, gender, sexual orientation, ethnic background, language proficiency, immigration status, socioeconomic status, or disability. Organisation for Economic Co-operation and Development (OECD) (2008) acknowledges that a fair and inclusive system that makes the advantages of education available to all is one of the most powerful levers to make society more equitable. Equity in education has two dimensions. The first is fairness, which basically means making sure that personal and social circumstances, for example, gender, socio-economic status or ethnic origin, should not be an obstacle to achieving educational potential. Then the second dimension is inclusion, in other words ensuring a basic minimum standard of education for all, for instance, that everyone should be able to read, write and do simple arithmetic. The two dimensions are closely intertwined: tackling school failure helps to overcome the effects of social deprivation which often causes school failure. Both equity and fairness are issues for OECD countries. Children from poorer homes in most OECD countries are between three and four times more likely to be among the poorest scorers in mathematics at age 15. However, three key policy areas that can affect equity in education are: the design of education systems, practices in and out of school, and how resources are allocated (OECD, 2008).

As suggested by Levin (2003), equity in education is important for the following reasons:

- There is surely a human right imperative for all people to have a reasonable opportunity to develop their capacities and to participate fully in society. The right to education is recognized, for example, in the United Nations Declaration on the Rights of the Child.

- Insofar as opportunity is not distributed fairly there will be an underutilization of talent; some people will not develop their skills and abilities with consequent loss not only to them but to the society generally. It is not known how many outstanding scientists, writers, artists, or teachers are lost because a significant number of people are not able to obtain the necessary learning.
- Higher levels of education are associated with almost every positive life outcome, not only with improved employment and earnings but also with health, longevity, successful parenting, civic participation, and many others. Insofar as societies contain significant numbers of people without adequate skills to participate socially and economically, there will be higher social costs for security, health, income support and child welfare.
- Social cohesion, or trust, is itself an important factor supporting successful countries. Greater inequality is associated with lower levels of social cohesion and trust thus hampering countries' capacities in many areas.

Thus, equity based education refers to reassessment and redistribution of resources such as human, institutional and financial, in education with the goal of reducing or eliminating systematic inequality in outcomes. Equity is fairness, or equal opportunity to achieve the same outcomes regardless of conditions and barriers. Equity considers needs and disparities and seeks to level opportunity to achieve the same outcome (Omoeva, 2017).

Basically, education systems have equity as one of their guiding principles. Jurado de los Santos, Antonio-José Moreno-Guerrero & Costa (2020) highlight that the conceptualization of the term equity is twofold: on the one hand, those normative references that confirm the fact that the principles of quality and equity are inseparable. This conceptualization of equity is based on two principles: quality education for all citizens, seeking to develop to the maximum the individual, social, intellectual, cultural, and emotional capacities, always within a framework of effective equality of opportunity; and the shared effort of the entire education community in caring for the diversity of learners. On the other hand, the term equity is associated with social well-being, based on the principle of personalized and universal education. Equity is conceived in the education system as part of social justice in which each person, by virtue of being a person, receives what he or she needs from the common goods to compensate for the initial inequalities and, thus, rescind the biases related to personal, social, or cultural factors (Jurado de los Santos, Antonio-José Moreno-Guerrero & Costa, 2020).

Jurado de los Santos, Antonio-José Moreno-Guerrero and Costa, (2020) argues that equity in education should not only be seen as compensation or readjustment of common goods in order to alleviate initial limitations, but should also go beyond this by seeking to ensure that this equity is manifested in such important aspects as equal opportunities in access to studies regardless of gender, social origin, or ethnic origin. Equity in education also seeks to ensure that equity is reflected in academic results and quality, which will allow learners to access higher education and thus break the inequality gap (Jurado de los Santos, Antonio-José Moreno-Guerrero & Costa, 2020).

OECD (2018) points out that equity in education means that schools and education systems provide equal learning opportunities to all students. Consequently, learners of different socio-economic status, gender or immigrant and family background achieve similar levels of academic performance in key cognitive domains, such as reading, mathematics and science, and similar levels of social and emotional well-being in areas such as life satisfaction, self-confidence and social integration, during their education. Equity does not mean that all learners obtain equal education outcomes, but rather that differences in learners' outcomes are unrelated to their background or to economic and social circumstances over which the learners have no control. Equity in education also demands that learners from different backgrounds are equally likely to earn desirable post-secondary education credentials, such as university degrees, that will make it easier for them to succeed in the labor market and to realize their goals as adult members of society. Equity is a fundamental value and guiding principle of education policy, but it is not necessarily actualized in education systems around the world (OECD, 2018). OECD (2018) reveals that at the moment, the international community is committed to the right to education, which was first established in Article 26 of the Universal Declaration of Human Rights of 1948 and is now mandated in national legislation. Equity in education is also a specific target of the Sustainable Development Goals set by the United Nations in 2015 (UNESCO, 2015).

Having looked at the concept of equity based education as revealed by consulted literature, it is important to articulate the difference between equality and equity as these two terms are usually used interchangeably by some authorities. Hence, the subsequent section focuses on the difference between the two concepts.

DIFFERENCE BETWEEN EQUALITY AND EQUITY

It is critical to note that the term equity is different from equality. According to Jurado de los Santos, Antonio-José Moreno-Guerrero and Costa (2020) equality refers to having the same resources and opportunities, in order to satisfy the needs of each individual. This principle is a long-term objective of a just society where children, regardless of ethnic origin, socio-economic class, or gender, should have access to the same resources and opportunities. In addition to these egalitarian aspects, equality must be made effective in the treatment and non-discrimination of people with disabilities, also promoting non-sexist and non-stereotypical attitudes.

The term equity on the other hand, means a system where common goods are redistributed to create systems and schools that share a greater likelihood of being more equal. This educational approach manifests itself in an equitable system where additional resources are provided so that learners have the opportunity to excel academically and socially. From the highlighted revelation, equity requires an unequal distribution of resources in the hope that sustained equity will temporarily favor and promote more equal educational opportunities for students, in which all reach the maximum possible development of their individual and social, intellectual, cultural and emotional capacities. Students should receive a quality education adapted to their needs, thus making equity and quality the two sides of the same coin. This proposition would imply that differences between people would not be a risk factor for discrimination, exclusion, or social, labor or educational disadvantage, but rather an opportunity to improve them and to meet their needs. These approaches can promote egalitarian thinking on learner performance and achievement when inequality in this sense is not necessarily unfair, as differences in learner outcomes may be due to differences in learners' efforts, motivations, interests, talents, or even luck (Jurado de los Santos, Antonio-José Moreno-Guerrero & Costa, 2020).

Metsämuuronen and Lehikko (2022) state that even though the concepts of equity and equality are often used interchangeably, from the philosophical viewpoint, equity is a value and principle that has to do with justness and fairness, while equality can be interpreted as the degree or the state of being equal, especially regarding one's status, rights, and opportunities. Similarly, an example indicator of equality is gender parity or equality between genders: equality between males and females—to simplify the issue—makes sense in the context of the expectation that the genders should be treated equally. Scholars have identified four types of equality which are: numerical equality (give all the same load); proportional equality (give all what they can carry) formal equality (give the like cases the same load) and moral equity (everyone deserves the same dignity and the same respect) (Metsämuuronen & Lehikko, 2022). It should be noted that no single form of equality is superior to other.

The foregoing discussion has highlighted the difference between equity and equality. It is prudent to find out what several authorities have identified as the factors that influence equity in education. Hence, the next section spells out the factors that influence equity in education.

FACTORS THAT INFLUENCE EQUITY IN EDUCATION

Reviewed literature has revealed that there are various factors that influence equity in education. UNESCO (2017) highlights that many factors can work either to facilitate or to inhibit inclusive and equitable practices within education systems. Some of those factors are: teacher skills and attitudes, infrastructure, pedagogical strategies and the curriculum. These are all variables which education ministries either control directly, or over which they can at least exert considerable influence. It is also documented that in the United States currently, the poorest learners are nearly four times as likely to fail in Mathematics than their wealthiest peers. If the achievement gap is to be closed completely, current inequities in funding, access to high-level curriculum, access to good teachers, and how school discipline is imposed should be addressed (Barth, 2016). This section, therefore, focuses on factors such as funding, access to high-level curriculum, teacher quality and discipline among others.

Funding

The distribution of funds among schools is a distinct indicator of equity in education. Barth (2016) asserts that money is the clearest indicator of educational equity between districts. The largest share of school revenue comes from state and other stakeholders and the funds are not adequate to meet the needs of all schools. How the funds are distributed within states can manifest in sizable revenue gaps between districts based on the poverty rates of the students they serve. UNESCO (2017) points out that it may be necessary to set up or strengthen monitoring systems to ensure that funding and other resources are used appropriately and effectively. Even though levels of funding differ from country to country, many of the challenges and the strategies are similar. Establishing sustainable partnerships between the government and other potential funders is also worthwhile

Access to High-Level Curriculum

Achieving educational equity demands more than distributing funds more fairly. Learners should also be guaranteed of equal access to high-level curriculum. Literature reveals that the curriculum is the central means for enacting the principles of equity within an education system. Developing a curriculum that will include all learners may well involve broadening the definition of learning used by teachers and education decision-makers. As long as learning is defined narrowly as the acquisition of knowledge presented by a teacher, schools will likely be locked into rigidly organized curricula and teaching practices. In contrast, inclusive curricula are based on the view that learning occurs when students are actively involved, taking the lead in making sense of their experiences (UNESCO, 2017). Access to high-level curriculum needs to start long before high school. It is documented that good early education is especially beneficial to children from low-income or non-English speaking families by helping them start school with the same skills as their classmates from more advantaged circumstances (Barth, 2016).

When learners of color do not see their own cultures and experiences reflected in the curriculum, or worse, they receive a curriculum that denounces their culture, they can become detached and disinterested through subtractive schooling. School districts can carefully analyze their curriculum and eliminate biases. Culturally relevant education (including culturally relevant/sustaining pedagogy and culturally responsive teaching) can act as gateways to a more inclusive, challenging educational experience. Cultural responsive teaching involves using ethnically diverse cultural knowledge, experiences, frames of reference, and performance styles to help better reach students. (Regional Equity Assistance Centers, 2017). Upper secondary education needs to be attractive not just to an academically-inclined elite, but also to offer good quality pathways without dead ends and effective links to the world of work. Offering at-risk students good career guidance and counselling, as well as making the curriculum more flexible and diverse is helpful. Additional learning support at the end of secondary school may also help to encourage students to stay in school (Organisation for Economic Co-operation and Development, 2008).

A rigorous K-12 curriculum is critical to preparing college and career ready learners. The emphasis should be on deep learning, collective effort, reflection, and respect for others. Regarding content, this curriculum includes but is not limited to college preparatory classes in English, Mathematics, Science, Social Studies, and World Languages (Regional Equity Assistance Centers, 2017). To operationalize equity, policies and practices must be established that open pathways to academic excellence for all students. Prerequisites must be integrated into the curriculum for positive academic learning (Regional Equity Assistance Centers 2017).

To achieve equity in education, the teacher's role becomes one of guiding and facilitating engagement and learning, rather than instructing. This makes it possible for a diverse group of learners to be educated together, since the learners need not to be at the same point in their learning, or receive the same instruction from their teacher. Rather, they can work at their own pace and in their own way, within a common framework of objectives and activities. This approach also fosters a sense of belonging to a community and a shared understanding of key values and global citizenship – a sense of being a part of a broader community and common humanity (UNESCO, 2017).

It is noteworthy to highlight that to achieve equity in education schools should connect the academic curriculum to what learners already know. By acknowledging the heritage and communities in which learners develop and grow, teachers help learners of diverse backgrounds feel comfortable in their classroom environment (Hanover Research, 2017).

Teacher Quality

As for teacher quality, it has been observed that teachers have more influence on learner learning than any other school factor. Besides, the effect of high-performing teachers has been shown to be similar notwithstanding school characteristics, making teacher quality a major element in equity plans (Barth, 2016). There is no single way to define teacher quality. Experience, credentials and academic background have all been shown to have an effect on learner learning in varying degrees. In addition, new "growth" or "value-added" measures have been developed to relate learner gains to individual teachers. In truth, all of these indicators matter (Barth, 2016). Providing adequate professional supports to educators and school leaders is a critical basic requirement for increasing educational equity in schools. An equity focus for professional learning opportunities specifically refers to a paradigm shift from isolated and deficit-based professional development to an asset-based, job-embedded approach. This type of development is accessible to each professional and grounded in the real-time context and scope of their role. It can be understood as a differentiated approach to ensure maximum capacity building for equitable practice in classrooms, schools, and offices (Regional Equity Assistance Centers, 2017).

To create an equitable learning environment, educators must be culturally competent and possess the ability to communicate and work effectively across cultural lines. The most effective way to develop cultural competency among staff is to provide long-term, sustained professional development that enriches teachers' cultural understanding (Hanover Research, 2017). Excellent teaching should be developed, nurtured, and sustained through the creation of robust professional learning communities that support educators in their process of meeting and exceeding a clearly articulated vision for excellent teaching (Regional Equity Assistance Centers, 2017).

Posti-Ahokas and Janhonen-Abruquah (2021) confirm that societal structures, access and academic achievement as well as structures within classrooms influence the social justice outcomes of education. Social justice can be approached from both its distributive and relational dimensions. Positioning oneself in relation to these dimensions is a challenge for teachers. Studies on early-career teachers have shown polarised positions of commitment and resistance to social justice. Thus, for early-career teachers, the focus may often be on the micro level and on the techniques in which their own classrooms are sites for enacting more socially just relationships and practices. In Finland, teachers' role in advancing social justice is emphasised. The high level of autonomy that teachers have, for instance, decisions on teaching methods and material in instructional delivery, makes teachers' attitudes, behaviours and actions with regard to justice or injustice powerful (Posti-Ahokas & Janhonen-Abruquah, 2021). The complexity of pedagogical conversation in teacher education about politically and emotionally charged issues of equity and social justice requires pedagogies that extend beyond content knowledge construction and skills development (Gorski as cited in Posti-Ahokas & Janhonen-Abruquah, 2021).

OECD (2018) confirms that changing practices inside the classroom can help reduce cognitive and socio-emotional gaps related to socio economic status. By providing schools with services such as specialized teacher support and training, teachers may be better equipped with the skills to identify and address learning difficulties, develop more customized and effective teaching methods, and foster self-esteem and positive attitudes among disadvantaged learners. Often, programmes that conduct more frequent assessments and monitor individual performance help teachers identify struggling learners and track learners progress more effectively. These activities should be coupled with greater enthusiasm for personalized learning and the use of technologies that facilitate it (OECD, 2018).

Discipline

Discipline is another important factor which impacts on achievement of equity in education. There is evidence that discipline policies that make heavy use of out-of school suspensions might place learners at risk of academic failure. Learners with multiple suspensions have a higher likelihood of dropping out of school, and can even lead to worse outcomes such as substance abuse and delinquency in the community. Such policies can produce a harmful school climate for learners overall (Barth, 2016). Hence, there is need for schools to adopt positive discipline management strategies to ensure that there is equitable provision of education to all learners. Furthermore, the design of education systems, practices in and out of school, and how resources are allocated have been identified by Organisation for Economic and Co-operation Development (2008) as key policy areas that can affect equity in education.

Teachers should establish and maintain behavior standards for respectful treatment in the classroom. Consequences for misbehavior must be implemented consistently and equitably in order to avoid the cultural misunderstandings that sometimes lead to disciplinary interventions (Hanover Research, 2017).

Schools and communities can look at discipline referral rates, both for mandatory referrals and discretionary referrals, as well as the severity of punishment. School administrators and educators are all too familiar with the statistics showing which learners in the school population are most likely to be sent to the principal's office, suspended, and expelled. These learners are typically male, and males of color, followed by males of a low socioeconomic status. These interactions between learners and teachers can be assessed quantitatively using an equity lens. For example, discipline can be assessed from the classroom level to building level in counting how many learners are disciplined, for what reasons, and further disaggregated if the learner is male/female, white/a student of color, English speaker/English learner, is able/disabled, rich/poor, of the dominate religion/another religion. Learner codes of conduct can be examined by the school community to determine any unjust or unfair policies that may implicitly or explicitly target learners of color (Regional Equity Assistance Centers, 2017).

Equitable disciplinary policies should be considered in schools if equity in education is to be achieved. According to Hanover Research (2017), the following guidelines should be adopted to ensure equitable discipline policies are implemented in schools.

1. Experts should encourage schools to implement positive disciplinary programs, such as restorative justice and collaborative problem solving. Through restorative justice, learners gather in circles with adults and the learner(s) they offended to focus on the practical consequences of misbehavior, rather than the specific rule that was broken. The response to misbehavior seeks to ensure the offending student understands the consequences of his or her actions, allows the student to restore balance to the situation created by the misconduct, and holds the learner accountable for his or her actions. Offending learner works with their victims to repair the harm they have caused and reintegrate back into the school community. Using the collaborative problem solving (CPS) model, adults work together with children to solve problems in mutually satisfactory and realistic ways. The CPS approach involves four steps indicated below:
   a. Identify and understand the learner's concern about the problem to be solved and reassure him or her that the problem will not be resolved through the imposition of adult will.
   b. Identify and share the adults' concerns about the same issue.
   c. Invite the learner to brainstorm solutions together with the adult.
   d. Work with the learner to assess potential solutions and choose one that is both realistic and mutually satisfactory (Hanover Research, 2017).
2. Experts should emphasize the importance of creating a positive school climate to facilitate equitable disciplinary practices. In a 2014 guidance document, the U.S. Department of Education advises schools to focus on preventing discipline incidents by promoting a positive school climate and setting clear expectations for student behavior. Many schools achieve both goals, in part, through implementing a multi-tiered system of Positive Behavioral Interventions and Supports (PBIS). Researchers recommend that schools implemented a three-tiered consequence system, whereby the punishment that learners receive is proportionate to the offense. For the consequence system to serve as a preventative mechanism, teachers should clearly communicate to learners what the

school expectations are and what consequences learners will experience if they misbehave. In addition, staff should have a clear understanding of their role within the system to ensure equitable and consistent application of consequences (Hanover Research, 2017).

3. Schools should set clear expectations for learner learning and behavior. It has been noted that some learners are more vulnerable to low expectations because of societal biases and stereotypes associated with their racial and/or ethnic identity. Hence, teachers should communicate expectations using both explicit directions and non-verbal cues. For example, it is recommended that teachers outline the criteria and standards that will be used to evaluate leaners' work, and provide learners with anonymous samples of prior learner work. In addition, teachers should maintain eye contact with both high- and low-achieving learners while communicating expectations for learning and participation. Similarly, teachers who ask difficult questions of both low- and high- achieving learners communicate equitable expectations and help learners develop oral response skills (Hanover Research, 2017).

OECD (2018) adds that school characteristics and learners' attitudes and behaviors towards school tend to be more strongly associated with academic resilience than learners' demographic background. The share of nationally and core-skills resilient learners is greater in schools with a better disciplinary climate, and among learners who do not skip school and who have greater motivation to achieve. Disadvantaged learners who are socially and emotionally resilient also tend to do better academically. This implies that helping disadvantaged learners develop positive attitudes and behaviors towards themselves and their education can also benefit these learners' academic development. Academic resilience can also promote social and emotional resilience, creating a cycle of positive reinforcement (OECD, 2018).

The forgoing section presented factors that influence equity in education which include funding, access to high-level curriculum, teacher quality and discipline. The discussion revealed that funding is a distinct indicator of equity in education, hence, establishing sustainable partnerships between the government and other potential funders is advisable. As for access to high-level curriculum, it has been indicated that learners should be guaranteed of equal access to high-level curriculum. Curriculum is seen as the central means for enacting the principles of equity within an education system. Regarding teacher quality, the argument shows that teachers have more influence on learner learning than any other school factor. Teacher experience, credentials and academic background have all been identified as having an impact on student learning in varying degrees. Concerning the aspect of discipline, it has been shown that equitable disciplinary policies should be considered in schools if equity in education is to be achieved. Suggested guidelines include encouraging schools to implement positive disciplinary programs, such as restorative justice and collaborative problem solving; emphasizing the importance of creating a positive school climate to facilitate equitable disciplinary practices and setting clear expectations for student learning and behavior. The succeeding section looks at the strategies for achieving equity based education.

STRATEGIES FOR ACHIEVING EQUITY BASED EDUCATION

Achieving equity based education calls for governments and school systems to adopt numerous strategies such as free and compulsory primary and secondary education for children, providing access to excluded groups of learners, improving the quality of teaching, adopting various forms of assessment strategies, increased resource allocation, creating equitable learning environments and creating an equity framework. These strategies are discussed in the subsequent sections.

Free and Compulsory Primary and Secondary Education for Children

The most substantial intervention to achieve equity-based education on a universal scale has been to provide free and compulsory primary and secondary education for children. (Ismail, 2015). The right of all children to education is asserted in numerous international treaties and texts, and has been affirmed by both legally binding and non-binding instruments. States therefore have an obligation to respect, protect and fulfil the right of all learners to education (UNESCO, 2017). Thus, new approaches since the Dakar Global Forum on Education for All in 2000 have given greater prominence to rights-based approaches to educational service provision for basic education. These place more stress on equitable access to reasonable quality primary schooling as a right that is widely denied to large proportions of the population of many developing countries. This is seen as unacceptable since both governments and development partners have obligations to deliver on commitments they have made in the United Nations Charter and Declaration of Human Rights to promote universal access to education (Lewin, 2007).

However, the findings of a study by OECD (2018) indicate that expansion of access to education does not automatically result in greater equity in educational attainment. Educational expansion opens opportunities for education to more learners. Who these new learners are, however, can determine whether expansion improves equity. For expansion to result in greater equity, disadvantaged learners need to benefit as much as or more than advantaged learners. Findings show that, in recent decades, the children of families with higher levels of education were more likely than the children of families with lower levels of education to benefit from educational expansion. Previous studies suggest that, unless special policies are put into place to assist disadvantaged students in accessing tertiary education, wealthy and middle-class families will maintain their relative advantage (Raftery & Hout, as cited in OECD, 2018).

Providing Access to Excluded Groups of Learners

Providing access to excluded groups of learners by participation to be inclusive of gender, religion, age, race, indigenous groups, or marginalized groups is another noteworthy strategy for achieving equity based education. (Ismail, 2015). In an equitable classroom environment, learners of all backgrounds, for example, race, nationality and gender have the same opportunities to learn and develop their knowledge (Hanover Research, 2017). Hanover Research, (2017) further suggests the following strategies to assist schools in meeting their equity goals. The proposed strategies support the excluded groups of learners to access education. The strategies include:

- Acknowledging students and their cultural heritage,
- Preparation for advanced courses should begin in middle school,
- Schools should conduct targeted outreach to ensure that qualified students are aware of their eligibility and the benefits of taking rigorous courses,
- Enhance outreach efforts for low-income and minority parents.

This prompts two conclusions: early tracking and streaming need to be justified in terms of proven benefits; and school systems using early tracking should postpone it to a later stage to reduce inequities and improve outcomes.

Organisation for Economic Co-operation and Development (2008) argues that selecting learners on the basis of academic achievement tends to create great social differences between schools. It also increases the link between socio-economic status and performance – it tends to accelerate the progress of those who have already gained the best start in life from their parents – and is also associated with stronger performance at the top end of the scale in mathematics and science. Hence, academic selection needs to be used with caution because of the risks it poses to equity. The assumption is that if selection is carefully done the excluded groups of learners stand a chance to access education as well.

With regards to providing equitable education to learners with disability, Sarangapani (2020) affirms that deficit perceptions regarding children with disabilities and negative attitudes towards inclusion have also been noted across the South Asian region. These also may be attributed to cultural stereotypes and prejudices carried by teachers into the classroom. Thus, attitudes that function as barriers to inclusion include fear of reducing overall academic performance and fear of negative effects on learners with higher abilities. Learners with severe disabilities are considered problems and therefore purportedly need segregation. Inclusion tends to be rendered in moral and ethical terms, requiring sympathy and kindness; overall, teachers are found to hold stereotyped views of occupational options for these learners. Numerous teachers report that they lack capacity and resources to be inclusive (Sarangapani, 2020). Hence, such practices hinder achievement of equity in education. OECD (2018) attests that if education systems around the world were to deliver truly equitable opportunities for all learners to succeed in school, no differences in learner performance related to socio economic status would be found.

Ainscow (2020) stresses that the importance of including disabled children is an essential strand within the international policy agenda. There is emphasis in the United Nations' Convention on the Rights of Persons with Disabilities (United Nations, 2008), which states: 'The right to inclusive education encompasses a transformation in culture, policy and practice in all educational environments to accommodate the differing requirements and identities of individual students, together with a commitment to remove the barriers that impede that possibility.' The Convention defines non-inclusion, or segregation, as the education of students with disabilities in separate environments, that is, in separate special schools, or in special education units located with regular schools. It compels to ending segregation within educational settings by ensuring inclusive classroom teaching in accessible learning environments with appropriate support. This means that education systems must provide a personalized educational response, rather than expecting the student to fit the system (Ainscow, 2020).

Improving the Quality of Teaching

Globally, as a way of achieving equity based education, most countries are focusing on improving the quality of teaching which includes teacher training, encouraging progressive teaching methods rather than more didactic models that emphasize technical rationality. Additional interventions for teachers have ranged from incentives in particular for rural teachers, workshops, in-house training, and professional development programmes (Ismail, 2015).

As they conduct instruction, teachers should accommodate diverse learning styles. Experts note that students of different cultural backgrounds may be more comfortable with specific modes of learning. In addition, school leaders should support equitable instruction by maintaining high expectations for student achievement and encouraging peer-driven discussions about how to support struggling students (Hanover Research, 2017).

Hanover Research, (2017) further advises that for schools to improve the quality of teaching they should:

- Communicate high expectations for all teachers and students,
- Not accept excuses for the lack of achievement by subgroups of students,
- Change school schedules, curriculum, and use of staff time to support the learning of struggling students,
- Expect teachers to change classroom practices to support struggling students,
- Encourage respectful dialogue among members of staff regarding their role in helping all students learn,
- Challenge educators' underlying assumptions concerning the role of parents, socio-economic status, race, and background in student learning, and
- Provide an ongoing system of staff development to enhance teacher skills and knowledge about teaching struggling students.

As a result, in classrooms where facilities are better, more 'learner-centric' activities are evident, in contrast to lower grades and in schools catering to lower socio-economic groups where traditional instructional methods dominate (Sarangapani, 2020). Thus, the highlighted elements if appropriately implemented would lead to achievement of equity in education.

Adopting Various Forms of Assessment Strategies

Reviewed literature point out that schools should adopt various forms of assessment strategies which include oral and written forms of assessments and to scaffold assessments, as well as to allow for cumulative and formative assessment models. (Ismail, 2015). According to OECD (2008) it is possible to improve classroom attainment with methods such as formative assessment – a process of feeding back information about performance to student and teacher and adapting and improving teaching and learning in response, particularly with students at risk.

Accordingly, student success in an integrated schooling environment should be monitored and measured across several indicators, including valid measures for academic growth, course grades, grade retention, graduation rates, dropout rates, college readiness indicators, rigorous course success, and educational attainment beyond high school. By examining these indicators using cross-sectional data, improvements can then be targeted through the co-constructive approach to increase equity for all disaggregated student groups (Regional Equity Assistance Centers, 2017). It is also essential to develop and use national assessment systems that comply with international human rights norms, so that education will fulfil the objectives that human rights conventions established (UNESCO, 2017). As a result, in an effective education system, all students are assessed on an on-going basis in terms of their progress through the curriculum. This allows teachers to respond to a wide range of individual learners. This means that teachers and other professionals must be well informed about their students' characteristics and attainments, while also assessing broader qualities, such as their capacity for cohesion and cooperation (UNESCO, 2017).

Increased Resource Allocation

Other measures to improve education performance and learning opportunities that could be implemented by schools encompass increased resource allocation, such as providing basic infrastructure for water and electricity, classroom facilities, improved instructional materials, calls for greater parent and community involvement, and incentives for teachers and school heads (Ismail, 2015).

School districts may exacerbate the inequities by distributing fewer resources to their high-need schools. Some school districts may tend to focus on providing sufficient resources to their more afflu-ent schools, whether to appease parents, stem White flight, or for other reasons. A recent study showed that some districts allocate $300 to $500 more to schools enrolling fewer percentages of underserved students. (Regional Equity Assistance Centers, 2017). There is need for a comprehensive review of re-source distribution policies and resource allocations in the schools across a district can help monitor any potential or resulting resource inequities. (Regional Equity Assistance Centers, 2017). Extra resources also need to be channelled through schools to help disadvantaged students. This should help overcome the effect of social background and help to tackle poor performance. The stigma arising from labelling of particular schools as "for disadvantaged children" should be avoided (Organisation for Economic Co-operation and Development, 2008).

Creating Equitable Learning Environments

To improve educational equity, schools should create equitable learning environments that enhance eq-uity in classroom instruction; engage families by creating welcoming environments for diverse families and supporting high-mobility learners and ensure that the move to their new school does not disrupt their education (Hanover Research, 2017). Ainscow, Dyson, Goldrick and West (2013) highlight that:

- Schools have to collaborate in ways that create a whole-system approach
- Equity-focused local leadership is needed in order to coordinate collaborative
- Development in schools must be linked to wider community efforts to tackle inequities experi-enced by children.
- National policy has to be formulated in ways that enable and encourage local actions
- Moves to foster equity in education must be mirrored by efforts to develop a fairer society.

In schools where diversity and culture are valued, the child's sense of identity and self-worth are validated, and social learning and academic achievement are much more likely to occur.

Positive school culture is an essential aspect of school improvement efforts that can lead to student engagement and achievement. A positive school culture employs techniques to engage states, districts, and schools in shared responsibility for implementing equitable practices and eliminating marginalizing practices that perpetuate prejudice and segregation (Regional Equity Assistance Centers, 2017). Students who are in learning environments where they feel safe and accepted will increase their motivation to learn and take advantage of extracurricular programs and summer enrichment programs. Establishing short- and long-term learning goals with constructive feedback will provide students with increased capacity for self-assessment and equitable opportunities for achievement (Regional Equity Assistance Centers, 2017).

Creating an Equity Framework

Developing policies that are inclusive and equitable requires the recognition that students' difficulties arise from aspects of the education system itself, including: the ways in which education systems are organized currently, the forms of teaching that are provided, the learning environment, and the ways in which students' progress is supported and evaluated (UNESCO, 2017).

Integrating the principles of equity and inclusion into education policy involves:

- Valuing the presence, participation and achievement of all learners, regardless of their contexts and personal characteristics.
- Recognizing the benefits of student diversity, and how to live with, and learn from, difference.
- Collecting, collating and evaluating evidence on children's barriers to education access, to participation and to achievement, with particular attention to learners who may be most at risk of underachievement, marginalization or exclusion.
- Building a common understanding that more inclusive and equitable education systems have the potential to promote gender equality, reduce inequalities, develop teacher and system capabilities, and encourage supportive learning environments. These various efforts will, in turn, contribute to overall improvements in educational quality.
- Engaging key education and community stakeholders to foster the conditions for inclusive learning, and to foster a broader understanding of the principles of inclusion and equity.
- Implementing changes effectively and monitoring them for impact, recognizing that building inclusion and equity in education is an on-going process, rather than a one-time effort.
- Bringing the principles of equity and inclusion into education policy also requires engaging other sectors, such as health, social welfare and child protection services, to ensure a common administrative and legislative framework for inclusive and equitable education. (UNESCO, 2017).

Ainscow (2020) confirms that progress in relation to inclusion and equity requires an effective strategy for implementation. Particularly, it requires new thinking which focuses attention on the barriers experienced by some children that lead them to become marginalized as a result of contextual factors. The consequence is that overcoming such barriers is the most important means of development forms of education that are effective for all children. As such, inclusion becomes a way of achieving the overall improvement of education systems, which leads to attainment of equity in education. Accordingly, OECD (2018) affirms that in education systems with greater equity in learner performance, more disadvantaged learners perform among the best learners in their own country.

The forgoing sections reviewed literature on the strategies for achieving equity based education which encompass free and compulsory primary and secondary education for children, providing access to excluded groups of learners, improving the quality of teaching, adopting various forms of assessment strategies, increased resource allocation, creating equitable learning environments and creating an equity framework. The next section discusses the challenges encountered in achieving equity based education.

CHALLENGES ENCOUNTERED IN ACHIEVING EQUITY BASED EDUCATION

Worldwide, the education systems are faced with the challenge of achieving equity. Literature reveals that there are about 70 million children who are not attending school in economically poorer countries. Whereas in wealthier countries many young people leave school with no worthwhile qualifications, others are placed in various forms of special provision away from mainstream educational experiences, and some simply choose to drop out since the curriculum seems irrelevant to their lives (Ainscow, Dyson, Goldrick & West, 2013).

According to United Nations Girls' Education Initiative (UNGEI), (2010) some children especially, those from poor families; living in remote rural communities; girls; children infected with or affected by HIV; children engaged in child labour or those with disabilities; children from ethnic or other minority groups and those in countries affected by conflict or natural disaster are at risk of not attending or completing school.

Additionally, the basic structure of education systems affects equity. Traditionally, education systems have grouped learners according to achievement. Confirmation from studies of secondary and primary schools suggests that such categorization can increase inequalities and inequities, particularly if it takes place early in the education process (Organisation for Economic and Co-operation Development, 2008).

Literature observations suggest that in many contexts equity inspired sustainable development goals (SDGs) are not always realized and where they have been attained political and economic changes can reverse equity gains. The key reasons cited for not achieving equity are that not everyone has equal resources and structural poverty excludes those who are poor or cultural and religious practices are discriminatory against gender, age, diversity, or disability (Ismail, 2015).

The views of scholars in above consulted literature have highlighted the challenges encountered in achieving equity based education. The next section underscores the solutions and recommendations of the chapter.

SOLUTIONS AND RECOMMENDATIONS

- It is recommended that schools, states and other stakeholders which include: parents/caregivers; teachers and other education professionals; teacher trainers and researchers; national, local and school-level administrators and managers; policy-makers and service providers in other sectors, for example, health, child protection and social services; civic groups in the community; and members of minority groups that are at risk of exclusion should work towards eliminating inequities in the education systems globally.
- To enhance the equity in education, governments need to mobilize human and financial resources, to assist schools to minimize inequities in the education systems.
- Schools should also promote routines and practices that encourage educational leadership. This leadership should favor the entire educational community, focusing mainly on teachers, parents, and learners.
- Schools that provide guidance and career counselling to learners should complement efforts in the classroom, and help learners assess their progress and think strategically about goals and aspirations.

- Whereas advantaged learners tend to enjoy the benefits of stronger support networks and mentorship outside of the classroom, hence requiring less from their school environments, this is often not the case for disadvantaged learners. Therefore, schools and teachers should understand the obstacles that disadvantaged learners face, and apportion resources to initiatives that have been proven successful, so that they help learners overcome the obstacles.

FUTURE RESEARCH DIRECTION

While this chapter has focused on strategies for achieving equity based education, it is proposed that an empirical study be conducted.

CONCLUSION

In conclusion, this chapter focused on strategies for achieving equity based education. The concept of equity based education has been examined. Factors that influence equity in education which include funding, access to high-level curriculum, teacher quality and discipline have been discussed. The discussion further revealed that funding is a distinct indicator of equity in education, hence, establishing sustainable partnerships between the government and other potential funders is advisable. The chapter also revealed numerous equity strategies such as free and compulsory primary and secondary education for children, providing access to excluded groups of learners, improving the quality of teaching, adopting various forms of assessment strategies, increased resource allocation, creating equitable learning environments and creating an equity framework. The chapter suggested solutions and recommendations, and provided future research directions.

REFERENCES

Ainscow, M. (2016). Collaboration as a strategy for promoting equity in education: Possibilities and barriers. *Journal of Professional Capital and Community*, *1*(2), 1–20. doi:10.1108/JPCC-12-2015-0013

Ainscow, M. (2020). Promoting inclusion and equity in education: Lessons from international experiences. *Nordic Journal of Studies in Educational Policy*, *6*(1), 7–16. doi:10.1080/20020317.2020.1729587

Ainscow, M., Alan Dyson, A., Sue Goldrick, S., & West, M. (2013). Promoting equity in education. *Revista de Investigación Educacional*, *11*(3), 32–43.

Barth, P. (2016). Educational Equity: What does it mean? How do we know when we reach it? Center for Education Equality.

Center for Public Education Hanover Research. (2017). *Closing the Gap: Creating Equity in the Classroom K-12 Education. Hanover Research highlights classroom strategies, tips, and approaches to close the equity gap*

Ismail, S. (2015). Equity and Education. In: James D. Wright (ed.), International Encyclopaedia of the Social & Behavioural Sciences, (2nd edition), 7, pp. 918–923. Elsevier. doi:10.1016/B978-0-08-097086-8.92099-3

Levin, B. (2003). *Approaches to Equity in Policy for Lifelong Learning.* Education and Training Policy Division, OECD, for the Equity in Education Thematic Review.

Lewin, K. M. (2007). *Improving access, equity, and transitions in education: Creating a research agenda. Consortium for Research into Educational Access Transition and Equity (CREATE),* [Working Paper No. 1]. University of Sussex.

Metsämuuronen, J., & Lehikko, A. (2022). Challenges and Possibilities of Educational Equity and Equality in the Post-COVID-19 Realm in the Nordic Countries. *Scandinavian Journal of Educational Research*, 1–22. doi:10.1080/00313831.2022.2115549

OECD. (2018). *Equity in Education: Breaking Down Barriers to Social Mobility*, PISA, OECD Publishing, Paris.

Omoeva, C. (2017). Mainstreaming Equity in Education. Paper Commissioned by the International Education Funders Group. Education Policy and Data Center / Education Equity Research Initiative.

Organisation for Economic and Co-operation Development (2008). *Policy Brief: Ten Steps to Equity in Education.* OECD.

Posti-Ahokas & Janhonen-Abruquah. (2021). Towards equity literacy: Exploratory enquiry with Finnish student teachers. *European Journal of Teacher Education*, ●●●, 1–19. doi:10.1080/02619768.2021.1952977

Regional Equity Assistance Centers. (2017). *Equity Based Framework for Achieving Integrated Schooling: A Framework for School Districts and Communities for Designing Racially and Economically Integrated Schools.* IDRAEC. https://www.idraeacsouth.org/wp-content/uploads/2018/12/Equity-Based-Framework-for-Achieving-Integrated-Schooling-112718
.pdf

Sarangapani, P. M. (2020). Chapter written for the section titled 'Teachers, Teaching and Teacher Education' Section, Padma M. Sarangapani and Yusuf Sayed in 'Handbook of Education Systems in South Asia'. Springer Major Reference Work, pp. 1-19

Sturgis, C., & Jones, A. (2017). In pursuit of equality: A framework for equity strategies in competency-based education. Vienna, VA: International Association for K–12 Online Learning United Nations. (2008). Convention on the rights of persons with disabilities. New York: UN.

UNESCO. (2014). *Education for All Global Monitoring Report 2013/4: Teaching and Learning: Achieving Quality for All.* UNESCO.

UNESCO. (2015). *Education for All 2000-2015: achievements and challenges.* UNESCO.

UNESCO. (2017). *A guide for ensuring inclusion and equity in education.* UNESCO.

UNESCO. (2018). *Handbook on Measuring Equity in Education.* UNESCO Institute for Statistics.

United Nations Girls' Education Initiative (UNGEI) (2010). *Equity and Inclusion in education: A guide to support education sector plan preparation, revision and appraisal.* New York: UN

Chapter 8
The State of Inclusive Education in Secondary Schools in Zimbabwe Decades After Independence and the Salamanga Declaration

Edson Nyasha Muresherwa
University of the Free State, South Africa

Loyiso C. Jita
University of the Free State, South Africa

ABSTRACT

This chapter explores the state of inclusive education in the secondary schools in Zimbabwe decades after independence and the Salamanca Declaration. The thrust of the chapter is very important at a time when inclusive education is increasingly being viewed as a critical element of basic education and a step towards social justice. The chapter shows that inclusive education has remained an illusion at a time when the inclusive framework is expected to have fully developed and to be bearing fruit. This paradox is explained in terms of the historical, cultural, and economic context prevailing in the country. This Zimbabwean context focuses public education on political and economic goals only, disregarding equity and social justice objectives. It is therefore recommended that the purpose of education be redefined to fully embrace the needs of 'all' and the social justice logics, bearing in mind the context of the local environment.

INTRODUCTION

In this chapter, the authors explore the state of inclusive education in Zimbabwean secondary schools, more than 42 years after independence and 28 years after the ratification of the Salamanca Statement

DOI: 10.4018/978-1-6684-6386-4.ch008

and Framework for Action on Special Needs Education. The Salamanca Statement and Framework for Action on Special Needs Education is sometimes referred to as the Salamanca Declaration, the Salamanca Statement or simply as the Salamanca (Magnusson, 2019). The Salamanca Statement and the advent of independence in 1980 mark key milestones in the history of Zimbabwe's public education system in general and the inclusive education agenda in particular. The aim of the chapter is to explore the extent to which the country has embraced the inclusive framework and to establish whether the brand of inclusive education embraced in the country is culturally affirming. In addition, the chapter also recommends the measures that may be taken to make inclusive education practices, both in Zimbabwe and beyond, more responsive to the needs of the local people. Given the time-lapse from the attainment of independence in 1980 and the ratification of the Salamanca Declaration in 1994 to date and the focus of these milestones on the inclusive agenda, it is reasonable to expect that by now the inclusive education framework should have been fully developed to bear fruits in the education system in Zimbabwe, including in secondary schools. The inclusive education framework was defined by Musengi and Chireshe (2013) as the only means to humanise the classroom and by Polat (2011) as a step towards social justice. Astuti and Sudrajat (2020, p. 178) also viewed inclusive education as one way through which countries may achieve social justice in education. At this stage into the history of an independent Zimbabwe, it has become plausible to begin interrogating some of the social policies and practices adopted at independence as a form of social impact assessment (Vanclay, 2020). The aim here is to establish how culturally affirming (responsive) (Williams et al., 2021) these policies and practices are and to inform future policies and practices. With regard to the inclusive framework, the situation on the ground seems to show persistent misalignment between formulations and realisation (Haug, 2017; Muresherwa & Jita, 2021; Musengi & Chireshe, 2013) of inclusive education in the country. This situation persists regardless of the promises (Musengi & Chireshe, 2013 and the timespan since independence in 1980 and ratification of the Salamanca Statement in 1994 to date.

The present chapter is informed by the complexity theory of inclusive education (Schuelka & Engsig, 2020; Walton & Engelbrecht, 2022) and uses Tomasevski's (2004) four-fold model as a conceptual framework to explore and explain the state of inclusive education in Zimbabwe, with special reference to the situation in the secondary schools. Tomasevski's (2004) model focuses on four elements: i) availability, ii) accessibility, iii) acceptability, and iv) adaptability, in this case of inclusive education thought and practice in the secondary schools of Zimbabwe. In combination, these four elements speak to the issues of access, equity, quality and relevance of education (Anlimachie, 2015) and therefore comprise key performance indicators for inclusive education interventions that may be used for social impact assessment. The issues at stake in this chapter are "considered relevant at a time when inclusive education and secondary school education are increasingly being viewed as components of the basic education framework internationally" (Muresherwa & Jita, 2021, p. 1743). This chapter is also relevant at a time when the role of the traditional family system as an agent of primary socialisation (Hunter-Jones, 2014) is slowly but surely disintegrating and the public education system is expected to fill the gap being left behind (Haralambos & Holborn, 2013). This is a time when inclusive education has also firmly entrenched itself as a key element within the general field of public education and educational research (Walton & Engelbrecht, 2022). In particular, inclusive education is increasingly being viewed as the only fair and socially just way of grouping learners for instruction (Mafa, 2012; Musengi & Chireshe, 2013). Therefore, Polat (2011) and Astuti and Sudrajat (2020) saw the adoption of inclusive practices by schools and/or education systems as a step towards social justice. The term *social justice* "refers to the principles of equality and equity in all aspects of life for all members of a community" (Farid, 2022,

p. 3). Mantras such as "For all in all places", "Of all at all times", and "Never wilfully against anybody" are always given priority in issues relating to social justice (Boakari 2010), such as inclusive education. The grounding assumption in this chapter is that, for it to be seen as worth its salt and to effectively act as a step towards social justice, the brand of inclusive education embraced in any given country or community should be culturally affirming (Allen et al., 2013) and not serve as basis for social alienation (Kee & Lai, 2022). This link between inclusive education, social justice and culturally affirming education in secondary schools, though important, has not been fully explored (Forlin, 2013).

This chapter on the state of inclusive education in Zimbabwe decades after independence and the Salamanca Declaration therefore seeks to contribute to the growing discourse of inclusive instructional practice as an instrument for social justice and culturally affirming education internationally. It is needless to point out that the protracted war of liberation in Zimbabwe was fought to institute a governance system which is grounded on the key principles of growth with equity (inclusivity) and social justice. This chapter is grounded on the question "How far, so far?" with regard to inclusive education, decades after independence and the ratification of the Salamanca Statement. These milestones undoubtedly provide a baseline for understanding inclusive education interventions in the country. According to Nevill and Savage (2022), "[t]he term 'inclusive education' specifically came to the forefront globally with the ratification of The Salamanca Statement and Framework for Action on Special Needs Education by the United Nations Educational, Scientific and Cultural Organization (UNESCO) in 1994" (p. 2). The Salamanca Declaration represents an agreement of participants from 92 governments and non-governmental organisations, of which Zimbabwe was a member. This agreement enjoins all progressive governments internationally to embrace an inclusive approach to education, either in policy or law, as a matter of urgency. All children are enrolled in regular schools, unless there are compelling reasons for doing the contrary (UNESCO, 1994). The question of "How far, so far?" with regard to inclusive education in Zimbabwe as asked in this chapter is therefore very well placed and relevant, coming as it does decades after independence and the Salamanca Declaration.

Unless otherwise stated, this chapter is informed by the findings of a qualitative multiple case study, *Challenges and opportunities to instructional leadership in inclusive secondary schools of Zimbabwe* (Muresherwa, 2020) recently completed by the first author under the supervision of the second author. Specifically, the present chapter comprises conceptual issues on the state of inclusive education in the secondary schools of Zimbabwe at a time when, under normal circumstances, the inclusive framework is expected to have blossomed and developed to fruition. This research is informed by a combination of existing literature on the concept of inclusive education, both in Zimbabwe and beyond, and research findings by the authors. As such, this chapter seeks to explore and explain the paradox that, regardless of the existence of a seemingly supportive policy and political environment, successful practices of inclusive education have remained a mirage in the secondary schools of Zimbabwe (Mafa, 2012; Musengi & Chireshe, 2013; Muresherwa & Jita, 2021) decades after the Salamanca Declaration and independence from colonial rule. This means that the chapter is informed by literature from earlier writers on the inclusive education framework to explore and explain the gap between formulations and realisations of inclusive education in the secondary schools of Zimbabwe at a time when the country is expected to have fully matured and to be fully embracing the inclusive framework in all its institutions as the foundation for social justice. In line with this paradox, the chapter also proffers possible solutions and recommendations which, if adopted, may have the potential to make inclusive education in the secondary schools of Zimbabwe and beyond more relevant, effective and responsive to the needs of the community. This conceptual chapter is grounded on a combination of scientific enquiry and a comprehensive review of existing literature on policy and practice of inclusive education. The chapter therefore points to possible directions for future research on inclusive education in the secondary schools of Zimbabwe, and in other countries sharing similar socio-political and socio-economic contexts.

It ought to be highlighted at this point that similar gaps between policy and practice of inclusive education (Donohue & Bornman, 2014; Haug, 2017; Jansen, 2002; Muresherwa & Jita, 2021) have been observed in various countries other than Zimbabwe. In addition, these gaps between formulations and realisations of inclusive education have been found in countries of both the developed and developing world (Walton & Engelbrecht, 2022). In the developed world, mismatch between policy and practice of inclusive education has been reported in countries such as Australia, Italy, the United States of America, Canada, New Zealand and China, whilst in the developing world, such countries include Zambia, Malawi, Angola and South Africa (Anastasiou et al., 2015; Ballard, 1999; Forlin, 2013; Siziba, & Kaputa, 2022). This geographical distribution of the mismatch between formulations and realisations of inclusive education makes the present chapter very relevant. The uniqueness of the present chapter is that it focuses on inclusive education in secondary schools. This is an area which has not been fully explored, especially in Africa. Most research in Africa, including in Zimbabwe (cf. Chimhenga, 2016; Hashmi et al., 2017; Mafa, 2012; Musengi & Chireshe, 2013; Opoku et al., 2021; Samkange, 2013; Siziba & Kaputa, 2022) has focused on inclusive education in primary schools. More so, the present chapter focuses on inclusive education "[a]s involving all groups that risk exclusion and not on inclusive education as concerned with disability and special educational needs" only (Ainscow & César, 2006, p. 234). Furthermore, this chapter focuses on a developing country with a strong colonial history, which may be unique to the countries in Southern Africa. These are countries in which colonial oppression was deeply entrenched and bloody and protracted wars were fought for the people to regain their political independence and majority rule.

The present chapter is predicated on the view that whilst the phenomenon concerning misalignment between the policy and practice of inclusive education may be widespread, the explanations for the observed gaps in the countries of the developed world and the secondary schools in post-colonial countries of the developing world, especially those in Southern Africa, may differ in significant ways (Walton & Engelbrecht, 2022). The situation in developed countries such as Canada, the United States of America and Australia have been fully explored and, hence, readily understood and explained. Nonetheless, the gap between policy and practice of inclusive education from the perspective of developing countries, such as those on the African continent, has not been fully explored (Forlin, 2013). The reasons for this dearth of knowledge about the state of inclusive education in developing countries has not been fully documented, and hence exclusionary practices by schools have continued, with serious ramifications on the purpose of education and social justice in these countries (Walton & Engelbrecht, 2022). In the Zimbabwean situation, this lack of knowledge is particularly evident in secondary schools (Muresherwa & Jita, 2021), which, until recently, have not been considered to be part of the basic education framework. It is against this background that this chapter seeks to explore the state of inclusive education in Zimbabwe decades after the enactment of the Salamanca Declaration in 1994 and the attainment of political independence in 1980.

The chapter seeks to create an understanding of the issues, controversies and dilemmas associated with inclusive education in Zimbabwe and to proffer possible solutions and recommendations which, if embraced, may serve to make inclusive education a reality in the secondary schools in the country and other countries sharing a similar history. This would make inclusive education more relevant, effective and responsive to the needs of the local people. The issue here is that, as global citizens, people in these countries should not be left behind by the international wave and/or discourse on promoting social justice and culturally affirming education interventions through equity-based instructional practices (Williams et al., 2021). The ratification of the Salamanca Declaration and attainment of independence are considered to be key milestones in the history of Zimbabwe's public education in general and inclusive education in particular.

Whilst it is beyond doubt that there is discrepancy between formulations and realisations of the inclusive framework (Mafa, 2012; Musengi & Chireshe, 2013; Muresherwa & Jita, 2021; Siziba & Kaputa, 2022), the nature, causes and extent of this misalignment in the secondary schools of Zimbabwe have not been clearly understood. The central objective of this chapter is therefore to close this gap by exploring and offering an explanation of the origin, nature and extent of the "perceived" misalignment between policy and practice of inclusive education, focusing on the secondary schools of Zimbabwe. The authors' effort to produce an entire book chapter dedicated to the state of inclusive education in the secondary schools of Zimbabwe at a time when many researchers have written about inclusive education in general and the inclusive framework internationally (Walton & Engelbrecht, 2022) should not be seen as academic arrogance (Muresherwa & Jita, 2021). Instead, this effort should be viewed as an attempt by the authors to domesticate and acculturate the inclusive framework, and to fully understand the challenges to and opportunities for inclusive education in the secondary schools of Zimbabwe. The aim here is to proffer recommendations that may make inclusive education interventions in the country more effective and culturally affirming, that is, responsive to the needs of the local people. This is also a step towards social justice (Polat, 2011).

The chapter also seeks to motivate other writers to come up with inclusive theories and frameworks that are relevant and applicable to local conditions, and thereby avoid the temptation of universalising this evidently context-based concept, which Walton and Engelbrecht (2022) defined as complex. The concept of inclusive education in an African setting, for example, may not need to be viewed as concerned with disability and "special educational needs" only. Instead, without demeaning and de-emphasising the role of inclusive education as concerned, especially with children with disabilities, in an African, post-colonial and developing-country perspective, inclusive education should be seen as an educational practice that involves all groups that risk exclusion. This should include those with a particular political stance and those with low intellectual ability. This is because, in these countries, many social groups were previously excluded from some social institutions and social activities, such as education. Such exclusion was, for example, based purely on racial grounds, leaving new governments to always feel duty-bound to redress such deficiencies at the slightest opportunity availed to them. Inclusive education interventions in these countries should therefore seriously consider embracing all the groups that risk exclusion, if the objective of social justice were to be realised (Muthukrishna & Engelbrecht, 2018). Clearly, inclusive education under these circumstances should be viewed as a special type of special needs education and not as its synonym only.

This chapter is also based on the key assumption that although inclusive education is grounded on the basic principles of equity, equality and social justice, individual learners' needs and exceptionalities that this framework seeks to address are contextual, complex, culturally defined and therefore fluid and transitory (Walton & Engelbrecht, 2022). As a result, the definitions of special needs, disabilities or even exceptionalities and therefore the inclusive–exclusive education dichotomy may vary across geographical, historical and social contexts. Such contexts may comprise the socio-political, socio-economic and socio-historical environment in which school systems find themselves. These contexts, in turn, determine and shape the cultural, psychological, professional, political and institutional perspectives with which educational stakeholders and agents understand and/or practise the inclusive education framework. This means that any theory that seeks to describe and explain the state of inclusive education in any given geographical or social setting should be grounded on a deep understanding of the socio-political, socio-historical, socio-cultural and socio-economic contexts of the involved region, province or country. This means that, in assessing the state of inclusive education in any given country, for example Zimbabwe, and the extent to which inclusivity has moved it towards attaining its social justice objectives (Rigby, 2014), the impact of the historical, cultural and economic contexts of the country should never be ignored. This also means that to be seen as worth its salt, the brand of inclusive education embraced in any country should be seen to be culturally affirming and not to be at odds with the cultural expectations and socio-economic needs of the people involved. This view also means that regardless of varying definitions of exceptionalities as a result of the varying and complex nature of inclusive instructional contexts, full inclusive education should be defined to involve all groups that are at risk of exclusion. This is because public education should be based on social justice as opposed to purely entrepreneurial (Rigby, 2014) and/or political logics (Erll, 2012) only. Performance indicators for the inclusive frameworks as a step towards social justice (Polat, 2011) are grounded on the principles of equal access, equity, quality and relevance of education (Anlimachie, 2015; Tomasevski, 2004). *Access* in this context comprises both physical access to learning institutions and epistemic access to the curriculum (Hudson, 2019; Mhlolo, 2015).

THE SOCIO-HISTORICAL CONTEXT OF THE INCLUSIVE AGENDA IN ZIMBABWE

"Zimbabwe is a former British colony that was known as Rhodesia from 1965 to 1979" (Shizha & Kariwo, 2012, p. 1). Before 1964, the country was known as Southern Rhodesia, to distinguish it from Northern Rhodesia, that is, present-day Zambia, which was also part of the Federation of Rhodesia and Nyasaland, comprising three countries, namely present-day Zimbabwe, Zambia and Malawi (Shizha & Kariwo, 2012). The history of education, hence the inclusive education–exclusive education dichotomy in Zimbabwe, can be traced to the country's political history, beginning from the colonial era through the early years of independence to date (Gondo et al., 2019). Zimbabwe was a British colony from 1890 to 1980 (Raftopoulos & Mlambo, 2009). Undoubtedly, this history has set the foundation of the socio-political perspectives, socio-economic mind-set and cultural memories (Erll, 2012) which have shaped people's understanding of the nature and purpose of public education and the inclusive–exclusive education narratives in the country until today. Without any reservation, the colonial era should be credited for setting the foundation of formal education as it is known in Zimbabwe today. Throughout the colonial period, the colonial government had an insatiable hunger and thirst to offer a British-type education to white children in order to make them internationally competitive, informed and knowledgeable. However, it is also blamed for restricting the majority of African children to an inferior type of education. As a result of this dualistic view, the country embraced a two-tiered system of education during the entire colonial period. This dualistic system of education comprised what came to be known as the F1 and F2 subsystems of public education. On the one hand, the F2 subsystem focused on churning out learners who majored in technical subjects such as woodwork, metalwork, fashion and fabrics, and home economics, amongst other vocational subjects. Given the type of curriculum that they were afforded, the majority of the F2 graduates, on leaving school, would naturally find themselves involved in manual and/or technical jobs. A few of them found their way to apprenticeship training in various trades related to the vocational education framework that they were exposed to during their secondary school level of education. On the other hand, the F1 school system produced students who were meant for white-collar jobs. Socially, the graduates from the F1 schools were purposefully and consciously designed to become employers and/ or managers for the businesses that employed their counterparts from the F2 school system.

Whilst the F2 schools enrolled the children of black Zimbabweans only, the F1 schools enrolled mainly children from the white community (Bhurekeni, 2020).With regard to Africans, the F1 schools employed a bottleneck system by enrolling African learners that were considered to be exceptionally gifted on an intellectual level only. These learners would enjoy the privilege of being admitted into what was referred to as group 'A' schools, that is, exclusive schools that focused mainly on educating white people. These privileged learners were seen to be so intellectually gifted that under normal circumstances, they had the chance to proceed to 'A' level and then to the only university available in the country during the time, that is, the University of Rhodesia, now the University of Zimbabwe (Masaka, 2016). These were just a few African learners who would be trained as African lawyers, medical doctors, architects, engineers and surveyors, amongst other highly regarded white-collar professions of the time. The school curriculum was structured in such a way that the majority of African learners in the F2 system were offered subjects such as arithmetic, English language and general science. These subjects were less demanding and, therefore, considered inferior to the syllabi for the same subjects which were offered to learners in F1 schools. In fact, African children were regarded as perpetual minors, only capable of learning arithmetic, basic English language and hygiene, with their white counterparts afforded the opportunity to learn more thought-provoking subjects that prepared them for a fuller and happier life in adulthood. For denying the majority of African children access to the F1 class of schools and the related curriculum, this colonial education system began to bear the seeds of exclusionary pressure that seem to have persisted in the education system up to this day. The exclusive schools that emerged from the colonial education system were referred to as group 'A' schools to distinguish them from the rest of the schools that accommodated the majority of the African children. The main criterion for discriminating one group of learners from the other was race, purported to be the basis for intellectual ability, thereby creating an inclusive–exclusive dichotomy of education during the colonial period (Mapako & Mareva, 2013). However, this approach to education was based on the desire to maintain the supremacy of the white race over Africans and capitalist competition for resources and to enable the colonial administration system to survive.

Abdi (2007) apparently agreed with the negative perception concerning African education, coupled with the desire by white colonial masters to destroy indigenous knowledge systems. Abdi (2007) submitted that the process of colonialism regarded the indigenous ways of learning which were rooted in the cultural and historical practices of oral societies to be relics of the past, with no place in the "civilised and enlightened" society that colonialism sought to build. This education system was blamed for lacking innovative alternatives that would make Africans attractive and acceptable in the new modalities of colonial relationships. Abdi (2007) thus went further to assert that the white colonial masters desired to subjugate the African population and to create the type of person desired in the new order. As a result, they designed colonial pedagogies which focused on educational objectives that were premised on promoting an inferiority complex amongst Africans to their European colonialist counterparts, cultural dislodgment, epistemological domination, and implanting mediocrity. Clearly, this system did not stem from the interests of the African child (Masaka, 2016; Shizha & Kariwo, 2012), equity, equal opportunities or social justice (Rigby, 2014), but from the desire to maintain the supremacy of the white race over Africans, and hence was detested by nationalist leaders. Abraham (2020), citing earlier work from

Rodney (1989), supported this view and described the colonial education system such as implanted in Zimbabwe as a "[s]chooling for subordination, exploitation, the creation of mental confusion, and the development of underdevelopment" (p. 48). Bhurekeni (2020) shared the view that the African child during the colonial period suffered deficiencies in accessing knowledge at the same level as those undertaking a European education curriculum, because there was a dual and discriminatory system of education, one for Africans and another one for white people.

It may be important to appreciate at this stage that, whilst education for white people was sponsored by the state, the education for Africans was mainly sponsored by missionaries for "compassionate" reasons and as part of fulfilling the social concern objectives (Ireland, 2022) of their missionary work (Maurice, 2022). The state only adopted a regulatory and auxiliary role in the education of Africans, especially in the F2 school system. Following the growth of black consciousness and nationalist movements in the 1960s in the backdrop of an increased effort by the white Zimbabwean community to portray their race as a superior race, education for Africans came to be viewed negatively by the indigenous African population (Bhurekeni, 2020).This negativity was also focused on those schools which were run by missionaries. In fact, in the minds of the African people of colonial Zimbabwe, then Rhodesia, the education for African children was seen from the perspective of white people serving their key interests. These interests included racial supremacy, dominance over the African majority by the white minority groups and Christian conversion of Africans in order to make them more malleable and to readily accept their role as being inferior to the white race. From the perspective of the Africans, the white missionaries believed that, through the formal education system, they were bringing "light" and "civility" to "barbaric" communities in the dark continent of Africa. In addition, the African nationalist believed that the education system for Africans was fostering the belief amongst African learners that the African learners' worldview was myopic and superstitious (Bhurekeni, 2020) and, hence, this deficiency needed to be addressed. Clearly, this type of thinking was seen to socialise Africans to deny themselves and wish that they were different, a situation which would perpetuate white supremacy, colonialism and domination of Africans by the white race. (Peterson, 2000).

Whether wrongly or correctly, the nationalist leaders, most of whom were educated through this dualistic system of education, therefore strongly detested this exclusionary nature of the F1 category of the colonial school system. They were therefore determined to fight and dismantle it, leaf, root and stem, at the slightest opportunity. However, it is important to appreciate that, before the advent of colonialism, there was no formal education to talk about in Zimbabwe. The African nationalists nonetheless believed that the white colonial masters destroyed the African way of learning and implanted a system which made African learners accept their role in society as hewers of wood and fetchers of water for "their" white colonial masters (Bassey, 1999). The negativity associated with colonial education, especially from the perspective of the state, was to a large extent very plausible. However, this negative thought associated with white Zimbabweans and their participation in education should not be taken as a blanket statement applying to all members of this community. This view is particularly valid if one considers the role that was played by white missionaries such as John Mark Pemberton and Garfield Todd and his wife, Merriam Todd, amongst other Churches of Christ/Christian Churches, in building the foundation of what we call formal education in Zimbabwe today. The good work of church institutions such as the Roman Catholic, Anglican, Reformed, United Methodist, Lutheran and United Baptist churches should also not go unnoticed as people seek to understand and explain the state of inclusive education and inclusive instructional practices in Zimbabwe. It is beyond doubt that, whilst the education system served the purpose of subjugating the African people in Zimbabwe and to make them accept their position in society as inferior to other races, some missionaries had a strong drive to ameliorate the life of vulnerable communities through educational interventions, in line with their social concern objectives. Some of the works of these missionaries still stand tall for all to see up to this day. The schools they established, such as Masvingo Christian College and Biriiri, Dadaya, Gokomere, Kutama, Mashoko and Mutambara mission schools, are still actively involved in educating the nation. In fact, the story of public education in Zimbabwe cannot be complete without talking about the missionary work of such key figures as Garfield and Merriam Todd and their Dadaya School, for example. What this means is that no matter how emotive and Afrocentric the narrative of education in Zimbabwe may be made to appear, the positive side of the good works and efforts of foundational institutions such as Churches of Christ/Christian Churches, Roman Catholic, Anglican, Reformed Church, Lutheran, Baptist and Methodist should never be ignored.

This reality shows that for all intents and purposes, the story and state of inclusive education in Zimbabwe today cannot be explained outside the socio-political, socio-cultural and socio-economic perspectives emerging from that historical context. From the perspective of the nationalist leaders who ushered in independence in 1980, and of the black majority, the two-tiered education system premised on racial discrimination, racial segregation and white supremacy was considered undesirable. As a result, this had no place in the new democratic dispensation and hence had to be dismantled. In the backdrop of these negativities towards the dual education system, there was surely a prima-facie case for reforming education to embrace a more equitable (inclusive) and socially just educational framework at the advent of independence in 1980. The dual education system had to be eradicated leaf, root and stem. It was assumed to be following an apartheid (separate development) approach as it excluded African children from accessing "quality" education offered through group 'A' type of schools. In addition, it was a private preserve of white people and only a handful Africans who were seen to be intellectually gifted. The advent of independence in 1980 therefore set the foundation of a new trajectory in the history of education which should be understood by those seeking to understand and explain the state of inclusive education in Zimbabwe today, decades after independence and the Salamanca.

Since the new government in 1980 was grounded on the principles of equity (inclusivity), equality and social justice, the colonial education system had to be dismantled entirely. It was regarded to be skewed in favour of children from the minority former white colonial rulers. In the minds of the nationalist leaders, this exclusionary colonial education system had to be replaced by a more equitable (inclusive) and hence socially just education system which allows all children, that is, black and white, gifted or otherwise, access to "quality" education in inclusive settings. This type of thinking led to the abandonment of the F2 system in favour of the F1 education system. The situation on the ground today seems to show that whilst there was a need to re-dress the colonial imbalances (Forlin, 2013), complete eradication of the F2 education system might have been an overreaction on the part of the founding fathers of independent Zimbabwe. By completely abandoning the F2 education system, which focused on vocational skills which are useful in real life, in favour of the F1 system, which prepares learners for white-collar jobs, the political fathers in Zimbabwe seem to have created another form of exclusion involving denying epistemic access (Hudson, 2019) to relevant and quality education to some learners in the education system. This practice of denying some learners epistemic access to education jives in the face of promoting social justice through education interventions. This view is further explored in the following section that focuses on the growth trajectory and the state of inclusive education in Zimbabwe, in the backdrop of the socio-historical and socio-economic contexts, including the cultural memories discussed above.

GROWTH TRAJECTORY AND STATE OF INCLUSIVE EDUCATION IN ZIMBABWE

This section of the chapter on the state of inclusive education in Zimbabwe is informed by the socio-historical context of public education and cultural memories (Erll, 2012) on racial discrimination and racial segregation in the country, as discussed above. The section focuses on the issues, controversies and dilemmas surrounding inclusive education thought and practice in the country today. In this vein, this section seeks to unpack what may be viewed as the conundrum of the inclusive education agenda in the country.

Issues, Controversies and Problems of the Inclusive Framework in Zimbabwe

Whilst Zimbabwe did not immediately make sweeping changes to the education system inherited from the colonial masters at the advent of independence in 1980, no time was taken before the F2 education system was scrapped in favour of the F1 system of education. According to Shizha (2007), following the attainment of political independence by Zimbabwe in 1980, the young nation was quick to abandon the F2 education system in favour of the F1 system. This move was premised on the understanding that the colonial education system restricted African children to an inferior type of education. This means that the most immediate form of inclusive education in the minds of nationalist leaders was about providing African children physical access into the F1 school system. When the opportunity presented itself in 1980, the nation therefore embraced the F1 system of education, which previously was considered a private preserve for children from the white community as the ideal education system for all. Several other educational reforms focusing on aspects of education which are not directly related to inclusive education, for example syllabus changes, followed this initial reform much later. Eradication of the two-tiered education system meant that learners across the social divide were now also exposed to the same type of curriculum, regardless of race differences amongst them. Shizha (2007) referred to this type of inclusive education as political inclusion. The climax of this type of inclusive education in the Zimbabwean context is epitomised by the nationalisation of the examination system in 1994 (Abraham, 2003). The scrapping of the F2 education system in favour of the F1 system thus marked the beginning of an inclusive drive in the public education system in Zimbabwe.

The new Zimbabwean government, in addition to embracing this political inclusion, also described by Shizha (2007) as the most immediate and necessary reform for the young nation, also advocated for providing education for children with disabilities, at least on paper. This focus was on aligning public education with the equity, equality and social justice principles upon which the young democracy was grounded. At a national level, the education for learners with disabilities was enshrined in the Disabled Persons' Act of 1992. Reforms during the early years of independence were also based on the desire by the political leadership in the country to establish a socialist state based on the philosophy of growth with equity, equal rights and social justice principles, as also informed by the Education for All (EFA) agenda and United Nations Convention on the Rights of Persons with Disabilities (CRPD). It should be appreciated, however, that both the EFA agenda and the CRPD in their original perspectives did not directly speak to the inclusive agenda but to giving access to all, including people with disabilities. The CRPD, for example, adopted a special needs approach to the education of children with disabilities, in particular. The EFA focused on providing physical access to educational amenities to 'all' learners. These conventions and regulations were informed by human rights principles. This approach promoted institutionalised education for children with disabilities and capitalistic competition amongst learners without special needs designations. It can be argued that inclusive education during the formative years of Zimbabwe's independence focused on the politically sensitive and socially emotive issues of affording "learners" physical access to schools and the curriculum previously reserved for children from the white community only that is political inclusion (Shizha, 2007). The focus for most learners with exceptionalities other than those who risked exclusion on the grounds of race, tribe, and place of origin, national origin, political opinion, colour, creed or gender was on providing access to schools and the curriculum previously reserved for white people. The question of inclusive education for learners with exceptionalities, other than those listed in the Education Act as cited above, those outside dismantling the F2 education system and affording everyone who could afford it to have access to education in former group 'A' schools, was de-emphasised in this new rights-based approach to education. Clearly, what seemed important was to provide access to education for 'all', in a non-racial environment, as long as one's parents were able to pay the fees asked for in a given school. Issues of epistemic access to relevant education appeared to not be of concern to the new government, since the new government seemed to be attracted by the political and entrepreneurial logics (Rigby, 2014) of public education.

Whilst there are other documents informing the inclusive education framework during the formative years of Zimbabwe's independent history, the Salamanca Statement (UNESCO, 1994) marks a key milestone on inclusive education in Zimbabwe and beyond. This is a policy product of the Salamanca Conference which was held in the city of Salamanca, Spain in 1994. In fact, the Salamanca Declaration is considered to be the ground-breaking and most important single document that has ever been promulgated to advance the cause for special education in general and inclusive education in particular, internationally (Francisco et al., 2020; Miles & Singhal, 2010). The Salamanca Declaration provides the philosophical foundations, principles and the framework for policy and practice on inclusive education as a special type of special needs education globally. Specifically, the Salamanca Declaration combines the principles of special needs education, advanced by various conventions and statements on the rights of people with disabilities, with the issues of the EFA agenda entrenched in the Jomtien Declaration of 1990. This combination of the special needs education framework with the EFA agenda produced a hybrid statement that informs the inclusive framework as it is known across the globe today (Magnússon, 2019). In Zimbabwe, as is the case with many other progressive countries internationally (Mafa, 2012; Musengi & Chireshe, 2013), participation in the Salamanca Conference and the subsequent ratification of the Salamanca Declaration are considered to be key milestones in the country's history of education and the practice of inclusive education. Together with the attainment of independence in 1980, the ratification of the Salamanca Declaration forms the basis for understanding the growth trajectory and practice of inclusive education in the public education system in Zimbabwe. Undoubtedly, this situation in Zimbabwe also has implications in other countries that share a common history, for example those grounded in the foundation of colonialism.

In the perspective of the nationalist leaders, the young Zimbabwe had to embrace the inclusive framework as a matter of policy and hence their participation in both the Jomtien 1990 and the Salamanca Conference of 1994. In fact, the EFA agenda was in line with the manifesto of the new ruling party, ZANU-PF. This founding manifesto of independent Zimbabwe, as is the case with the subsequent manifestoes of ZANU-PF, also spoke to issues of equity (inclusivity), equal rights and social justice. Specifically, inclusive education was considered a legal right, at least on paper. Typically, this interest in the inclusive education agenda by the founding fathers of independent Zimbabwe meant that the inclusive agenda had to be reflected on all the socio-political and socio-economic blueprints that sought to usher in a new dispensation, different from what had prevailed in the country's dark period of colonial bondage. Although grounded on the smouldering ashes of the lived experiences of political and racial injustices of the colonial past, the new education system had to be built on the foundations of equity, equality of all races and social justice, as opposed to racial supremacy, racial segregation and racial discrimination.

Various outstanding and successive economic blueprints in the country's post-colonial history resulted from the new focus on humanity described above. Included are the Transitional National Development Plan (TNDP) (1982–1990), the Economic Structural Adjustment Programme (ESAP) (1991–1995), the Zimbabwe Programme for Economic and Social Transformation (ZIMPREST) (1996–2000), the Short Term Emergency Recovery Programme (STERP) 1 & 2 (2009–2012), Zimbabwe Agenda for Sustainable Socio-Economic Transformation (ZIMASSET) (2013–2018) and, more recently, the National Development Strategy 1 (NDS 1) (2021–2025) (Demillo, 2021). All these blueprints had a focus on the growth with equity (inclusivity), equality and social justice principles. The success or otherwise of these blueprints is beyond the scope of this chapter. What is material in this chapter is that all these blueprints, like the successive manifestoes of the ruling party, ZANU-PF, also spoke to the inclusive education agenda since independence in 1980. The NDS 1, that is the country's most current economic blueprint, for example, talks about the need to afford the citizenry an "improved access to quality, equitable and inclusive education" (Government of Zimbabwe, 2020, p. 154).

In addition to the economic blueprints reviewed above, and to further entrench and operationalise the inclusive framework, Zimbabwe made an effort to enact its own home-grown inclusive-related social policies (Mafa, 2012; Muresherwa & Jita 2021; Musengi & Chireshe, 2013). These social policies, such as the economic blueprints cited above, are also grounded on the founding and subsequent ZANU-PF manifestoes, which focus on issues of equity (inclusivity), equality and social justice. The most important social policies that have been enacted in Zimbabwe to speak to the inclusive framework include the Education Act of 1987 (as amended) and the Disabled Persons Act of 1992. Specifically, section 4, subsection 2 of the Education Act (Government of Zimbabwe, 1987) states that "every child has the right to access education at the nearest school and should not be discriminated against by the imposition of onerous terms and conditions in regard to admission to any school on the ground of race, tribe, place of origin, national origin, political opinion, colour, creed or gender". The Disabled Persons Act, which Mafa (2012) and Musengi and Chireshe (2013) also viewed as speaking to the inclusive framework, focuses on making "provisions for the welfare and rehabilitation of disabled persons; to provide for the appointment and functions of a Director for Disabled Persons' Affairs and the establishment and functions of a National Disability Board; and to provide for matters connected with or incidental to the foregoing" (Government of Zimbabwe, 1992, p. 1). Interestingly, inclusive education is not mentioned directly in this act. The assumption would be, however, that this issue is implied where the act talks about "[p]roviding for matters related to the foregoing" (Government of Zimbabwe, 1992, p. 1), wherein the matters in question have not been spelt out.

Undoubtedly, the social policies cited above vaguely provide process indicators for the interventions that should be embraced towards the realisation of the goals of inclusive education and therefore social justice in education. An analysis of these social policies shows that they seem to loosely speak to the inclusive framework (Musengi & Chireshe, 2013). Where these social policies specifically speak to the inclusive framework, the focus seems to be on physical inclusion only, without much recourse to what Mhlolo (2015) and Hudson (2019) defined as epistemic inclusion. Further analysis of the inclusive-related policies in Zimbabwe also shows that, in some cases, the issues involved are discordant, thereby creating a situation devoid of a comprehensive theory upon which inclusive education thought and practice in the country can be grounded. For example, the Education Act speaks to inclusive education in the context of involving 'all' groups that are vulnerable for exclusion (Ainscow & César, 2006), whilst the Disabled Persons Act focuses on providing for the welfare and rehabilitation of persons with disabilities. No reference to epistemic inclusion is made in these foundational policies for the inclusive framework. A particularly striking deficiency on the part of the Education Act is that disability and low intellectual ability are not directly mentioned on the list of "onerous" (Government of Zimbabwe, 1987) factors that should not be taken as grounds for excluding prospective learners from accessing education in any school of their choice. The list of these grounds includes one's "race, tribe, place of origin, national origin, political opinion, colour, creed or gender" (Government of Zimbabwe, 1987). Issues to do with disability and low ability to learn (Slee, 2018) are strikingly absent from the list.

Clearly, this list of onerous factors points to the political bias of the inclusive agenda (Slee, 2001) in the perspective of policy-makers in the country. This bias further points to the view that inclusive education, at least during the formative years of the country's independence, was driven by the political desire of the founding fathers of independent Zimbabwe to afford all children physical access to schools and a common curriculum to 'all', rather than a pedagogic understanding of the different needs of learners. The bias was mainly on the basis of legal and political rights and not social justice. Another conspicuous deficiency is that the Disabled Persons Act, though it is the most important single policy instrument speaking directly to issues of people with disabilities in the country, does not directly speak to inclusive education. If anything, this act speaks only loosely to inclusive education, preferring to focus on providing for the welfare and rehabilitation of persons with disabilities and not inclusive education in particular. These omissions point to the view that, at least during the formative years of the history of public education in independent Zimbabwe, inclusive education focused on physical inclusion of children who risked exclusion from some school on the grounds of race, tribe, place of origin, political opinion, colour, creed or gender only. This approach seemed oblivious to the issues related to disability and learners with low ability to learn due to operations of the differential- and multiple-intelligence hypotheses (Chen & Gardner, 2018). Clearly, the EFA agenda and Disabled Persons Act focus on different types of exceptionalities. Whilst the Disabled Persons Act speaks to disability issues, the EFA agenda (Mathwasa & Sibanda, 2021) addresses the issues of 'all'. However, the 'all' concept in the founding document of the EFA agenda is not clearly defined (Magnússon, 2019), thereby giving room to different interpretations. Slee (2001) thus lamented that "[t]he absence of a language for inclusive education that stipulates its vocabulary and grammar increases the risk for political misappropriation" (p. 167) of the key concept and practice of inclusive education and the related concept of 'all' ". According to Slee (2001), this is because the issue of "[l]anguage and meaning ... lies at the heart of the inclusive educational project" (p. 170). The situation in Zimbabwe seems to be exacerbated by the fact that the Disabled Persons Act of 1992 is administered by the Ministry of Social Welfare and not the Ministry of Primary and Secondary Education (MoPSE), the custodian of public education in the country. The assumption in this chapter is that the concept 'all' in Zimbabwe is used, in its strictest sense, to refer to all learners at risk for exclusion from some schools, for one reason or the other.

In addition to statutory regulations relating to inclusive education cited above, a number of ministerial-level statements and policy circulars, such as the Education Secretary's Policy Circular No. P36 of 1990, have also been formulated by the Ministry of Education, now the MoPSE, to speak directly and operationalise the inclusive framework. Needless to say, Circular No. P36, being a ministerial circular and not an act of parliament or statutory instrument, may not on its own wield legal authority which is enforceable at law. In recent years, however, the New Constitution of 2013 and the Zimbabwe New

Curriculum Framework (ZNCF) for the MoPSE (2015–2022) have also provided renewed energy in the drive for the inclusive agenda. On the face of it, although with glaring gaps and policy inconsistencies, the situation on the ground seems to show that various policies and the political environment in Zimbabwe support the inclusive agenda (Mafa, 2012; Muresherwa & Jita, 2021; Musengi & Chireshe, 2013). It is against this background that former State President Robert Mugabe in his acceptance remarks of the ZNCF 2015–2022 document expressed the wishful statement that:

Over the years I have called for a relevant, quality and inclusive education in the school curriculum whose hallmarks are competencies desired in life and work. Simultaneously, such education must remain accessible and affordable to all. (Zimbabwe. MoPSE, 2015, p. i)

This pronouncement by the founding president, Robert Mugabe, indicates that throughout his reign, stretching over 36 years, he always wished that all schools in Zimbabwe could embrace an inclusive approach to education (Muresherwa & Jita, 2021). Reference to such terms as "relevant", "quality" and "all" by the then president suggests that the political leadership in the country perceived inclusive education in the perspective of 'all' groups that risk exclusion from some schools for one reason or the other. In particular, his use of the term "relevant" to describe the education that he wished to implement in the country also shows that he was conscious of the need for promoting epistemic inclusion as opposed to physical inclusion only. The former comprises inclusive education which goes beyond providing physical access to learners that risk physical exclusion from some schools, for one reason or the other, to embracing inclusive education which ensures that each learner enrolled in any given school benefits from the learning experiences and the curriculum offered in that particular school (Hudson, 2019; Mhlolo, 2015).

Based on the citation above, it is evident that the political leadership in the country has been cognisant of the need to create an appropriate balance between the issues of providing learners with physical access to educational institutions in which they wish to enrol, and of affording all learners epistemic access to quality education in non-selective settings. However, the concept of 'all' in this Zimbabwean education context also seems to lack a clear definition. Assuming that the concept of 'all' in the above quotation derives from the broad sense of the concept (Miles & Singhal, 2010) as is the case in the Jomtien Declaration (Inter-Agency Commission, 1990), it is not immediately clear why full inclusion (Musengi & Chireshe, 2013) is still a pipe dream in the country, as the above quotation from the former president also seems to suggest. Given the support by the former president, as implied in the quotation above, it is again not immediately clear why inclusive practices in Zimbabwe seem to ignore the issues of epistemic inclusion (Mhlolo, 2015) in favour of physical inclusion only. Apparently, the former state president seemed to be aware of the need for the education system to afford all learners epistemic quality (Hudson, 2019) education.

Undoubtedly, the statement by President Mugabe cited above points to the view that inclusive education in whatever form had not been fully realised by the time the ZNCF 2015–2022 was officially launched. The statement is thus a wish, suggesting that the situation on the ground contradicted political views and the policy environment prevailing in the country, which on the face of it favoured an inclusive approach to education. The situation on the ground, as literature has shown, firmly points to misalignment between formulations and realisations (Forlin, 2013; Haug, 2017; Muresherwa & Jita, 2021) of inclusive education. Apparently, in agreement with this policy vis-à-vis practice misalignment, the Permanent Secretary's Circular No. 13 of 2015 had this to say about access of prospective learners to education in some schools in the country:

The Ministry has noted [with concern] that some schools are enrolling learners into Form 1, through an application of their own entrance tests and assessments ... This practice is discriminatory and violates the provisions of the Constitution of Zimbabwe and the Education Act. It is against this background that Cabinet directed the Ministry to address the issues ... with a view to making education more accessible to all learners. (Zimbabwe. MoPSE, 2015, p. 1)

The quotation above clearly confirms the exclusionary character of the education system in Zimbabwe, and the misalignment between formulations and realisations of inclusive education (Muresherwa & Jita, 2021), which the former president, Robert Mugabe, also alluded to as noted earlier in this chapter. Musengi and Chireshe (2013) also concurred with the view that full inclusion in Zimbabwe has remained a pipe dream regardless of policy and a political environment which seem to support the inclusive framework. Furthermore, the Secretary's Circular, as cited above, seems interested in providing physical access only, as opposed to epistemic inclusion. This view is particularly evident where the permanent secretary (see quotation above) views the use of school-based entrance tests and assessments to be discriminatory and a violation of the provisions of the Constitution of Zimbabwe and the Education Act. Entrance tests in this sense deny some low-ability prospective learners physical access to some schools in the country. The circular does not mention issues relating to affording learners epistemic access to the curriculum. Whilst affording all learners physical access to schools is important, it still needs to be appreciated that this does not on its own fully address issues of the inclusive–exclusive dichotomy (Ballard, 1999; Miles & Singhal, 2010) in public education as a means to social justice.

The Secretary's Circular No. 13, the statement by the former president cited above, and the ZNCF 2015–2022 are strikingly silent about inclusive education of learners with disabilities. The Secretary's Circular, in particular, seems to focus on inclusive education from the perspective of providing physical access to low-ability learners who risk being deselected from some schools when they fail to pass learner selection tests and assessments. However, by focusing on inclusion of all children who risk exclusion as a result of low ability to learn, the Secretary's Circular No. 13 seems to be bringing to the fore the fact that inclusive education must also focus on 'all' (Ballard, 1999). Unfortunately, it seems that the circular does not say much about bridging the gap between the notion of inclusive education as concerned with disability and special educational needs (Francisco et al., 2020) with inclusive education, which involves all groups that risk exclusion for one reason or the other (Ainscow & César, 2006).

In the backdrop of this broad perspective of the notion of 'all', for example, in the Salamanca Conference Resolution, an outcome of the Return to Salamanca Conference (2009), it was stated that:

We understood inclusive education to be a process where mainstream schools and early years' settings are transformed so that all children/students are supported to meet their academic and social potential and which involves removing barriers in environment, communication, curriculum, teaching, socialisation and assessment at all levels. (Mathwasa & Sibanda, 2021, p.3)

The definition above highlights that inclusive education is about 'all' learners in the broad sense of the concept. In addition, this type of inclusive education should go beyond providing physical access only (Mhlolo, 2015) to also affording learners epistemic access to the curriculum (Hudson, 2019). Clearly, the quotation above is cognisant of the differential- and multiple-intelligence principles (Chen & Gardner, 2018). This is particularly evident where the conference report talks about the need to support learners to meet their academic and social potential. However, the discussion above shows that the education system in Zimbabwe is experiencing pressure to maintain an exclusionary trajectory, which seems to be more attractive to school authorities than the inclusive framework. Where inclusive education policies appear to be enforced, especially by the state, the focus is on political inclusion of learners who risk exclusion from some schools on the grounds of place of origin, race, tribe, national origin, political opinion, colour, creed or gender. Exclusion of learners on the grounds of disability and low ability to learn appears to be an issue, at least on paper. However, reference to entrance tests and assessments in the Secretary's Circular No. 13 and the statement by the then state president, as cited above, are affirmations that some schools in the country have remained selective and therefore exclusionary. It seems that this exclusionary pressure has continued to be felt, even at a time when on the face of it, both the policy and the political environment are speaking to the inclusive agenda.

Empirical evidence from the authors' research has established that, whilst the MoPSE and the political leadership in the country seem to be worried that some secondary schools are excluding some prospective learners by using school-based tests and assessments (Zimbabwe. MoPSE, 2015), other schools, especially those run by church-related responsible authorities, have gone on to embrace the inclusive framework (Muresherwa & Jita, 2021). In fact, some school heads in the secondary schools of Zimbabwe believe that the MoPSE does not fully support inclusive education, especially involving learners with disabilities and those with low ability to learn. They prefer, then, to adopt a lip-service approach to these types of inclusive education. Without any coercion from the MoPSE, some of these school heads embraced the inclusive framework in their schools as a result of motivation from the responsible authorities and through motivation from within. For example, one school head, Mr Sithole (pseudonym), who participated in the study; *Challenges and opportunities to instructional leadership in inclusive secondary schools of Zimbabwe* articulated that:

Truly speaking, inclusive education in this school is a project of the church. Children with physical disabilities and OVC [orphans and vulnerable children] are at the heart of the RA [responsible authority]. Izvi hamutombodi kuudzwa (This, you don't need to be told. You can just see). The support being given to the school, teachers and even to children with special needs is a textbook example of the fact that inclusive education is at the heart of the church. However, I don't see the MoPSE doing the same by way of rewarding and recognising schools that have embraced the inclusive education full time. (Muresherwa, 2020, p. 166)

In a similar vein, Mr Simango (pseudonym), another school head, had this to say concerning the inclusive framework as embraced in his school:

... From its very beginning, this school was built with the disadvantaged in mind. As I indicated before, this school was built at the end of the war of liberation in order to accommodate children who had been disadvantaged by the war, including returning refugees and children who were injured during the war and were returning home following the end of the war in 1980. Open Gate School (not its real name) has been non-selective from the word go. As we define our purpose as a church school, we therefore stand guided by this original vision and purpose for the church to build this community-based school ... The church does not expect us to select out learners we admit in this school, for whatever reason ... We just serve children as they come. (Muresherwa, 2020, p. 142)

The excerpts above shows that some responsible authorities of church-run schools motivate their school heads to embrace the inclusive framework and thus realise the objectives for which their respective schools were built. At an individual level, Mr Moyo (pseudonym) had this to say about inclusive education at his school:

As a person living with a disability myself, I feel I am what I am because of the people who accepted me as I am. As much as possible, I should help people in similar circumstance to develop and live their own independent life as healthy, responsible and productive citizens who own and control their destiny. You know what? Even as a parent, when you have a child with a disability, and you find people who stand with you, you will feel very light in your heart. I remember my own parents felt relieved when, as a child with a disability, I was accepted as a person worth school authorities' attention. I therefore am convinced beyond any doubt that the purpose of my life is to bring hope to the life of people in similar circumstances as mine. ... Through embracing a non-selective approach, I feel I am responding to the needs of the community that I serve. (Muresherwa, 2020, p. 188)

The verbatim excerpt above shows that although Zimbabwe has not fully embraced inclusive education in secondary schools, there are several schools that have adopted different versions and mixes of the inclusive framework, and for various reasons. The excerpts above, for example, also show that some of these secondary schools have embraced the inclusive framework for reasons other than motivation by the MoPSE. For example, the responsible authorities of some of these schools are at the core of promoting an inclusive approach to instruction. In addition, resources of biography (Jita, 2010) and early socialisation for the respective school heads also played a part in the schools' adoption of the inclusive framework (Muresherwa & Jita, 2021). Mr Moyo, for example, is a person living with a disability. On the other hand, Mr Simango grew up with a brother who had a physical disability (Muresherwa & Jita, 2021). These circumstances socialised the two school heads to readily embrace the inclusive framework. This is despite the fact that, in practice, the MoPSE, the official representative of the state and custodian of education in the country, did not seem to support full inclusion. The MoPSE seems to prefer politically driven physical inclusion of learners who risk exclusion on the grounds of race, tribe, place of origin, national origin, political opinion, colour, creed or gender. Mr Moyo expressed the view that the MoPSE does not actively support full inclusion as embraced in his school. He expressed his views thus:

Whilst this is the key ministry in terms of education in this country, the MoPSE seems not to have a genuine interest in full inclusion beyond the regulation it has put in place ... Surely, there is nothing on the ground by way of practice to show its interest. The Ministry appears to be interested in examination results and inclusion of Black children in former Whites only schools; something like what happened at X High School (a secondary school formerly reserved for white learners, prior independence). For the Ministry, inclusion as we practise it here is only a paper thing. There is nothing meaningful to show on the ground. (Muresherwa, 2020, p. 188)

The quotation above shows that, according to Mr Moyo, the MoPSE favours physical inclusion of African children in former group 'A' schools as opposed to epistemic inclusion of all learners with exceptionalities, including children with disabilities and those with low ability to learn. In further clarifying his position, Mr Moyo explained that:

I think, as a nation, we got it wrong where we confused work with employment and took education as the route to employment only. The reality is that if your school does not guarantee that every learner or at least most of them get full 'O' level certificates, forget it. You will never be taken seriously, even by the MoPSE. In addition, your school will never be taken as first choice by parents seeking to place their children, unless if such parents feel their particular child is not good enough or when they are unable to pay fees asked for in what they may be seeing as better schools ... People feel that sending their children to a poorly performing school (academically) is to risk their future employment prospects. (Muresherwa, 2020, p. 202)

Clearly, school heads in inclusive secondary schools in Zimbabwe believe that they are practising their brand of inclusive education in a non-supportive environment. The thinking amongst these school heads that participated in the above study on the challenges to and opportunities for instructional leadership in inclusive secondary schools in Zimbabwe is that key stakeholders in education focused on entrepreneurial objectives, as opposed to social justice logics of education (Muresherwa, 2020). In an apparent agreement with Mr Moyo's views as cited above, Mr Sithole expressed:

You may have noticed that even the best school head in the district was determined, basing on the performance of her school in examinations, not to provide access to education to children who are often excluded from other schools. Not even in terms of the quality of education offered. I see the criteria of selecting and rewarding schools basing on examination results only as reinforcing exclusion of children with exceptionalities from some schools. ... In fact, I don't see the MoPSE genuine in its drive for full inclusion. This explains why I say inclusion in this school is a project of the responsible authority and not the MoPSE. (Muresherwa, 2020, p. 164)

It is evident from the above discussion that, decades after the attainment of independence in 1980 and the enactment of the Salamanca Declaration in 1994, full inclusion in the secondary schools of Zimbabwe is still a wishful goal. The situation on the ground is that, like any other progressive country, Zimbabwe has embraced the inclusive framework, at least on paper. For example, the country is a signatory to international conventions and regulations on inclusive education. These regulations and conventions include the Jomtien Declaration (1990), the Salamanca (1994) and the CRPD (2006). In addition, the country has also enacted its own home-grown inclusive-related social policies. These include the Education Act of 1987 (as amended), the Disabled Persons Act of 1992, and more recently, the New Constitution of 2013 as well as the ZNCF 2015–2022. The MoPSE has also produced ministry-level circulars that speak to the inclusive framework. Key amongst these circulars is the Education Secretary's Policy Circular No. P36 of 1990. Clearly, Zimbabwe has created a policy environment that supports the inclusive framework. In addition to creating this favourable policy environment, the country also has a political environment that supports an inclusive approach to education. For example, former President Mugabe and current President Emerson Mnangagwa have been supportive of the inclusive framework. During his 36-year reign, President Mugabe presided over the enactment of a number of laws that favour an inclusive approach to education, for example the Education Act of 1987 as amended, the New Constitution of 2013 and the ZNCF 2015–2022. The new economic blueprint, the NDS 1, which was put in place by the new president, Emerson Mnangagwa, to steer the country into the future, also speaks to the inclusive education framework. Paradoxically, in the backdrop of this policy and the political environment that, on the face of it, seem to support the inclusive framework, inclusive education in Zimbabwe is still a fantasy decades after independence and the Salamanca Declaration. Clearly, it is evident from the discussion in this chapter that there is misalignment between formulation and realisation of inclusive education in Zimbabwe. This discrepancy still exists more than 42 years after independence in 1980 and the Salamanca Declaration in 1994. On the face it, is not immediately clear why full inclusion has remained elusive in the country at a time when the inclusive framework is expected to have developed, blossomed and born fruits for all to see. However, the discussion above points to the "keys" that may be used to unlock, unpack and therefore understand this conundrum of the policy–practice gap in inclusive education thought and practice in secondary schools in Zimbabwe. The issues relating to this closed book are further discussed below.

Deconstructing the Policy–Practice Gap in Inclusive Education in Zimbabwe

The central argument in this chapter is that regardless of policy and a political environment that seem to favour the inclusive framework, this goal is still a fantasy in the secondary schools of Zimbabwe decades after independence and the Salamanca. The existing literature and the recent study by (Muresherwa 2020) used to inform this chapter concur on the existence of this discrepancy between formulations and realisations of inclusive education in this country. This gap between formulations and realisations of inclusive education has also been observed in earlier literature (Mafa, 2012; Musengi & Chireshe, 2013). At an international level, Forlin (2013) and Haug (2017) also observed similar gaps in other countries, including those in the Global North. Writing specifically about the state of inclusive education in Zimbabwe, Musengi and Chireshe (2013), for example, maintained that inclusive education has remained just an aspiration in the backdrop of policy and a political environment that on the face of it seem to support an inclusive education agenda. This type of thinking has prompted some critics of the inclusive framework to advance the view that inclusive education is a dead concept that is suitable only for the academic dustbin (Muresherwa & Jita, 2021).

Although they are also disillusioned by this policy–practice gap, the more moderate writers still have faith in inclusive education as the only democratic and socially just approach to grouping learners for instruction (Mafa, 2012; Musengi & Chireshe, 2013) and therefore to humanise the classroom (Suyatno & Wantini, 2018). Others have also believed that inclusive education is not dead and that, if anything, it only smells funny (Slee, 2018). Meltz et al. (2014) viewed the inclusive education framework as a case of beliefs that are competing for implementation. This view, which is also shared by this chapter, seems to dispute the one-size-fits-all perspective of the inclusive agenda. It is true that the state of inclusive education in Zimbabwe is characterised by a mismatch between policy and practice (Muresherwa & Jita, 2021), which makes the inclusive policy to appear like political symbolism (Donohue, & Bornman, 2014; Jansen, 2002). However, in the Zimbabwean context, this policy-practice gap may be explained in terms of the socio-political, socio-cultural and socio-economic context in which the country's education system found itself throughout the history of formal education in the country. This context of the educational environment in the country shapes the political, cultural, psychological and institutional perspectives through which policy-makers construct and understand what inclusive education in that particular environment ought to be. These stakeholders therefore act upon this understanding to make policies and influence policy implementation in a particular direction.

The colonial history of Zimbabwe and the growth of the nationalist movements that culminated in the attainment of political independence in 1980, for example, have created an enduring political perspective that has serious ramifications on the state of inclusive education in the country up to this day. This political perspective, in turn, exerted pressure over the minds of the founding fathers of independent Zimbabwe to redress colonial imbalances regarding access to education for the erstwhile segregated African children. These are learners who were denied access to schools and a curriculum considered to be the private preserve of the children of the white community. As a result of this pressure to redress colonial imbalances, inclusive education in the formative years of independence focused on affording African children physical access to the former exclusive schools and curriculum. It can thus be said that the inclusive education framework that emerged was a vestige of colonialism and aimed at affording African children physical access to schools and the curriculum that previously were reserved mainly for the children from the white Zimbabweans. Issues of epistemic inclusion were not a priority as the new government was absorbed in trying to address the emotive and politically sensitive issues of providing all learners physical access to educational institutions. This type of inclusive education which is shaped by cultural memories (Erll, 2012) grounded on the colonial past is defined by Shizha (2007) as political inclusion and has persisted up to this day.

Closely related to the issues of socio-political context as a factor for shaping inclusive education practices are the issues relating to the socio-economic and cultural contexts. These contexts have helped to define the purpose of public education in the community and are therefore key drivers of inclusive education, or lack of it, in the Zimbabwean context. Instead of being taken as a social artefact used for socialising the young and developing them into mature adults that are capable of living their own independent lives as healthy, responsible and productive citizens who control their own destiny (Muresherwa & Jita, 2021), education in Zimbabwe has been commodified and marketised (Florian, 2014). Education has thus come to be viewed as an instrument for sorting, sifting and selecting students for employment, which is sometimes confused with work. This association between education and employment has resulted in schools focusing on preparing learners to pass theory-based public examinations and not on any other learning outcomes that may be relevant for their future life. This practice seems to be based on the assumption that children are the same in every respect and are capable of learning and passing exactly the same subjects. This assumption is oblivious of the differential- and multiple-intelligence hypotheses (Chen & Gardner, 2018), upon which the concept of individual and special needs of learners should be grounded. However, an understanding of the operation of the differential- and multiple-intelligence hypotheses seems to pressure some school heads to ensure high pass rates for their schools. They are therefore pressed to avoid admitting prospective learners whose performance in public examinations is not guaranteed (Muresherwa & Jita, 2021). This view is in agreement with Forlin's (2013) proposition that commitment to inclusive education in some schools is being undermined by the focus of education systems on the economic goals of education only. It is for this reason that the Zimbabwean Secretary for Education was against "... some schools ... enrolling learners into Form 1 through an application of their own entrance tests and assessments ..." (Zimbabwe. MoPSE, 2015, p. 1).

Clearly, policy-makers saw the practice by some school heads to de-select learners by use of own tests and assessments to be discriminatory and a violation of the provisions of the Constitution of Zimbabwe and the Education Act. The Cabinet therefore tasked the Secretary for Education to intervene and ban this practice in the spirit of affording every learner access to any school of their choice in the community (Zimbabwe. MoPSE, 2015). However, the MoPSE seems to be failing to enforce the policy on inclusive education for learners with low ability to learn and for children with disabilities, and therefore the inclusive education policy for these learners appears to be political symbolism (Donohue & Bornman, 2014; Jansen, 2002). Where such learners are afforded physical inclusion in some schools, for example, issues of epistemic access to quality and relevant education are not addressed, in an environment where some educational stakeholders, unlike school heads, seem to be oblivious of the differential- and multiple-intelligence hypotheses and therefore the different needs of learners. This implies that the state of inclusive education in Zimbabwe is characterised by pressure on some school heads to de-select learners with low ability to learn, in the backdrop of a political environment that on the face of it seems to support the inclusive framework. This pressure can be explained by the schools' focus on the economic goals of education, in the backdrop of high unemployment rates in the country.

As a result of focusing on the economic goals of education only, the performance of schools in Zimbabwe is measured in terms of the pass rate of learners in public examinations only. Given this background, school heads are tempted to avoid admitting learners that they feel are not capable of passing public examinations. This exclusion helps to protect the school heads' personal images and that of their schools, which may be damaged when learners perform poorly in public examinations. This practice of de-selecting learners whose performance in public examinations is not guaranteed has resulted in exclusion of some learners from certain schools. School authorities fear that the pass rate for their schools would be negatively affected by a non-selective learner admissions policy. This view is in line with Muresherwa and Jita's (2021) conclusion that "[i]nclusive education may itself be a 'marginalising' social activity within the education system" (p. 1753) and may best be avoided by school authorities who are risk-averse. This conclusion is also supported by Howley et al. (2019), who observed that "[p]rincipals who take an interest in marginalised students confront power arrangements that structure inequity throughout society as a whole and schooling in particular, where they may also risk marginalisation" (p. 6). Overemphasis on the economic goals of education to the detriment of other goals, such as socialisation goals, has therefore resulted in some schools de-selecting learners whose performance in public examinations is not guaranteed. In the Zimbabwean context, this challenge is exacerbated by the fact that inclusive-related policies are only loosely framed and do not specifically compel any entity to embrace all learners, especially those with disabilities and low intellectual ability, unless the inclusive framework is supported by church organisations (Muresherwa & Jita, 2021). On the part of the MoPSE and the Government of Zimbabwe in general, inclusive education seems to focus more on political perspectives than anything else, although public policy speaks to issues of full inclusion. This situation makes it appear that the inclusive education policy for children with disabilities and those with low ability to learn (Slee, 2018) is mere political symbolism without any mechanism for enforcement.

Specific factors have made social policies to focus rather loosely on inclusive education of learners with disabilities and with low ability to learn. This includes the desire by political leadership in Zimbabwe to redress colonial imbalances by affording African children access to former group 'A' schools. It also includes the pressure to commercialise and marketise education (Rigby, 2014) in an environment where education is viewed as an instrument for sifting, sorting and selecting learners for employment (Muresherwa & Jita, 2021). This fact that inclusive policies in Zimbabwe speak rather loosely to inclusive education of learners with disabilities (Musengi & Chireshe, 2013) and those with low ability to learn (Muresherwa & Jita, 2021) is therefore key to explaining the state of inclusive education in Zimbabwe, in which there appears to be misalignment between policy and practice. As a result of this laxity, for example, the concept of inclusive education has not been fully operationalised beyond the loosely defined EFA perspective as well as the disability and/or special needs education perspective. The country has thus failed to come up with a comprehensive theory concerning what inclusive education ought to be and what it is not, in order to inform practice in a Zimbabwean context. This situation has caused the state to focus mainly on affording African children access to former group 'A' schools, leaving inclusive education of learners with disabilities and with low ability to learn to be the responsibility of church-related schools and their responsible authorities. These church-related responsible authorities have been at the driving seat for special needs education for many years, as part of their missionary work, which focuses on evangelism and social concerns (Ireland, 2022). The Reformed Church in Zimbabwe, for example, established special schools for learners with exceptionalities, and the Mashoko Christian Mission has established inclusive schools in the mould of Masvingo Christian College, in the city of Masvingo, Zimbabwe.

An analysis of the founding documents of the inclusive framework in Zimbabwe has suggested that the discrepancy between what inclusive education ought to be and what it is not can be traced back to the Salamanca Declaration that that, on the one hand, talks to inclusive education as involving all groups that are vulnerable and therefore risk exclusion (Ainscow & César, 2006), whilst on the other hand, the same document also talks about inclusive education as being concerned with disability and special educational needs (Magnússon, 2019). This observation seems to point to the weaknesses of the Salamanca Declaration. However, a further analysis of this seminal document and the international reality on the ground suggests that the apparent tension is actually the strength of this seminal document for inclusive education. Whilst the political project of the Salamanca has its roots firmly in special education (Magnússon, 2019), as is reflected in its title, the declaration is structured in such a way that countries should be able to define and/or redefine their own version of the inclusive framework, depending on the context of the local situation. Since each country or region is composed of unique people with a unique history and therefore unique needs, it makes sense for inclusive education policies and definitions of special needs, disabilities and exceptionalities to differ (Towle, 2015). The loosely defined concept of the inclusive framework in the Salamanca Declaration therefore seems to be a conscious effort by the parties involved to enable individual countries to come up with context-based definitions and theories of inclusive education that speak to the local conditions. Like any other country, Zimbabwe may also redefine and refine the concept of inclusive education, bearing in mind the various characteristics of the local context and keeping in line with the key principles of equity, equality, social justice and 'all'. The final definitions of inclusive education in this Zimbabwean context should also recognise the historical context in which the country is grounded and the purpose of education in society.

CONCLUSION

This chapter has shown that Zimbabwe, like many other progressive countries globally, has made inroads to embrace the inclusive education framework as an instrument for promoting social justice and, hence, giving shape and meaning to learners' lives (Ward & Stewart, 2008). After attaining independence in 1980, Zimbabwe became party to international conventions and declarations on inclusive education (Musengi & Chireshe, 2013) and has remained so up to this day. In addition, the country also promulgated its own home-grown social policies that speak to inclusive education and has a political leadership that, on the face of it, supports the inclusive framework. However, regardless of policy and a political environment that seem to favour an inclusive approach to education, inclusive education in secondary schools in the country is still unfinished business. This situation exists decades after the country gained independence in 1980 and ratification of the Salamanca Declaration in 1994. What this means is that there is misalignment between policy and practice of inclusive education. This misalignment between policy and practice of inclusive education is explained in terms of a number of factors. These factors stem from the socio-historical, socio-cultural and socio-economic environment informing the formal education system throughout the history of the country. This discrepancy may also be explained in terms of the complexity theory (Schuelka & Engsig, 2020; Walton & Engelbrecht, 2022). This theory is, in part, manifested by the unending debate on the disability and/or special educational needs perspective of inclusive education vis-à-vis the EFA concerns of inclusive education thought and practice which have virtually refused to die (Miles & Singhal, 2010).

This chapter has shown, for example, that the need to redress colonial imbalances in education has made the nationalist leaders to focus on inclusive education that afforded African children physical access to schools that previously accommodated learners from the white community only. This desire by the founding fathers of independent Zimbabwe to redress colonial imbalances therefore made inclusive education in the country to focus on issues to do with political inclusion only, within a narrow sense of 'all'. The situation has continued to this day whereby the state remains focused on affording physical access to schools by 'all' groups that risk to be excluded from some schools on the grounds of race, tribe, place of origin, national origin, political opinion, colour, creed or gender (Government of Zimbabwe, 1987). Issues of disability and "special educational needs" (Ainscow & César, 2006) are conspicuously absent from this list of onerous factors and therefore in the adopted definition of 'all'. However, the Education Act, the founding document for inclusive education, defines these factors in a way that suggest that they are the only grounds that should not be used for excluding learners from any school in the country. This reality seems to have made full inclusion to be elusive.

In line with the complexity theory (Schuelka & Engsig, 2020; Walton & Engelbrecht, 2022), which informs this chapter, it can be said that a complex mix of factors has shaped societal perspectives on the purpose of education in society and inclusive education thought and practice in Zimbabwe. These factors include the socio-economic, socio-cultural and socio-political contexts which emerged at the advent of independence in 1980 and have persisted up to this day. This educational context in independent Zimbabwe is characterised by high unemployment rates and capitalist competition for resources. For example, societal perspectives on the purpose of education in the country regard it mainly as an instrument for preparing the young for formal employment in a country faced with a high unemployment rate and thus created a social culture that emphasises only the economic goals of education (Reid, 2011). Employment in Zimbabwe seems to be confused with work. This association between education and employment which is confused with work seems to have made schools in Zimbabwe to de-select learners whose performance in public examinations is not guaranteed. The de-selection is caused by the fact that school performance and the performance of teachers, including school heads, is now measured in terms of the extent to which they prepare learners for examinations, and therefore employment only. Clearly, this practice of de-selecting learners with low ability to learn has created a form of exclusion in Zimbabwe that affects these learners. This is a form of exclusion that may not be common in some countries with different historical and economic contexts to that of Zimbabwe and may not have been perceived when the Salamanca Declaration was enacted. However, writing in Australia, Singhal (2018) submitted that this type of exclusion is one of the most subtle forms of educational exclusion which, if left unabated, may have serious ramifications on the life of the learners affected. This view is also echoed by Muresherwa and Jita (2021), who added that where learners with low intellectual ability are allowed physical access to schools, they are often denied epistemic access to the curriculum that focuses on examination pass rate only. Apparently, the assumption in this practice is that all children are capable of learning and passing the same subjects. The prevailing situation in the country confirms that, as is the case with many other countries internationally, inclusive education in Zimbabwe is still unfinished business (Musengi & Chireshe, 2013; Phasha et al., 2017). Paradoxically, this situation exists decades after independence and the Salamanca Declaration, in the backdrop of policy and a political environment that on the face of it seem to support the inclusive framework.

In light of this conclusion, it is recommended that in order to make inclusive education more effective and responsive to the needs of the local people, that is, more culturally affirming, the purpose of education and therefore that of inclusive education in society should be reconstructed and redefined in the perspective of the African context in general and the Zimbabwean context in particular. In this context, inclusive education should not be compartmentalised in the perspective of political inclusion, disability education or "special educational needs" only. Instead, inclusive education should be defined to embrace all learners that risk exclusion for one reason or the other. This also means that education should not focus on economic goals or the entrepreneurial logics only (Rigby, 2014). Instead, education should be reconceptualised to embrace the social justice logic, as an agent for socialising the young and developing them to become mature adults who are capable of living their own independent and fuller lives as healthy, responsible and productive citizens who control their own destiny (Muresherwa 2020). This view should recognise that each learner, regardless of the circumstances surrounding their life, should be allowed to access quality education which enables them to grow and become an adult capable of living a meaningful life or as a parent whose own children look up to them for livelihood. This means that inclusive education should be redefined to embrace both the concept of 'all' and that of special needs, or exceptionalities, bearing in mind the operations of both the differential and the multiple-intelligence hypotheses. This perspective of inclusive education should afford learners both physical access to schools and epistemic access to the curriculum. As such, all learners should benefit from their learning experiences, each according to their needs, as they also prepare for adult life, independent of their own parents. Undoubtedly, this approach would ensure realisation of equity and social justice goals of education in the country.

The current practice in Zimbabwe focuses inclusive education on physical access only, whilst disregarding the issues of epistemic access. This approach to inclusive education places schools at the risk of practising what Slee (2018) defines as exclusion within inclusion. This phenomenon is characterised by a lack of epistemic access to the curriculum, coupled with a high failure rate in public examinations. Since independence in 1980, for example, the national pass rate for ordinary level examinations in Zimbabwe has averaged around 20%. This high failure rate relegates more than 80% of the candidates who sit for examinations each year into the academic dustbin (Muresherwa & Jita, 2021). Undoubtedly, allowing learners to leave school without any useful skills in life is an indicator of lack of epistemic access to the curriculum by the learners in the Zimbabwean school system and an antithesis of social justice. The Student Christian Movement of Zimbabwe (2013) described this high failure rate as the manifestation of a neglected generation. In agreement with this view, Muresherwa (2020) asked the question: "When will we learn?" (p. 255). It is felt that this question should continue to call for answers if public education in general and/or inclusive education in particular should effectively realise its purpose as an instrument for social justice that also gives shape and meaning to learners' lives (Ward & Stewart, 2008). In this endeavour, researchers may also focus their attention on the extent to which Christian churches are supported by the MoPSE in their quest to realise their missionary objectives of evangelism and asocial concern (Ireland, 2022) through participation in inclusive education interventions as a step towards social justice (Polat, 2011).

REFERENCES

Abdi, A. A. (2007). Oral societies and colonial experiences: Sub-Saharan Africa and the de facto power of the written word, education, decolonisation, development and perspectives from Asia, Africa and the Americas. *International Journal of Education*, *37*(1), 39–56.

Abraham, G. Y. (2020). A post-colonial perspective on African education systems. *African Journal of Education and Practice*, *6*(5), 40–54.

Abraham, R. (2003). The localization of 'O' level art examinations in Zimbabwe. *Studies in Art Education*, *45*(1), 73–87. doi:10.1080/00393541.2003.11651757

Ainscow, M., & César, M. (2006). Inclusive education ten years after Salamanca: Setting the agenda. *European Journal of Psychology of Education*, *21*(3), 231–238. doi:10.1007/BF03173412

Allen, A., Scott, L. M., & Lewis, C. W. (2013). Racial micro-aggressions and African American and Hispanic students in urban schools: A call for culturally affirming education. *Interdisciplinary Journal of Teaching and Learning*, *3*(2), 117–129.

Anastasiou, D., Kauffman, J. M. S., & di Nuovo, J. M. (2015). Inclusive education in Italy: Description and reflections on full inclusion. *European Journal of Special Needs Education*, *30*(4), 429–443. doi:10.1080/08856257.2015.1060075

Anlimachie, M. A. (2015). Towards equity in access and quality in basic education in Ghana: Comparative strategies for the rural and urban milieu. *American Journal of Social Issues and Humanities*, *5*(2), 400–426.

Astuti, D. S., & Sudrajat. (2020). Promoting inclusive education for social justice in Indonesia. In *2nd International Conference on Social Science and Character Educations (ICoSSCE 2019)* (pp. 178–183). Atlantis Press. https://www.researchgate.net/publication/339259762_Promoting _Inclusive_Education_for_Social_Justice_in_Indonesia

Ballard, K. (1999). *Inclusive education in an exclusive society: Some challenges to ideology and practice* [Inaugural lecture]. University of Otago.

Bassey, M. O. (1999). *Western education and political domination in Africa: A study in critical and dialogical pedagogy*. Greenwood Publishing Group.

Bhurekeni, J. (2020). Decolonial reflections on the Zimbabwean primary and secondary school curriculum reform journey. *Educational Research for Social Change*, *9*(2), 101–115. doi:10.17159/2221-4070/2020/v9i2a7

Boakari, F. M. (2010). Killing an inconvenient truth: Social justice and forms of oppression in modern society. *Verbum Incarnatum: An Academic Journal of Social Justice*, *4*(1), 1–32.

Chen, J. Q., & Gardner, H. (2018). Assessment from the perspective of multiple-intelligences theory: Principles, practices, and values. In D. P. Flanagan & E. M. McDonough (Eds.), *Contemporary intellectual assessment: Theories, tests, and issue* (4th ed., pp. 164–173). The Guilford Press.

Chimhenga, S. (2016). The implementation of inclusive education for children with disabilities in primary schools: A theoretical probability or practical possibility. *Asian Journal of Educational Research, 4*(4), 28–35.

Demillo, Q. (2021). School as a service enterprise in the Philippines. *Academia Letters. Article, 3535.* Advance online publication. doi:10.20935/AL3535

Donohue, D., & Bornman, J. (2014). The challenges of realising inclusive education in South Africa. *South African Journal of Education, 34*(2), 1–14. doi:10.15700/201412071114

Erll, A. (2012). Cultural memory. In M. Middeke, T. Müller, C. Wald, & H. Zapf (Eds.), *English and American Studies* (pp. 238–242). JB Metzler. doi:10.1007/978-3-476-00406-2_15

Farid, M. S. (2022). Social justice and inclusive education in Holy Cross education in Bangladesh: The case of Notre Dame College. *Religions, 13*(10), 980. doi:10.3390/rel13100980

Florian, L. (2014). What counts as evidence of inclusive education? *European Journal of Special Needs Education, 29*(3), 286–294. doi:10.1080/08856257.2014.933551

Forlin, C. (2013). Changing paradigms and future directions for implementing inclusive education in developing countries. *Asian Journal of Inclusive Education, 1*(2), 19–31.

Francisco, M. P. B., Hartman, M., & Wang, Y. (2020). Inclusion and special education. *Education Sciences, 10*(9), 1–17. doi:10.3390/educsci10090238

Gondo, R., Maturure, K. J., Mutopa, S., Tokwe, T., Chirefu, H., & Nyevedzanayi, M. (2019). Issues surrounding the updated secondary school curriculum in Zimbabwe. *European Journal of Social Sciences Studies, 4*(2), 59–76. doi:10.5281/zenodo.2605499

Government of Zimbabwe. (1987). *Education Act of 1987* [Chapter 25:04]. Government of Zimbabwe.

Government of Zimbabwe. (1992). *Disabled Persons Act* [Chapter 17:01]. Government of Zimbabwe.

Government of Zimbabwe. (2020). *National Development Strategy 1: Towards A Prosperous & Empowered Upper Middle Income Society by 2030.* Government of Zimbabwe.

Haralambos, M., & Holborn, M. (2013). *Sociology: Themes and perspectives* (8th ed.). Harper Collins.

Hashmi, S., Khan, I. K., & Khanum, N. (2017). Inclusive education in government primary schools: Teacher perceptions. *Journal of Education and Educational Development, 4*(1), 32–47. doi:10.22555/joeed.v4i1.1331

Haug, P. (2017). Understanding inclusive education: Ideals and reality. *Scandinavian Journal of Disability Research, 19*(3), 206–217. doi:10.1080/15017419.2016.1224778

Howley, C., Howley, A., Yahn, J., VanHorn, P., & Telfer, D. (2019). Inclusive instructional leadership: A quasi-experimental study of a professional development program for principals. *Mid-Western Educational Researcher, 31*(1), 3–23.

Hudson, B. (2019). Epistemic quality for equitable access to quality education in school mathematics. *Journal of Curriculum Studies, 51*(4), 437–456. doi:10.1080/00220272.2019.1618917

Hunter-Jones, P. (2014). Changing family structures and childhood socialisation: A study of leisure consumption. *Journal of Marketing Management, 30*(15–16), 1533–1553. doi:10.1080/0267257X.2014.930503

Inter-Agency Commission. (1990). *World conference on education for all: Meeting basic learning needs.* World Declaration on Education for All and Framework for Action to Meet Basic Learning Needs, Jomtien, Thailand. Inter-Agency Commission.

Ireland, J. (2022). Proclaiming mercy, practicing salvation: St. Basil's practical theology of evangelism and social action. *Journal of the Evangelical Missiological Society, 2*(1), 1–14. https://journal-ems.org/index.php/home/article/view/31

Jansen, J. D. (2002). Political symbolism as policy craft: Explaining non-reform in South African education after apartheid. *Journal of Education Policy, 17*(2), 199–215. doi:10.1080/02680930110116534

Jita, L. C. (2010). Instructional leadership for the improvement of science and mathematics in South Africa. *Procedia: Social and Behavioral Sciences, 9*, 851–854. doi:10.1016/j.sbspro.2010.12.247

Kee, T., & Lai, A. (2022). Learning motivation and psychological empowerment of Socio-economically disadvantaged learners–an empirical study on inclusive project-based learning during Covid-19. *International Journal of Inclusive Education*, 1–20. doi:10.1080/13603116.2022.2112771

Mafa, O. (2012). Challenges of implementing inclusion in Zimbabwe's education system. *Online Journal of Education Research, 1*(2), 14–22.

Magnússon, G. (2019). An amalgam of ideals: Images of inclusion in the Salamanca Statement. *International Journal of Inclusive Education, 23*(7–8), 677–690. doi:10.1080/13603116.2019.1622805

Mapako, F. P. & Mareva, F. (2013). The concept of free primary school education in Zimbabwe: Myth or reality. *Basic Education, 1*(1), 135 – 145.

Masaka, D. (2016). *The impact of Western colonial education in Zimbabwe's traditional and postcolonial educational system(s)* [Unpublished PhD dissertation]. University of South Africa.

Mathwasa, J., & Sibanda, L. (2021). Inclusion in early childhood development settings: A reality or an oasis. In O. A. de la Rosa, L. M. V. Angulo, & C. Giambrone (Eds.), *Education in childhood*. IntechOpen. doi:10.5772/intechopen.99105

Maurice, P. M. (2022). The impact of Christianity on the social-economic life of sub-Saharan Africa. *ShahidiHub International Journal of Theology & Religious Studies, 2*(1), 72–88.

Meltz, A., Herman, C., & Pillay, V. (2014). Inclusive education: A case of beliefs competing for implementation. *South African Journal of Education, 34*(3), 1–8. doi:10.15700/201409161049

Mhlolo, M. K. (2015). Examining covert impediments to inclusive education for the mathematically gifted learners in South Africa. In *9th Mathematical Creativity and Giftedness Conference*. Central University of Technology.

Miles, S., & Singhal, N. (2010). The education for all and inclusive education debate: Conflict, contradiction or opportunity? *International Journal of Inclusive Education, 14*(1), 115. doi:10.1080/13603110802265125

Muresherwa, E. (2020). *Challenges and opportunities to instructional leadership in inclusive secondary schools of Zimbabwe* [Doctoral dissertation]. University of the Free State.

Muresherwa, E., & Jita, L. C. (2021). Instructional leadership in inclusive secondary schools of Zimbabwe: Balancing multiple and competing expectations. *Universal Journal of Educational Research, 9*(10), 1742–1755. doi:10.13189/ujer.2021.091003

Musengi, M., & Chireshe, R. (2013). Inclusion of deaf students in mainstream rural primary schools in Zimbabwe: Challenges and opportunities. *Studies of Tribes and Tribals, 10*(2), 107–116. doi:10.1080/0972639X.2012.11886648

Muthukrishna, N., & Engelbrecht, P. (2018). Decolonising inclusive education in lower income, Southern African educational contexts. *South African Journal of Education, 38*(4), 1–11. doi:10.15700aje.v38n4a1701

Nevill, T., & Savage, G. (2022). The changing rationalities of Australian federal and national inclusive education policies. *Australian Educational Researcher*, 1–19. doi:10.100713384-022-00555-y

Opoku, M. P., Cuskelly, M., Pedersen, S. J., & Rayner, C. S. (2021). Attitudes and self-efficacy as significant predictors of intention of secondary school teachers towards the implementation of inclusive education in Ghana. *European Journal of Psychology of Education, 36*(3), 673–691. doi:10.100710212-020-00490-5

Peterson, B. (2000). *Monarchs, missionaries and African intellectuals: African theatre and the unmaking of colonial marginality*. NYU Press.

Phasha, N., Mahlo, D., & Dei, G. J. S. (Eds.). (2017). *Inclusive education in African contexts: A critical reader*. Springer. doi:10.1007/978-94-6300-803-7

Polat, F. (2011). Inclusion in education: A step towards social justice. *International Journal of Educational Development, 31*(1), 50–58. doi:10.1016/j.ijedudev.2010.06.009

Raftopoulos, B., & Mlambo, A. S. (2009). *The hard road to becoming national*. Department of History, University of the Western Cape.

Rigby, J. G. (2014). Three logics of instructional leadership. *Educational Administration Quarterly, 50*(4), 610–644. doi:10.1177/0013161X13509379

Samkange, W. (2013). Inclusive education at primary school: A case study of one primary school in Glen View/Mufakose education district in Harare, Zimbabwe. *International Journal of Social Sciences & Education, 3*(4), 953–963.

Schuelka, M. J., & Engsig, T. T. (2020). On the question of educational purpose: Complex educational systems analysis for inclusion. *International Journal of Inclusive Education,* 1–18. https://doi.o doi:rg/10.1080/13603116.2019.1698062

Shizha, E. (2007). Critical analysis of problems encountered in incorporating indigenous knowledge in science teaching by primary school teachers in Zimbabwe. *The Alberta Journal of Educational Research, 53*(3), 302–319.

Shizha, E., & Kariwo, M. T. (2012). *Education and development in Zimbabwe: A social, political and economic analysis*. Sense Publishers.

Singhal, P. (2018, January 9). Open up selective schools for more 'inclusive' education, says Rob Stokes. *The Sydney Morning Herald*. https://www.smh.com.au/education/open-up-selective-schools-f or-more-inclusive-education-says-rob-stokes-20180109-h0fk94. html#:~:text=Education%20Minister%20Rob%20Stokes%20says%20op ening%20up%20selective,not%20%22create%20a%20rigid%2C%20sepa rated%20public%20education%20system%22

Siziba, K., & Kaputa, T. M. (2022). Management of learners with conduct disorders in Nkayi rural district primary schools in Zimbabwe. *Journal of Research in Social Science and Humanities*, *3*(1), 19–24. doi:10.47679/jrssh.v3i1.38

Slee, R. (2001). Social justice and the changing directions in educational research: The case of inclusive education. *International Journal of Inclusive Education*, *5*(2–3), 167–177. doi:10.1080/13603110010035832

Slee, R. (2018). *Inclusive education isn't dead, it just smells funny*. Routledge. doi:10.4324/9780429486869

Suyatno, S., & Wantini, W. (2018). Humanizing the classroom: Praxis of full day school system in Indonesia. *International Education Studies*, *11*(4), 115–125. doi:10.5539/ies.v11n4p115

The Student Christian Movement of Zimbabwe. (2013). *Poor O-level results: A manifestation of a neglected generation*. http://kubatana.net

Tomasevski, K. (2004). *Manual on rights-based education: Global human rights requirements made simple*. UNESCO Bangkok. https://unesdoc.unesco.org/ark:/48223/pf0000135168

Towle, H. (2015). *Disability and inclusion in Canadian education*. desLibris.

UNESCO. (1994). *The Salamanca Statement and Framework for Action on Special Needs Education*. Adopted by the World Conference on Special Needs Education; Access and Quality, Salamanca, Spain, 7–10 June 1994. UNESCO.

Vanclay, F. (2020). Reflections on social impact assessment in the 21st century. *Impact Assessment and Project Appraisal*, *38*(2), 126–131. doi:10.1080/14615517.2019.1685807

Walton, E., & Engelbrecht, P. (2022). Inclusive education in South Africa: Path dependencies and emergences. *International Journal of Inclusive Education*, 1–19. doi:10.1080/13603116.2022.2061608

Ward, T., & Stewart, C. (2008). Putting human rights into practice with people with an intellectual disability. *Journal of Developmental and Physical Disabilities*, *20*(3), 297–311. doi:10.100710882-008-9098-4

Williams, K. L., Russell, A., & Summerville, K. (2021). Centering blackness: An examination of culturally-affirming pedagogy and practices enacted by HBCU administrators and faculty members. *Innovative Higher Education*, *46*(6), 733–757. doi:10.100710755-021-09562-w

Zimbabwe Ministry of Primary and Secondary Education (MoPSE). (2015). *Secretary's Circular Minute No. 13 of 2015: Guidelines on enrolment of Form 1 students*. Government Printers.

KEY TERMS AND DEFINITIONS

Colonial Education System: A school system implemented in the country during the colonial era.

Epistemic Inclusion: Inclusive instructional practice in which learners benefit from the education experiences and the curriculum afforded them.

Formulations of Inclusive Education: Policies on inclusive education.

Inclusive Instructional Leadership: An approach to school leadership in which learners with special needs are made to learn side by side with their peers without special needs designations.

Instructional Leadership: An approach to school leadership which focuses on student learning.

Missionary Education: Education which is accessed by learners from schools that are run by churches.

Physical Inclusion: Inclusive instructional practices which focus on allowing learners physical access to schools even if they may not benefit from the learning experiences and/or the curriculum afforded them.

Social Concern: A missionary objective that focuses on ameliorating the social life of the people being preached to by missionaries.

Social Justice: Justice relating to distribution of opportunities, wealth, and privileges within a community. This type of justice is often contrasted with legal justice.

Section 3
Inclusive Education

Chapter 9
Inclusive Pedagogies and Social Justice for Transforming Teaching and Learning in South African Classrooms:
Inclusive Pedagogies in Education

Matshidiso Joyce Taole
University of South Africa, South Africa

ABSTRACT

This chapter looks at inclusive pedagogies and social justice for transforming teaching and learning in South African classrooms. Learners should not be marginalised or be made to feel that they do not belong. Therefore, teachers need to utilize inclusive pedagogies to ensure that learners' individual needs are met. The first section of this chapter defines the concepts of inclusive education and social justice, followed by the contextualisation of inclusive education in South Africa. The section that follows then engages the reader with issues of inclusive education globally. Finally, the chapter concludes with a discussion on instructional strategies that promote inclusive pedagogies and social justice.

INTRODUCTION

Education is key for the development of a country and the pursuit of social justice for its citizens. Education is regarded as a basic human right. The South African Constitution (RSA, 1996) protects children's right to education, and internationally, treaties such as the United Nations Convention on Children's Rights aim to address social justice, inequality, and human rights issues. However, the right to education is not practiced equitably among citizens owing to barriers to inclusivity (United Nations, 2016).

Inclusion and social justice play an important role in ensuring that quality education is accomplished and that learners are provided access to quality education (Polat, 2011; Hytten & Bettez, 2011). However, schools have not been seen to be acting in the best interest of the child and have systematically failed to

DOI: 10.4018/978-1-6684-6386-4.ch009

plan for and accommodate the varying learners' needs (Kelly, 2012). Schools are seen as perpetuating the inequalities that exist in societies and disadvantaged children continue to be short-changed. Therefore, new policies and practices must be introduced to ensure that the school is ready for the child (Shyman, 2012) and that every learner is given the necessary support to attain the learning outcomes.

Inclusivity and social justice have dominated the discourse on educational reforms to provide quality education and ensure access to education. The two concepts, inclusive education, and social justice are interlinked as they address issues of equity, quality, access, the participation of all stakeholders, and learners' achievement.

Murungi (2015) regards the discourse on inclusive education as the most celebrated, yet controversial, in the current educational reforms and in respect of the right to education. Inclusive education is also contained in the UN Sustainable Development Goals (SDGs), which were developed in 2012. SGD 4 focuses on education and its aim is to ensure inclusive and equitable quality education and promote lifelong learning opportunities for all (UNESCO, 2016). SDG 4 talks about the equitable, inclusive, and good quality education that is needed to fully realize children's right to education. Inclusion in education pertains directly to giving opportunities to all learners to learn, irrespective of their differences. Inclusion suggests that all learners should be accepted and valued, irrespective of their differences (Ainscow, 2013). Learners can contribute meaningfully to their learning experiences if they are provided with the opportunity to learn despite their diverse backgrounds.

This chapter looks at inclusive pedagogies and social justice for transforming teaching and learning in South African classrooms. Learners should not be marginalized or be made to feel that they do not belong. Therefore, teachers need to utilize inclusive pedagogies to ensure that learners' individual needs are met. The first section of this chapter defines the concepts of inclusive education and social justice, followed by the contextualization of inclusive education in South Africa. The section that follows then engages the reader with issues with inclusive education in the South African context. Finally, the chapter concludes with a discussion on instructional strategies that promote inclusive pedagogies and social justice.

CONCEPTUALIZING INCLUSIVE EDUCATION AND SOCIAL JUSTICE

The concept of "inclusive education" is not consistently or universally defined, as it means different things to different people, depending on the context (Booth et al., 2006; Murungi, 2015). Inclusive education generally refers to the type of education that does not discriminate against learners according to their race, gender, culture, or any other aspect (Makoelle & Malindi, 2014). Polat (2011, pp 50-51) maintains that inclusive education is about changing values, attitudes, policies, and practices within the school setting and beyond. Polat (2011) further contends that inclusive education deals with issues of social justice, inequality, and human rights. Inclusive education has the potential to enhance social skills among learners with and without disabilities and promote mutual understanding and acceptance among them (Shah, 2007). It aims at transforming the education space to rid it of practices that perpetuate inequalities and human injustices and to promote social justice. Research has shown that more needs to be done than merely placing learners in a particular classroom and assuming that they will learn, and more needs to be done than focusing solely on disabled learners (Celoria, 2016; Murungi, 2015; Polat, 2011). Celoria (2016) and Schugurensky (2010) argue that inclusion is about social justice, which places much emphasis on equity, solidarity, and human dignity. Inclusive education is not about access, but about the transformation of an education sector that discriminates against learners. It questions merit-based school cultures and promotes the equitable distribution of resources in a meaningful and nurturing environment (Meltz et al., 2014).

It should be pointed out that the concept of inclusive education has been used largely in the context of individuals with disabilities. According to Schugurensky (2010), labelling learners as disabled is not only discriminating against them but can also be perceived as a repressive social culture. Murungi (2015) argues that the conceptualization of the term as referring specifically to learners with disabilities is limiting to the overall goal of universal access to primary education, both under the South African Constitution and in terms of international declarations.

Polat (2011, pp 51) refers to inclusion as the

"inclusion of all regardless of race, ethnicity, disability, gender, sexual orientation, language, socio-economic status, and any other aspect of an individual's identity that might be perceived as different".

The definition above confirms that inclusion should go beyond disability and accommodate all diversity that exists in classrooms. Inclusivity, therefore, needs to incorporate issues of access, participation, achievement, and quality. Inclusion in the classrooms requires teachers' collaboration with different stakeholders such as parents and other professionals who deal with children (Pantić & Florian, 2015). Polat (2011) believes that more emphasis should be placed on quality in the attainment of inclusive education and argues that if the quality is neglected, the education system will be highly compromised, and this could jeopardize the attempts to meet the goals of equity and justice within the education system. Murungi (2015) argues that for education to be inclusive, it must meet the needs and circumstances of every learner in society.

SOCIAL JUSTICE

Social justice, just like inclusive education, is fluid, multidimensional, and conceptualized differently by different scholars (Sen, 2011; Hytten & Bettez, 2011). The social context will dictate the conceptualization of the concept (Rodgers & Knafl, 2000). For example, social justice will have different meanings in education, religion, and law. Individuals' different social contexts will dictate their conceptualization of social justice.

In an attempt to unpack this multi-layered concept, Samier (2020) conceptualized it as equitable education providing fair access. He further mentions that social justice in education can also involve the equitable and fair representation of knowledge and value traditions. Pearce and Cumming-Potvim (2017) aver that social justice as a process aims at ensuring that systems and structures are fair and free from challenges that could jeopardize the attainment of humans' basic rights. Buettner-Schmidt & Lobo (2012) understand social justice to involve the equitable sharing of burdens and benefits by citizens and participation in societal issues resulting in living in harmony with each other. Therefore, social justice is attained when individuals participate in issues that affect their well-being. As a result, issues of equity and equality should be considered within a social justice framework (Polat, 2011). Hytten and Bettez (2011:8-9) argue that social justice in education is associated with concepts such as democratic education, multiculturalism, poststructuralism, feminism, queer theory, anti-oppressive education, cultural studies, critical pedagogy, postcolonialism, globalization, and critical race theory. Social justice cannot be achieved in education if learners are still discriminated against based on their gender, background, and race (Ryan, 2006).

The Principles of Social Justice

Alfattal (2015) identified equality, a safe environment, equity, rights, and participation as principles of social justice:

Equality

Equality implies that all individuals have the right to resources and should benefit from public goods, irrespective of their differences. This extends to the political sphere and implies that every citizen should be afforded the opportunity to participate in decisions that affect them.

Safe Environment

Learners must feel accepted and accommodated in the school environment, irrespective of their backgrounds. Respect and tolerance go a long way in ensuring that every learner feels that he/she belongs to a particular organization and that his/her views are respected. When learners feel safe and accepted, their confidence and motivation to learn increase (Alfattal, 2015).

Equity

Equity means that learners are provided with equitable opportunities to learn. This implies that resources should be channelled to where they are needed most. For example, learners who are experiencing challenges should be provided with additional support such as remedial services and academic support where necessary.

Rights

Khechen (2013) maintains that rights are divided into two categories, namely moral rights, and legal rights. Moral rights mean that individuals are given the right to participate in decisions that affect them. Legal rights are rights that are protected by the law. This may be a binding contract between individuals or the laws that are passed by states or governments.

Participation

Participation in the context of social justice means that individuals are consulted, and their views are considered when decisions that affect them are taken (Khechen, 2013). When individuals are consulted, they feel included and own the process and will endeavour to see that it succeeds. Furthermore, participation is emancipation, as individuals will feel empowered and valued.

Teaching for Social Justice

Teaching for social justice is a multidimensional and ambiguous concept (Dover, 2009; Kelly, 2012). Dover (2009) maintained that there was a paucity of research that documented the idea of teaching for social justice, the definition, context, and assessment. Teachers have a moral duty to ensure that they provide learning activities that accommodate all learners, and they are obliged by their duty of care towards all learners that are in their classrooms. Teachers need to be concerned with diversity because it is a fact that learners are not the same, and that they differ in their learning styles, culture, language, gender, and/or intellectual capability. Yet, more often than not, learners are discriminated against based on their differences. It is therefore clear that education is not provided on an equitable basis, as learners are discriminated against based on their background. Zang et al. (2018) maintain that social justice cannot be isolated from teaching practices and theories and must be threaded throughout the educational enterprise. They further point out that the practice of social justice will lead to the transformation of educational systems. Dover (2013) acknowledges that teachers have the mammoth task of addressing inequity in the educational system, but they need to be supported to be able to execute that task. Dover (2013) argues that schools that are situated in affluent areas have more resources and qualified teachers than schools situated in disadvantaged communities. Schools, therefore, tend to reproduce the inequalities that exist in society.

Sleeter (2014) posits that teaching for social justice involves preparing learners to be critical thinkers and challenge the inequalities and inequity that exist in their environments. Dover (2013) identified six principles of teaching for social justice, namely culturally responsive education, multicultural education, critical pedagogy, social justice education, and democratic education.

Shyman (2012) contends that to ensure social justice for all citizens, inclusive pedagogies that protect learners from acts of curricular discrimination and subjugation should be introduced in schools. Following the line of reasoning put forward by Paul Freire (1970), Shyman (2012) asserts that when educational systems discourage critical inquiry among learners, that system is guilty of oppressive violence. To achieve critical consciousness among learners, the playfield should be levelled, which means that every learner must be allowed to perform maximally (Shyman, 2012).

THE CONTEXT OF INCLUSION IN SOUTH AFRICA

The current state of affairs in education, and poor implementation of inclusive education in particular in the South African context, can be blamed on the legacy of apartheid. During apartheid, White and Black learners were taught in separate schools. Although much has been achieved to reduce segregation in the schools, there are still pockets of segregation where the language of instruction is used as the deciding factor for enrolling Black learners in White-dominated schools. Learners with disabilities were taught in separate schools.

At the dawn of democracy in South Africa, that is, immediately after the democratic elections in 1994, many educational reforms took place, including the introduction of a policy on inclusive education. Inclusion in South Africa is foregrounded in the Constitution of the Republic of South Africa, Act No. 108 of 1996, under section 29 (the Bill of Rights), which grants everyone the right to "basic education" (RSA, 1996). Section 29 of the Constitution emphasized that no one should be discriminated against on any grounds, directly or indirectly. Inclusive education was documented at the policy level in 2001 in the *Education White Paper 6: Special Education: Building an inclusive education and training system* (Department of Education, 2001). White Paper 6 underscored that all learners have the potential to learn when given the support that they need. The white paper aimed at transforming the education system by strengthening support to teachers to cope with learners with barriers to learning and by developing district-based support for teachers and learners (DBE, 2014). The White Paper 6 policy focused on values such as social justice, human rights, respect for human rights, and equality (Ngcobo & Muthukrishna, 2011). Inclusive education was introduced in the South African education system in the Foundation Phase (Grades R-3); the Intermediate Phase (Grades 4-6), the Senior Phase (Grades 7-9), and the Further Education and Training (FET) Phase (Grades 10-12) in 2001in the quest to provide quality education and providing adequate learner support. The inclusive education policy not only focused on disability, but covered issues of context, such as the provisioning of resources, levels of poverty, inflexible curriculums, and inaccessible environments (Walton & Lloyd, 2011). The inclusion policy was aimed at addressing barriers to learning and further emphasized the diversity that exists among learners and the valuing of learners' needs (Dalton et al. 2012). Importantly, the policy recognized that, in addition to the formal structures such as the school, the home and community play important roles in the provisioning of inclusive education.

To achieve access, equity, and social justice in education, Full-Service schools were introduced. According to the inclusive education and special education progress report, there are 715 Full-Service schools in the country (DBE, 2017). Full-Service schools are defined as mainstream institutions that provide quality education to learners by supplying the full range of learning needs in an equitable manner (DBE 2010). According to the DBE (2010), Full-Service schools have the following key features:

- They are schools that ensure that learners have a sense of acceptance and inclusion in the classroom.
- They represent good practice in inclusive education.
- Ensure curriculum inclusion by using different teaching methods
- They provide different kinds of support without referring learners to outside professionals
- They promote collaboration among teachers and between teachers and parents

In addition, District-Based Support Teams (DBST) and School-Based Support Teams (SBST) were introduced to train and support teachers in the implementation of inclusive education. These teams assist teachers in developing inclusive learning programme and differentiating their teaching and assessment. However, the study by Nel et al (2016) found that few schools are benefitting from the services.

Furthermore, the Department of Education published two policy guidelines to aid in the implementation of inclusive education in schools. These guidelines were the National Strategy on Screening, Identification, Assessment, and Support (SIAS) (DBE, 2014) and Responding to Learner Diversity in the Classroom through Curriculum and Assessment Policy Statements (CAPS) (DBE, 2011).

The SIAS policy aims at ensuring that all learners of school-going age who experience barriers to learning, including those who are disabled, will be able to access inclusive, quality, free, primary and secondary education on an equal basis with other young people in the communities in which they live. In addition, the policy sets out clear guidelines on how learners with barriers to learning can be identified, assessed, and given appropriate support to enhance their participation and inclusion in school, making teachers and parents central to the support processes.

Responding to Learner Diversity in the Classroom through Curriculum and Assessment Policy Statements (CAPS) (DBE, 2011) ensures that learners can demonstrate their learning by writing, making, doing, and saying. Using these modalities will ensure that learners are provided with different possibilities for different kinds of expression and production. For example, when writing learners can tabulate their ideas, write full sentences, write a paragraph, or write a report. Making involves doing a sketch, a visual portrait, or a model. Doing encompasses performance, routine, demonstration of a skill problem solving, and saying includes discussions, debates, role-playing and conferencing.

These two guidelines encouraged the early detection of learning challenges, outlined measures to be taken to remedy the situation, and guided teachers and principals in planning learning experiences to meet the needs of the diverse learners in the classrooms. Despite all the policies and the establishment of support models such as DBS and SBS, implementation of inclusive education is still a challenge in South Africa as teachers still need continuous support for them to implement inclusive education successfully (Dreyer, 20wana & Dreyer, 2018). Dreyer (2017) argues that legislation alone cannot bring the desired changes in the education system, but policies and practices must be contextually responsive.

Issues With Inclusive Education in South Africa

Although inclusive education is widely advocated in educational spaces, its full implementation is yet to be realized in South Africa. Although education for social justice is discussed in various educational platforms in an attempt to transform the education system, it remains an elusive idea (Fiske & Ladd, 2004), thus prolonging the damages wrought by apartheid education prior to 1994.

Although the introduction of White Paper 6 on inclusive education in South Africa is laudable, its implementation is fraught with challenges (Donohue & Bornman, 2014; Makoelle & Malindi, 2014). The challenges include: the need to develop role players' capacity in dealing with inclusion issues and address issues that relate to teachers' morale (Engelbrecht & Green, 2007); teachers' attitude (Makoelle & Malindi, 2014; Mahlo 2017,); no implementation of the policy and, if implemented, this is done with some inconsistencies (Meltz et al., 2014); teachers not using inclusive teaching strategies, but relying on the old methods they have been taught (Basson, 2011); teachers not open to change (Meltz et al. 2014); lack of meaningful transformation in the education system (Dreyer, 2017); inadequate teacher training that will enable them to address learners barrier to learning (Dreyer, 2017; Mahlo, 2017) and teachers having inadequate knowledge of curriculum differentiation (Dalton et al. 2012).

According to Donohue and Bornman (2014), the context of the school influences how inclusive education is implemented. While children with disabilities are integrated into the mainstream, teachers' attitudes are seen as the main hindrance to how inclusive education is implemented in schools (Bornman & Rose, 2010). Although teachers believe that learners should be included in the classroom, they believe that disabled learners should be separated from learners in mainstream schools (Campbell, Gilmore & Cuskelly, 2003). However, Donohue and Bornman (2014) argue that teachers' attitudes could change if they were to receive appropriate service support and be given the necessary resources that they need. For example, a learner with a hearing impairment might need a hearing aid to be able to function at the level of his/her peers in the classroom. In some instances, the teacher-learner ratio is the barrier to inclusive education. Learners with disabilities might require individualized instruction and that cannot happen if classes are overcrowded.

Donohue and Bornman (2014) contend that the challenges of implementing inclusive education could be attributed to the apartheid legacy that resulted in the separation of different cultures, languages (there are currently 11 official languages), ethnic groups, and extreme poverty. Donohue and Bornman

(2014) further add that the policy is not clear on the goals of inclusion and the measures that should be taken to achieve the goals.

INSTRUCTIONAL STRATEGIES THAT PROMOTE INCLUSIVE PEDAGOGIES AND SOCIAL JUSTICE

Teachers are seen as agents of social justice and inclusion (Pantić & Florian, 2015). How they respond to learners' differences, how they interact with learners, their beliefs about learning and learners' learning, their attitude toward learners and learning, and how they respond to learners experiencing challenges in their learning will influence the outcome of the educational goals. Teachers have the responsibility to provide instruction that meets learners' needs, thus decreasing the learning challenges that learners might experience in the teaching and learning process (Dalton et al. 2012). Teachers are positioned to mitigate against elements that breed inequality within classrooms. However, they can only execute that duty if they are adequately prepared. Florian & Camedda (2020) argue that for teachers to be adequately prepared, inclusive education should be a core element in their training, rather than a specialist topic. This means that every teacher needs to be comfortable teaching in an inclusive classroom. Learners should not be taught as if their needs and expectations were the same. Unfortunately, teachers tend to treat learners as if they were the same, in an attempt to be fair to all learners. However, treating learners the same way could be disadvantaging some of the learners, as their expectations would not be met.

Teachers can use inclusive pedagogies to deal effectively with diverse learners in their classrooms. Tchatchoueng (2014) argues that teachers need to bear in mind two things when choosing an inclusive teaching strategy: they need to ensure that the learners' needs are met and that opportunities are created for all learners to perform at their maximum potential. This suggests that teachers need to design learning experiences that would respond to varying learners' needs. Tchatchoueng (2014) further points out that a teaching-learning strategy should consider learners' prior knowledge, interest, and abilities. As Dreyer (2017) argues, teachers' attitudes and their pedagogical knowledge have a direct influence on their practices.

Inclusive pedagogy is defined by Pantić and Florian (2015, pp 334) as "an approach that attends to individual differences between learners while actively avoiding the marginalization of some learners and/or the continued exclusion of particular groups". According to UNESCO (2020), learners can be excluded from different dimensions such as the physical, social, psychological, and systematic dimensions. The physical dimension involves access to facilities. The social dimension relates to the opportunities given to learners to participate in decisions that affect them. The psychological dimension involves learners perceiving themselves as disadvantaged or marginalized. The systematic dimension involves putting policies in place that discriminate against learners, for example, language policies, and policies against refugees or migrant children that prevent learners from exercising their right to education.

For Corbett (2001), inclusive pedagogy involves using different teaching approaches to ensure that learners are given the opportunity to learn. Nilholm and Alm (2010) in turn suggest that inclusive pedagogy allows learners to be engaged in the learning material, and to try to negotiate meaning. They further explain that the learning material needs to match learners' interests and relate to the learners' background knowledge for them to engage meaningfully with it. Florian (2015) posits that inclusive pedagogy aims at providing alternative teaching strategies, thus ensuring that discrimination and marginalization are greatly reduced in the classroom. Inclusive pedagogies include teachers' actions, their philosophy about what teaching is and how learners learn, and the social processes and influences (Moriña, 2020). Moriña argues that inclusive pedagogy may reduce dropout rates and improve the academic success of all students.

Teachers still lack the necessary skills to use inclusive pedagogies. Teaching them new approaches will enable them to utilize different teaching approaches that address learners' needs and improve the quality of schooling for all learners (Pantić & Florian, 2015). Training whether in-service or pre-service is a viable option to ensure that teachers stay abreast with the changes in the education system and ensuring that social justice is promoted in the classroom. Mahlo (2017) emphasized that teachers are faced with new demands every day, therefore, it is imperative to train them continuously especially when new policies are introduced as new policies increase the demands made on teachers. Teachers are sometimes ill-prepared to deal with the diversity in their classrooms and provide support for the unique learning needs in their classrooms. Because learning takes place in different contexts, for teachers to be adequately prepared to support learners in those contexts, teacher training should be diverse and multifaceted (Spear & Da costa 2018). Spear and Da costa (2018) further mention that training should be based on how to teach (methodology), and how to interact with learners (emotional and affective components) thus connecting with learners emotionally. Lawyer et al., (2020) argue that teacher training should train teachers to be able to recognize inequalities in its different forms. Additionally, they maintain that teachers should be prepared to be able to address inequality within the classrooms in order to promote social change among students.

While it is recognized that teaching occurs in complex and diverse circumstances, there are several instructional strategies that the teacher can use to apply inclusive pedagogies and practices in classrooms. These strategies are not conclusive but can serve as a starting point in ensuring that marginalization in the classroom is minimized and teaching promotes social justice.

Co-Teaching

Co-teaching is one of the inclusive pedagogies that can be used in the classroom to ensure that all learners are allowed to learn, irrespective of their academic and social background. Co-teaching is a collaboration between two or more teachers to ensure that the learning outcomes are met (Badiali & Titus, 2010). It aims at accommodating the variety of learners' needs that are found in the classroom. The collaboration happens in the classroom and teachers work together from the planning stage to the lesson presentation and assessment stages. The teachers share responsibility for a particular group of learners, ensuring that they learn and receive the necessary support. Co-teaching provides mediation and learning opportunities for learners (Neifeald & Nissim, 2019); it provides individualised support, and enhances student teachers' understanding of culturally responsive pedagogy (Cobb & Sharma, 2015). In research conducted by Graziano and Navarrete (2012), teachers have reported benefiting from co-teaching exercises and said that good practices are shared. The aim of co-teaching is to ensure that learners are supported. For co-teaching to succeed, the teachers need to work together when planning the learning activities and sharing responsibilities, and they should trust each other's decisions in the teaching and learning process (Friend & Cook, 2007).

Friend & Cook (2007) proposed different types of co-teaching, as discussed below:

1.   One teaches, one observes: In this method, the two teachers decide in advance that one of the teachers will be observed during the lesson. The observations will provide data that can be analysed to further improve instruction.

2. One teaches, one assist: The responsibility of teaching relies upon one individual and the other teacher provides unobstructed assistance to the learners. The other teacher could, for instance, assist by sharing resources in the classroom.

3. Parallel teaching: The two teachers share the learning content and teach simultaneously in the same classroom. They separate the class into two groups.

4. Station teaching: Two teachers share the learning content and divide the learners into groups. They then teach the groups of students separately and switch to delivering content to another group.

5. Alternative teaching: In this method, there are two groups of learners, a large group and a small group. The two teachers alternate between these groups and teach them separately.

6. Team teaching: The two teachers teach simultaneously, and they teach the same content. To avoid chaos, the two teachers can decide who will cover a particular area at what stage. For example, one teacher can teach and the other can do a demonstration for the learners. Role-playing can be used as a teaching approach in this method. Turn-taking plays an important role in this method, to make sure that effective learning is taking place.

These models have their own merits and demerits. Teachers need to decide on the model that will best suit their contexts. However, team teaching and alternative teaching have been found to increase learner involvement and enhance their social skills. Like any other teaching approach, co-teaching has its challenges and not all teachers are comfortable implementing it (Friend & Cook, 2007). This is because it is not easy for some teachers to work together, change their teaching styles and share teaching responsibilities. Most teachers have worked for a long time in their own space and the presence of another teacher can present a threat to the autonomy they used to have. Co-teaching requires intensive planning by both teachers, and this can be a time-consuming exercise. Furthermore, learners with disabilities feel overwhelmed by the expectation to perform at the level of mainstream learners (Gürgür & Uzuner, 2010). Friend and Cook (2007) maintain that for co-teaching to work, teachers should be thoroughly trained for the roles they are expected to play, and they should be given administrative support. Administrative support includes support with planning, the provision of resources, and assistance with time-management skills. As Cobb and Sharma (2015) mention, a collaboration between two teachers creates more possibilities for using different co-teaching approaches. When two teachers give each other feedback about their lessons, that creates opportunities for reflection that is rooted in social justice thinking.

Differentiated Teaching and Assessment

Meeting the varied needs of students is a challenge for teachers (Stanford et al., 2010). Differentiating teaching and assessment is a prevalent strategy that ensures inclusion and social justice. Shyman (2012) regards differentiated instruction as a pedagogy of social liberation, because learners are given instructional access and freedom to learn. Stanford et al. (2010) consider differentiated instruction as responsive teaching because all efforts are geared toward ensuring that the needs of the learners are accommodated. Traditionally, differentiated instruction was popular in classes with learners with disabilities. However, differentiation could be used for all learners to ensure that they are supported in their learning endeavors. Differentiation takes support to a different level, where the focus is not only on learners' learning styles but on how different individuals store, process and retrieve information in the learning process (Shyman, 2012). While differentiating their instruction, the teacher whose intention is to teach for social justice will pay attention to the needs of the learner holistically, try to meet the learners where they are, and try to understand the challenges that they might face.

Although learners are accommodated in one classroom, they have varying learning needs. Therefore, teachers must not use a "one-size-fits-all" technique in teaching and learning. Learners should be encouraged to make a meaningful contribution to the learning experience by taking into consideration what they already know about the subject and the different abilities that they have. This means that the learning activities should be aligned with the different needs of the learners. Differentiating learning activities involves giving learners different tasks according to their different skills. Shyman (2012, pp 65) defines differentiated instruction as follows:

Differentiated instruction is the process of varying and modifying the methods of instruction, curricular materials, and pedagogical methodology to meet the diverse learning needs of students without sacrificing the integrity of the curricular information itself.

This suggests that instruction can be differentiated by modifying what is to be learned (the content); the methods (how the learners will learn); the assessment (how the learners will demonstrate what they have learned); and the learning environment where learning should take place (Chandra-Handa, 2009). There are various reasons why instruction should be differentiated. Teachers get to know learners' strengths and needs; it improves the teacher-learner relationship; creates a good teaching environment; and it ensures that the learners are prepared for learning (Stanford et al., 2010). For example, learners who experience barriers to learning might have difficulty working independently and may require additional support. The teacher can convert independent activities to group activities so that learners can support each other and can also provide instructions to help learners achieve the learning outcomes. Furthermore, Stanford et al. (2010) argue that technology can be used for differentiating instruction. For example, the teacher can use PowerPoint, podcasts, and/or blogs. Stanford et al. add that the use of technology will motivate learners, improve their technological skills, and reduce the load on the part of the teacher. Furthermore, differentiation using technology promotes communication between the teacher and the learners, and the learners take responsibility and are engaged in their learning Learners should not all be expected to do the same assessment under the same conditions, as that does not take diversity into account. They should be given different opportunities to demonstrate their competence in a particular subject or concept. For example, in the composition writing task, learners can be asked to present a task using different formats such as using diagrams, illustrations, and/or cartoons instead of written descriptions so that learners can have a sense of inclusion in the classroom. In addition., the teacher can allow group, peer, or teacher assessment. differentiation can be done in the nature of questions asked in the assessment tasks. For example, the teacher can use multiple choice questions, problem -solving tasks and provide tasks that require short answers

It should be mentioned that this is a mammoth task on the part of the teacher, but it can be done when the resources are available, and teachers are supported. Moreover, although every attempt should be made to ensure that learners are engaged and challenged during the learning process, differentiation should not have to be done in every lesson (Bannister-Tyrrell & Pringle, 2021).

Collaborative Learning

Collaborative learning is a contested concept among researchers and is used interchangeably with the term "cooperative learning". It is likely that the lack of consensus among researchers is because collaborative learning serves different gains and purposes for different individuals. Despite the contested definition of the term, the researchers agree that in collaborative learning learners learn together in groups, the learning is learner-centered, learners take responsibility for their learning, and learning is a shared experience (Laal & Ghodsi, 2012; Resta & Laferrière, 2007). Collaborative learning is a teaching method that involves groups of learners working together to achieve a common goal (Laal & Ghodsi, 2012). It is a learner-centred method that provides learners with the opportunity to work together. Collaborative learning represents a shift from the traditional method where the teacher is in control, to a method where learners work together to achieve the learning outcomes. Teachers can also work together with the learners to ensure that learning is monitored and takes place systematically. Teachers who utilize this method of learning challenge the idea that teachers are the know-all figures in education and instead believe that learners have an important contribution to make towards teaching and learning. For example, the teacher can use flexible grouping to enable learners to work together and learn from each other. Flexible grouping is encouraged so that the learner is not labelled as belonging to a particular group as that can affect his/her performance. Instead, groupings should depend on the task at hand.

The Merits of Collaborative Learning

According to Laal & Ghodsi (2012), collaborative learning has social, psychological, academic, and assessment benefits for the learner.

- *Social Benefits*

The social benefit includes building a community of practice among learners in which they will be supporting each other. This could lead to improved relationships between teachers and learners and among learners themselves.

- *Psychological Benefits*

Laal & Ghodsi (2012) argue that collaborative learning provides psychological benefits to learners because it builds their self-esteem, and self-confidence fosters a good relationship between teachers and learners.

- *Academic Benefits*

Collaborative learning tends to foster creative thinking and problem-solving skills among learners. Learners take leadership in solving problems that they encounter.

- *Assessments Benefits*

Laal & Ghodsi (2012) assert that collaborative learning makes the use of different assessment techniques possible. Using a variety of assessment methods ensures that the teacher accommodates diversity in the classroom.

Peer Teaching

Peer tutoring is a learner-centred teaching approach which can be used with learners of varying ages or learners of the same age (Ali et al. 2015). In this approach, learners are involved in teaching each other and the teacher plays the role of the monitor. This does not mean that the learners are replacing the teacher. The method works well when the peer tutor has understood the concepts clearly before teaching his/her peers. Peer tutoring can be done in two ways – through spontaneous peer tutoring, where learners help one another unprompted, or through guided peer tutoring. Spontaneous peer tutoring is not planned or guided by the teacher. The learner initiates the tutoring process when he/she sees the need. Guided tutoring, on the other hand, happens under the guidance of the teacher, and the teacher plans the activities for the learner.

Ali et al. (2015) have identified three types of peer tutoring: reciprocal peer tutoring (RPT), class-wide peer tutoring (CWPT), and cross-age peer tutoring (CAPT). In reciprocal peer tutoring, the learners take turns in taking the role of the tutor and that of the learner. This type of peer tutoring boosts learners' confidence, as they get the opportunity to be a tutor.

In class-wide peer tutoring, the teacher divides the learners into small groups, and each learner gets the chance to share his/her ideas with the other learners. Every learner is given a task and is expected to take responsibility for the completion of the task and share it with the other learners.

Cross-age peer tutoring allows advanced learners or older learners to teach young learners. Advanced learners tend to have more experience and are knowledgeable. They get the opportunity to share their knowledge with young learners, which also solidifies their own knowledge.

The Value of Peer Tutoring

1. Peer tutoring allows learners to share their knowledge with other learners.
2. It allows direct communication between learners, which enhances the attainment of learning outcomes.
3. It provides learners with individualised instruction, which they may otherwise not get from their teacher.
4. The tutor gets the opportunity to reinforce what he/she has learned.
5. It provides a flexible learning environment where learners are free to interact with their peers, without the teacher's interference.
6. Tutors develop a sense of responsibility, as they have to assist fellow learners.
7. It develops the tutors' interpersonal and communication skills.
8. Learners learn from each other, which enhances their confidence and motivation, and it improves their cooperative learning skills (Ali et al., 2015).

For peer tutoring to be effective, the tutors should be thoroughly trained, and they should be rotated. Rotation will ensure that the tutor does not become overwhelmed, as he/she is also a learner and expects to be taught. For example, teachers can promote social justice using peer teaching through collaborative learning that uses small learners groups to accomplish a common goal. Learners will become active learners and be able to solve problems.

The inclusive pedagogies that have been discussed in this chapter are learner-centered and focus on learners' needs and enhance their development. The learner-centered methods promote social justice in the learners' everyday life by ensuring that learners feel included, and teachers hold high expectations for all learners. It should be mentioned that when using learner-centered approaches, teachers draw on learners' experiences and engage them thus enhancing their communication and collaboration skills. The methods discussed will ensure that learners feel that they belong and will break the common classroom systems of teacher autonomy, thus challenging the traditional method of teaching. Teachers design learning activities for all learners. In addition, the teaching materials used are varied and presented in different formats thus making learning accessible to all.

SUMMARY

In this chapter, inclusive education was discussed in relation to social justice in both global and local contexts. The discussion started with the conceptualization of inclusive education, social justice, and inclusive pedagogies. This was followed by a discussion of the context of inclusion in South Africa. Teaching for social justice and the challenges of inclusive education were described. Literature reviews on different inclusive pedagogies for teaching in contemporary classrooms were also provided. It became clear that educators need to classify learners in such a way that their unique abilities, talents, or limitations are adequately addressed in the learning environment. Therefore, it is imperative that teachers acknowledge that learners are different and have their own, diverse individual needs. Furthermore, learner differences may influence how they learn. It is important for teachers to make provision for the diverse learning needs of all learners by planning and implementing approaches and strategies which respond to these needs.

REFERENCES

Ainscow, M. (2013). From special education to effective schools for all: widening the agenda. In Handbook of Special Education (2nd ed.). Sage Publications.

Alfattal, D. (2015). *Principles for Social Justice in Education*. https://www.linkedin.com/pulse/principles-social-justice-education-eyad-alfattal

Ali, N., Answer, M., & Abbas, J. (2015). Impact of peer tutoring on learning of students. *Journal for Studies in Management and Planning, 1*(2), 61–66.

Badiali, B., & Titus, N. E. (2010). Co-Teaching: Enhancing Student Learning Through Mentor-Intern Partnerships. *School-University Partnerships, 4*(2), 74–80.

Bannister-Tyrrel, M., & Pringle, E. (2021). Differentiation in an Australian multigrade classroom. In L. Cornish & M. J. Taole (Eds.), *Perspectives on multigrade teaching: Research and practice in South Africa and Australia* (pp. 185–212). Springer. doi:10.1007/978-3-030-84803-3_10

Basson, R. (2011). Adaptation, evaluation and inclusion. *Africa Education Review, 8*(2), 193-208. doi :10.1080/18146627.2011.602822

Booth, T., Ainscow, M., & Dyson, A. (2006). *Improving schools, developing inclusion.* Routledge.

Bornman, J., & Rose, J. (2010). *Believe that all can achieve: Increasing classroom participation in learners with special support needs.* Van Schaik.

Buettner-Schmidt, K., & Lobo, M.L. (2012). Social justice: A concept analysis. *Public Health Nursing, 34*(2), 76-184. doi:10.1111/j.1365-2648.2011.05856.x

Campbell, J., Gilmore, L., & Cuskelly, M. (2003). Changing student teachers' attitudes towards disability and inclusion. *Journal of Intellectual & Developmental Disability, 28*(4), 369–379. doi:10.1080/1366 8250310001616407

Celoria, D. (2016). The preparation of inclusive social justice education leaders. *Educational Leadership and Administration: Teaching and Program Development, 27,* 199–219.

Chandra-Handa, M. (2009). Learner-centred differentiated model: A new framework. *Australasian Journal of Gifted Education, 18*(2), 55–56.

Cobb, C., & Sharma, M. (2015). I've got you covered: Adventures in social justice-informed co-teaching. *The Journal of Scholarship of Teaching and Learning,* 41–57. doi:10.14434/josotl.v15i4.13339

Corbett, J. (2001). Teaching approaches which support inclusive education: A connective pedagogy. *British Journal of Special Education, 28*(2), 55–59. doi:10.1111/1467-8527.00219

Dalton, E. M., Mckenzie, J. A., & Kahonde, C. (2012). The implementation of inclusive education in South Africa: Reflections arising from a workshop for teachers and therapists to introduce universal learning design. *African Journal of Disability, 1*(1), 1–13. doi:10.4102/ajod.v1i1.13 PMID:28729974

Department of Basic Education. (2010). *Guidelines for inclusive teaching and learning.* Government Printer.

Department of Basic Education. (2011). *Guidelines for responding to learner diversity in the classroom through Curriculum and Assessment Policy Statements.* Government Printer.

Department of Basic Education. (2017). *Inclusive education and special education: DBE progress report; with Deputy Minister.* https://pmg.org.za/committee-meeting/24505/

Department of Basic Education. (2014). *Policy on screening, identification, assessment and support.* Government Printer.

Department of Education. (2001). *Education White Paper 6. Special needs education: Building an inclusive education and training system.* Government Printer.

Department of Education. (2008). *National strategy on screening, identification, assessment and support: School pack.* Government Printer.

Donohue, D., & Bornman, J. (2014). The challenges of realizing inclusive education in South Africa. *South African Journal of Education, 34*(2), 1–14. doi:10.15700/201412071114

Dover, A. G. (2009). Teaching for social justice and K-12 student outcomes: A conceptual framework and research review. *Equity & Excellence in Education, 42*(4), 506–524. doi:10.1080/10665680903196339

Dover, A. G. (2013). Teaching for social justice: From conceptual frameworks to classroom practices. *Action in Teacher Education, 35*(2), 89–102. doi:10.1080/01626620.2013.770377

Dreyer, L. M. (2017). Constraints to quality education and support for all: A Western Cape case. *South African Journal of Education, 37*(1), 1–11. doi:10.15700aje.v37n1a1226

Engelbrecht, P., & Green, L. (2007). Responding to the challenges of inclusive education: an introduction. In P. Engelbrecht & L. Green (Eds.), *Responding to the challenges of inclusive education in Southern Africa* (pp. 8–88). Van Schaik.

Engelbrecht, P., Oswald, M., & Forlin, C. (2006). Promoting the implementation of inclusive education in primary schools in South Africa. *British Journal of Special Education, 33*(3), 121–129. doi:10.1111/j.1467-8578.2006.00427.x

Fiske, E. B., & Ladd, H. F. (2004). *Elusive equity: Education reform in post-apartheid South Africa.* Brookings Institute/HSRC Press.

Florian, L. (2015). Inclusive pedagogy: A transformative approach to individual differences but can it help reduce educational inequalities? *Scottish Educational Review, 47*(1), 5–14. doi:10.1163/27730840-04701003

Florian, L., & Camedda, D. (2020). Enhancing teacher education for inclusion. *European Journal of Teacher Education, 43*(1), 4–8. doi:10.1080/02619768.2020.1707579

Freire, P. (1970). *Pedagogy of the oppressed.* Seabury Press.

Friend, M., & Cook, L. (2007). *Interactions: Collaboration skills for professionals* (5th ed.). Pearson.

Grant, C. A., & Agosto, V. (2008). Teacher capacity and social justice in teacher education. In M. Cochran-Smith, S. Feiman-Nemser, D. J. McIntyre, & K. E. Demers (Eds.), *Handbook of research on teacher education: Enduring questions in changing contexts* (3rd ed., pp. 175–200). Routledge.

Graziano, K. J., & Navarrete, L. A. (2012). Co-teaching in a teacher education classroom: Collaboration, compromise, and creativity. *Issues in Teacher Education, 21*, 109–115.

Gürgür, H., & Uzuner, Y. (2010). A phenomenological analysis of the views on co-teaching applications in the inclusion classroom. *Educational Sciences: Theory and Practice, 10*(1), 278–331.

Hytten, K., & Bettez, S. C. (2011). Understanding education for social justice. *Educational Foundations, 25*(1-2), 7–24.

Kelly, D. (2012). Teaching for social justice. *Our Schools/Our Selves, 21*(2), 135-154.

Khechen, M. (2013). *Social justice: Concepts, principles, tools and challenges.* Economic and Social Commission for Western Asia (ESCWA).

Laal, M., & Ghodsi, S. M. (2012). Benefits of collaborative learning. *Procedia: Social and Behavioral Sciences, 31*, 486–490. doi:10.1016/j.sbspro.2011.12.091

Lawyer, G., Shahan, C., Holcomb, L., & Smith, D. H. (2020). First Comes a Look at the Self: Integrating the Principles of Social Justice into a Teacher Preparation Program. *Odyssey: New Directions in Deaf Education, 21*, 66–70.

Mahlo, D. (2017). Teaching learners with Diverse Needs in the Foundation Phase in Gauteng Province, South Africa. *SAGE Open Journal*, 1-9. doi:10.1177/2158244017697162

Makoelle, T. M., & Malindi, M. J. (2014). Multi-grade teaching and inclusion: Selected cases in the Free State Province of South Africa. *International Journal of Educational Sciences, 7*(1), 77–86. doi:1 0.1080/09751122.2014.11890171

Meltz, A., Chaya, H., & Pillay, V. (2014). Inclusive education: A case of beliefs competing for implementation. *South African Journal of Education, 34*(3), 1–8. doi:10.15700/201409161049

Mfuthwana, T., & Dreyer, L. M. (2018). Establishing inclusive schools: Teachers' perceptions of inclusive education teams {special issue}. *South African Journal of Education, 38*(4), 1–10. doi:10.15700aje. v38n4a1703

Miles, S., & Singal, N. (2010). The Education for All and inclusive education debate: Conflict, contradiction or opportunity? *International Journal of Inclusive Education, 14*(1), 1–15. doi:10.1080/13603110802265125

Moriña, A. (2020). Approaches to Inclusive Pedagogy: A Systematic Literature Review. *Pedagogy, 140*(4), 134–154. doi:10.15823/p.2020.140.8

Mphanda, E. G. (2018). *From main-stream to full-service schools: an exploration of teachers' attitudes towards the inclusion of learners living with physical disabilities in South African schools* [Doctoral dissertation]. University of Pretoria.

Murungi, L. N. (2015). Inclusive basic education in South Africa: Issues in its conceptualization and implementation. *Potchefstroom Electronic Law Journal, 18*(1), 3160–3195. doi:10.4314/pelj.v18i1.07

Neifeald, E., & Nissim, Y. (2019). Co-teaching in the "academia class": Evaluation of advantages and frequency of practices. *International Education Studies, 12*(5), 1913-9039. doi:10.5539/ies.v12n5p86

Nel, N. M. (2016). Teachers' perceptions of education support structures in the implementation of inclusive education in South Africa. *KOERS – Bulletin for Christian Scholarship, 81*(3).

Ngcobo, J., & Muthukrishna, N. (2011). The geographies of inclusion of students with disabilities in an ordinary school. *South African Journal of Education, 31*(3), 357–368. doi:10.15700aje.v31n3a541

Nieuwenhuis, J. (2010). Social justice in education revisited. *Education Inquiry, 1*(4), 269–287. doi:10.3402/edui.v1i4.21946

Nilholm, C., & Alm, B. (2010). An inclusive classroom: A case study of inclusiveness, teacher strategies, and children experiences. *European Journal of Special Needs Education, 25*(3), 239–252. doi:10 .1080/08856257.2010.492933

North, C. E. (2006). More than words? Delving into the substantive meaning(s) of "social justice" in education. *Review of Educational Research, 76*(4), 507–535. doi:10.3102/00346543076004507

Pantić, P., & Florian, L. (2015). Developing teachers as agents of inclusion and social justice. *Education Inquiry*, *6*(3), 27311. doi:10.3402/edui.v6.27311

Pather, S. (2011). Evidence on inclusion and support for all learners in mainstream schools in South Africa: Off the policy radar? *International Journal of Inclusive Education*, *15*(10), 1103-1117. doi:10.1080/13603116.2011.555075

Pearce, J., & Cumming-Potvin, W. (2017). English classrooms and curricular justice for the recognition of LGBT individuals: What can teachers do? *The Australian Journal of Teacher Education*, *42*(9), 77–92. doi:10.14221/ajte.2017v42n9.5

Polat, F. (2011). Inclusion in education: A step towards social justice. *International Journal of Educational Development*, *31*(1), 50–58. doi:10.1016/j.ijedudev.2010.06.009

Resta, P., & Laferrière, T. (2007). Technology in support of collaborative learning. *Educational Psychology Review*, *19*(1), 65–83. doi:10.100710648-007-9042-7

Roche, S. (2016). Education for all: Exploring the principle and process of inclusive education. *International Review of Education*, *62*(2), 131–137. doi:10.100711159-016-9556-7

Rodgers, B. L., & Knafl, K. A. (2000). *Concept development in nursing. Foundation, techniques and applications* (2nd ed.). Saunders.

RSA (Republic of South Africa). (1996). *The Constitution, Act No. 108 of 1996*. Government Printer.

Ryan, J. (2006). Inclusive leadership and social justice for schools. *Leadership and Policy in Schools*, *5*(1), 3–17. doi:10.1080/15700760500483995

Samier, E. A. (2020). Missing non-western voices on social justice for education: A postcolonial perspective on traditions of humanistic marginalized communities. *Handbook on promoting social justice in education*, 105-126.

Schugurensky, D. (2010). The heteronymous university and the question of social justice: In search of a new social contract. In J. Zajda (Ed.), *Globalization, education, and social justice*. Springer. doi:10.1007/978-90-481-3221-8_4

Sen, A. (2011). *The idea of justice*. Harvard University Press.

Shah, S. (2007). Special or mainstream: The views of disabled students. *Research Papers in Education*, *22*(4), 425–442. doi:10.1080/02671520701651128

Shyman, E. (2012). Differentiated instruction as a pedagogy of liberation. *The International Journal of Critical Pedagogy*, *4*(1), 65–75.

Slee, R. (2001). Inclusion in practice: Does practice make perfect? *Educational Review*, *53*(2), 113–123. doi:10.1080/00131910120055543

Sleeter, C. E. (2014). Deepening social justice teaching. *Journal of Language & Literacy Education*, *42*(6), 512–535.

Stanford, P., Crowe, M. W., & Flice, H. (2010). Differentiating with technology. *Teaching Exceptional Children Plus, 6*(4), 1–9.

Stangvik, G. (2010). Special education in society and culture: Comparative and developmental perspectives. *European Journal of Special Needs Education, 25,* 349-358. .2010.513539 doi:10.1080/08856257

Tchatchoueng, J. (2014). Inclusive education in the classroom: Practical applications. In Schooling, society and inclusive education: An Afrocentric perspective (pp. 195-217). Oxford University Press.

UNESCO. (2012). *Addressing exclusion in education: a guide to assessing education systems towards more inclusive and just societies.* UNESCO.

UNESCO. (2016). *Global education monitoring report.* UNESCO.

UNESCO. (2020). *Towards inclusion in education: Status, trends and challenges. UNESCO Salamanca Statement 25 years on.* UNESCO.

Walton, E., & Lloyd, G. (2011). An analysis of metaphors used for inclusive education in South Africa. *Acta Academica, 43*(3), 1–31.

Zhang, Y., Goddard, J. T., & Jakubiec, B. A. (2018). Social justice leadership in education: A suggested questionnaire. *Research in Educational Administration and Leadership, 3*(1), 53–86. doi:10.30828/real/2018.1.3

KEY TERMS AND DEFINITIONS

Co-Teaching: This involves two teachers working together to ensure that students have a worthwhile learning experience. The two teachers decide on how to collaborate.

Differentiation: This is ensuring that learners are provided with various opportunities to learn. It can happen at different levels during the teaching and learning process that is at the level of content and the level of assessment.

Inclusive Pedagogies: These are teaching methods that promote learners' participation in the teaching and learning experiences.

Inclusive Teaching: This is teaching that appreciates the diversity that exists among learners and provides opportunities for all learners to learn despite their diversity.

Social Justice in Education: This is education that does not discriminate and provides equal opportunities for learners to learn, taking into account their different backgrounds and protecting their basic human rights

Chapter 10
A Systematic Review of the Literature on the Problems and Suggestions for Inclusive Education in Turkey

Ismail Hakki Hakki Mirici
ⓘ https://orcid.org/0000-0002-0906-0259
Hacettepe University, Turkey

Özge Gümüş
ⓘ https://orcid.org/0000-0003-4621-842X
Adiyaman University, Turkey

Burcu Şentürk
ⓘ https://orcid.org/0000-0001-8951-3256
Bartin University, Turkey

ABSTRACT

Inclusive education, without excluding anyone regardless of his/her physical features, gender, or any other reasons, is considered a powerful instrument in achieving an inclusive society. The study aims to investigate the literature on inclusive education in K-12 classes in Turkey. In the study, document analysis method, one of the qualitative research designs, was adopted. The data were collected online via typing variations of the key words "problems, suggestions of inclusive education in Turkey" into several databases including Google Scholar, ProQuest, EBSCOhost, ERIC, and the search engine of the Higher Education Institution's thesis archive for the years of 2009-2022. The results have revealed that there are needs for a better inclusive education in Turkey, such as improving of educational facilities and reducing class sizes, developing inclusive education policies and approaches, increasing the quantity and quality of special education personnel, and more financial support.

DOI: 10.4018/978-1-6684-6386-4.ch010

INTRODUCTION

Inclusive activities in a particular society are closely interconnected with the attitude of that community (Sorkos, 2020). The main effective educational sources of a community are well educated teachers. Majority of schools cannot enroll students with special needs due to not having teachers skillful at implementing special education requirements in educational activities (Buchner & Thompson, 2021). Therefore, in the teacher education programs, inclusive education courses may play a significant role to increase awareness about inclusive activities in a society in every means of activities from educational to social activities (Lancaster & Brain, 2007; Loreman & Earle, 2007). There are various definitions of inclusion, which has been discussed and accepted recently in the contemporary world, stemming from the principle of equality in education, which is a requirement of democratization, and the view that individuals should be educated in the least restrictive environment. The goal of inclusion is to educate children with special needs alongside their peers in normal education settings by providing additional educational services to meet the requirements of the children. Inclusion; it envisages that individuals with special needs should be placed in normal school programs as much as possible, depending on the type and degree of their needs and the opportunities provided by the resources to be used, and they should be educated together with their peers in equal educational conditions (Karacaoglu, 2008). Like individuals without special needs designations, individuals with special needs have the right to have the equal opportunities in education. Education of individuals with special needs can be carried out in two ways; one of them is separate education and the other is inclusive education. Separate education is carried out by special education personnel and programs developed taking into account the disability situation. Inclusive education, on the other hand, is the education of individuals with special needs and normal development in the same class by normal classroom teachers (Batu et al., 2005).

Giving people with special needs the knowledge and skills they require through special needs education is another crucial element in enabling them to live independently in social situations (Eripek, 2003). For the education of students with special needs, the least restrictive educational setting is advised. By placing kids in this learning setting with their chronological age peers, it is intended to best suit their requirements (Kircaali-iftar, 1998). According to Mitchell (2004), policies that promote inclusive education allow all students to be treated equally regardless of their level of functioning or other personal traits. In its broadest sense, inclusive education refers to "education for all," including people from disadvantaged backgrounds including poverty, racial and ethnic minorities, rural areas, and other groups. According to Singh (2009), inclusive education is largely about "belonging, membership, and acceptance" both philosophically and practically (p. 13). Villa and Thousand (2000) added to this issue by arguing that building an atmosphere that promotes and includes all learners is the foundation of high-quality education rather than solely relying on student placement.

The Salamanca Statement (1994) of United Nations Educational, Scientific and Cultural Organization (UNESCO), which describes inclusive education from the standpoint of the United Nations (UN), plays a significant role in Turkey's inclusion education initiatives. Although its emphasis on children's rights and perspective is rooted in earlier declarations, the Salamanca Statement has also had the greatest impact on educational practices globally. According to UNESCO's definition, inclusive education is primarily concerned with concerns of human rights, equality, and the fight for a society devoid of discrimination. According to the Salamanca Statement, UNESCO's role as the principal leader is to:

1. ensure that special needs education is discussed in every forum that deals with education for all;

2. mobilize the support of teaching organizations in matters related to improving teacher preparation for provision for special educational needs;
3. encourage the academic community to strengthen research;
4. network and establish regional centers of information; and
5. raise money by developing an enlarged program for inclusive schools and community assistance initiatives within its upcoming Medium-Term Plan (1996-2002).

The basis of the concept of inclusion is the aim of special needs students going to the same school with their peers and being in the same classroom environment and providing the students or teachers with the support special education services they need (Kargin, 2004). Similarly, Atici (2014) stated that the purpose of inclusive education is to enable individuals in need of special education to be aware of their personal abilities and to increase their participation in social life, regardless of their disadvantaged situations. In this sense, inclusive education is a very important practice in terms of not only academic success but also social success of individuals in need of special education. The study of Karacaoglu (2008) supports other studies; He stated that the purpose of inclusive education is to make it easier for children without special needs designations to live in society without being isolated from children with normal development, and to enable them to develop desired behaviors by using their interests and abilities. The achievement of the above-mentioned goals of inclusive education depends on the realization of some conditions. Akkoyun (2007) stated that families, teachers and school administrators should act together in cooperation and that the desired success can be achieved in inclusive education as a result of taking all the necessary precautions for inclusive students.

Turkey's national laws, particularly those pertaining to the education of children with disabilities, are thought to be compliant with international law (Duskun, 2016). The United Nations Convention on the Rights of Persons with Disabilities was ratified by Turkey's Ministry of National Education (MoNE) in 2006; the MoNE also engages in anti-discrimination activities and troubleshooting. These actions have had a significant influence on the development of law. Additionally, Turkey set up special needs students' educational services in 1997 (MoNE Inclusive Education Project 2016-2018). Although the Constitution and several other laws prohibit discrimination based on gender, comprehensive plans have not been created to make educational environments inclusive of females and children of various sexual orientations. This is true despite the fact that extensive education projects—particularly for Syrian migrants—have been implemented recently (MoNE Inclusive Education Project 2016-2018). The objectives of inclusive education, however, cannot be met by policy makers, administrators, teachers, typically developing students, and parents if their beliefs and attitudes about inclusive education are not examined through the lens of social justice and diversity, according to approaches that see inclusive education as a part of human rights and participatory democracy. Legislation containing regulations does not guarantee that issues will be resolved. The teachers and school administrators should be informed, and the applications should be closely watched, in order to solve the difficulties in general. Additionally, the families who are in charge of their children's upbringing and education must be notified, and applications must be made while taking into consideration the views of the parents regarding what can be done to ensure that pupils' academic lives are not interrupted.

There are differences in the desired implementation of the strategies and ideas regarding inclusive education in each country. So, the problems regarding inclusive education practices encountered in K-12 classes and also suggestions presented in the studies to enhance inclusive education practices may vary from one country to another. The present study focuses on the problems and suggestions for inclusive education in K-12 classes in Turkey.

Inclusive Education in Turkey

The proportion of special needs pupils attending inclusive schools in Turkey has been rising. Currently only 54% of special education pupils were enrolled in regular education classes in 2001 (MoNE Inclusive Education Project 2016-2018). In 2008, it was 61 percent; in 2016, it was 70 percent (Disabled & Elderly, 2016). According to these statistics, general education teachers have a greater proportion of disabled pupils in their classes. Unless they took any special education classes in college, these teachers lack sufficient training in special education. Turkish general education teachers believed that a self-contained classroom would be preferable for kids with special needs, according to a study that surveyed general and special education teachers about their thoughts on inclusive education. It was due to general education instructors' inadequate preparation for teaching special needs children in an inclusive classroom (Karnas & Bayar, 2013b). When it comes to special education services, collaboration between teachers and parents is essential. Effective communication between teachers and with families is lacking. Despite the fact that some general education and special education teachers think cooperation is crucial, they don't frequently work together (Karnas & Bayar, 2013a). Additionally, Turkish parents with disabled children lack knowledge and education. They lack the special education policy knowledge necessary to participate in their children's education. As a result, these parents are unaware of how crucial it is for them to be involved in their children's education. They think that educators always make the wiser choices. Due to these factors, parents rarely participate in or alter their children's education. If teachers and parents don't work together, kids may receive an inclusive education that is unsuccessful.

Universities and colleges with special education programs have grown in number during the past twenty years (Council of Higher Education, 2017). As a result, the number of instructors who have graduated from special education programs has increased significantly. As a result, the state might encourage general education teachers who have received brief special education training and are now working with students who have special needs to return to their regular classroom settings. The state should then offer instructors who have completed a special education major a teaching position in an inclusive classroom. The elementary education, scientific education, math education, and social sciences education curricula in university programs were not developed to encourage inclusive education. There aren't many universities that provide special education courses. Teachers who graduated from these universities were not prepared to educate kids with special needs because the number of students with special needs in general education classrooms has been rising (Karnas & Bayar, 2013b). To facilitate inclusive education, it is essential that university education departments enhance the curriculum. One of the most crucial elements needed for successful inclusive education is collaboration (Fisher, Frey, & Thousand, 2003). School districts should create training programs that emphasize the significance of collaboration among teachers and between teachers and parents due to the lack of collaboration among instructors as well as between teachers and families (Karnas & Bayar, 2013a).

In Turkey, there are more studies concerning students with disabilities than the studies on inclusive education. The class of the inclusive student should be created by examining the competencies of the teachers in the classes where inclusive education is practiced and their educational status on this subject. On the other hand, arrangements should be made to ensure and control the size of the classes, the number of inclusive students in the classes and the equal distribution of inclusive students to the classes. By checking the adequacy of the support services of the school where inclusive education is applied, priority can be given to the appointment of a guidance teacher in case of a need for practice in a school without a guidance teacher, or a support service should be provided with a traveling guidance teacher. Various study methodologies and the challenges experienced by underprivileged students are discovered to be featured in some studies, while the curriculum and textbooks are seen to be scrutinized in other studies. It is noted that instructors and their attitudes toward inclusive education are among the most significant stakeholders in this field (Duskun, 2016). Currently, it is believed that looking at inclusive education research can help practitioners by exposing the view of inclusive education and the trend in these studies.

This study aims to report the systematic review of the literature on the problems and suggestions of inclusive education in K-12 classes in Turkey by analysis the studies conducted between 2012 and 2022. Investigating the problems and suggestions that emerged in inclusive education and identified by previous research can help us minimize the problems that emerged in new conditions and adapt more effectively. This chapter may serve as a basis for future research in providing some possible paths towards effective inclusive education and designing effective inclusive education programs. To this end, we attempted to locate all studies on the problems and suggestions of inclusive education in K-12 classes in Turkey appearing between 2012 and 2022 to address the following research questions:

Research Question One (RQ1): What are the problems faced in inclusive education in K-12 classes?
Research Question Two (RQ2): What suggestions are presented in the studies of inclusive education in K-12 classes in Turkey appearing between 2012 and 2022?

METHOD

Research Design

In the study, qualitative method was adopted based on document analysis. Other details about the research method are as follows:

Samples and Data collection

Several databases including Google Scholar, ProQuest, EBSCOhost, ERIC, and the search engine of the Higher Education Institution's thesis archive were searched for "inclusive + education + in Turkey" "problems in inclusive education in Turkey" "suggestions for inclusive education in Turkey" and their variations. On the initial pool of reports, the following inclusion criteria were followed: (1) inclusive education in Turkey was a main focus of the report, and (2) the problems and suggestions in inclusive education in Turkey were included. For completeness, book reviews and poster presentations were excluded. Those studies included were peer-reviewed and data-driven empirical reports either published as journal articles, book chapters, or theses. Eventually, a total of 44 Reports appearing between 2009 and April 2022 satisfied the inclusion criteria.

Table 1. Coding Scheme Used in the Study

Basic Information	a. author(s)	b. title	c. year
Publication Outlet	a. article	b. book chapter	c. thesis
Type of research	a. empirical	b. conceptual	
(If empirical) Context	a. number of part.	b. age of part.	
(If empirical) Design	a. method	b. statistical analysis	
Purpose and methodology	a. purpose	b. results (if empirical)	c. arguments (if conceptual)
Problems and Suggestions	a. problems faced	b. suggestions provided	

Data Analysis

Based on the coding scheme included in Table 1, two coders coded systematically the reports satisfying the inclusion criteria. The coders coded each report in relation to its publication outlet (whether it is article, book chapter, thesis), type of research (empirical or conceptual), context if empirical (no of participants + age of participants), design if empirical (method + statistical analysis), outcome (purpose + results (if empirical) + arguments (if conceptual)), a brief overview of the problems and suggestions drawn from the reports.

To sort the data into categories in terms of problems and suggestions in inclusive education in Turkey, content analysis was implemented to analyze the data (Ryan & Bernard, 2000). The three analyzers identified and created their code list, then grouped the reports and recontextualized them based on the coding scheme and then in terms of their problems and suggestions. To reach an agreement on the tabulation of the finalized codes and subcodes, they checked and reviewed by more-focused re-reding (Bowen, 2009). The reports were carefully read and the ones that have direct relevance to the RQs were identified. Then, the findings of the studies were synthesized to address the RQs. Additionally, the main findings of each report regarding the RQs were summarized. Subsequently, related to each category (problems and suggestions), a cross analysis of the data was implemented.

RESULTS

A summary of the reports on inclusive education in K-12 classes in Turkey based on the coding scheme adopted in this review is provided in Table 2, involving the authors, research outlet, research design, the purposes, main findings, the observed problems, and suggestions.

As shown in table 2, a total of 44 reports which, in one way or the other, attempted to examine inclusive education and its conceptual underpinnings were examined. This also comprises the total number of the articles that were accessed from the various websites visited during the data collection process.

Most of the literature has relied on a qualitative approach or phenomenology utilizing interviews; for this reason, to get effect-sizes for a meta-analytic synthesis was impossible. Only one study employed experimental research design (Kirkic & Sayan, 2021). A few studies additionally used mixed methods (n= 2). Two reports were unpublished PhD dissertations, in addition to three MA thesis and one book chapter. The rest of the reports were journal articles (n= 38).

Table 2. Summary of the Literature on Inclusive Education in K-12 Classes in Turkey

Authors	Publication Outlet	Type of Research	Context	Design	Purpose	Results/Arguments	Problems Encountered	Suggestions
Coskun, Tosun & Macaroglu (2009)	Article	Empirical	37 primary classroom teachers	Mixed methods	To determine classroom teachers' ways to choose, develop, and use of instructional materials for inclusion students in their classes	§ Inefficiency of teachers to develop and use instructional materials for inclusion students	§ Inefficiency of teachers to develop and use instructional materials for inclusion students	§ Inclusion of some courses about "special education" and "its applications" in the teacher training programs
Ciyer (2010)	PhD Dissertation	Empirical	6 teachers 4 administrators 2 policy makers from MONE 4 academic advisors	Qualitative case study (Document analysis and qualitative survey)	To examine key international policies, resolutions, and their effect on inclusive education programs in Turkey from the perspective of current practitioners in the Turkish education system	§ There are various complexities, tensions, and inadequacies in the conceptualization of inclusive education in Turkish public primary schools.	§ Societal values and beliefs § Negative attitudes about raising a child with a disability § Cost, lack of funds, and family poverty § Inadequate educational infrastructure § Physical barriers for children with disabilities § Class size § Lack of educational professionals § Insufficient teacher preparation and in-service training programs § Lack of collaboration/ communication among education professionals § Lack of communication with parents § Lack of instructional adaptations § Evaluation/Measurement bias	§ Modifying deeply held attitudes at both personal and institutional levels § Providing clearly constructed inclusive education policies and approaches § Offering appropriate training to key stakeholders § Making adequate resources available
Demir & Acar (2011)	Article	Empirical	45 classroom teachers	Qualitative survey	To receive the opinions of classroom teachers who had had at least one inclusion student in their classrooms during their professional lives	§ Majority of the participants do not support inclusion. § There are various problems teachers experience with inclusive education.	§ Lack of guidance services § Lack of administrative support § Overcrowded classrooms § Lack of equipment § Lack of knowledge of inclusion § Lack of cooperation with families § Lack of social acceptance	§ Exclusive practices § More in-service training § Individualized instruction
Sadioglu, Bilgin, Batu & Oksal (2013)	Article	Empirical	23 elementary school teachers	Qualitative descriptive research	To display a detailed investigation of the views of the elementary teachers in the specification of defects in the inclusive education applications and in the evaluation of success	§ Elementary teachers generally have a negative opinion regarding the inclusive education applications in Turkey. § The teachers are inadequate in this subject and need a great deal of sustenance particularly expert support.	§ Inadequacy of teachers in terms of inclusive education § Insufficiency of pre-service and in-service training in terms of inclusive education § Insufficiency of physical conditions of classrooms for inclusive education	§ Presence of separate teaching environments and part-time inclusive education § Organization of qualified and effective pre-service and in-service training § Material support
Akalin, Demir, Sucuoglu, Bakkaloglu & Iscen (2014)	Article	Empirical	40 preschool teachers	Phenomenology	To examine the needs of preschool teachers with regard to supporting the development of children with disabilities in their classes	§ Teachers mainly need knowledge, skills, experience, and support when assessing the performance of children with special needs, working with their parents, preparing individualized education programs (IEPs), adapting and modifying their curriculum, and dealing with behavioral problems.	§ Lack of knowledge, skills, experience and support	§ Functional teacher training programs
Melekoglu (2014)	Book chapter	Conceptual			To focus on the development, as well as the current state of special education in Turkey		§ The current quality of education and assessment processes being practiced needs to be improved. § Almost no support services in the school for children with special needs nor in-service assistance to the teachers of students in inclusive classrooms § The majority of teachers of inclusive classrooms are against inclusion practices, and teachers, administrators, nondisabled peers, and their families often manifest negative attitudes toward children with special needs and their families.	§ Establishing a new model of training special education personnel § Resolving the academic personnel shortage needs at universities § Establishing effective inclusive education § Early diagnosis and intervention of young students with special needs § Developing better family participation and support § Job training and placement of individuals with disabilities § Dealing with the current deficiency in laws and policies about special education § Dissemination of research-based practices § Transition of individuals with disabilities to independent living

continued on following page

Table 2. Continued

Authors	Publication Outlet	Type of Research	Context	Design	Purpose	Results/Arguments	Problems Encountered	Suggestions
Sakiz & Woods (2014)	Article	Empirical	4 class teachers 4 school counsellors	Qualitative survey	To examine school staff views on inclusion in their schools	§ School staff held positive beliefs towards educating disabled students in regular schools and believed in the contribution of this to both disabled students and their non-disabled peers. § Special educational paradigms existed in mainstream schools and shaped professional practice. § There was a lack of conceptual and methodological knowledge of inclusion among stakeholders, indicating a need for awareness raising and development. § Disabled students were far from being fully included within classroom practice. § There was a lack of collaboration among school staff, inadequate family engagement and a strong need for effective school leadership in inclusion. § There were individual efforts by the school staff to develop inclusive practices.	§ Lack of knowledge of inclusion § Lack of real inclusion § Lack of collaboration among school staff § Inadequate family engagement	§ Awareness raising and development for school staff § More collaboration among school staff § Awareness raising for families § More family engagement § More effective school leadership
Sakiz & Woods (2015)	Article	Conceptual			To investigate the inclusion of students with disabilities in the Turkish context		§ An incomplete understanding of the philosophy of inclusion § Negative attitudes towards inclusion § The number of students per staff member § Teachers' lack of knowledge of inclusion § Ineffective assessment procedures § Insufficient curriculum	§ A better understanding of inclusion § Clarification of the roles of the school staff § More pre-service courses on inclusion § Increase in the number of mainstream schools, teachers, counsellors, and technological facilities § In-service training activities § More financial support § Better assessment procedures § Development of the curriculum § More research on inclusion § Governmental and educational efforts to include more students with disabilities in mainstream schools
Diken, Rakap, Diken, Tomris & Celik (2016)	Article	Conceptual			To describe Turkish special education laws and regulations that support inclusive education and teaching in natural environment To summarize current inclusive practices in early childhood in Turkey To summarize and synthesize the available research on early childhood inclusion in Turkey To discuss challenges and suggestions for future directions to enhance early childhood inclusion in Turkey		§ Negative opinions or attitudes toward early childhood inclusion § Lack of information and training in inclusive and special education § Having minimal or no support from school administrations § Having difficulties in preventing and addressing challenging behaviors of young children with disabilities § Inability to make necessary adaptations in classroom environments to serve young children with disabilities § Lack of cooperation with experts § Lack of resources § Teachers' willingness for inclusion § Attitudes of school administration § Characteristics of children with disabilities § Inadequate physical environment § Insufficient support services	§ Individualized instruction to participate in activities designed to support their development and learning § Professional development efforts designed to support inclusive practices § Supporting families of young children with disabilities § Preparing and implementing individualized education programs § Arranging classroom environment § Collaborating with other professionals § More courses in teacher training programs § More pre-service and in-service trainings
Sakiz (2016)	Article	Empirical	27 educational administrators	Qualitative survey	To investigate the extent to which inclusive education is seen by administrators as a factor that enables constructive educational change	§ Participants had various conceptualizations of educational change. § Inclusive education was conceived as an opportunity (though difficult to implement) to realize educational change towards educational improvement. § The current competitive and centralized system left little space to utilize inclusive education to catalyse positive educational change.	§ The competitive education system § Teachers' lack of knowledge and experience of inclusion § Lack of understanding of inclusion § Curriculum § Assessment practices	§ Mainstreaming § Reorganization of schools § Individualized instruction § Trainings §

continued on following page

Table 2. Continued

Authors	Publication Outlet	Type of Research	Context	Design	Purpose	Results/Arguments	Problems Encountered	Suggestions
Yilmaz & Batu (2016)	Article	Empirical	17 teachers	Qualitative survey	To investigate teachers' perspectives on inclusion	§ There are various problems for the inclusion on students with special needs.	§ Class size § Assessment issues § Lack of knowledge of stakeholders § Negative attitudes from peers towards students with special needs	§ Decreasing class size § Reorganizing the physical environment § Better assessment procedures § Awareness raising for stakeholders § More support room services
Ugurlu (2017)	PhD Dissertation	Empirical	397 Turkish general and special educators at in-service and pre-service level	Survey	To validate the Turkish version of International Survey of Inclusion To understand the attitudes, knowledge, and skills of Turkish special and general educators with respect to students with learning disabilities and emotional behavioural disorders and education of such students in inclusive settings	§ The Turkish version of the International Survey of Inclusion was both valid and reliable. § Turkish educators had positive attitudes toward inclusive education. § Turkish educators mostly defined inclusion as placing students with disabilities in the same educational environment with their peers without disabilities.	§ Lack of emphasis on transition planning in Turkey § Lack of knowledge of instructional strategies used for students with severe intellectual disabilities § Infavorable attitudes toward inclusion of students with autism and severe intellectual disabilities § Lack of a data collection system § Ineffectiveness of teacher trainings in Turkey	§ Collaboration between special and general education teachers § Increasing knowledge of disabilities and inclusive education § Better teacher training
Yaman (2017)	MA Thesis	Empirical	30 teachers	Qualitative survey	To find out the ideas upon inclusive education of primary school teachers who have inclusive students in their classes at schools having inclusive application	§ Various problems and suggestions were detected in inclusive education.	§ Class sizes § Low attendance for in-service trainings § Unprofessional in-service trainings § Inadequacy in preparing a separate inclusive education § Inadequate support from administrative personnel counselling service and other staff at schools § Unsuitable physical environment for students with special needs § Insufficient coordination with the families of mentally incompetent students	§ Improving the physical circumstances § Providing suitable tools and materials for students with special needs § Including parents, teachers and all the school staff into inclusive education programs § Cooperation of parents, teachers and school staff § Employing inclusive education experts and forming inclusive education classes at school § Preparing pedagogical diagnosis reports according to the students' needs
Esmer, Yilmaz, Günes, Tarim & Delican (2017)	Article	Empirical	10 teachers	Phenomenology	To reveal classroom teachers' experiences about training of inclusive students	§ There is not enough cooperation through classroom teachers and other stakeholders and teachers appear to have various problems which personal and professional in this process.	§ Social acceptance § Lack of knowledge of inclusion § Lack of cooperation with stakeholders	§ Training for parents, peers, and teachers § More cooperation among stakeholders
Birol & Zor (2018)	Article	Empirical	15 classroom teachers	Qualitative survey	To determine the problems that classroom teachers experienced with students who had special learning difficulties	§ The education levels of the teachers regarding the specific learning difficulties are inadequate and that they confront with various problems in the implementation of the education programs, classroom management and classroom communication.	§ Inadequate knowledge regarding inclusion § Classroom management issues	§ Forming support classrooms § Appointing permanent teachers to support classrooms § Making it compulsory to go rehabilitation centers § Providing financial support § Educating parents about inclusive education
Hauwadhanasuk, Karnas & Zhuang (2018)	Article	Conceptual			To investigate the transitional process of special education programs, services, and public policy toward inclusive education in China, Thailand and Turkey To present the development of educational plans that promote inclusive education and practices in these countries	§ The special education development and its process in China, Thailand, and Turkey are challenging. § The education policies in Thailand and Turkey have addressed issues regarding children with disabilities and appear to move toward inclusion for individuals with disabilities.	§ Insufficiency of special education in Turkey § Parents' lack of knowledge and awareness concerning inclusive education	§ Collaboration between educators and governmental officials from all over the world to promote and support educational plans that deal with the positive aspects of inclusive education
Kahya & Hosgörür (2018)	Article	Conceptual		Comparative educational research	To compare inclusive education in Turkey and Argentina utilizing Bereday's (1964) comparative education model	§ While inclusive education policies in Turkey focus on disabled students and students with learning difficulties, in Argentina they focus on disadvantaged groups in order to provide educational equality.	§ Neglect of disadvantaged groups in inclusive education in the Turkish educational system	§ Inclusion of disadvantaged groups in in education
Kutay (2018)	Article	Conceptual		Literature review	To discuss the concept of inclusion in Turkish education system	§ Teachers who have students with SENs in their classrooms believe in usefulness of inclusive education, but they need to be supported by additional services such as resource rooms, counselling, teaching assistants.	§ Lack of support services for inclusive education	§ Provision of support services for inclusive education

continued on following page

Table 2. Continued

Authors	Publication Outlet	Type of Research	Context	Design	Purpose	Results/Arguments	Problems Encountered	Suggestions
Ozokcu (2018)	Article	Empirical	457 classroom teachers	Descriptive survey	To investigate classroom teachers' attitudes towards inclusion practices in terms of demographic variables	§ Classroom teachers do not have favorable attitudes towards inclusion practices. § No significant difference was found among the participants' total scores on the scale according to their gender and educational level. § A significant difference was found according to their ages, level of interaction with individuals with special needs, level of attending special education courses, level of knowledge about laws and policies, level of self-confidence in working with disabled individuals, and level of experience in working with disabled students.	§ Infavorable attitudes towards inclusion § Lack of knowledge on legislation	§ More communication with inclusive students § More undergraduate courses on special education § Awareness raising on legislation § Raising teachers' self-confidence in working with inclusive students
Tekinarslan, Sivrikaya, Keskin, Ozlu & Rasmussen (2018)	Article	Empirical	125 parents with children in inclusive education	Descriptive research	To determine the needs of parents with children in inclusive education	§ Parents have needs for social support, information, assistance and adaptation § The mothers have higher needs than the fathers. § No significant correlation between needs and the gender of the child	§ Lack of social support for parents with children in inclusive education § Lack of information for parents with children in inclusive education	§ Arrangements and adjustments for parents in inclusive education environments
Yilmaz & Melekoglu (2018)	Article	Empirical	Laws, articles, and theses	Qualitative case study	To descriptively examine the situation of inclusive education related legal regulations and laws in practice in Turkey and Europe	§ Although inclusive education is based on laws and regulations in Turkey, United Kingdom, Sweden, Denmark, Spain, Greece and Lithuania, problems and shortcomings are observed in implementation. § On the contrary, in Italy and Ireland, it can be said that there is no problem in the implementation of regulations.	§ Class size § Lack of support personnel § Lack of individualized instruction § Lack of in-service training § Lack of governmental support services	§ Arranging class size § Supporting classrooms with support teachers educated in the field of special education § Having schools, the responsibility to prepare individualized education plan for students and evaluate the achievement of the targeted goals at the end of the school year § In-service training to principals and teachers § Preparing internet based educational software to reach the information easily, § Getting support of the non-governmental organizations for works related to special education
Aktan, Budak & Botabeknova (2019)	Article	Empirical	301 primary school students	Mixed methods	To examine the social acceptance levels of the students in primary schools to the inclusive students	§ Significant differences in social acceptance levels according to gender, having special needs individuals in their surroundings, having inclusive students in their classes	§ Definition of inclusive students with their academic and social problem behaviors § Low social acceptance levels of inclusive students by their peers	§ Improvement in teacher skills to cause a change in social acceptance levels for inclusive students § Awareness raising in parents and students for inclusive education
Gezer & Aksoy (2019)	Article	Empirical	19 preschool teachers	Phenomenology	To evaluate preschool teachers' perceptions of their roles within the context of inclusion education	§ Teachers are unaware of some of their roles in relation to inclusive education assigned by relevant legislation.	§ Unawareness of teachers of their roles in relation to inclusive education. § Lack of knowledge, awareness and skills on the nature and requirements of inclusive education and teachers' roles and skills	§ Training and support for teachers
Ilik & Hacieminoglu (2019)	Article	Empirical	37 science teachers	Qualitative survey	To investigate the problems of the elementary science teachers having students with special needs in the inclusive education applications.	§ More than half of the science teachers have not received any training on inclusion. § Half of the participants pay individualized attention to students with special needs.	§ Inadequacy of pre-service training on inclusion § Inadequacy of support services § Classroom management problems § Communication with parents § Lack of materials	§ Resource rooms § Collaboration among teachers § More undergraduate courses on inclusion § More in-service trainings § Awareness raising for parents

continued on following page

Table 2. Continued

Authors	Publication Outlet	Type of Research	Context	Design	Purpose	Results/Arguments	Problems Encountered	Suggestions
Kaptan (2019)	MA Thesis	Empirical	35 teachers	Qualitative survey	To receive the opinions of teachers who provide education in the first and second level schools in Konya in order to determine the conditions of the support education rooms and the difficulties faced by teachers who provide support education room services	§ Teachers reported that physical environment of support education rooms, materials and technological equipment were insufficient. § They stated that time management is negatively affected due to the implementation of support education rooms during the school hours. § They reported that during support education students had difficulty in being motivated so they negatively reacted to the education.	§ Insufficient physical environment of support education rooms § Insufficient technological equipment § Time management problems due to support room education § Students' lack of motivation for support room education § Limited communication with families § Lack of communication with other institutions and organizations	§ Modification of support rooms § Increasing the quantity and quality of support room materials and technological equipment § Better time management for support room services § Trainings and seminars for awareness-raising § Better communication with families
Kaysili, Soylu & Sever (2019)	Article	Empirical	12 teachers 5 administrators 10 parents	Case study	To answer how sociocultural clashes between Turkish kids and Syrians interrupt inclusive education of Syrian refugees	§ There are various barriers in front of inclusion of Syrian refugees in Turkish education system.	§ Language barrier § Lack of communication among stakeholders § Lack of family participation § Insufficiency of economic and cultural resources	§ A collective and holistic approach to inclusion
Keser & Tanriverdi (2019)	Article	Empirical	62 teachers	Qualitative Survey	To determine the special education support services regarding inclusive practices for students with special needs	§ Support services are limited and inconsistent with inclusive practices.	§ Lack of knowledge concerning special education support services § Insufficient support services for individuals with special needs and their families § Inadequate support services provided for mainstreaming practices	§ Redefining inclusion and inclusive practices § Restructuring support services for special education § Reorganization of teacher training programs according to inclusive principles § In-service training for teachers § Coordination of support services
Ramo Akgun, Ristovska & Canevska (2020)	Article	Empirical		Document analysis	To compare the training and qualifications of future special educators and rehabilitators in higher education systems in the Netherlands, Austria, Italy, Germany, Finland, Russia, Lithuania and Spain in order to obtain positive application methods regarding the competences of special educators and rehabilitators	§ The education of special educators and rehabilitators varies in different countries and it is contextualized or adapted to the tradition, history, and norms of each society.	§ Lack of in-service training for special education teachers § Inadequate pre-service training	§ Development of the network of resource centers § Increasing of the competences of the regular teachers § Increasing the competences of the special educators and rehabilitators for work in the regular inclusive conditions § Specializing after the graduate studies
Burunsuz & Ince (2020)	Article	Empirical	12 teachers	Phenomenology	To determine the teachers' opinions on the implementation of Individualized Education Program (IEP) for teachers working in elementary education schools	§ The teachers encountered various problems such as shortage of time for the application process of the IEP, lack of awareness of parents, inadequate training and seminars, lack of knowledge, problems experienced during the reporting period.	§ Shortage of time for the application process of the IEP § Lack of awareness of parents § Inadequate training and seminars § Lack of knowledge	§ Training on IEPs § Support services § Cooperation with families
Gülec-Aslan (2020)	Article	Empirical	8 preschool teachers	Phenomenology	To explore the experiences of eight preschool teachers in Turkey for including children with Autism Spectrum Disorders	§ The teachers experience various difficulties and use various methods, though limited, to handle these difficulties.	§ Overcrowded classrooms § Insufficiency of equipment § Negative reactions of typically developing children and their families § Characteristics of students with ASD § Insufficiency of teacher competencies	§ Development of teachers' professional competencies to cope with difficulties in inclusion § Establishment of support rooms for inclusion students § Informing typically developing peers and their families about the student with ASD § Support services such as resource rooms and assisting staff § Reducing class sizes § Pre-service and in-service training and seminars
Ilik & Deniz (2020)	Article	Empirical	50 pre-service teachers	Descriptive Survey	To examine branch teacher candidates' observations relating to inclusive education practices in Turkey	§ The majority of the branch teachers have positive approach towards inclusive students. § They take the inclusive students into consideration while planning and teaching the course. § They enable their participation in the class and assign them tasks in which the students could take responsibility. § They attend to them in and out of the class.	§ Lack of support services § Overcrowded classes	§ More support services § Reducing class size

continued on following page

Table 2. Continued

Authors	Publication Outlet	Type of Research	Context	Design	Purpose	Results/Arguments	Problems Encountered	Suggestions
Katitas & Coskun (2020)	Article	Empirical	120 teachers	Phenomenology	To determine the perceptions of teachers in Turkey towards inclusive education through metaphors.	§ Suitable educational support should be given to the students with special needs according to their individual needs. § It is important for students with special needs to share the same learning environment in an integrity without separating them from their peers who had 'normal' academic and social development.	§ Insufficient patience for inclusive students § Improper educational support § Lack of affection for inclusive students § Lack of understanding of inclusive education § Lack of understanding of characteristics of inclusive students § Inequal access to opportunities	§ Proper educational support § More patience § Individualized instruction § More positive attitudes and behaviors § Acceptance of differences of inclusive students
Kirkiç & Sayan (2020)	Article	Empirical	40 preschool students	Experimental research	To examine the development of students who receive inclusive education in schools providing early childhood education	§ The results of the study were significantly higher for inclusion students who were trained in the support room than inclusion students without support room education in terms of the development of the psychomotor, cognitive, language and self-care skills.	§ Lack of support rooms for inclusion students	§ Establishment of support rooms for inclusion students
Mete (2020)	Article	Empirical	12 high school students		To determine the problems of students in an inclusive classroom environment in high school during the classes and to suggest some solutions to these problems	§ Although some of the students in an inclusive classroom environment stated that they received support from their families, it was observed that the cooperation with the individuals involved in the process did not fully take place.	§ Lack of individualized training programs § Lack of social acceptance § Lack of appropriate teaching methods and materials § Inappropriate physical environment § Inappropriate assessment procedures	§ Individualized training programs § Teaching adaptations for students with special needs § Restructuring of the curriculum § Arrangements in physical environment § Technical equipment, rehabilitation activities, material, and teacher support
Uygur, Aycicek, Dogrul & Yanpar Yelken (2020)	Article	Empirical	38 teachers working in Mersin province, Turkey 11 school administrative staff 11 faculty members working at the Education Faculty	Qualitative survey	To determine the views of teachers, school administrative staff having educational leadership roles, and faculty members on integration of technology and the role of educational leadership for sustainable inclusive education	§ The faculty members do not consider that inclusive education practices reach an adequate level of sustainability. § Technological infrastructures of schools are inadequate for sustainable inclusive education practices.	§ Inadequate inclusive education practices § Inadequate technological infrastructure for inclusive education	§ Adding a sustainable inclusive education course in teacher education programs § Integration of technology into sustainable inclusive education
Aktan (2021)	Article	Empirical	28 teachers	Holistic single case study	To determine the opinions of teachers for inclusive education interventions in Turkey	§ Most of the teachers have negative views on inclusive education due to the current conditions.	§ Professional deficiencies of teachers § Insufficient support services § Insufficient cooperation among partners § Crowded classes § Unqualified schools in terms of physical infrastructure § Lack of expert support § Leaving all responsibility to teachers during interventions	§ Improving professional competencies of teachers § Strengthening human resources in special education services § Increasing the number of staff § Enriching the content of special education courses in undergraduate programs § Preparing the infrastructure of schools for inclusive education interventions
Bayram & Ozturk (2021)	Article	Empirical	313 social studies teachers	Survey	To determine the opinions and attitudes of social studies teachers towards inclusive education	§ Teachers generally have positive opinions about inclusive education. § They do not have an adequate and efficient level of knowledge and in-class practices.	§ The curriculum § Social structure and politics § Physical, technological, and hardware § Education system § Teachers' lack of knowledge and skills § Negative attitudes and behaviours towards disadvantaged students § School administration and management	§ The implementation of a flexible learning system to meet the diverse and complex needs of each student § Support services § Individualized curriculum § Adaptation of assessment criteria § Training of teachers
Celik, Isler & Saka (2021)	Article	Empirical	1900 teachers 400 school headteachers	Qualitative survey	To unpack the challenges that refugee children, mainly from Syria, face in integrating into primary and secondary public schools in Turkey To propose some tentative resolutions, drawing from the experiences of refugee parents, teachers, and headteachers.	§ The study confirms students' barriers in schooling with regard to psychosocial factors, cultural adaptation, language learning, systemic barriers, and family relations.	§ Psychosocial barriers § Adaptation barriers § Language and communication barriers § Systemic barriers § Family-related barriers	§ In-service training on how to support inclusivity in educational settings § Coordination and collaboration among stakeholders § Awareness raising for parents § Language training § Awareness raising for students, teachers, headteachers, and parents

continued on following page

Table 2. Continued

Authors	Publication Outlet	Type of Research	Context	Design	Purpose	Results/Arguments	Problems Encountered	Suggestions
Gelir (2021)	Article	Empirical	Turkish preschool education program	Document analysis	To examine the Turkish preschool education program from the perspective of educational inclusivity	§ Although the existing program does not refer explicitly to taking an inclusive approach toward immigrant children, the findings show that three of the program's features are oriented toward inclusivity. § Achievements in developmental education indicate that the program implicitly has an inclusive perspective.	§ The program does not explicitly mention inclusivity in early years education. § Lack of knowledge of inclusion	§ More experimental studies to examine the ways in which teachers implement inclusive practices in the classroom § Pedagogical changes (e.g., revised and adapted classroom activities emphasizing inclusive education) in early years education to guide preschool teachers toward best practice in inclusive education § A new definition of inclusive education for immigrant children
Karadag Yilmaz & Yeganeh (2021)	Article	Empirical	20 primary school teachers	Qualitative survey	To determine the perceptions and practices of teachers about inclusive education To propose solutions to the problems experienced by the teachers in the light of the study findings	§ The teachers experienced a lack of conceptual clarity regarding the definition of inclusive education. § A great majority of them focused on the main philosophy of inclusiveness. § Few of them attempted to relate inclusiveness to instructional practices. § The teachers did not perform activities directed to the application of inclusive education in their classes.	§ Lack of understanding of inclusion § Lack of inclusive activities in the classroom § Lack of materials § Crowded classrooms § Inadequate in-service training	§ Ensuring stakeholder participation § Diversifying instructional practices § Changes in the instructional environment § Changes in instructional materials § Changes in evaluation § Offering one-to-one teaching § Assigning individual homework § Organizing group works § Developing enriched education plan § Offering compensatory teaching to assist inclusive students § Conducting language studies with refugee students § Offering professional in-service training for teachers § Decreasing the number of students in classes § Improvement of schools' physical conditions § Fostering school-community cooperation § Offering training for families § Reducing the intensity of the curriculum
Karsli-Calamak & Kilinc (2021)	Article	Empirical	2 Turkish as a second language teachers	Phenomenology	To understand the evolving experiences of teachers of Syrian refugee students in relation to inclusive education in Turkey	§ Teachers' notions around particular themes exemplify Fraser's three-dimensional social justice framework dimensions – redistribution, recognition, and representation – and their practices are accordingly moving on a continuum of inclusivity-oriented to exclusion-oriented actions.	§ Lack of economic resources § Lack of educational resources § Exclusion-oriented actions § Misrecognition of refugee students' cultural and historical backgrounds § Misrecognition of refugee students' linguistic diversity	§ Efforts to ensure social justice in recognition of refugee students, redistribution of resources, and representation
Kiziloglu (2021)	MS Thesis	Empirical		Documentation and policy analysis	To discover the reasons behind why thousands of Syrian children are out of school, and how child labour creates the biggest reason behind the out of schooling problem of Syrian children living in Turkey	§ The migration related schooling problems of Syrian children in Turkey can be solved with short-term policies and strategies, § Problems and obstacles related to poverty resulting with child labour are harder to overcome and need special focus through longer term, comprehensive and multisectoral policy making.	§ Dropout of school § Absenteeism § Language barrier § Discrimination by peers or teachers § Physical access to education § Financial barriers § Child labour	§ Granting access to schools § Teacher training § Parent training § Ensuring social cohesion § Eliminating child labour § Financial assistance § Stronger advocacy and monitoring mechanisms § Better coordination among stakeholders
Vural, Piskin & Durmusoglu (2021)	Article	Empirical	20 preschool teachers	Qualitative survey	To determine the problems that preschool teachers experience in the inclusive education processes To define the educational practices of teachers for students who benefit from inclusive education	§ Preschool teachers do not feel professionally competent in inclusive education. § They do not receive enough practical training in undergraduate education. § Teachers have some problems with children, families, administrators, and legislation in the learning and teaching process regarding inclusive education.	§ Classroom management § Lack of materials § Crowded classes § Assessment § Lack of experience § Insufficient undergraduate education § Lack of individualized instruction § Lack of cooperation with families § Lack of support services	§ Having more support staff § Reducing class size § More cooperation with families § Better environmental conditions § More materials § Revision of teacher training programs § Better diagnosis § Awareness raising for families § Awareness raising for administrators

continued on following page

Table 2. Continued

Authors	Publication Outlet	Type of Research	Context	Design	Purpose	Results/Arguments	Problems Encountered	Suggestions
Yazcayir & Gurgur (2021)	Article	Empirical	15 parents	Phenomenology	To examine how special education provided for students within inclusive education has continued at home during the pandemic	§ All students, including those with special needs, have continued their schooling via distance education provided by Turkish Ministry of National Education through EBA TV and the official website of the Ministry. § Participants have reported that some teachers conducted online lessons and shared worksheets with all students via the WhatsApp group.	§ Inclusive students' unwillingness to participate in online lessons § No support services during the pandemic § Lack of communication with families § Lack of communication with students	§ More communication with families § More feedback for inclusive students § Teacher guidance and follow-up § Individualized instruction § More support services

Generally, these studies aimed to investigate the current state of inclusive education in Turkey focusing on opinions and attitudes of students with special needs, their peers, teachers, parents, and school administrators, revealing the commonly experienced issues in inclusive education. Additionally, based on the identified problems, a majority of these reports came up with certain suggestions for the planning, development, and utilization of inclusive practices.

As explained above, the aim of this investigation was not to provide a comprehensive review of all aspects related to inclusive education in Turkey. Instead, we had two specific foci:

the problems identified in inclusive education in K-12 classes and the suggestions presented in these reports. The findings based on the two purposes of our review are discussed in the sections that follow.

The Problems Identified in Inclusive Education in K-12 Classes in Turkey

The problems identified in inclusive education literature in Turkey were categorized under the following sub-themes in Table 3.

The answer to our first research question is related to the main problems identified in the reviewed studies. As observed in Table 3, the problems are categorized under the following sub-themes: (1) educational system-related, (2) teacher-related, (3) educational environment-related, (4) community-related, (5) teacher training-related, and (6) student-related problems. The most commonly experienced group of problems regarding inclusion in the Turkish education system is educational-system related problems (f = 88). Among these issues, the most frequently mentioned one is lack of support services (f = 17) such as school counselling, support rooms, support personnel etc. The second most frequent issue observed is educational personnel's lack of communication (f = 13) with the families of children with special needs due to economic, motivational, and time-related constraints. Lack of necessary equipment and materials (f = 12) required for the effective inclusion of students with special needs into mainstream schools and classes is another commonly experienced problem in this theme. The other codes which represent educational system-related problems for inclusion are assessment and diagnostic issues (f = 8), lack of collaboration among educational professionals (f = 8), lack of real inclusion (f = 7) due to ineffective utilization of inclusive practices, improper methodology (f = 6), insufficient curriculum (f = 6), lack of administrative support (f = 5), insufficient number of educational professionals (f = 2), lack of individualized instruction (f = 2), lack of educational transition planning (f = 1), and competitive educational atmosphere (f = 1).

The second most frequent theme involves teacher-related problems for inclusive education (f = 42). Although this theme accounts for the second biggest number of problems related to inclusive education, it encapsulates the most frequently mentioned code, which is teachers' lack of knowledge, skills, and experience regarding inclusion (f = 30). Teachers in inclusive education practices stated that they are not sufficiently supported from outside. However, in order for this application to achieve the desired success, they have to take responsibility in other relevant organizations, especially in RAMs. The classroom teachers stated that they had difficulties in finding the necessary tools, equipment and materials in addition to the physical inadequacies of the environment in inclusive education practices. The Special Education Services Directive states that a development unit should be established in order to prepare Individual Education Programs (IEP) for inclusive students in schools and an education support room should be opened in schools by providing special equipment and educational materials (MoNE, 2006). The other teacher-related issues which appear to be interfering with the proper utilization of inclusive practices in Turkish K-12 classes are teachers' negative attitudes towards children with special needs (f = 6), classroom management issues stemming from the existence of students with special needs in mainstream classes (f = 3), time management issues (f = 2), and low level of attendance for in-service trainings by educational professionals (f = 1).

The third theme regards the educational environment-related problems (f = 24) that create challenges in the utilization of inclusive education in Turkey. The most outstanding of these problems is related to class size (f = 11); in other words, the overcrowded classes in Turkish public K-12 schools makes it very challenging to implement inclusive practices, since teachers have limited time to pay special attention to kids with special needs. This result was revealed in most of the studies (e.g., Bilen, 2007), emphasizing that the majority of teachers made it difficult to implement inclusive education in large classrooms. The crowded classrooms prevent the inclusion student from receiving the more attention and support they need, as the classroom teacher cannot spare enough time for the mainstreaming student (Yigen, 2008). In the Special Education Regulation (Art. 23), it is stated that classes with two individuals in need of special education at primary education level should not exceed 25 students, and classes with one individual should not exceed 35 students. However, it is not considered appropriate to have more than 2 inclusive students in inclusive classrooms (MoNE, 2006). Another issue that makes it difficult for disabled children to attend classes in mainstream schools is insufficient physical conditions (f = 11) such as the unavailability of elevators or wheelchair ramps. The final educational environment-related problem mentioned in the reviewed studies is the lack of support rooms (f = 2) where children with special needs can receive individualized instruction and support.

Community-related problems (f = 21) make up the fourth theme under problems for inclusive education in Turkey. The negative beliefs and attitudes towards children with special needs held by different sectors of the community resulting in a lack of social acceptance of these children (f = 7) forms the most frequent community-related issue. This may be related to the second code in this theme, which is the community members' lack of knowledge of inclusion (f = 5). The other problems that relate to the community are economic issues (f = 4), cultural issues (for the inclusion of Syrian kids) (f = 3), inadequate legislation (f = 1), and dropout of school due to child labor (Syrians) (f = 1).

An obvious issue that interferes with inclusion is the lack of proper teacher training activities in Turkey (f = 16). The most frequently mentioned problem is the lack/inadequacy of in-service training programs and activities (f = 9) such as seminars, conferences, and trainings. The inadequacy of the pre-service teacher training courses and activities (f = 7) that can professionally develop prospective teachers in proper utilization of inclusive practices is the second most frequently mentioned teacher training-related issue. It is observed in the reviewed reports that there are also student-related problems (f = 15) regarding inclusion. Foremost among them is the negative attitudes towards children with special needs by their

Table 3. Themes of the Problems Identified in Inclusive Education Literature in Turkey

Sub-themes	Code	Frequency
Educational system-related problems	Lack of support services	17
	Lack of communication with families	13
	Lack of equipment and materials	12
	Assessment and diagnostic issues	8
	Lack of collaboration among educational professionals	8
	Lack of real inclusion	7
	Improper methodology	6
	Insufficient curriculum	6
	Lack of administrative support	5
	Insufficient number of educational professionals	2
	Lack of individualized instruction	2
	Lack of educational transition planning	1
	Competitive educational atmosphere	1
	Total	88
Teacher-related problems	Lack of knowledge, understanding, skills, and experience about inclusion	30
	Negative attitudes towards children with special needs	6
	Classroom management issues	3
	Time management issues	2
	Low attendance for in-service trainings	1
	Total	42
Educational environment-related problems	Overcrowded classes	11
	Insufficient physical conditions	11
	Lack of support rooms	2
	Total	24
Community-related problems	Negative beliefs and attitudes towards children with special needs resulting in a lack of social acceptance	7
	Lack of knowledge of inclusion	5
	Economic issues	4
	Cultural issues (Syrians)	3
	Inadequate legislation	1
	Dropout of school (Syrians)	1
	Total	21
Teacher training-related problems	Insufficient in-service training	9
	Insufficient pre-service education	7
	Total	16
Student-related problems	Negative attitudes towards children with special needs by their peers	5
	Language barrier (Syrians)	4
	Characteristics of children with special needs	3
	Lack of motivation of inclusive students to receive support services	2
	Absenteeism due to child labor	1
	Total	15

Table 4. Themes of the Suggestions Provided in Inclusive Education Literature in Turkey

Sub-themes	Code	Frequency
Educational system-related suggestions	Developing better support services for teachers and students with special needs	14
	Preparing and utilizing individualized instruction	10
	Establishing better communication and collaboration among educational professionals	9
	Providing necessary equipment and materials	9
	Developing assessment and diagnosis of children with special needs	7
	Awareness raising for educational professionals about inclusion	7
	Ensuring the utilization of inclusive practices	6
	Development of the curriculum for better inclusive education	3
	Establishing better administrative support	1
	Developing vocational training programs for children with special needs	1
	Developing better communication with children with special needs	1
	Total	68
Teacher training-related suggestions	Offering more comprehensive in-service trainings	21
	Reorganization of pre-service teacher training programs	14
	Awareness raising for teachers about inclusion	10
	Providing teachers with graduate education on special education	1
	Developing teacher training personnel infrastructure	1
	Total	47
Community-related suggestions	Awareness raising for the community about inclusion	15
	Establishing better communication and collaboration with families	12
	Providing families with support services	2
	Providing families with financial assistance	1
	Total	30
Educational environment-related suggestions	Development of educational facilities	12
	Reducing class sizes	7
	Development of educational personnel capacity	3
	Total	22
Policy-related suggestions	Developing inclusive education policies and approaches	7
	Increasing the quantity and quality of special education personnel	5
	More financial support for inclusive education	2
	Developing research-based practices	1
	Better collaboration with non-governmental organizations to support inclusive education	1
	Developing the capacity of Counseling and Research Centers	1
	Ensuring school participation for immigrant children by preventing child labor	1
	Total	11
Student-related suggestions	Awareness raising for the peers about inclusion	7
	Total	7

peers (f = 5). Language barrier (of Syrians) (f = 4), characteristics of children with special needs (f = 3), lack of motivation of inclusive students to receive support services (f = 2), and absenteeism due to child labor (f = 1) are the other student-related issues that make it challenging for the proper utilization of inclusion. Among these one of the most challenging factors that complicates the inclusive education practices is the difference in the disability status of the students, and the most challenging is the education of students with mental disabilities. Most of the students in the teachers' classrooms have intellectual disability. There are also inclusion students with both mental and physical disabilities. In general, there is no great imbalance in the distribution of inclusive students by gender. Although most of the teachers stated that receiving additional support from Rehabilitation Research Centers according to the type of disability of the students within the scope of the inclusive education application, it has a very positive effect on their social and academic development, or that it will affect the social and academic development of the students, but most of the inclusion students do not receive any additional training from the Rehabilitation Research Centers according to the type of disability. Most of the students within the scope of the Inclusion Education Practice in the classrooms of the teachers participating in the research do not receive any additional support training from the Rehabilitation Research Centers regarding their disability

The Suggestions Provided for the Problems in Inclusive Education in K-12 Classes in Turkey

The suggestions provided in inclusive education literature in Turkey to eliminate the problems faced during inclusion practices were categorized under the following sub-themes in Table 4.

The second research question is related to suggestions provided in the reviewed reports to overcome problems regarding inclusive education in Turkey. As shown in Table 4, as a result of the systematic review of the 44 reports, we formed six sub-themes under which suggestions for the problems mentioned before were compiled: (1) educational system-related, (2) teacher training-related, (3) community-related, (4) educational environment-related, (5) policy-related, and (6) student-related suggestions. The most frequently stated suggestions are related to the educational system in Turkey (f = 68). The reports mostly suggested the development of better support services for teachers and students with special needs (f = 14). These support services involve support rooms, support personnel, and support activities. Preparing and utilizing individualized instruction (f = 10) came up as another valuable suggestion, since it has been established that children with special needs require individualized programs and interventions. It was also mentioned in many reports that there is room for improvement to facilitate better communication and collaboration among educational professionals (f = 9) to ensure better utilization of inclusive practices. The lack of necessary equipment and materials should be eliminated by the provision of these tools (f = 9). To better implement inclusive education, assessment and diagnosis tools that can enable the placement of children with special needs into mainstream education should be developed or improved (f = 7). It was also evident from the reports that awareness-raising activities for educational professionals about inclusion should also be an indispensable part of the inclusive education practices (f = 7). Other educational system-related suggestions are ensuring the utilization of inclusive practices (f = 6), development of the curriculum for better inclusive education (f = 3), establishing better administrative support (f = 1), developing vocational training programs for children with special needs (f = 1), and developing better communication with children with special needs (f = 1).

Teacher training-related suggestions formed the second most frequently mentioned group of propositions (f = 46). The authors of the reviewed reports mostly suggested the development of more comprehensive in-service trainings (f = 21). Then, they emphasized the need to reorganize pre-service teacher training programs (f = 14) so as to include more courses on special education. It was also suggested that there is a requirement for more comprehensive awareness raising activities for teachers about inclusion (f = 10). The other teacher training-related suggestions involve providing teachers with graduate education on special education (f = 1) and developing teacher training personnel infrastructure in undergraduate programs on special education (f = 1).

The need to create a community which better understands the case of children with special needs and inclusive education formed another theme (f = 30) in the suggestions. The reports mostly offer awareness-raising activities for the community about inclusion (f = 15). It is also contended that establishing better communication and collaboration with families (f = 12) will aid the utilization of inclusive educational practices. The other suggestions that are believed to contribute to inclusion are providing families with support services (f = 2) and financial assistance (f = 1).

The reviewed reports also put forward some educational environment-related suggestions (f = 22) to better implement inclusive education practices. Among these suggestions is the need to develop educational facilities (f = 12) to make them more inclusive education friendly. This can be achieved by making some structural adaptations in school buildings and classrooms such as wheelchair ramps which will enable disabled kids to more easily access educational services. Reducing class sizes (f = 7) is another educational environment-related suggestion that can contribute to the easier access of children with special needs to special education services provided by teachers. Finally, the development of educational personnel capacity (f = 3) at mainstream schools is also believed to help with inclusive educational issues.

It is also discovered in the review of the reports that higher-level policy-related interventions (f = 14) can also be made for better inclusive implementations. The most obvious of these interventions is the need to develop inclusive education policies and approaches that are more user-friendly (f = 7). Increasing the quantity and quality of special education personnel (f = 5) is another suggestion that is believed to contribute to the provision of special education services for inclusive students. The other suggestions put under this theme are more financial support for inclusive education (f = 2), developing research-based practices (f = 1), better collaboration with non-governmental organizations to support inclusive education (f = 1), developing the capacity of Counseling and Research Centers (f = 1), and ensuring school participation for immigrant children by preventing child labor (f = 1).

As a suggestion for the student-related problems detected in the studies, the analysis of the reports emphasizes the need for activities that can create awareness for the peers of children with special needs about inclusion (f = 7). Since inclusive students are being educated in the same environment with their normally developing peers, it is of prime importance to create cohesion between inclusive students and their peers.

In short, the results have revealed the problems and relevant suggestions about inclusive education in Turkey by systematically analyzing 44 research reports conducted within the past 13 years. The review produced six sub-themes in the problems and six sub-themes in the suggestions regarding inclusive education. A further inquiry into the codes revealed that the most commonly encountered educational system-related problems are lack of support services, lack of communication with families, and lack of equipment and materials. As for teacher-related problems, the most commonly stated ones are teachers' lack of knowledge, understanding, skills and experience about inclusion and teachers' negative attitudes towards children with special needs. The third sub-theme, educational environment-related problems, involves overcrowded classes and insufficient physical conditions. Community-related issues cover problems such as negative beliefs and attitudes towards children with special needs, lack of knowledge of inclusion on the part of the member of the community, and economic/cultural issues. The most outstanding teacher training-related problems are insufficient in-service and pre-service training. Finally, student-related problems involve negative attitudes towards children with special needs by their peers, language barrier (Syrians), and characteristics of children with special needs.

The most frequently mentioned suggestions under the first sub-theme are developing better support services for teachers and children with special needs, preparing and utilizing individualized instruction, establishing better communication and collaboration among educational professionals, providing necessary equipment and materials, developing assessment and diagnosis of children with special needs, and awareness raising for educational professionals about inclusion. Teacher training-related suggestions are offering more comprehensive in-service trainings, reorganization of pre-service teacher training programs, and awareness raising for teachers about inclusion. The most outstanding community-related suggestions are awareness raising for the community about inclusion and establishing better communication and collaboration with families. The most frequently observed educational environment-related suggestions are development of educational facilities and reducing class sizes. Policy-related suggestions involve developing inclusive education policies and approaches, increasing the quantity and quality of special education personnel, and more financial support for inclusive education. Finally, the student-related suggestion about inclusion is awareness raising for the peers of inclusive students.

All in all, it can be stated that the current review is a valuable contribution to the literature on inclusive education, since it accomplished to compile the problems related to inclusion in Turkey and suggestions for the elimination of these problems. There are some other review studies in the literature (e.g., Sari et al., 2020); however, none of these reports systematically analyzed the literature to find out the main challenges and potential solutions in the field of inclusive education in Turkey. In this respect, the current review diversifies from the previous ones and can be considered a starting point for further experimental and procedural interventions.

DISCUSSION, CONCLUSION AND SUGGESTIONS

When all studies were examined in line with the two main themes (the problems of inclusive education in K-12 classes in Turkey and the suggestions for inclusive education in K-12 classes in Turkey presented in the literature), six sub-themes in the problems and six sub-themes in the suggestions regarding inclusive education were observed. A further inquiry into the codes revealed that it has been concluded that although there are many studies to determine the existing problems of inclusive education in K-12 classes in Turkey, there are few studies carried out to find out the ways of eliminating the problems related to inclusion. Only one research study (Kirkic & Sayan, 2021) attempted to experimentally uncover the ways to deal with problems related to inclusive education. Having said this, the current review tried to uncover the problems related to inclusion in Turkey and the suggestions provided in the relevant literature to cope with these problems and challenges. The most commonly experienced group of problems regarding inclusion in the Turkish education system is educational-system related problems. Regarding these problems, lack of support services, lack of communication with families, and lack of equipment and materials are the ones which are the most commonly encountered (e.g., Deniz, 2018). The studies which have been carried out so far all reach the same conclusion: it is crucial that support services, including reorganized physical settings, educational materials and resources, social support from assistant teachers, and special education, should be available in the classroom and at the school level. They all have showed that it is an important issue that teachers teach the lesson according to the curriculum, but the participation of both student groups in the lesson activities together shows that IEP remains on paper and that the environment and materials in physical education and sports lessons are not suitable for inclusive students. Moreover, numerous researchers have concluded from their reviews that, to achieve inclusive practices, the availability of support services at the classroom and school levels, including modified physical environments, educational materials and resources, and social support from assistant teachers, special education teachers, and therapists, must be significantly increased (e.g., Eripek, 2003; Buchner & Thomspon, 2021). Shortly, further studies should focus on studying the ways to develop better support services for teachers and children with special needs, to enable teachers to prepare and utilize individualized instruction, to establish better communication and collaboration among educational professionals, to provide necessary equipment and materials, and to develop assessment and diagnosis of children with special needs, and awareness raising for educational professionals about inclusion.

The most commonly stated teacher-related problems are teachers' lack of knowledge, understanding, skills and experience about inclusion and teachers' negative attitudes towards children with special needs. In line with this finding, Carrington (1999) concluded that teachers' attitudes and values did have an impact on how they implemented inclusive education principles in their classrooms in the course of his study on inclusive practices. Among the factors that Carrington (1999) listed as having an impact on inclusive education practices include the relationship between special education professionals and general education teachers, the administrators' attitudes toward inclusive education, and teachers' level of confidence in selecting and putting into practice effective teaching methods. Moreover, Kircaali-İftar (1998) states that one of the most important conditions for the success of inclusive education practices is the full acceptance of students with special needs into the regular class. Students in the classroom should understand that the differences that the inclusive student has (such as hearing, learning or speaking difficulties, etc.) are similar to the individual differences that exist in each person. In addition, there should be no doubts that the inclusive student has the same right to be in that class as other students. Students should know that the help they provide to the mainstreaming student will contribute to their academic and social development. In the study conducted by Diker et al. (2009), the fact that elementary teachers were unable to receive sufficient support from RAM (Counseling and Research Center) was expressed by indicating that these institutions did not work properly and that they were not able to receive support from these institutions. When the teacher-related problems are taken into account, it is not surprising to find out that the most outstanding teacher training-related problems are insufficient in-service and pre-service training. Teacher training-related suggestions should focus on ways to offer more comprehensive in-service trainings, reorganization of pre-service teacher training programs, and awareness raising for teachers about inclusion. Conducted studies indicated that teachers were in need of detailed information regarding inclusive education applications (Yikmis, et al., 1998; Metin et al., 2009), and that the related training given increased the proficiency of the teachers (Mrsnik, 2003) and provided a positive change in the attitudes of the teachers (Batu et al., 1998; Metin et al., 2009; Yikmiş et al., 1998b). As for the most commonly encountered educational environment-related problems, in order to combat overcrowded classes and insufficient physical conditions, class sizes should be reduced and also classroom settings or educational facilities should be developed in accordance with students with special requirement. Students with special requirement should be regularly observed (Timucin, 1998; Horne & Timmons, 2009).

Negative beliefs and attitudes towards children with special needs, lack of knowledge of inclusion on the part of the member of the community, and economic/cultural issues are among the most commonly encountered community-related problems. The most outstanding community-related suggestions are awareness raising for the community about inclusion and establishing better communication and collaboration with families. Important point here is that school and parents should be in constant communication to improve the inclusion practices. For this reason, school administrators and teachers should be given in-service training on inclusive education practices and also student groups and their parents, namely both groups should participate in these training activities. Additionally, effective cooperation between the Rehabilitation Research Centers and the school and the teacher should be ensured and controlled at every stage. The achievement of academic and social goals determined in the individualized education programs of Rehabilitation Research Centers and schools should be followed and evaluated based on the pre-established success criteria.

Student-related issues cover problems such as negative attitudes towards children with special needs by their peers, language barrier (Syrians), and characteristics of children with special needs. As for one issue of this problem, Polat (2020) found that peers make fun of those with special needs, do not include them in the games, apply physical and verbal violence. Students without special needs and inclusion students are proposed to have expectations such as having private teachers, namely teachers who are more moderate, playing games with their peers, their peers being more respectful and understanding, having various courses for physical education and sports, materials and gymnasium. Inclusion of these students in games in these lessons is utmost importance without isolating themes from their peers in the games, or other activities ensuring their active participation. So, training should be given on mainstreaming practices, especially on the awareness rising of parents and students, the presence of experts in the institution, the appointment of assistant teachers, the increase of artistic and sports activities. Inclusion practices should be designed to provide gains such as the development of empathy skills of students with normal development, gaining awareness and living in the same environment with different individuals.

In conclusion, in order to improve inclusion practices and combat the problems of inclusion, all parties should be in collaboration with each other and trainings to all parties should be given on mainstreaming practices. It is necessary to have a special education expert in every school where inclusive education is applied and for the schools without an expert mobile special education expert practice should be exercised in a more planned and effective manner to provide help when necessary.

REFERENCES

Akalin, S., Demir, S., Sucuoglu, B., Bakkaloglu, H., & Iscen, F. (2014). The needs of inclusive pre-school teachers about inclusive practices. *Eurasian Journal of Educational Research*, *54*(54), 39–60. doi:10.14689/ejer.2014.54.3

Akkoyun, K. A. (2007*). The Mainstreaming of the Guidance Research Center Staff His Views on Education* [Unpublished master's thesis]. Abant İzzet Baysal University, Bolu, Turkey.

Aktan, O. (2021). Teachers' Opinions towards Inclusive Education Interventions in Turkey. *Anatolian Journal of Education*, *6*(1), 29–50. doi:10.29333/aje.2021.613a

Aktan, O., Budak, Y., & Bakygul Botabekova, A. (2019). Determination of social acceptance levels of primary school students towards inclusive students: A mixed method study. *Elementary Education Online*, *18*(4), 1520–1538.

Atıcı, R. (2014, Spring). Challenges faced by inclusive students during their school life. *Turkish Studies - International Periodical for the Languages, Literature and History of Turkish or Turkic, 9*(5), 279–291.

Batu, E. S., & Kircaali-Iftar, G. (2005). *Inclusion*. Kök Publications.

Batu, S., Kircaali Iftar, G., & Uzuner, Y. (1998). *The opinions and suggestions of teachers in a vocational high school for girls, where special needs bodies are integrated* [Paper presentation]. *8th National Special Education Congress*, Edirne, Turkey.

Bayram, B., & Oztürk, M. (2021). Opinions and practices of social studies teachers on inclusive education. *Education in Science, 206*(46), 355–377.

Birol, Z. N., & Aksoy Zor, E. (2018). Views of classroom teachers on the problems they have with their students with special learning disabilities. *Journal of Gazi Faculty of Education, 38*(3), 887–918.

Bowen, G. A. (2009). Document analysis as a qualitative research method. *Qualitative Research Journal, 9*(2), 27–40. doi:10.3316/QRJ0902027

Buchner, T., & Thompson, S. A. (2021). From plot twists, progress, and the persistence of segregated education: The continuing struggle for inclusive education in relation to students with intellectual disabilities. *Journal of Policy and Practice in Intellectual Disabilities, 18*(1), 4–6. doi:10.1111/jppi.12378

Burunsuz, E., & Ince, M. (2020). Teachers' views on the implementation of the individualized education program of teachers working in primary schools. *Mediterranean Journal of Educational Research, 31*(14), 530–544. doi:10.29329/mjer.2020.234.25

Carrington, C. (1999). *No place like home: Relationships and family life among lesbians and gay men.* University of Chicago Press. doi:10.7208/chicago/9780226094847.001.0001

Celik, R. (2016). Curriculum elements of a politically liberal education in a developing democracy. *Educational Philosophy and Theory, 48*(14), 1464–1474. doi:10.1080/00131857.2016.1160356

Celik, S., Kardas Işler, N., & Saka, D. (2021). Refugee education in Turkey: Barriers and suggested solutions. *Pedagogy, Culture & Society*, 1–19. Advance online publication. doi:10.1080/14681366.2021.1947878

Cengiz Sayan, E. (2020). *Preschool teachers' opinions about inclusive education* [Unpublished master's thesis]. Pamukkale University Graduate School of Educational Sciences, Denizli, Turkey.

Choi, S., & Lee, S. W. (2020). Enhancing teacher self-efficacy in multicultural classrooms and school climate: The role of professional development in multicultural education in the United States and South Korea. *AERA Open, 6*(4), 1–17. doi:10.1177/2332858420973574

Ciyer, A. (2010). *Developing inclusive education policies and practices in Turkey, A study of the roles of UNESCO and local educators* [Unpublished doctoral dissertation]. Arizona State University, Tempe, AZ.

Coskun, Y. D., Tosun, U., & Macaroglu, E. (2009). Classroom teachers' styles of using and development materials of inclusive education. *Procedia: Social and Behavioral Sciences, 1*(1), 2758–2762. doi:10.1016/j.sbspro.2009.01.489

Demir, M. K., & Acar, S. (2011). Opinions of experienced classroom teachers about inclusive education. *Kastamonu Journal of Education, 19*(3), 719–732.

Diken, I. H., Rakap, S., Diken, O., Tomris, G., & Celik, S. (2016). Early childhood inclusion in Turkey. *Infants and Young Children, 29*(3), 231–238. doi:10.1097/IYC.0000000000000065

Diker Coskun, Y., Tosun, U., & Macaroglu, E. (2009). Classroom teachers' styles of using and development materials of inclusive education. *Procedia: Social and Behavioral Sciences, 1*(1), 2758–2762. doi:10.1016/j.sbspro.2009.01.489

Duskun, Y. (2016). *Inclusive education situation analysis in secondary education in Turkey.* Education Reform Initiative.

Emin, M. N. (2019). *Construction of future: Education of Syrian children in Turkey.* Seta Publishing.

Eripek, S. (2003). *Special education in preschool period.* Anadolu University Open Education Faculty Publication.

Ersoy, O., & Avcı, N. (2000). Children with special needs and their education. Special Education. Yapa Publications.

Esmer, B., Yılmaz, E., Gunes, A. M., Tarim, K., & Delican, B. (2017). Classroom teachers' experiences towards inclusive students' education. *Kastamonu Journal of Education, 25*(4), 1601–1618.

Fisher, D., Frey, N., & Thousand, J. (2003). What do special educators need to know and be prepared to do for inclusive schooling to work? *Teacher Education and Special Education, 26*(1), 42–55. doi:10.1177/088840640302600105

Gelir, I. (2021). Examining the Turkish preschool education program from an inclusive perspective. *HAYEF: Journal of Education, 18*(1), 55–65. doi:10.5152/hayef.2021.20028

General Directorate of Disabled and Elderly Services. (2016). *Statistical information of disabled and senior individuals.* Retrieved from http://eyh.aile.gov.tr/data/ 56179f30369dc5726c063e73/Bulletin_July2016.pdf

Gezer, M. S., & Aksoy, V. (2019). Perceptions of Turkish preschool teachers about their roles within the context of inclusive education. *International Journal of Early Childhood Special Education, 11*(1), 31–42. doi:10.20489/intjecse.583541

Gol, H., & Sakiz, H. (2020). Designing the guidance program of pre-school education in line with the principles of inclusive education. *Qualitative Social Sciences, 2*(2), 90–115.

Gulec Aslan, Y. (2020). Experiences of Turkish preschool teachers for including children with autism spectrum disorders: Challenges faced and methods used. *International Journal of Psychology and Educational Studies, 7*(2), 37–49. doi:10.17220/ijpes.2020.02.004

Hauwadhanasuk, T., Karnas, M., & Zhuang, M. (2018). Inclusive education plans and practices in China, Thailand, and Turkey. *Educational Planning, 25*(1), 29–48.

Horne, P., & Timmons, V. (2009). Making it work: Teachers' perspectives on inclusion. *International Journal of Inclusive Education, 13*(3), 273–286. doi:10.1080/13603110701433964

Ilik, S. S., & Deniz, S. (2020). Observations of prospective teachers from different branches about inclusion practices during teaching practice. *Kastamonu Education Journal, 28*(1), 338–351. doi:10.24106/kefdergi.3611

Ilik, S. S., & Hacieminoglu, E. (2019). Evaluation of elementary science teachers' perceptions regarding inclusive education application. *Journal of Education and Training Studies, 7*(1), 19–29. doi:10.11114/jets.v7i10.4396

Kahriman, P. D., & Bal, M. (2019). Identifying pre-school teachers' opinions on the language development process of children in inclusive education. *National Education, 48*(1), 737–754.

Kahya, O., & Hosgorur, V. (2018). Comparing inclusive education in Turkey and Argentina. *International Online Journal of Education & Teaching, 5*(1), 82–92.

Kaptan, O. (2019). *Determining the difficulties faced by the teachers who teach in the support training room for individuals with special needs in mainstreaming schools* [Unpublished master's thesis]. Necmettin Erbakan University, Konya, Turkey.

Karacaoglu, I. (2008). *Investigation of the relationship between primary school teachers' perceptions of school climate and their attitudes towards inclusion* [Unpublished master's thesis]. Yeditepe University Graduate School of Educational Sciences, Istanbul, Turkey.

Karadag Yilmaz, R., & Yeganeh, E. (2021). Who and how do I include? A case study on teachers' inclusive education practices. *International Journal of Progressive Education, 17*(2), 406–429. doi:10.29329/ijpe.2021.332.25

Kargin, T. (2004). Inclusion: Definition, Development and Principles. Ankara University Faculty of Educational Sciences Journal of Special Education, 5(2). doi:10.1501/Ozlegt_0000000080

Karnas, M., & Bayar, A. (2013a). *The collaboration between general and special education teachers and principal's role in this process* [Paper presentation]. Vth International Congress of Educational Research: Peace, Memory & Education, Canakkale, Turkey.

Karnas, M., & Bayar, A. (2013b). *Turkish elementary teachers' perspective of students with disabilities in general education classrooms* [Paper presentation]. Vth International Congress of Educational Research: Peace, Memory & Education Research, Çanakkale, Turkey.

Karsli-Calamak, E., & Kilinc, S. (2021). Becoming the teacher of a refugee child: Teachers' evolving experiences in Turkey. *International Journal of Inclusive Education, 25*(2), 259–282. doi:10.1080/13603116.2019.1707307

Katitas, S., & Coskun, B. (2020). What is meant by inclusive education? Perceptions of Turkish teachers towards inclusive education. *World Journal of Education, 10*(5), 18–28. doi:10.5430/wje.v10n5p18

Kaysili, A., Soylu, A., & Sever, M. (2019). Exploring major roadblocks on inclusive education of Syrian refugees in school settings. *Turkish Journal of Education, 8*(2), 109–128. doi:10.19128/turje.496261

Keser, F., & Tanriverdi, A. (2019). Determining support services received by individuals with special needs living in Mardin and İstanbul. *The Journal of International Social Research, 12*(62), 1058–1066. doi:10.17719/jisr.2019.3118

Kırcaali-Iftar, G. (1998). Individuals with special needs and special education. In S. Eripek (Ed.), *Special education* (pp. 1–14). Anadolu University Publications.

Kirkic, K. A., & Sayan, A. (2020). Investigation of the effect of the education given in the support education rooms on the development of preschool inclusion students. *Turkish Studies*, *15*(2), 1121–1136. https://doi.org/10.29228/TurkishStudies.29348

Kiziloglu, Y. (2021). *Potentialities for and limits to inclusion by education: The case of Syrian children's education in Turkey and child labor* [Unpublished master's thesis]. Middle East Technical University, Ankara, Turkey.

Kutay, V. (2018). Inclusive education in Turkey. *Studies in Educational Research and Development*, *2*(2), 144–162.

Lancaster, J., & Bain, A. (2007). The design of inclusive education courses and the self-efficacy of preservice teacher education students. *International Journal of Disability Development and Education*, *54*(2), 245–256. https://doi.org/10.1080/10349120701330610

Loreman, T., & Earle, C. (2007). The development of attitudes, sentiments and concerns about inclusive education in a content-infused Canadian teacher preparation program. *Exceptionality Education Canada*, *17*(1/2), 85–106.

Melekoglu, M. A. (2014). Special education in Turkey. *Special Education International Perspectives: Practices Across the Globe. Advances in Special Education*, *28*, 529–557. https://doi.org/10.1108/S0270-401320140000028024

Mete, P. (2020). The views of students in an inclusive classroom environment in high school on the course learning process. *Elementary Education Online*, *19*(2), 552–564.

Metin, N., Gulec, H., & Sahin, C. (2009). *Determining the competencies of primary school teachers after in-service training for the integration of mentally handicapped children* [Paper presentation]. *1st International Turkey Educational Research Congress*, Canakkale, Turkey.

Mitchell, D. R. (Ed.). (2004). *Special educational needs and inclusive education: Inclusive education* (Vol. 2). Taylor & Francis.

Mrsnik, K. O. (2003). *A case study of the effects of the interactive change model for inclusion on the development of teacher efficacy and teachers' willingness to implement inclusive practices* [Unpublished doctoral dissertation]. Cleveland State University.

Ozokcu, O. (2018). Investigating classroom teachers' attitudes towards inclusion. *Inonu University Journal of the Faculty of Education, 19*(3), 418-433. doi:10.17679/inuefd.472639

Polat, S. (2020). Multicultural structure of schools and intercultural education. In *Empowering multiculturalism and peacebuilding in schools* (pp. 61–85). IGI Global.

Ramo, A. N., Karovska, R., Rashikj, A., & Canevska, O. (2020). Training and competencies of special educators in Turkey and other countries. *Turkish Studies -Education, 15*(6), 4459-4473. doi:10.47423/TurkishStudies.4

Ryan, G. W., & Bernard, H. R. (2000). Data management and analysis methods. In N. Denzin & Y. Lincoln (Eds.), Handbook of qualitative research (pp. 769–802). Sage.

Sadioglu, O., Bilgin, A., Batu, S., & Oksal, A. (2013). Problems, expectations, and suggestions of elementary teachers regarding inclusion. *Educational Sciences: Theory and Practice, 13*(3), 1760–1765.

Sakiz, H. (2016). Thinking change inclusively: Views of educational administrators on inclusive education as a reform initiative. *Journal of Education and Training Studies, 4*(5), 64–75.

Sakiz, H., & Woods, C. (2014). From thinking to practice: School staff views on disability inclusion in Turkey. *European Journal of Special Needs Education, 29*(2), 135–152. https://doi.org/10.1080/08856 257.2014.882058

Sakiz, H., & Woods, C. (2015). Achieving inclusion of students with disabilities in Turkey: Current challenges and future prospects. *International Journal of Inclusive Education, 19*(1), 21–35. https://doi. org/10.1080/13603116.2014.902122

Sari, T., Nayir, F., & Kahraman, U. (2020). A Study on inclusive education. *Journal of Education and Future Year, 18*, 69-82.

Singh, R. (2009). Meeting the challenge of inclusion—from isolation to collaboration. *Inclusive education across cultures: Crossing boundaries, sharing ideas*, 12-29.

Sorkos, G., & Hajisoteriou, C. (2020). Sustainable intercultural and inclusive education: Teachers' efforts on promoting a combining paradigm. *Pedagogy, Culture & Society, 29*(4), 1–20. https://doi.org/ 10.1080/14681366.2020.1765193

Tarnoto, N. (2016). Permasalahan-permasalahan yang dihadapi sekolah penyelenggara pendidikan inklusi pada tingkat SD. *Humanitas. Jurnal Psikologi Indonesia, 13*(1), 50–61.

Tekinarslan, I. C., Sivrikaya, T., Keskin, N. K., Ozlu, O., & Ucar Rasmussen, M. (2018). Determining the needs of parents with children in inclusive education. *Elementary Education Online, 17*(1), 82–101.

Terzi, L. (2008). Justice and equality in education: A capability perspective on disability and special educational needs. *Continuum.*

Terzi, L. (2014). Reframing inclusive education: Educational equality as capability equality. *Cambridge Journal of Education, 44*(4), 479–493.

Timucin, E. (1998). *Inclusion in Turkey, existing practices and what needs to be done to achieve inclusion* [Paper presentation]. *8th National Special Education Congress*, Edirne, Turkey.

Ugurlu, H. E. (2017). *Inclusion of students with learning and behavior problems: knowledge, attitudes, and inclusive practices in Turkey* [Unpublished master's thesis]. University of Massachusetts, Amherst, MA.

Unal, R., & Aladag, S. (2020). Investigation of problems and solution proposals in the context of inclusive education practices. *Journal of Interdisciplinary Education: Theory and Practice, 2*(1), 23–42.

UNESCO. (1994). *The Salamanca Statement and Framework for Action on Special Needs Education.* Retrieved from http://www.unesco.org/education/pdf/SALAMA_E.PDF

UNESCO. (2009). *Policy Guidelines on Inclusion in Education.* Retrieved from http://www.inclusive-education-in-ction.org/iea/dokumente/up load/72074_177849e.pdf

UNESCO. (2011). *UNESCO and Education.* Retrieved from https://unesdoc.unesco.org/images/0021/002127/212715e.pdf

UNICEF. (2019). *Syrian children in Turkey.* Retrieved from https://www.unicefturk.org/yazi/acil-durum-turkiyedeki-suriy eli-cocuklar

Uygur, M., Aycicek, B., Dogrul, H., & Yanpar Yelken, T. (2020). Investigating stakeholders' views on technology integration: The role of educational leadership for sustainable inclusive education. *Sustaniablity, 12,* 10354. doi:10.3390/su122410354

Villa, R. A., Thousand, J. S., & Chapple, J. W. (2000). Preparing educators to implement inclusive practices. In R. A. Villa & J. S. Thousand (Eds.), *Restructuring for caring and effective education: Piecing the puzzle together* (2nd ed., pp. 531–557). Paul H. Brookes.

Vural, D., Piskin, N. B., & Durmusoglu, M. C. (2021). Problems and practices experienced by preschool teachers in inclusive education. *International Journal of Curriculum and Instructional Studies, 11*(2), 287–308. https://doi.org/10.31704/ijocis.2021.014

Westwood, P. (2013). *Inclusive and adaptive teaching: meeting the challenge of diversity in the classroom.* Routledge.

Yaman, A. (2017). *Determining the opinions of classroom teachers on the development and implementation of individualized education programs for students educated with the inclusion model* [Unpublished master's thesis]. Necmettin Erbakan University, Konya, Turkey.

Yazcayir, G., & Gurgur, H. (2021). Students with Special Needs in Digital Classrooms during the COVID-19 Pandemic in Turkey. *Pedagogical Research, 6*(1), em0088. doi:10.29333/pr/9356

Yikmiss, A., Sahbaz, U., & Peker, S. (1998). *The effect of in-service training programs on teachers' attitudes towards inclusion* [Paper presentation]. *8th National Special Education Congress,* Edirne, Turkey.

Yildirim, E., & Merey, Z. (2020). Inclusive Education. In I. Kozikoglu (Ed.), *Current approaches in education* (pp. 1-16). Pegem. Retrieved from www.onceokuloncesi.com/.../9b084d96d5254342f0e3f88ae24e/4a3.doc

Yilmaz, E., & Batu, E. S. (2016). Opinions of primary school teachers from different branches about individualized education program, legal regulations and inclusion practices. *The Journal of Special Education, 17*(3), 247–268.

Yilmaz, E., & Melekoglu, M. A. (2018). Evaluation of the status of inclusive education in law and practice in Turkey and the European context. *Osmangazi Journal of Educational Research, 5*(1), 1–17.

Chapter 11
Bringing the Margins to the Forefront:
Exploring Social Justice and Identity With Preservice Teachers

Deborah Bruns
https://orcid.org/0000-0002-9794-3659
Southern Illinois University, USA

Heidi R. Bacon
https://orcid.org/0000-0001-5958-212X
Southern Illinois University, USA

ABSTRACT

Focusing on content, pedagogy, and dispositions, individually and collectively, with preservice teachers contributes to understanding the intersectionality of identities and structural inequities. In this chapter, the authors describe their backgrounds as an entry point to teaching about social justice and identity in their courses. They share guiding theoretical perspectives used to ground their practice and build classroom communities with preservice teachers. The authors emphasize content, applied assignments, and activities to build an understanding of social justice and equity and bring students closer to understanding their life experiences and their impact when working with students and families. This chapter offers a means to bring the margins to the forefront in preservice teacher education to affect lasting change in how preparation can better address educational inequities in schools and communities.

INTRODUCTION

In our work with preservice teachers, we, Deborah and Heidi, have noticed a reticence to engage with topics of social justice and identities. These topics often raise a range of feelings and perspectives. They are familiar and easily observed. Students make their feelings and opinions known during class discus-

DOI: 10.4018/978-1-6684-6386-4.ch011

sions, in online forums, and through course artifacts. Students' beliefs tend to be strongly held and surface when reading about or discussing working class and marginalized students and families. Despite the challenges of engaging with these topics, they are important to consider, unpack, discuss, and analyze when preparing teachers to work with children and families.

The historical impact of marginalization calls for meaningful change to challenge the status quo. Despite the demographic shift in U.S. schools, the preponderance of teachers including those in urban schools are typically white, female, and often ill-prepared to work with diverse learners (Durand & Tavaras, 2021; Sleeter, 2017). Zeichner (2019) explains that teacher preparation 1.0 focused on clinical practice, while 2.0 emphasized instructional strategies and classroom management with the aim of raising test scores. Although strategies, curricula, and materials are important, they must reflect a critical orientation and practice within a social justice framework (Nieto, 2011; Zeichner, 2019). Moreover, Zeichner and Nieto (2011) argue, and we agree, that teacher educators must prepare teachers to work with students' families, draw on community resources and expertise, and commit to practicing the values consistent with equity and social justice.

Preparing socially just minded teachers is inclusive and centered on the collective (see Milner, 2008; Sleeter 2017). Being inclusive is a matter of access that promotes community and belonging while honoring individuals' lived experiences (Cobb & Krownapple, 2019). As actions are socially, culturally, and historically mediated, inclusion as a means of social justice entails awareness of intersectional identities (Artiles et al., 2006). But defining inclusion and what it means for students, with and without disabilities, can be complicated especially in relation to social justice. To this end, Pugach et al. (2021) advance the following definition of social justice:

[It] embraces the complex, intersectional identities of individuals, and the rich histories of communities, in the redistribution of resources and educational opportunities for all students, through a transformative process that disrupts the marginalization of non-dominant social groups [emphasis in original]. (p. 238)

We situate Pugach et al.'s definition of social justice within Cochran-Smith's (2010) framework of social justice as a theory of practice, which "characterizes the relationship of teaching and learning, the nature of teachers' work, and the knowledge, strategies, and values that inform teachers' efforts for social justice" (p. 446). It is the *how* and *why* of developing a social justice mindset with the potential to impact both the present and the future.

To effect meaningful change, Zeichner (2019) calls for teacher educators and teacher education programs to demonstrate a commitment to social justice that elevates the voices of marginalized leaners and students with disabilities. Although these ideas are not new, they have not generated a continuous dialogue or solidarity among teacher educators who focus on diversity, disability, multi-cultural education, and social justice (Pugach et al., 2021). Creating a conversation that focuses on content, pedagogy, and dispositions, individually and collectively, can contribute to understanding the intersectionality of identities and structural inequities, overrepresentation in special education, and the persistence of deficit discourses and tropes (Artiles, 2022). Thus, to bring about transformative and *lasting* change, we approach instruction intentionality to provide the necessary depth and breadth and to raise awareness and build and deepen understanding about equity and justice (Arao, & Clemens, 2013; Francis et al., 2017; Kavanagh, & Danielson, 2020; Kinloch et al., 2021; McDonald, & Zeichner, 2009).

Transformational change in teacher education is rooted in discussion and reflection and includes taking action through purposeful practice (see Dana & Yendol-Hoppey, 2020). It involves curiosity and desire and grows over time through experience. Like O'Connor and Daniello (2019), we explicitly name the social justice ends to which we work and highlight how we get there. In our courses, the curriculum is not static. We provide concrete strategies that can open minds, shift discourses, and influence preservice teachers' practice. We hope this combination of theoretical perspectives and exploration of content, course activities, and practices can contribute to growing informed, empathetic teachers who will work to disrupt systemic and structural inequities and advocate for students, families, and communities. As students typically don't know what they don't know, they need opportunities to examine their existing funds of knowledge, the historical and cultural knowledge present in families and communities (González al., 2005), learn about people unlike themselves, and, ultimately, embrace the unfamiliar.

In this chapter, we share our backgrounds and how we came to focus on social justice and equity in two of our teacher preparation courses that we believe align with the ideas outlined above. We begin with an overview of the theoretical perspectives that ground our practice and explain our positionality and the setting in which we work. We describe how we build classroom communities with preservice teachers and prepare them to be *in* community with children and families. We further explain how we work with students to identify local resources and community assets, conduct ethnographic interviews, and communicate with parents and community members in a space that enables them to explore their own multiple and dynamic identities. The chapter concludes with implications for practice and a call to action.

Bringing Who We Are Into What and How We Teach

We are teacher educators who teach across two university initial licensure programs. Deborah is a special education professor, and Heidi teaches courses in language, literacies, and culture. Our teaching employs a critical stance, and we weave social justice and identities into the framework of the focal courses highlighted in this chapter. It reflects the stance of reality as dynamic and a commitment to better serving the needs of students, families, and communities (Nieto, 2011; Kinloch et al., 2021).

The first course, a home-school coordination course in special education, is taught by Deborah, and the second, a child, family, and community engagement course, is taught by Heidi. We pool our experiences teaching early childhood and elementary education majors at a rural Midwestern university. Our students are typically first-generation and place-based who often come with little knowledge beyond their geographical locale, its inhabitants, and its local traditions. Our backgrounds, who we are, have shaped the *how* and *why* of what we teach and our approach to working with marginalized children and families.

Navigating Worlds and Differences

As the first in her family to complete high school and attend college, education was always emphasized in Deborah's home. Her parents grew up in Eastern Europe during World War II and left during the Hungarian Revolution in 1956. As a first generation American, she navigated two worlds. Although her parents sought to assimilate, Deborah did not speak English until kindergarten. Her grandmothers played a large role in caregiving in her early years. They refused to learn English so Hungarian was spoken in the home until Deborah entered school. Deborah's peers helped her learn English, as she had no siblings and most of her family's social circle were also Hungarian immigrants.

Deborah completed her undergraduate and master's degrees in special education. During the latter, she worked full time as an educational therapist with young children with significant developmental delays and health needs in a medical facility in Manhattan. Deborah met many local parents and families from outside the United States (e.g., South Korea, India, Mexico) and learned a number of life lessons from their experiences. She felt fortunate that her circumstances were different than those of her parents and the families with whom she worked. For example, her mother and father had several narrow escapes from the Nazis as young children. They also talked about food shortages they experienced as children and when Hungary was invaded by Russian soldiers. Deborah's parents instilled the importance of appreciating what one has, no matter how much or how little. Many families with whom Deborah worked lived in poverty, experienced substance use, and were sometimes involved in illegal activities. In contrast to her experiences and worldview, she learned that one does not have to agree with the choices people make to empathize or collaborate with families on behalf of children with a disability.

Deborah lived in Queens, New York City (NYC) until relocating to the Midwest to work on her doctorate. It was quite a shift in terms of adjusting to the slower pace and learning that most of the country functions differently than the hustle and bustle of NYC. As such, her pedagogy leans toward exploration of the unfamiliar while drawing parallels to her upbringing and the intersection of one's background, context, and cultural milieu as described by Artiles (2019), Nieto (2011), and, and Pugach et al. (2021).

After moving to Southern Illinois, Deborah was struck by the depth and breadth of social and educational inequities. Despite witnessing many instances of haves and have nots in NYC, there were programs and agencies to step in and address food insecurity and other needs. In rural Illinois, however, assistance tends to be spotty, and public transportation is limited or non-existent. When agencies cut back or eliminate programs and services, there are often no temporary measures to mitigate gaps in service. As such, families may need to travel several hours to access needed resources.

Heidi is the only child of German parents who immigrated to the U.S. after World War II. The child of a Holocaust survivor, she is a first-generation citizen and a first-generation college student. Her mother had the equivalent of a high school education in Germany, but the war interrupted any plans to continue her education. Heidi's father began his apprenticeship as a tool and die maker in his early teens and eventually achieved the status of master craftsman before he was forcibly interned. As such, Heidi was a late in life child whose only extended family in the U.S. was considerably older. She grew up in a large Midwestern industrial city, and although her family followed many German customs and ate traditional foods, Heidi's parents assimilated to life in the U.S. and spoke English in the home.

Heidi's parents likely experienced post-traumatic stress due to their war experiences and eventually divorced when she was in her teens. She found herself without a home living in the margins of society. A high school dropout, she married early, divorced, and supported herself by working a series of restaurant jobs. Heidi later remarried, obtained her GED, and began taking courses at the local community college. She later relocated with her husband and children to the Southwestern United States where she lived for 16 years.

As a non-traditional working wife and mother, Heidi earned her associate's, bachelor's, post-baccalaureate teaching certificate, master's, and doctoral degrees. Along the way, she began volunteering as an adult literacy tutor. As a volunteer tutor and high school teacher at a charter school, Heidi too witnessed structural and systemic poverty and educational inequities that supported opportunities for some while denying them to others. The majority of her students came from racialized and marginalized communities. The adults and students with whom she worked were mostly first, second, or third-generation immigrants and Spanish dominant bilinguals (see Bacon, 2016; Bacon & Byfield, 2018; Bacon & Kaya, 2018; Bacon et al., 2019).

The charter school where Heidi taught for eight years had a Learn and Serve service-learning grant, and regardless of how many or few resources her students had, they and their families made time to support the school's service mission. Service-learning was a student/family/school engagement activity (Bacon, 2016) . Heidi's work at the charter school and her leadership on a community-wide literacy initiative laid the foundation for becoming a teacher educator. Over the years, she worked with many families who valued, cared about, and sacrificed for their children's education, and these experiences led her to focus her teaching and research on grassroots advocacy and activism to advance educational equity for women, children, and families.

Contextualizing Our Experience

We have lived in Southern Illinois for 20 and eight years, respectively. The region where we live and work is included in the Delta Regional Authority, a federal poverty designation (see Delta Regional Authority link: http://dra.gov/about-dra/mission-and-vision). Illinois counties in the Delta Regional Authority have some of the highest poverty rates in the country with limited access to social, health, and municipal services. As noted, public transportation is limited or non-existent. Population estimates across the 8 counties in Southern Illinois number 241,766 with an average white only population of 65.2% in the least densely populated county (5085) to 91.3% in the most densely populated county (66, 879) (U.S. Census Bureau Facts, 2021). Although this demographic data is limited in scope, the statistics cited are representative of a mostly white, rural population.

The region has a long history of racial strife dating back to Reconstruction as evidenced by the presence of former and active sundown towns, which Loewen (2005) describes as "any or organized jurisdiction that for decades kept African Americans or other groups from living in it and was thus 'all-white' on purpose" (p. 4). Sundown towns appeared and proliferated at the end of the Civil War, and some have maintained their historical legacy. The loss of coal and manufacturing jobs in recent decades has further impacted the region (see Russell, 2012), leading to a backlash against immigrants and marginalized groups (see Bacon & Byfield, 2018). Given the region's history, racialized ideologies and discourses often become normalized (Bacon & Byfield, 2018). We therefore raise these issues because students who enter the university with little exposure to diversity frequently struggle to understand individuals whose experiences are different from their own.

CREATING A CONTEXT FOR SOCIAL JUSTICE AND IDENTITY

Sociocultural theory grounds our perspectives on practice. We build from Scribner and Cole (1981, as cited in Kavanagh & Danielson, 2020) who conceive of practice as socially and culturally mediated ways of "knowing, being, and doing" (p. 71). Through this lens, Moll (2014) reminds us that education "makes us not only what we are but who we are, and who we think we are" (p. 1), connecting identities and practice. Teachers typically tend to enact practices grounded in their personal histories, but the practice of teaching can also enable them to become agents who challenge social structures and norms (Kavanagh & Danielson, 2020). Kavanagh and Danielson (2020) point out that teaching within a social justice framework involves disrupting the macro and microstructures that perpetuate social inequities and oppression.

Within this grounding, we employ a multiperspectival approach that draws on ecological theory, multicultural perspectives, and funds of knowledge to frame our teaching around social justice in teacher preparation. Cochran-Smith (2010) defined a multiperspectival approach as "critical perspectives" combined with "anti-oppressive practices" (p. 449). Thus, we conceptualize knowledge, learning, and practice as socially situated, constructed, and shared with students, families, and communities (Lynch & Prins, 2022). These perspectives are nonjudgmental and value the primary language, knowledge, and cultures of children and families. We are mindful that to "achieve socially just teaching, the intricacies of students' multiple and intersecting identities—disability among them—need to be acknowledged and understood in relationship to all other markers, and in relationship to the institutional and political structures within which they exist (Pugach et al., 2021, p. 238). As students and families rely on schools to provide opportunities for academic and social success, it is important to consider how systems and institutional influence children and families and impact school curriculum and interactions (see Bronfenbrenner, 1997; Lynch & Prins, 2022; Milner et al., 2022).

Ecological Systems Framework

Bronfenbrenner's (1977) ecological framework is central to teacher preparation and Deborah and Heidi's courses, as it encourages preservice teachers to self-examine past and current systems that impact their development as individuals in a sociocultural context. It also assists them in developing an understanding of the systems affecting children in their care. Bronfenbrenner's (1977) theory posits the need to examine the relationships, influences, services, and supports placing the person at its center. The first level (microsystem) examines the interplay of family, community, and school, a key tenet for developing relationships with families. The mesosystem emphasizes communication and interaction among these entities. This framework is undergirded by the direct and indirect impacts of these systems on the child.

Discussing the availability of resources in the exosystem, for example, heightens awareness of disparities in health and medical services, after school programs, and employment opportunities for young adults, parents, and extended family members. Unique needs associated with the exosystem, such as disability specific programs and organizations, respite care and assistive equipment, are present across the educational continuum. It is therefore essential for preservice teachers to consider the exosystem in today's multicultural, multiracial, and multiethnic world.

Family Systems Framework

An additional perspective is provided by Turnbull and Turnbull (1990) family systems framework, which views the family as an interrelated social system with unique characteristics and needs. This is especially relevant when a family has a member with a disability who requires additional care, adjustments to the daily schedule, and may not be able to follow the traditional path of leaving home to pursue higher education or work. In their framework, Turnbull and Turnbull discuss family characteristics such as composition, socioeconomic status, and geographic location in addition to family interactions and functions. In this framework, family functions attend to needs such as self-esteem, socialization, and daily care. Cohesion and adaptability are also key when families are faced with meeting challenges related to unemployment, loss of a family member, or medical crises. The overriding element is how family members, individually and collectively, interact, influence, and affect one another.

These frameworks are critical for preservice teachers who will need to value and build on families' strengths and assets to better serve their students. Preservice teachers also need knowledge to provide supports and tools for self-advocacy that align with each family's needs, preferences, and priorities. As families change over time, preservice teachers must develop their capacity to initiate and nurture relationships to meet families where they are.

Funds of Knowledge

In addition, preservice teachers must consider their students' funds of knowledge. A funds of knowledge approach is premised on the foundation that people have a wealth of knowledge gained through experience, which can be documented through first-hand research with families (González & Moll, 1994). It is a means of using knowledge about students' homes as pedagogical resources to affirm their culturally mediated practices and provide a "theoretical orientation for understanding students' households, family practices, and cultural resources" (Moll, 2014, p. 117). As such, funds of knowledge can counter cultural models or simplified notions or stereotypical views (see Gee, 2015) about students from marginalized families that often permeate the educational landscape and negatively impact expectations and outcomes.

Allowing deficit perspectives to persist perpetuates binaries of advantaged and disadvantaged children and families (Dyson, 2015) and further pathologizes disability and human differences in schools and society (Smagorinsky et al., 2019). Compton-Lilly and Delbridge (2019) draw on Bourdieu's construct of social capital to define academic social capital as the networks and alliances that "support relationships with educators and community members who have access to resources and opportunities" (p. 533). They encourage educators to listen to families and learn from them to challenge cultural models, provide needed supports, and advocate for change. Adopting a socially just mindset begins with recognizing the limitations of the knowledge one holds, being willing to work through conflict, responding to differences with humility and respect, and actively listening to families to disrupt deficit orientations and discourses embedded in schools, communities, and organizations.

Practicing Core Values

As this chapter is centered on values consistent with a commitment to social justice teaching, in this section, we highlight the core values of the Council for Exceptional Children (CEC), the leading organization for special education professionals, which impact children both with and without disabilities. The CEC's core values are visionary thinking, integrity, and inclusiveness. Importantly, the emphasis on inclusivity, a recurring theme in teaching for social justice, encompasses diversity and addresses students with varying abilities and those who interact with them in educational settings, as marginalized students and English learners are often overrepresented in special education (Cooc, & Kiru, 2018; Ford, & Russo, 2016; Morgan et al., 2018; Sullivan, 2011). These core values are embedded in the CEC Code of Ethics and Standards for Professional Standards (see https://exceptionalchildren.org/standards/ethical-principles-and-practice-standards) and inform special education courses with applications for family studies courses.

CEC is at the forefront of research and practice with a strong focus on collaboration. As such, there is an emphasis on working with families to address their children's diverse educational, social and behavioral needs and also to "respectfully and effectively communicate considering the background, socioeconomic status, language, culture, and priorities of the family" (https://exceptionalchildren.org/topics/working-families).

Grounding Practice in a Social Justice Framework

Taken together, Bronfenbrenner (1977) and Turnbull and Turnbull (1990) along with a funds of knowledge approach and CEC Standards frame our positioning in our respective courses. Each brings discipline-specific content, relevant personal experiences, and a social justice lens to their pedagogy. This multiperspectival framing informs the theoretical basis woven into their teaching and enables preservice students to build a foundation for the range of applied activities. We intentionally structure discussions to build student understanding of these theoretical underpinnings and provide increasingly complex applications with which students engage. The sections that follow offer an overview of each course including examples of key ways that social justice is addressed in brave and exploratory spaces.

Our teaching and practices are guided by these theoretical perspectives and underlying social justice frameworks. Teaching in public schools requires an ethic of care (see Noddings, 2012) to address disparities related to race, class, ethnicity, disability, sexual orientation, and access to technology. We include technology because the Covid-19 pandemic underscored the lack of access to learning activities for students living in rural and low-socioeconomic status communities, which significantly limited ongoing communication with families and educational team members, including social workers and therapists, who support underserved families and students with disabilities in need of services.

Engaging students requires a balance of encouragement and the ability to create brave spaces (Arao & Clemens, 2013) for discussion around topics not typically broached in students' homes, K-12 schools, community organizations, or places of worship. Brave spaces, a framework for having conversations about difficult topics, emphasizes courage and risk-taking, and as Arao and Clemens (2013) make clear, recognizing and deconstructing identity, oppression, power, and privilege is challenging and requires bravery rather than safety.

Courses and field experiences offer opportunities to engage in critical dialogue and in-depth reflection with opportunities for brave spaces discussions that illustrate a range of diversity-related factors and influences. Moreover, they provide spaces to conduct local work and collaborate with community members, which is necessary for developing equity-focused, culturally competent teachers (Sleeter, 2017). As described below, our courses emphasize awareness and identification of resources to assist children and families with financial, social-emotional, and daily needs and involve reflection, dialog, action, and praxis (see Freire, 2000) with the understanding that learning is a life-long and life-wide process.

PRACTICAL ACTIVITIES AND APPLICATIONS

We address the aims described above individually and collectively by focusing on topics related to social justice and identity that can engender more equitable learning spaces. To this end, at the start of the semester, we employ community building activities for students to examine their identities and assets. We do this because as Artiles (2019) notes, "*What teachers bring* [emphasis is original] to their participation in practice calls attention to the roles of identities," which serve different purposes and have consequences (p. 2).

In Deborah's class, preservice teachers are asked to introduce their families, biological or otherwise, and describe what makes them unique. They learn about peers in their cohort and begin discussions about similarities and differences in family composition with an emphasis on educational attainment and socioeconomic background. This exercise is complimented by discussion of comparisons when there is a child with a disability present, which can impact sibling relationships and microsystem level variations including school placement options (see Bronfenbrenner, 1977; Turnbull & Turnbull, 1990).

In Heidi's course, preservice teachers introduce themselves by creating stick figures to identify what is in their heads and their hearts, their roots (feet), and their talents (hands). The students share in pairs and then across the class. At the close of the activity, students feel connected and note that they have been in classes with one another for several semesters but never knew each other on a deeper level. They also consider their funds of knowledge and share in small groups, e.g., language spoken in the home; family values and traditions; division of labor and chores; family outings and activities; educational activities such as homework, bedtime stories, or devotions; scientific knowledge such as health and wellness or recycling; and other knowledges (González et al., 2005). When students finish sharing, they are asked to reflect on how they might come to know their future students' funds of knowledge, which provides a framework for learning in the course. These types of activities build classroom community and engage preservice teachers in practicing active listening and reflection.

In each course, preservice teachers are reminded of culture as knowledge, communication, a system of tools, practices, and participation (Duranti, 1997) in familial and community contexts. They begin to think about how collaborating with families is a key component of effective teaching. In the special education course, case studies push students to examine their perspectives on working with a multi-generational family from an unfamiliar culture (the Philippines), a parent with an intellectual disability, and a child claiming physical abuse. There are no right answers. This is a space for asking questions, brainstorming solutions, and gaining knowledge about resources. Students often comment on how the case studies move them out of their comfort zone and offer real-life situations for discussions that encourage risk-taking and raise awareness of inequities.

For example, Deborah provides a case study focused on a student with hearing loss and some academic delays. Their mother is described as working in retail and having limited financial resources. The educational team is encouraging placement in the state School for the Deaf, which is located approximately 100 miles away. Much of the discussion focuses on the limited availability of needed services closer to home, the feasibility of the student living so far from family, and the mother's concerns about travel and other expenses associated with an out-of-home placement. As students consider this case study, they carefully weigh and balance the ecological and family systems at play in this scenario.

In the child, family, and community engagement course, preservice teachers complete a community resource directory, identify a family who is culturally or linguistically different from their own, conduct two ethnographic interviews, map the assets in the family's community, and complete a case study narrative of their research. They gain first-hand research experience and deepen their understanding of children and families and the importance of community. Students in both courses report these course experiences are eye-opening and perspective changing. In the following paragraphs we emphasize the need for open communication and how we involve students in enhancing their relational and communicative competence.

Communicating With Parents, Caregivers, and School Personnel

The importance of communication cannot be overstated. Wynter-Hoyte et al. (2022) remind us that language matters because words, phrases, and manners of speaking can perpetuate stereotypes and cultural models. Preservice teachers need to learn, implement, and evaluate their spoken and written communication with parents, teachers, administrators, and related service providers. To achieve optimal outcomes for school-age students with and without disabilities, communicating with parents, especially a non-responsive parent, a parent who speaks a language other than English, or other factors impacting the ongoing two-way exchange of information must be learned and practiced. Communication is subtle and, therefore, essential to developing "a shared sense of goals and aspirations" (Edwards, 2016, p. 107) and to broadening one's perspectives and beliefs about students and their families using an asset-based funds of knowledge approach (Wynter-Hoyte et al., 2022).

In the family, school, and community engagement course, Heidi helps preservice teachers think about different ways to communicate with parents and caregivers including daily conversations when parents pick up or drop off children, telephone calls that inform families as to what students are doing well in addition to problems encountered, electronic conversation using email, blogs, newsletters, and apps such as Class Dojo or Remind, personal notes, and bulletin boards. Not only do students refresh and expand their knowledge of communication styles and explore communicating through different modalities, but they also discover different ways to learn about families through questionnaires and inventories.

Heidi invites local practitioners with expertise in elementary and special education to talk with preservice teachers. The resulting conversations are open question and answer sessions that provide opportunities for preservice teachers to ask difficult questions they may be uncomfortable raising in their clinical placements or with their supervisors. Heidi also asks a Head Start family engagement coordinator who specializes in father and father figure involvement to share her perspectives and experiences with the class. Having guest speakers reiterate the importance of learning about families, communicating with families, and meeting families where they are raises awareness of the importance of effective communication and can ameliorate common misperceptions about low socioeconomic status families and father involvement in their children's lives. Preservice teachers in the course take away the idea that everyone benefits from communication and interactions that foster home-school relationships.

The topic of communication requires an understanding of recommendations for specific contexts coupled with applications. Education discourse includes acronyms and unfamiliar terms that are generally inaccessible to parents. Moreover, for parents with less than positive school experiences, school can be intimidating and a less-than-welcoming place. Edwards (2016) calls on educators to recognize the "ghosts" of past experiences that signal whether parents feel welcome in schools and classrooms (p.106). She further notes that when teachers and school personnel engage in open, respectful communication with parents, parents are more likely to trust and work with their children's schools, which can begin to break down social barriers and address social and systemic inequities.

In special education, it is important for preservice teachers to refrain from using educational jargon with parents. In Deborah's course, she provides examples of word choice and input from parents of students with disabilities. She also uses simulations for students to gain experience with this aspect of information exchange, which requires them to self-reflect, self-evaluate, and realize the work involved in building or refining how they interact with parents, family members, and the range of professionals in school settings. For example, a parent guest speaker describes a situation in which this occurs. After the parent leaves, Deborah has several students role play what was shared. She, then, asks students to provide feedback about the exchanges. As the semester progresses, students are better able to use parent-friendly language and convey a positive and welcoming tone.

Although strategies can be modeled and feedback provided, a deeper level of skill development is needed. Deborah also pushes her students to examine their communication patterns in terms of wait time for a response, use of paraphrasing, and answering questions. There have also been many instances of one or more students correcting another's use of an insensitive or derogatory term. This leads to discussion of why such terms are used and the conscious need to shift away from such terminology. Often students do not realize the undertones of classism or racism. The serendipitous nature of these opportunities translates to being at the ready to talk about these issues and their on impact on equity in terms of shifting the status quo for students and classroom practices. These teachable moments occur with regularity as preservice students grapple with difficult topics around societal views on disability and marginalization.

Much discussion relates to assisting parents at IEP meetings. Students are provided with a range of scenarios from case studies, parent guest speakers and course materials with both recommendations for positive communication and how information should not be offered or provided (e.g., use of educational jargon). The latter often has more of an impact than the former especially when shared by a parent. Parents sharing experiences of being talked down to, not receiving answers to questions about their child's placement, accommodations or only receiving negative reports from school staff gets preservice teachers' attention. For example, as evidenced in end-of-semester thank you letters written during the final course session, students share their commitment to provide positive communication in easy-to-understand language, so parents feel part of their child's educational team. It is a means of reaching and communicating with parents from diverse backgrounds and overcoming invisible feelings from parents' past school experiences.

Identifying and Applying Resources

Any discussion of social justice requires an examination of resources. For preservice special education students, knowledge of local, state, and national resources is required. They need to build their knowledge of a range of programs, organizations, and services for students with a disability and their families. Families may require resources to meet basic needs such as assistance to pay the monthly electric bill or find free or low-cost events for families to do together. Families also need disability specific information and supports. Deborah emphasizes ways to search for resources online and through networking with community leaders, social service agencies, and businesses. The overarching point is to ask what is available and share who, when, and how to contact providers. Additionally, parents should not feel singled out or shamed. For example, in an assignment which includes developing a weekly newsletter, Deborah asks students to include a local or state resource with a few sentences about it and contact information. This strategy gives parents access to the information including the one or two (or more) who may need assistance with paying their monthly energy bill or who need a winter coat for their child.

Deborah encourages students to push themselves to expand their circle of contacts to help create a network focused on assistance and support because one person cannot do it alone. Learning about the depth and breadth of a school social worker's responsibilities is one way to build a network of individuals interested in students and families' well-being. There are many discussions during the course about professionals who work with children or families along with different agencies, programs and organizations. The focal point of these conversations is acknowledging "you don't know what you don't know" and to always look for resources whether it is locating a piece of adaptive equipment, someone with specialized expertise or low or no cost family activities. These practices can heighten awareness of possible needs especially for families at the margins (Pugach et al., 2021).

Heidi teaches students how to map community assets and resources (see Kretzmann & McKnight, 1993). Students begin by mapping their personal assets. Then they expand outward to map the community of the person or family they intend to interview. Students must identify a minimum of 15 community resources using their personal knowledge, the internet, and information obtained from service providers. They describe each community resource in their own words and include pictures, hours, directors, and contact information. Students also include a Google map of the community and resources in their directory. They share their directories in small groups and reflect on their learning in a written reflection. Student reflections indicate that the assignment familiarized them with resources they had not considered such as places and spaces for children and families that offer a range of services and free programming.

Preservice teachers in Heidi's class also learn how to conduct observations using an observation protocol. They observe a community event capturing what they observed and what stood out to them. Before conducting their individual or family interviews, students walk or drive the neighborhood with an eye toward personal safety to get a feel for the community. They learn about conducting interviews and develop interview questions. During the interviews, students are encouraged to ask questions about the neighborhood and its resources to gain an idea of the individual or family's perspectives, needs, and lived experiences. The ethnographic case study builds on the funds of knowledge approach emphasized in the course, offering a real-life application for course learning and positions students as learners and researchers (González & Moll, 1994) and fostering a culturally responsive pedagogical approach to familiarizing preservice teachers with students' communities in ways that identify community networks and affirm a community's culture (Nieto, 2011; Sleeter, 2011).

As a culminating project in the child and family studies course, students work in groups to plan and conduct an event for children and families in a school or community setting. Students identify a specific purpose for their event, obtain permissions to hold the event, produce a flyer or other means of advertising the event, and seek resources from the local community. They are given class time for planning and a course release day to conduct their events, which are typically held at students' clinical placement sites, the local Boys & Girls Club, the public library, child-care facilities, and local churches. These applied projects open avenues for understanding the critical role of community in school, family, and community engagement and highlight the importance of planning, communication, and collaboration in partnership with the university preparation program.

Both courses emphasize students looking into the programs and organizations with which they are unfamiliar. Even though they may never personally need or use these resources and programs, the knowledge gained from course activities such as those described above can be a game changer for a child or family Being knowledgeable about community resources and knowing how to locate them enhanced students' media and technology skills. In addition to using search engines and Google maps, they also critically examined websites, video, and other media, which can be overwhelming. Deborah and Heidi help students refine their searches to locate both local and regional resources and programs to meet a family's specific needs. They also ask guiding questions that assist students in determining the practical value of a given website or portal. In their reflections, students report learning how to find, evaluate, and utilize resources that may not be readily apparent. Experiences such as these provide them with valuable skills for the workplace and other professional settings.

To address equity and social justice in teacher preparation, there must be discussion of ways to foster self-determination and advocacy for students and their families. For students with disabilities, receiving and accepting assistance is a first step, but active participation is the sought after outcome in the disability community. Given the history of treatment of individuals with disabilities and their families, Deborah's course includes content on the pivotal role of parents in passing the Individuals with Disabilities Education Act (2004) (20 U.S.C. § 1400). Educational services were initially developed and implemented by parents. They banded together to fight for access to instruction and related services in the public schools. This legacy is the basis for knowledge of resources with the power to change lives.

Heidi teaches preservice teachers how to advocate for children and families in their clinical placements and future teaching. Much of her work with preservice teachers focuses on the need to suspend judgment, challenge assumptions, and practice deep respect and caring. These discussions are difficult but worthwhile, as students express gaining confidence to interact with parents, form relationships with them, and value the role parents play in their children's lives along with gaining some understanding of potential challenges, especially for parents at the margins. Preservice teachers come to understand that incorporating funds of knowledge in their practice can help them establish home, school, and community connections and make classroom learning meaningful. Lastly, they convey their appreciation for learning about and experiencing different kinds of community from classrooms to neighborhoods and beyond and what it means to be in community with others.

IMPLICATIONS FOR PRACTICE

Our work in our respective classes along with the theoretical perspectives and worldviews shared in this chapter offers several implications for practice. As we reflect on our writing, we elaborate on the following key ideas for foregrounding social justice and equity into preservice preparation programs and professional practice. In doing so, we highlight the need for preservice teachers to entertain - delve into tough - difficult topics and have critical discussions. Course activities that contribute to producing caring, respectful, empathetic, and informed teachers are essential. And last, preservice teachers require opportunities to apply and reflect on course concepts in authentic ways.

Professional development and growth require the ability to engage in critical conversations. According to hooks (2010), creating community requires mutual risk-taking to embrace how we know and learn together. Arao and Clemons' (2013) brave spaces can help create classroom spaces for students to ask tough questions about controversial topics, focus on the topic rather than individuals, and critique and shape their thinking in dialogue with one another. Student-centered classrooms that incorporate reading and discussion enable preservice teachers to get comfortable with the uncomfortable, go beneath the surface, shape their thinking, and challenge common assumptions, which can lead to a shift in beliefs, knowledge, and practice with the possibility of immediate, short, and long-term change.

Similarly, careful planning of course content, activities, and applied learning can contribute to producing better informed and empathetic teachers. Teaching preschoolers to young adults with disabilities is more than teaching content. It is finding new ways to provide content in relevant ways and connecting with families and communities to assist in meeting students' current and future needs. It is also necessary to have an open mind as a prerequisite to offering and providing supports.

Families are complex and differ in beliefs, perspectives, and abilities (Edwards, 2016). Effective communication requires knowledge of each family's circumstances and preferences. Developing a social justice mindset entails learning about one's students and their families, joining professional and activist organizations, and becoming active in schools and communities (Nieto, 2011). It is relational work that is grounded in a funds of knowledge approach to classrooms and communities and a fundamental means of demonstrating one's commitment to advancing equitable practices in teacher education (Zeichner, 2019).

Assisting preservice students to examine their own background prepares them to go beyond the familiar. Yet, this requires brave spaces. Deborah and Heidi have continued to modify their courses to address changes in the social and political context and societal shifts. This is critical, as the current times in which live and work demand courage to challenge the status quo and embrace diversity in thought and action.

As described previously, the thank you letters in the special education course illustrate how preservice students gain an understanding of parents' lived experiences and use this information to inform their practice both in the preparation program and in their future teaching. As in Heidi's classes, there is a corresponding increase in confidence and empathy when preservice teachers are asked to self-evaluate their knowledge at the beginning and end of each course, especially with regard to equitable sharing of information and working with families who often face financial, social, or other difficulties and challenges.

A further step in this process is the emphasis on self-examination and reflection. Being able to understand and take on the perspective of others begins the process of introspection and self-reflection. There is no way to understand social justice without doing the work to recognize and appreciate what, oftentimes, is beyond the knowledge and experience of preservice teachers in our courses (Francis et al., 2017; Kinloch et al., 2021). One's context should be acknowledged to delve into the circumstances of others, especially those who are or have been marginalized, which entails a willingness to say, "I don't know." Both Deborah and Heidi came to their university with limited familiarity with living in a rural area and have had to (re)examine their own beliefs, practices, and identities to learn from and with their students. We share our stories of uncomfortable learning experiences, challenges faced, and successes experienced, which often surprises students who tend to consider their instructors in terms of difference rather than commonalities.

Finally, the importance of applied activities, discussions, and assignments coupled with opportunities to debrief and process cannot be stressed enough. In their work on practice-based pedagogies, Kavanagh and Danielson (2020) consider how "challenging practices that exclude children and raising questions about whose interests are being served" can be (re)conceptualized as "instructional practices in and of themselves" (p. 100). Social justice is not a discrete topic for one class session. It must be infused and integrated throughout, examined from various perspectives, and enacted in practice. Deborah and Heidi make a point of modeling the discourses and dispositions of equity focused educators to communicate more effectively in ways that honor and respect students, families, and communities.

Our two courses take similar paths to immersive experiences for preservice teachers. Through difficult conversations, applied assignments, and self-reflection, preservice teachers broaden their worldview and learn what it means to interact with families and (re)imagine classrooms and communities as affirming spaces (see Kinloch et al., 2021; Nieto, 2011). Preparing students to interact with parents and professionals orients them to a broader view of justice, one that eschews bias, welcomes diversity, and supports equitable practice. It is how we demonstrate our commitment to social justice (Pugach et al., 2021; Zeichner, 2019).

CONCLUDING THOUGHTS

An understanding of theory is critical though not always recognized when working with children and families. Reading, math, and curricular approaches are typically grounded in theories. But working with children and families is also grounded in a rich theoretical framework. As we have shown, identity and social justice work with preservice teachers is not an easy process especially in a rural context. Reflecting on our work and telling our stories has led us to wonder about future possibilities (see Kinloch et al., 2021; Nieto, 2011), and so, we pose the following questions for further reflection and action:

How can educators reach beyond names, categories, and deficit discourses to center affirming equity-focused practices?

How might educators join together to create learning environments that foster community and translate into commitment, advocacy, and action?

What might this look like in practice across content areas, learning contexts, and regions?

How can teacher educators collectively teach the values consistent with a social justice mindset to demonstrate our commitment to social justice?

Taken together, we believe the elements discussed in this chapter can bring the margins to the forefront in preservice teacher education and call upon teachers and teacher educators to refine and expand this work and effect lasting change.

REFERENCES

Arao, B., & Clemens, K. (2013). From safe spaces to brave spaces: A new way to frame dialogue around diversity and social justice. In L. M. Landreman (Ed.), *From the art of effective facilitation* (pp. 135–150). Stylus.

Artiles, A. J. (2019). Understanding practice and intersectionality in teacher education in the age of diversity and inclusion. *Teachers College Record, 121*(6), 1–6. doi:10.1177/016146811912100612

Artiles, A. J. (2022). Interdisciplinary notes on the dual nature of disability: Disrupting ideology-ontology circuits in racial disparities research. *Literacy Research: Theory, Method, and Practice, 71*(1), 1–20. doi:10.1177/23813377221120106

Artiles, A. J., Harris-Murri, N., & Rostenberg, D. (2006). Inclusion as social justice: Critical notes on discourses, assumptions, and the road ahead. *Theory into Practice, 45*(3), 260–268. doi:10.120715430421tip4503_8

Bacon, H. R. (2016). Creating community connections and partnerships for transformative social change. *LEARNing Landscapes, 10*(1), 81–94. doi:10.36510/learnland.v10i1.719

Bacon, H. R., Byfield, L., Kaya, J., & Humaidan, A. Y. A. (2019). Re-storying lives and literacies: Narratives of transformational resistance. *Journal of Latinos and Education.* Advance online publication. doi:10.1080/15348431.2019.1685527

Bacon, H. R., & Byfield, L. G. (2018). Navigating discourses in academia: Challenging the status quo. *English Teaching, 17*(2), 90–102. doi:10.1108/ETPC-05-2017-0083

Bacon, H. R., & Kaya, J. (2018). Imagined communities and identities: A spacio–temporal discourse analysis of one women's literacy journey. *Linguistics and Education, 46*, 82–90. doi:10.1016/j.linged.2018.05.007

Bronfenbrenner, U. (1977). Toward an experimental ecology of human development. *The American Psychologist, 32*(7), 513–531. doi:10.1037/0003-066X.32.7.513

Cobb, F., & Krownapple, F. (2019). *Belonging through a culture of diversity: The keys to successful equity implementation*. Mimi and Todd Press.

Cochran-Smith, M. (2010). Toward a theory of teacher education for social justice. In A. Hargreaves, A. Lieberman, M. Fullan, & D. Hopkins (Eds.), *Second international handbook of educational change* (pp. 445–467). Springer. doi:10.1007/978-90-481-2660-6_27

Compton-Lilly, C., & Delbridge, A. (2019). What can parents tell us about poverty and literacy learning? Listening to parents over time. *Journal of Adolescent & Adult Literacy, 62*(5), 531–539. doi:10.1002/jaal.923

Cooc, N., & Kiru, E. W. (2018). Disproportionality in special education: A synthesis of international research and trends. *The Journal of Special Education, 52*(3), 163–173. doi:10.1177/0022466918772300

Dana, N. F., & Yendol-Hoppey, D. (2020). *The reflective educator's guide to classroom research: Learning to teach and teaching to learn through practitioner inquiry* (4th ed.). Corwin.

Durand, T. M., & Tavaras, C. L. (2021). Countering complacency with radical reflection: Supporting white teachers in the enactment of critical multicultural praxis. *Education and Urban Society, 53*(2), 146–162. doi:10.1177/0013124520927680

Duranti, A. (1997). *Linguistic anthropology*. Cambridge University Press. doi:10.1017/CBO9780511810190

Dyson, A. H. (2015). The search for inclusion: Deficit discourse and the erasure of childhood. *Language Arts, 92*(3), 199–207.

Edwards, P. A. (2016). *New ways to engage parents: Strategies and tools for teachers and leaders, K–12*. Teachers College Press.

Ford, D. Y., & Russo, C. J. (2016). Historical and legal overview of special education overrepresentation: Access and equity denied. *Multiple Voices for Ethnically Diverse Exceptional Learners, 16*(1), 50–57.

Francis, B., Mills, M., & Lupton, R. (2017). Towards social justice in education: Contradictions and dilemmas. *Journal of Education Policy, 32*(4), 414–431. doi:10.1080/02680939.2016.1276218

Freire, P. (2000). Pedagogy of the oppressed (30th anniversary ed.). Continuum.

Gee, J. P. (2015). *Social linguistics and literacies: Ideology in discourses* (5th ed.). Routledge. doi:10.4324/9781315722511

González, N., Moll, L. C., & Amanti, C. (Eds.). (2005). Funds of knowledge: Theorizing practices in households, communities, and classrooms. Lawrence Erlbaum Associates.

hooks, b. (2010). *Teaching critical thinking: Practical wisdom*. Routledge.

Individuals With Disabilities Education Act, 20 U.S.C. § 1400 (2004).

Kavanagh, S. S., & Danielson, K. A. (2020). Practicing justice, justifying practice: Toward critical practice teacher education. *American Educational Research Association, 57*(1), 69–105. doi:10.3102/0002831219848691

Kinloch, V., Nemeth, E. A., Butler, T. T., & Player, G. D. (2021). *Where is the justice: Engaged pedagogies in schools and communities.* Teachers College Press.

Kretzmann, J. P., & McKnight, J. L. (1993). *Building communities from the inside out: A path toward finding and mobilizing a community's assets.* The Asset-Based Community Development Institute: DePaul University Steans Center.

Loewen, J. W. (2005). *Sundown towns: A hidden dimension of American racism.* The New Press.

Lynch, J., & Prins, E. (2022). *Teaching and learning about family literacy and family literacy programs.* Routledge.

McDonald, M., & Zeichner, K. M. (2009). Social justice teacher education. In W. Ayers, T. Quinn, & D. Stovall (Eds.), *Handbook of social justice in education* (pp. 613–628). Routledge.

Milner, H. R. IV. (2008). Critical race theory and interest convergence as analytic tools in teacher education policies and practices. *Journal of Teacher Education, 58*(4), 332–346. doi:10.1177/0022487108321884

Milner, H. R. IV, Fittz, L., Best, B., & Cunningham, H. B. (2022). What if special education could be seen as a site for justice? *Journal of Emotional and Behavioral Disorders, 30*(2), 159–166. doi:10.1177/10634266221087990

Moll, L. C. (2014). *L. S. Vygotsky and education.* Routledge.

Moll, L. C., & González, N. (1994). Lessons from research with language minority children. *Journal of Reading Behavior, 25*(4), 439–456. doi:10.1080/10862969409547862

Morgan, P. L., Farkas, G., Cook, M., Strassfeld, N. M., Hillemeier, M. M., Pun, W. H., Wang, Y., & Schussler, D. L. (2018). Are Hispanic, Asian, Native American, or language-minority children overrepresented in special education? *Exceptional Children, 84*(3), 261–279. doi:10.1177/0014402917748303

Nieto, S. (2011). The light in their eyes: Creating multicultural learning communities (10th anniversary ed.). Teachers College Press.

Noddings, N. (2012). The caring relation in teaching. *Oxford Review of Education, 38*(6), 771–781. doi:10.1080/03054985.2012.745047

O'Connor, M. T., & Daniello, F. (2019). From implication to naming: Reconceptualizing school-community partnership literature using a framework nested in social justice. *School Community Journal, 29*(1), 297–316l.

Pugach, M. C., Matewos, A. M., & Gomez-Najarro, A. (2021). Disability and the meaning of social justice in teacher education research: A precarious guest at the table? *Journal of Teacher Education, 72*(2), 237–250. doi:10.1177/0022487120929623

Russell, H. K. (2012). *The state of Southern Illinois: An illustrated history.* Southern Illinois University Press.

Scribner, S., & Cole, M. (1981). *The psychology of literacy.* Harvard University Press. doi:10.4159/harvard.9780674433014

Sleeter, C. E. (2011). An agenda to strengthen culturally responsive teaching. *English Teaching*, *10*(2), 7–23. https://education.waikato.ac.nz/research/files/etpc/files/2011v10n2art1.pdf

Sleeter, C. E. (2017). Critical race theory and the whiteness of teacher education. *Urban Education*, *52*(2), 155–159. doi:10.1177/0042085916668957

Smagorinsky, P., Tobin, J., & Lee, K. (2019). Introduction. In P. Smagorinsky, J. Tobin, & K. Lee (Eds.), *Disability studies in education* (pp. 1–22). Peter Lang.

Sullivan, A. L. (2011). Disproportionality in special education identification and placement of English language learners. *Exceptional Children*, *77*(3), 317–334. doi:10.1177/001440291107700304

Turnbull, A. P., & Turnbull, H. R. (1990). *Families, professionals, and exceptionality: A special partnership* (2nd ed.). Charles E. Merrill.

U. S. Census Bureau. (2021). *QuickFacts*. https://www.census.gov/quickfacts/fact/table/US/PST045221

Wynter-Hoyte, K., Braden, E., Myers, M., Rodriguez, S. C., & Thornton, N. (2022). *Revolutionary love: Creating a culturally inclusive literacy classroom*. Scholastic.

Zeichner, K. M. (2019). *The struggle for the soul of teacher education*. Routledge.

Section 4
Educator Training

Chapter 12
Diversity in the Classroom:
How Teacher Perceptions and Teacher–Child Interactions Matter

Derya Ası
https://orcid.org/0000-0002-7647-3029
University of Dundee, UK

Tracey Joyce
https://orcid.org/0000-0002-7705-538X
University of Dundee, UK

ABSTRACT

In early years settings and schools, the population of children from diverse ethnic backgrounds has been increasing all over the world. Along with this increase, there is growing interest and concern in meeting the needs of these children and their families throughout their early years and school experience. Within any mainstream culture it is assumed that an ethnically diverse population should be able to be successfully integrated; however, it is not always clear how this could be achieved. Adaptation and integration to a new culture or school environment may be best achieved via effective communication between students, parents, and professionals. In this chapter, teacher beliefs and attitudes and how these affect communication will be discussed. The power of teacher-child relationships will be highlighted and suggestions will be made about effective practices to promote communication and build relationships.

INTRODUCTION

Living in a multicultural community has many benefits and also many challenges. Significantly, it has been shown to have an influence on the social and mental wellbeing of children and their parents (European Union, 2013a, Gopalkrishnan, 2018, European Commission/EACEA/Eurydice, 2019). Some of the challenges of cultural and linguistic diversity from the early years of childhood have been emphasized in previous studies (Souto-Manning & Mitchell, 2010, Oades-Sese et al., 2011, Gay, 2013) and it has been shown that children from ethnically diverse backgrounds' behavioural, emotional, and cognitive devel-

DOI: 10.4018/978-1-6684-6386-4.ch012

opment can be negatively influenced by such challenges (NAEYC, 2009, Daglar, Melhuish, & Barnes, 2011, Oades-Sese et al., 2011, Garner, et.al., 2014, Belhadj Kouider Koglin, & Petermann, 2014, Doan, Marcelo, & Yates, 2019). Along with the increasing number of children from diverse ethnic backgrounds in many countries over the years, there has also been arising concerns about effective teaching of those children as ethnically diverse students are at higher risk of leaving school earlier compared to native-born peers (OECD, 2012, European Commission/EACEA/Eurydice, 2019). Because of these concerns, schools are increasingly aware of the need to provide secure, confident, and encouraging learning environments for all children in order to increase inclusivity and engagement in the education process (OECD, 2012, Darling-Hammond, 2020). We suggest a better understanding of ethnically diverse populations by those involved in early years and schools would offer better experiences for children, their families and all professionals working in the education field to spread social justice across communities more effectively (Hannon & O'Donnell, 2022)

Teachers have a key role in contributing to creating a secure context for all children and supporting them in adapting to the school context. Within this role, they are expected to have the skills to recognise the difficulties children might experience and be able to provide improved opportunities for them in collaboration with the school's management team and wider stakeholders. Teachers also have the role of interpreting the indicators and behaviours of children and to encourage their motivation for better engagement in academic learning and to foster their social adaptation within the school environment (OECD, 2010, Darling-Hammond, 2020). Their interactions with children can model how effective communication can be managed with others and this can have an impact on creating welcoming interactions within the classroom context (Geerlings, Thijs, & Verkuyten, 2017). This may be particularly relevant when working with ethnically diverse children as teachers might have some additional concerns while working them (OECD, 2010). Teachers may feel they do not have the knowledge or experience to manage ethnically diverse classrooms effectively. Teachers might also have some implicit or explicit attitudes which could affect their ability to create harmonious and welcoming classroom environments. As indicated by Greenwald, Nosek, and Banaji (2003), some of these attitudes may not be expressed explicitly by individuals. The reasons for this may be that they are aware of the issues but are not willing to express them, or they cannot express these because they do not know exactly how they think or feel. Thus, while it is possible to ask people's overt opinions about different ethnic groups, if they do not recognise their own hidden attitudes and associations, which may come from prejudiced beliefs, the answers given may not reflect reality.

There are good examples of how schools have been performing well with their ethnically diverse student population across many countries (OECD, 2010, Goodwin & Stanton, 2022). On the other hand, there is evidence of how student drop-out rates have been increasing during the transition to upper levels of education for ethnically diverse students (Herweijer, 2009). The reasons for this increase in drop-out rates have been attributed to the nature and the frequency of the support provided for students from diverse backgrounds as well as changing academic demands (Baker et.al., 2001). Therefore, it is important to provide adequate opportunities and resources for all, but more specifically for ethnically diverse children as early as possible. It is recognised that this targeted provision is dependent on the teachers' skills and understanding (Gazeley & Dunne, 2013), and, we argue, effective child-teacher relationships are the core factors in supporting culturally diverse students. Therefore, in this chapter we focus on how understanding and support of ethnic diversity can be promoted across early years and school settings via enhanced child-teacher interactions.

BACKGROUND

Promoting Successful Engagement of All Children Into School Context via Recognition of Different Cultures

According to Ladson-Billings (1995), cultural awareness and implementing culturally responsive practices should not be confined to academic instruction but should also cover students' cultural heritage and background within all aspects of the learning environment. A greater understanding of cultural heritage can be developed and enhanced via teacher/child relationships. Therefore, school policies and teaching practices should allow for the implementation of this kind of approach (Horenczyk & Tatar, 2002 Coronel & Gómez-Hurtado, 2015). Key to this is the importance of understanding that cultural requirements may have a powerful impact on behaviour patterns and expectations of children and families. In some cultures, asking questions or initiating communication with an adult may not be appreciated, whereas in other cultures students are expected to take the initiative and be curious. In cultures with a collectivistic nature the emphasis on social and relational components within communication might be much stronger (Kagitcibasi, 2010, Beyazkurk & Kesner, 2005). Therefore attitudes, practices, and values of the differing cultures should be understood by both parties for effective communication (Shor & Bernhard, 2003). If it is expected that ethnically diverse individuals should be able to be successfully integrated within the mainstream culture, then it should also be noted that adaptation may be best achieved via effective and respectful communication between students, parents, and professionals within schools.

To enable this, teachers need to have an understanding of the distinct cultural components of their students and the factors affecting their community life. This would enhance effective design and management of the learning environments and help meet the needs of students (Milner & Tenore, 2010). Notably, flexibility and creativity are the crucial aspects in creating such environments (Biasutti, Concina, & Frate, 2020). In that sense, ethnic diversity can be seen as an opportunity to create a welcoming and respectful classroom environment in which difference is viewed positively. Creative and adaptable environments also promote better inclusion of children into classroom processes enabling other children to explore and understand diverse cultures and respect for others (Byrd, 2016).

For promoting culturally responsive practices in the settings, in addition to culturally sensitive and inclusive school policies, teachers also need to recognise their own cultural biases which might be either unconscious or conscious. There are indications that teachers might not be confident how to implement culturally responsive practices and how to identify potential biases within their own, and others, educational practices (Malo-Juvera, Correll, & Cantrell, 2018, Herzog-Punzenberger et al., 2020). This lack of confidence might be an issue for teachers and practitioners. One method to help support the development of teachers confidence and understanding is to be exposed to diverse classroom environments as a part of systemic practice (Price-Dennis & Souto-Manning, 2011, Darling-Hammond et al., 2020). This is not only important for the individual person but also for the society as a whole, as a lack of understanding in variations across ethnic identities and cultures might lead to biased attitudes and prejudices. Within an early years or school environment a prejudiced approach might hinder the academic performance of ethnically diverse children. Results from a previous study based on teacher ratings of children from different racial groups showed interesting results (Yates & Marcelo, 2014). While the ratings of the teachers in terms of children's imagination and expressive play did not differ between the racial groups (Black and non-Black), the attributions of teachers regarding school preparedness and peer acceptance were lower and the perceived child-teacher relationship ratings were more conflictual for Black children.

Therefore, it is essential to understand potential biases and challenges that ethnically diverse children might come across throughout their education journey (Glock, 2016). Exposure from the very beginning of their teacher-practitioner training period at university/college and within everyday practice in diverse educational settings would be beneficial for teachers in terms of self-reflection, recognising own biases, and understanding the strengths and challenges of ethnic diversity (Malo-Juvera, Correll, & Cantrell, 2018). It is evident that contact with other individuals from diverse cultural backgrounds would be helpful to make stronger connections with others and to reduce potential biased intergroup attitudes which is not only valid for one ethnic group but for humanity as a whole (Sparkman & Hamer, 2020).

When cultural diversity and potential biases are recognised by teachers, culturally responsive practices can be promoted successfully across classroom practices. However, it is difficult to understand every aspect of cultural diversity. We cannot expect teachers to have an in-depth knowledge of every aspect of all cultures. Instead, the most crucial factors are for teachers to see this as an opportunity for learning rather than a challenge or difficulty and to appreciate that anyone can become a part of a minority ethnic group if s/he does not come from the dominant culture (Rogoff, 2011), even in one's own homeland. Therefore, it is crucial for a teacher to think about how classroom practices and learning/instructional activities can be enhanced based on culturally relevant/sustaining pedagogy (Ladson-Billings, 2014, Paris, 2021). This would help to contribute towards cultural enrichment of classroom practices thus expanding the idea of social justice at various levels of community (Paris, 2012). Teachers who display interest, are open and respectful, and communicate with people from diverse ethnic backgrounds are more likely to better understand how new strategies can be integrated in the ongoing practices. A lack of such cultural sensitivity and responsiveness of teachers may result in misunderstandings and biased perceptions regarding ethnically diverse groups which, in turn, may lead to ineffective support for those children with diverse background (Han & Thomas, 2010). In contrast, a better understanding, or a willingness to learn more about differing cultures and backgrounds would make a strong foundation from which to build positive relationships.

Factors Affecting Teachers' Beliefs and Attitudes About Ethnically Diverse Children

Many previous studies indicate that it is crucial to understand teachers' points of view as they are seen as starting point to promote social competency and academic success of children (Pianta, 1999, Howes, 2000, Pianta, Stuhlman, & Hamre, 2002, Pianta & LaParo, 2003). It is also important to know what challenges teachers face and the insights they have in relation to teaching children from cultural backgrounds different than their own. Although the role of teachers in promoting school success of ethnically diverse children is crucial, there are very few studies evaluating teachers' implicit and explicit perceptions of native and ethnic minority students (Van den Bergh et al., 2010, Peček, Macura-Milovanović, & Vujisić-Živković, 2014). The studies investigating teachers' hidden beliefs and attitudes towards their students mostly focus on expressions of explicit beliefs via face-to-face interviews or self-reporting measures (Payne, Burkley, & Stokes, 2008). However, it is difficult for any person to express their beliefs without any bias. Teachers' own ethnic background might also influence their beliefs. Any prejudiced attitudes, explicit or implicit, may affect the understanding of any ethnic group which may, in turn, affect the expectations and behaviours of students and teachers. These expectations and attitudes may also be extended to parents of those students (Van den Bergh et al., 2010, Redding, 2019).

Teachers' attitudes towards ethnicity may also be related to their beliefs regarding the levels of academic success in the classroom. If students show underachievement academically, they may not meet teachers' (and the schools') expectations of success. Teachers may have anxiety, due to external pressures on them, that their class will not achieve a high performance, or success rate, because of those academically underachieving students (Wubbels, Den Brok, Veldman, & Van Tartwijk, 2006, Ready & Wright, 2011, Adair, 2015, Banerjee & Lamb, 2016). In a Dutch study, researchers found that the range of biased attitudes varied across different classrooms. However, teacher's performance was found to be consistently related to their biased evaluations and implicit attitudes, specifically regarding ethnically diverse children, such as lower intelligence and poor academic performance (Van den Bergh et al., 2010). Another finding reported differences between the perceptions of Dutch teachers who have elevated level of biased attitudes and those with low level of biased attitudes towards ethnically diverse students. They found lower achievement status in classrooms where teachers were highly prejudiced towards ethnic diversity students compared to classrooms with less prejudiced teachers. Although teachers' explicit attitudes toward those students might be influenced by academic achievement, there is also a bias in evaluating ethnically diverse children's performance (Glock, 2016).

Another factor in influencing teachers' attitudes could be the motivation and enthusiasm of the teachers themselves. Teaching can be highly stressful and demanding (Glock et al., 2019). Sometimes, teachers might have difficulties in sustaining their own motivation because they might experience emotional exhaustion which influences their professional commitment and the quality of interactions with children (Ansari et al., 2020). In addition, they may not know how to create a diverse approach to capture all the needs of children and, specifically, ethnically diverse children (Herzog-Punzenberger et al., 2020). However, teachers should not wait until they experience a diverse classroom to develop these skills. By being prepared for this in advance they are more likely to be welcoming to all children regardless of background, rather than feel apprehensive or challenged. Therefore, it is worthwhile to recognise teachers' motivation and enthusiasm to learn about themselves and their own attitudes, which can then be translated into more inclusive education methods. To achieve this, it is not sufficient for teachers to only participate in courses, training, or workshops. A professional framework based on competencies driven by ethnically and culturally sensitive principles is required (Muniz, 2020).

Effective Interactions vs. Disciplinary Actions for Ethnically Diverse Children

Schools in general, and teachers in particular, want children to be more adaptive, in terms of keeping the rules, having good relationships with peers and being successful academically. If children fail to achieve these, discipline strategies may be implemented which in fact, lead to the reverse (Gregory, Skiba, & Noguera, 2010). Discipline strategies may change according to regulations within schools. Strategies used by teachers range from a mild warning about behaviour, to temporary or permanent suspension. Research suggests more extreme discipline strategies (such as suspension) are more likely to be applied to ethnically diverse students (Gregory et al., 2010, Okonofua & Eberhardt, 2015). Once suspension from the school towards ethnic students increases, the achievement gap between the ethnically dominant group of students and the student from diverse backgrounds is also likely to increase. This is due to the frequent disciplinary actions which lead to students missing learning opportunities. This, in turn, leads to a decrease in school success and the sense of belonging and inclusion of students. Therefore, disciplinary actions and the way teachers treat their students determine school success and influence the commitment of students.

Instead of using disciplinary actions, it is proposed that any kind of relationship including sensitive and corresponding interactions can function as a protecting and enriching factor to promote children's competencies (Pianta, 1999, Baker, 2006, Darling-Hammond, 2020). From this point of view, a motivating, creative classroom environment and positive relationship experiences can support children to adjust to a cultural context that differs from their home context and help to meet expectations. It can also assist in dealing with increasing pressures for school success and being comfortable at school (Su, 2005). Close child-teacher relationships together with high quality classroom organisation could contribute towards better behavioural adaptation, greater social competence with their peers and engagement in learning environments (Howes, Phillips, & Whitebook, 1992; Pianta, 1999; Howes, Shivers, & Ritchie, 2004, Cadima et al., 2015, Baysu et al., 2021, Grütter et al., 2021). In other words, closer teacher-child relationships lead to a better transition to school, increases in adaptation, academic success and a sense of belonging.

When it comes to ethnically diverse students, potential expectations may rise in meeting requirements (Ready & Wright, 2011). Some teachers may keep students' motivation high by giving various pathways for enhanced learning and to enable better performance (Wubbels et al., 2006). Expectations and perceptions are important at this point. If teachers have biased attitudes about ethnic diversity, they are likely to make negative attributions for those students coming from diverse backgrounds. Even students themselves can make negative attributions about their own skills which may inhibit them from actively engaging in learning experiences (Adair, 2015). However, earlier research shows how teacher support can affect the academic performance of students and their commitment to school (Birch & Ladd, 1997, Pianta, 1999, Rucinski, Brown, & Downer, 2018, Darling-Hammond et al., 2020). For this reason, teachers, working at any grade level, with competencies such as initiating and sustaining positive student-teacher relationships, effective strategies in managing students' behaviours, continuous monitoring, keeping students' attention on appropriate tasks and creating a positive and culturally sensitive atmosphere within the classroom would contribute to better engagement of students and enhance their learning experiences. Instead of making assumptions about the ethnicity of children and their cultural expectations, recognising that every child comes from a different background and is unique should be the focus of all teachers. By having positive relationships with individual children, teachers may better understand the complexity and diversity of cultural backgrounds. This will enhance ways to communicate with those children and will also help to break down any barriers between children and teachers to ensure a connection is made.

Conflictual relationships stemming from teachers' biased views of ethnic diversity can lead to increased risks throughout school life, meaning that perceived conflict can widen the gap between students from ethnically diverse backgrounds and native students (Van der Bergh et.al., 2010, Vervaet et al., 2016). From this point of view, close relationships with teachers may function as a protective mechanism for ethnically diverse students (Pianta, 1999, Baker, 2006, Verschueren & Koomen, 2012, Baysu et al., 2021). It is critical for teachers to understand how close and supportive relationships are significantly important for diverse students when adapting to unfamiliar settings, specifically when considering integration into another culture that is diverse from the original family background (Thijs, Westhof, & Koomen, 2012). The more experience teachers can have with ethnically diverse children and the closer relationships they have, the less likely conflicts will occur. Also, working with ethnically diverse students would influence teachers' perceptions, leading to changes in teaching beliefs and methods and the teacher-child relationship (Su, 2005).

As stated by Wubbels et al. (2006) "ethnically diverse classrooms put heavier demands on teachers to manage than less diverse classrooms". Ethnic diversity is therefore one of the critical factors to focus on for both pre-service and in-service teacher training in organising classroom settings, learning environments and interpersonal relationships. Regarding preservice teachers' views, there are some variations about how diversity issues were perceived. In Clarke and Drudys study (2006), preservice teachers' attitudes were found to be resistant to meeting the needs of students in a diverse classroom, however this depended on the subject area. Although there was agreement about the involvement of diverse students in schools, preservice teachers also expressed concerns about having diverse students in their classes. This returns to the idea that teachers are not confident about how to engage with ethnically and linguistically diverse students and their parents (Peček, Macura-Milovanović, & Vujisić-Živković, 2014). Respecting and appreciating diversity is among the basic steps of social emotional learning skills. Therefore, it is critical, specifically for a teacher, to appreciate diversity (Kress & Elias, 2006). It is important to enrich teacher training programmes to increase awareness about cultural heritage, via engaging in direct experiences regarding various cultural practices, in order to improve teaching skills and strategies within classrooms. This enables teachers to consider cultural, linguistic, and individual needs of the children more effectively and to see this as an opportunity to develop and extend their teaching practices.

Shifting Negative Perceptions to Positive Ones: Improving Self-Awareness of Teachers Through Supervision

Unconscious bias has been discussed widely as an explanation for racism. If people are made aware of their biases, does it mean they will acknowledge these, accept them and have the willingness to change their behaviour? Noon (2017) questions the assumption that once biases have been identified, that changes to attitudes will follow. Implicit attitudes are described as automatic reactions to an object or situation and therefore are less likely to be adapted to be socially acceptable in any particular context (Glock et al., 2019). For this reason, there is a risk that unconscious bias could be used as an excuse for prejudiced attitudes in that sense. As it is not intended, making any change in attitudes and/or behaviours may be out with the individuals' control. Therefore, acknowledging that there may be some biases that might hinder effective communication is important. It might be difficult finding ways to eliminate those attitudes, however, one can still try to find ways to reduce the influence of these attitudes and beliefs on their behaviour, rather than reducing the prejudice itself (FitzGerald et al., 2019).

According to Jowsey (2019), there are stages in order to reach a higher level of recognition of diverse cultures and to deal with potential biases. First, at 'the surface competency zone', individuals need to understand how people behave and organise their daily practices within diverse cultures. This means one needs to have culture-specific knowledge. This may indicate a cultural awareness at surface level such as greeting people in their own languages or asking children and families to bring traditional food from their culture to the school. The second stage is 'the bias twilight zone' in which individuals look for hidden aspects of their ideas regarding diverse cultures which suggests increasing self-awareness and critical consciousness of biases that might influence behaviours and attitudes towards ethnically diverse individuals. Full competency is not a painless process; it is difficult to face one's own biases. This is called 'the confronting midnight zone'. Considering the three stages approach of Jowsey is key in pulling out hidden attitudes that might hinder communication with people from ethnically diverse backgrounds. The most crucial step is to recognise one's attitudes and hidden beliefs, face them and then revise them to display more bias free behaviours (Jowsey, 2019). Self-reflection on one's own experiences can assist this process. However, for those who do not have previous experiences or engagement with diverse communities that may prove more challenging. By exposing oneself to aspects of differing communities, self-reflection can be enhanced.

There are many ways of perceiving relationships to achieve enhanced and bias-free communication. Indeed, teachers may learn how to transform any negative perceptions into positive ones (Alvarez-Hevia, 2017). In order to achieve this, teachers need to know how to deal with their attitudes and potential negative emotions. Using self-reflection and self-criticality in terms of cultural consciousness to enhance experiences of all children as well as promoting better outcomes for ethnically diverse students is key (Gay & Kirkland, 2003). Teachers can reflect on their own beliefs and teaching practices by considering how cultural diversity can embrace all children in the context. Rather than only recognising the cultural difference, engaging in a respective and collaborative communication is another way to promote more inclusive practices in the classroom (Willis, 2021). Spending scheduled time with the children individually might be a helpful strategy to enhance this communication. In order to improve perceptions of both teachers and children, a relationship-based intervention programme called "Banking Time' could be used to enhance child–teacher relationships (Pianta, 1999; Pianta & Hamre 2001a, b, c). This is identified as one of the leading interventions in the field to promote positive interactions between teachers and children via face-to-face sessions initiated by teachers. There is a considerable amount of evidence indicating that teachers participating in Banking Time intervention groups had reported more positive relationship perceptions about children in their classrooms (Williford & Pianta, 2020, Driscoll & Pianta, 2010) Similarly, children reported how their relationships had improved via Banking Time sessions (Sahin Asi, 2019). In this intervention, the main idea is to share positive experiences during designated sessions. Although the teacher is the starting point to organise the sessions, the child leads the session without any instruction or interruption by the teacher. The teacher focuses on the child, what the child plays and/or says and tries to understand feelings of the child. This is used to create a key message to the child, called 'relational themes', such as 'I am here for you', to best explain the importance of the relationship between them. In this way, the child can see the teacher as a supportive adult hence, they both can get to know each other. This method helps to break down barriers and helps teachers find a connection between them and the individual child from which the basis of the relationship can grow.

Reflecting on the current or previous experiences of teachers would also be helpful to recognise alternatives in enhancing communication across ethnically diverse classrooms. Black (2021) emphasizes the importance of using clear lenses about cultural awareness while communicating with people from various cultural backgrounds:

'........(student)'s written reflection made me angry, I felt personally attacked, and I was in denial. These feelings instigated a cycle in which I evaded my racial awareness; I did not believe that I treated (student) and the other Black students any differently than the way I treated my white students.....At this point in my teaching career, I was utterly unwilling (and unable at the time) to view myself as anything other than a colorblind teacher who treated all her students fairly....(pp.122)'

For this reason, a supervision model might be helpful in teacher training programs and/or via in-service training programs to increase awareness teachers about their feelings and attitudes so that they can have better understanding how to manage an ethnically diverse classroom. In order to achieve this, teachers and/or teacher candidates might be supervised via case studies or reflective strategies for a particular period to enhance their skills in building and sustaining healthy relationships with their students. Weekly organised supervisory meetings or mentoring groups and/or individually planned sessions with a supervisor would be specifically helpful. During the supervision period, using reflective techniques, teachers might talk about their experiences, feelings, or struggles they experience. For example, saying if they think about a particular child at home, if so, in what ways, or describing a specific time at which they and a child had a positive experience (Pianta, 1999). These reveal the teacher's perceptions about any particular child and help the teacher become aware of her/his own thoughts, feelings, and/or attitudes. This might be a way to help them realise unspoken thoughts or feelings about children and increase self-awareness of teachers to improve sensitivity and responsiveness during interactions with their students.

CONCLUSION

There is a necessity to promote respect for diversity in educational settings since cultural variations will always be there. Increasing cross-cultural exchanges may help teachers to understand a variety of cultural practices and how these contribute towards various parts of society, more specifically school contexts (Greenfield, Suzuki, & Rothstein-Fisch, 2006). In this way, it may be possible to achieve a balance and understanding between distinct groups and to help manage diversity challenges in society. It is also crucial for teachers to recognise the experiences and expectations of families in order to have a broader sense of children. Teachers should prioritise time to get to know individual children and families they work with (Byrd, 2016). By doing so, teachers can better assess how each family is shaped, better understand cultural differences, and the potential support ethnically diverse families may benefit from. If teachers have more contact with parents, this is likely to increase the empathetic behaviour of teachers towards ethnically diverse children and their families. Correspondingly, parents and students may display more positive attitudes towards the school, which in turn may lead to more collaboration with teachers and the school management (Gay, 2002, Christenson, 2004). It could also lead to better outcomes academically and a more positive self-concept and feeling of belonging (Hughes & Kwok, 2007, Toldson & Lemmons, 2013).

A teacher may feel they have a role to protect students against school failure, maladjustment into school context and prejudiced attitudes as well. On the other hand, teachers who are not ethnically sensitive enough may evaluate their students' competencies negatively because of their biased attitudes (Vervaet et al., 2016) thus hindering academic success and social competencies of their students (Gregory et al., 2010, Van der Bergh et al., 2010). As discussed earlier, people's attitudes become more positive when they have more positive exposure to diverse cultures (Glock et al., 2019, Malo-Juvera, Correll, & Cantrell, 2018). This is possible in school environments with a significant cultural mix. However, in settings with limited diversity there could be a danger this could lead to a "stop and point" approach where individuals from diverse cultures are highlighted and could lead to more discrimination as they are being presented as "different." Teachers who are prepared for the likelihood of children from diverse backgrounds entering the classroom and who ensure the environment and resources reflect differing cultures, may also be warmer and more welcoming in their relationships with children as they are open to difference and change. Being prepared for the likelihood of children from diverse backgrounds entering the classroom may require additional initial input, such as resources or training however, enabling a more inclusive learning environment should be viewed as an essential part of the role, not an additional task. Teaching can be a stressful and highly demanding profession; however, it should be kept in mind that it is a fundamental right for *all* children to receive the best quality teaching possible.

Research has shown that an overall positive emotional climate may support high quality one-to-one relationships, however more supportive interactions at individual level are crucial (Rucinski et al., 2018). Spending quality time with individual children could be an effective strategy to challenge stereotypes and prejudices, on both sides, and lead to a more inclusive learning environment (Reddings, 2019). To achieve this, teachers need to be enabled to take time to reflect on their own attitudes. This should be an expectation of professional development. Identifying, challenging, and changing these attitudes is essential to provide a fair and equitable approach to learning for all students.

What is learnt from literature is that teachers may have prejudiced attitudes, as all humans do. However, it is important to be aware of how these attitudes may affect communication with children and to know that they are a crucial factor in determining the well-being of children. Making time to get to know each other to help make connections with individuals and to overcome potential biases should be a priority. For this reason, school is an important resource that can be utilized not only by children but also by families and teachers in order to better understand each other, to respect diversities and to find a way for living in harmony and peace.

REFERENCES

Adair, J. K. (2015). *The impact of discrimination on the early schooling experiences of children from immigrant families*. Migration Policy Institute.

Alvarez-Hevia, D. M. (2017). The Emotional Learning of Educators Working in Alternative Provision. *Educational Studies*, *54*(3), 303–318. doi:10.1080/00131946.2017.1356307

Ansari, A., Pianta, R. C., Whittaker, J. V., Vitiello, V. E., & Ruzek, E. A. (2020). Preschool Teachers' Emotional Exhaustion in Relation to Classroom Instruction and Teacher-child Interactions. *Early Education and Development*, *33*(1), 107–120. doi:10.1080/10409289.2020.1848301

Baker, J. A. (2006). Contributions of teacher–child relationships to positive school adjustment during elementary school. *Journal of School Psychology*, *44*(3), 211–229. doi:10.1016/j.jsp.2006.02.002

Banerjee, P. A., & Lamb, S. (2016). A Systematic Review of Factors Linked to Poor Academic Performance of Disadvantaged Students in Science and Maths in Schools. *Cogent Education*, *3*(1), 1178441. doi:10.1080/2331186X.2016.1178441

Baysu, G., Hillekens, J., Phalet, K., & Deaux, K. (2021). How Diversity Approaches Affect Ethnic Minority and Majority Adolescents: Teacher–Student Relationship Trajectories and School Outcomes. *Child Development*, *92*(1), 367–387. doi:10.1111/cdev.13417 PMID:32786088

Belhadj Kouider, E., Koglin, U., & Petermann, F. (2014). Emotional and behavioral problems in migrant children and adolescents in Europe: A systematic review. *European Child & Adolescent Psychiatry*, *23*(6), 373–391.

Biasutti, M., Concina, E., & Frate, S. (2020). Working in the classroom with migrant and refugee students: The practices and needs of Italian primary and middle school teachers. *Pedagogy, Culture & Society*, *28*(1), 113–129. https://doi.org/10.1080/14681366.2019.1611626

Birch, H., & Ladd, G. W. (1997). The Teacher-Child Relationship and Children's Early School Adjustment. *Journal of School Psychology, 35*(1), 61–79.

Black, A. D. (2021). Starting with the Teacher in the Mirror: Critical Reflections on Whiteness from Past Classroom Experiences. *The Clearing House: A Journal of Educational Strategies, Issues and Ideas, 94*(3), 116–127. doi:10.1080/00098655.2021.1907142

Byrd, C. M. (2016). Does Culturally Relevant Teaching Work? An Examination from Student Perspectives. *SAGE Open, 6*(3). https://doi.org/10.1177/2158244016660744

Cadima, J., Doumen, S., Verschueren, K., & Buyse, E. (2015). Child engagement in the transition to school: Contributions of self-regulation, teacher–child relationships and classroom climate. *Early Childhood Research Quarterly, 32*, 1–12.

Christenson, S. L. (2004). The Family-School Partnership: An Opportunity to Promote the Learning Competence of All Students. *School Psychology Review, 33*(1), 89–104.

Clarke, M., & Drudy, S. (2006). Teaching for diversity, social justice, and global awareness. *European Journal of Teacher Education, 29*(3), 371–386.

Coronel, J. M., & Gómez-Hurtado, I. (2015). Nothing to do with me! Teachers' perceptions on cultural diversity in Spanish secondary schools. *Teachers and Teaching, 21*(4), 400–420.

Daglar, M., Melhuish, E., & Barnes, J. (2011). Parenting and preschool child behavior among Turkish immigrant, migrant, and non-migrant families. *European Journal of Developmental Psychology, 8*(3), 261–279.

Darling-Hammond, L., Flook, L., Cook-Harvey, C., Barron, B., & Osher, D. (2020). Implications for educational practice of the science of learning and development. *Applied Developmental Science, 24*(2), 97–140. doi:10.1080/10888691.2018.1537791

Doan, S. N., Marcelo, A. K., & Yates, T. M. (2019). Ethnic-racial discrimination, family ethnic socialization and Latinx children's emotion competence. *Culture and Brain, 7*, 190–211. https://doi.org/10.1007/s40167-019-00079-w

Driscoll, K. C., & Pianta, R. C. (2010). Banking time in head start: Early efficacy of an intervention designed to promote supportive teacher-child relationships. *Early Education and Development, 21*(1), 38–64.

European Commission/EACEA/Eurydice. (2019). *Integrating Students from Migrant Backgrounds into Schools in Europe: National Policies and Measures. Eurydice Report*. Publications Office of the European Union.

European Union. (2013). *5th Annual Report on Immigration and Asylum*. https://ec.europa.eu/dgs/home-affairs/e-library/documents/policies/legal-migration/general/docs/5th_annual_report_on_immigration_and_asylum_en.pdf

FitzGerald, C., Martin, A., Berner, D., & Hurst, S. (2019). Interventions designed to reduce implicit prejudices and implicit stereotypes in real world contexts: A systematic review. *BMC Psychology*, *7*, 29. https://doi.org/10.1186/s40359-019-0299-7

Garner, P. W., Mahatmya, D., Brown, E. L., & Vesely, C. K. (2014). Promoting Desirable Outcomes Among Culturally and Ethnically Diverse Children in Social Emotional Learning Programs: A Multilevel Heuristic Model. *Educational Psychology Review*, *26*, 165–189. https://doi.org/10.1007/s10648-014-9253-7

Gay, G. (2002). Preparing for culturally responsive teaching. *Journal of Teacher Education*, *53*(2), 106–116.

Gay, G. (2013). Teaching To and Through Cultural Diversity. *Curriculum Inquiry*, *43*(1), 48–70.

Gay, G., & Kirkland, K. (2003). Developing Cultural Critical Consciousness and Self-Reflection in Preservice Teacher Education. *Theory into Practice*, *42*(3), 181–187. doi:10.120715430421tip4203_3

Gazeley, L., & Dunne, M. (2013). Initial Teacher Education programmes: Providing a space to address the disproportionate exclusion of Black pupils from schools in England? *Journal of Education for Teaching*, *39*(5), 492–508. doi:10.1080/02607476.2013.844956

Geerlings, J., Thijs, J., & Verkuyten, M. (2017). Student-teacher relationships and ethnic outgroup attitudes among majority students. *Journal of Applied Developmental Psychology*, *52*, 69–79. doi:10.1016/j.appdev.2017.07.002

Glock, S. (2016). Does ethnicity matter? The impact of stereotypical expectations on in-service teachers' judgments of students. *Social Psychology of Education*, *19*, 493–509. https://doi.org/10.1007/s11218-016-9349-7

Glock, S., Kovacs, C., & Pit-ten Cate, I. (2019). Teachers' attitudes towards ethnic minority students: Effects of Schools' cultural diversity. *The British Journal of Educational Psychology*, *89*, 616–634.

Goodwin, A. L., & Stanton, R. (2022). Lessons from an Expert Teacher of Immigrant Youth: A Portrait of Social Justice Teaching. *Equity & Excellence in Education*, *55*(1-2), 23–36. doi:10.1080/10665684.2021.2021652

Gopalkrishnan, N. (2018). Cultural Diversity and Mental Health: Considerations for Policy and Practice. *Frontiers in Public Health*, *6*, 179. https://doi.org/10.3389/fpubh.2018.00179

Greenfield, P. M., Suzuki, L. K., & Rothstein-Fisch, C. (2006). Cultural pathways through human development. In K. A. Renninger & I. E. Sigel (Eds.), Handbook of Child Psychology: Vol. 4. *Child Psychology in Practice*. John Wiley & Sons, Inc.

Greenwald, A. G., Nosek, B. A., & Banaji, M. R. (2003). Understanding and using the Implicit Association Test: I. An improved scoring algorithm. *Journal of Personality and Social Psychology*, *85*(2), 197–216.

Gregory, A., Skiba, R. J., & Noguera, P. A. (2010). The achievement gap and the discipline gap: Two sides of the same coin? *Educational Researcher*, *39*(1), 59–68.

Grütter, J., Meyer, B., Philipp, M., Stegmann, S., & van Dick, R. (2021). Beyond Ethnic Diversity: The Role of Teacher Care for Interethnic Relations. *Frontiers in Education*, *5*, 586709. doi:10.3389/feduc.2020.586709

Han, H. S., & Thomas, M. S. (2010). No Child Misunderstood: Enhancing Early Childhood Teachers' Multicultural Responsiveness to the Social Competence of Diverse Children. *Early Childhood Education Journal, 37,* 469–476.

Hannon, L., & O'Donnell, G. M. (2022). Teachers, parents, and family-school partnerships: Emotions, experiences, and advocacy. *Journal of Education for Teaching, 48*(2), 241–255. doi:10.1080/0260747 6.2021.1989981

Herzog-Punzenberger, B., Altrichter, H., & Brown, M. (2020). Teachers responding to cultural diversity: Case studies on assessment practices, challenges, and experiences in secondary schools in Austria, Ireland, Norway, and Turkey. *Educational Assessment, Evaluation and Accountability, 32,* 395–424. https://doi.org/10.1007/s11092-020-09330-y

Horenczyk, G., & Tatar, M. (2002). Teachers' attitudes toward multiculturalism and their perceptions of the school organizational culture. *Teaching and Teacher Education, 18,* 435–445.

Howes, C., Phillips, D. A., & Whitebook, M. (1992). Thresholds of quality: Implications for the social development of children in center–based childcare. *Child Development, 63,* 449–460.

Howes, C., Shivers, E. M., & Ritchie, S. (2004). improving social relationships in childcare through a researcher-program partnership. *Early Education and Development, 15,* 57–78.

Hughes, J., & Kwok, O. (2007). Influence of Student–Teacher and Parent–Teacher Relationships on Lower Achieving Readers' Engagement and Achievement in the Primary Grades. *Journal of Educational Psychology, 99*(1), 39 51.

Jowsey, T. (2019). Three zones of cultural competency: Surface competency, bias twilight, and the confronting midnight zone. *BMC Medical Education, 19*(1), 306. https://doi.org/10.1186/s12909-019-1746-0

Kagitcibasi, C. (2010). *Family, Self and Human Development across Cultures: Theory and Applications.* Koc University Publications.

Kress, J. S., & Elias, M. J. (2006). School-based social and emotional learning programs in Handbook of Child Psychology: Vol. 4: Child Psychology in Practice (6th ed.). John Wiley & Sons, Inc.

Ladson-Billings, G. (1995). Toward a theory of culturally relevant pedagogy. *American Educational Research Journal, 32*(3), 465–491.

Malo-Juvera, V., Correll, P., & Cantrell, S. A. (2018). mixed methods investigation of teachers' self-efficacy for culturally responsive instruction. *Teaching and Teacher Education, 74,* 146–156. https://doi.org/10.1016/j.ijintrel.2020.08.001

Milner, H. R., & Tenore, F. B. (2010). Classroom Management in Diverse Classrooms. *Urban Education, 45*(5), 560–603.

NAEYC. (2009). Developmentally Appropriate Practice in Early Childhood Programs Serving Children from Birth through. *Age (Dordrecht, Netherlands), 8.* Retrieved December 15, 2016, from https://www.naeyc.org/files/naeyc/file/positions/position%20 statement%20Web.pdf

Noon, M. (2017). Pointless Diversity Training: Unconscious Bias, New Racism and Agency. *Work, Employment and Society, 32*(1), 198–209.

Oades-Sese, G. V., Esquivel, G. B., Kaliski, P. K., & Maniatis, L. (2011). A longitudinal study of the social and academic competence of economically disadvantaged bilingual preschool children. *Developmental Psychology, 47*(3), 747–764. https://doi.org/10.1037/a0021380

Okonofua, J. A., & Eberhardt, J. L. (2015). Two Strikes: Race and the Disciplining of Young Students. *Psychological Science, 26*(5), 617–624. https://www.jstor.org/stable/24544011

Paris, D. (2012). Culturally Sustaining Pedagogy: A Needed Change in Stance, Terminology, and Practice. *Educational Researcher, 41*(3), 93–97. doi:10.3102/0013189X12441244

Paris, D. (2021). Culturally Sustaining Pedagogies and Our Futures. *The Educational Forum, 85*(4), 364–376. doi:10.1080/00131725.2021.1957634

Payne, B. K., Burkley, M. A., & Stokes, M. B. (2008). Why Do Implicit and Explicit Attitude Tests Diverge? The Role of Structural Fit. *Journal of Personality and Social Psychology, 94*(1), 16–31.

Peček, M., Macura-Milovanović, S., & Vujisić-Živković, N. (2014). The cultural responsiveness of teacher candidates towards Roma pupils in Serbia and Slovenia–case studies. *Journal of Education for Teaching, 40*(4), 359–376.

Pianta, R. C. (1999). *Enhancing relationships between children and teachers*. American Psychological Association.

Pianta, R. C., & La Paro, K. (2003). Improving early school success. *Educational Leadership*, (April), 24–29.

Pianta, R. C., Stuhlman, M. W., & Hamre, B. K. (2002). How schools can do better: Fostering stronger connections between teachers and students. *New Directions for Youth Development, 93*, 91–107.

Price-Dennis, D., & Souto-Manning, M. (2011). (Re)Framing Diverse Pre-service Classrooms as Spaces for Culturally Relevant Teaching. *The Journal of Negro Education, 80*(3), 223–238. Retrieved June 16, 2021, from https://www.jstor.org/stable/41341130

Ready, D. D., & Wright, D. L. (2011). Accuracy and inaccuracy in teachers' perceptions of young children's cognitive abilities: The role of child background and classroom context. *American Educational Research Journal, 48*(2), 335–360.

Redding, C. (2019). A Teacher Like Me: A Review of the Effect of Student–Teacher Racial/Ethnic Matching on Teacher Perceptions of Students and Student Academic and Behavioral Outcomes. *Review of Educational Research, 89*(4), 499–535. https://doi.org/10.3102/0034654319853545

Rogoff, B. (2011). Developing destinies: a Mayan midwife and town. Oxford University Press. Retrieved November 2, 2022, from, https://doi.org/10.1093/acprof:oso/9780195319903.001.0001.

Rucinski, C. L., Brown, J. L., & Downer, J. T. (2018). Teacher–child relationships, classroom climate, and children's social-emotional and academic development. *Journal of Educational Psychology, 110*(7), 992–1004. https://dx.doi.org/10.1037/edu0000240

Sahin Asi, D. (2019). How Banking Time intervention works in Turkish preschool classrooms for enhancing student–teacher relationships. *ICEP, 13*(3). doi:10.1186/s40723-019-0059-4

Shor, R., & Bernhard, J. K. (2003). A comparative study of conflicts experienced between immigrant parents in Canada and in Israel, and professionals in educational institutions about appropriate responses to children's misbehavior. *Intercultural Education, 14*(4), 385–396.

Souto-Manning, M., & Mitchell, C. H. (2010). The Role of Action Research in Fostering Culturally Responsive Practices in a Preschool Classroom. *Early Childhood Education Journal, 37*, 269. https://doi.org/10.1007/s10643-009-0345-9

Sparkman, D. J., & Hamer, K. (2020). Seeing the human in everyone: Multicultural experiences predict more positive intergroup attitudes and humanitarian helping through identification with all humanity. *International Journal of Intercultural Relations, 79*, 121–134. doi:10.1016/j.ijintrel.2020.08.007

Su, Y. L. (2005). *Understanding Teachers' Experiences Working with Young Children from Diverse Cultural and Linguistic Backgrounds* [Unpublished doctoral dissertation]. Virginia Polytechnic Institute and State University.

Thijs, J., Westhof, S., & Koomen, H. (2012). Ethnic incongruence and the student–teacher relationship: The perspective of ethnic majority teachers. *Journal of School Psychology, 50*, 257–273.

Toldson, I. A., & Lemmons, B. P. (2013). Social demographics, the school environment, and parenting practices associated with parents' participation in schools and academic success among Black, Hispanic, and White students. *Journal of Human Behavior in the Social Environment, 23*(2), 237–255.

Van den Bergh, L., Denessen, E., Hornstra, L., Voeten, M., & Holland, R. W. (2010). The implicit prejudiced attitudes of teachers: Relations to teacher expectations and the ethnic achievement gap. *American Educational Research Journal, 47*(2), 497–527.

Verschueren, K., & Koomen, H. M. Y. (2012). Teacher–child relationships from an attachment perspective. *Attachment & Human Development, 14*(3), 205–211.

Vervaet, R., D'hondt, F., Van Houtte, M., & Stevens, P. A. J. (2016). The ethnic prejudice of Flemish teachers: The role of ethnic school composition and of teachability. *Cultural Diversity & Ethnic Minority Psychology, 22*(4), 552–562. https://doi.org/10.1037/cdp0000085

Williford, A. P., & Pianta, R. C. (2020). Banking Time: A Dyadic Intervention to Improve Teacher-Student Relationships. In A. Reschly, A. Pohl, & S. Christenson (Eds.), Student Engagement. Springer. https://doi.org/10.1007/978-3-030-37285-9_13.

Willis, A. S. (2021). Teachers' cultural, social and emotional capabilities: How teacher compassion and humility is an antecedent to student confidence. *Pedagogy, Culture & Society*. Advance online publication. doi:10.1080/14681366.2021.1884122

Wubbels, T., Den Brok, P., Veldman, I., & Van Tartwijk, J. (2006). Teacher interpersonal competence for Dutch secondary multicultural classrooms. *Teachers and Teaching, 12*(4), 407–433.

Yates, T. M., & Marcelo, A. K. (2014). Through race-colored glasses: Preschoolers pretend play and teachers' ratings of preschooler adjustment. *Early Childhood Research Quarterly, 29*, 1–11.

Chapter 13
Teacher Identity and Language Ideology via Critical Pedagogy

Juland Dayo Salayo
https://orcid.org/0000-0001-5540-7885
University of Santo Tomas, Philippines

Merry Ruth M. Gutierrez
Philippine Normal University, Philippines

ABSTRACT

This qualitative research aims to determine how language teachers' ontological beliefs on critical pedagogy build teacher identity and language ideology. Participants included 18 public junior high school teachers. Results revealed that critical language pedagogy (CLP) constructed teacher identities against its trajectory. These identities include the lack of familiarity and misunderstanding of CLP, resistance to a critical teaching approach, dependency on the official textbook or learning modules, and confidence in their traditional practices. Similarly, distorted critical language ideologies were also determined, such as language as an apolitical entity, CLP as a threat to social and cultural harmony, L1 as a threat to L2 learning, and the perceived dominance of American English. Both identities and ideologies are attributed to social conflicts and sociopolitical activities that produce oppression and marginalization. Hence, it is recommended that the education sector provide an opportunity to fully understand the role of criticality through dialogue, reflection, and praxes.

INTRODUCTION

Critical pedagogy (CP), associated with Paulo Freire, aims to concretize the process of transforming the oppressed into humanized and empowered individuals. Its criticality roots in constructing a just, democratic and liberated society where every member experiences "political, economic, and cultural control" (p. 77). With such a goal, CP rejects the dominance, violations, marginalization, oppression, and inequalities by developing social consciousness (Aliakbari & Faraji, 2011). In language teaching, its criticality is still influenced by the Freirean ideology of teaching for social justice, which is supported

DOI: 10.4018/978-1-6684-6386-4.ch013

by "democratic values associated with equality, freedom, and solidarity" (p. 247). Several approaches are highlighted in achieving such critical language teaching, which include the following: problem-posing, dialogic engagement, praxes (reflection and action), and critical thinking (Crookes, 2021). In Henry Giroux's principal features of critical language pedagogy (CLP), he emphasized the students' subjectivities and voice which is their political nature, in search for truth, equality, and justice through language use (Pennycook, 2017).

While critical pedagogy, generally, has been explored in different contexts across the globe, language teacher identity through CLP remains underrated in research; hence, it is interesting to know how critical language teachers construct their identities, specifically with the influence of radical teaching, which aims transformational achievement and social consciousness (Kubota, 2017). With the complexities of teachers' identities, it was suggested by Higgins (2017) to investigate further teachers' experiences [in using additional language] and their language ideologies for the class. With such intricacies and limitations of critical studies concerning teachers' identities and language ideologies, this study determined to respond to those established gaps, specifically in the Philippine context, where education remains conservative.

Teacher Identity

It has been established by several studies that teacher identity undoubtedly builds relations between and among teachers and students, including their relation to the institutions and the formation of language teaching and learning ideologies (Toohey, 2017). However, language teacher identity is not confined to a single ground of understanding because of its multifaceted, dynamic, and adaptive characteristics, which are shaped and linked by their internal and external worlds (Cheung, 2017). Its complexity lies in the multiple influences of the social, historical, and political realities acquired or inherited, such as physical appearance, actions, decisions, perceptions through human interactions, and experiences and associations, which further produce several more identities that construct self-image concerning social reality. In pedagogy, teachers' teaching experiences and their philosophical stance on language teaching could also serve as a reference for building language teacher identities (Matsuda, 2017). These complexities that shaped identity caused Menezes de Oliveira e Paiva (2017, pp. 260-261) to define teacher identity as a fractal system because it constantly "changes, self-organizes, and adapts to the environment." Hence, this complex interactive system produces complex human identities associated with gender, social, political, and religious affiliations and associations to their communities, including the "imagined community of English speakers."

In language education, teacher identities are "cognitive, social, emotional, ideological, and historical" (Barkhuizen, 2017, p. 4), which defines language teachers as influenced by executing language learning, interacting with other members of their academic and professional community, philosophical underpinnings that guide them in pedagogical practices, their perception of themselves and their society, and the influences of their past to define their present self.

These complexities were addressed by Nelson (2017) as an identity-related dilemma, but this conflicting understanding is believed to provide language education with even more excitement brought upon by social changes.

Previous studies and narratives on teacher identities were conducted, which were associated with or correlated to different factors or variables. For instance, English language teachers' professional identity and autonomy were investigated to determine their impact on instructional success. Having participating Iranian EFL teachers, using the Teacher Autonomy Questionnaire (TAQ), the Teacher Professional

Identity Scale (TPIS), and the Characteristics of Successful Language Teachers Questionnaire (CSLTQ), significant correlations among the stated factors were established. Hence, teacher identity and autonomy can contribute to the respondents' instructional success. These professional identities include "external influential factors, self-expectation, pedagogy, teachers' duties, teaching knowledge and expertise, as well as instructors' citizenship behavior" (Derakhshan et al., 2020, p. 18).

Pedagogical applications and practices were considered to determine the pre-service teachers' professional identity in Estonia. To establish and understand such identity, the study focused on developing professional identity through teacher knowledge and analytical skills, which support their teaching job. Besides, personal identity was also highlighted by stressing their beliefs, values, and experiences. Finally, pedagogies were employed to support the integration of professional and personal identities (Leijen et al., 2014).

During the pandemic, another perspective of language teachers' identity, including their emotions and well-being, was identified in the context of Kazakhstan as influenced by its complex "geopolitical, institutional and sociocultural tensions" (Chen, 2021, p. xiii). With this, teachers' access to ICT during remote emergency teaching and acquiring the necessary skills to address the needs of the learners and community has been dramatically affected. In effect, teachers become emotionally challenged because of the failure to meet the pedagogical standards and the community expectations, including the administration, parents, and other stakeholders. Additionally, they have developed such poor self-worth as their lack of familiarity and skills with the virtual platform made them helpless to continue the traditional classroom practices, which are not intended for the new learning environment. Such confusion and frustrations deprofessionalized their identity and diminished their self-efficacy (Kozhabayeva & Boivin (2021).

Language Ideologies

Such limitations on the concretization of language teacher identities parallel the challenges of concretizing language ideology. Although generally, the latter pertains to the systems of beliefs and behavior about the aspects of lived experiences that connect one's relationship with any human experience. From a more critical perspective, it reflects and values the cultural orientations of what language is, how it operates and what it does in the social world; hence, it builds the so-called 'symbolic power' (Blommaert, 2006, Bourdieu, 1991, cited in Mooney & Evans, 2015). Similarly, it was emphasized that language ideologues are permeated with political, cultural, and moral interests, which construe language use concerning their role and position in the social, political, and cultural world (Irvine & Gal, 2009; Woolard, 2020). In this case, language ideologies are not limited to language only but their association, relation, and implication to the material world as phenomena and identities (Woolard, 2020). Sustaining the ideologies as a universal understanding, Hall and Cunningham (2020, p. 2) stated that these are a "set of beliefs, attitudes, and behaviors which develop in individuals through socialization into cultural groups," which may be contributory in either developing resistance to or supporting social hegemony.

Like teacher identity, previous studies and narratives on language ideologies were also associated with different factors to build its concept further and understand significant issues and approaches. Some of these include political economy (Friedrich, 1989), linguistic differentiation (Irvine & Gal, 2009), language policy (Spolsky & Shohamy, 2000), language prejudice (Lippi-Green, 2004), and neoliberalism (Holborow, 2007), among others. Behind some narratives on ideological stance and social consciousness, such as Collins (1999), the development of critical language ideology is concretely established

Table 1. Gee's (2000) Four Ways to View Identity

Perspective	Description	Process	Power	Source of Power
Nature-identity	A state	Developed from	Forces	In nature/biological
Institutional-identity	A position	Authorized by	Authorities	Within institution
Discourse-identity	An individual trait	Recognized in	The discourse/dialog	Of/with 'rational' individual
Affinity-identity	Experiences	Shared in	The practice	Of affinity groups

in modern-day language and education research. However, there is an apparent scarcity of language ideology concerning critical pedagogy.

Theoretical Frameworks

Gee's Identity Theory. Generally, teacher identity can hardly be concretized because it is not permanently attributed to an individual because of his/her relation to the "social, material and technological world" (Barkhuizen, 2017, p. 5). In a sense, identity can be developed by human beliefs and reflection as defined by their role in society. On the contrary, society can also be a powerful influence to dictate and shape one's identity according to social, political, cultural, or even moral orientations and affiliations. In this case, identity can change because of a contestant's human interaction, learning acquisition, and institutional engagement, which sustains or affects the complex and dynamic formation of identities.

The Identity framework by Gee (2000) is adopted for this study to support the research objectives. Accordingly, four significant components *(see Table 1)* clarify understanding and analyzing social contexts of one's identity, which shows the different perspectives, descriptions, processes, and influences of building one's identity. These consist of nature-identity, institutional-identity, discourse-identity, and affinity identity.

The first component is nature-identity, which refers to the state of being that characterizes an individual's natural or biological traits. Hence, human nature defines us as dictated by acquired biological characteristics, which answer "Who am I?" The second component pertains to the institutional-identity, which is determined or influenced by authorial power, such as the state where one is affiliated, such as citizenship, education, employment, and others. Through this, our identity is influenced by the role or position human plays in his/her world, which answer, "How do my institutional affiliations assign the role that describes me?" Next is discourse-identity, which defines one's trait or character through his/her dialog, language use, preference, and style as he/she interacts with others. Hence, such identity can be produced from the recognition of others through human interaction. This may answer, "How does my language define me as a social agent?" Finally, affinity-identity is assigned by one's community as a product of his/her association or participation in shared community activities. This may answer, "How does my interaction with community practices define me?"

The complexity and dynamism of human identities are primarily produced by the interdependence of one identity with the others as it is evitable that human behavior, beliefs, and practices may be influenced by either personal or outside world as human goals toward development and improvement arise through learning, interaction, and association.

Language relativity. On top of the diverse views on language beliefs, this study is anchored to the theory or principle of language [linguistic] relativity, which hypothesizes that language structure, including their vocabulary, reflects the speakers' cognition of their world. Aligned explicitly with the idea of Benjamin Lee Whorf and Edward Sapir, this linguistic relativity "advocate the position that language limits, or at least influences, the way a speech community conceives of its worldview and reality" (Chapman & Routledge, 2009, p. 116). Giving clarity to the relationship between language and culture and thinking, Chapman and Routledge (2009, p. 117) further quoted Sapir's position on language and society:

Language is a guide to 'social reality.' Though language is not ordinarily thought of as a vital interest to the students of social science, it powerfully conditions all our thinking about social problems and processes. Human beings do not live in the objective world alone, not alone in the world of social activity as ordinarily understood, but are very much at the mercy of the particular language which has become the medium of expression for their society. It is quite an illusion to imagine that one adjusts to reality essentially without the use of language and specific problems of communication or reflection. The fact of the matter is that the 'real world' is to a large extent unconsciously built up on the language habits of the group. No two languages are ever sufficiently similar to be considered as representing the same social reality. The worlds in which different societies live are distinct worlds, not merely the same world with different labels attached.

In this study, society and culture become the central consideration in constructing language ideology through critical pedagogy. Participants' ontological engagements with their actual community are translated into more concrete views of the language and their world. In the end, it is not just the position of the language in the society that is investigated, but rather the language itself as a reflection of social activities and interactions socially, culturally, historically, and politically. Hence, language is the result of their social reality.

Research Problems

With a provocative stance to build an abstract language teachers' identity and language ideology via critical pedagogy, this study aims to determine how teachers of English in a government school in the Philippines perceived and characterized the employment of critical language pedagogy in Filipino ESL classrooms that build language ideology and teachers' identity as perceived by the participants. Specifically, this answered this question: *How do language teachers' ontological beliefs on critical pedagogy build teacher identity and language ideology in their ESL classes?*

METHODOLOGY

This present study is qualitative research, which intends to uncover the meaning of a particular phenomenon; hence qualitative researchers' interest evolves around "understanding how people interpret their experiences, how they construct their worlds, and what meaning they attribute to their experiences" (Merriam & Tisdell, 2016, p. 6). The goal of determining the participants' perception of identity and ideology through critical pedagogy is anchored to the phenomenological-ontological-interpretive or constructivist approach, which aims to describe, understand and interpret the multiple realities that characterize the beliefs, experiences, and practices of the participants about language teaching.

To achieve such a goal, this qualitative study was conducted on eighteen (18) public school teachers who taught English classes in Junior High Schools in the Province of Cavite, South of Metro Manila, the Philippines. They taught English subjects for Grades 7, 8, 9, and 10. They were volunteered participants in response to the released call for participation and personal invitation for this research purpose. Necessary consent from the participants was provided to voluntarily participate with an assurance of protecting their identity as demanded by the ethical standards. Junior high school teachers were considered because of their direct engagements with the young learners whose critical thinking is highly encouraged to be developed as a foundation for becoming critical citizens of the nation. Additionally, it is interesting to determine if the Philippine K to 12 highlighted skills in communication, critical thinking, problem-solving, career and life, and understanding self and society (Department of Education, 2009) are supported by the ontological beliefs and practices of the participants in their ESL classes.

After the experts validated the instrument and interview questionnaire for critical language teaching and learning, the researchers personally approached the participants to participate in this present study and scheduled specific times for both semi-structured interviews (SSI) and unstructured interviews (USI). Both structured and unstructured types of interviews were conducted to avoid possible limitations of the participants to provide a richness of information. Accordingly, semi-structured interviews produce multiple themes, and free responses "uncover knowledge through interaction, conversations, and subjects from different life experiences" (Kakilla, 2021, p. 1). With seemingly related or overlapping definitions with the previous, unstructured interview "elicits people's social reality" to understand the complex behavior of the participants through the natural flow of conversation or inquiry (Zhang & Wildermuth, n.d., p. 1). Hence, the goal of unveiling their ontological beliefs toward critical pedagogy would be elaborated and produce the necessary information to establish the status of critical language teaching in basic education.

Some participants were interviewed physically, while others participated online, including through phone interviews. After collecting the necessary data through the interview recordings, the researcher transcribed it, then coded the data for content and thematic analysis and interpretation. The researchers clarified through e-mail, online chat, and phone calls to address item ambiguities beyond the researchers' understanding. Results were further confirmed by scholars in education, language studies, and philosophy.

RESULTS AND DISCUSSION

Critical pedagogy in language learning is an underrated field, especially regarding research. With several classroom myths concerning radical and revolutionary teaching, a conservative community like the Philippines considers this teaching approach inappropriate, especially for young learners. Commonly, people believe that any act of radical thinking is detrimental to the value formation of young learners; hence, they may end up with a philosophical formation that disadvantages the nation's security, peace, and order. In the article of McShane and Hess (2021), conservative principles were highlighted, which either directed or contradicted with philosophical and practical elaborations in the Philippine context. Among those principles which highly define conservative in the local context is that schools are formative rather than performative grounds. While education aims to help learners to be critical thinkers and responsible citizens, the idea of conservative has extended its impact to enrich their ideological stance, but with limited opportunities to practically convert theories into practice. Such limitations are culturally influenced that learners need to submit themselves to the wisdom of the adults or the teachers in the learning community. In the end, the goal of transformative education heavily lies on an ideological agenda rather than active engagement in transforming themselves and their society. What makes this worst is the limited opportunity for the learners to question those discomforts that affect their learning.

Van der Galien (2006) argued that one of the challenges of conservative education is that schools are funded locally, which may result in unfair opportunities for improvement as the poor local government may not address the needs of their local schools. While Philippine education is generally nationally-funded, the local government's role significantly influences the school's overall entity. On a positive note, partnership, collaboration, and cooperation with local stakeholders are important ways to improve learning. On the other hand, the implementation of the local school board is highly controlled by the local government. This reality may strengthen the argument of Durban and Catalan (2012) that there is really "too much politics in [Philippine] education" (p. 7).

The issue of conservatism may also be attributed to the curriculum's misalignment to the learners' needs and overloaded subjects and competencies. This reality heavily burdens young learners and may be detrimental to developing nationalism and patriotism (Durban & Catalan, 2012). These academic burdens could also produce a conservative stand where learners acquire learning according to the demand of the academic frame, such as achievement of competencies, with the limited realization of the social functions of education. These and many more related issues on education have called for the review of the recently implemented K to 12 programs in the Philippine education by President Ferdinand "Bong Bong" Marcos, Jr. to improve the quality of the country's education, especially in Science and English as a second language (Maralit, 2022).

In this study, the interview of 18 public school teachers demonstrated those myths and misconceptions remain myths and misconceptions that damage the purity of critical pedagogy's agenda. However, this problematic status of critical pedagogy further builds teachers' identity and language ideology that deserves further investigations and solutions.

From Ontological Beliefs to Teacher Identity via Critical Pedagogy

Consistent with Gee's identity framework, participants of this study also revealed their different identities associated with their ontological beliefs on employing critical language pedagogy in ESL classrooms. These dominant identities, as shown in Table 2, consist of the following: unfamiliarity with and misunderstanding the critical pedagogy as an approach to language teaching, dependence on the official textbooks or modules, which affects their teaching creativity, perceived resistance of the authority toward criticality, confidence in their conventional practices in language teaching, and confidence in their job as producers of knowledge.

Initially, teachers believed they were already practicing criticality in their daily classroom teaching routines. It is common for teachers to include 'achieving critical thinking skills as one of the learning objectives. Besides, 'critical reading,' 'critical engagement,' and 'critical writing' were overly used in their weekly learning plans, either in the learning objectives, activities, or assessments. However, the achievement of criticality can hardly be concretized because learners remain passive participants in the classroom. Most often than not, teachers complain that students do not want to speak using English as the target or focus language of the subject. Many of them worry about the results of the examinations, which are only sometimes favorable to the target goals of the assessment. Generally, English class be-

Table 2. Constructed teacher identities via critical language pedagogy (CLP)

Constructed Teacher Identities	Perspectives	Influences / Causes
Lack of familiarity and misunderstanding of CLP	Nature-identity	Social, cultural, and political orientation; submission to authority; lack of training in critical approaches; resistance to criticality
Perceived resistance of the authority to the critical teaching approach	Institutional-identity	Established power of the authority; unquestioned authority; gap between the administration and the teachers; observed administrations' identity
Dependency on the official textbook or learning modules	Institutional-identity	Standardized learning materials and sources; lack of time for creative constructions of critical references and materials due to teachers' workloads; lack of training in material development and preparation
Confidence and trust in the traditional practices	Affinity-identity	Fossilized praxes (dependency on the positive outcome of the old practices and measurements); lack of motivation
Resistant to CLP	Nature-identity	Personal beliefs/perceptions about critical teaching approaches; social, cultural, and political orientations

comes either a ground of 'silence' as learners mostly listen and agree with the dominant presence of the teachers or the ground of L1 production in an L2 class. As a result, English can produce a wider gap between and among learners' differences associated with their social and cultural orientations.

When critical pedagogy was introduced to them, they expressed **their unfamiliarity with and misunderstanding of critical pedagogy (nature-identity)**. According to one of the participants, their criticality measurement is the learners' activeness in the class by responding to the teachers' questions, engaging with the class activities, topping the assessments, and observing the rules and mechanics of good grammar, which is the central and ultimate goal of language learning. Suppose the learner follows and observes grammar rules, correct use of punctuations, and appropriate use of vocabulary in different tasks. In that case, they could be critical thinkers as far as language learning is concerned. This lack of awareness and misunderstanding of critical pedagogy can be attributed to the social, educational, cultural, and political orientations of their locale and their submission to the authority, which significantly affect their recognition of criticality and the development of critical thinking skills. However, in the study of Aliakbari and Amori (2014), awareness of the language instructors' critical pedagogy is attributed to age, gender, educational background, and work experiences. The more the participants grow in age, degree, and experience, the more likely they show better appreciation and understanding of critical approaches in teaching. Regarding gender, female participants responded better to critical pedagogy items, which contradicted their previous study revealing that male participants are superior. In the end, scholars and researchers agree that critical pedagogy is unfamiliar, underrated, and explored discipline in [language] education and research (Aliakbari & Amoli, 2014; Ghaemi & Sadeghi, 2015; Mahmoodarabi & Khodabakhsh (2015).

These decade-long struggles of the public school teachers are influenced by the education practice that the teachers remain apolitical with many social and political issues, including sharing their political views on social media, such as teachers' participation in different political issues and activities like the election. This has been reiterated by the education czar, Leonor M. Briones, that teachers' neutrality is supported by DO 048, which states the "prohibition against electioneering and partisan political activity, citing that it is in violation of Article IX-B Section 2(b), Paragraph 4 of the 1987 [Philippine] Constitution" (Soriano, 2021, para. 6). However, this legal reference of the education chief is opposed by Urayjan Borlaza stating that being apolitical is a danger to the freedom of expression stipulated by the constitution, while Kristhean Navales highlighted the "teacher's job of teaching critical thinking and identifying what is wrong from right based on verifiable facts will never become apolitical" (para. 11). Supporting his arguments is his reference to Commission of Election and Civil Service Commission's Joint Circular 1, s. 2016 "expressing one's views on current political problems or issues cannot be deemed as a partisan political activity" (Bautista, 2021, para. 7). Borlaza (in Bautista, 2021, paras. 8 & 10) further states:

'Public expressions, opinions or discussions of probable issues in a forthcoming election, or on attributes of or criticisms against probable candidates to be nominated in a forthcoming political party convention' is also excluded from what is considered as electioneering ... It's an act of charity to the nation when we, teachers, become faithful to our vocation to free the young from ignorance and disinformation even in the realm of social media.

This example opposes, and even worsens, the primary reason for critical pedagogy in critiquing the "unquestioned practices with concrete ways of introducing change through the individual teacher" (Johnson, 1999, cited in Aliakbari & Amoli, 2014, p. 128), which allows individuals to shape their position as significant key players of economic, social, political, and personal changes and reforms. In another significant discussion, the popularity of Freirean ideology still needs to gain wide recognition and be fully integrated into formal schooling because Freire's identity is usually identified with other radical thinkers such as Marx, Lenin, Mao, and Guevarra. They are considered threats to a repressive society (Cortez, 2013). While they all agree on a radical approach to attaining social equality, Freire emphasized the role of the learner to be the subject, not just a mere object; hence, a learner must serve as a co-producer of knowledge (*see Table 3*).

Further, despite the available studies and narratives on critical pedagogy, relatively limited attention and interest have been observed, which affect teachers' beliefs and associated aspects of criticality in language teaching (Mahmoodarabi & Khodabakhsh, 2015). Contributory to this is highlighted by Abraham (2014) as he stated that "critical pedagogy is criticized for a focus on the macro-level system, for not having a model for classroom implementation and for being abstract" (p. 1); hence, the lack of applicability in ESL classroom centers on the call for the teachers to "do the work of empowering, to be the agents of empowerment, without providing much in the way of concrete guidance for that work" (Gore, 1992, cited in Riasati & Mollaei, 2012).

Another issue is their **'perceived resistant of the authority toward critical classroom approach.'** While they fully understand that the education agency calls for 'criticality, learner empowerment, student-centeredness, inclusivity, and other associated terms, the very concept of critical teaching is believed to be unfavorable to the taste of the administration because of the possibility of developing radical learners whose ideology is not aligned to the mission, vision, objectives, and philosophy of education. It is associated with nature-identity because it is a common thinking of the teachers to follow what the administration wants them to do. In this case, it becomes their nature to become submissive and passive to the policy and authority of the school administration; otherwise, they could be misinterpreted and labeled negatively, or worse, the enemy of the institution. These common perceptions in the education community have resulted from the authority's established power and unquestioned position, the gap between the administrations and the teachers, and the observed administrations' identity. This reality further supports the perceived problems that Kumaravadivelu (2010) identified among Asian [learners], who show excessive obedience to authority, passivity, and lack of critical thinking.

Having been oriented with the basic concepts of critical pedagogy, they believe there are no available learning resources to help them execute such criticality through critical activities and learning materials. This is because they depend highly **on the official textbooks or modules (institutional-identity)** provided by the education agency or by the teacher-in-charge responsible for creating grade-level modules. In this case, teachers' creativity as a possible source of creating critical instruction is also affected because they rely too much on a single institutionalized source. One of the participants honestly stated that they are not even allowed to use other sources; otherwise, the results of the standardized examinations for their students may be affected because they need to follow the prescription on using the required reference. One of the participants even said, *"We are not allowed to use any other materials except the one prepared by the grade level coordinator or the one assigned by the department head. Furthermore, even if we use or recommend other good materials, it may affect the student's assessment results because their examinations are highly controlled by the competencies and activities in the provided module."*

In a way, this dependency on the official textbook is the result of the classic observation of the standardized learning materials and resources, lack of time for creative constructions of critical references and materials due to teachers' workloads, including those additional clerical works, and research, and the lack of training about material development and preparation.

Among those identified identities of the participants, it is the last associated with **affinity-identity, and confidence in their conventional practices**, which they believed to have provided positive results to their former students. From the participants' point of view, this confidence in old practices may result from the already fossilized practices, which do not respond anymore to the demands and needs of contemporary learners. Lack of motivation, caused by the challenges of teaching, also resulted in sustaining the knowledge they know. Hence, its effectiveness should be continued.

In this case, the participants silently continue and support what Paulo Freire would like to debunk in classroom instruction, the banking model of education (Freire, 1993), *see Table 3*. Through this, teachers believed that they all have the responsibility to produce knowledge because of the perceived emptiness of the learners. They should speak and discuss the target lessons for their learners to learn. While they recognize the idea of learners' voices as a source of learning, the teacher always considers the learners' perceived limitations. This is evident by their silence as a form of response or participation, taking time to respond to classroom inquiries, or asking to reply using their home language or first language. In the end, teachers would instead dominate the discussion than experience frustrations from the learners' reactions or immediate feedback. Sadly, this teacher's dominance in the classroom fails to promote components of critical pedagogy, such as dialogue in the learning space, as an opportunity for the learners to critique and question this dominance by struggling to activate this participation and produce authentic knowledge based on experiences and social engagements. Further, such a teacher's dominance is a silent but explicit act of favoring oppression by silencing learners' opportunity to produce their voices. In many observations, classrooms, and generally, education across levels recognize the dominant and biased teacher talks, which sustain teachers' power in the overall classroom management and lesson execution, with limited students' participation, and responses (Hardman & Abd-Kadir, 2010).

Freire's banking model of education has characterized education for a long time. It is rejected and proven detrimental in constructing student empowerment and centeredness. However, its danger cannot be detached from the local practices, as it remains the silent framework of classroom instruction, leaving the teacher as the "omniscient" persona in class surrounded by empty spectators in class in the presence

Table 3. Freire's (1993) Banking System of Education

Teachers	Students
Teach	Are taught
Know everything	Know nothing
Think	Are thought about
Talk	Listen
Discipline	Are disciplined
Choose and enforce their choice	Comply
Act	Follow the action of the teachers
Choose the suggested contents or topics strictly	(not consulted) adapt the chosen program content
Establish authority which appears to be detrimental to the freedom of learning	No authority
Subjects of the learning process	Objects of the learning process

of their students. As a result, teachers remain "unquestioned authorities who were only responsible for delivering knowledge to students, and students, in turn, were doomed to listening meekly" (Izadinia, 2009, p. 7). Interestingly, but sadly, anyone involved in education is even afraid of the question of young learners. They often do not even entertain learners' inquiries, highlighting that the classroom or school is a perfect venue to address their inquiries. Without dialogue and such ambiguous circumstances, learners may find answers elsewhere to satisfy the necessary information (Tony Blaire Institute for Global Change, 2017).

Interestingly, another teacher's identity is worthy of being grounded, which is their **resistance to adopting critical pedagogy**. This identity may be associated either with nature-identity because it is typical behavior of Filipinos to express respect to the authority through submission or institutional-identity because of the institutional practices of constructing and imposing policies as 'final and irrevocable.' Either way, too much standardization and observing the top-down approach in basic education has resulted in a problematic teachers' identity as agents of reforms and transformations. While resistance is one of the keywords of critical pedagogy emphasizing the refusal to accept inequalities and dominance in their society, which produce divisions and differences between and among the powerful and powerless, this new resistance becomes an enemy of this classroom approach as teachers show hesitation to the teaching criticality as a possible source of social conflicts. This identified teachers' resistance to CLP, which highlights their identity in connection to language teaching, is influenced by their personal beliefs that the critical approach may be too radical or revolutionary for young learners; hence, this approach can put the lives of the learners at risk. Additionally, the participants' most evident reasons are still their social, cultural, and political orientations, which mute them to criticality convert language learning into social justice and transformation.

From Ontological Beliefs to Language Ideology via Critical Pedagogy

Language ideologies generally refer to the system of beliefs and practices in the use of language and its relation to the world's realities. Commonly, beliefs, either personal, social, political, cultural, or even moral, control human thinking and decision because of the power of language as a tool for integral and

Table 4. Observed language ideologies via critical pedagogy (CP)

Observed Language Ideologies *via* Critical Pedagogy (CP)	Influences
Language is apolitical or neutral.	Local conflicts; historical, social, political, and cultural struggles of the community against the dominant elements of the society; oppressions against the "perceived weak" members of the community, i.e., poor; women, LGBTQA+, migrants, Etc.
CLP is a threat to social and cultural harmony.	Local conflict; historical, social, political, and cultural struggles of the community against the dominant elements of the society; oppressions against the "perceived weak" members of the community, i.e., poor, women, LGBTQA+, migrants, Etc.; institutionalized authority
Learners' L1 is a threat to L2 acquisition.	Colonial mentality; the strong influence of the Western world on Philippine education, specifically, American English to L2 learning; discrimination between and among local/regional languages; perceived "low class" of local/regional languages' power of language in employment, business, politics, Etc.
The English language is an advantage in building a better future for learners.	Power of language in employment, business, politics, Etc.; English standard of intelligence and social identity
American English is the best form of English language learning.	Colonial mentality; the strong influence of the Western world on Philippine education, specifically, American English to L2 learning; discrimination between and among local/regional languages; perceived "low class" of local/regional languages' power of language in employment, business, politics, Etc.

meaningful human interaction. With the introduction of critical pedagogy and its possible employment in the classroom instructions, interesting language ideologies were summarized in Table 4, such as **language as apolitical or neutral**, critical language learning as a threat to social and cultural harmony of the society, learners' L1 as a threat to learning the target L2, English as an advantage to the future of the learners, and the American English as the best form of learning the language.

Primarily, critical language threatens social and cultural harmony in society; hence, it is inappropriate for young learners, making language learning apolitical or neutral. Most participants believed that language acquisition for young learners is for more than just knowing and questioning social inequalities. Otherwise, the security of the learners may be at risk because of the possibility of engaging themselves in different conflicts and anomalies that characterize governance, leadership, community engagement, and others. Hence, the focus mainly of language learning is for them to know the basic and general language rules and mechanics to develop language skills in writing, reading, speaking, and listening. While it is true that these are the foundations of solid language learning, the ultimate goal of understanding the functions of the language is not within their objective, and that is using the language as a tool in addressing social conflicts and inequities to shape democracy and liberation for all.

Additionally, the understanding of the "voice" is not toward empowering them as the possible source of democratizing society and liberating people from dominance, oppression, and marginalization. Their voice is limited to communicating using the language with emphasis on correct grammar and pronunciation, which defeats the purpose of critical language pedagogy to produce language citizenship necessary to equalize their environment. In the end, teachers affirmed the value of language as apolitical or neutral because of its lack of role in conscientizing social realities, which affects the learners' quality of learning. This reality of cultural stereotyping in language learning usually points to Asian classrooms. Among those perceived problems identified by Kumaravadivelu (2010) are obedience to authority, passivity in class, and lack of critical thinking.

Having been influenced by American education, implementing an English-Only policy in the classroom has become a common practice as an effective way to learn the language effectively. While this is partly evident in some educational communities, this policy tends to produce 'silence' in the classroom because learners are afraid of committing mistakes, which can be a source of immediate judgments, insults, and laughter. With this, **the learners' first language (L1) is considered a threat to acquiring the second language (L2)**, which is English in the case of Filipinos. This belief leaves the lack of role of the learners' first or home language as a cultural artifact in penetrating their second target language.

Very interestingly, English as a language is commonly considered a learner's advantage to knowledge acquisition and eventually their tool for a better future. Most of the participants stated:

"English is being studied to be employed."

"English helps us to communicate confidently."

"English helps the students to clinch an advantage in the world where English dominates."

"It is a tool to achieve success."

"English helps learners to reach their target."

Finally, the dominance of American English in Filipino ESL classrooms still matters a lot despite the recognition of Philippine English as one of the significant varieties of World Englishes. Accordingly, participants fully understand that there is Philippine English. However, they have admitted to needing a complete understanding of Philippine English, which means that they wanted to understand how it is different from American English, which they believed is an international language that serves as the standard for language education. For the participants, Americanizing their language classroom constitute an advantage; hence, it becomes a measurement of excellent language learning. For many, English, as a dominant and sought-after language, is primarily influenced by the continuous spirit of colonialism of the Western world in local education, especially in the Philippines. Hence, the perceived power of American English as an international language becomes the standard of language learning and intelligence measurement, which weakens local languages to penetrate national and international engagements in business, politics, economy, Etc.

This idea parallels the study of Robert Philipson (cited in Hewings & Tagg, 2012), which established the linguistic imperialism that produces political inequities between English and other languages in the global community. As a result, English sustains its dominance in the world as it favors language policies, school curriculums, and language ideology. Besides inequities, such linguistic hegemony or dominance marginalizes other non-dominant languages (Ljungdahl, 2004) and threatens linguistic diversity (Fergusson, 2006, cited in Hewings & Tagg, 2012).

As a result, ideological identification of the language through critical pedagogy becomes even more complex and conflicting as their beliefs go against their practices or vice versa. For instance, they always wanted their students to be active and critical. However, these become limited to language rules in constructing good sentences and paragraphs and communicating classroom discourse using good English. As a result, language appears to be just an educational slogan with an aesthetic function to beautify the community's judgment toward learning and education. It is also interesting that education promotes critical thinking among learners. However, the school is afraid to be critically questioned on the policies and practices that affect the learners' quality of learning.

There are numerous beliefs and principles the respondents shared as far as the role of English is concerned. While most look at language as a way to be globally competitive and unify society, most have expressed language as a mere tool for self-expression to survive in future functions such as employment which focuses on overseas work. True enough, we mean language to express ideas or perhaps 'to send a message.' However, at least by now, it must be clear to our understanding that most of the time, language suppresses voice, reflection, and creativity (Benjamin, 2006) instead of empowering the learners. Therefore, language teaching and learning should produce democracy and emancipation (Ledwith, 1997) for social action (Corbett, 2007; National Writing Project, 2009) and political empowerment and education (Corbett, 2007; Crookes, 2009(a), 2009(b)).

CONCLUSION

Critical pedagogy in language teaching is genuinely an underexplored discipline, approach, and practice in education and research. While critical pedagogies radically call for the promotion of this approach to achieve social equity and liberation through conscientization, conservative society plays an influential role in silencing its own goal to empower learners and society. With the identified teacher identity and language ideologies *via* criticality, the status of Freirean ideology in education is defeated. This is because of the misunderstanding of the concept as a threat to social harmony and peace and order, which are expected to develop in the education premises. Additionally, the fossilized institutional practices remain powerful to continue the classic praxes and policies, which do not respond to the demands and needs of today's learning and learners. Results of this present current further implicate meaningful implementation of critical pedagogy in language teaching across culture. Hence, an opportunity to professional development can widely be provided. Through this initial effort to know the status of critical language pedagogy through identity and ideologies, future researchers are encouraged to investigate this topic further for complete understanding and, possibly, implementation of the fundamental goal of critical pedagogy. It is also interesting to investigate more of the critical language pedagogy in the actual instructions and other specific areas of language through curriculum, assessment, textbook, instructional aids, teachers' and learners' roles, and strategies and approaches.

REFERENCES

Abraham, G. Y. (2014). *Critical pedagogy: Origin, vision, action & consequences*. Retrieved from https://www.diva-portal.org/smash/get/diva2:768785/FULLTEXT01.pdf

Aliakbari, M., & Amoli, F. A. (2014). Teachers' awareness of critical pedagogy: A case study of Iranian EFL teachers. *European Online Journal of Natural and Social Sciences*, *3*(1), 128–134.

Aliakbari, M., & Faraji, E. (2011). Basic principles of critical pedagogy. In *2nd International Conference on Humanities, Historical, and Social Sciences IPEDR*, 17. IACSIT Press.

Barkhuizen, G. (2017). Language teacher identity research. In G. Barkhuizen (Ed.), Reflections on Language Teacher Identity Research. Routledge/Taylor & Francis Group.

Bautista, J. (2021). *Critical thinking can't be apolitical, teachers tell DepEd.* Retrieved from https://newsinfo.inquirer.net/1507433/critical-thinking-cant -be-apolitical-teachers-tell-deped

Benjamin, A. (2006). *Writing put to the test: Teaching for the high stakes essay.* Eye on Education.

Chapman, S., & Routledge, C. (2009). *Key ideas in linguistics and the philosophy of language.* Edinburgh University Press. doi:10.1515/9780748631421

Chen, J. (2021). *Emergency Remote Teaching and Beyond: Voice from World Language Teachers and Researchers.* Springer. doi:10.1007/978-3-030-84067-9

Cheung, Y. L. (2017). Writing teacher identity: Current knowledge and future research. In G. Barkhuizen (Ed.), Reflections on Language Teacher Identity Research. Routledge/Taylor & Francis Group.

Collins, C. (1999). *Language, ideology and social consciousness: A Critique of J.C. Scott.* Routledge.

Corbett, J. (2007). *An intercultural approach to English language teaching.* Multilingual Matters.

Cortez, F. G. F. (2013). The Philippine engagement with Paulo Freire. *Kritike, 7*(2), 50–70. doi:10.25138/7.2.a.4

Crookes, G. V. (2009a). The practicality and relevance of second language critical pedagogy. Language Teaching. Cambridge University Press. Doi:10.1017/So261444809990292

Crookes, G. V. (2009b). *Values, philosophies, and beliefs in TESOL: Making statements.* Cambridge University Press.

Crookes, G. V. (2021). Critical language pedagogy: An introduction to principles and values (Anniversary Article). *ELT Journal, 75*(3), 247–255. doi:10.1093/elt/ccab020

Department of Education. (2009). *K to 12 Basic Education Curriculum.* Retrieved from https://www.deped.gov.ph/k-to-12/about/k-to-12-basic-educati on-curriculum/

Derakhshan, A., Coombe, C., Arabmofrad, A., & Taghizadeh, M. (2020). Investigating the Effects of English Language Teachers' Professional Identity and Autonomy in Their Success. *Issues in Language Teaching, 9*(1), 1–28. doi:10.22054/ilt.2020.52263.496

Durban, J. M., & Catalan, R. D. (2012). Issues and concerns of Philippine education through the years. *Asian Journal of Social Sciences & Humanities, 1*(2).

Freire, P. (1993). *Pedagogy of the oppressed (Twentieth Anniversary Edition).* Continuum.

Friedrich, P. (1989). Language, ideology, and political economy. *American Anthropologist, 91*(2), 295–312. doi:10.1525/aa.1989.91.2.02a00010

Gee, J. P. (2000). Chapter 3 : Identity as an Analytic Lens for Research in Education. *Review of Research in Education, 25*(1), 99–125. doi:10.3102/0091732X025001099

Ghaemi, F., & Sadeghi, P. (2015). Critical pedagogy: Concept and principles. *International Journal of Engineering Education, 4*(2), 244–249.

Hall, C. J., & Cunningham, C. (2020). Educators' beliefs about English and languages beyond English: From ideology to ontology and back again. *Linguistics and Education, 57*, 100817. Advance online publication. doi:10.1016/j.linged.2020.100817

Hardman, F., & Abd-Kadir, J. (2010). Classroom discourse towards a dialogic pedagogy. 254-263. In D. Wyse, R. Andrews, & J. Hoffman (Eds.), The Routledge International Handbook of English, Language and Literacy Teaching (1st ed.). Routledge. doi:10.4324/9780203863091

Hewings, A., & Tagg, C. (Eds.). (2012). *The politics of English: Conflict, competition, coexistence.* Routledge and The Open University.

Higgins, C. (2017). Towards sociolinguistically informed language teacher identities. In G. Barkhuizen (Ed.), Reflections on Language Teacher Identity Research. Routledge/Taylor & Francis Group.

Holborow, M. (2007). Language, ideology, and neoliberalism. *Journal of Language and Politics, 6*(1), 51–73. doi:10.1075/jlp.6.1.05hol

Irvine, J. T., & Gal, S. (2009). Language ideology and linguistic differentiation. *Linguistic anthropology. REAd (Porto Alegre), 1*, 402–434.

Izadinia, M. (2009). Critical pedagogy: An introduction. In Power in the EFL Classroom: Critical Pedagogy in the Middle East. Cambridge Scholars Publishing.

Kakilla, C. (2021). *Strengths and weaknesses of semi-structured interviews in qualitative research: A critical essay.* doi:10.20944/preprints202106.0491.v1

Kozhabayeva, K., & Boivin, N. (2021). Emergency remote teaching in the Kazakhstan context: Deprofessionalization of teacher identity. In J. Chen (Ed.), *Emergency Remote Teaching and Beyond: Voice from World Language Teachers and Researchers.* Springer. doi:10.1007/978-3-030-84067-9_6

Kubota, R. (2017). Critical language teacher identity. In G. Barkhuizen (Ed.), Reflections on Language Teacher Identity Research. Routledge/Taylor & Francis Group.

Kumaravadivelu, B. (2010). Problematizing cultural stereotypes in TESOL. TESOL Quarterly, 37(4), 709-719.

Ledwith, M. (1997). *Participating in transformation.* Venture Press/British Association of Social Workers.

Leijen, A., Kullasepp, K., & Anspal, T. (2014). Pedagogies of developing teacher identity. *Advances in Research on Teaching, 22*, 311–328. doi:10.1108/S1479-368720140000022019

Lippi-Green, R. (2004). Language ideology and language prejudice. *Language in the USA: Themes for the twenty-first century*, 289–304.

Ljungdahl, L. (2004). *The English language and linguistic imperialism: The Trojan Horse?* Retrieved from https://opus.lib.uts.edu.au/bitstream/10453/6369/1/2004001444.pdf

Mahmoodarabi, M., & Khodabakhsh, M. R. (2015). Critical pedagogy: EFL teachers' views, experience, and academic degrees. *English Language Teaching, 8*(6), 100–110. doi:10.5539/elt.v8n6p100

Maralit, K. (2022). Review K to 12 program, Marcos orders DepEd. *The Manila Times*. https://www.manilatimes.net/2022/06/22/news/national/review-k-to-12-program-marcos-orders-deped/1848275

Matsuda, P. K. (2017). Second language writing teacher identity. In G. Barkhuizen (Ed.), Reflections on Language Teacher Identity Research. Routledge/Taylor & Francis Group.

McShane, M. Q., & Hess, F. M. (2021). *Three conservative principles of education.* American Enterprise Institute. Retrieved from https://www.aei.org/op-eds/three-conservative-principles-for-education/

Menezes de Oliveira e Paiva, V.L. (2017). Language teaching identity: A fractal system. In G. Barkhuizen (Ed.), Reflections on Language Teacher Identity Research. Routledge/Taylor & Francis Group.

Merriam, S.B. & Tisdell, E.J. (n.d.). *Qualitative research: A guide to design and implementation* (4th ed.). Jossey-Bass: A Wiley Brand.

Mooney, A., & Evans, B. (2015). *Language, society & power: An introduction.* Routledge. doi:10.4324/9781315733524

National Writing Project. (2009). Writing for a change: Boosting literacy and learning through social action. Jossey-Bass: A Wiley Imprint.

Nelson, C. D. (2017). Identity dilemmas and research agenda. In G. Barkhuizen (Ed.), Reflections on Language Teacher Identity Research. Routledge/Taylor & Francis Group.

Pennycook, A. (2017). *The cultural politics of English as an international language.* Routledge. doi:10.4324/9781315225593

Pennycook, A. (2017). *The cultural politics of English as an international language.* Routledge. doi:10.4324/9781315225593

Riasati, M. J., & Mollaei, F. (2012). Critical pedagogy and language learning. *International Journal of Humanities and Social Science, 2*(21).

Soriano, L. (2021). DepEd to teachers; be neutral in politics. *The Post.* Retrieved from https://thepost.net.ph/news/nation/deped-to-teachers-be-neutral-in-politics/

Spolsky, B., & Shohamy, E. (2000). Language practice, language ideology, and language policy. *Language policy and pedagogy: Essays in honour of A. Ronald Walton,* 1–41.

Tony Blaire Institute for Global Change. (2017). *Difficult dialogue in the classroom.* Available at https://institute.global/sites/default/files/inline-files/Difficult-Dialogue.pdf

Toohey, K. (2017). Tangled up with everything else: Toward new conceptions of language, teachers, and identities. In G. Barhuizen (Ed.), Reflections on Language Teacher Identity Research. Routledge/Taylor & Francis Group.

van der Galien, M. (2006). *Conservatives and education.* The Moderate Voice. Retrieved from https://themoderatevoice.com/conservatives-and-education/

Woolard, K. A. (2020). Language ideology. In J. Stanlaw (Ed.), The International Encyclopedia of Linguistic Anthropology. doi:10.1002/9781118786093.iela0217

Zhang, Y., & Wildemuth, B. M. (n.d.). *Unstructured interviews.* Available at https://www.ischool.utexas.edu/~yanz/Unstructured_interviews.pdf

Chapter 14
Teachers' Commodified Relationships With Racial Justice Through Professional Development

Lena Shulyakovskaya
University of Toronto, Canada

Arlo Kempf
University of Toronto, Canada

ABSTRACT

This chapter explores teachers' interpretations of racial justice-oriented professional development (PD). Findings emerge from surveys and interviews conducted with 74 teachers in Toronto, Canada. Data reveals that teachers' ideological positions have a direct relationship to their understanding of racial justice. Three patterns of thought emerged: 1) The majority of teachers interpreted racial justice to be a commodity that they expected be given to them. 2) Some teachers interpreted racial justice as a way to "save" racialized Others, and 3) a small number of teachers recognized racial justice to be an ongoing process of self-reflection. In this chapter, the authors argue white supremacist logics at the systemic level influence what racially just strategies and activities teachers imagine in terms of individual teachers' institutionalized ideological stances. Most importantly, the authors demonstrate how many teachers' uncritical interpretations of racial justice serve to reinforce white supremacy already present in the organizational norms of Canada's K-12 schooling.

INTRODUCTION

This chapter explores secondary teachers' interpretations of racial justice-oriented professional development (PD). Findings were drawn from survey and interview responses of 74 teachers from eight secondary schools in Toronto, Ontario, Canada. The qualitative interview and survey data presented here on

DOI: 10.4018/978-1-6684-6386-4.ch014

professional development are part of a wider mixed-methods study examining relationships between classroom conditions (understood here to include class size, composition, pedagogical delivery mode) and teachers' ability to successfully engage in racially just teaching. Findings on racial justice-oriented PD suggest teachers' ideological positionality can have a direct relation to teachers' understandings of racial justice within the various conditions of their classrooms. Participants described participating in various PD sessions that ranged in delivery modes and required time commitments. While some PD was self-directed and elective, most was mandatory. Some PD sessions were developed locally by staff at their schools, some at the board level, and others were presented by third parties. In this study, we were not concerned with the content or quality of racial justice-oriented PD sessions, rather, we wanted to explore teachers' interpretations of those PD sessions. Despite the variety in the types of PD sessions the participants received, three overarching themes emerged.

This chapter focuses on three emergent thematic findings that offer a rough typology of teacher engagement with and reflection on racial justice-oriented professional development: 1) The majority of teachers interpreted racial justice to be a commodity that they expected be given to them; 2) Some teachers interpreted racial justice as a way to "save" racialized Others; and 3) A small number of teachers recognized racial justice to be an ongoing process of self-reflection. The first two findings demonstrated that the majority of participants interpreted racial justice as something they needed "to do" (e.g., follow a specific activity, a lesson, or another resource) rather than "be" racially just. By equating doing racial justice to being racially just, teacher participants insisted that they needed to be explicitly shown the activities or lesson plan exemplars in order for them to know how to incorporate racial justice into the curriculum.

In this chapter, we interrogate the concerning insistence that teachers must be explicitly shown how to do racial justice in order to be racially just. Using Critical Race Theory (CRT) as our guiding theoretical framework, we argue white supremacist logics at the systemic level influence what racially just strategies and activities teachers imagine in terms of individual teachers' institutionalized ideological stances. Most importantly, we illustrate how the impact of racial justice-oriented PD, based on teacher interpretations, can serve to reinforce extant white supremacist logics in the organizational norms of Canada's K-12 schooling.

The first major section of this chapter offers an overview of the context and purpose of this work in terms of education policy, race, and classroom conditions. Next, we sketch our engagements with CRT as our guiding theoretical framework, with a focus on CRT in education. It is followed by a review of relevant literature on organizational PD surrounding issues of equity, diversity, and inclusion, with a focus on in-service and pre-service teachers. We then offer an overview of our methodology and methods. The final section offers our findings and implications in three areas: Commodification of racial justice, white saviourism and othering, and (critical) self-reflection. We end with a brief conclusion.

Definitions

Several phrases are threaded throughout the chapter, such as "racialization," "othering," "doing racial justice," and "critical consciousness." To limit misinterpretations of those key phrases, we offer definitions that are consistent with prior literature referenced in this chapter.

- *Racialized* - a person or a group of people who are socially assigned race and racial character that are "non-white," also known as racially minoritized or racially marginalized persons and groups (Parekh et al., 2016).
- *Othering* - an "us versus them" process of stereotyping and essentializing a person or a group of people, turning people into abstract entities known as Others (Ross & Rivers, 2018).
- *To do racial justice* - refers to teacher misconception that racial justice is a tangible activity or lesson plan or other resource that needs to be done or followed in their classrooms (Ladson-Billings, 2011).
- *Critical consciousness* - an in-depth understanding of how social, political, and economic forces work and the ability to recognize one's location and social conditioning within those interlocking forces in a way that feeds critical motivation for just social change (Freire, 1970/2017).

CONTEXT AND PURPOSE

This chapter seeks to deepen scholarly understanding about secondary teachers' experiences and interpretations of racial justice-oriented professional development. Racial inequity in K-12 schooling is a problem across Canada in terms of ongoing issues of equitable access to quality schooling (Gallagher-Mackay et al., 2021; Nîtôtemtik, 2020) as well as racially equitable treatment and outcomes in schooling (James, 2019; Maynard, 2017; Robson et al., 2018;). Race-based disadvantages have been clearly established in research in the Ontario context for over a decade (Clandfield et al., 2014; Dei, 2017; Ontario Ministry of Education, 2013; St. Denis, 2011). More specifically, the phenomena surrounding race and teacher-student relationships are well-documented in Canada and the United States (Crosby & Monin, 2017; Dee, 2005; Dei, 2000; Dei et al., 1997), and targeting racism has become an explicit policy priority in the education sector (Ontario Ministry of Education, 2017, 2021; Toronto District School Board, 2017, 2022a). Recent changes to education policy for K-12 schooling in Ontario make this research particularly timely and urgent. The study was conducted in the context of Canada's rapidly developing anti-racism policies in education, Ontario's de-streaming initiatives, the province's proposed increases to class sizes, and changes to pedagogical delivery modes due to the COVID-19 pandemic, which Kendi (2020) called the racial pandemic within a viral pandemic.

In spring 2019, the Ontario Ministry of Education announced a series of policy changes for K-12 schooling in the province. Among the more noteworthy shifts was the decision to increase class sizes, including the move to increase the secondary school average class size across the province from 22 in 2018-2019 to 28 by 2022-2023 (Lapierre, 2019; Ontario Ministry of Education, 2019). As a direct result of Ontario Ministry of Education policy changes, including the decision to increase class sizes, the Toronto District School Board (TDSB) made changes which led to a number of larger than usual secondary classes during the 2019-2020 school year. Due to the COVID-19 pandemic, the 2020-2021 school year saw a mix of online and in-person models in use for teachers throughout Ontario. This project sought to identify the ways in which PD for racial justice was understood, engaged, grappled with, and taken up by teachers, as well as how PD impacted teachers' ability to successfully support students when there were significant differences among students in terms of academic skills, abilities, and challenges in the same class.

THEORETICAL FRAMEWORK

This chapter is guided by the theoretical offerings of Critical Race Theory and, specifically, considerations of the ways in which CRT in education draws attention to the systemic operations of racism and white supremacy in schooling. Informed by the foundational works of legal scholars Bell (1973), Higginbotham (1978), and others, Yosso (2005) framed CRT as a "framework that can be used to theorize, examine and challenge the ways race and racism implicitly and explicitly impact on social structures, practices and discourses" (p. 37). Understanding racism as endemic and baked into the fundamental core of society, CRT requires a careful consideration of racism and white supremacy at the structural, institutional, and systemic levels - looking beyond the domain of individual actions, opinions, and decisions (Crenshaw et al., 1995). In this framing, racism and white supremacy are simultaneously commonplace and enduring. This contrasts with liberal conceptions of race as waning in the face of race progress over time. CRT also asserts that racism and white supremacy are part and parcel of our system's normal functionality rather than deviations from an otherwise just set of operations (Bell, 1972). Crenshaw (1988, 1991) powerfully formulated the now widely known concept of intersectionality, arguing that the combined racism and sexism experienced by Black women offered a unique understanding of the ways oppression can operate as an amalgam. These and other foundational scholars have informed subsequent generations of critical race theorists beyond legal studies.

CRT scholarship in education emerged in the early 1990s and has evolved over the past thirty years into a key theoretical tool for understanding the operations of racism and white supremacy in education (Delgado, 1991; Delgado, & Stefancic, 2001; Ladson-Billings & Tate, 1995; Ledesma & Calderón, 2006, 2015; Parker & Gillborn, 2020). Kohli (2014) and Solórzano and Bernal (2000) theorized CRT methods in education. Kohli (2014) sketched five elements of CRT's basic perspectives, research methods, and pedagogy that included: "centrality and intersectionality of race and racism... challenge to the dominant ideology... commitment to social justice... the importance of experiential knowledge... and the use of interdisciplinary perspectives" (p. 369). Kohli (2014) and others thus offer important sign posts for CRT-informed work in education. CRT was particularly important for this study as we sought to de-centre individual classroom practices as the sole or even primary place to look to understand the workings of racism in schools, and focus instead on the ways these practices were products of systemic logics, decisions, and policies. Findings presented here on racial justice-oriented PD explore the intersections of the individual, structural, institutional, and systemic operations of race as called for by CRT.

LITERATURE REVIEW

Professional development training to advance equity, diversity, and inclusion (EDI) in the workplace has grown in popularity in recent years (Ahmed, 2012; Hiranandani, 2012; Kempf, 2020; Trenerry & Paradies, 2012; Vaught & Castagno, 2008). Such training ranged from unconscious bias training (Kempf, 2020) to cultural competency training (Trenerry & Paradies, 2012; Vaught & Castagno, 2008) to general reminders about the existence of racism and discrimination (Hiranandani, 2012). The supposed goal of such EDI training was to bring awareness to societal inequities with the hope that employees (largely presumed to be white), once equipped with that new knowledge, would undergo an attitudinal change and, thus, create welcoming environments for the historically marginalized (Hiranandani, 2012). However, such EDI training, whether through facilitation or through training interpretation by staff, tended to perceive discrimination as an individual rather than a systemic issue (Gorski, 2016; Hiranandani, 2012; Kempf, 2020; Trenerry & Paradies, 2012) and left it up to individuals to fix deeply structural oppressions (Vaught & Castagno, 2008).

Individual vs. the System

By 2010, decades of research demonstrated that organizations made only minor progress toward more equitable practices (Sawchuk, 2010), and EDI training not only had limited impact on improving equity, diversity, or inclusion at the organizational level (Hiranandani, 2012; Trenerry & Paradies, 2012), but also served to reinforce existing inequitable power dynamics at the individual level (Vaught & Castagno, 2008). Hiranandani (2012) and Vaught and Castagno (2008) questioned the imposition and effectiveness of EDI training developed according to organizational needs within existing organizational structures. Such EDI training was often developed and presented by facilitators with privileged social identities and in a manner that fit existing organizational regulations and practices (Vaught & Castagno, 2008). Yet, it was those very organizational regulations and practices that created the need for EDI training in the first place (Ahmed, 2011), suggesting an "inherent and problematic tension in attempting to address a systemic and structural problem... solely through individual transformation" (Vaught & Castagno, 2008, p. 98).

If racism is not understood as a systemic phenomenon, such as being located in "the economic, political, and social arrangements of modern society, then it follows that its origins are in people's minds" (Wellman, 1993, p. 42). By focusing EDI training on individual staff members who were assumed to simply lack awareness of oppression instead of focusing on the broader white supremacist system of which each organization with its regulations and practices was a product (Ahmed, 2011), organizations were able to present themselves as neutral and just workplaces where individual staff simply needed to be persuaded that minoritized Others could be beneficial for the economic well-being of the organization (Hiranandani, 2012), while "avoiding the possibility of institutional change and reorganization" (Wellman, 1993, p. 59). Actually, Trenerry and Paradies (2012) assured that even if EDI training was able to change employees' behaviours and even attitudes to be more equitable, those changes would only be temporary if organizational structures and policies that shaped ongoing employee actions and interactions did not change to reflect anti-oppression.

Despite the evidence that EDI training had limited impact at best (Hiranandani, 2012) and reinforced white supremacy at worst (Aitken & Radford, 2018; Vaught & Castagno, 2008), organizational commitments to providing EDI training for their staff remained strong. The K-12 education system, made up of mostly white teachers and known for the reproduction of white supremacy (Ladson-Billings, 2011; Wellman, 1993), was often front and centre in conversations about systemic oppression (Aitken & Radford, 2018; Parekh et al., 2016) due to schools' political roles in socially shaping society and their potential to remedy social inequities (Donald, 2009; King, 1991).

In 2014, the education system was called to action in redressing institutional racism toward Indigenous peoples in, what is now called, Canada - "it is precisely because education was the primary tool of oppression of Aboriginal people, and miseducation of all Canadians, that we have concluded that education holds the key to reconciliation" (Sinclair, 2014, p. 7). In 2015, the *Calls to Action* report was officially released by the Truth and Reconciliation Commission of Canada (TRC) to guide Canadian institutions and individuals toward reconciliation. Out of the 94 calls to action, the 57th call to action specifically called on federal, provincial, territorial, and municipal governments to provide professional development and training for public servants, which included teachers at publicly funded schools:

Provide education to public servants on the history of Aboriginal peoples, including the history and legacy of residential schools, the United Nations Declaration on the Rights of Indigenous Peoples, Treaties and Aboriginal rights, Indigenous law, and Aboriginal-Crown relations. This will require skills-based training in intercultural competency, conflict resolution, human rights, and anti-racism. (Calls to Action, 2015, p. 7)

Immediately following the release of the report, ministries of education across the country, along with school districts, announced their reconciliation commitments that have since undergone several iterations (e.g., Alberta Education, 2022; British Columbia Ministry of Education and Child Care, n.d.; Ottawa-Carleton District School Board, 2021; Saskatchewan Ministry of Education, 2022; Toronto District School Board, 2021), with some even introducing new teaching quality standards to ensure teachers' practices reflected schools' reconciliation commitments (e.g. Alberta Education, 2020; British Columbia Ministry of Education and Child Care, 2019). Just as the final report of the TRC was not the first report to call for change in Canada's relationship with Indigenous peoples and Indigenous Nations (e.g., the 1991 Royal Commission on Aboriginal Peoples), the 94 calls to action were also not the first time North America's K-12 schooling as an institution and school employees as individuals were urged to take a critical look at how their practices reflected and reproduced colonial social inequities (e.g., Battiste & Barman, 1995; Donald, 2009; King, 1991; Ladson-Billings, 2011; Smith, 1999; Vaught & Castagno, 2008).

In the fall of 1986 and 1988, King explored pre-service teachers' views on racial justice in the classroom and in society, in general. The responses came from two different cohorts at the same elite, private, Jesuit, American university from pre-service teachers, most of whom were described as white and coming from privileged monocultural backgrounds (King, 1991). The two cohorts shared similarities in how people going into the teaching profession conceptualized racial justice. The findings were later shared in King's (1991) article and revealed that the majority of pre-service teachers viewed racial inequity as a consequence of something that happened in the past (e.g., enslavement) that influenced individual white people's prejudices and discrimination in the present, "without recognizing the structural inequity built into the social order" (p. 138) which socialized individual teachers in that present moment to hold certain ideologies, including how they conceptualized racial justice. In addition to the misrecognition of the broader social system of oppression, some white pre-service teachers in King's (1991) study expressed feeling tired of being made to feel guilty for being white, demonstrating activated defenses upon exposure to difficult knowledge.

Over three decades after King's (1991) study and three years after the release of the *Calls to Action* (2015), the majority of pre-service teacher participants at two public secular universities in Canada, who were described as non-Indigenous, expressed similar sentiments toward teaching for reconciliation (Aitken & Radford, 2018). Similar to the pre-service teachers in King's (1991) study, the pre-service teachers in Aitken and Radford's (2018) study appeared anxiously motivated to help their students learn about "the dark past," while distancing themselves from personal privileges accrued from ongoing colonialism in the present.

Furthermore, by suggesting the use of "neutral language" and "making it lighter," the majority of pre-service teachers in Aitken and Radford's (2018) study were preoccupied with ensuring their students did not feel blamed. Therefore, the main concern of teaching for reconciliation appeared to be for those students (and teachers) who may have felt guilty rather than the victims of colonialism (Aitken & Radford, 2018). Similar to King's (1991) study, some pre-service teachers in Aitken and Radford's (2018) study expressed frustration at being made to feel guilty for being white and tried to position themselves as victims of (imagined) Indigenous peoples' dislike of their presence in Canada, demonstrating activated defensiveness and resulting evasion of associations with the aggressor.

Similar to the pre-service teachers from King's (1991) and Aitken and Radford's (2018) studies, the in-service teachers from Vaught and Castagno's (2008) study expressed racialized interpretations of their districts' anti-bias and anti-racism professional development. Vaught and Castagno's (2008) interview data from two large racially diverse districts in the United States demonstrated that the majority of white teacher participants resisted being thought of as having white privilege by re-defining "race" as "cultural difference;" instead treating white privilege as an individual situational experience based on sheer numbers of people (e.g., a white teacher in a school that had a predominantly racialized student population was not believed to possess white privilege). Without recognizing white privilege as a structural phenomenon that afforded them systemic power over racialized Others, the majority of white teacher participants had no recognition of how "their authority as White teachers of children of color was highly powerful and determinative... [and] seemed unaware of the fact that White institutions create power hierarchies with or without the immediate presence of White students" (Vaught & Castagno, 2008, p. 101).

Interestingly, while the majority of white pre-service and in-service teachers treated their individual selves as disconnected from the collective identity of whiteness, they, nonetheless, recognized people of colour as members of collectives (Aitken & Radford, 2018; King, 1991; Vaught & Castagno, 2008). By viewing themselves as separate from the broader social order, yet recognizing racialized students as victims of "the past," teachers believed they were condemning racism (Vaught & Castagno, 2008) and, as heroic isolates (Goldin et al., 2021; Gorski, 2016; Ladson-Billings, 2011), wanted to know exactly how to do racial justice in their classrooms (Aitken & Radford, 2018; Ladson-Billings, 2011).

Ladson-Billings (2011) observed that well-meaning pre-service and in-service teachers would "quickly reject teaching for social justice by insisting that there are no practical exemplars that make such teaching possible" (p. 34). By the same token, "in describing what teaching for reconciliation involves, the emphasis is on knowing what to do - rather than needing to learn, or needing to better understand their ambivalences" (Aitken & Radford, 2018, p. 45). Despite teachers' concerns with the lack of available exemplars, the internet actually overflowed with lesson plans for teachers to use, and a number of ministries, unions, and community groups provided continuously updated vetted resources and lesson plans to assist teachers in teaching for anti-colonialism (e.g., Alberta Education, 2012, 2015; Manitoba Education and Early Childhood Learning, 2013; Saskatchewan Teachers' Federation, 2022; Saskatchewan Ministry of Education, 2017; Toronto District School Board, 2022b; University of Ontario Institute of Technology, 2022). In fact, it could have been the amplification rather than the absence of anti-colonial narratives that made it difficult for teachers "to relinquish the more comfortable stories of Canada that they have been told and grown accustomed to telling" (Donald, 2009, p. 4). Lindstrom et al. (2022) characterized difficult knowledge as "that which we do not want to know - that about which we want to remain ignorant and therefore resist knowing" (p. 6). Thus, it was activated defenses - the refusal to let go of "the comfortable good" and rejection of "the uncomfortable bad" that made these teachers feel as though it was impossible to teach for reconciliation, even though lesson plans and resources for their students may have been available.

On the other hand, in Vaught and Castagno's (2008) study, teacher participants talked about their school districts having provided them with "cultural competency cheat sheets" at which teachers could look in order to know how to interact with children who did not come from the dominant white North American culture. Thus, "rather than have White teachers understand racism, the leadership hoped to have them understand the *different* perceptions, or worldviews, of 'culturally' (i.e. racially) different people" (Vaught & Castagno, 2008, p. 106). However, according to Ladson-Billings (2011), such practices had high potential to reinforce stereotypes by presenting essentialized views of Others, without exposing or questioning the very culture that racialized and oppressed them.

In contrast to insistence on practical exemplars and "cheat sheets," Ladson-Billings (2011) affirmed that teaching for racial justice or injustice was rooted in teachers' socio-political ideologies that influenced their actions, and instead of focusing racial justice on "the specific lessons and activities that we select to fill the day, we must begin to understand the ways our theories and philosophies are made to manifest in the pedagogical practices and rationales we exhibit in the classroom" (p. 34). Gorski (2016) further confirmed that the trouble with teaching for equity was not with the lack of practical exemplars or the lack of teachers' good intentions, but it was ideological because no set of curricular topics or teaching strategies could turn a classroom with a deficit view of its students and their families into an equitable space for them.

While the concept of "cultural difference" and the need to learn about "different worldviews" was generally embraced by the teachers (Ladson-Billings, 2011), the importance of educating students to develop critical consciousness (Freire, 1970/2017) about the wider white supremacist capitalist system of which schools and teachers were a social product was a much harder concept for teachers to accept (King, 1991; Ladson-Billings, 2011; Vaught & Castagno, 2008).

Counterculture Against Academic Disenfranchisement

The phenomenon of teachers helping reproduce white supremacy, however unknowingly, became very well-known among racialized communities and fuelled counterculture discourse through hip hop. Hip hop originated among African American, Latinx, and Afro-Caribbean youth in the Bronx, giving rise to countless songs sharing messages about systemic oppression that featured teachers, alongside cops, as antagonists in those stories (e.g., J. Cole, 2007; Kendrick Lamar, 2015; Nas, 2001; Scarface, 2017). We included hip hop in this literature review for two reasons. First, we argue that CRT is significantly strengthened and enriched when it is inter-disciplinary. With scholarly literature and hip hop songs coming from two vastly different disciplines, we wanted to provide a more comprehensive review of what narratives existed about racial (in)justice issues in schools. Secondly, hip hop emerged as a youth movement in response to structural oppression and social alienation, and served as an act of resistance against the status quo (Ross & Rivers, 2018). Despite its associations with popular culture around the globe, Baszile (2009) reminded scholars to consider why, how, and among whom hip hop was most popular – "mainly among alienated or disenfranchised youth. Ironically enough, it is this group of students that is so often at the center of our concerns about schooling and academic achievement" (p. 7).

Hip hop communicates connections between race and status within society (Ross & Rivers, 2018), and serves as an articulation of the tensions between marginalized students, school curriculum, and teaching (Baszile, 2009). Therefore, discussions about racial (in)justice in schools are incomplete "if we fail to locate them within the racialized social crisis of our time, but our understanding of that crisis will also be incomplete if we fail to learn the lessons that young people are trying to teach through their dance, dress, speech and visual imagery" (Lipsitz, 1994, p. 18). From messages about pedagogies and curriculum marginalizing the already marginalized students: "Teacher-teacher, I'm trying to unteach ya. All the shit they taught y'all, they got you all in the bleachers" (Jay Z., 2013, Verse 4, lines 7-8) to the messages about the school to prison pipeline: "That school shit is a joke. The same people who control the school system, control the prison system, and the whole social system... Fuckin' with the teachers had, callin' 'em racist. I tried to show them crackers some light, they couldn't face it" (dead prez, 2000, Intro., Verse 1, lines 8-9) - from the perspectives of racialized students, such stories of teachers resisting and refusing to understand the broader socio-political context stood in stark contrast to the messages of heroic saviourship many teacher participants in scholarly literature tended to express. The performativity of schools' attempts at equitable practices was brought up in Coolio's (1995) "Gangsta's Paradise" - a song that quickly became a hip hop classic but was, ironically, used as a soundtrack for *Dangerous Minds*, a movie that featured a "heroic" white teacher "saving" racialized students.

They say I gotta learn, but nobody's here to teach me

If they can't understand it, how can they reach me?

I guess they can't, I guess they won't

I guess they frontin', that's why I know my life is out of luck, fool." (Verse 3, lines 5-8)

In an interview with *Rolling Stone*, Coolio (2015) expressed that he initially thought it was going to be a "hood song" that white people would not like because of its messaging. While lyrics may, of course, be subjective and Coolio (1995) did not explicitly mention teachers or schools in the verse above, within the historical context of hip hop, the antagonistic "they" that had the power to tell the protagonist what to do ("They say I gotta learn"), yet abandoned the said learner ("but nobody's here to teach me"), together with Coolio's (2015) interview, it may be inferred that the artist did, in fact, send out a message about the failed education system and white teachers not understanding the reality of racialized students. The verse concluded with a powerful line that gave reason ("that's why I know") for the racialized learner's failure. That reason was white teachers' performativity ("I guess they frontin'") when in fact they did not understand the reality ("I guess they can't") and refused to understand the reality ("I guess they won't").

Ladson-Billings (2011) assured that teachers' social justice fronting was the result of most of them not having had "developed a sociopolitical consciousness of their own" (p. 41). Developing critical consciousness was important because without a critical awareness of one's social conditioning, teachers recreated white supremacy despite their laudable intentions (Shim, 2017). While EDI training that brought awareness to systemic oppressions could potentially address teachers' lack of critical consciousness, teachers' racial attitudes were difficult to change (Shah & Coles, 2020), and "becoming aware of racial phenomena does not guarantee that teachers will interpret them in antiracist ways" (Shah & Coles, 2020, p. 587). In fact, in the face of difficult knowledge, teachers interpreted elements of their EDI training by adapting them to fit a pre-existing racial frameworks (Vaught & Castagno, 2008). Additionally, it was difficult to know whether teacher ideologies were shifting and becoming more anti-racist or if teachers were simply learning to 'talk the talk' (Shah & Coles, 2020). Having courageous conversations about white supremacy and racism, and making statements about the need to be reflective in their practice going forward did not mean that teachers actually engaged in the practice of critical self-reflection (Shim, 2017).

The analyses of teacher participants from prior literature, as in hip hop, should not be viewed as teacher bashing, but should, instead, expose the tension between the individual and the system when attempting to do EDI work within the education system (Vaught & Castagno, 2008). Teachers are institutional actors, and teacher thinking and acting is a reflection of existing norms within the institution

(Vaught & Castagno, 2008). However, an institution is not an unpeopled entity and teachers should not walk away from EDI training "secure that their own racism is indeed part of something far larger, in which they play no agentive role and for which they bear no responsibility" (Kempf, 2020, p. 121). The institution of K-12 education should be understood as a bigger entity made up of multiple smaller parts that work interactively together, feeding on one another in order to keep going - "Becoming part of an institution, which we can consider as the demand to share in it or have a share of it, requires not only that one inhabits its buildings but that one follows its lines" (Ahmed, 2012, p. 40). For this reason, personal awareness training that saw teachers solely as individuals rather than members of social groups was insufficient as it did not lead to systemic awareness and failed to recognize structural and systemic elements of oppression (Vaught & Castagno, 2008).

The interactivity between individual staff members who knew how to "talk the talk" and the inertia of the broader education system allowed school districts to say all the right things as they announced renewed commitments to anti-racism in light of events that happened during the COVID-19 pandemic, such as the murders of George Floyd and Breonna Taylor, the discovery of child remains at the sites of former residential schools, and ever-increasing incidence of anti-Asian hate (e.g., Calgary Board of Education, 2020; Edmonton Public School, 2021; Peel District School Board, 2022; Toronto District School Board, 2021). Yet, "giving form to institutional goals involves following a set of conventions" (Ahmed, 2012, p. 24) that rely "upon existing structures, and assum[e] that those structures are just and equitable" (Vaught & Castagno, 2008, p. 107). Actually, "presuming oneself to be objective tends to increase the role of implicit bias" (Kempf, 2020, p. 119), and therefore, racism may be revealed not in what is not done in the present (as exhibited in anti-racism goals for the future), but in exactly how things are done in the present. If anti-racism is something that is added to organizations, then it confirms the racism that is already in place (Ahmed, 2012). Research studies decades apart (e.g., Aitken & Radford, 2018; King, 1991; Ladson-Billings, 2011; Vaught & Castagno, 2008), together with countless counterculture messages (e.g., Coolio, 1995; dead prez, 2000; J. Cole, 2007; Jay Z., 2013; Kendrick Lamar, 2015; Nas, 2001; Scarface, 2017;) demonstrated that EDI training for pre-service and in-service teachers exposed a lack of systemic awareness and ongoing rejection of critical consciousness. "Perhaps the habits of the institutions are not revealed unless you come up against them" (Ahmed, 2012, p. 26) over and over.

Following school boards' renewed commitments to anti-racism that came out in the middle of the COVID-19 pandemic, mandatory racial justice-oriented PD for teachers is expected, and may even increase in frequency. At this point, it remains to be explored how in-service teachers engage with racial justice in their classrooms. Currently, there is a lack of literature that explores how teachers interpret racial justice-oriented professional development in the Canadian context, and what institutional and organizational norms those interpretations reflect.

METHODOLOGY AND METHODS

This chapter reports on the qualitative findings from a mixed-method study with secondary teachers in Toronto, Ontario, Canada. The research sought to understand the ways in which (as well as the degrees to which) secondary teachers understood, engaged, implemented, and valued racial justice-oriented professional development.

Setting

In terms of setting, Toronto is the largest city in Canada and one of the most ethnically and racially diverse cities in the world. According to Census Canada (2016), almost half of Toronto's residents were born outside of Canada, with approximately 85% of those residents identifying as people of colour. Overall, 52% of Toronto's residents identify as people of colour (City of Toronto, 2016). The student population of the TDSB is even more racially diverse with more than 70% identifying with a race other than white (Parekh et al., 2016; Toronto District School Board, 2017). The racial identity of teachers is a lot more difficult to establish, however, a rough estimation based on the data collected by an outside consulting firm in 2006 stated that only 22% of TDSB's teachers identified as a "visible minority" (Parekh et al., 2016).

Data Collection

The data presented here were collected during two consecutive research phases. Phase one included an electronic survey of teachers at eight public secondary schools in Toronto. Located across the city, these eight schools offered a widely representative sample of Toronto secondary students in terms of racial identity, socio-economic status, gender, language, and academic pathways. Survey questions were Likert-scale fixed choice and were divided into four parts: 1) Class size and teaching practice, 2) Professional development, 3) Delivery mode and teaching practice, 4) Demographics and teaching background of respondents. At the end of the survey, participants could indicate if they were interested in a follow-up interview. Phase two consisted of qualitative interviews with survey participants who expressed interest in sharing their thoughts and insights in a Zoom or phone interview. We conducted in-depth open-ended interviews with 15 teachers from across the eight schools, focusing on the following themes: 1) Professional biography and demographics; 2) Class size and teaching; 3) Delivery mode and teaching (online, blended, in-person). In focus here, are the qualitative comments on professional development from the survey, as well as from the interview data.

The qualitative interview approach engages the significance of experiential knowledge as empirically informative and relevant, and following Critical Race Theory, lifts up the epistemic agency of the subject/participant as a knower (Bernal 2002 & Ladson-Billings 2000). Following Haraway's (1988) thesis that no knowledge is total or complete, and that indeed all knowledge is contested, qualitative approaches avoid claims of total or final truths, and engage instead with the messy reality of layers of knowing, degrees of knowing, continuums of understanding, that emerge from subjective histories, reflections, and experiential meanings required to understand teachers' experiences and perspectives. In the case of in-depth open-ended interviews, further explanation and prompting are available in service of thick description as argued by Geertz (1973) and others.

Participants

The 201 participants (N=201) in this study were all in-service secondary school teachers. In terms of the proportions of white and BIPOC racial identification, participant demographics roughly matched those of teachers across the Toronto District School Board, as reported by Parekh et al. (2016): 23% identified as Black, Indigenous, or person of colour (BIPOC) and 72% identified as white. The remaining 5% of teacher participants chose to not disclose their racial identities. This chapter presents findings from the 15 interviews, as well as from a subset (N=59) of survey respondents who reported participating in racial justice-oriented PD, and who offered qualitative comments on that PD. Thus, the qualitative contributions from 74 teachers serve as the data for this analysis.

Out of the 74 participants, 47 identified as women, 23 identified as men, 1 identified as male but not man, and 3 did not disclose their gender identities. In terms of racial identities of the 74 participants, 12 identified as BIPOC, 48 identified as white, and 14 chose not to disclose their racial identities. Gender identity distributions were similar between BIPOC and white teachers. Participants ranged from working class to wealthy, however, the majority came from middle class socio-economic backgrounds. Participants varied in age, with the youngest being in their early 20s and the oldest in their late 60s. There was also a broad representation of teaching experience that ranged from first-year teachers to veteran teachers of over 40 years. However, we recognize the limitations of sample size and representativeness, and hasten to suggest that findings are not generalizable, but rather inferential and question generating.

Data Analysis and Researcher Subjectivity

Following transcription of the interviews and collation of the qualitative comment data from the surveys, using open verbal code generation, we analyzed the texts with a focus on theme identification (Ryan & Bernard, 1994). Organizing and leveling our codes, we then identified meta-themes within the transcripts (Miles & Huberman, 1994) in the following areas: correlations between teacher subject positionality and teacher reflections on PD, teacher perceptions of personal and professional responsibility, teacher perceptions of personal and school accountability, teachers perceptions of barriers and supports, and teacher perspectives on opportunities for teaching for racial justice. After highlighting these themes within the transcripts (Miles & Huberman, 1994) we fashioned responses by theme into individual vignettes, which we cross-analyzed for comparison (Creswell, 1998; Merriam, 1998).

Our cross-case analysis identified divergences and convergences within teacher responses, for example divergent conceptions of responsibility to direct one's own racial justice learning and practice (Taylor, Bodgan, & Walker 2000). These findings were then analyzed in light of the relevant literature, as well as in relation to the CRT's insistence that analyses of race go beyond individual anecdote to identity patterns at the institutional (as well as systemic) level, revealing the mutually constituting nature of race and schooling (Parker & Gillborn, 2020). These considerations helped to narrow our analytical focus on three partially divergent key themes which we take up in our findings section below: racial justice as a perceived commodity, racial justice as a way to "save" racialized Others, and racial justice as a process of self-reflection. As with social research contained by a fairly narrow timeframe such as this (three - four months), findings had to be carefully contextualized not only in terms of place (Toronto) but time - a matter that bore somewhat uniquely on this research in the context of a country like Canada undergoing particularly rapid developments in race conversations in education.

As researchers, we are conscious of our own identities as being relevant to the research process. I (Lena) am a first-generation immigrant, living on the traditional lands of the Niitsitapi (Blackfoot Confederacy) and the peoples of the Treaty 7 region in Southern Alberta, as well as the Métis Nation of Alberta Region 3. I am a mixed-race cisgender woman, and also, a teacher. The analysis provided in this chapter is not simply a reflection of participant ideologies, but a reflection of researcher ideologies as well based on what we paid attention to and what we did not notice. The analysis of what teachers had to say about racial justice, especially those who identified as people of colour, mixed-race, or English language learners served as an ongoing reminder to critically examine my own internalized oppression and socially conditioned need to self-preserve by assimilating into dominant cultures, internal racial identity struggles, and my own K-12 institutionalization as a teacher. I (Arlo) am a settler, living on Williams Treaty Territory. I am a white cisgender man. I am also a former high school teacher in Toronto. The discourses we trace here are familiar, and as a reflection of my own relationships to whiteness, understandable in highly personal ways. The criticisms we offer here are thus cautions for me too. While I have the language and critical training to problematize the ways many white folks work to not see and engage race, I am neither above nor beyond the critiques that arise from these analyses. Finally, we both recognize that our analysis and engagement with the data are necessarily informed by our respective subjectivities.

FINDINGS AND DISCUSSION

In this section, we discuss the findings from the qualitative data in this study. The data consisted of optional short answers left in the survey, as well as in-depth open-ended interviews. Overall, there were 102 responses that contributed to this study on racial justice-oriented PD. However, we had to exclude survey responses of 28 participants from the qualitative analysis as they could not be coded due to their uncertain meaning. For example, when discussing experiences with racial justice-oriented PD, those responses included "Somewhat useful, but it was much whitebashing," "I didn't find it helpful," or "Somewhat limited." Such comments were too ambiguous and short to confidently tease out meaning. Therefore, the responses of the remaining 74 participants formed the basis for the findings in this study. Out of the 74 participants, 15 participated in in-depth open-ended interviews. Out of the 74 participants, 12 racially identified as BIPOC, 48 racially identified as white, and 14 chose to not disclose their racial identities.

The responses in this study expressed teachers' desires to have all their students succeed and demonstrated that teacher participants condemned inequity and racism. However, only a few teacher participants recognized their own responsibilities for racially just teaching, while everyone else (the majority of whom identified as white) distanced themselves from their privileges and power. The interview and survey data revealed three patterns of thought in how teacher participants interpreted racial justice-oriented professional development: 1) The majority of teachers interpreted racial justice to be a commodity that they expected be given to them; 2) Some teachers interpreted racial justice as a way to "save" racialized Others; and 3) A small number of teachers recognized racial justice to be an ongoing process of self-reflection. By equating doing racial justice to being racially just, teacher participants in the first two findings insisted that they needed to be explicitly shown the activities or lesson plan exemplars or other resources in order for them to know how to incorporate racial justice into the curriculum. These two groups of participants illustrated teachers' good intentions of wanting to help racialized students, while being unaware of their own institutionally conditioned patterns of thinking and acting that reinforced hegemonic whiteness. The teacher participants in the third finding recognized racial justice to be an ongoing process of teachers' self-reflection required in order to understand how one's social conditioning based on their social location translated into teaching practice.

In this section, we discuss the three patterns of thought the findings surfaced and point to the importance of teachers' critical self-reflection needed to develop critical consciousness within oneself and within students in order to affect meaningful social change. To ensure confidentiality, participants were assigned pseudonyms and their school names were erased.

Racial Justice as a Commodity

While all teacher participants in this study condemned racism and, unlike participants in previous studies (e.g., Aitken & Radford, 2018; Ladson-Billings, 2011; King, 1991; Vaught & Castagno, 2008) who interpreted racism to be an individual issue rather than a systemic phenomenon, most of these teachers expressed an awareness of racism as systemic. Nevertheless, beyond statements about racism being systemic there seemed to be little recognition of the interconnectedness between systemic racism, the current organization of Canadian schools, and teachers as individuals. Without that recognition, the white supremacist world economic system and the whiteness of Canada's K-12 institutions faded into the background as "just the way things are," allowing racial justice to get commodified as most things under capitalism.

Out of the 74 participants, 48 interpreted racial justice to be a commodity. Out of those 48 participants, 5 identified as BIPOC, 31 identified as white, and 11 did not disclose their racial identities. The following three quotes are illustrative of the vast majority of teacher participants' attempts at commodifying racial justice.

"It was not particularly useful from a pragmatic sense. The PD was more about acknowledging systemic racism. Practically addressing it in a classroom setting? Not so much" (Avery, white man, middle class, anglophone).

"It was a year long focus with some great sessions and workshops...but no time to really implement anything and it felt like nothing tangible was given...more theory and discussion" (Blake, white woman, middle class, anglophone).

"Most PD on this subject focuses on raising awareness, and offers little if any specific implementation recommendations" (Cai, white woman, middle class, anglophone).

For Avery, racial justice had to be something practical. Blake did not want theory or discussion, but instead required *"tangible"* racial justice. Cai did not need awareness but wanted to be specifically told how racial justice could be utilized. Therefore, these three teachers, as well as many other participants, interpreted racial justice to be a commodity in the form of a lesson plan or some kind of resource that needed to be given to them by a PD presenter, administrator, or someone else in order for them to do racial justice in the classroom. Without that commodity, they deemed racial justice-oriented PD useless.

Teachers who commodified racial justice also demonstrated the implicit whiteness of the teaching force with its lack of personal experience with systemic racism, even in a city like Toronto. The following quotes by Emerson and Finn were illustrative of teachers' initial lack of awareness of systemic racism and them being *"made conscious of this"* or having *"been told that the racial inequity exists."*

"I have been told that the racial inequity exists but have not been given explicit instruction on how to address the inequity" (Emerson, white woman, middle class, anglophone).

"We were made conscious of this [racial inequity], but never specific approaches. And even if the[re] are, they never are adequately specific to deal with individual subjects. Teachers are smart, they already know most of this and such PD is just a big waste of time" (Finn, white man, middle class, anglophone).

Even though Emerson and Finn acknowledged new awareness of racial inequity, they viewed themselves and the organization of schooling with its subjects as disconnected from that inequity, insisting that they just needed to be given *"explicit instruction"* and *"specific approaches"* that are adequate for already existing individual subjects. Neither of the five participants above nor the majority of teachers in this study recognized themselves (as individuals) as part of the broader system of racism. They expressed an openness to racial justice under the condition that they are given a lesson plan exemplar or other instructions, while keeping their personal selves innocently separate from the bigger collective of whiteness that reproduced the status quo through their ways of thinking about schooling.

Since training that involved difficult knowledge often activated defenses (Friere, 1970/2017; Olesen, 2007; Shim, 2017) and, no matter how anti-racist, was filtered through individual teachers' already existing racial frameworks (Vaught & Castagno, 2008), many of the teacher participants in this study followed the pattern of thought observed in prior literature that was discussed earlier in the chapter.

Dysconscious Racism

Even if some teacher participants may have insinuated that racial justice PD made them more aware of the reproduction of systemic racism in their classrooms, they distanced their individual selves from that racist reproduction and insisted that the barrier to racial justice in their classrooms was, indeed, the lack of specific practical exemplars. The assumption that teachers were already good, just, and informed people who *"already know most of this"* prevented these teachers from even considering the myriad of ways they could be upholding racial injustices, outside of a particular resource - through their interactions, through their thinking about students and their families, thinking about their colleagues, thinking about the curriculum and the functioning of their schools, to which things they paid attention and which they ignored, justifications that they made in various situations, among many others. Yet, the message most of the participants communicated was that it was a lesson plan exemplar or a particular subject-specific resource that was needed in order to resolve institutional racism in their classrooms.

Such tendencies and inabilities to recognize own whiteness within past and present white supremacy revealed, what King (1991) referred to as, "dysconscious racism" - not unconsciousness, but an impaired consciousness that takes for granted the system of racial privilege and "tacitly accepts dominant White norms and privileges" (p. 135). Dysconscious racism allows white norms of Canada's K-12 education system to be taken for granted "by not being the object of perception" (Ahmed, 2012, p. 21) despite teachers' desires, that may very well be internally felt as sincere, to enact racial justice. Due to this impaired consciousness, teacher participants re-enacted hegemonic whiteness through their inability to "distinguish between racist justification of the status quo (which limit their thought, self-identity, and responsibility to take action) and socially unacceptable individual prejudice or bigotry (which [teachers] often disavow)" (King, 1991, p. 140).

The Neutral STEM Teacher

Of particular note were concerns of math and science teachers who expressed uncertainty about how racial justice could be incorporated into what were usually considered "neutral" subjects. In discussing racial justice in their classrooms and their interpretations of racial justice-oriented PD, similar to the participants in the above section, there was impaired consciousness of the whiteness ingrained into the math and science curriculum. Unfortunately, none of the participants asking for STEM exemplars questioned the curriculum or wondered why what and how they were teaching seemed to be so out of sync with racial justice in the first place, sustaining the status quo and concealing the white norms of Canada's K-12 curriculum.

In the following example, Grayson deemed invisible his own whiteness as well as that of the science curriculum by presuming neutrality of that subject.

"Because I teach science it's [racial justice] not sort of the sort of thing that I do as part of the job I guess. The opportunity isn't there unless I make it happen" (Grayson, white man, middle class, anglophone).

To Grayson, racial justice was an add-on to an otherwise neutral science curriculum. Within that assumed science neutrality, he could create opportunities for racial justice if he so chose. Yet, he did not realize the power and privilege one had to have in order to be able to *"make [racial justice] happen"* - a statement that, indeed, pointed to the opposite of neutrality and to very clear racial power dynamics. Similar to Grayson, in the following quote, Harper made invisible the curriculum, her teaching, and her own identity by commodifying racial justice as a thing that needed to fit into the current organization of schools, all the while, ironically, acknowledging the need for racially just teaching.

"Equity has been a core topic during in-school PD over the past several years. The PD is seldom (if ever) accompanied by classroom ready resources, and never by subject area resources specific to mathematics instruction (my core teachable)… There is a clear, indisputable need to address inequality, however leveled, class ready, subject specific, curriculum aligned resources are scant in most subjects and near non-existent in mathematics. Thus, it is unrealistic for teachers in terms of implementation" (Harper, white woman, middle class, anglophone).

To Harper, racially just teaching was located in a particular math-specific resource. While Harper acknowledged the *"indisputable need to address inequality,"* it was unclear where she thought that inequality originated and what upheld it, as she assumed schools to be neutral places by not considering the current curriculum or school organization. She could not imagine schools or her teaching any differently, that was the invisible "natural" order of things. By perceiving inequality as existing somewhere else, outside of school, Harper believed that a *"leveled, class ready, subject specific, curriculum aligned"* resource in an otherwise neutral environment with neutral teachers was going to address that indisputable need for equity.

The following two participants, Izzy and Jamie, expressed an openness to changing or adjusting their lessons, but again, just as other teachers already mentioned, considered their own personal selves as separate from STEM educational inequity.

"I did not find [PD] helpful. I teach science and it would be beneficial to have specific examples so that I can understand how to make my lessons better" (Izzy, white woman, middle class, anglophone).

"The problem with almost all workshops that I've attended is that it's too general and not targeted to the subject I teach – science" (Jamie, white woman, working class, anglophone).

Izzy and Jamie perceived racial justice-oriented PD to be too general. Because the whiteness of teachers and of Canada's K-12 schooling was not an object of perception due to its invisibility, these participants did not see the applicability of *"general"* racial justice as they did not know how to apply it to something that they could not see. Therefore, they wanted something *"specific"* and *"targeted"* to their subjects in order to be able to actually *"understand how to make my lessons better."* Racial justice, once again, could only be seen as a lesson, an activity, or a tangible resource.

By insisting that racial injustice laid in how they were not doing things in the classroom due to forces outside of their control (because they were not given an exemplar or a resource), these teachers absolved themselves from the racial injustice that could lay in how they were already doing things that were under their control. In that sense, "we might want to consider racism as a form of doing or even a field of positive action, rather than a form of inaction" (Ahmed, 2012, p. 45). Considering racial justice to be a commodity that was simply added onto the (invisible) existing social order, individual teachers were able to evade, consciously, unconsciously, or dysconsciously, confronting their own privileges accrued from ongoing racial injustices - the very structural injustices that led to the academic marginalization of their own racialized students.

Since white privilege within the white supremacist system is easily camouflaged, leading to impaired consciousness of many who benefit from it (King, 1991), sudden recognition, however slight, of racial power and privilege over racialized Others may activate emotional defenses that may stall learning (Freire, 1970/2017; Olesen, 2007) due to the disruption of one's established self-image as a "good hardworking white person" (Ladson-Billings, 2011; Shim, 2017). Therefore, these white teacher participants commodified racial justice by changing the meaning of the term to fit their pre-existing self-conceptions within their pre-existing racial frameworks. That is, of course, ironic because white people are the only racial group provided with the systemic privilege to determine racial meaning (Vaught & Castagno, 2008). It is vital to recognize in such instances that by developing a commodified relationship with racial justice, these teachers "were not just individually but simultaneously creating meaning themselves; they were tapping into and recreating meanings that already existed within the district's structural practices and within the larger society" (Vaught & Castagno, 2008, p. 102) situated within contemporary capitalism. "In their unrestricted eagerness to possess, the oppressors develop the conviction that it is possible for them to transform everything into objects of their purchasing power... For them *to be* is *to have*" (Freire, 1970/2017, p. 32). This capitalist world dynamic was observed playing out in these presumed educational efforts toward justice, where *to be* racially just meant *to have* racial justice (in the form of a lesson exemplar or a particular resource). According to Wellman (1993), racist thinking is a dynamic and is "reflected in its changing content. As political and economic forces move subordinate groups into new and different social positions, or if racial hegemony is challenged, the racial thinking of whites changes to accommodate these new realities" (p. 56). So, just like that, the white supremacist social order morphs to adapt to new social conditions under the guise of racial justice.

Racial Justice as Othering

Another pattern of thought that emerged in this study was with teacher participants expressing deficit views of racialized students. Just like the group of teachers who commodified racial justice, these teachers' comments demonstrated dysconscious racism as they clearly admitted to academic disparity between racialized and white students, but the white norms of the school curriculum, together with individual teachers and their practices were so invisible to these teachers that it led to an uncritical and limited conception of racial justice that only served to other racialized students. Even though a number of teacher participants referenced racism and academic barriers as being systemic, it was unclear how they actually understood the said system since they did not question why and how BIPOC students came to be marginalized in the first place.

Out of the 74 participants, 14 interpreted racial justice to be an act of saving racialized Others. Out of those 14 participants, 3 identified as BIPOC, 8 identified as white, and 3 did not disclose their racial identities. In the quote below, Leigh pointed out the school board's hypocrisy of leaving individual teachers to solve the problem that, they were informed during their PD, was, in fact, systemic. She also seemingly acknowledged the system by referring to the students as "racialized" - as in, it is not them that had a "race" but rather were racialized, assigned race based on the social construct of race, by someone else. Interestingly, she did not acknowledge who did the racializing and put the barriers in place for those students. While Leigh attempted to demonstrate her openness to racial justice and her comments could be interpreted as wanting to help solve the systemic problem, she nevertheless saw the students as racialized Others who were perceived to have inherently different academic abilities than their white peers.

"There was a lack of specific guidance that was relevant to the science curriculum, and the general training was vague in that it clearly indicated racial disparities in student outcomes, identified that systemic barriers exist for racialized students, but basically left it up to us to solve the systemic problem without any specific guidance. E.g. it would be beneficial for racialized students to study grade 9 astronomy before chemistry, because there is some evidence that this increases engagement, is actionable vs. students are falling behind, and it's your job to fix it" (Leigh, white woman, middle class, anglophone).

By speculating if academic engagement of racialized students would be better if they did astronomy before chemistry, reasons for academic disparities were placed on the students who, even in this supposed openness, were perceived to be inherently different from white students. Without questioning (white) curricular standards, school organization, and teachers' practices and biases that led to the disparities in academic achievement, Leigh presented racialized students as a biologically different monolith whose brains could not process the content in the same order as white students' brains, and simply required shifting around of the same science units, allowing white norms to disappear into the background. Therefore, the problem of racial injustice was assumed to be with how racialized students' brains operated rather than being the problem with how and what teachers taught and why the system racialized BIPOC students.

Structural Hosts of K-12

Similar to the teacher participants who commodified racial justice, these teachers acknowledged the disadvantages faced by racialized groups while ignoring their own racial advantages. Additionally, when discussing racialized students in connection to the curriculum or talking about the need to provide them with equitable support, the teacher participants noticed the negative aspects associated with coming from a marginalized community but failed "to account for White people's beliefs and attitudes that have long justified societal oppression and inequity" (King, 1991, p. 138).

In the two examples below, Mason and Noah indirectly (and perhaps, unintentionally) pointed out the whiteness of those who decided how equity and racial justice were to be implemented. Mason did not question the whiteness that leveled students' academic skills and abilities, and Noah assumed himself to be neutral and colourblind as he attempted *"to read"* every student in a we-are-all-just-the-human-race manner of assessment.

"The focus [of PD] was on granting students from underserved communities as opposed to providing them the equitable support necessary to develop their academic skills and abilities to the level of their more privileged peers" (Mason, white man, middle class, anglophone).

"To be honest, I didn't learn anything that I didn't already know. I make a point 'to read' every one of my students. That means, I endeavour to make meaning of their behaviour, their facial expressions as they approach the challenges, what or how they say things, what they write and how they read. My students are humans like me, so I endeavour to read their feelings and chat to them about what the[y are] thinking & feeling, regardless of race, income, or gender identification" (Noah, white man, middle class, anglophone).

It is important to notice how explicitly talking about who was disadvantaged and who needed to be brought up *"to the level of their more privileged peers,"* Leigh's, Mason's, and Noah's comments revealed the implicit whiteness already in place. As a result of such thinking, the problem of whiteness gets "redescribed here not as an institutional problem but as a problem with those who are not included by it" (Ahmed, 2012, p. 35). Of course it is very important that all students have access to equitable support to develop academic skills and to also recognize the shared humanity across all social groups; however, it is also very important to recognize whose standard is being used to level and compare others. As these participants described students who were excluded from academic success within the current system, they inadvertently exposed the whiteness of those who decided how to include Others - "those who are already given a place are the ones who are welcoming rather than welcomed, the ones who are in the structural position of hosts" (Ahmed, 2012, p. 42). Therefore, such comments from teachers beg the question - when thinking of equitable educational practices, are teachers actually looking to de-centre whiteness and genuinely value different knowledge systems and ways of being; or, are they looking for more effective ways to assimilate racialized students into whiteness?

Racial Justice as Ongoing (Critical) Self-Reflection

Unlike the vast majority of teachers in this study, the smallest number of teacher participants interpreted racially just teaching to be something that came from the self. Instead of focusing outwardly and looking for racial justice in this or that lesson exemplar or this or that racialized group of students, this small number of teachers looked inwardly and expressed that racial justice was about self-reflection. Despite so few teachers expressing the importance of self-reflection, the practice of critical self-reflection was the most important step toward racially just teaching that any teacher could take (Freire, 1970/2017; Ladson-Billings, 2011; Lindstrom et al., 2022; Shim, 2017).

Out of the 74 participants, 12 teachers communicated that racial justice was not something that a person "did" and, instead, had to be a process of ongoing reflection that led to "being" more racially just. Out of those 12 participants, 4 identified as BIPOC (33% of all BIPOC teacher participants) and 8 identified as white (17% of all white teacher participants). Quinn and Rylee expressed that the more general approach to racial justice (the source of complaints for previous participants) allowed them to learn more about the way the world functioned and served as an entry point for teachers to start reflecting on interconnections between their biases and teaching practices.

"The PD has been more of a generalized approach with the intention of ongoing examination of our own biases with regard [to] our own practice" (Quinn, white woman, middle class, anglophone).

"I think the conversations are great and I learn from them. But take that with a grain of salt. I am open to learning and so I think the PD helps. Sometimes there were 'realistic' things aka resources that I could directly use in my classes. But even if there aren't resources, the info from a PD can help you grow and become more aware of the world" (Rylee, East Asian woman, middle class, anglophone).

Rylee specifically pointed out that even without particular resources to take to the classroom, the new knowledge allowed her to grow as a person. Quinn and Rylee interpreted racial justice as ongoing learning and personal examination - an interpretation that was also shared by Skylar during his interview when reflecting on some past experiences. Skylar recalled times when he was, unintentionally, engaging with and academically pushing students who spoke English more fluently versus those who were just beginning to learn the language. Looking back, he realized that by disengaging from the students who were just beginning to learn English, he was negatively affecting their sense of belonging, learning engagement, and overall academic success.

"It wasn't intentionally marginalizing students but if you're not aware of it, the ball is going to keep, it's like a snowball effect, it's going to keep rolling downhill unless you stop it, it's going to get bigger and it's going to get worse" (Skylar, white man, middle class, anglophone).

Skylar believed that without ongoing reflection on one's biases, teachers were bound to marginalize students in various ways, without even realizing it. Another participant, Taylor, also expressed that racial justice had to be a *"self-diagnostic and personal"* process so that teachers could correct issues as they learned more about themselves. However, Taylor indicated that racial justice-oriented PD did not provide teachers with opportunities to self-reflect or with any additional services such as equity-oriented counselling to help them properly process difficult knowledge that was presented and resulting difficult emotions.

"It needs to be self-diagnostic and personal... We need to do this work personally and focus so that we can keep private and reflect on ourselves to correct any issues we discover with the opportunity to talk to a counsellor afterwards one-on-one with equity sensitivity training. Doing group PD to let us know 'there is a problem' and not allow for group sharing and discussion of individual cases doesn't fix anything" (Taylor, mixed-race woman, working class, anglophone).

Skylar and Taylor, desiring to affect social change in their classrooms in a meaningful way, articulated struggles similar to those described by Lindstrom et al. (2022). According to Lindstrom et al. (2022), as teachers struggle to understand how to decolonize themselves, "they must also seek effective ways to conceptualize the links between the meso-level of the discipline [academic subject] and the micro-level of the classroom" (p. 2). Additionally, Taylor's sentiment aligned with what King (1991) observed in that simply presenting teachers with facts about systemic inequities did not necessarily enable "teachers to examine the beliefs and assumptions that may influence the way they interpret these facts" (p. 142). The "critical" part in "critical self-reflection" is what helps teachers realize the mediating effects of their individual social locations between the broader social order, institutional norms including curriculum, organizational norms, and their actions in the classroom. Such a critical lens is important not only because it develops a deeper understanding of marginalized students as "targets, rather than causes, of these unjust conditions" (Gorski, 2016, p. 380) but because "to surmount the situation of oppression, people must first critically recognize its causes, so that through transforming action they can create a new situation" (Freire, 1970/2017, p. 21). This alternative and difficult way of looking at (and into) oneself and at one's relationship with knowledge (Lindstrom et al., 2022) uncovers the political role of schooling (King, 1991). During that process, teachers realize that discomfort is actually a sign of taken for granted colonialism (Lindstrom et al., 2022) and recognize that, even if they were provided with lesson exemplars, a lesson or a resource could only be as anti-oppressive as the teacher delivering it (Gorski, 2016).

However, even this group of teachers, while reflective of their own practices, did not explicitly reference inequities as stemming from the broader systemic organization, making it unclear whether their interpretations of racial justice PD led them to challenge personal power only, making them feel personally responsible for fixing injustices or allowed them to recognize their pedagogies as a product of social conditioning based on their intersecting social identities as well as their jobs as subordinated workers in an otherwise white hierarchical institution. While self-reflection on individual power was necessary for personal growth, Vaught and Castagno (2008) warned that training teachers to examine their own privileges "without training them to understand how individual experiences and behaviors are both drawn from and constituent of structural privilege and power assumes that change can occur effectively on the individual level" (p. 102).

Partial Recognition of the System?

When writing about the importance of teachers' critical consciousness in understanding the interconnections between systemic inequities and academic outcomes, Gorski (2016) contemplated if it was still, perhaps, possible for teachers "to eradicate outcome disparities most closely related to the barriers and challenges experienced by people experiencing poverty by ignoring those barriers and challenges - the symptoms of economic injustice" (p. 382). If prior literature (e.g., Freire, 1970/2017; Hiranandani, 2012; Ladson-Billings, 2011; Ray, 2019; Vaught & Castagno, 2008; Wellman, 1993), including Gorski's (2016) conclusion, and ongoing oppressions unmasked further under the conditions of COVID-19 are any indication, then no, attempting to alleviate the symptoms of injustices without understanding the actual cause does not lead to transformational change because the cause remains unaffected - "there simply is no way to eradicate educational outcome disparities while sidestepping structural injustice" (Gorski, 2016, p. 383) and any training that keeps the supposed social transformation at the individual level "is formulated to discourage direct responses to inequity" (p. 384).

A developing recognition of the broader system was observed during Grayson's interview. He was coded under commodity for the purposes of data presentation as he initially started with statements indicative of the neutrality of the science classroom, seeing no academic barriers in relation to his students' race, and, as discussed in the section about commodities, considered racial justice to be a commodity that could be added onto the "normal" order in his classroom. However, as he continued to reflect on questions about schools' structural formations like class size and academic streaming, he recognized that the school was structured in a way that further marginalized students who were already in disadvantaged positions due to (interconnecting) societal inequities outside of school:

"if a kid only shows up twice a week, I mean, I can't dedicate that much time to them when I've got kids that are in the 45% range, and the school wants me to try to get them credits (Pause) I even hate saying it that way - the school wants me to..."

Shortly after, Grayson expressed a recognition that the less academically successful students tended to come from economically marginalized households and that those homes also tended to be racialized:

"Insofar as some of the students who are less academically successful, they tend to come from lower socio-economic status homes and they tend to be from families that would identify as minority. So in that sense, I guess, now that you put it that way, there is a difference in a large classroom."

In the above quote, Grayson recognized that the students who were not receiving his support (due to the school expecting him to focus on the 45% range) were generally the economically marginalized students who were likely to be racialized. He realized that in a large class, he was not attending to them because of that focus on the 45% range. Thinking about class size, Grayson may not have acknowledged the Eurocentricity of a particular science lesson, but he nevertheless began to recognize racial injustice in some of the structural elements that contributed to ongoing academic marginalization in his classroom:

"I had never thought about this stuff because I do teach science and, and, I mean, it doesn't really matter what culture a kid is from - an atom is an atom, you know, a food web is a food web. So, I was, I was thinking exactly of what happened in this particular question where initially I was like 'No, I don't see a difference in terms of how a person's race might affect them,' but now that you asked this question, it's like 'Well, wait a minute, yeah, there is.'"

Even though some teachers in this theme reflected on their personal conditioning as barriers to racially just teaching without necessarily explicitly referencing systemic barriers, Grayson began to reflect on systemic barriers to racially just teaching, without necessarily acknowledging personal conditioning. Similar to Grayson, Ulric expressed a partial awareness of the system. While Ulric condemned ongoing marginalization of racialized students by the K-12 education system and also recognized himself as contributing to the K-12 inequities in his classroom due to large class sizes and a lack of supports (such as, not having enough educational assistants) that prevented him from attending to the most vulnerable students more effectively, he nonetheless failed to consider the bigger oppressive capitalist system that extended beyond K-12.

"Ultimately, the lens that I'm really, I really look at equity in STEM education and in math education specifically - is about how do we increase post-secondary enrollment and achievement of people from racialized communities, more specifically, our Black students and Indigenous students who are woefully underrepresented in STEM fields, and in STEM post-secondary areas of study? How do we increase that representation?" (Ulric, white man, middle class, anglophone).

Ulric's comment served as a reminder about internal and external dynamics involved in fighting and sustaining oppressions while being a small but important interconnecting part of the existing capitalist machine; and, that even supposed anti-racist teachers aware of educational injustices and their individual roles in them usually have to work with the institution and follow its prescriptions, inadvertently trying to assimilate students into becoming part of the establishment - to break out of the cycle of poverty, racialized students have to get into post-secondary, become "higher-skilled" workers.

Thus, even this equity lens was institutionalized. But the interests of institutions and the interests of those seeking liberation are inherently incompatible. The very presence of "high-skilled" workers means there have to be "low-skilled" workers who are exploited as such because "the existing social order cannot provide for unlimited (or equal) opportunity... Thus, elimination of the societal hierarchy is inevitable if the social order is to be reorganized" (King, 1991, p. 139). However, the elimination of existing social order may not have been what Ulric, or the majority of other teachers in this study were thinking about when they indicated the need for racially just teaching.

Taken together, all the comments from this group of teacher participants prompted important points for further consideration about what it means for racially just thinking to be institutionalized and how much further (if at all) in the fight toward liberation that takes these teachers compared to those who commodify racial justice or attempt to "save" racialized Others. While it was clear that teachers from this group knew change was necessary based on what they learned about themselves or newly discovered insights into the organization of schooling, there was vagueness around whether racial justice, to them, meant to bring down the oppressive institution or to diversify the workforce in order to "maximize talent and creativity and foster innovation, which can ultimately lead to increased profits and positive public image for a successful business enterprise" (Hiranandani, 2012, p. 1) - essentially making racial justice more so about the fight for financial gain within the same capitalist system that rests upon wealth accumulation, concentrated power, and exploitation, using racialized Others as necessary tools required at this stage of economic growth.

The Master's Tools

Based on the ambivalences expressed by the participants in this study, it was unclear what school leadership tried to accomplish with racial justice-oriented PD for their teachers. Are the institution and institutional leaders actually devising training to bring themselves down? According to some participants, the answer to that question would be a big "no." Vega and Waverly added comments indicating that racial justice-oriented PD simply served as a public relations gimmick for schools and districts.

"It's a token gesture" (Vega, white woman, middle class, anglophone).

"I find that the PD simply pays lip service and seems to be provided to meet some kind of 'requirement.' Possibly so that schools/boards can say 'we offered that'" (Waverly, white woman, middle class, anglophone).

While many of the previous participants pointed out schools' and districts' hypocrisy in making individual teachers responsible for an issue that their PD told them was systemic, Vega and Waverly also pointed out the performativity of such racial justice-oriented PD sessions.

It is a great paradox to have oppressive institutions proclaim commitments to anti-oppression and attempt to lead that liberation. The oppressive group, those granted with systemic privileges and power over Others, "can free neither others nor themselves. It is therefore essential that the oppressed wage the struggle to resolve the contradiction in which they are caught" (Freire, 1970/2017, p. 30).

Only one participant in the entire study, Xav, articulated a critically conscious approach to racial justice, saying that the racialized students had to be the ones leading justice movements with the support (not the lead) of those with more power, the support that could be something as simple as not staying in the way.

"And the easiest thing that the rest of the [school] community could do is stay out of it. That's a lot to ask - teachers are very controlling of the environment that they work in, and they want to be in charge, and 'I should be able to go to every locked door and have keys and access.' And there's something about that that needs to just fall to the wayside... So allowing young people to congregate, they start to share part of themselves, including race and ethnicity... And that's like a big way that we can support them - it's like literally see them and listen to them and hear them for who they are. And then they'll tell us what they need. And then we have to be able to actually follow through" *(Xav, white woman, middle class, anglophone).*

According to Xav, it was important for the marginalized to have the space to come together on their own, and share their stories in order to build togetherness and deepen understanding of their lived experiences as opposed to having those with more power, like teachers, controlling and supervising environments intended for counter-hegemony. Xav insisted that those with more power had to actually be open to seeing and hearing the marginalized *"for who they are,"* and use their power to listen to the marginalized about what and how to do things to progress justice rather than decide for them. Unfortunately, teachers were not allowing the marginalized students to congregate on their own terms and instead wanted *"to be in charge."* Xav's comments were consistent with Freire's (1970/2017) concept of critical consciousness in that one of the fundamental dimensions of oppression was to keep the oppressed divided in order to prevent their unification - "concepts such as unity, organization, and struggle are immediately labeled as dangerous. In fact, of course these concepts *are* dangerous - to the oppressors - for their realization is necessary to actions of liberation" (p. 114).

While teachers prevented students from congregating, a little higher up the ladder within K-12 institutional hierarchy, some teachers, like Yancey, Zein, and Ash expressed that school leaders prevented them from congregating with other teachers, or deepening their own understanding of racial justice and implementing their ideas.

"No release time from teaching was given to strategize and work with colleagues to plan" *(Yancey, white woman, middle class, anglophone).*

"I received lots of links and attachments but there was no time to follow through in understanding" *(Zein, Black woman, middle class, anglophone).*

"It [racial justice] is difficult to implement depending on admin's expectations of teachers in their schools. Admin expectations trump all" *(Ash, undisclosed identity).*

Even though Ash's responses were coded as part of the first group that interpreted racial justice to be a commodity, the three participants above echoed an earlier comment by Taylor who shared that the organization of racial justice-oriented PD did not allow teachers to properly process new knowledge in a meaningful way that would result in social change. Therefore, the current organization of schools assures that teachers, too, are isolated from one another, weakening their potential to deepen their knowledge from racial justice-oriented PD, but "giving them the impression that they are being helped" (Freire, 1970/2017, p. 114) by sending them *"links and attachments"* and holding PD sessions *"so that schools/boards can say 'we offered that.'"* Such comments by teacher participants exposed the structural limitations of trying to develop critical consciousness under the unchanging practices of the institution and revealed school districts' gross misappropriation of racial justice.

According to Freire (1970/2017), an oppressive institution cannot have its leaders be the thinkers for others' doing, while denying them (students and subordinated workers like teachers) the opportunity to critically reflect on their situations. Neither can leaders lead without serious ongoing self-reflection themselves (Freire, 1970/2017).

The leaders cannot treat the oppressed as mere activists to be denied the opportunity of reflection and allowed merely the illusion of acting, whereas in fact they would continue to be manipulated... By imposing their word on others, they falsify that word and establish a contradiction between their method and their objectives. If they are truly committed to liberation, their action and reflection cannot proceed without the action and reflection of others." (Freire, 1970/2017, p. 99)

If they are truly committed to liberation... so, before racial justice PD is presented to teachers and before teachers are told to change their practices based on that PD, school leaders have to honestly and critically reflect on what exactly they want to achieve with racial justice-oriented professional development. Therefore, "any evaluation of a school's or school system's commitment to equity begins, not with an accounting of this or that policy or practice intervention, but rather with an accounting of the ideological positions of the institutional leaders" (Gorski, 2016, p. 381).

In this section, we presented themes that emerged out of optional qualitative short answers from the survey and in-depth open-ended interviews. The responses from 74 teacher participants were coded into three themes: 1) The majority of teachers interpreted racial justice to be a commodity that they expected be given to them; 2) Some teachers interpreted racial justice as a way to "save" racialized Others; and 3) A small number of teachers recognized racial justice to be an ongoing process of self-reflection. There was a tendency among teacher participants to equate doing racial justice (in the form of a lesson or activity, or following a particular resource) to being racially just, which allowed those teachers to commodify the concept of racial justice whilst reinforcing, however unknowingly and unintentionally, white racial supremacy of Canada's schools. Additionally, some teacher participants othered their racialized students by misconstruing systemic racism as the problem with racialized students' academic abilities rather than the oppressive racist system that led to academic disenfranchisement. Finally, only a small number of teacher participants recognized racial justice to be an act of ongoing critical self-reflection. Only one participant explicitly connected the importance of self-reflection to critical consciousness that was required for true liberation of the oppressed.

LIMITATIONS

This study had some limitations. First, 74 participants were a relatively small sample to draw any general conclusions. However, participants were distributed among the eight schools that, together, provided a representative workplace context for Toronto teachers. Additionally, our study was situated within prior literature discussed in this chapter.

Secondly, the nature of the survey did not allow for any follow-up or clarifying questions to the participants' short answers. Unless participants signed up to be interviewed (only 15 participants did), short answers were analyzed at face value, potentially misrepresenting some of the short answers that could carry more nuanced opinions and reflections that could have surfaced during an interview, as was the case with Grayson.

Thirdly, because this theme of racial justice-oriented PD was not the main focus of the study originally, some of the comments carried more uncertainty in terms of analysis as they may have been incomplete. Although the majority of participants in the first two groups (commodification and othering) communicated enough information for a more accurate analysis, some of the teacher participants in the self-reflection group may have received an incomplete analysis. Specifically, Quinn, Rylee, Skylar, and Taylor may have, indeed, approached racial justice PD with critical consciousness or may have begun to develop critical consciousness as a result of their interpretations of PD content. Unfortunately, the comments they shared in regard to PD were not enough to know with certainty if they were referring to their personal privileges and power at the individual level only, which would indicate only a partial recognition of the system, or if they were realizing their power as systemic oppressors at the classroom level, as well as beginning to understand their own institutional oppression as marginalized others or subordinated workers within a hierarchical machine that conditioned them to participate in the oppression of others.

Finally, a major limitation of this study was the incomplete racial demographic count for the participants, which prevented us from making any inferences, of an exploratory nature, about racial justice-oriented PD interpretations in relation to the racial identities of the interpreting teachers. Out of the 74 participants, 14 did not disclose their racial identities. While certain biased inferences could be made based on the comments some of those participants left to the racial identity question, such as "human race," "none of your business," "I don't identify racially," or "irrelevant," we could not properly analyse such racial identifications. Therefore, a future study should explore potential relationships between the racial identification of teachers and their interpretations of racial justice-oriented PD.

CONCLUSION

This study explored teachers' interpretations of racial justice-oriented professional development. Teacher participants came from eight high schools in Toronto. The eight schools provided a representative workplace context for the Toronto teachers in terms of various student demographics. There were 74 teacher participants whose qualitative contributions, either through written short answers in the survey or in-depth open-ended interviews, contributed to the data in this study.

The focus of the analysis was on teachers' interpretations of racial justice-oriented PD and, therefore, we were not concerned with the exact resources, presentations, webinars, or workshops that were provided to the teachers. The 74 participants described a variety of PD sessions in which they participated that ranged from those developed and provided by groups of teachers at their schools, school librarians, department heads, administrators, school board staff, third parties; ranged from in-person to online during school hours, evenings, and during the summer months; some were self-directed, most were mandatory. A future study may want to explore how particular resources or workshops affected teacher interpretations, however, our focus in this study was not on the specifics of racial justice-oriented PD but on teachers' interpretations of their (various) PD sessions. Despite the variety of racial justice-oriented PD in which the teacher participants in this study participated, three themes emerged from the data:

1) The majority of teachers interpreted racial justice to be a commodity that they expected be given to them; 2) Some teachers interpreted racial justice as a way to "save" racialized Others; and 3) A small number of teachers recognized racial justice to be an ongoing process of self-reflection. These themes are particularly important since the original focus of this research study was not on professional development. The short answers in the survey were completely optional and none of the interview questions asked about professional development. The fact that 102 out of a total of 201 participants chose to share their interpretations of PD (74 of which were coded for this study) revealed a noteworthy importance of PD to teachers' work.

Interview and survey data demonstrated that regardless of an awareness of systemic racism, the vast majority of teachers in the study did not acknowledge the connection between the system and their individual selves. When responding to questions about racial justice in their classroom, they attempted to distance themselves from the collective identity of whiteness and concealed the white norms of Canada's K-12 schooling. Ironically, that only served to reinforce their own whiteness and that of Canada's schools since they were the only race granted the systemic ability to ignore own race. The majority of teacher participants equated doing particular lessons or using specific resources to being racially just, and thus, interpreted racial justice to be a commodity that they expected to be given to them in the form of a curriculum-aligned lesson exemplar or a resource. A smaller group of participants interpreted racial justice to be a way to save racialized Others and assimilate them more effectively into the existing whiteness of Canada's education system. Only a small group of participants recognized racial justice to be a process of learning how to be racially just through ongoing self-reflection. However, it was unclear how critical the self-reflection of those participants was as they did not explicitly share views indicative of critical consciousness. Despite the potential weakness with the critical consciousness analysis, Quinn, Rylee, Skylar, and Taylor served as examples that demonstrated how some teachers desired to bring systemic oppressions to their consciousness yet struggled against the mixed messaging surrounding racial justice-oriented PD. Although, in rare cases, that mixed messaging encouraged teachers to seek out their own professional development outside of work hours in order to gain clarification, for the most part, such PD strengthened white supremacy by commodifying racial justice or reinforcing the othering of racialized students.

Overall, this study demonstrated that teachers tapped into white supremacist racial meanings that already existed and were available to them institutionally, reproducing inequitable racial power dynamics under the guise of racial equity. That being the case, school leaders need to consider not only their objectives but also the impacts of current racial justice-oriented PD, and reflect on whether their goal is liberation or assimilation. Living, studying, and working in a capitalist society with schools constantly facing budget cuts, there may be a lot of money wasted on PD if the outcome is the reinforcement of white supremacy. Instead, that money could go directly to the students based on what the students communicate they need. That is, of course, assuming that the goal of school leadership's racial justice commitments is racial justice. If the goal is to liberate the academically marginalized, ideas for racial justice have to come from some of the most oppressed in the system - racialized students themselves. After all, "Who are better prepared than the oppressed to understand the terrible significance of an oppressive society? Who suffer the effects of oppression more than the oppressed? Who can better understand the necessity of liberation?" (Freire, 1970/2017, p. 19).

Furthermore, future research needs to examine school leaders' attitudes, justifications, and overall ideological stances on why they think teachers need to receive PD on racial justice. Keeping in mind Xav's words: *"we have to be able to actually follow through,"* and the accountability of schools and school districts to their publicly proclaimed devotions to anti-racism, it is vital to explore at what point on this path to the liberation of the oppressed (if there is a certain point, or if it has already been reached), do white district leaders, administrators, and teachers become more afraid of racialized people's critical consciousness than of their own capitalist subjugation?

REFERENCES

Ahmed, S. (2012). Institutional life. In *On Being included: Racism and diversity in institutional life* (pp. 19–50). Duke University Press. doi:10.1215/9780822395324-002

Aitken, A., & Radford, L. (2018). Learning to teach for reconciliation in Canada: Potential, resistance and stumbling forward. *Teaching and Teacher Education*, *75*, 40–48. doi:10.1016/j.tate.2018.05.014

Alberta Education. (2012). *Walking together: First Nations, Métis, and Inuit perspectives in curriculum.* Government of Alberta. https://www.learnalberta.ca/content/aswt/

Alberta Education. (2015). *Guiding voices.* Government of Alberta. https://www.learnalberta.ca/content/fnmigv/index.html#relationships

Alberta Education. (2020, October 1). *Teaching quality standard.* Government of Alberta. https://open.alberta.ca/publications/teaching-quality-standard-2020

Alberta Education. (2022). *Education for reconciliation.* Government of Alberta. https://www.alberta.ca/education-for-reconciliation.aspx

Baszile, D. T. (2009). Deal with it we must: Education, social justice, and the curriculum of hip hop culture. *Equity & Excellence in Education*, *42*(1), 6–19. doi:10.1080/10665680802594576

Battiste, M., & Barman, J. (1995). *First nations education in Canada: The circle unfolds.* UBC Press.

Bell, D. (1973). *Race, racism, and American law.* Little Brown.

Bell, D. (1992). *Faces at the bottom of the well: The permanence of racism.* Basic Books.

Bernal, D. D. (2002). Critical race theory, Latino critical theory, and critical raced-gendered epistemologies: Recognizing students of color as holders and creators of knowledge. *Qualitative Inquiry*, *8*(1), 105–126. doi:10.1177/107780040200800107

British Columbia Ministry of Education and Child Care. (2019, June 19). *New teaching standard strengthens Truth and Reconciliation in the classroom.* Government of British Columbia. https://news.gov.bc.ca/releases/2019EDUC0053-001275

British Columbia Ministry of Education and Child Care. (n.d.). *Report on actions taken to support the truth and reconciliation commission of Canada's calls to action.* Government of British Columbia. https://www2.gov.bc.ca/gov/content/education-training/k-12/a dministration/program-management/indigenous-education/action s-taken-on-reconciliation

Calgary Board of Education. (2020, June 25). *CBE shares our commitment to anti-racism and equity.* https://cbe.ab.ca/news-centre/Pages/cbe-shares-our-commitmen t-to-anti-racism-and-equity.aspx

Clandfield, D., Curtis, B., Galabuzi, G.-E., Gaymes San Vicente, A., Livingstone, D. W., & Smaller, H. (2014). *Restacking the deck: Streaming by class, race and gender in Ontario schools.* Canadian Centre for Policy Alternatives. https://policyalternatives.ca/sites/default/files/uploads/pu blications/National%20Office/2014/02/osos114_cover_TOC_Intro .pdf

J. Cole. (2007). School daze [Song]. On *The Come Up* [Album]. By Any Means Management.

Coolio. (1995). Gangsta's paradise [Song]. On *Gangsta's Paradise* [Album]. MCA Records.

Crenshaw, K. (1988). Race, reform and retrenchment transformation and legitimation in antidiscrimination law. *Harvard Law Review, 1331*(7), 1379–1380. doi:10.2307/1341398

Crenshaw, K. (1991). Mapping the margins: Intersectionality, identity politics, and violence against women of color. *Stanford Law Review, 43*(6), 1241–1299. doi:10.2307/1229039

Crenshaw, K., Gotanda, N., & Thomas, K. (Eds.). (1995). *Critical race theory: The key writings that formed the movement.* The New Press.

Creswell, J. W. (1998). *Qualitative inquiry and research design: Choosing among five designs.* Sage.

Crosby, J. R., & Monin, B. (2007). Failure to warn: How student race affects warnings of potential academic difficulty. *Journal of Experimental Social Psychology, 43*(4), 663–670. doi:10.1016/j.jesp.2006.06.007

dead prez. (2000). They school [Song]. On *Let's Get Free* [Album]. Loud Records.

Dee, T. (2005). A teacher like me: Does race, ethnicity or gender matter? *The American Economic Review, 95*(2), 158–165.

Dei, G. J. S. (2000). *Removing the margins: The challenges and possibilities of inclusive schooling.* Fernwood.

Dei, G. J. S. (2017). *Reframing blackness and black solidarities through anti-colonial and decolonial prisms.* Springer.

Dei, G. J. S., Mazzuca, J., & McIsaac, E. (1997). *Reconstructing 'dropout': A critical ethnography of the dynamics of black students' disengagement from school.* University of Toronto Press.

Delgado, R. (1991). Affirmative action as a majoritarian device: Or, do you really want to be a role model? *Michigan Law Review, 89*, 1224–1232.

Delgado, R. (Ed.). (1995). *Critical race theory: The cutting edge.* Temple University Press.

Delgado, R., & Stefancic, J. (2001). *Critical race theory: An introduction.* NYU Press.

Donald, D. T. (2009). Forts, curriculum, and Indigenous Métissage: Imagining decolonization of Aboriginal-Canadian relations in educational contexts. *First Nations Perspectives, 2*(1), 1–24. https://www.mfnerc.org/wp-content/uploads/2012/11/004_Donald.pdf

Edmonton Public Schools. (2021, June 22). *Anti-racism and equity.* https://www.epsb.ca/ourdistrict/policy/h/haabbpanti-racismandequity/

Epstein, D. (2015). Coolio's "Gangsta's Paradise" *Rolling Stone.* https://www.rollingstone.com/music/music-news/coolios-gangstas-paradise-the-oral-history-of-1995s-pop-rap-smash-50357/

Freire, P. (2017). *Pedagogy of the oppressed.* Penguin Classics. (Original work published in English 1970)

Gallagher-Mackay, K., Srivastava, P., Underwood, K., Dhuey, K., McCready, L., Born, K. B., Maltsev, K., Perkhun, P., Steiner, R., Barrett, K., & Sander, B. (2021). COVID-19 and education disruption in Ontario: Emerging evidence on impacts. *Ontario COVID-19 Science Advisory Table.* doi:10.47326/ocsat.2021.02.34.1.0

Geertz, C. (1973). *The interpretation of cultures.* Basic.

Goldin, S., Duane, A., & Khasnabis, D. (2021). Interrupting the weaponization of trauma-informed practice: "Who were you really doing the 'saving' for? *The Educational Forum, 86*(1), 5–25. https://doi.org/10.1080/00131725.2022.1997308

Gorski, P. C. (2016). Poverty and the ideological imperative: A call to unhook from deficit and grit ideology and to strive for structural ideology in teacher education. *Journal of Education for Teaching, 42*(4), 378–386. https://doi.org/10.1080/02607476.2016.1215546

Haraway, D. (1988). Situated knowledges: The science question in feminism and the privilege of partial perspectives. *Feminist Studies, 14*(3), 575–599.

Harris, C. I. (1993). Whiteness as property. *Harvard Law Review, 106,* 1707–1791.

Higginbotham, A. L., Jr. (1978). In the matter of color: Race and the American legal process 1, the Colonial Period. New York: Oxford University Press.

Hiranandani, V. (2012). Diversity management in the Canadian workplace: Towards an antiracism approach. *Urban Studies Research.* doi:10.1155/2012/385806

James, C. (2019). *We rise together.* Peel District School Board. https://www.peelschools.org/aboutus/equity/Documents/We%20Rise%20Together%20report%20-%20Carl%20E%20James%20June%202019.pdf

Jay Z. (2013). F.U.T.W. [Song]. On *Magna Carta Holy Grail* [Album]. Roc-A-Fella, Roc Nation, UMD, The Island Def Jam Music Group.

Kempf, A. (2020). If we are going to talk about implicit race bias, we need to talk about structural racism in teaching and learning about race. *Taboo: The Journal of Culture & Education, 19*(2), 115–132.

Kendi, I. X. (2020). The Coronavirus is exposing our racial divides. *The Atlantic.* https://www.theatlantic.com/ideas/archive/2020/04/coronavirus-exposing-our-racial-divides/609526/

Kendrick Lamar. (2015). Momma [Song]. On *To Pimp a Butterfly* [Album]. TDE, Aftermath, Interscope.

King, J. E. (1991). Dysconscious racism: Ideology, identity, and the miseducation of teachers. *The Journal of Negro Education, 60*(2), 133–146. https://doi.org/10.4135/9781446220986.n29

Kohli, R. (2014). Unpacking internalized racism: Teachers of color striving for racially just classrooms. *Race, Ethnicity and Education, 17*(3), 367–387.

Ladson-Billings, G. (2000). Racialized discourses and ethnic epistemologies. In N. K. Denzin & Y. S. Lincoln (Eds.), *Handbook of qualitative research* (2nd ed., pp. 257–277). Sage Publications, Inc.

Ladson-Billings, G. (2003). It's your world, I'm just trying to explain it: Understanding our epistemological and methodological challenges. *Qualitative Inquiry, 9*(5), 5–12.

Ladson-Billings, G. (2011). Practicing culturally relevant pedagogy. In J. Landsman & C. W. Lewis (Eds.), *White teachers/diverse classrooms: Creating inclusive schools, building on students' diversity, and providing true educational equity.* Stylus Publishing, LLC.

Ladson-Billings, G. (2014). Culturally relevant pedagogy 2.0: A.K.A. the remix. *Harvard Educational Review, 84*(1), 87–84. https://doi.org/10.17763/haer.84.1.p2rj131485484751

Ladson-Billings, G., & Tate, W. (1995). Toward a critical race theory of education. *Teachers College Record, 97*(1), 47–67. https://doi.org/10.1177/016146819509700104

Ledesma, M. C., & Calderón, D. (2015). Critical race theory in education: A review of past literature and a look to the future. *Qualitative Inquiry, 21*(1), 206–222.

Lindstrom, G., Easton, L., Yeo, M., & Attas, R. (2022). The disrupting interview: A framework to approach decolonization. *International Journal for Academic Development,* 1–13. doi:10.1080/1360144X.2022.2103560

Lipsitz, G. (1994). We know what time it is: Race, class and youth culture in the nineties. In A. Ross & T. Rose (Eds.), Microphone fiends: Youth music & youth culture (pp. 17–28). Routledge. https://doi.org/10.4324/9780203699768.

Lynn, M. (2002). Critical race theory and the lives of black male teachers in the Los Angeles Public Schools. *Equity & Excellence in Education, 35*(2), 119–130.

Lynn, M. (2006). Race, culture, and the education of African-Americans. *Educational Theory, 56*(1), 107–119.

Lynn, M., & Jennings, M. E. (2009). Power, politics, and critical race pedagogy: A critical race analysis of black male teachers' pedagogy. *Race, Ethnicity and Education, 12*(2), 173–196.

Manitoba Education and Early Childhood Learning. (2013). *From apology to reconciliation*. Government of Manitoba. https://www.edu.gov.mb.ca/k12/cur/socstud/far/doc/full_doc.pdf

Matsuda, M., Lawrence, C., Delgado, R., & Crenshaw, K. (1993). *Words that wound: Critical race theory, assaultive speech, and the first amendment*. Westview.

Maynard, R. (2017). *Policing Black lives: State violence in Canada from slavery to the present*. Fernwood Publishing.

Merriam, S. B. (1998). *Qualitative research and case study applications in education*. Jossey-Bass.

Miles, M. B., & Huberman, A. M. (1994). *Qualitative data analysis* (2nd ed.). Sage.

Nas. (2001). What goes around [Song]. On *Stillmatic* [Album]. III Will, Columbia.

Nîtôtemtik, T. (2020). Let's talk gaps in education for on and off reserve First Nations Peoples. *Alberta Law Type Pad*. https://ualbertalaw.typepad.com/faculty/2020/10/lets-talk-gaps-in-education-for-on-off-reserve-first-nations-peoples.html

Olesen, H. S. (2007). Theorising learning in life history: A psychosocietal approach. *Studies in the Education of Adults*, *39*(1), 38–53. https://doi.org/10.1080/02660830.2007.11661539

Ontario Ministry of Education. (2013). *Culturally responsive pedagogy towards equity and inclusivity in Ontario schools*. Queen's Printer for Ontario.

Ontario Ministry of Education. (2017). *Ontario's education equity action plan*. https://www.ontario.ca/page/ontarios-education-equity-action-plan

Ontario Ministry of Education. (2021). *Annual progress report 2021: Ontario's anti-racism strategic plan*. https://www.ontario.ca/page/annual-progress-report-2021-ontarios-anti-racism-strategic-plan

Ottawa-Carleton Disctrict School Board. (2021). *National truth and reconciliation day and orange shirt day*. https://www.ocdsb.ca/our_schools/indigenous_education/national_truth

Parekh, G., Flessa, J., & Smaller, H. (2016). The toronto district school board: A global city school system's structures, processes, and student outcomes. *London Review of Education*, *14*(3), 65–84. https://doi.org/10.18546/LRE.14.3.06

Paris, D. (2012). Culturally sustaining pedagogy: A needed change in stance, terminology, and practice. *Educational Researcher*, *41*(3), 93–97.

Parker, L., & Gillborn, D. (Eds.). (2020). *Critical race theory in education*. Routledge.

Peel District School Board. (2022, June 22). *The Peel District School Board approved the most comprehensive anti-racism policy ever announced by a school board in Ontario.* https://www.peelschools.org/news/The-Peel-District-School-Board-approved-the-most-comprehensive-Anti-Racism-Policy-ever-announced-by-a-school-board-in-Ontario2022-06-29-19:10:49.09 1418+00

Ray, V. (2019). A theory of racialized organizations. *American Sociological Review, 84*(1), 26–53. https://doi.org/10.1177/0003122418822335

Robson, K., Anisef, P., Brown, R. S., & George, R. (2018). Underrepresented students and the transition to post-secondary education: Comparing two Toronto cohorts. *Canadian Journal of Higher Education, 48*(1), 39–59. https://doi.org/10.47678/cjhe.v48i1.187972

Ross, A. S., & Rivers, D. J. (2018). *The sociolinguistics of hip-hop as critical conscience: Dissatisfaction and dissent.* doi:10.1007/978-3-319-59244-2

Ryan, G. W., & Bernard, H. R. (2003). Techniques to identify themes. *Field Methods, 15*, 85–109.

Saskatchewan Ministry of Education. (2017, May). *Supporting reconciliation in Saskatchewan schools.* Government of Saskatchewan. https://www.edonline.sk.ca/webapps/blackboard/content/listContent.jsp?course_id=_3514_1&content_id=_129667_1&mode=reset

Saskatchewan Ministry of Education. (2022, March 9). *$140,000 in provincial funding help Saskatchewan schools support for Truth And Reconciliation.* Government of Saskatchewan. https://www.saskatchewan.ca/government/news-and-media/2022/march/09/140000-in-provincial-funding-help-saskatchewan-schools-support-truth-and-reconciliation

Saskatchewan Teachers' Federation. (2022). *Residential schools and reconciliation.* https://www.stf.sk.ca/professional-resources/emma-stewart-resources-centre/resources/related-links/residential-schools-and

Sawchuk, P. (2010). Equity in organizations: Issues of gender, race, disability and class. In J. Bratton (Ed.), *Work and organizational behavior* (2nd ed., pp. 276–293). Palgrave Mcmillan.

Scarface. (2017). Black still [Song]. On *Deeply Rooted: The Lost Files* [Album].

Shah, N., & Coles, J. A. (2020). Preparing teachers to notice race in classrooms: Contextualizing the competencies of preservice teachers with antiracist inclinations. *Journal of Teacher Education, 71*(5), 584–599. https://doi.org/10.1177/0022487119900204

Shim, J. M. (2017). Play of the unconscious in pre-service teachers' self-reflection around race and racism. *Journal of Curriculum Studies, 49*(6), 830–847. https://doi.org/10.1080/00220272.2017.1320429

Sinclair, M. (2014). Education: Cause and solution. *Manitoba Teacher, 93*(3), 6–10. http://www.mbteach.org/pdfs/mbt/2014/Dec14_MBT.pdf

Smith, D. G. (1999). Globalization and education: Prospects for postcolonial pedagogy in a hermeneutic mode. *Interchange, 30*(1), 1–10.

Solórzano, D., & Bernal, D. (2001). Examining transformational resistance through a critical race and LatCrit framework: Chicana and Chicano students in an urban context. *Urban Education, 36*(3), 308–342.

St. Denis, V. (2011). Silencing Aboriginal curricular content and perspectives through multiculturalism: "There are other children here. *Review of Education, Pedagogy & Cultural Studies, 33*(4), 306–317.

Taylor, S. J., Bogdan, R., & Walker, P. (2000). Qualitative research. In A. E. Kazdin (Ed.), *Encyclopedia of psychology* (Vol. 6, pp. 489–491). American Psychological Association and Oxford University Press.

Toronto District School Board. (2017). *Enhancing equity task force.* https://www.tdsb.on.ca/Portals/0/community/docs/EETFReportPdfVersion.pdf

Toronto District School Board. (2021, May 31). *Tragic discover in British Columbia.* https://www.tdsb.on.ca/News/Article-Details/ArtMID/474/ArticleID/1653/Statement-Re-Tragic-Discovery-in-British-Columbia

Toronto District School Board. (2022a). *Equity, anti-racism and anti-oppression.* https://www.tdsb.on.ca/About-Us/Equity-Anti-Racism-and-Anti-Oppression

Toronto District School Board. (2022b). *Resources for Indigenous resources.* https://www.tdsb.on.ca/Community/Indigenous-Education/Resources

Trenerry, B., & Paradies, Y. (2012). Organizational assessment: An overlooked approach to managing diversity and addressing racism in the workplace. *Journal of Diversity Management, 7*(1), 11–26.

Truth and Reconciliations Commission of Canada. (2015). *Truth and reconciliation commission of Canada: Calls to action.* https://www.trc.ca/websites/trcinstitution/File/2015/Findings/Calls_to_Action_English2.pdf

University of Ontario Institute of Technology. (2022). *Indigenous K-12 teacher resources.* https://guides.library.ontariotechu.ca/indigenous_k-12/textbooks-curriculum

Vaught, S. E., & Castagno, A. E. (2008). "I don't think I'm a racist:" Critical Race Theory, teacher attitudes, and structural racism. *Race, Ethnicity and Education, 11*(2), 95–113. https://doi.org/10.1080/13613320802110217

Wellman, D. (1993). Portraits of white racism (2nd ed.). Cambridge University Press. https://doi.org/doi:10.1017/CBO9780511625480.

Yosso, T. J. (2005). Whose culture has capital? A critical race theory discussion of community cultural wealth. *Race, Ethnicity and Education, 8*(1), 69–91.

Chapter 15
Hiring Practices for Teachers From Underrepresented Backgrounds

William Clark
University of Pittsburgh, Bradford, USA

ABSTRACT

When considering the many cases brought before the Supreme Court of the United States, one that had the greatest impact on the field of education when it came to diversity, equity, and inclusion was Brown v. Board of Education (1954). The outcome of Brown (1954) did bring changes in the operations of public schools with the concept of "separate but equal" no longer being the standard. The ruling, which was not always received with open arms, brought student diversity into schools across the country. This chapter will present the concept of hiring practices for teachers from underrepresented backgrounds by looking at several areas such as hiring for diversity, recruitment, interviews, and retention. Each of these areas must be considered if the current hiring practices for underrepresented populations are to be impacted. Scholars studying staffing in education consider human capital management to be strategic when it involves recruiting, developing, and retaining effective teachers who make a positive contribution to student learning.

INTRODUCTION

Brown v. Board of Education (1954) is one of the cases that has had the greatest impact on Education. In Brown v. Board of Education of Topeka, it was ruled unanimously that racial segregation of children in public schools was unconstitutional. Prior to this landmark ruling, schools were segregated based on race. Brown (1954) was one of the cornerstones of the civil rights movement and helped establish the precedent that "separate-but-equal" education and other services were not, in fact, equal at all. The ruling, which was not always received with open arms, brought student diversity into schools across the country. Some arguments brought forward by advocates for integration were grounded in the principles of social justice, morality, and democracy. In addition, it was believed that the outcome would be positively associ-

DOI: 10.4018/978-1-6684-6386-4.ch015

ated with increases in the black teacher workforce (Oakley et al., 2009). However, some black teachers felt that integration would discourage racial pride, that black students would not express themselves naturally, and that black students would not want to be where they were merely tolerated (Oakley et al., 2009; Rosenthal, 1957). Other teachers felt that integration would end the culture of leadership of black teachers, and there would be a loss of incentive for black students to want to become teachers (Rosenthal, 1957). Finally, an unintended consequence of the Brown decision was that it impacted the teachers who taught in the black schools because of the mandated the desegregation it provided no protections for the 82,000 black teachers in the U.S. segregated schools (Rosenthal, 1957) who were deemed unqualified to teach white children. Despite the mixed reactions from across the racial spectrum, this case changed the face of the American education system.

Schools may overlook the fact that scores from subgroups are broken out and reviewed year over year. Having teachers on staff that represent the student subgroups (Teachers of Color and People with Disabilities) may help students identify with a teacher and therefore improve test scores. With government mandated consequences for schools that fail to educate disadvantaged students and the rapidly increasing levels of diversity and disenfranchisement among nonwhite students, it is imperative that schools identify strategies to meet the ever-increasing academic needs of their nonwhite students (Barney, 2007).

While society generally has become more diverse, the teaching profession has remained relatively homogenous, a feature made more noticeable over time and increasingly subject to criticism (Ryan et al., 2009). Diversity in society has changed since Brown (1954) but the faculties within public schools across the country have not kept pace. One of the many criticisms of a homogenous faculty stems from the belief that students of difference are disadvantaged in school when the teacher workforce is unrepresentative of their differences (Jack, 2016).

Another consideration with a homogenous teacher workforce is that students need to be exposed to a variety of instructional approaches and a variety of teachers from various backgrounds that may be different than their own (Boser, 2014). There is a growing body of research indicating that teacher diversity can make a difference in student performance and their interest in school (Clotfelter et al., 2006; Egalite et al., 2015). For example, Egalite et al. (2015) utilized a large data set from the Florida Department of Education to obtain achievement variations as students were assigned to teachers of different races. Results showed significant positive effects in reading when black and white students were assigned to teachers consistent with their race. These findings, coupled with federal mandates from the US Department of Education, have ramped up calls for increasing teacher diversity in American classrooms to improve student outcomes and erase the achievement deficit between students from minority backgrounds and their white counterparts (Bartanen & Grissom, 2021). On the other hand, there may be benefits for white students who are immersed in a classroom with a racially diverse teacher, including more prosocial attitudes and better preparation of white students for employment in diverse work settings (Wells et al., 2016). Students' exposure to diverse teachers and students, and the novel ideas and challenges that such exposure brings, leads to improved cognitive skills, including critical thinking and problem solving (Wells et al., 2016). Therefore, it is crucial to explore ways to diversify the teacher workforce. Unfortunately, there is limited research in this particular area. The purpose of this chapter is to discuss the concept of hiring practices and retention for teachers from underrepresented backgrounds by looking at several areas such as hiring for diversity, recruitment, interviews, and retention. Each of these areas must be considered if the current hiring practices for underrepresented populations are to be impacted. Hiring teachers from the underrepresented is the first step towards diversifying the teacher workforce but retention of these new hires cannot be overlooked. Scholars studying staffing in education consider human capital management to be strategic when it involves recruiting, developing, and retaining effective teachers who make a positive contribution to student learning (Heneman and Milanoski, 2004; Odden, 2011).

UNDERREPRESENTED GROUPS

Existing research indicates that the groups considered underrepresented in the teacher workforce come from a variety of areas (i.e., teacher of color, Internationally Educated Teachers (IETs); teachers who identify as LGBT, and teachers who have disabilities) (Abawi & Eizadird 2020; Brecher et al., 2006; Markel & Barclay 2009; Ryan et al., 2009).

IETs are often multilingual individuals with years of professional experience and graduate degrees, qualities that should surely be an advantage to them in a competitive employment market; yet the opposite appears to be true (Schmidt, 2015). The National Center for Education Statistics (NCES) reported that in the Fall of 2019, there were 5.1 million students who were English Language Learners. This statistic demonstrates the urgency to hire IETs. However, there seems to be an underlying issue since these teachers come from backgrounds and geographic locations that may not provide schools with the correct fit for their institutions (Taie & Goldring, 2020). In addition, employers and the general public hold on to this faulty assumption that immigrants from "third world countries" hold inferior "human capital" despite having gone through rigorous teacher training in their native countries (Ryan et al., 2009). Considering the wealth of experience IETs have, they should be seen as an untapped resource for schools who will bring outside experience to the classroom.

Teachers of color are significantly underrepresented in the teacher workforce especially in the rural schools. Currently, teachers of color comprise only 20% of the U.S. public school teacher population, while students of color represent about 52% of public-school students (McFarland et al., 2018). The United States is not the only country dealing with the issue of underrepresented teachers. Canadian surveys indicate that the racialized teacher population has also not kept pace with the racialized student populations (Moll, 2001).

Teachers who identify as LGBTQ+ serve as another underrepresented population where the amount of research and data seems to be an area where further research needs to be conducted. There are no official statistics on how many teachers identify as gay or lesbian. Drawing on information from four recent national and two state-level population-based surveys, the analyses suggest that there are more than eight million adults in the U.S. who are lesbian, gay, or bisexual, comprising 3.5% of the adult population. Despite the legal and social changes in society and the enactment of formal mandates to provide union assistance, the isolation and invisibility that many LGBT+ educators still feel prevent them from recognizing their rights (Young, 2014).

Teachers with disabilities are also underrepresented when considering the teachers within the school systems. The 2000 United States Census showed that people with disabilities represented about 19.3% of the 257.2 million individuals age 5 or older (Markel and Barclay, 2009). Persons with disabilities (PWD) continue to be underemployed, which leads to the increased likelihood that such individuals live in poverty. Stereotyping is a problem PWDs typically face. In some cases, other employees categorize these individuals as having diminished capacity. When looking at the current teaching population one in four teachers have some type of disability which in turn means nearly 900,000 teachers may have some disability-related limitation in need of reasonable accommodations (Chan et al., 2022).

HIRING FOR DIVERSITY

As previously discussed, the teacher workforce does not reflect the demographic profile of the student population. Thus, schools need to take a more active role in recruitment to attract and retain teachers from underrepresented groups. The first step to addressing issues with hiring teachers from underrepresented populations is looking into the hiring process. Teacher hiring is arguably one of the most important levers available to school leaders who have autonomy in this area (Engel & Curran, 2016). Schools should have strategic hiring practices in place that are aligned with the teacher recruitment aspect of a district's plan (Engel & Curran, 2016). Areas of consideration would include the process of recruiting, interviewing, and retention.

Recruitment

Principals are the gate keepers to the process of hiring new staff so looking at how principals go about hiring teachers, and the factors that weigh most heavily when making decisions is important for two reasons. First, since principals are central to the entire teacher-hiring process, it is critical to engage them in discussions about their hiring practices. Doing so will bring to light their views in regard to the hiring process that facilitates or inhibits teachers from diverse backgrounds. Second, schools need to reflect the principles of equity entrenched in social policy that claims discrimination to be unacceptable (Jack, 2016). The critical step to hiring can be heard in comments from the Former US Secretary of Education John King (2016) when he stated: "We need a teaching force that is as diverse as our students. More and more research outlines that diversity is not just a nicety – it is a real contributor to better outcomes in our schools, workplaces, and communities (King 2016, p. 1).

Currently, districts across the country face two basic constraints that prevent them from maximizing their hiring choices. The first constraint is the scarcity of resources: there are limits to the resources that decision makers have available to them in the search process. The second is ambiguity in the information available (application packets that are used to base decision-making), as well as the ambiguity in the organizational preferences that should guide administrators in deciding which candidate maximizes their choice options (Reimann, 2016).

An important step for principals to consider with respect to a diverse teacher workforce include making sure that underrepresented teachers within their current teaching ranks are involved in the recruitment and interviews of new hires to ensure a diverse portrayal in these selection pools. Incorporating this approach would allow for greater attention to the important issues at hand; recognizing that all students benefit from a diverse teacher workforce; a closer examination of policies and practices that limit or thwart hiring a diverse teacher workforce; ensuring opportunities for teachers to develop supportive communities of practice; and recognizing the insider/outsider positions of many historically marginalized teachers (Andrews et al, 2019). There is a small, emerging body of research that indicates that "fit interview" (an interview committee focused on hiring individuals that fit in with the existing staff) may be blocking the career paths of job seekers from underrepresented backgrounds based on race, gender, and class (Quadlin, 2018). School principals may take the interview process as an attempt to find the best Candidate "fit". Harris and colleagues argued that principals look for candidates who appear to match the work ethic of the existing staff, including their commitment to teaching disadvantaged students. "Candidate fit" means their ability to keep the White people racially comfortable and their likelihood of leaving Whiteness (or the status quo) undisturbed (Sensoy & DiAngelo 2017). This, the relationship between the social location of those responsible for hiring (namely administrators) in relation to that of the applicant must be acknowledged, discussed, and contested to effectively engage in a constructive dialogue to eliminate barriers, including historical and ongoing biases an applicant may face during the recruitment, promotion, and retention process (Abawi, 2018).

Despite our best efforts, everyone brings some biases to the table, those that can be seen and those that cannot be seen. Abawi (2021) states that one cannot be bias-free because of the situatedness of the complex, power relations both at the individual and institutional levels and between the person in a position of power and authority (hiring committee and administrators) and the applicant. The predominant assumption of bias-free hiring is that one can divorce themselves from their unconscious biases and preconceptions of groups who are dissimilar to them in order to recruit the so-called "most qualified applicant" (Abawi, 2018). These biases can be seen when considering some research points postulated through Critical Whiteness Studies (CWS), such as the focus on problematizing the normality of hegemonic whiteness. In doing so, whiteness deflects, ignores, or dismisses their role, and their racialization and privilege in race dynamics (Matias et al., 2014). CWS acknowledges the dangers of whiteness, especially when whites assume the role of the Determiner (with a capital D) in regard to what is and what is not racist. A diverse interview committee can help to avoid CWS issues and allow for a more open and diverse outcome.

The need for diversity in the hiring process has been championed by the National Education Association. NEA believes that as our country and classroom demographics continue to change, it is critical to ignite a national discussion on the importance of addressing teacher diversity.

We must:

1. Examine the compelling need to recruit and retain teachers of color. 2) Analyze recommendations and best practices in the recruitment and retention of minority teachers that support high student achievement. 3) Explore how NEA members and affiliates can take a more central leadership role in collaborating with other stakeholders to recruit and retain a diverse teacher workforce. 4) Advocate for state and federal policies that first recruit then retain teachers who are diverse and highly qualified (Dilworth & Coleman, 2014).

In Canada, the Ministry of Education's Policy Program Memorandum (PPM 119) created a Developing and Implementing Equity and Inclusive Education Polices for Ontario Schools.

Boards should make every effort to identify and remove discriminatory biases and systemic barriers that may limit the opportunities of individuals from diverse communities for employment, mentoring, retention, promotion, and succession planning in all board and school positions. The board's work force should reflect the diversity within the community so that students, parents, and community members are able to see themselves represented. (2009, p. 5)

When a district posts a position, the wording can determine what type of candidates could be attracted to school. One possible solution could be to add the following to a job posting: (such-and-such school) is an affirmative action/equal opportunity employer. Women, minorities, (people who are first-generations college and of poverty- and working-class origins), veterans and persons with disabilities are strongly encouraged to apply (Oldfield, 2007). Schools need to change the wording of posts if they want to make a sincere effort to make their postings inclusive in order to attract individuals from underrepresented groups.

Schools need to approach hiring by considering where they want to focus their time and energy. Some early research from Wise, Darling-Hammond, and Berry (1987) describe low-cost data, medium-cost data, and high-cost data that can be used in the hiring process. Low-cost data is used during the early stages of the hiring process and includes transcripts, resumes, and application forms. Medium-cost data includes such items as reference reviews, telephone contacts, formal interviews, and teacher tests. High-cost data includes teacher observation. Each of these elements needs to be reviewed by the interview committee to determine if bias is contained within any of the stages. A study conducted by Barney (2007) looked at Iowa urban districts regarding the recruitment and hiring of teachers from ethnically underrepresented backgrounds. The following conclusions were drawn: a) all the districts appeared to put a lot of value on the importance of teacher diversity; b) most of the strategies utilized by the selected districts tended to attract the same populations that they have always attracted thus yielding minimal diversity; c) there was a consistent failure among the studied districts to formalize, implement, and enforce a plan for recruiting and hiring of teachers from underrepresented backgrounds; d) the barriers identified for the most part seemed too man-made, system driven, or deeply connected to the manner in which institutions do business; e) many of those recurrent and common barriers could be addressed through collaborative efforts of school districts, universities and colleges, and by utilizing the community organizational needs of the 21st Century. As schools consider the recruitment process, these elements must be considered to establish an effective recruitment and hiring process for the underrepresented populations.

As part of the screening process, schools need to consider the elements in the application packet that are most critical to the position. According to Mason and Schroeder (2010), a trend in interviews of favoring professional rather than personal attributes is the likely result of two factors. First, professional attributes (e.g., grade point average) can be evaluated more objectively than personal attributes (e.g., enthusiasm). Second, professional attributes provide more defensible grounds for the acceptance or rejection of a candidate.

Based upon the research of Mason and Schroeder (2010) to reduce uncertainty, the hiring practices of administrators should include:

1. Principals and/or the interview team need to develop a teacher characteristic profile of what is needed or wanted in a candidate for a particular vacancy before the selection process begins.
2. Principals need to develop a criteria for examining paperwork that is consistent and reduces the level of uncertainty.
3. Principals need to hire their own staff for their own schools while conducting their own screening of paperwork.
4. Principals need to hire new teachers as soon in the hiring process as possible, when the choice of potential candidates is sizeable and quality is ensured.
5. Principals need to create a "hiring team" to facilitate hiring, reduce bias and provide input into the hiring process.

When considering the hiring practices of schools, the goal to attract individuals from underrepresented groups needs to be addressed as positions are posted and during the gathering of information prior to the interviewing process.

Interviews

The interview process needs to be reviewed by school administrators to assure that any elements of bias are removed. The employment interview provides an arena where negative stereotypes held by the interviewers regarding such characteristics as age, race, gender, and disability can lead to biases in their evaluations of applications (Brecher et al., 2006). To avoid bias, schools need to create a "structured interview" that allows for a highly organized interview process using formats and questions that have been clearly vetted. The term "structured", when referring to an interview, can be broadly defined as "any enhancement of the interview that is intended to increase the psychometric properties by increasing standardization or otherwise assisting the interviewer in determining what questions to ask and how to evaluate responses" (Campion et al., 1997).

Members of the interview committee need to be aware of any potential personal bias they may bring into the interview process. This can be done by having interview committee members take an Implicit Association Test (IAT) that can check attitudes and beliefs about topics. When thinking of the hiring committee, which is designed to represent a diverse mix of people, school principals should remain cognizant of any hidden motives that individuals bring to the interview process. Having some key guideposts can help the interview committee move through the interview process smoothly. These include: 1) what are our goals regarding implicit bias, 2) which biases should we be on the lookout for, 3) which of those biases may be specific to recruitment, 4) what methods and technologies are at our disposal and what's our plan? (Leske, 2016). Having teachers and school principals working together during the interview process provides a strong representation of a united front and allows for staff ownership of the process and any selected teacher. The make-up of the interview committee needs to have a diverse pool of educational leaders and "...needs to pay attention to creating diverse search committees and rethinking how they operate" (Pendleton, 2022).

Committee members need to feel that the process is inclusive and that their voice is relevant to the overall selection of the finalist. Crutchfield (2022) provides 8 strategies that search committees can use to become inclusive. 1) Build rapport and trust within the committee. Start with some getting-to-know-you exercises that encourage personal insights that connect the work of the committee. 2) Early on, establish rules for how the decisions will be made. Create a Community Agreement – a document that outlines committee behavior, such as listening, being respectful, and not talking over other people. 3) Provide training and resources on inclusive hiring practices. Training may come from the Human Resources department on how the institution values diversity and provides advice on best practices. 4) Actively counteract structural hierarchies. Committees know that the final decision comes to management and the Board, but the members of the committee should feel they have an equal voice. 5) Recognize biases and beware of "fit". Let each person's record speak for itself. How does each candidate add to the diversity of the team. 6) Screen and interview stretch candidates. Instead of looking for reasons to exclude candidates look for reasons to include them. 7) Access diversity at every point in the process. At each step in the process the committee should pause and look at the diversity of its pool. 8) Design an interview process that reflects inclusive values. Committee members need to conduct themselves in a professional manner during the interview process. Crutchfield's eight strategies can serve as a guide for schools and search committees.

Racialized participants felt that the policies to address hiring the underrepresented populations were just as Ahmed (2012) referred to as "happy talk", and that the policies effectively held empty promises that were baseless, that there was no way to know whether or not policies were being monitored and how hiring selection occurred. In some countries, such as Canada, policies have been put in place to guide the hiring process of the underrepresented populations. Overall, in the last decade, equity, and inclusive education policies have surged across the province to address the lack of teacher representation in Ontario's publicly funded schools. While the implementation of these policies is commendable, the policies reinforce surface level, recognition-based, celebratory conceptions of equity and inclusive hiring policies (Abawi and Eizadirad, 2020). According to Abawi (2022), policy governance is diluted and offloaded from the shoulder of government and onto school boards, who then place the enactment responsibilities in the hands of administrators.

In some schools, principals are the sole decision maker for hiring. The empirical results suggest that school districts where principals are responsible for hiring teachers are more efficient than school districts with traditional centralized hiring processes which allows the hiring to take place at central office outside the building where the teacher will be placed (Naper, 2009). In this situation where the principal has the responsibility, that individual has some creative authority in how they structure and conduct interviews. For example, a principal can make it a priority to hire for social justice in their school by focusing on a) raising student achievement, b) improving the school structure, c) recentering and enhancing staff capacity, and d) strengthening school culture and community (Theoharis, 2007). Because of this, interview questions should be directed towards these areas to determine what the teacher candidate brings to the school to enhance the specific social justice strategy that the principal has enacted within the school building.

When considering the interview team, the administration should emphasize the impact these individuals have on the candidates they may attract as well as on who they may retain. If the target diversity population is higher, the need for diversity among the managers should be higher. Matching diversity between two levels – public managers (administration) and target population (teachers)– produces the most positive and consistent relationship between ethnicity and performance (Pitts, 2005). Sensoy and DiAngelo (2017) state that the committee must consider the following: committee balance in terms of bodies as well as perspectives; developing a response to stand by decisions that will be read by some faculty as biased; not underestimating the role of the committee chair; and drawing on the expertise in your faculty and accounting for extra service load.

Before starting the interview, or even advertising the position, the school administrator should take the time to review the position with respect to the job responsibilities and, if needed, create a revised job description. While applicants are waiting for the interview to start, a copy of the job description can be provided for them to review to determine if they are a good fit for the job. Organizations should have clearly written and updated job descriptions so the "essential duties" of the job are easily understandable and legally defensible. The job description should make clear what qualifications are truly necessities and which qualifications are desirable, but not necessary (Brecher et al., 2006).

When considering the interview questions, the team should consider those aspects that they feel capture the elements of what will help determine the best candidate for the position. Caution must be taken to make sure questions are not inappropriate. Bias-free hiring removes any interview bias that may interfere with this assessment, including questions that do not access the candidate against job duties for the position. Tana Charity Village (2014) provides six categories of questions that should be avoided: questions unrelated to the duties of the job, culturally-biased questions, questions that the seasoned candidates can easily answer, questions on organizational fit, things you should be telling them, and puzzles, riddles, and other tricks.

The interview should be an interactive process where the candidate gets to know the school and team conducting the interview can determine if the candidate can fulfill the elements of the job description. Levashina et al. (2014) stated the employment interview is a personally interactive process of one or more people asking questions orally to another person and evaluating the answers for the purpose of determining the qualifications of that person to make employment decisions. The content of the interview structure should include components of a) basing questions on a job analysis; b) asking the same questions of each applicant; c) limiting prompting, follow up, and elaboration on questions; d) using specific types of questions based upon the job description; e) using longer interviews or a larger number of questions; f) controlling ancillary information; and g) not allowing for questions from the applicant until after the interview (Levashina et al., 2014).

Once the interview is completed, the panel should take time to evaluate responses to questions. The scoring should be done by each member individually with a total score that is based on the rubric created. The evaluation dimension includes the components of a) rating each answer or using multiple scales; b) using anchored rating scales; c) taking notes; d) using multiple interviewers; e) using the same interviewer(s) across all applicants for the position being filled; f) not discussing applicants/answers between interviews; g) providing interviewer training; and h) using statistical rather than clinical prediction (Levashina et al., 2014). When conducting the interviews, the committee needs to be aware of the role that they play in the selection process. The responsibility falls first on committees to keep in mind the different types of leaders present in interviews and that, while style is important, results matter most (Mamlet, 2017). Committees need to 1) remember their charge – find people that will succeed in the position, 2) don't be quick to judge – give the candidates the whole 75 minutes or more, 3) keep in mind that different people present themselves differently – be on alert for unjustified overconfidence, 4) consider the potential for double standards – noticing "I" statements from a female compared to a male candidate, 5) beware of dazzlers – people who interview well, and 6) look at the big picture – incorporate information gathered throughout the process (Mamlet, 2017).

Principals were asked about the positive and negative characteristics for which they look during the interview session. For positive attributes, most of the responses dealt with personal rather than professional traits. Excitement (25%), appearance (20%), and confidence (20%) - all personal attributes were most often mentioned. Other personal attributes of note were love of children (17%), communication skills (15%), a willingness to learn (10%), and a cooperative attitude (10%). Professional attributes included content/pedagogical knowledge (15%) and professionalism (13%) (Mason and Schroeder, 2010).

The interview process is where the school decides who will become the teacher of choice. Having a structured interview process creates an opportunity to be consistent in the approach used for all candidates. A key aspect to this is a well-structured scoring rubric, which allows for consistent ranking of candidates. The most important outcome of the interview process is the fact that schools need to retain teachers who are a good fit for the institution as well as well-rounded, insightful educators.

Retention

Once teachers are hired, keeping them in their positions does take some effort on behalf of school administration. Administrators and school boards need to understand that each new teacher is an investment of over a million dollars given their salary and benefits if the teacher stays in the district for their entire career. Taking the time to make sure teachers feel comfortable and confident in the school system will be an investment well earned.

Most schools are required to have a mentor program or teacher induction program for new hires. These initiatives are associated with reduced attrition rates (Borman & Dowling, 2008). During the induction process, schools must consider what elements can assist with teacher retention. Early research on retention plans was developed by Rosenholt in 1989. Rosenholt supplied the ten essential components of a retention plan.

1. Carefully selected initial assignments which avoid placing the new teacher in the most difficult schools nor with the most difficult situations.
2. Opportunities to participate in decision-making, coupled with autonomy in many classroom choices.
3. Clearly setting administrative goals.
4. Regular, clear feedback and specific suggestions for improvement.
5. Encouragement from administrators and colleagues.
6. A non-threatening environment which encourages questions.
7. Opportunities for discussion with experienced colleagues.
8. Encouragement to experiment and discuss the results with colleagues.
9. Clearly set school rules for student behavior.
10. Opportunities to interact with parents (Rosenholtz, 1989).

There are several research facts based upon research that show the importance of supporting teachers as they start their career. According to the National Education Association (NEA http;//wwwnea.org/tools/17054.htm), induction plans are important because data shows that 50% of new teachers will leave the profession within their first five years of teaching. Another issue school administrator's need to consider, teachers generally need to acquire five years of experience to become fully effective at improving student performance (Rivkin et al., 2005). If staff are leaving during this five-year period, schools are losing out because they have invested in staff through salaries, benefits, and professional development. But research shows both new hires and seasoned teachers may leave the profession for different reasons. Young teachers leave the profession either from dissatisfaction with teaching or for family reasons such as children and older teachers leave teaching for retirement (Hughes, 2012).

There is some research that supports the need for administration to consider teacher retention with the underrepresented population. Some studies have shown underrepresented teachers have lower attrition rates than do White teachers (Kukla-Acevedo, 2009). The odds of a teacher leaving his or her current post were reduced if there is a perceived support from the school's administration (Kukla-Acevedo, 2009). This allows the teacher to feel valued and assured that they are being heard. Teachers' perceptions of principal support and effectiveness are among the most important factors in teachers' decisions to remain in or leave their institutions (Bartanen & Grissom, 2021). Relationships between principals and teachers who share demographic backgrounds translates in different teacher employment outcomes, including lower turnover propensities among teachers who share race, ethnicity, and gender with their supervisors (Grissmon et al., 2015).

What factors do teachers need in order to consider staying in the profession or in the district in which they are employed? Some of the items seem so simple but may not be attainable in the eyes of teachers if these issues are not on the radar of the school's administration. The first element is that a teachers' decisions to remain in the profession are impacted by their perceptions of their effectiveness with their students (Hughes, 2012). A second element is helping administrators understand their level of influence and guiding them toward building a positive working relationship with teachers; empowering teachers would enhance teacher retention (Hughes, 2012). The new teachers need to get involved in various aspects of the school operations and let their voices be heard concerning school-related issues. The most disconcerting fact regarding the issue of full commitment to recruiting and retaining Black males within the teacher preparation programs is that research has shown males and minorities are less likely to leave the field than non-minorities (Ingersoll, 2001).

Because of the pandemic, teachers have been under extreme stress as education has moved from a traditional classroom to online learning and then back to the traditional classroom or a combination of a hybrid and traditional models. Teachers were in need of Professional Development (PD) in online learning during COVID. Many districts scrambled to provide PD so staff could continue to instruct students. COVID would have been perfect time to provide PD across all levels in order to keep teachers apprised on diversity, equity, and inclusion. Both preservice and practicing teachers need tools for recognizing our cultural positionality so that we can adjust our practice accordingly (Garcia and O'Donnell-Allen, 2014).

In many cases, the shift from traditional to online learning led to stress and anxiety. A 2021 research study found that burnout stems from three key components brought on by anxiety and stress: exhaustion, cynicism, and inefficacy (Beachboard, 2022). School leaders can help struggling teachers overcome these by valuing competence, autonomy, and the need for relatedness to students and fellow teachers. The first key value competence relates to a person's desire to gain mastery in their work. The second is that autonomy allows teachers an opportunity to voice their thoughts on school culture and have choices in school decision making. The third is that relatedness allows teachers to have senses of belonging and connection with other people in their building to support their identity (Beachboard, 2022).

What can schools and colleges do to address the diversity issue within their own system rather than continue to do what they have always done? Einstein has been credited with defining insanity as "doing the same thing over and over again while expecting different results", and the continued use of traditional recruitment strategies to attract diverse candidates is consistent with this thinking. Although there were some discussions of specific activities to attract diverse populations, only one of the strategies identified by districts "grow your own approach" appeared to result in direct increases in the number of nonwhite teachers working in selected districts (Barney, 2007). Another thought to consider at the college level is that, in addition to taking classes, students should be required to fulfill some sort of "Diversity Practicum" or applied practicum that would immerse them in a diverse experience. These may include having the student enter a diverse community to serve in an outreach program, gain work placement in an agency that works directly with diverse populations, or extended volunteer experiences in a community agency (Barney, 2007).

CONCLUSION

One cautionary note about diversity is that it deals not only with skin color but also with other attributes as well. Jackson et al. (2003) estimate that nearly 90% of diversity studies have focused on the visible differences between people, a pattern that maintains a narrow conceptualization of diversity. According to the National Education Association (NEA), actions to increase teacher diversity tend to fall into four categories: a) early prospective teacher identification initiatives, b) aggressive recruitment activities, c) financial aid/support, and d) social and economic support (Barney, 2007).

Schools may look at a variety of areas to address the need for hiring the underrepresented population. Sometimes the easiest solution may be having an administrator who comes from the underrepresented group. A strategy for increasing the number of teachers of color in a school is to hire a principal or color who will more likely hire and retain those teachers (Bartanen & Grissom, 2021)

A potential tool for schools to consider is conducting a book read for administrators and teachers who conduct the interviews. Abawi's (2021) book on The Effectiveness of Educational Policy for Bias-Free Teacher Hiring would be one such resource to consider. The Equity Hiring Toolkit includes a) belief about teacher representation, b) perspectives of teacher and administrative representation, c) experiences of race and racism in hiring, d) implementation of equity and inclusive education policies, e) challenging nepotism and favoritism in hiring, and f) conceptions of bias free hiring.

A suggestion to consider would be to follow the strategy from the Ontario Faculty of Education by providing an option for applicants to self-identify and by encouraging administrators to take part in a transformative critical leadership practice and action to self-examine how their social location impacts how they hire teachers (Abwai, 2021). The Center for American Progress: Strategies to Improve Teacher Workforce has establish detailed strategies that have been implemented in different states to diversify the teaching population: 1) alternative certification programs (Troops to Teachers, Teach for America, Urban Education Enrichment Program, New York Teaching Fellow, Boston Teacher Residing Program, and UCLA's Center X Teacher Education Program), 2) the "Grow-Your-Own-Programs" that involve school district partnerships with universities, and 3) Early Outreach Programs that are responsible for attracting minority high school students to the teaching profession (Abawi, 2020). The federally funded Troops for Teachers program is designed to assist retiring and separating military veterans to become teachers in their next careers (Borman & Dowling, 2008). The UCLA's Center for X Teacher Education Program has a nontraditional approach to multicultural, urban teacher education and induction that supports "social justice" educators, engages a diverse group of faculty and teacher candidates in long-term learning communities integrates technical dimensions of teaching with cultural and political dimensions, and provides learning that builds on strengths of urban communities and schools (Achinstein et. al., 2010).

With schools across the country in need of staff to fill critical positions, the time is right to create a new and more effective hiring process. Recrafting the hiring process will take time and effort but the benefit for the students will be the greatest payoff. Taking time at each step in the process of recruitment, interviews, and retention to pause and think of the impact on underrepresented populations would be a positive step for change in the hiring process.

REFERENCES

Abawi, Z., & Eizadirad, A. (2020). Bias-free or biased hiring? Racialized teachers' perspectives on educational hiring practices in Ontario. *Canadian Journal of Educational Administration and Policy*, *193*, 18–31. https://journalhosting.ucalgary.ca/index.php/cjeap/article/view/68280

Abawi, Z. E. (2018). *Troubling the teacher diversity gap: The perpetuation of whiteness through practices of bias free hiring in Ontario School Boards* [Doctoral dissertation]. University of Toronto, Canada. https://www.proquest.com/docview/2029284663?pq-origsite=gscholar&fromopenview=true

Abawi, Z. E. (2021). *The effectiveness of educational policy for bias-free teacher hiring*. Routledge. doi:10.4324/9781003145462

Achinstein, B., Ogawa, R. T., Sexton, D., & Freitas, C. (2010). Retaining teachers of color: A pressing problem and a potential strategy for "hard-to-staff" schools. *Review of Educational Research, 80*(1), 71–107. doi:10.3102/0034654309355994

Ahmed, S. (2012). *On being included: Racism and diversity in institutional life.* Duke University Press.

Barney, W. (2007, July). *Guess who's not coming to dinner: A review of the policies and practices of three urban Iowa School districts to recruit teachers from underrepresented populations.* University of Northern Iowa.

Bartanen, B., & Grissom, J. A. (2021). School principal race, teacher racial diversity, and student achievement. *Journal of Human Resources.*

Beachboard, C. (2022, February 25). How school leaders can build hope and prevent teacher burnout. *Edutopia.*

Borman, G. D., & Dowling, N. M. (2008). Teacher attrition and retention: A meta-analytic and narrative review of the research. *Review of Educational Research, 78*(3), 367–409. doi:10.3102/0034654308321455

Boser, U. (2014, May). *Teacher diversity revisited: A new state-by-state analysis.* Center for American Progress. https://eric.ed.gov/?id=ED564608

Brecher, E., Bragger, J., & Kutcher, E. (2006). The structured interview: Reducing biases toward job applicants with physical disabilities. *Employee Responsibilities and Rights Journal, 18*(3), 155–170. doi:10.100710672-006-9014-y

Brown v. Board of Education, 347 U.S. 483 (1954).

Campion, M. A., Pamler, D. K., & Campion, J. E. (1997). A review structured in the selection interview. *Personnel Psychology, 79*(3), 655–702. doi:10.1111/j.1744-6570.1997.tb00709.x

Carter Andrews, D. J., He, Y., Marciano, J. E., Richmond, G., & Salazar, M. (2021). Decentering whiteness in teacher education: Addressing the questions of who, with whom, and how. *Journal of Teacher Education, 72*(2), 134–137. doi:10.1177/0022487120987966

Chan, P. E., Hakala, A., Katsiyannis, A., Counts, J., & Carlson, A. (2022). Litigation on accommodating teachers with disabilities. *Journal of Disability Policy Studies, 33*(2), 112–121. doi:10.1177/10442073211036899

Clotfelter, C. T., Ladd, H. F., & Vigdor, J. L. (2007). *How and Why Do Teacher Credentials Matter for Student Achievement?* No. w12828. NBER. https://www.nber.org/papers/w12828

Crutchfield, A. (2022, March). 8 Ways for Search Committees to be Inclusive. *The Chronicle of Higher Education.* https://www.chronicle.com/article/8-ways-for-search-committees-to-be-inclusive

Dilworth, M. E., & Coleman, M. J. (2014). *Time for a change: Diversity in teaching revisited.* http://hdl.handle.net/10919/84025

Egalite, A. J., Kisida, B., & Winters, M. A. (2015). Representation in the classroom: The effect of own-race teachers on student achievement. *Economics of Education Review, 45*, 44–52. doi:10.1016/j.econedurev.2015.01.007

Engel, M., & Curran, C. (2016). Toward understanding principals' hiring practices. *Journal of Educational Administration, 54*(2), 173–190. doi:10.1108/JEA-04-2014-0049

Garcia, A., & O'Donnell-Allen, C. (2014, July). Wobbling in public: Supporting new and experienced teachers. *English Journal, 103*(6), 65–70. doi:10.1177/23813369166615537

Grissom, J. A., Kern, E. C., & Rodriguez, L. A. (2015). The "representative bureaucracy" in education: Educator workforce diversity, policy outputs, and outcomes for disadvantaged students. *Educational Researcher, 44*(3), 185–192. doi:10.3102/0013189X15580102

Heneman, H. III, & Milanowski, A. (2004). Alignment of human resource practices and teacher performance competency. *Peabody Journal of Education, 79*(4), 108–125. doi:10.120715327930pje7904_6

Hughes, G. (2012, June). Teacher retention: Teacher characteristics, schools characteristics, organizational characteristics, and teacher efficacy. *The Journal of Educational Research, 105*(4), 245–255. doi:10.1080/00220671.2011.584922

Ingersoll, R. (2001). Teacher turnover and teacher shortages: An organizational analysis. *American Educational Research Journal, 38*(3), 499–534. doi:10.3102/00028312038003499

Jack, D. (2016). *Hiring for diversity: Changing the face of Ontario's teacher workforce* [Doctoral dissertation]. University of Toronto, Canada. https://www.proquest.com/docview/1819293922?pq-origsite=gscholar&fromopenview=true

Jackson, S. E., Joshi, A., & Erhardt, N. L. (2003). Recent research on team and organizational diversity: SWOT analysis and implications. *Journal of Management, 29*(6), 801–830. doi:10.1016/S0149-2063(03)00080-1

King, J. (2016). The invisible tax on teachers of color. *The Washington Post*, pp. 1-4.

Kukla-Acevedo, S. (2009). Leavers, movers, and stayers: The role of workplace conditions in teacher mobility decisions. *The Journal of Educational Research, 102*(6), 443–452. doi:10.3200/JOER.102.6.443-452

Leske, L. (2016, November). How search committees can see bias in themselves. *The Chronicle of Higher Education.* https://www.chronicle.com/article/how-search-committees-can-see-bias-in-themselves/

Levashina, J., Hartwell, C. J., Morgeson, F. P., & Campion, M. A. (2014). The structured employment interview: Narrative and quantitative review of the research literature. *Personnel Psychology, 67*(1), 241–293. doi:10.1111/peps.12052

Mamlet, R. (2017, February). Gender and the job interview. *The Chronicle of Higher Education.* https://www.chronicle.com/article/gender-in-the-job-interview/

Markel, K. S., & Barclay, L. A. (2009). Addressing the underemployment of persons with disabilities: Recommendations for expanding organizational social responsibility. *Employee Responsibilities and Rights Journal, 21*(4), 305–318. doi:10.100710672-009-9125-3

Mason, R., & Schroeder, M. (2010). Principal hiring practices: Toward a reduction of uncertainty. *The Clearing House: A Journal of Educational Strategies, Issues and Ideas, 83*(5), 186–193. doi:10.1080/00098650903583727

Matias, C. E., Vieska, K. M., Garrison-Wade, D., Madhavi, T., & Galindo, R. (2014). What is critical whiteness doing in our nice field like the critical race theory? Applying CRT and CRW to understand the white imagination of white teacher candidates. *Equity & Excellence in Education, 47*(3), 289–304. doi:10.1080/10665684.2014.933692

McFarland, J., Hussar, B., Wang, X., Zhang, J., Wang, K., Rathburn, A., & Mann, F. (2018). *The condition of education 2018* (NCES 2018 – 144) [Data set]. U.S. Department of Education: National Center for Educational Statistics. https://nces.ed.gov/pubsearch/pubsinfo. asp?pubid=2018144

Moll, M. (2001). Teacher diversity: An elusive goal. *PD & Research News, 1*(4), 3–4.

Naper, L. (2010). Teacher hiring practices and educational efficiency. *Economics of Education Review, 29*(4), 658–688. doi:10.1016/j.econedurev.2009.11.002

National Center for Education Statistics. (2013). Number and percentage distribution of teachers in public and private elementary and secondary schools, by selected teacher characteristics: Selected years, 1987-88 through 2011-12. *Digest of Education Statistics.* https://eric.ed.gov/?id=ED556349

National Education Association. (2003). *NEA and teacher recruitment: An overview.* https://www.new. org/recruit/minority

Oakley, D., Stowell, J., & Logan, J. R. (2009). The impact of desegregation on black teachers in the metropolis, 1970–2000. *Ethnic and Racial Studies, 32*(9), 1576–1598. doi:10.1080/01419870902780997 PMID:24039318

Oldfield, K. (2007, July). Expanding economic democracy in American higher education: A two-step approach to hiring more teachers from poverty and working-class backgrounds. *Journal of Higher Education Policy and Management, 29*(2), 217–230. doi:10.1080/13600800701351785

Ontario College of Teachers. (2015). *Transition to Teaching 2014.* Ontario College of Teachers.

Ontario Ministry of Education. (2009). *Equity and inclusive education in Ontario schools: Guidelines for policy development and implementation.* https://www.edu.gov.on.ca/eng/policyfunding/inclusiveguide.p df

Pendleton, C. (2022, November). How a search committee can be the arbiter of diversity. *The Chronicle of Higher Education.* https://www.chronicle.com/article/how-a-search-committee-can -be-the-arbiter-of-diversity

Pitts, D. (2005, March). Diversity, representation, and performance: Evidence about race and ethnicity in public organizations. *Journal of Public Administration: Research and Theory, 15*(4), 615–631. doi:10.1093/jopart/mui033

Plessy v. Ferguson, 163 US 537 (1896)

Quadlin, N. (2018). The mark of a women's record: Gender and academic performance in hiring. *American Sociological Review, 83*(2), 331–360. doi:10.1177/0003122418762291

Reimann, C. B. (2016). *District teacher hiring practices.* Michigan State University. https://www.proquest.com/docview/1868871917?pq-origsite=gscholar&fromopenview=true

Rivkin, S., Hanushek, E., & Kain, J. (2005). Teachers, schools, and academic achievement. *Econometrica, 73*(2), 417–458. doi:10.1111/j.1468-0262.2005.00584.x

Rosenholtz, S. J. (1989). *Teachers' workplace: The social organization of schools.* Longman.

Rosenthal, J. O. (1957). Negro teachers' attitude toward desegregation. *The Journal of Negro Education, 26*(1), 63–71. doi:10.2307/2293328

Ryan, J., Pollock, K., & Antonelli, F. (2009). Teacher diversity in Canada: Leaky pipelines, bottlenecks, and glass ceilings. *Canadian Journal of Education, 32*(3), 591–617.

Schmidt, C. (2015). Herculean efforts are not enough: Diversifying the teaching profession and the need for systemic change. *Intercultural Education, 26*(6), 584–592. doi:10.1080/14675986.2015.1109776

Sensoy, Ö., & DiAngelo, R. (2017). "We are all for diversity, but...": How faculty hiring committees reproduce whiteness and practical suggestions for how they can change. *Harvard Educational Review, 87*(4), 557–580. doi:10.17763/1943-5045-87.4.557

Tale, S., & Goldring, R. (2020). *Characteristics of Public and Private Elementary and Secondary School Teachers in the United States: Results from the 2017-18 National Teacher and Principal Survey. First Look.* NCES 2020-142. National Center for Education Statistics. https://eric.ed.gov/?id=ED604223

Tana Charity Village. (2014, May 21). *Bias-free hiring: Interview questions not to ask.* https://charityvillage.com/bias_free_hiring_interview_questions_not_to_ask/

Theoharis, G. T. (2007). Social justice educational leaders and resistance: Toward a theory of social justice leadership. *Educational Administration Quarterly, 43*(2), 221–258. doi:10.1177/0013161X06293717

Wells, A. S., Fox, L., & Cordova-Cobo, D. (2016). How racially diverse schools and classrooms can benefit all students. *Education Digest, 82*(1), 17.

Wise, A. E., Darling-Hammond, L., & Berry, B. (1987). *Effective teacher selection: From recruitment to retention* (R-3462-NIE/CSTP) [Report]. The RAND Corporation. https://www.rand.org/pubs/reports/R3462.html

Young, L. (2014, March 28), *Coming Out From Shadows: A History of Gay and Lesbian Educators in the United States.* New Teaching and Learning Spaces.

Compilation of References

Abawi, Z. E. (2018). *Troubling the teacher diversity gap: The perpetuation of whiteness through practices of bias free hiring in Ontario School Boards* [Doctoral dissertation]. University of Toronto, Canada. https://www.proquest.com/docview/2029284663?pq-origsite=gscholar&fromopenview=true

Abawi, Z. E. (2021). *The effectiveness of educational policy for bias-free teacher hiring.* Routledge. doi:10.4324/9781003145462

Abawi, Z., & Eizadirad, A. (2020). Bias-free or biased hiring? Racialized teachers' perspectives on educational hiring practices in Ontario. *Canadian Journal of Educational Administration and Policy, 193*, 18–31. https://journalhosting.ucalgary.ca/index.php/cjeap/article/view/68280

Abdi, A. A. (2007). Oral societies and colonial experiences: Sub-Saharan Africa and the de facto power of the written word, education, decolonisation, development and perspectives from Asia, Africa and the Americas. *International Journal of Education, 37*(1), 39–56.

Abraham, G. Y. (2014). *Critical pedagogy: Origin, vision, action & consequences.* Retrieved from https://www.diva-portal.org/smash/get/diva2:768785/FULLTEXT01.pdf

Abraham, G. Y. (2020). A post-colonial perspective on African education systems. *African Journal of Education and Practice, 6*(5), 40–54.

Abraham, R. (2003). The localization of 'O' level art examinations in Zimbabwe. *Studies in Art Education, 45*(1), 73–87. doi:10.1080/00393541.2003.11651757

Aceves, T. C., & Orosco, M. J. (2014). *Culturally responsive teaching* (Document No. IC-2). University of Florida. https://ceedar.education.ufl.edu/tools/innovation-configurations/

Achinstein, B., Ogawa, R. T., Sexton, D., & Freitas, C. (2010). Retaining teachers of color: A pressing problem and a potential strategy for "hard-to-staff" schools. *Review of Educational Research, 80*(1), 71–107. doi:10.3102/0034654309355994

Adair, J. K. (2015). *The impact of discrimination on the early schooling experiences of children from immigrant families.* Migration Policy Institute.

Ahmed, S. (2012). Institutional life. In *On Being included: Racism and diversity in institutional life* (pp. 19–50). Duke University Press. doi:10.1215/9780822395324-002

Ahmed, S. (2012). *On being included: Racism and diversity in institutional life.* Duke University Press.

Ainscow, M. (2013). From special education to effective schools for all: widening the agenda. In Handbook of Special Education (2nd ed.). Sage Publications.

Ainscow, M. (2016). Collaboration as a strategy for promoting equity in education: Possibilities and barriers. *Journal of Professional Capital and Community, 1*(2), 1–20. doi:10.1108/JPCC-12-2015-0013

Ainscow, M. (2020). Promoting inclusion and equity in education: Lessons from international experiences. *Nordic Journal of Studies in Educational Policy, 6*(1), 7–16. doi:10.1080/20020317.2020.1729587

Ainscow, M., Alan Dyson, A., Sue Goldrick, S., & West, M. (2013). Promoting equity in education. *Revista de Investigación Educacional, 11*(3), 32–43.

Ainscow, M., & César, M. (2006). Inclusive education ten years after Salamanca: Setting the agenda. *European Journal of Psychology of Education, 21*(3), 231–238. doi:10.1007/BF03173412

Aitken, A., & Radford, L. (2018). Learning to teach for reconciliation in Canada: Potential, resistance and stumbling forward. *Teaching and Teacher Education, 75*, 40–48. doi:10.1016/j.tate.2018.05.014

Akalin, S., Demir, S., Sucuoglu, B., Bakkaloglu, H., & Iscen, F. (2014). The needs of inclusive preschool teachers about inclusive practices. *Eurasian Journal of Educational Research, 54*(54), 39–60. doi:10.14689/ejer.2014.54.3

Akkoyun, K. A. (2007*). The Mainstreaming of the Guidance Research Center Staff His Views on Education* [Unpublished master's thesis]. Abant İzzet Baysal University, Bolu, Turkey.

Aktan, O. (2021). Teachers' Opinions towards Inclusive Education Interventions in Turkey. *Anatolian Journal of Education, 6*(1), 29–50. doi:10.29333/aje.2021.613a

Aktan, O., Budak, Y., & Bakygul Botabekova, A. (2019). Determination of social acceptance levels of primary school students towards inclusive students: A mixed method study. *Elementary Education Online, 18*(4), 1520–1538.

Alberta Education. (2012). *Walking together: First Nations, Métis, and Inuit perspectives in curriculum.* Government of Alberta. https://www.learnalberta.ca/content/aswt/

Alberta Education. (2015). *Guiding voices.* Government of Alberta. https://www.learnalberta.ca/content/fnmigv/index.html#relationships

Alberta Education. (2020, October 1). *Teaching quality standard.* Government of Alberta. https://open.alberta.ca/publications/teaching-quality-standard-2020

Alberta Education. (2022). *Education for reconciliation.* Government of Alberta. https://www.alberta.ca/education-for-reconciliation.aspx

Alfattal, D. (2015). *Principles for Social Justice in Education.* https://www.linkedin.com/pulse/principles-social-justice-education-eyad-alfattal

Aliakbari, M., & Amoli, F. A. (2014). Teachers' awareness of critical pedagogy: A case study of Iranian EFL teachers. *European Online Journal of Natural and Social Sciences, 3*(1), 128–134.

Aliakbari, M., & Faraji, E. (2011). Basic principles of critical pedagogy. In *2nd International Conference on Humanities, Historical, and Social Sciences IPEDR*, 17. IACSIT Press.

Ali, N., Answer, M., & Abbas, J. (2015). Impact of peer tutoring on learning of students. *Journal for Studies in Management and Planning, 1*(2), 61–66.

Allee-Herndon, K. A., Kaczmarczyk, A. B., & Buchanan, R. (2021). Is it "just" planning? Exploring the integration of social justice education in an elementary language arts methods course thematic unit. *Journal for Multicultural Education*, *15*(1), 103–116. doi:10.1108/JME-07-2020-0071

Allen, A., Scott, L. M., & Lewis, C. W. (2013). Racial micro-aggressions and African American and Hispanic students in urban schools: A call for culturally affirming education. *Interdisciplinary Journal of Teaching and Learning*, *3*(2), 117–129.

Allen, J. K. (2017). Exploring the role teacher perceptions play in the underrepresentation of culturally and linguistically diverse students in gifted programming. *Gifted Child Today*, *40*(2), 77–86. doi:10.1177/1076217517690188

Allison, A. C., & Ferreira, R. J. (2017). Implementing cognitive behavioral intervention for trauma in schools (CBITS) with Latino youth. *Child & Adolescent Social Work Journal*, *34*(2), 181–189. doi:10.100710560-016-0486-9

Almomani, S. (2022). Only Half the Story: How Stigma and Discrimination Shape the Lives of Children with Disabilities. *World Forgotten Children Foundation*. https://www.worldforgottenchildren.org/blog/only-half-the-story-how-stigma-and-discrimination-shape-the-lives-of-children-with-disabilities/147?utm_source=IGI+Global+Products+and+P ublishing+Opportunities&utm_campaign=edc41ebff8-EMAIL_CAMPAI GN_2018_04_30_COPY_01&utm_medium=email&utm_term=0_bcbd627034 -edc41ebff8-50311603

Al-Qaysi, N. (2018). The Impact of Child Protection Policy on Omani Classrooms. *International Journal of Information Technology and Language Studies*, *2*(1), 1–11.

Alvarez-Hevia, D. M. (2017). The Emotional Learning of Educators Working in Alternative Provision. *Educational Studies*, *54*(3), 303–318. doi:10.1080/00131946.2017.1356307

American Psychiatric Association. (2013). *Diagnostic and statistical manual of mental disorders* (5th ed.)., doi:10.1176/ appi.books.9780890425596

Anastasiou, D., Kauffman, J. M. S., & di Nuovo, J. M. (2015). Inclusive education in Italy: Description and reflections on full inclusion. *European Journal of Special Needs Education*, *30*(4), 429–443. doi:10.1080/08856257.2015.1060075

Anlimachie, M. A. (2015). Towards equity in access and quality in basic education in Ghana: Comparative strategies for the rural and urban milieu. *American Journal of Social Issues and Humanities*, *5*(2), 400–426.

Annamma, S. A., Connor, D., & Ferri, B. (2013). Dis/ability critical race studies (DisCrit): Theorizing at the intersections of race and dis/ability. *Race, Ethnicity and Education*, *16*(1), 1–31. doi:10.1080/13613324.2012.730511

Ansari, A., Pianta, R. C., Whittaker, J. V., Vitiello, V. E., & Ruzek, E. A. (2020). Preschool Teachers' Emotional Exhaustion in Relation to Classroom Instruction and Teacher-child Interactions. *Early Education and Development*, *33*(1), 107–120. doi:10.1080/10409289.2020.1848301

Anyon, Y., Jenson, J. M., Altschul, I., Farrar, J., McQueen, J., Greer, E., Downing, B., & Simmons, J. (2014). The persistent effect of race and the promise of alternatives to suspension in school discipline outcomes. *Children and Youth Services Review*, *44*, 379–386. doi:10.1016/j.childyouth.2014.06.025

Arao, B., & Clemens, K. (2013). From safe spaces to brave spaces: A new way to frame dialogue around diversity and social justice. In L. M. Landreman (Ed.), *From the art of effective facilitation* (pp. 135–150). Stylus.

Arı, R. (2018). Eğitim Psikolojisi. Nobel Yayıncılık. [Education psychology. Nobel Publishing].

Aronson, B., & Laughter, J. (2016). The theory and practice of culturally relevant education: A synthesis of research across content areas. *Review of Educational Research*, *86*(1), 163–206. doi:10.3102/0034654315582066

Artiles, A. J. (2013). Untangling the racialization of disabilities: An intersectionality critique across disability models. *Du Bois Review*, *10*(2), 329–347. doi:10.1017/S1742058X13000271

Artiles, A. J. (2019). Understanding practice and intersectionality in teacher education in the age of diversity and inclusion. *Teachers College Record*, *121*(6), 1–6. doi:10.1177/016146811912100612

Artiles, A. J. (2022). Interdisciplinary notes on the dual nature of disability: Disrupting ideology-ontology circuits in racial disparities research. *Literacy Research: Theory, Method, and Practice*, *71*(1), 1–20. doi:10.1177/23813377221120106

Artiles, A. J., Harris-Murri, N., & Rostenberg, D. (2006). Inclusion as social justice: Critical notes on discourses, assumptions, and the road ahead. *Theory into Practice*, *45*(3), 260–268. doi:10.120715430421tip4503_8

Asio, J. M. R., Bayucca, S. A., & Jimeniez, E. C. (2020). Child Protection Policy Awareness of Teachers and Responsiveness of the School: Their Relationship and Implications. *Shanlax International Journal of Education*, *9*(1), 1–10. doi:10.34293/education.v9i1.3384

Astuti, D. S., & Sudrajat. (2020). Promoting inclusive education for social justice in Indonesia. In *2nd International Conference on Social Science and Character Educations (ICoSSCE 2019)* (pp. 178–183). Atlantis Press. https://www.researchgate.net/publication/339259762_Promoting_Inclusive_Education_for_Social_Justice_in_Indonesia

Ataman, A. (2008). Okullar, Öğretmenler, Öğrenciler ve Özel Eğitim. N. Erol, (Ed.), Koruyucu Aile, Evlat Edinme Hizmetleri ve Ruh Sağlığı içinde (pp.227-231). Ankara Üniversitesi Çocuk/Ergen Ruh Sağlığı ve Hastalıkları Anabilim Dalı Yayınları, 6. [Schools, Teachers, Students and Special Education. N. Erol, (Ed.), In Foster Family, Adoption Services and Mental Health (pp.227-231). Ankara University Child/Adolescent Psychiatry Department Publications, 6.].

Atıcı, R. (2014, Spring). Challenges faced by inclusive students during their school life. *Turkish Studies - International Periodical for the Languages, Literature and History of Turkish or Turkic*, *9*(5), 279–291.

Avant, D. W. (2016). Using response to intervention/multi-tiered systems of supports to promote social justice in schools. *Journal for Multicultural Education*, *10*(4), 507–520. doi:10.1108/JME-06-2015-0019

Aydın, İ. (2003). Risk Altındaki Çocukların Eğitimde Alternatif Okullar: ABD Örneği. *Kriminoloji.* [Alternative Schools in the Education of Children at Risk: The Case of the USA. *Criminology.*] https://www.kriminoloji.com/Risk_Altindaki_Cocuklarin_Egitimi-Inayet_Aydin.htm

Bacete, F. J. G., Marande, G., & Mikami, A. Y. (2019). Evaluation of a multi-component and multi-agent intervention to improve classroom social relationships among early elementary school-age children. *Journal of School Psychology*, *77*, 124–138. doi:10.1016/j.jsp.2019.09.001 PMID:31837721

Bacon, H. R. (2016). Creating community connections and partnerships for transformative social change. *LEARNing Landscapes*, *10*(1), 81–94. doi:10.36510/learnland.v10i1.719

Bacon, H. R., & Byfield, L. G. (2018). Navigating discourses in academia: Challenging the status quo. *English Teaching*, *17*(2), 90–102. doi:10.1108/ETPC-05-2017-0083

Bacon, H. R., Byfield, L., Kaya, J., & Humaidan, A. Y. A. (2019). Re-storying lives and literacies: Narratives of transformational resistance. *Journal of Latinos and Education*. Advance online publication. doi:10.1080/15348431.2019.1685527

Bacon, H. R., & Kaya, J. (2018). Imagined communities and identities: A spacio–temporal discourse analysis of one women's literacy journey. *Linguistics and Education, 46*, 82–90. doi:10.1016/j.linged.2018.05.007

Badiali, B., & Titus, N. E. (2010). Co-Teaching: Enhancing Student Learning Through Mentor-Intern Partnerships. *School-University Partnerships, 4*(2), 74–80.

Bağla, A. G., Arıkan, M., Kılıç, R. Ö., Orulluoğlu, F., Kuyucu, İ., Özğan, M., Öngü, B., Özdemir, T., Gerger, A. S., Baykan, A. Y., Tutar, E. F., Korkmaz, D., Ursavaş, S., Sümbüloğlu, V., & Soran, Ö. (2017). Sağlık Çalışanları, Öğretmenler Ve Üniversite 1. Sınıf Öğrencilerinin Çocuk İstismarı Ve İhmali İle İlgili Bilgi Düzeylerinin Değerlendirilmesi. *Balıkesir Sağlık Bilimleri Dergisi,* 6(1):1-10. (Evaluation of Knowledge Levels of Healthcare Professionals, Teachers and First Year University Students about Child Abuse and Neglect. *Balıkesir Journal of Health Sciences, 6*(1), 1–10.

Baker, J. A. (2006). Contributions of teacher–child relationships to positive school adjustment during elementary school. *Journal of School Psychology, 44*(3), 211–229. doi:10.1016/j.jsp.2006.02.002

Bal, A., Afacan, K., & Cakir, H. I. (2018). Culturally responsive school discipline: Implementing learning lab at a high school for systemic transformation. *American Educational Research Journal, 55*(5), 1007–1050. doi:10.3102/0002831218768796

Bal, A., & Trainor, A. A. (2016). Culturally responsive experimental intervention studies: The development of a rubric for paradigm expansion. *World Yearbook of Education, 2017*(2), 237–277. doi:10.3102/0034654315585004

Ballard, K. (1999). *Inclusive education in an exclusive society: Some challenges to ideology and practice* [Inaugural lecture]. University of Otago.

Banerjee, P. A., & Lamb, S. (2016). A Systematic Review of Factors Linked to Poor Academic Performance of Disadvantaged Students in Science and Maths in Schools. *Cogent Education, 3*(1), 1178441. doi:10.1080/2331186X.2016.1178441

Banks, C. A. M., & Banks, J. A. (1995). Equity pedagogy: An essential component of multicultural education. *Theory into Practice, 34*(3), 152–158. doi:10.1080/00405849509543674

Banks, J. A. (1993). Approaches to multicultural curricular reform. In J. A. Banks & C. A. M. Banks (Eds.), *Multicultural education: Issues and perspectives* (2nd ed., pp. 355–365). Allyn & Bacon.

Bannister-Tyrrel, M., & Pringle, E. (2021). Differentiation in an Australian multigrade classroom. In L. Cornish & M. J. Taole (Eds.), *Perspectives on multigrade teaching: Research and practice in South Africa and Australia* (pp. 185–212). Springer. doi:10.1007/978-3-030-84803-3_10

Barber, S., & Ramsay, L. (2020), Literally speechless? Refugees to Canada overcome preliteracy and trauma through a literacy of the heart. *English 4-11 online article.* https://englishassociation.ac.uk/wp-content/uploads/2019/07/Barber-and-Ramsay-Sept-2020-1.pdf

Barber, S. (2021). Achieving holistic care for refugees: The experiences of educators and other stakeholders in Surrey and Greater Vancouver, Canada. *British Educational Research Journal, 47*(4), 959–983. doi:10.1002/berj.3730

Barkhuizen, G. (2017). Language teacher identity research. In G. Barkhuizen (Ed.), Reflections on Language Teacher Identity Research. Routledge/Taylor & Francis Group.

Barney, W. (2007, July). *Guess who's not coming to dinner: A review of the policies and practices of three urban Iowa School districts to recruit teachers from underrepresented populations.* University of Northern Iowa.

Bartanen, B., & Grissom, J. A. (2021). School principal race, teacher racial diversity, and student achievement. *Journal of Human Resources.*

Barth, P. (2016). Educational Equity: What does it mean? How do we know when we reach it? Center for Education Equality.

Bassey, M. O. (1999). *Western education and political domination in Africa: A study in critical and dialogical pedagogy.* Greenwood Publishing Group.

Basson, R. (2011). Adaptation, evaluation and inclusion. *Africa Education Review, 8*(2), 193-208. doi:10.1080/18146 627.2011.602822

Baszile, D. T. (2009). Deal with it we must: Education, social justice, and the curriculum of hip hop culture. *Equity & Excellence in Education, 42*(1), 6–19. doi:10.1080/10665680802594576

Battiste, M., & Barman, J. (1995). *First nations education in Canada: The circle unfolds.* UBC Press.

Batu, E. S., & Kircaalí-Iftar, G. (2005). *Inclusion.* Kök Publications.

Batu, S., Kircaali Iftar, G., & Uzuner, Y. (1998). *The opinions and suggestions of teachers in a vocational high school for girls, where special needs bodies are integrated* [Paper presentation]. *8th National Special Education Congress,* Edirne, Turkey.

Bautista, J. (2021). *Critical thinking can't be apolitical, teachers tell DepEd.* Retrieved from https://newsinfo.inquirer.net/1507433/critical-thinking-cant-be-apolitical-teachers-tell-deped

Bayındır, N. (2021). Risk Altındaki Çocukların Tespiti Ve Korunmasına Yönelik Öğretmen Adaylarının Görüşleri. *21. Yüzyılda Eğitim ve Toplum, 10* (28): 167-182. [Opinions of Pre-service Teachers on the Identification and Protection of Children at Risk. *Education and Society in the 21st Century, 10* (28): 167-182].

Bayram, B., & Oztürk, M. (2021). Opinions and practices of social studies teachers on inclusive education. *Education in Science, 206*(46), 355–377.

Baysu, G., Hillekens, J., Phalet, K., & Deaux, K. (2021). How Diversity Approaches Affect Ethnic Minority and Majority Adolescents: Teacher–Student Relationship Trajectories and School Outcomes. *Child Development, 92*(1), 367–387. doi:10.1111/cdev.13417 PMID:32786088

Bayuca, S. A. (2020). Teachers' Awareness and School's Responsiveness to the Child Protection Policy: Basis for a Development Plan. [IJAMR]. *International Journal of Academic Multidisciplinary Research, 4*(6), 59–65. doi:10.2139srn.3640895

Beachboard, C. (2022, February 25). How school leaders can build hope and prevent teacher burnout. *Edutopia.*

Beckett, C., Bredenkamp, D., Castle, J., Groothues, C., O'Connor, T. G., & Rutter, M. (2002). Behavior patterns associated with institutional deprivation: A study of children adopted from Romania. *Journal of Developmental and Behavioral Pediatrics, 23*(5), 297–303. doi:10.1097/00004703-200210000-00001 PMID:12394517

Beißert, H., Staat, M., & Bonefeld, M. (2022). The Role of Gender for Teachers' Reactions to Social Exclusion Among Students. *Front. Educ., 7,* 819922. doi:10.3389/feduc.2022.819922

Belhadj Kouider, E., Koglin, U., & Petermann, F. (2014). Emotional and behavioral problems in migrant children and adolescents in Europe: A systematic review. *European Child & Adolescent Psychiatry, 23*(6), 373–391.

Bell, D. (1973). *Race, racism, and American law.* Little Brown.

Bell, D. (1992). *Faces at the bottom of the well: The permanence of racism.* Basic Books.

Bencik-Kangal, S. (2017). Ahlak Gelişimi. Nilgün Baysal Metin (Ed.), Doğum Öncesinden Ergenliğe Çocuk Gelişimi içinde (pp. 197-226). 2. Baskı. Ankara: Pegem Akademi. [Moral Development. Nilgün Baysal Metin (Ed.), In Child Development from Prenatal to Adolescence (pp. 197-226). 2nd Edition. Ankara: Pegem Academy].

Benjamin, A. (2006). *Writing put to the test: Teaching for the high stakes essay*. Eye on Education.

Bennett, S. V., Gunn, A. A., Gayle-Evans, G., Barrera, E. S. IV, & Leung, C. B. (2018). Culturally responsive literacy practices in an early childhood community. *Early Childhood Education Journal*, *46*(2), 241–248. doi:10.100710643-017-0839-9

Berger, E. (2019). Multi-tiered approaches to trauma-informed care in schools: A systematic review. *School Mental Health*, *11*(4), 650–664. doi:10.100712310-019-09326-0

Bernal, D. D. (2002). Critical race theory, Latino critical theory, and critical raced-gendered epistemologies: Recognizing students of color as holders and creators of knowledge. *Qualitative Inquiry*, *8*(1), 105–126. doi:10.1177/107780040200800107

Bernal, E. M. (2001). Three ways to achieve a more equitable representation of culturally and linguistically different students in GT programs. *Roeper Review*, *24*(2), 82–88. doi:10.1080/02783190209554134

Bhurekeni, J. (2020). Decolonial reflections on the Zimbabwean primary and secondary school curriculum reform journey. *Educational Research for Social Change*, *9*(2), 101–115. doi:10.17159/2221-4070/2020/v9i2a7

Bianco, M., & Harris, B. (2014). Strength-based RTI: Developing gifted potential in Spanish-speaking English language learners. *Gifted Child Today*, *37*(3), 169–176. doi:10.1177/1076217514530115

Bianco, M., Harris, B., Garrison-Wade, D., & Leech, N. (2011). Gifted girls: Gender bias in gifted referrals. *Roeper Review*, *33*(3), 170–181. doi:10.1080/02783193.2011.580500

Biasutti, M., Concina, E., & Frate, S. (2020). Working in the classroom with migrant and refugee students: The practices and needs of Italian primary and middle school teachers. *Pedagogy, Culture & Society*, *28*(1), 113–129. https://doi.org/10.1080/14681366.2019.1611626

Birch, H., & Ladd, G. W. (1997). The Teacher-Child Relationship and Children's Early School Adjustment. *Journal of School Psychology*, *35*(1), 61–79.

Birol, Z. N., & Aksoy Zor, E. (2018). Views of classroom teachers on the problems they have with their students with special learning disabilities. *Journal of Gazi Faculty of Education*, *38*(3), 887–918.

Black, A. D. (2021). Starting with the Teacher in the Mirror: Critical Reflections on Whiteness from Past Classroom Experiences. *The Clearing House: A Journal of Educational Strategies, Issues and Ideas*, *94*(3), 116–127. doi:10.1080/00098655.2021.1907142

Blitz, L. V., Yull, D., & Clauhs, M. (2020). Bringing sanctuary to school: Assessing school climate as a foundation for culturally responsive trauma-informed approaches for urban schools. *Urban Education*, *55*(1), 95–124. doi:10.1177/0042085916651323

Boakari, F. M. (2010). Killing an inconvenient truth: Social justice and forms of oppression in modern society. *Verbum Incarnatum: An Academic Journal of Social Justice*, *4*(1), 1–32.

Booth, T., Ainscow, M., & Dyson, A. (2006). *Improving schools, developing inclusion*. Routledge.

Borman, G. D., & Dowling, N. M. (2008). Teacher attrition and retention: A meta-analytic and narrative review of the research. *Review of Educational Research*, *78*(3), 367–409. doi:10.3102/0034654308321455

Bornman, J., & Rose, J. (2010). *Believe that all can achieve: Increasing classroom participation in learners with special support needs.* Van Schaik.

Boser, U. (2014, May). *Teacher diversity revisited: A new state-by-state analysis.* Center for American Progress. https://eric.ed.gov/?id=ED564608

Boullier & Blair, M. (2018). Adverse childhood experiences. *Pediatrics and Child Health, 28*(3), 132–137. doi:10.1016/j.paed.2017.12.008

Bourdieu, P. (1986). *The forms of capital.* J. Handbook of Theory and Research for the Sociology of Education. Greenwood.

Bowen, G. A. (2009). Document analysis as a qualitative research method. *Qualitative Research Journal, 9*(2), 27–40. doi:10.3316/QRJ0902027

Bowlby, J. (1952). *Maternal care and mental health* (2nd ed.). World Health Organization., https://darkwing.uoregon.edu/~eherman/teaching/texts/Bowlby%20Maternal%20Care%20and%20Mental%20Health.pdf

Brandon, R. R., Higgins, K., Jones, V. T., & Dobbins, N. (2021). African American parents with children with disabilities: Gathering home-school reflections. *Intervention in School and Clinic, 57*(2), 119–125. doi:10.1177/10534512211001837

Braun, G., Kumm, S., Brown, C., Walte, S., Hughes, M. T., & Maggin, D. M. (2020). Living in Tier 2: Educators' perceptions of MTSS in urban schools. *International Journal of Inclusive Education, 24*(10), 1114–1128. doi:10.1080/13603116.2018.1511758

Breault, R. A. (2016). Emerging issues in duoethnography. *International Journal of Qualitative Studies in Education: QSE, 29*(6), 777–794. doi:10.1080/09518398.2016.1162866

Brecher, E., Bragger, J., & Kutcher, E. (2006). The structured interview: Reducing biases toward job applicants with physical disabilities. *Employee Responsibilities and Rights Journal, 18*(3), 155–170. doi:10.100710672-006-9014-y

British Columbia Ministry of Education and Child Care. (2019, June 19). *New teaching standard strengthens Truth and Reconciliation in the classroom.* Government of British Columbia. https://news.gov.bc.ca/releases/2019EDUC0053-001275

British Columbia Ministry of Education and Child Care. (n.d.). *Report on actions taken to support the truth and reconciliation commission of Canada's calls to action.* Government of British Columbia. https://www2.gov.bc.ca/gov/content/education-training/k-12/administration/program-management/indigenous-education/actions-taken-on-reconciliation

Bronfenbrenner, U. (1977). Toward an experimental ecology of human development. *The American Psychologist, 32*(7), 513–531. doi:10.1037/0003-066X.32.7.513

Brown v. Board of Education, 347 U.S. 483 (1954).

Browne, K. (2008). Çocuk İstismarı ve İhmalini Önleme Konusunda Dünya Sağlık Örgütü Tarafından Yürütülen Bilgilendirme ve Eğitim Paketi, (İ. Altınoğlu-Dikmeer, Trans.). *Koruyucu Aile, Evlat Edinme Hizmetleri ve Ruh Sağlığı, Prof. Dr. Mualla Öztürk Anısına XX. Sempozyum Sunumları* içinde (pp.251-257). Üniversitesi Tıp Fakültesi Yayınları. [Information and Education Package Conducted by the World Health Organization on the Prevention of Child Abuse and Neglect, (İ. Altınoğlu-Dikmeer, Trans.). *In Foster Family, Adoption Services and Mental Health, Prof. Dr. In Memory of Mualla Öztürk XX. Symposium Presentations* (pp.251-257). University Faculty of Medicine Publications].

Buchner, T., & Thompson, S. A. (2021). From plot twists, progress, and the persistence of segregated education: The continuing struggle for inclusive education in relation to students with intellectual disabilities. *Journal of Policy and Practice in Intellectual Disabilities, 18*(1), 4–6. doi:10.1111/jppi.12378

Buettner-Schmidt, K., & Lobo, M.L. (2012). Social justice: A concept analysis. *Public Health Nursing, 34*(2), 76-184. doi:10.1111/j.1365-2648.2011.05856.x

Burton, C. B. (1986). Children's Peer Relationships. *ERIC Publications*. https://files.eric.ed.gov/fulltext/ED265936.pdf

Burunsuz, E., & Ince, M. (2020). Teachers' views on the implementation of the individualized education program of teachers working in primary schools. *Mediterranean Journal of Educational Research, 31*(14), 530–544. doi:10.29329/mjer.2020.234.25

Byrd, C. M. (2016). Does Culturally Relevant Teaching Work? An Examination from Student Perspectives. *SAGE Open, 6*(3). https://doi.org/10.1177/2158244016660744

Cadima, J., Doumen, S., Verschueren, K., & Buyse, E. (2015). Child engagement in the transition to school: Contributions of self-regulation, teacher–child relationships and classroom climate. *Early Childhood Research Quarterly, 32*, 1–12.

Caldera, A., Whitaker, M. C., & Conrad Popova, D. A. (2019). Classroom management in urban schools: Proposing a course framework. *Teaching Education, 31*(3), 343–361. doi:10.1080/10476210.2018.1561663

Calgary Board of Education. (2020, June 25). *CBE shares our commitment to anti-racism and equity.* https://cbe.ab.ca/news-centre/Pages/cbe-shares-our-commitment-to-anti-racism-and-equity.aspx

Callahan, C. M., Moon, T. R., Oh, S., Azano, A. P., & Hailey, E. P. (2015). What works in gifted education: Documenting the effects of an integrated curricular/instructional model for gifted students. *American Educational Research Journal, 52*(1), 137–167. doi:10.3102/0002831214549448

Callahan, R. M. (2005). Tracking and high school English learners: Limiting opportunity to learn. *American Educational Research Journal, 42*(2), 305–328. doi:10.3102/00028312042002305

Cammarota, J. (2007). A social justice approach to achievement: Guiding Latina/o students toward educational attainment with a challenging, socially relevant curriculum. *Equity & Excellence in Education, 40*(1), 87–96. doi:10.1080/10665680601015153

Cammarota, J. (2011). The value of a multicultural and critical pedagogy: Learning democracy through diversity and dissent. *Multicultural Perspectives, 13*(2), 62–69. doi:10.1080/15210960.2011.571546

Campbell, J., Gilmore, L., & Cuskelly, M. (2003). Changing student teachers' attitudes towards disability and inclusion. *Journal of Intellectual & Developmental Disability, 28*(4), 369–379. doi:10.1080/13668250310001616407

Campion, M. A., Pamler, D. K., & Campion, J. E. (1997). A review structured in the selection interview. *Personnel Psychology, 79*(3), 655–702. doi:10.1111/j.1744-6570.1997.tb00709.x

Card, D., & Giuliano, L. (2015). *Can universal screening increase the representation of low income and minority students in gifted education?* National Bureau of Economic Research. doi:10.3386/w21519

Carrington, C. (1999). *No place like home: Relationships and family life among lesbians and gay men.* University of Chicago Press. doi:10.7208/chicago/9780226094847.001.0001

Carter Andrews, D. J., He, Y., Marciano, J. E., Richmond, G., & Salazar, M. (2021). Decentering whiteness in teacher education: Addressing the questions of who, with whom, and how. *Journal of Teacher Education, 72*(2), 134–137. doi:10.1177/0022487120987966

CASEL. (2020). CASEL's SEL framework: What are the core competence areas and where are they promoted? *CASEL.* https://casel.org/casel-sel-framework-11-2020/

Celik, R. (2016). Curriculum elements of a politically liberal education in a developing democracy. *Educational Philosophy and Theory, 48*(14), 1464–1474. doi:10.1080/00131857.2016.1160356

Celik, S., Kardas Işler, N., & Saka, D. (2021). Refugee education in Turkey: Barriers and suggested solutions. *Pedagogy, Culture & Society*, 1–19. Advance online publication. doi:10.1080/14681366.2021.1947878

Celoria, D. (2016). The preparation of inclusive social justice education leaders. *Educational Leadership and Administration: Teaching and Program Development, 27*, 199–219.

Cengíz Sayan, E. (2020). *Preschool teachers' opinions about inclusive education* [Unpublished master's thesis]. Pamukkale University Graduate School of Educational Sciences, Denizli, Turkey.

Cenoz, J., & Gorter, D. (2020). Teaching English through pedagogical translanguaging. *Special Issue: World Englishes and Translanguaging, 39*(2), 300–311.

Center for Public Education Hanover Research. (2017). *Closing the Gap: Creating Equity in the Classroom K-12 Education. Hanover Research highlights classroom strategies, tips, and approaches to close the equity gap*

Chafouleas, S. M., Johnson, A. H., Overstreet, S., & Santos, N. M. (2016). Toward a blueprint for trauma-informed service delivery in schools. *School Mental Health, 8*(1), 144–162. doi:10.100712310-015-9166-8

Chafouleas, S. M., Pickens, I., & Gherardi, S. A. (2021). Adverse childhood experiences (ACEs): Translation into action in K12 education settings. *School Mental Health, 2*(2), 213–2214. doi:10.100712310-021-09427-9

Chandra-Handa, M. (2009). Learner-centred differentiated model: A new framework. *Australasian Journal of Gifted Education, 18*(2), 55–56.

Chan, P. E., Hakala, A., Katsiyannis, A., Counts, J., & Carlson, A. (2022). Litigation on accommodating teachers with disabilities. *Journal of Disability Policy Studies, 33*(2), 112–121. doi:10.1177/10442073211036899

Chapman, S., & Routledge, C. (2009). *Key ideas in linguistics and the philosophy of language.* Edinburgh University Press. doi:10.1515/9780748631421

Chen, J. (2021). *Emergency Remote Teaching and Beyond: Voice from World Language Teachers and Researchers.* Springer. doi:10.1007/978-3-030-84067-9

Chen, J. Q., & Gardner, H. (2018). Assessment from the perspective of multiple-intelligences theory: Principles, practices, and values. In D. P. Flanagan & E. M. McDonough (Eds.), *Contemporary intellectual assessment: Theories, tests, and issue* (4th ed., pp. 164–173). The Guilford Press.

Cheung, Y. L. (2017). Writing teacher identity: Current knowledge and future research. In G. Barkhuizen (Ed.), *Reflections on Language Teacher Identity Research.* Routledge/Taylor & Francis Group.

Chimhenga, S. (2016). The implementation of inclusive education for children with disabilities in primary schools: A theoretical probability or practical possibility. *Asian Journal of Educational Research, 4*(4), 28–35.

Choi, J. H., McCart, A. B., & Sailor, W. (2020). Reshaping educational systems to realize the promise of inclusive education. *FIRE: Forum for International Research in Education, 6*(1). doi:10.32865/fire202061179

Choi, S., & Lee, S. W. (2020). Enhancing teacher self-efficacy in multicultural classrooms and school climate: The role of professional development in multicultural education in the United States and South Korea. *AERA Open*, *6*(4), 1–17. doi:10.1177/2332858420973574

Christenson, S. L. (2004). The Family-School Partnership: An Opportunity to Promote the Learning Competence of All Students. *School Psychology Review*, *33*(1), 89–104.

Chuang, S., Rasmi, S., & Friesen, C. (2011). Service Providers' Perspectives on the Pathways of Adjustment for Newcomer Children and Youth in Canada. In S. S. Chuang & R. P. Moreno (Eds.), *Immigrant children: Change, adaptation, and cultural transformation* (pp. 149–170). Lexington Books.

Çiftçi-Topaloğlu, Z. (2013). *4-5 yaş çocuklarının sosyal yetkinlik, saldırganlık, kaygı düzeyleri ile anne-babalarının ebeveyn özyeterliği algısı arasındaki ilişkilerin incelenmesi.* [Yayınlanmamış yüksek lisans tezi. Pamukkale Üniversitesi, Türkiye]. [*Investigation of the relationships between the social competence, aggression and anxiety levels of 4-5 year old children and their parents' perception of parental self-efficacy.* [Unpublished master's thesis. Pamukkale University, Turkey].]

Ciyer, A. (2010). *Developing inclusive education policies and practices in Turkey, A study of the roles of UNESCO and local educators* [Unpublished doctoral dissertation]. Arizona State University, Tempe, AZ.

Clandfield, D., Curtis, B., Galabuzi, G.-E., Gaymes San Vicente, A., Livingstone, D. W., & Smaller, H. (2014). *Restacking the deck: Streaming by class, race and gender in Ontario schools.* Canadian Centre for Policy Alternatives. https://policyalternatives.ca/sites/default/files/uploads/publications/National%20Office/2014/02/osos114_cover_TOC_Intro.pdf

Clarke, M., & Drudy, S. (2006). Teaching for diversity, social justice, and global awareness. *European Journal of Teacher Education*, *29*(3), 371–386.

Clotfelter, C. T., Ladd, H. F., & Vigdor, J. L. (2007). *How and Why Do Teacher Credentials Matter for Student Achievement?* No. w12828. NBER. https://www.nber.org/papers/w12828

Cobb, C., & Sharma, M. (2015). I've got you covered: Adventures in social justice-informed co-teaching. *The Journal of Scholarship of Teaching and Learning*, 41–57. doi:10.14434/josotl.v15i4.13339

Cobb, F., & Krownapple, F. (2019). *Belonging through a culture of diversity: The keys to successful equity implementation.* Mimi and Todd Press.

Cochran-Smith, M. (2010). Toward a theory of teacher education for social justice. In A. Hargreaves, A. Lieberman, M. Fullan, & D. Hopkins (Eds.), *Second international handbook of educational change* (pp. 445–467). Springer. doi:10.1007/978-90-481-2660-6_27

Coffey, H., & Fulton, S. (2018). The responsible change project: Building a justice-oriented middle school curriculum through critical service-learning. *Middle School Journal*, *49*(5), 16–25. doi:10.1080/00940771.2018.1509560

Collins, C. (1999). *Language, ideology and social consciousness: A Critique of J.C. Scott.* Routledge.

Compton-Lilly, C., & Delbridge, A. (2019). What can parents tell us about poverty and literacy learning? Listening to parents over time. *Journal of Adolescent & Adult Literacy*, *62*(5), 531–539. doi:10.1002/jaal.923

Connor, D., Cavendish, W., Gonzalez, T., & Jean-Pierre, P. (2019). Is a bridge even possible over troubled waters? The field of special education negates the overrepresentation of minority students: A DisCrit analysis. *Race, Ethnicity and Education*, *22*(6), 723–745. doi:10.1080/13613324.2019.1599343

Cooc, N., & Kiru, E. W. (2018). Disproportionality in special education: A synthesis of international research and trends. *The Journal of Special Education, 52*(3), 163–173. doi:10.1177/0022466918772300

Coolio. (1995). Gangsta's paradise [Song]. On *Gangsta's Paradise* [Album]. MCA Records.

Cooper, C. R. (2011). *Bridging multiple worlds: Cultures, identities, and pathways to college.* Oxford University Press. doi:10.1093/acprof:oso/9780195080209.001.0001

Cooper, C. R. (2014). Cultural brokers: How immigrant youth in multicultural societies navigate and negotiate their pathways to college identities. *Learning, Culture and Social Interaction, 3*(2), 170–176. doi:10.1016/j.lcsi.2013.12.005

Corbett, J. (2001). Teaching approaches which support inclusive education: A connective pedagogy. *British Journal of Special Education, 28*(2), 55–59. doi:10.1111/1467-8527.00219

Corbett, J. (2007). *An intercultural approach to English language teaching.* Multilingual Matters.

Coronado, J. M., & Lewis, K. D. (2017). The disproportional representation of English language learners in gifted and talented programs in Texas. *Gifted Child Today, 40*(4), 238–244. doi:10.1177/1076217517722181

Coronel, J. M., & Gómez-Hurtado, I. (2015). Nothing to do with me! Teachers' perceptions on cultural diversity in Spanish secondary schools. *Teachers and Teaching, 21*(4), 400–420.

Cortez, F. G. F. (2013). The Philippine engagement with Paulo Freire. *Kritike, 7*(2), 50–70. doi:10.25138/7.2.a.4

Coskun, Y. D., Tosun, U., & Macaroglu, E. (2009). Classroom teachers' styles of using and development materials of inclusive education. *Procedia: Social and Behavioral Sciences, 1*(1), 2758–2762. doi:10.1016/j.sbspro.2009.01.489

Cossar, J., Brandon, M., & Jordan, P. (2014). "You've got to trust her and she's got to trust you": Children's views on participation in the child protection system. *Child & Family Social Work, 21*(1), 103–112. doi:10.1111/cfs.12115

Council of Europe. (2022). *Report on child consultations informing the elaboration of the Council of Europe Strategy for the Rights of the Child 2022-2027.* COE. https://rm.coe.int/council-of-europe-child-consultations-to-inform-the-elaboration-of-the/1680a697d5

Cramer, E. D. (2015). Inequities of intervention among culturally and linguistically diverse students. *Perspectives on Urban Education Journal, 12*(1).

Cramer, E. D., Little, M., & Alvarez McHatton, P. (2018). Equity, equality, and standardization: Expanding the conversations. *Education and Urban Society, 50*(5), 483–501. doi:10.1177/0013124517713249

Crenshaw, K. (1988). Race, reform and retrenchment transformation and legitimation in antidiscrimination law. *Harvard Law Review, 1331*(7), 1379–1380. doi:10.2307/1341398

Crenshaw, K. (1989). Demarginalizing the intersection of race and sex: A Black feminist critique of antidiscrimination doctrine, feminist theory and antiracist politics. *University of Chicago Legal Forum, 1989*(1). https://chicagounbound.uchicago.edu/uclf/vol1989/iss1/8

Crenshaw, K. (1991). Mapping the margins: Intersectionality, identity politics, and violence against women of color. *Stanford Law Review, 43*(6), 1241–1299. doi:10.2307/1229039

Crenshaw, K. (2017). *On intersectionality: Essential writings.* The New Press.

Crenshaw, K., Gotanda, N., & Thomas, K. (Eds.). (1995). *Critical race theory: The key writings that formed the movement.* The New Press.

Creswell, J. W. (1998). *Qualitative inquiry and research design: Choosing among five designs.* Sage.

Crick, N. R., & Dodge, K. A. (1994). A review and reformulation of social information-processing mechanisms in children's social adjustment. *Psychological Bulletin, 115*(1), 74–101. doi:10.1037/0033-2909.115.1.74

Crocco, M. S., & Costigan, A. T. (2007). The narrowing of curriculum and pedagogy in the age of accountability urban educators speak out. *Urban Education, 42*(6), 512–535. doi:10.1177/0042085907304964

Crookes, G. V. (2009a). The practicality and relevance of second language critical pedagogy. Language Teaching. Cambridge University Press. Doi:10.1017/So261444809990292

Crookes, G. V. (2009b). *Values, philosophies, and beliefs in TESOL: Making statements.* Cambridge University Press.

Crookes, G. V. (2021). Critical language pedagogy: An introduction to principles and values (Anniversary Article). *ELT Journal, 75*(3), 247–255. doi:10.1093/elt/ccab020

Crosby, L. M. S. W., Shantel, D., Penny, B., & Thomas, M. A. T. (2020). Teaching through collective trauma in the era of COVID-19: Trauma-informed practices for middle level learners. *Middle Grades Review, 6*(2), 5. https://scholarworks.uvm.edu/mgreview/vol6/iss2/5

Crosby, J. R., & Monin, B. (2007). Failure to warn: How student race affects warnings of potential academic difficulty. *Journal of Experimental Social Psychology, 43*(4), 663–670. doi:10.1016/j.jesp.2006.06.007

Crutchfield, A. (2022, March). 8 Ways for Search Committees to be Inclusive. *The Chronicle of Higher Education.* https://www.chronicle.com/article/8-ways-for-search-committees-to-be-inclusive

Cüceloğlu, D. (2002). İletişim Donanımları. 'Keşke'siz Bir Yaşam İçin İletişim. 46. Baskı. Remzi Kitabevi. [Communication Skills. Communication for a Life Without 'I Wish'. 46th Edition. Remzi Bookstore].

Cummins, J. (2021). *Rethinking the education of multilingual learners: A critical analysis of theoretical concepts.* Bristol, Blue Ridge Summit: Multilingual Matters. https://doi-org.myaccess.library.utoronto.ca/10.21832/9781800413597

Cummins, J., & Early, M. (2011). *Identity texts: The collaborative creation of power in multilingual schools.* Trentham Books.

Dachyshyn, D., & Kirova, A. (2011). Classroom challenges in developing an intercultural early learning program for refugee children. *The Alberta Journal of Educational Research, 57*(2), 220–233.

Daggett, W. R. (2000). Moving from standards to instructional practice. *NASSP Bulletin, 84*(620), 66–72. doi:10.1177/019263650008462008

Daglar, M., Melhuish, E., & Barnes, J. (2011). Parenting and preschool child behavior among Turkish immigrant, migrant, and non-migrant families. *European Journal of Developmental Psychology, 8*(3), 261–279.

Dahl, A., & Killen, M. (2018). A Developmental Perspective on the Origins of Morality in Infancy and Early Childhood. *Frontiers in Psychology, 9*, 1736. doi:10.3389/fpsyg.2018.01736 PMID:30294291

Dalton, E. M., Mckenzie, J. A., & Kahonde, C. (2012). The implementation of inclusive education in South Africa: Reflections arising from a workshop for teachers and therapists to introduce universal learning design. *African Journal of Disability, 1*(1), 1–13. doi:10.4102/ajod.v1i1.13 PMID:28729974

Dana, N. F., & Yendol-Hoppey, D. (2020). *The reflective educator's guide to classroom research: Learning to teach and teaching to learn through practitioner inquiry* (4th ed.). Corwin.

Darling-Hammond, L., Flook, L., Cook-Harvey, C., Barron, B., & Osher, D. (2020). Implications for educational practice of the science of learning and development. *Applied Developmental Science*, 24(2), 97–140. doi:10.1080/10888691.2 018.1537791

De Boer, A., Pijl, S. J., Post, W., & Minnaert, A. (2013). Peer Acceptance and Friendship of Students with Disabilities in Regular Education: The Role of Child, Peer, and Classroom Variables. *Social Development*, 22(4), 831–844. doi:10.1111/j.1467-9507.2012.00670.x

De Leeuw, R. R., De Boer, A. A., & Minnaert, A. E. M. G. (2018). Student voices on social exclusion in general primary schools. *European Journal of Special Needs Education*, 33(2), 166–186. doi:10.1080/08856257.2018.1424783

dead prez. (2000). They school [Song]. On *Let's Get Free* [Album]. Loud Records.

Dee, T. (2005). A teacher like me: Does race, ethnicity or gender matter? *The American Economic Review*, 95(2), 158–165.

Dei, G. J. S. (2000). *Removing the margins: The challenges and possibilities of inclusive schooling*. Fernwood.

Dei, G. J. S. (2017). *Reframing blackness and black solidarities through anti-colonial and decolonial prisms*. Springer.

Dei, G. J. S., Mazzuca, J., & McIsaac, E. (1997). *Reconstructing 'dropout': A critical ethnography of the dynamics of black students' disengagement from school*. University of Toronto Press.

Delgado, R. (1991). Affirmative action as a majoritarian device: Or, do you really want to be a role model? *Michigan Law Review*, 89, 1224–1232.

Delgado, R. (Ed.). (1995). *Critical race theory: The cutting edge*. Temple University Press.

Delgado, R., & Stefancic, J. (2001). *Critical race theory: An introduction*. NYU Press

Demillo, Q. (2021). School as a service enterprise in the Philippines. *Academia Letters. Article*, 3535. Advance online publication. doi:10.20935/AL3535

Demir, M. K., & Acar, S. (2011). Opinions of experienced classroom teachers about inclusive education. *Kastamonu Journal of Education*, 19(3), 719–732.

Department of Basic Education. (2010). *Guidelines for inclusive teaching and learning*. Government Printer.

Department of Basic Education. (2011). *Guidelines for responding to learner diversity in the classroom through Curriculum and Assessment Policy Statements*. Government Printer.

Department of Basic Education. (2014). *Policy on screening, identification, assessment and suppor*t. Government Printer.

Department of Basic Education. (2017). *Inclusive education and special education: DBE progress report; with Deputy Minister*. https://pmg.org.za/committee-meeting/24505/

Department of Education. (2001). *Education White Paper 6. Special needs education: Building an inclusive education and training system*. Government Printer.

Department of Education. (2008). *National strategy on screening, identification, assessment and support: School pack*. Government Printer.

Department of Education. (2009). *K to 12 Basic Education Curriculum*. Retrieved from https://www.deped.gov.ph/k-to-12/about/k-to-12-basic-education-curriculum/

Derakhshan, A., Coombe, C., Arabmofrad, A., & Taghizadeh, M. (2020). Investigating the Effects of English Language Teachers' Professional Identity and Autonomy in Their Success. *Issues in Language Teaching, 9*(1), 1–28. doi:10.22054/ilt.2020.52263.496

Diken, I. H., Rakap, S., Diken, O., Tomris, G., & Celik, S. (2016). Early childhood inclusion in Turkey. *Infants and Young Children, 29*(3), 231–238. doi:10.1097/IYC.0000000000000065

Dilsiz, H. ve Mağden, D. (2015). Öğretmenlerin Çocuk İstismar Ve İhmali Konusunda Bilgi Ve Risk Tanıma Düzeylerinin Tespit Edilmesi [Determination of Teachers' Knowledge and Risk Recognition Levels on Child Abuse and Neglect]. *Hacettepe University Faculty Of Health Sciences Journal, 1*(2), 678–694.

Dilworth, M. E., & Coleman, M. J. (2014). *Time for a change: Diversity in teaching revisited.* http://hdl.handle.net/10919/84025

Doan, S. N., Marcelo, A. K., & Yates, T. M. (2019). Ethnic-racial discrimination, family ethnic socialization and Latinx children's emotion competence. *Culture and Brain, 7*, 190–211. https://doi.org/10.1007/s40167-019-00079-w

Dodge, K. A. (1986). *A social information processing model of social competence in children.* Lawrence Erlbaum.

Dodge, K. A., Lansford, J. E., Burks, V. S., Bates, J. E., Pettit, G. S., Fontaine, R., & Price, J. M. (2003). Peer Rejection and Social Information-Processing Factors in the Development of Aggressive Behavior Problems in Children. *Child Development, 74*(2), 374–393. doi:10.1111/1467-8624.7402004 PMID:12705561

Donald, D. T. (2009). Forts, curriculum, and Indigenous Métissage: Imagining decolonization of Aboriginal-Canadian relations in educational contexts. *First Nations Perspectives, 2*(1), 1–24. https://www.mfnerc.org/wp-content/uploads/2012/11/004_Donald.pdf

Dong, Q., Garcia, B., Pham, A. V., & Cumming, M. (2020). Culturally responsive approaches for addressing ADHD within multi-tiered systems of support. *Current Psychiatry Reports, 22*(6), 1–10. doi:10.100711920-020-01154-3 PMID:32378025

Donohue, D., & Bornman, J. (2014). The challenges of realising inclusive education in South Africa. *South African Journal of Education, 34*(2), 1–14. doi:10.15700/201412071114

Dover, A. G. (2009). Teaching for social justice and K-12 student outcomes: A conceptual framework and research review. *Equity & Excellence in Education, 42*(4), 506–524. doi:10.1080/10665680903196339

Dover, A. G. (2013). Teaching for social justice: From conceptual frameworks to classroom practices. *Action in Teacher Education, 35*(2), 89–102. doi:10.1080/01626620.2013.770377

Dreyer, L. M. (2017). Constraints to quality education and support for all: A Western Cape case. *South African Journal of Education, 37*(1), 1–11. doi:10.15700aje.v37n1a1226

Driscoll, K. C., & Pianta, R. C. (2010). Banking time in head start: Early efficacy of an intervention designed to promote supportive teacher-child relationships. *Early Education and Development, 21*(1), 38–64.

Durand, T. M., & Tavaras, C. L. (2021). Countering complacency with radical reflection: Supporting white teachers in the enactment of critical multicultural praxis. *Education and Urban Society, 53*(2), 146–162. doi:10.1177/0013124520927680

Duranti, A. (1997). *Linguistic anthropology.* Cambridge University Press. doi:10.1017/CBO9780511810190

Durban, J. M., & Catalan, R. D. (2012). Issues and concerns of Philippine education through the years. *Asian Journal of Social Sciences & Humanities, 1*(2).

Duskun, Y. (2016). *Inclusive education situation analysis in secondary education in Turkey.* Education Reform Initiative.

Dyson, A. H. (2015). The search for inclusion: Deficit discourse and the erasure of childhood. *Language Arts, 92*(3), 199–207.

Eagle, J. W., Dowd-Eagle, S. E., Snyder, A., & Holtzman, E. G. (2015). Implementing a multi-tiered system of support (MTSS): Collaboration between school psychologists and administrators to promote systems-level change. *Journal of Educational and Psychological Consultation, 25*(2-3), 160-177. doi:10.1080/10474412.2014.929960

Ecker-Lyster, M., & Niileksela, C. (2017). Enhancing gifted education for underrepresented students: Promising recruitment and programming strategies. *Journal for the Education of the Gifted, 40*(1), 79–95. doi:10.1177/0162353216686216

Edmonton Public Schools. (2021, June 22). *Anti-racism and equity*. https://www.epsb.ca/ourdistrict/policy/h/haabbpanti-racismandequity/

Edwards, P. A. (2016). *New ways to engage parents: Strategies and tools for teachers and leaders, K–12*. Teachers College Press.

Egalite, A. J., Kisida, B., & Winters, M. A. (2015). Representation in the classroom: The effect of own-race teachers on student achievement. *Economics of Education Review, 45*, 44–52. doi:10.1016/j.econedurev.2015.01.007

Eilers, N. (2021). Critical disability studies and 'Inclusive' early childhood education: The ongoing divide. *Journal of Disability Studies in Education, 1*(1-2), 64–89. doi:10.1163/25888803-00101004

Ekinci, C., & Ve Tösten, R. (2018). Koruma Altında Bulunan 13-18 Yaş Arası Çocukların Okul Algısı. *Sosyal Bilimler Enstitüsü Dergisi, 12*: 360 – 378. (School Perception of Protected Children aged 13-18. *Journal of Social Sciences Institute, 12*: 360 – 378). ISSN: 2147-8406.

Emin, M. N. (2019). *Construction of future: Education of Syrian children in Turkey*. Seta Publishing.

Engelbrecht, P., & Green, L. (2007). Responding to the challenges of inclusive education: an introduction. In P. Engelbrecht & L. Green (Eds.), *Responding to the challenges of inclusive education in Southern Africa* (pp. 8–88). Van Schaik.

Engelbrecht, P., Oswald, M., & Forlin, C. (2006). Promoting the implementation of inclusive education in primary schools in South Africa. *British Journal of Special Education, 33*(3), 121–129. doi:10.1111/j.1467-8578.2006.00427.x

Engel, M., & Curran, C. (2016). Toward understanding principals' hiring practices. *Journal of Educational Administration, 54*(2), 173–190. doi:10.1108/JEA-04-2014-0049

Epstein, D. (2015). Coolio's "Gangsta's Paradise" *Rolling Stone*. https://www.rollingstone.com/music/music-news/coolios-gangstas-paradise-the-oral-history-of-1995s-pop-rap-smash-50357/

Erbay, E. (2019). Çocuk Hakları. 2. Basım. Yeni İnsan Yayınevi. [Children's Rights. 2nd Edition. Yeni İnsan Publisher].

Erípek, S. (2003). *Special education in preschool period*. Anadolu University Open Education Faculty Publication.

Erll, A. (2012). Cultural memory. In M. Middeke, T. Müller, C. Wald, & H. Zapf (Eds.), *English and American Studies* (pp. 238–242). JB Metzler. doi:10.1007/978-3-476-00406-2_15

Erol, N. (2004). Yuva ve Yetiştirme Yurtları Sorunun mu Yoksa Çözümün mü Parçası? Uslu, R. (Ed.). Koruma Altındaki Çocuklar içinde (pp:133-140). Ankara Üniversitesi Tıp Fakültesi Çocuk Ruh Sağlığı ve Hastalıkları Anabilim Dalı Yayını. No:IX. [Are Kindergartens and Orphanages Part of the Problem or the Solution? Uslu, R. (Ed.). In Protected Children (pp:133-140). Ankara University Faculty of Medicine, Department of Child Psychiatry and Diseases Publication. No: IX].

Erol, N. (2008). Evlat Edinme ve Okul Sorunları. N. Erol (Ed.). Koruyucu Aile, Evlat Edinme Hizmetleri ve Ruh Sağlığı içinde (pp.219-225). Ankara Üniversitesi Çocuk/Ergen Ruh Sağlığı ve Hastalıkları Anabilim Dalı Yayınları. No: 6 [Adoption and School Problems. N. Erol (Ed.). In Foster Family, Adoption Services and Mental Health (pp.219-225). Ankara University Child/Adolescent Psychiatry Department Publications. No: 6].

Ersoy, O., & Avcı, N. (2000). Children with special needs and their education. Special Education. Yapa Publications.

Ertürk-Kara, H. G., & Yıldız, T. G. ve Fındık, E. (2018). Erken Çocukluk Döneminde Öz Düzenleme İzleme, Değerlendirme ve Destekleme Yöntemleri. Anı Yayıncılık. [Self-Regulation Monitoring, Evaluation and Support Methods in Early Childhood. Anı Publishing].

Esmer, B., Yılmaz, E., Gunes, A. M., Tarim, K., & Delican, B. (2017). Classroom teachers' experiences towards inclusive students' education. *Kastamonu Journal of Education*, 25(4), 1601–1618.

Esquierdo, J. J., & Arreguín-Anderson, M. (2012). The "invisible" gifted and talented bilingual students: A current report on enrollment in GT programs. *Journal for the Education of the Gifted*, 35(1), 35–47. doi:10.1177/0162353211432041

European Commission/EACEA/Eurydice. (2019). *Integrating Students from Migrant Backgrounds into Schools in Europe: National Policies and Measures. Eurydice Report*. Publications Office of the European Union.

European Union. (2013). *5th Annual Report on Immigration and Asylum*. https://ec.europa.eu/dgs/home-affairs/e-library/documents/policies/legal-migration/general/docs/5th_annual_report_on_immigration_and_asylum_en.pdf

Ezzani, M. D., Mun, R. U., & Lee, L. E. (2021). District leaders focused on systemic equity in identification and services for gifted education: From policy to practice. *Roeper Review*, 43(2), 112–127. doi:10.1080/02783193.2021.1881853

Farid, M. S. (2022). Social justice and inclusive education in Holy Cross education in Bangladesh: The case of Notre Dame College. *Religions*, 13(10), 980. doi:10.3390/rel13100980

Feuerverger, G. (2011). Re-Bordering spaces of trauma: Auto-ethnographic reflections on the immigrant and refugee experience in an inner-city high school in Toronto. *International Review of Education*, 57(3-4), 357–375. http://dx.doi.org.proxy.bib.uottawa.ca/10.1007/s11159-011-9207-y. doi:10.100711159-011-9207-y

Fisher, D., Frey, N., & Thousand, J. (2003). What do special educators need to know and be prepared to do for inclusive schooling to work? *Teacher Education and Special Education*, 26(1), 42–55. doi:10.1177/088840640302600105

Fiske, E. B., & Ladd, H. F. (2004). *Elusive equity: Education reform in post-apartheid South Africa*. Brookings Institute/HSRC Press.

FitzGerald, C., Martin, A., Berner, D., & Hurst, S. (2019). Interventions designed to reduce implicit prejudices and implicit stereotypes in real world contexts: A systematic review. *BMC Psychology*, 7, 29. https://doi.org/10.1186/s40359-019-0299-7

Florian, L. (2014). What counts as evidence of inclusive education? *European Journal of Special Needs Education*, 29(3), 286–294. doi:10.1080/08856257.2014.933551

Florian, L. (2015). Inclusive pedagogy: A transformative approach to individual differences but can it help reduce educational inequalities? *Scottish Educational Review*, 47(1), 5–14. doi:10.1163/27730840-04701003

Florian, L., & Camedda, D. (2020). Enhancing teacher education for inclusion. *European Journal of Teacher Education*, 43(1), 4–8. doi:10.1080/02619768.2020.1707579

Fondren, K., Lawson, M., Speidel, R., McDonnell, C. G., & Valentino, K. (2020). Buffering the effects of childhood trauma within the school setting: A systematic review of trauma-informed and trauma-responsive interventions among trauma-affected youth. *Children and Youth Services Review, 109*, 104691. doi:10.1016/j.childyouth.2019.104691

Ford, D. Y. (2010). Multicultural issues: Underrepresentation of culturally different students in gifted education: reflections about current problems and recommendations for the future. *Gifted Child Today, 33*(3), 31–35. doi:10.1177/107621751003300308

Ford, D. Y. (2013). Multicultural issues: Gifted underrepresentation and prejudice—learning from Allport and Merton. *Gifted Child Today, 36*(1), 62–67. doi:10.1177/1076217512465285

Ford, D. Y. (2014). Why education must be multicultural: Addressing a few misperceptions with counterarguments. *Gifted Child Today, 37*(1), 59–62. doi:10.1177/1076217513512304

Ford, D. Y., & Grantham, T. C. (2003). Providing access for culturally diverse gifted students: From deficit to dynamic thinking. *Theory into Practice, 42*(3), 217–225. doi:10.120715430421tip4203_8

Ford, D. Y., Moore, J. L., & Harmon, D. A. (2005). Integrating multicultural and gifted education: A curricular framework. *Theory into Practice, 44*(2), 125–137. doi:10.120715430421tip4402_7

Ford, D. Y., & Russo, C. J. (2014). No Child Left Behind ... unless a student is gifted and of color: Reflections on the need to meet the educational needs of the gifted. *Journal of Law and Society, 15*(2), 213–241.

Ford, D. Y., & Russo, C. J. (2016). Historical and legal overview of special education overrepresentation: Access and equity denied. *Multiple Voices for Ethnically Diverse Exceptional Learners, 16*(1), 50–57.

Ford, D. Y., & Trotman Scott, M. (2013). Culturally responsive response to intervention: Meeting the needs of students who are gifted and culturally different. In M. R. Coleman & S. K. Johnsen (Eds.), *Implementing RTI with gifted students: Service models, trends and issues* (pp. 209–228). Proofrock Press.

Foreman, J. L., & Gubbins, E. J. (2015). Teachers see what ability scores cannot: Predicting student performance with challenging mathematics. *Journal of Advanced Academics, 26*(1), 5–23. doi:10.1177/1932202X14552279

Foreman, M. (2009). *A child's garden: A story of hope.* Candlewick Press.

Forlin, C. (2013). Changing paradigms and future directions for implementing inclusive education in developing countries. *Asian Journal of Inclusive Education, 1*(2), 19–31.

Francis, B., Mills, M., & Lupton, R. (2017). Towards social justice in education: Contradictions and dilemmas. *Journal of Education Policy, 32*(4), 414–431. doi:10.1080/02680939.2016.1276218

Francisco, M. P. B., Hartman, M., & Wang, Y. (2020). Inclusion and special education. *Education Sciences, 10*(9), 1–17. doi:10.3390/educsci10090238

Freire, P. (2000). Pedagogy of the oppressed (30th anniversary ed.). Continuum.

Freire, P. (1970). *Pedagogy of the oppressed.* Bloomsbury Academic.

Freire, P. (1993). *Pedagogy of the oppressed (Twentieth Anniversary Edition).* Continuum.

Friedrich, P. (1989). Language, ideology, and political economy. *American Anthropologist, 91*(2), 295–312. doi:10.1525/aa.1989.91.2.02a00010

Friend, M., & Cook, L. (2007). *Interactions: Collaboration skills for professionals* (5th ed.). Pearson.

Gagné, A., Wattar, D., & Rajendram, S. (2020), *Me Mapping activities: A guide for teachers*. Supporting English Learners (SEL) & Supporting the Academic and Social Integration of Children and Youth of Refugee Backgrounds (SAIRCY) Projects, Ontario Institute for Studies in Education, University of Toronto, Canada. https://sites.google.com/view/memapping/guides-for-teachers/full-activity-guides

Gagné, A. (Ed.). (2007). *Growing new roots: The voices of immigrant families and the teachers of their children. Resource book for educators and immigrant families.* OISE/UT., https://wordpress.oise.utoronto.ca/diversityinteaching/wp-content/uploads/sites/24/2012/11/VIF_ResBook.pdf

Gagné, A., Al-Hashimi, N., Little, M., Lowen, M., & Sidhu, A. (2018). Educator perspectives on the social and academic integration of Syrian refugees in Canada. *Journal of Family Diversity in Education, 3*(1), 48–76. doi:10.53956/jfde.2018.124

Gagné, A., Schmidt, C., & Markus, P. (2017). Teaching about refugees: Developing culturally responsive educators in contexts of politicised transnationalism. *Intercultural Education, 28*(5), 429–446. doi:10.1080/14675986.2017.1336409

Gallagher-Mackay, K., Srivastava, P., Underwood, K., Dhuey, K., McCready, L., Born, K. B., Maltsev, K., Perkhun, P., Steiner, R., Barrett, K., & Sander, B. (2021). COVID-19 and education disruption in Ontario: Emerging evidence on impacts. *Ontario COVID-19 Science Advisory Table.* doi:10.47326/ocsat.2021.02.34.1.0

Garcia, S. B., & Ortiz, A. A. (1988). Preventing inappropriate referrals of language minority students to special education: Occasional papers in bilingual education. *NCBE New Focus, 5,* 1-21. http://eric.ed.gov/?id=ED309591

Garcia, A., & O'Donnell-Allen, C. (2014, July). Wobbling in public: Supporting new and experienced teachers. *English Journal, 103*(6), 65–70. doi:10.1177/2381336916661537

Garner, P. W., Mahatmya, D., Brown, E. L., & Vesely, C. K. (2014). Promoting Desirable Outcomes Among Culturally and Ethnically Diverse Children in Social Emotional Learning Programs: A Multilevel Heuristic Model. *Educational Psychology Review, 26,* 165–189. https://doi.org/10.1007/s10648-014-9253-7

Gay, G. (2002). Preparing for culturally responsive teaching. *Journal of Teacher Education, 53*(2), 106–116.

Gay, G. (2013). Teaching To and Through Cultural Diversity. *Curriculum Inquiry, 43*(1), 48–70.

Gay, G. (2018). *Culturally responsive teaching: Theory, research, and practice* (3rd ed.). Teachers College Press.

Gay, G., & Kirkland, K. (2003). Developing Cultural Critical Consciousness and Self-Reflection in Preservice Teacher Education. *Theory into Practice, 42*(3), 181–187. doi:10.120715430421tip4203_3

Gazeley, L., & Dunne, M. (2013). Initial Teacher Education programmes: Providing a space to address the disproportionate exclusion of Black pupils from schools in England? *Journal of Education for Teaching, 39*(5), 492–508. doi:10.1080/02607476.2013.844956

Gee, J. P. (2000). Chapter 3 : Identity as an Analytic Lens for Research in Education. *Review of Research in Education, 25*(1), 99–125. doi:10.3102/0091732X025001099

Gee, J. P. (2015). *Social linguistics and literacies: Ideology in discourses* (5th ed.). Routledge. doi:10.4324/9781315722511

Geerlings, J., Thijs, J., & Verkuyten, M. (2017). Student-teacher relationships and ethnic outgroup attitudes among majority students. *Journal of Applied Developmental Psychology, 52,* 69–79. doi:10.1016/j.appdev.2017.07.002

Geertz, C. (1973). *The interpretation of cultures*. Basic.

Gelir, I. (2021). Examining the Turkish preschool education program from an inclusive perspective. *HAYEF: Journal of Education, 18*(1), 55–65. doi:10.5152/hayef.2021.20028

General Directorate of Disabled and Elderly Services. (2016). *Statistical information of disabled and senior individuals*. Retrieved from http://eyh.aile.gov.tr/data/ 56179f30369dc5726c063e73/Bulletin_July2016.pdf

Gezer, M. S., & Aksoy, V. (2019). Perceptions of Turkish preschool teachers about their roles within the context of inclusive education. *International Journal of Early Childhood Special Education, 11*(1), 31–42. doi:10.20489/intjecse.583541

Ghaemi, F., & Sadeghi, P. (2015). Critical pedagogy: Concept and principles. *International Journal of Engineering Education, 4*(2), 244–249.

Giessman, J. A., Gambrell, J. L., & Stebbins, M. S. (2013). Minority performance on the Naglieri Nonverbal Ability Test, Second Edition, versus the Cognitive Abilities Test, Form 6: One gifted program's experience. Gifted Child Quarterly, 57(2), 101–109. doi:10.1177/0016986213477190

Gilligan, R. (1998). The importance of schools and teachers in child welfare. *Child & Family Social Work, 3*(1), 13–25. doi:10.1046/j.1365-2206.1998.00068.x

Girvan, E. J., Gion, C., McIntosh, K., & Smolkowski, K. (2017). The relative contribution of subjective office referrals to racial disproportionality in school discipline. *School Psychology Quarterly, 32*(3), 392–404. doi:10.1037pq0000178 PMID:27736122

Glock, S. (2016). Does ethnicity matter? The impact of stereotypical expectations on in-service teachers' judgments of students. *Social Psychology of Education, 19*, 493–509. https://doi.org/10.1007/s11218-016-9349-7

Glock, S., Kovacs, C., & Pit-ten Cate, I. (2019). Teachers' attitudes towards ethnic minority students: Effects of Schools' cultural diversity. *The British Journal of Educational Psychology, 89*, 616–634.

Goldfeld, S., Beatson, R., Watts, A., Snow, P., Gold, L., Le, H. N. D., Edwards, S., Connell, J., Stark, H., Shingles, B., Barnett, T., Quach, J., & Eadie, P. (2022). Tier 2 oral language and early reading interventions for preschool to grade 2 children: A restricted systematic review. *Australian Journal of Learning Difficulties, 27*(1), 65–113. doi:10.1080/19404158.2021.2011754

Goldin, S., Duane, A., & Khasnabis, D. (2021). Interrupting the weaponization of trauma-informed practice: "Who were you really doing the 'saving' for? *The Educational Forum, 86*(1), 5–25. https://doi.org/10.1080/00131725.2022.1997308

Gol, H., & Sakiz, H. (2020). Designing the guidance program of pre-school education in line with the principles of inclusive education. *Qualitative Social Sciences, 2*(2), 90–115.

Gondo, R., Maturure, K. J., Mutopa, S., Tokwe, T., Chirefu, H., & Nyevedzanayi, M. (2019). Issues surrounding the updated secondary school curriculum in Zimbabwe. *European Journal of Social Sciences Studies, 4*(2), 59–76. doi:10.5281/zenodo.2605499

González, N., Moll, L. C., & Amanti, C. (Eds.). (2005). Funds of knowledge: Theorizing practices in households, communities, and classrooms. Lawrence Erlbaum Associates.

Goodwin, A. L., & Stanton, R. (2022). Lessons from an Expert Teacher of Immigrant Youth: A Portrait of Social Justice Teaching. *Equity & Excellence in Education, 55*(1-2), 23–36. doi:10.1080/10665684.2021.2021652

Gopalkrishnan, N. (2018). Cultural Diversity and Mental Health: Considerations for Policy and Practice. *Frontiers in Public Health, 6*, 179. https://doi.org/10.3389/fpubh.2018.00179

Gorski, P. C. (2016). Poverty and the ideological imperative: A call to unhook from deficit and grit ideology and to strive for structural ideology in teacher education. *Journal of Education for Teaching, 42*(4), 378–386. https://doi.org/10.1080/02607476.2016.1215546

Government of Zimbabwe. (1987). *Education Act of 1987* [Chapter 25:04]. Government of Zimbabwe.

Government of Zimbabwe. (1992). *Disabled Persons Act* [Chapter 17:01]. Government of Zimbabwe.

Government of Zimbabwe. (2020). *National Development Strategy 1: Towards A Prosperous & Empowered Upper Middle Income Society by 2030*. Government of Zimbabwe.

Gözübüyük, N. (2015). *Okul öncesi dönem çocuklarında davranış sorunlarının anne-baba tutumu ve öz-kontrol ile ilişkisinin incelenmesi.* [Yayınlanmamış yüksek lisans tezi, Adnan Menderes Üniversitesi, Türkiye]. (*Examination of the relationship between behavioral problems in preschool children and parental attitudes and self-control.* [Unpublished master's thesis, Adnan Menderes University, Turkey].]

Grant, C. A., & Agosto, V. (2008). Teacher capacity and social justice in teacher education. In M. Cochran-Smith, S. Feiman-Nemser, D. J. McIntyre, & K. E. Demers (Eds.), *Handbook of research on teacher education: Enduring questions in changing contexts* (3rd ed., pp. 175–200). Routledge.

Graves, S. L. Jr, Herndon-Sobalvarro, A., Nichols, K., Aston, C., Ryan, A., Blefari, A., Schutte, K., Schachner, A., Vicoria, L., & Prier, D. (2017). Examining the effectiveness of a culturally adapted social-emotional intervention for African American males in an urban setting. *School Psychology Quarterly, 32*(1), 62–74. doi:10.1037pq0000145 PMID:27124505

Graziano, K. J., & Navarrete, L. A. (2012). Co-teaching in a teacher education classroom: Collaboration, compromise, and creativity. *Issues in Teacher Education, 21*, 109–115.

Greenfield, P. M., Suzuki, L. K., & Rothstein-Fisch, C. (2006). Cultural pathways through human development. In K. A. Renninger & I. E. Sigel (Eds.), Handbook of Child Psychology: Vol. 4. *Child Psychology in Practice*. John Wiley & Sons, Inc.

Greenwald, A. G., Nosek, B. A., & Banaji, M. R. (2003). Understanding and using the Implicit Association Test: I. An improved scoring algorithm. *Journal of Personality and Social Psychology, 85*(2), 197–216.

Gregory, A., Skiba, R. J., & Noguera, P. A. (2010). The achievement gap and the discipline gap: Two sides of the same coin? *Educational Researcher, 39*(1), 59–68.

Grigore, M.G. (2014). Psycho-Socio-Professional Aspects of Foster Care in Romania. *Journal of Experiential Psychotherapy, 17*(4) (68); 30-46.

Grissom, J. A., Kern, E. C., & Rodriguez, L. A. (2015). The "representative bureaucracy" in education: Educator workforce diversity, policy outputs, and outcomes for disadvantaged students. *Educational Researcher, 44*(3), 185–192. doi:10.3102/0013189X15580102

Gross-Manos, D. (2015). Material deprivation and social exclusion of children: Lessons from measurement attempts among children in Israel. *Jnl Soc. Pol., 44*(1), 105–125. doi:10.1017/S0047279414000646

Grütter, J., Meyer, B., Philipp, M., Stegmann, S., & van Dick, R. (2021). Beyond Ethnic Diversity: The Role of Teacher Care for Interethnic Relations. *Frontiers in Education, 5*, 586709. doi:10.3389/feduc.2020.586709

Gulec Aslan, Y. (2020). Experiences of Turkish preschool teachers for including children with autism spectrum disorders: Challenges faced and methods used. *International Journal of Psychology and Educational Studies, 7*(2), 37–49. doi:10.17220/ijpes.2020.02.004

Gunawardena, C., Frechette, C., & Layne, L. (2019). *Culturally inclusive instructional design: A framework and guide to building online wisdom communities*. Routledge.

Gürgür, H., & Uzuner, Y. (2010). A phenomenological analysis of the views on co-teaching applications in the inclusion classroom. *Educational Sciences: Theory and Practice*, *10*(1), 278–331.

Hall, C. J., & Cunningham, C. (2020). Educators' beliefs about English and languages beyond English: From ideology to ontology and back again. *Linguistics and Education*, *57*, 100817. Advance online publication. doi:10.1016/j.linged.2020.100817

Han, H. S., & Thomas, M. S. (2010). No Child Misunderstood: Enhancing Early Childhood Teachers' Multicultural Responsiveness to the Social Competence of Diverse Children. *Early Childhood Education Journal*, *37*, 469–476.

Hankivsky, O. (2014). Rethinking care ethics: On the promise and potential of an intersectional analysis. *The American Political Science Review*, *108*(2), 252–264. doi:10.1017/S0003055414000094

Hannon, L., & O'Donnell, G. M. (2022). Teachers, parents, and family-school partnerships: Emotions, experiences, and advocacy. *Journal of Education for Teaching*, *48*(2), 241–255. doi:10.1080/02607476.2021.1989981

Haralambos, M., & Holborn, M. (2013). *Sociology: Themes and perspectives* (8th ed.). Harper Collins.

Haraway, D. (1988). Situated knowledges: The science question in feminism and the privilege of partial perspectives. *Feminist Studies*, *14*(3), 575–599.

Hardman, F., & Abd-Kadir, J. (2010). Classroom discourse towards a dialogic pedagogy. 254-263. In D. Wyse, R. Andrews, & J. Hoffman (Eds.), The Routledge International Handbook of English, Language and Literacy Teaching (1st ed.). Routledge. doi:10.4324/9780203863091

Harris, B., Plucker, J. A., Rapp, K. E., & Martínez, R. S. (2009). Identifying gifted and talented English language learners: A case study. *Journal for the Education of the Gifted*, *32*(3), 368–393. doi:10.4219/jeg-2009-858

Harris, C. I. (1993). Whiteness as property. *Harvard Law Review*, *106*, 1707–1791.

Harry, B., & Ocasio-Stoutenburg, L. (2020). *Meeting families where they are: Building equity through advocacy with diverse schools and communities*. Disability, Culture, and Equity.

Hashmi, S., Khan, I. K., & Khanum, N. (2017). Inclusive education in government primary schools: Teacher perceptions. *Journal of Education and Educational Development*, *4*(1), 32–47. doi:10.22555/joeed.v4i1.1331

Haug, P. (2017). Understanding inclusive education: Ideals and reality. *Scandinavian Journal of Disability Research*, *19*(3), 206–217. doi:10.1080/15017419.2016.1224778

Hauwadhanasuk, T., Karnas, M., & Zhuang, M. (2018). Inclusive education plans and practices in China, Thailand, and Turkey. *Educational Planning*, *25*(1), 29–48.

Haydan, H. (2008). "Who's got the chalk?": Beginning mathematics teachers and educational policies in New York City. *Forum on Public Policy: A Journal of the Oxford Round Table*. https://link.gale.com/apps/doc/A218606498/AONE?u=txshracd2488&sid=bookmark-AONE&xid=a882e526

Hays, P. A. (2008). *Addressing cultural complexities in practice: Assessment, diagnosis, and therapy* (2nd ed.). American Psychological Association. doi:10.1037/11650-000

Heneman, H. III, & Milanowski, A. (2004). Alignment of human resource practices and teacher performance competency. *Peabody Journal of Education*, *79*(4), 108–125. doi:10.120715327930pje7904_6

Hernández Finch, M. E. (2012). Special considerations with response to intervention and instruction for students with diverse backgrounds. *Psychology in the Schools*, *49*(3), 285–296. doi:10.1002/pits.21597

Hernández-Torrano, D., & Saranli, A. G. (2015). A cross-cultural perspective about the implementation and adaptation process of the schoolwide enrichment model: The importance of talent development in a global world. *Gifted Education International*, *31*(3), 257–270. doi:10.1177/0261429414526335

Herzog-Punzenberger, B., Altrichter, H., & Brown, M. (2020). Teachers responding to cultural diversity: Case studies on assessment practices, challenges, and experiences in secondary schools in Austria, Ireland, Norway, and Turkey. *Educational Assessment, Evaluation and Accountability*, *32*, 395–424. https://doi.org/10.1007/s11092-020-09330-y

Hewings, A., & Tagg, C. (Eds.). (2012). *The politics of English: Conflict, competition, coexistence*. Routledge and The Open University.

Higginbotham, A. L., Jr. (1978). In the matter of color: Race and the American legal process 1, the Colonial Period. New York: Oxford University Press.

Higgins, C. (2017). Towards sociolinguistically informed language teacher identities. In G. Barkhuizen (Ed.), Reflections on Language Teacher Identity Research. Routledge/Taylor & Francis Group.

Him, T. (2017). Öğretmen Adaylarının Çocuk İstismarı Ve İhmaline Yönelik Farkındalık Düzeyleri. (Awareness Levels of Pre-service Teachers about Child Abuse and Neglect). *Journal of International Social Research*, *10*(50), 541–546. doi:10.17719/jisr.2017.1687

Hiranandani, V. (2012). Diversity management in the Canadian workplace: Towards an antiracism approach. *Urban Studies Research*. doi:10.1155/2012/385806

Holborow, M. (2007). Language, ideology, and neoliberalism. *Journal of Language and Politics*, *6*(1), 51–73. doi:10.1075/jlp.6.1.05hol

hooks, b. (2010). *Teaching critical thinking: Practical wisdom*. Routledge.

Horenczyk, G., & Tatar, M. (2002). Teachers' attitudes toward multiculturalism and their perceptions of the school organizational culture. *Teaching and Teacher Education*, *18*, 435–445.

Horne, P., & Timmons, V. (2009). Making it work: Teachers' perspectives on inclusion. *International Journal of Inclusive Education*, *13*(3), 273–286. doi:10.1080/13603110701433964

Howes, C., Phillips, D. A., & Whitebook, M. (1992). Thresholds of quality: Implications for the social development of children in center–based childcare. *Child Development*, *63*, 449–460.

Howes, C., Shivers, E. M., & Ritchie, S. (2004). improving social relationships in childcare through a researcher-program partnership. *Early Education and Development*, *15*, 57–78.

Howley, C., Howley, A., Yahn, J., VanHorn, P., & Telfer, D. (2019). Inclusive instructional leadership: A quasi-experimental study of a professional development program for principals. *Mid-Western Educational Researcher*, *31*(1), 3–23.

Huang, F. L., & Cornell, D. (2018). The relationship of school climate with out-of-school suspensions. *Children and Youth Services Review*, *94*, 378–389. doi:10.1016/j.childyouth.2018.08.013

Hudson, B. (2019). Epistemic quality for equitable access to quality education in school mathematics. *Journal of Curriculum Studies*, *51*(4), 437–456. doi:10.1080/00220272.2019.1618917

Hughes, C. E., Shaunessy, E. S., Brice, A. R., Ratliff, M. A., & McHatton, P. A. (2006). Code switching among bilingual and limited English proficient students: Possible indicators of giftedness. *Journal for the Education of the Gifted*, *30*(1), 7–28. doi:10.1177/016235320603000102

Hughes, G. (2012, June). Teacher retention: Teacher characteristics, schools characteristics, organizational characteristics, and teacher efficacy. *The Journal of Educational Research*, *105*(4), 245–255. doi:10.1080/00220671.2011.584922

Hughes, J., & Kwok, O. (2007). Influence of Student–Teacher and Parent–Teacher Relationships on Lower Achieving Readers' Engagement and Achievement in the Primary Grades. *Journal of Educational Psychology*, *99*(1), 39–51.

Hunter-Jones, P. (2014). Changing family structures and childhood socialisation: A study of leisure consumption. *Journal of Marketing Management*, *30*(15–16), 1533–1553. doi:10.1080/0267257X.2014.930503

Hurt, J. W. (2018). "Why are the gifted classes so white?" Making space for gifted Latino students. *Journal of Cases in Educational Leadership*, *21*(4), 112–130. doi:10.1177/1555458918769115

Hytten, K., & Bettez, S. C. (2011). Understanding education for social justice. *Educational Foundations*, *25*(1-2), 7–24.

Ilik, S. S., & Deniz, S. (2020). Observations of prospective teachers from different branches about inclusion practices during teaching practice. *Kastamonu Education Journal*, *28*(1), 338–351. doi:10.24106/kefdergi.3611

Ilik, S. S., & Hacieminoglu, E. (2019). Evaluation of elementary science teachers' perceptions regarding inclusive education application. *Journal of Education and Training Studies*, *7*(1), 19–29. doi:10.11114/jets.v7i10.4396

Individuals With Disabilities Education Act, 20 U.S.C. § 1400 (2004).

Ingersoll, R. (2001). Teacher turnover and teacher shortages: An organizational analysis. *American Educational Research Journal*, *38*(3), 499–534. doi:10.3102/00028312038003499

Inter-Agency Commission. (1990). *World conference on education for all: Meeting basic learning needs.* World Declaration on Education for All and Framework for Action to Meet Basic Learning Needs, Jomtien, Thailand. Inter-Agency Commission.

Ireland, J. (2022). Proclaiming mercy, practicing salvation: St. Basil's practical theology of evangelism and social action. *Journal of the Evangelical Missiological Society*, *2*(1), 1–14. https://journal-ems.org/index.php/home/article/view/31

Irvine, J. T., & Gal, S. (2009). Language ideology and linguistic differentiation. *Linguistic anthropology. REAd (Porto Alegre)*, *1*, 402–434.

Ismail, S. (2015). Equity and Education. In: James D. Wright (ed.), International Encyclopaedia of the Social & Behavioural Sciences, (2nd edition), 7, pp. 918–923. Elsevier. doi:10.1016/B978-0-08-097086-8.92099-3

Izadinia, M. (2009). Critical pedagogy: An introduction. In Power in the EFL Classroom: Critical Pedagogy in the Middle East. Cambridge Scholars Publishing.

İzci, L., Sarı, K. S., & Uyanık, M. N. (2021). Aile Odaklı Hizmet Modeli Olarak Koruyucu Aile Uygulaması. *T.C. Aile ve Sosyal Hizmetler Bakanlığı Çocuk Politikaları Serisi*, 1(3):1-44. (Foster Family Practice as a Family Oriented Service Model. *TR Ministry of Family and Social Services Child Policy Series*, *1*(3), 1–44.

J. Cole. (2007). School daze [Song]. On *The Come Up* [Album]. By Any Means Management.

Jack, D. (2016). *Hiring for diversity: Changing the face of Ontario's teacher workforce* [Doctoral dissertation]. University of Toronto, Canada. https://www.proquest.com/docview/1819293922?pq-origsite=gscholar&fromopenview=true

Jackson, S. E., Joshi, A., & Erhardt, N. L. (2003). Recent research on team and organizational diversity: SWOT analysis and implications. *Journal of Management*, *29*(6), 801–830. doi:10.1016/S0149-2063(03)00080-1

James, C. (2019). *We rise together*. Peel District School Board. https://www.peelschools.org/aboutus/equity/Documents/We%20Ri se%20Together%20report%20-%20Carl%20E%20James%20June%202019. pdf

Jansen, J. D. (2002). Political symbolism as policy craft: Explaining non-reform in South African education after apartheid. *Journal of Education Policy*, *17*(2), 199–215. doi:10.1080/02680930110116534

Jay Z. (2013). F.U.T.W. [Song]. On *Magna Carta Holy Grail* [Album]. Roc-A-Fella, Roc Nation, UMD, The Island Def Jam Music Group.

Jita, L. C. (2010). Instructional leadership for the improvement of science and mathematics in South Africa. *Procedia: Social and Behavioral Sciences*, *9*, 851–854. doi:10.1016/j.sbspro.2010.12.247

Jitendra, A. K., Alghamdi, A., Edmunds, R., McKevett, N. M., Mouanoutoua, J., & Roesslein, R. (2021). The effects of tier 2 mathematics interventions for students with mathematics difficulties: A meta-analysis. *Exceptional Children*, *87*(3), 307–325. doi:10.1177/0014402920969187

Johnson, L., & Kendrick, M. (2021). Digital storytelling: Opportunities for identity investment for youth from refugee backgrounds. In L. Green, D. Holloway, K. Stevenson, T. Leaver, & L. Haddon (Eds.), *Routledge Companion to Digital Media and Children* (pp. 469–479). Routledge.

Jones, J. M. (2009). Counseling with multicultural intentionality: the process of counseling and integrating client cultural variables. In J. M. Jones (Ed.), *The psychology of multiculturalism in the schools: a primer for practice, training, and research* (pp. 191–213). NASP Publications.

Jones, J. M., Begay, K. K., Nakagawa, Y., Cevasco, M., & Sit, J. (2015). Multicultural counseling competence training: Adding value with multicultural consultation. *Journal of Educational & Psychological Consultation*, *25*, 1–26. doi:10.1080/10474412.2015.1012671

Jowsey, T. (2019). Three zones of cultural competency: Surface competency, bias twilight, and the confronting midnight zone. *BMC Medical Education*, *19*(1), 306. https://doi.org/10.1186/s12909-019-1746-0

Jung, P. G., McMaster, K. L., Kunkel, A. K., Shin, J., & Stecker, P. M. (2018). Effects of data- based individualization for students with intensive learning needs: A meta-analysis. *Learning Disabilities Research & Practice*, *33*(3), 144–155. doi:10.1111/ldrp.12172

K'naan & Guy. S. (2012). When I get older: The story behind "Wavin' Flag." Tundra Books.

Kabakulak, K. (2019). *Çocuk Evleri Hizmet Modeli Kapsamında Olan Lise Öğrencisi Çocukların Akademik Başarı Bileşenlerinin Keşfedilmesi.* [Yayınlanmamış yüksek lisans tezi, Selçuk Üniversitesi, Türkiye]. [*Exploring the Academic Achievement Components of High School Students in the Children's Houses Service Model.* [Unpublished master's thesis, Selcuk University, Turkey].].

Kagitcibasi, C. (2010). *Family, Self and Human Development across Cultures: Theory and Applications*. Koc University Publications.

Kahriman, P. D., & Bal, M. (2019). Identifying pre-school teachers' opinions on the language development process of children in inclusive education. *National Education*, *48*(1), 737–754.

Kahya, O., & Hosgorur, V. (2018). Comparing inclusive education in Turkey and Argentina. *International Online Journal of Education & Teaching*, *5*(1), 82–92.

Kakilla, C. (2021). *Strengths and weaknesses of semi-structured interviews in qualitative research: A critical essay.* doi:10.20944/preprints202106.0491.v1

Kalaycı, H. (2007). *Yetiştirme Yurdundaki Çocuklarda Sosyal Dışlanma Riski (Tokat ve Turhal Örneği).* [Yayınlanmamış doktora tezi, Sakarya Üniversitesi, Türkiye]. (*The Risk of Social Exclusion in Children in Orphanage* (The Case of Tokat and Turhal). [Unpublished doctoral dissertation, Sakarya University, Turkey].].

Kanu, Y. (2008). Educational needs and barriers for African refugee students in Manitoba. *Canadian Journal of Education, 31*(4), 915–940.

Kaptan, O. (2019). *Determining the difficulties faced by the teachers who teach in the support training room for individuals with special needs in mainstreaming schools* [Unpublished master's thesis]. Necmettin Erbakan University, Konya, Turkey.

Karacaoglu, I. (2008). *Investigation of the relationship between primary school teachers' perceptions of school climate and their attitudes towards inclusion* [Unpublished master's thesis]. Yeditepe University Graduate School of Educational Sciences, Istanbul, Turkey.

Karadag Yilmaz, R., & Yeganeh, E. (2021). Who and how do I include? A case study on teachers' inclusive education practices. *International Journal of Progressive Education, 17*(2), 406–429. doi:10.29329/ijpe.2021.332.25

Kargin, T. (2004). Inclusion: Definition, Development and Principles. Ankara University Faculty of Educational Sciences Journal of Special Education, 5(2). doi:10.1501/Ozlegt_0000000080

Karnas, M., & Bayar, A. (2013a). *The collaboration between general and special education teachers and principal's role in this process* [Paper presentation]. Vth International Congress of Educational Research: Peace, Memory & Education, Canakkale, Turkey.

Karnas, M., & Bayar, A. (2013b). *Turkish elementary teachers' perspective of students with disabilities in general education classrooms* [Paper presentation]. Vth International Congress of Educational Research: Peace, Memory & Education Research, Çanakkale, Turkey.

Karsli-Calamak, E., & Kilinc, S. (2021). Becoming the teacher of a refugee child: Teachers' evolving experiences in Turkey. *International Journal of Inclusive Education, 25*(2), 259–282. doi:10.1080/13603116.2019.1707307

Katitas, S., & Coskun, B. (2020). What is meant by inclusive education? Perceptions of Turkish teachers towards inclusive education. *World Journal of Education, 10*(5), 18–28. doi:10.5430/wje.v10n5p18

Kavanagh, K. M., & Fisher-Ari, T. R. (2020). Curricular and pedagogical oppression: Contradictions within the juggernaut accountability trap. *Educational Policy, 34*(2), 283–311. doi:10.1177/0895904818755471

Kavanagh, S. S., & Danielson, K. A. (2020). Practicing justice, justifying practice: Toward critical practice teacher education. *American Educational Research Association, 57*(1), 69–105. doi:10.3102/0002831219848691

Kaysili, A., Soylu, A., & Sever, M. (2019). Exploring major roadblocks on inclusive education of Syrian refugees in school settings. *Turkish Journal of Education, 8*(2), 109–128. doi:10.19128/turje.496261

Kee, T., & Lai, A. (2022). Learning motivation and psychological empowerment of Socio-economically disadvantaged learners–an empirical study on inclusive project-based learning during Covid-19. *International Journal of Inclusive Education,* 1–20. doi:10.1080/13603116.2022.2112771

Kelly, D. (2012). Teaching for social justice. *Our Schools/Our Selves, 21*(2), 135-154.

Kempf, A. (2020). If we are going to talk about implicit race bias, we need to talk about structural racism in teaching and learning about race. *Taboo: The Journal of Culture & Education, 19*(2), 115–132.

Kendi, I. X. (2020). The Coronavirus is exposing our racial divides. *The Atlantic.* https://www.theatlantic.com/ideas/archive/2020/04/coronavirus-exposing-our-racial-divides/609526/

Kendrick Lamar. (2015). Momma [Song]. On *To Pimp a Butterfly* [Album]. TDE, Aftermath, Interscope.

Kendrick, M., Early, M., Michalovich, A., & Mangat, M. (2022). Digital storytelling with refugee background youth: Possibilities for language and digital literacies learning. *TESOL Quarterly, 56*(3), 961–984. doi:10.1002/tesq.3146

Keser, F., & Tanriverdi, A. (2019). Determining support services received by individuals with special needs living in Mardin and İstanbul. *The Journal of International Social Research, 12*(62), 1058–1066. doi:10.17719/jisr.2019.3118

Khalifa, M. A., Gooden, M. A., & Davis, J. E. (2016). Culturally responsive school leadership: A synthesis of the literature. *Review of Educational Research, 86*(4), 1272–1311. doi:10.3102/0034654316630383

Khechen, M. (2013). *Social justice: Concepts, principles, tools and challenges.* Economic and Social Commission for Western Asia (ESCWA).

Killen, M., Mulvey, K. L., & Hitti, A. (2013). Social Exclusion in Childhood: A Developmental Intergroup Perspective. *Child Development, 84*(3), 772–790. doi:10.1111/cdev.12012 PMID:23170901

Kındıroğlu, Z., & Ve Yaşar-Ekici, F. (2019). The Relationship between Psychological Well-Being and Psychological Resilience Levels of Parents and Social Competence and Behaviors of Children. *Adıyaman University Journal of Educational Sciences, 9*(1), 138–157. doi:10.17984/adyuebd.458224

King, J. (2016). The invisible tax on teachers of color. *The Washington Post*, pp. 1-4.

King, J. E. (1991). Dysconscious racism: Ideology, identity, and the miseducation of teachers. *The Journal of Negro Education, 60*(2), 133–146. https://doi.org/10.4135/9781446220986.n29

Kinloch, V., Nemeth, E. A., Butler, T. T., & Player, G. D. (2021). *Where is the justice: Engaged pedagogies in schools and communities.* Teachers College Press.

Kırcaali-Iftar, G. (1998). Individuals with special needs and special education. In S. Eripek (Ed.), *Special education* (pp. 1–14). Anadolu University Publications.

Kirkic, K. A., & Sayan, A. (2020). Investigation of the effect of the education given in the support education rooms on the development of preschool inclusion students. *Turkish Studies, 15*(2), 1121–1136. https://doi.org/10.29228/Turkish-Studies.29348

Kirshner, B. (2007). Introduction: Youth activism as a context for learning and development. *The American Behavioral Scientist, 51*(3), 367–379. doi:10.1177/0002764207306065

Kiziloglu, Y. (2021). *Potentialities for and limits to inclusion by education: The case of Syrian children's education in Turkey and child labor* [Unpublished master's thesis]. Middle East Technical University, Ankara, Turkey.

Klingbeil, D. A., Van Norman, E. R., Nelson, P. M., & Birr, C. (2019). Interval likelihood ratios: Applications for gated screening in schools. *Journal of School Psychology, 76*, 107–123. doi:10.1016/j.jsp.2019.07.016 PMID:31759460

Kohli, R. (2014). Unpacking internalized racism: Teachers of color striving for racially just classrooms. *Race, Ethnicity and Education, 17*(3), 367–387.

Koşar, N. (1992). Sosyal Hizmetlerde Koruyucu Aile Hizmeti, Aile ve Çocuk Refahı Alanı. Hacettepe Üniversitesi Yayını. [Foster Family Service in Social Services, Family and Child Welfare Field. Hacettepe University Press].

Kovinthan Levi, T. (2019). Preparing pre-service teachers to support children with refugee experiences. *The Alberta Journal of Educational Research*, *65*(4), 285–304.

Kovinthan, T. (2016). Learning and teaching with loss: Meeting the needs of refugee children through narrative inquiry. *Diaspora, Indigenous, and Minority Education*, *10*(3), 141–155. http://dx.doi.org.proxy.bib.uottawa.ca/10.1080/15595692.2015 .1137282. doi:10.1080/15595692.2015.1137282

Kozhabayeva, K., & Boivin, N. (2021). Emergency remote teaching in the Kazakhstan context: Deprofessionalization of teacher identity. In J. Chen (Ed.), *Emergency Remote Teaching and Beyond: Voice from World Language Teachers and Researchers*. Springer. doi:10.1007/978-3-030-84067-9_6

Kraft, M. (2007). Toward a school-wide model of teaching for social justice: An examination of the best practices of two small public schools. *Equity & Excellence in Education*, *40*(1), 77–86. doi:10.1080/10665680601076601

Kramarczuk Voulgarides, C., Aylward, A., Tefera, A., Artiles, A. J., Alvarado, S. L., & Noguera, P. (2021). Unpacking the logic of compliance in special education: Contextual influences on discipline racial disparities in suburban school. *Sociology of Education*, *94*(3), 208–226. doi:10.1177/00380407211013322

Kress, J. S., & Elias, M. J. (2006). School-based social and emotional learning programs in Handbook of Child Psychology: Vol. 4: Child Psychology in Practice (6th ed.). John Wiley & Sons, Inc.

Kretzmann, J. P., & McKnight, J. L. (1993). *Building communities from the inside out: A path toward finding and mobilizing a community's assets*. The Asset-Based Community Development Institute: DePaul University Steans Center.

Kubota, R. (2017). Critical language teacher identity. In G. Barkhuizen (Ed.), Reflections on Language Teacher Identity Research. Routledge/Taylor & Francis Group.

Kukla-Acevedo, S. (2009). Leavers, movers, and stayers: The role of workplace conditions in teacher mobility decisions. *The Journal of Educational Research*, *102*(6), 443–452. doi:10.3200/JOER.102.6.443-452

Kumaravadivelu, B. (2010). Problematizing cultural stereotypes in TESOL. TESOL Quarterly, 37(4), 709-719.

Küsmez, B. (2020). Korunma İhtiyacı Olan Çocuklar İçin Kurumsal Ve Alternatif Hizmet Modelleri: Bir Değerlendirme. (Institutional and Alternative Service Models for Children in Need of Protection: An Evaluation). [IJSHS]. *International Journal of Social and Humanities Sciences*, *4*(3), 201–225.

Kutay, V. (2018). Inclusive education in Turkey. *Studies in Educational Research and Development*, *2*(2), 144–162.

Laal, M., & Ghodsi, S. M. (2012). Benefits of collaborative learning. *Procedia: Social and Behavioral Sciences*, *31*, 486–490. doi:10.1016/j.sbspro.2011.12.091

Ladd, G. W. (2006). Peer Rejection, Aggressive or Withdrawn Behavior, and Psychological Maladjustment from Ages 5 to 12: An Examination of Four Predictive Models. *Child Development*, *77*(4), 822–846. doi:10.1111/j.1467-8624.2006.00905.x PMID:16942492

Ladson-Billings, G. (1995). Toward a theory of culturally relevant pedagogy. *American Educational Research Journal*, *32*(3), 465–491.

Ladson-Billings, G. (2000). Racialized discourses and ethnic epistemologies. In N. K. Denzin & Y. S. Lincoln (Eds.), *Handbook of qualitative research* (2nd ed., pp. 257–277). Sage Publications, Inc.

Ladson-Billings, G. (2003). It's your world, I'm just trying to explain it: Understanding our epistemological and methodological challenges. *Qualitative Inquiry*, *9*(5), 5–12.

Ladson-Billings, G. (2011). Practicing culturally relevant pedagogy. In J. Landsman & C. W. Lewis (Eds.), *White teachers/ diverse classrooms: Creating inclusive schools, building on students' diversity, and providing true educational equity.* Stylus Publishing, LLC.

Ladson-Billings, G. (2014). Culturally relevant pedagogy 2.0: A.K.A. the remix. *Harvard Educational Review, 84*(1), 87–84. https://doi.org/10.17763/haer.84.1.p2rj131485484751

Ladson-Billings, G. (2014). Culturally relevant pedagogy 2.0: Aka the remix. *Harvard Educational Review, 84*(1), 74–84. doi:10.17763/haer.84.1.p2rj131485484751

Ladson-Billings, G., & Tate, W. (1995). Toward a critical race theory of education. *Teachers College Record, 97*(1), 47–67. https://doi.org/10.1177/016146819509700104

Lakin, J. M. (2016). Universal screening and the representation of historically underrepresented minority students in gifted education: Minding the gaps in Card and Guliano's research. *Journal of Advanced Academics, 27*(2), 139–149. doi:10.1177/1932202X16630348

Lancaster, J., & Bain, A. (2007). The design of inclusive education courses and the self-efficacy of preservice teacher education students. *International Journal of Disability Development and Education, 54*(2), 245–256. https://doi.org/10.1080/10349120701330610

Lawyer, G., Shahan, C., Holcomb, L., & Smith, D. H. (2020). First Comes a Look at the Self: Integrating the Principles of Social Justice into a Teacher Preparation Program. *Odyssey: New Directions in Deaf Education, 21*, 66–70.

Ledesma, M. C., & Calderón, D. (2015). Critical race theory in education: A review of past literature and a look to the future. *Qualitative Inquiry, 21*(1), 206–222.

Ledwith, M. (1997). *Participating in transformation.* Venture Press/British Association of Social Workers.

Leijen, A., Kullasepp, K., & Anspal, T. (2014). Pedagogies of developing teacher identity. *Advances in Research on Teaching, 22*, 311–328. doi:10.1108/S1479-368720140000022019

Leske, L. (2016, November). How search committees can see bias in themselves. *The Chronicle of Higher Education.* https://www.chronicle.com/article/how-search-committees-can-see-bias-in-themselves/

Levashina, J., Hartwell, C. J., Morgeson, F. P., & Campion, M. A. (2014). The structured employment interview: Narrative and quantitative review of the research literature. *Personnel Psychology, 67*(1), 241–293. doi:10.1111/peps.12052

Levin, B. (2003). *Approaches to Equity in Policy for Lifelong Learning.* Education and Training Policy Division, OECD, for the Equity in Education Thematic Review.

Levitas, R., Pantazis, C., Fahmy, E., Gordon, D., Lloyd, E., & Patsios, D. (2007). The Multi-Dimensional Analysis Of Social Exclusion (pp:86-95). https://dera.ioe.ac.uk/6853/1/multidimensional.pdf

Lewin, K. M. (2007). *Improving access, equity, and transitions in education: Creating a research agenda. Consortium for Research into Educational Access Transition and Equity (CREATE),* [Working Paper No. 1]. University of Sussex.

Linan-Thompson, S., Ortiz, A., & Cavazos, L. (2022). An examination of MTSS assessment and decision making practices for English learners. *School Psychology Review, 51*(4), 484–497. doi:10.1080/2372966X.2021.2001690

Lindstrom, G., Easton, L., Yeo, M., & Attas, R. (2022). The disrupting interview: A framework to approach decolonization. *International Journal for Academic Development,* 1–13. doi:10.1080/1360144X.2022.2103560

Lippi-Green, R. (2004). Language ideology and language prejudice. *Language in the USA: Themes for the twenty-first century*, 289–304.

Lipsitz, G. (1994). We know what time it is: Race, class and youth culture in the nineties. In A. Ross & T. Rose (Eds.), Microphone fiends: Youth music & youth culture (pp. 17–28). Routledge. https://doi.org/10.4324/9780203699768.

Ljungdahl, L. (2004). *The English language and linguistic imperialism: The Trojan Horse?* Retrieved from https://opus.lib.uts.edu.au/bitstream/10453/6369/1/2004001444.pdf

Loewen, J. W. (2005). *Sundown towns: A hidden dimension of American racism.* The New Press.

Lohman, D. F., & Gambrell, J. L. (2012). Using nonverbal tests to help identify academically talented children. *Journal of Psychoeducational Assessment, 30*(1), 25–44. doi:10.1177/0734282911428194

Loreman, T., & Earle, C. (2007). The development of attitudes, sentiments and concerns about inclusive education in a content-infused Canadian teacher preparation program. *Exceptionality Education Canada, 17*(1/2), 85–106.

Lynch, J., & Prins, E. (2022). *Teaching and learning about family literacy and family literacy programs.* Routledge.

Lynn, M. (2002). Critical race theory and the lives of black male teachers in the Los Angeles Public Schools. *Equity & Excellence in Education, 35*(2), 119–130.

Lynn, M. (2006). Race, culture, and the education of African-Americans. *Educational Theory, 56*(1), 107–119.

Lynn, M., & Jennings, M. E. (2009). Power, politics, and critical race pedagogy: A critical race analysis of black male teachers' pedagogy. *Race, Ethnicity and Education, 12*(2), 173–196.

Lyons, S. (2022). Let's Play! Cooperative Games In Early Childhood Programs. *Early Childhood Webinars.* https://www.earlychildhoodwebinars.com/wp-content/uploads/2022/05/Slides_Cooperative-Games-in-Early-Childhood-Programs_05_19_2022.pdf

MacLean, K. (2003). The impact of institutionalization on child development. *Development and Psychopathology, 15*(4), 853–884. doi:10.1017/S0954579403000415 PMID:14984130

MacNevin, J. (2012). Learning the way: Teaching and learning with and for youth from refugee backgrounds on Prince Edward Island. *Canadian Journal of Education, 35*(3), 48–63.

Mafa, O. (2012). Challenges of implementing inclusion in Zimbabwe's education system. *Online Journal of Education Research, 1*(2), 14–22.

Magnússon, G. (2019). An amalgam of ideals: Images of inclusion in the Salamanca Statement. *International Journal of Inclusive Education, 23*(7–8), 677–690. doi:10.1080/13603116.2019.1622805

Mahlo, D. (2017). Teaching learners with Diverse Needs in the Foundation Phase in Gauteng Province, South Africa. *SAGE Open Journal*, 1-9. doi:10.1177/2158244017697162

Mahmoodarabi, M., & Khodabakhsh, M. R. (2015). Critical pedagogy: EFL teachers' views, experience, and academic degrees. *English Language Teaching, 8*(6), 100–110. doi:10.5539/elt.v8n6p100

Makoelle, T. M., & Malindi, M. J. (2014). Multi-grade teaching and inclusion: Selected cases in the Free State Province of South Africa. *International Journal of Educational Sciences, 7*(1), 77–86. doi:10.1080/09751122.2014.11890171

Malo-Juvera, V., Correll, P., & Cantrell, S. A. (2018). mixed methods investigation of teachers' self-efficacy for culturally responsive instruction. *Teaching and Teacher Education, 74*, 146–156. https://doi.org/10.1016/j.ijintrel.2020.08.001

Malone, C. M., Wycoff, K., & Turner, E. A. (2021). Applying a MTSS framework to address racism and promote mental health for racial/ethnic minoritized youth. *Psychology in the Schools*, 1–15. doi:10.1002/pits.22606

Mamlet, R. (2017, February). Gender and the job interview. *The Chronicle of Higher Education*. https://www.chronicle.com/article/gender-in-the-job-interview/

Manitoba Education and Early Childhood Learning. (2013). *From apology to reconciliation*. Government of Manitoba. https://www.edu.gov.mb.ca/k12/cur/socstud/far/doc/full_doc.pdf

Mapako, F. P. & Mareva, F. (2013). The concept of free primary school education in Zimbabwe: Myth or reality. *Basic Education, 1*(1), 135 – 145.

Maralit, K. (2022). Review K to 12 program, Marcos orders DepEd. *The Manila Times*. https://www.manilatimes.net/2022/06/22/news/national/review-k-to-12-program-marcos-orders-deped/1848275

Markel, K. S., & Barclay, L. A. (2009). Addressing the underemployment of persons with disabilities: Recommendations for expanding organizational social responsibility. *Employee Responsibilities and Rights Journal, 21*(4), 305–318. doi:10.100710672-009-9125-3

Masaka, D. (2016). *The impact of Western colonial education in Zimbabwe's traditional and postcolonial educational system(s)* [Unpublished PhD dissertation]. University of South Africa.

Mason, R., & Schroeder, M. (2010). Principal hiring practices: Toward a reduction of uncertainty. *The Clearing House: A Journal of Educational Strategies, Issues and Ideas, 83*(5), 186–193. doi:10.1080/00098650903583727

Mathwasa, J., & Sibanda, L. (2021). Inclusion in early childhood development settings: A reality or an oasis. In O. A. de la Rosa, L. M. V. Angulo, & C. Giambrone (Eds.), *Education in childhood*. IntechOpen. doi:10.5772/intechopen.99105

Matias, C. E., Vieska, K. M., Garrison-Wade, D., Madhavi, T., & Galindo, R. (2014). What is critical whiteness doing in our nice field like the critical race theory? Applying CRT and CRW to understand the white imagination of white teacher candidates. *Equity & Excellence in Education, 47*(3), 289–304. doi:10.1080/10665684.2014.933692

Matsuda, P. K. (2017). Second language writing teacher identity. In G. Barkhuizen (Ed.), Reflections on Language Teacher Identity Research. Routledge/Taylor & Francis Group.

Matsuda, M., Lawrence, C., Delgado, R., & Crenshaw, K. (1993). *Words that wound: Critical race theory, assaultive speech, and the first amendment*. Westview.

Maurice, P. M. (2022). The impact of Christianity on the social-economic life of sub-Saharan Africa. *ShahidiHub International Journal of Theology & Religious Studies, 2*(1), 72–88.

Maynard, R. (2017). *Policing Black lives: State violence in Canada from slavery to the present*. Fernwood Publishing.

McBee, M. (2010). Examining the probability of identification for gifted programs for students in Georgia elementary schools: A multilevel path analysis study. *Gifted Child Quarterly, 54*(4), 283–297. doi:10.1177/0016986210377927

McBee, M. T. (2006). A descriptive analysis of referral sources for gifted identification screening by race and socioeconomic status. *Journal of Secondary Gifted Education, 17*(2), 103–111. doi:10.4219/jsge-2006-686

McCart, A., & Miller, D. (2020). Leading equity-based MTSS. In McLeskey, J., Billingsley, B., Brownell, M. T., Maheady, L., Lewis, T. J., Billingsley, B. S., & Maheady, L. J. (2019) What are high-leverage practices for special education teachers and why are they important? *Remedial & Special Education, 40*(6), 331–337. doi:10.1177/0741932518773477

McDonald, M., & Zeichner, K. M. (2009). Social justice teacher education. In W. Ayers, T. Quinn, & D. Stovall (Eds.), *Handbook of social justice in education* (pp. 613–628). Routledge.

McFarland, J., Hussar, B., Wang, X., Zhang, J., Wang, K., Rathburn, A., & Mann, F. (2018). *The condition of education 2018* (NCES 2018 – 144) [Data set]. U.S. Department of Education: National Center for Educational Statistics. https://nces.ed.gov/pubsearch/pubsinfo. asp?pubid=2018144

McShane, M. Q., & Hess, F. M. (2021). *Three conservative principles of education.* American Enterprise Institute. Retrieved from https://www.aei.org/op-eds/three-conservative-principles-for-education/

Me Mapping with Multilingual Learners. (n.d.) https://sites.google.com/view/memapping

Melekoglu, M. A. (2014). Special education in Turkey. *Special Education International Perspectives: Practices Across the Globe. Advances in Special Education, 28,* 529–557. https://doi.org/10.1108/S0270-401320140000028024

Meltz, A., Herman, C., & Pillay, V. (2014). Inclusive education: A case of beliefs competing for implementation. *South African Journal of Education, 34*(3), 1–8. doi:10.15700/201409161049

Menezes de Oliveira e Paiva, V.L. (2017). Language teaching identity: A fractal system. In G. Barkhuizen (Ed.), Reflections on Language Teacher Identity Research. Routledge/Taylor & Francis Group.

Mercier-Dalphond, G., & Helly, D. (2021). Anti-Muslim violence, hate crime, and victimization in Canada: A study of five Canadian cities. *Canadian Ethnic Studies, 53*(1), 1–22. doi:10.1353/ces.2021.0000

Merriam, S.B. & Tisdell, E.J. (n.d.). *Qualitative research: A guide to design and implementation* (4th ed.). Jossey-Bass: A Wiley Brand.

Merriam, S. B. (1998). *Qualitative research and case study applications in education.* Jossey-Bass.

Merriam, S., & Bierema, L. (2014). *Adult learning: Linking theory and practice.* John Wiley & Sons.

Mete, P. (2020). The views of students in an inclusive classroom environment in high school on the course learning process. *Elementary Education Online, 19*(2), 552–564.

Metin, N., Gulec, H., & Sahin, C. (2009). *Determining the competencies of primary school teachers after in-service training for the integration of mentally handicapped children* [Paper presentation]. *1st International Turkey Educational Research Congress,* Canakkale, Turkey.

Metsämuuronen, J., & Lehikko, A. (2022). Challenges and Possibilities of Educational Equity and Equality in the Post-COVID-19 Realm in the Nordic Countries. *Scandinavian Journal of Educational Research,* 1–22. doi:10.1080/00313831.2022.2115549

Mfuthwana, T., & Dreyer, L. M. (2018). Establishing inclusive schools: Teachers' perceptions of inclusive education teams {special issue}. *South African Journal of Education, 38*(4), 1–10. doi:10.15700aje.v38n4a1703

Mhlolo, M. K. (2015). Examining covert impediments to inclusive education for the mathematically gifted learners in South Africa. In *9th Mathematical Creativity and Giftedness Conference.* Central University of Technology.

Miles, J., & Bailey-McKenna, M.-C. (2016). Giving refugee students a strong head start: The LEAD program. *TESL Canada Journal, 33,* 109–128.

Miles, M. B., & Huberman, A. M. (1994). *Qualitative data analysis* (2nd ed.). Sage.

Miles, S., & Singhal, N. (2010). The education for all and inclusive education debate: Conflict, contradiction or opportunity? *International Journal of Inclusive Education*, *14*(1), 115. doi:10.1080/13603110802265125

Milner, H. R. IV. (2008). Critical race theory and interest convergence as analytic tools in teacher education policies and practices. *Journal of Teacher Education*, *58*(4), 332–346. doi:10.1177/0022487108321884

Milner, H. R. IV, Fittz, L., Best, B., & Cunningham, H. B. (2022). What if special education could be seen as a site for justice? *Journal of Emotional and Behavioral Disorders*, *30*(2), 159–166. doi:10.1177/10634266221087990

Milner, H. R., & Tenore, F. B. (2010). Classroom Management in Diverse Classrooms. *Urban Education*, *45*(5), 560–603.

Mitchell, D. R. (Ed.). (2004). *Special educational needs and inclusive education: Inclusive education* (Vol. 2). Taylor & Francis.

Moll, L. C. (2014). *L. S. Vygotsky and education*. Routledge.

Moll, L. C., & González, N. (1994). Lessons from research with language minority children. *Journal of Reading Behavior*, *25*(4), 439–456. doi:10.1080/10862969409547862

Moll, M. (2001). Teacher diversity: An elusive goal. *PD & Research News*, *1*(4), 3–4.

Montalvo, R., Combes, B. H., & Kea, C. D. (2014). Perspectives on culturally and linguistically responsive RtI pedagogics through a cultural and linguistic lens. *Interdisciplinary Journal of Teaching and Learning*, *4*(3), 203–219.

Montserrat, C. (2014). The Child Protection System from the Perspective of Young People: Messages from 3 Studies. *Soc. Sci.*, *3*(4), 687–704. doi:10.3390ocsci3040687

Mooney, A., & Evans, B. (2015). *Language, society & power: An introduction*. Routledge. doi:10.4324/9781315733524

Morgan, P. L., Farkas, G., Cook, M., Strassfeld, N. M., Hillemeier, M. M., Pun, W. H., Wang, Y., & Schussler, D. L. (2018). Are Hispanic, Asian, Native American, or language-minority children overrepresented in special education? *Exceptional Children*, *84*(3), 261–279. doi:10.1177/0014402917748303

Moriña, A. (2020). Approaches to Inclusive Pedagogy: A Systematic Literature Review. *Pedagogy*, *140*(4), 134–154. doi:10.15823/p.2020.140.8

Mphanda, E. G. (2018). *From main-stream to full-service schools: an exploration of teachers' attitudes towards the inclusion of learners living with physical disabilities in South African schools* [Doctoral dissertation]. University of Pretoria.

Mrsnik, K. O. (2003). *A case study of the effects of the interactive change model for inclusion on the development of teacher efficacy and teachers' willingness to implement inclusive practices* [Unpublished doctoral dissertation]. Cleveland State University.

Mulvey, K. L. (2016). Children's reasoning about social exclusion: Balancing many factors. *Child Development Perspectives*, *10*(1), 22–27. doi:10.1111/cdep.12157

Mulvey, K. L., Gönültaş, S., Irdam, G., Carlson, R. G., DiStefano, C., & Irvin, M. J. (2021). School and Teacher Factors That Promote Adolescents' Bystander Responses to Social Exclusion. *Frontiers in Psychology*, *11*, 581089. doi:10.3389/fpsyg.2020.581089 PMID:33505333

Münger, A. C., & Markström, A. M. (2019). School and Child Protection Services Professionals' Views on the School's Mission and Responsibilities for Children Living with Domestic Violence - Tensions and Gaps. *Journal of Family Violence*, *34*(5), 385–398. doi:10.100710896-019-00035-5

Mun, R. U., Ezzani, M. D., Lee, L. E., & Ottwein, J. K. (2021). Building systemic capacity to improve identification and services in gifted education: A case study of one district. *Gifted Child Quarterly, 65*(2), 132–152. doi:10.1177/0016986220967376

Mun, R. U., Hemmler, V., Langley, S. D., Ware, S., Gubbins, E. J., Callahan, C. M., McCoach, D. B., & Siegle, D. (2020). Identifying and serving English learners in gifted education: Looking back and moving forward. *Journal for the Education of the Gifted, 43*(4), 297–335. doi:10.1177/0162353220955230

Muresherwa, E. (2020). *Challenges and opportunities to instructional leadership in inclusive secondary schools of Zimbabwe* [Doctoral dissertation]. University of the Free State.

Muresherwa, E., & Jita, L. C. (2021). Instructional leadership in inclusive secondary schools of Zimbabwe: Balancing multiple and competing expectations. *Universal Journal of Educational Research, 9*(10), 1742–1755. doi:10.13189/ujer.2021.091003

Murungi, L. N. (2015). Inclusive basic education in South Africa: Issues in its conceptualization and implementation. *Potchefstroom Electronic Law Journal, 18*(1), 3160–3195. doi:10.4314/pelj.v18i1.07

Musengi, M., & Chireshe, R. (2013). Inclusion of deaf students in mainstream rural primary schools in Zimbabwe: Challenges and opportunities. *Studies of Tribes and Tribals, 10*(2), 107–116. doi:10.1080/0972639X.2012.11886648

Muthukrishna, N., & Engelbrecht, P. (2018). Decolonising inclusive education in lower income, Southern African educational contexts. *South African Journal of Education, 38*(4), 1–11. doi:10.15700aje.v38n4a1701

NAEYC. (2009). Developmentally Appropriate Practice in Early Childhood Programs Serving Children from Birth through. *Age (Dordrecht, Netherlands), 8*. Retrieved December 15, 2016, from https://www.naeyc.org/files/naeyc/file/positions/position%20statement%20Web.pdf

NAGC. (2011). *Identifying and serving culturally and linguistically diverse gifted students*. NAGC. http://www.nagc.org/sites/default/files/Position%20Statement/Identifying%20and%20Serving%20Culturally%20and%20Linguistically.pdf

NAGC. (n.d.) *Gifted Education in the U.S. National Association for Gifted Children*. NAGC. https://www.nagc.org/resources-publications/resources/gifted-education-us

Naglieri, J. A. (2008) *Naglieri nonverbal ability test* (2nd ed.) Pearson National Association for Gifted Children.

Nakeyar, C., Esses, V., & Reid, G. J. (2018). The psychosocial needs of refugee children and youth and best practices for filling these needs: A systematic review. *Clinical Child Psychology and Psychiatry, 23*(2), 186–208. doi:10.1177/1359104517742188 PMID:29207880

Naper, L. (2010). Teacher hiring practices and educational efficiency. *Economics of Education Review, 29*(4), 658–688. doi:10.1016/j.econedurev.2009.11.002

Nas. (2001). What goes around [Song]. On *Stillmatic* [Album]. III Will, Columbia.

National Academies of Sciences, Engineering, and Medicine (2022). *The Future of Education Research at IES: Advancing an Equity-Oriented Science*. The National Academies Press. . doi:10.17226/26428

National Center for Education Statistics. (2013). Number and percentage distribution of teachers in public and private elementary and secondary schools, by selected teacher characteristics: Selected years, 1987-88 through 2011-12. *Digest of Education Statistics*. https://eric.ed.gov/?id=ED556349

National Center for Learning Disabilities. (2011). *Multi-tier system of supports aka response to intervention (RTI).* NCLD. https://www.ncld.org/wp-content/uploads/2011/05/MTSS-brief-in-LJ-template.pdf

National Center for Learning Disabilities. (2020). *Significant disproportionality in special education: Current trends and actions for impact.* NCLD. https://www.ncld.org/wp-content/uploads/2020/10/2020-NCLD-Disproportionality_Trends-and-Actions-for-Impact_FINAL-1.pdf

National Center for School Mental Health. (2020). *School mental health quality guide: Mental health promotion services & supports (tier 1).* NCSMH, University of Maryland School of Medicine.

National Education Association. (2003). *NEA and teacher recruitment: An overview.* https://www.new.org/recruit/minority

National Writing Project. (2009). Writing for a change: Boosting literacy and learning through social action. Jossey-Bass: A Wiley Imprint.

Neifeald, E., & Nissim, Y. (2019). Co-teaching in the "academia class": Evaluation of advantages and frequency of practices. *International Education Studies, 12*(5), 1913-9039. doi:10.5539/ies.v12n5p86

Nel, N. M. (2016). Teachers' perceptions of education support structures in the implementation of inclusive education in South Africa. *KOERS – Bulletin for Christian Scholarship, 81*(3).

Nelson, C. D. (2017). Identity dilemmas and research agenda. In G. Barkhuizen (Ed.), Reflections on Language Teacher Identity Research. Routledge/Taylor & Francis Group.

Nelson, C. A., Fox, N. A., & Zeanah, C. H. (2014). *Romania's Abandoned Children.* Harvard University Press. doi:10.4159/harvard.9780674726079

Nevill, T., & Savage, G. (2022). The changing rationalities of Australian federal and national inclusive education policies. *Australian Educational Researcher,* 1–19. doi:10.100713384-022-00555-y

Ngcobo, J., & Muthukrishna, N. (2011). The geographies of inclusion of students with disabilities in an ordinary school. *South African Journal of Education, 31*(3), 357–368. doi:10.15700aje.v31n3a541

Nieto, S. (2011). The light in their eyes: Creating multicultural learning communities (10th anniversary ed.). Teachers College Press.

Nieuwenhuis, J. (2010). Social justice in education revisited. *Education Inquiry, 1*(4), 269–287. doi:10.3402/edui.v1i4.21946

Nilholm, C., & Alm, B. (2010). An inclusive classroom: A case study of inclusiveness, teacher strategies, and children experiences. *European Journal of Special Needs Education, 25*(3), 239–252. doi:10.1080/08856257.2010.492933

Nipedal, C., Nesdale, D., & Killen, M. (2010). Social group norms, school norms, and children's aggressive intentions. *Aggressive Behavior, 36*, 195–204. doi:10.1002/ab.20342 PMID:20301137

Nîtôtemtik, T. (2020). Let's talk gaps in education for on and off reserve First Nations Peoples. *Alberta Law Type Pad.* https://ualbertalaw.typepad.com/faculty/2020/10/lets-talk-gaps-in-education-for-on-off-reserve-first-nations-peoples.htm l

Noddings, N. (2012). The caring relation in teaching. *Oxford Review of Education, 38*(6), 771–781. doi:10.1080/03054985.2012.745047

Noon, M. (2017). Pointless Diversity Training: Unconscious Bias, New Racism and Agency. *Work, Employment and Society, 32*(1), 198–209.

Norris, J., & Sawyer, R. (2004). Null and hidden curricula of sexual orientation: A dialogue on the curreres of the absent presence and the present absence. In L. Coia, M. Birch, N. J. Brooks, E. Heilman, S. Mayer, A. Mountain, & P. Pritchard (Eds.), *Democratic responses in an era of standardization* (pp. 139–159). Educator's International Press, Inc.

North, C. E. (2006). More than words? Delving into the substantive meaning(s) of "social justice" in education. *Review of Educational Research*, *76*(4), 507–535. doi:10.3102/00346543076004507

O'Connor, M. T., & Daniello, F. (2019). From implication to naming: Reconceptualizing school-community partnership literature using a framework nested in social justice. *School Community Journal*, *29*(1), 297–316l.

Oades-Sese, G. V., Esquivel, G. B., Kaliski, P. K., & Maniatis, L. (2011). A longitudinal study of the social and academic competence of economically disadvantaged bilingual preschool children. *Developmental Psychology*, *47*(3), 747–764. https://doi.org/10.1037/a0021380

Oakley, D., Stowell, J., & Logan, J. R. (2009). The impact of desegregation on black teachers in the metropolis, 1970–2000. *Ethnic and Racial Studies*, *32*(9), 1576–1598. doi:10.1080/01419870902780997 PMID:24039318

OECD. (2018). *Equity in Education: Breaking Down Barriers to Social Mobility*, PISA, OECD Publishing, Paris.

Office of Special Education Programs. (2021). Individuals with Disabilities Education Act (IDEA) database. US Department of Education. https://www2.ed.gov/programs/osepidea/618-data/state-level-datafiles/index.html#bcc

Okilwa, N. S., & Robert, C. (2017). School Discipline Disparity: Converging Efforts for Better Student Outcomes. *The Urban Review*, *49*(2), 239–262. doi:10.100711256-017-0399-8

Okonofua, J. A., & Eberhardt, J. L. (2015). Two Strikes: Race and the Disciplining of Young Students. *Psychological Science*, *26*(5), 617–624. https://www.jstor.org/stable/24544011

Oldfield, K. (2007, July). Expanding economic democracy in American higher education: A two-step approach to hiring more teachers from poverty and working-class backgrounds. *Journal of Higher Education Policy and Management*, *29*(2), 217–230. doi:10.1080/13600800701351785

Olesen, H. S. (2007). Theorising learning in life history: A psychosocietal approach. *Studies in the Education of Adults*, *39*(1), 38–53. https://doi.org/10.1080/02660830.2007.11661539

Olszewski-Kubilius, P., & Thomson, D. (2015). Talent development as a framework for gifted education. *Gifted Child Today*, *38*(1), 49–59. doi:10.1177/1076217514556531

Omoeva, C. (2017). Mainstreaming Equity in Education. Paper Commissioned by the International Education Funders Group. Education Policy and Data Center / Education Equity Research Initiative.

Ontario College of Teachers. (2015). *Transition to Teaching 2014*. Ontario College of Teachers.

Ontario College of Teachers. (2017). *Accreditation resource guide*. OCT. https://www.oct.ca/-/media/PDF/Accreditation%20Resource%20Guide/Accreditation_Resource_Guide_EN_WEB.pdf

Ontario Ministry of Education. (2007). *English language learners - ESL and ELD programs and services - Policies and procedures for Ontario elementary and secondary schools, Kindergarten to Grade 12*. OME. https://www.edu.gov.on.ca/eng/document/esleldprograms/esleldprograms.pdf

Ontario Ministry of Education. (2008). *Supporting English language learners with limited prior schooling: A practical guide for Ontario educators - Grades 3 to 12*. OME. https://www.edu.gov.on.ca/eng/document/manyroots/ELL_LPS.pdf

Ontario Ministry of Education. (2009). *Equity and inclusive education in Ontario schools: Guidelines for policy development and implementation.* https://www.edu.gov.on.ca/eng/policyfunding/inclusiveguide.pdf

Ontario Ministry of Education. (2013). *Culturally responsive pedagogy towards equity and inclusivity in Ontario schools.* Queen's Printer for Ontario.

Ontario Ministry of Education. (2016). Supporting students with refugee backgrounds: A framework for responsive practice. *Capacity Building Series, Special Edition #45.* https://drive.google.com/file/d/1HBR_60cUuTX1sWZN-qhMMPF8MP8i_zmF/view

Ontario Ministry of Education. (2017). *Ontario's education equity action plan.* https://www.ontario.ca/page/ontarios-education-equity-action-plan

Ontario Ministry of Education. (2021). *Annual progress report 2021: Ontario's anti-racism strategic plan.* https://www.ontario.ca/page/annual-progress-report-2021-ontarios-anti-racism-strategic-plan

Opoku, M. P., Cuskelly, M., Pedersen, S. J., & Rayner, C. S. (2021). Attitudes and self-efficacy as significant predictors of intention of secondary school teachers towards the implementation of inclusive education in Ghana. *European Journal of Psychology of Education, 36*(3), 673–691. doi:10.100710212-020-00490-5

Organisation for Economic and Co-operation Development (2008). *Policy Brief: Ten Steps to Equity in Education.* OECD.

Ottawa-Carleton Disctrict School Board. (2021). *National truth and reconciliation day and orange shirt day.* https://www.ocdsb.ca/our_schools/indigenous_education/national_truth

Ozokcu, O. (2018). Investigating classroom teachers' attitudes towards inclusion. *Inonu University Journal of the Faculty of Education, 19*(3), 418-433. doi:10.17679/inuefd.472639

Özyürek, A. (2015). Okul öncesi çocukların sosyal beceri düzeyleri ile anne tutumları arasındaki ilişkinin incelenmesi. *Milli Eğitim Dergisi, 206,* 106-120. (Examination of the relationship between the social skill levels of preschool children and their mother attitudes. *Journal of National Education, 206,* 106–120.

Pantić, P., & Florian, L. (2015). Developing teachers as agents of inclusion and social justice. *Education Inquiry, 6*(3), 27311. doi:10.3402/edui.v6.27311

Parekh, G., Flessa, J., & Smaller, H. (2016). The toronto district school board: A global city school system's structures, processes, and student outcomes. *London Review of Education, 14*(3), 65–84. https://doi.org/10.18546/LRE.14.3.06

Parhar, N., & Sensoy, Ö. (2011). Culturally relevant pedagogy redux: Canadian teachers' conceptions of their work and its challenges. *Canadian Journal of Education / Revue Canadienne de l'éducation, 34*(2), 189-218.

Paris, D. (2012). Culturally sustaining pedagogy: A needed change in stance, terminology, and practice. *Educational Researcher, 41*(3), 93–97.

Paris, D. (2012). Culturally Sustaining Pedagogy: A Needed Change in Stance, Terminology, and Practice. *Educational Researcher, 41*(3), 93–97. doi:10.3102/0013189X12441244

Paris, D. (2021). Culturally sustaining pedagogies and our futures. [). Routledge.]. *The Educational Forum, 85*(4), 364–376. doi:10.1080/00131725.2021.1957634

Paris, D., & Alim, H. S. (Eds.). (2017). *Culturally sustaining pedagogies: Teaching and learning for justice in a changing world*. Teachers College Press.

Parker, L., & Gillborn, D. (Eds.). (2020). *Critical race theory in education*. Routledge.

Pather, S. (2011). Evidence on inclusion and support for all learners in mainstream schools in South Africa: Off the policy radar? *International Journal of Inclusive Education, 15*(10), 1103-1117. doi:10.1080/13603116.2011.555075

Payne, A. (2011). *Equitable access for underrepresented students in gifted education*. George Washington University Center for Equity and Excellence in Education. https://eric.ed.gov/?id=ED539772

Payne, A. A., & Welch, K. (2015). Restorative justice in schools: The influence of race on restorative discipline. *Youth & Society, 47*(4), 539–564. doi:10.1177/0044118X12473125

Payne, B. K., Burkley, M. A., & Stokes, M. B. (2008). Why Do Implicit and Explicit Attitude Tests Diverge? The Role of Structural Fit. *Journal of Personality and Social Psychology, 94*(1), 16–31.

Pearce, J., & Cumming-Potvin, W. (2017). English classrooms and curricular justice for the recognition of LGBT individuals: What can teachers do? *The Australian Journal of Teacher Education, 42*(9), 77–92. doi:10.14221/ajte.2017v42n9.5

Peček, M., Macura-Milovanović, S., & Vujisić-Živković, N. (2014). The cultural responsiveness of teacher candidates towards Roma pupils in Serbia and Slovenia–case studies. *Journal of Education for Teaching, 40*(4), 359–376.

Peel District School Board. (2022, June 22). *The Peel District School Board approved the most comprehensive anti-racism policy ever announced by a school board in Ontario*. https://www.peelschools.org/news/The-Peel-District-School-Board-approved-the-most-comprehensive-Anti-Racism-Policy-ever-announced-by-a-school-board-in-Ontario2022-06-29-19:10:49.09 1418+00

Pendleton, C. (2022, November). How a search committee can be the arbiter of diversity. *The Chronicle of Higher Education*. https://www.chronicle.com/article/how-a-search-committee-can-be-the-arbiter-of-diversity

Pennycook, A. (2017). *The cultural politics of English as an international language*. Routledge. doi:10.4324/9781315225593

Pereira, N. (2021). Finding talent among elementary English learners: A validity study of the hope teacher rating scale. *Gifted Child Quarterly, 65*(2), 153–166. doi:10.1177/0016986220985942

Pereira, N., & de Oliveira, L. C. (2015). Meeting the linguistic needs of high-potential English language learners: What teachers need to know. *Teaching Exceptional Children, 47*(4), 208–215. doi:10.1177/0040059915569362

Perry, B. D., & Slazavitz, M. (2018). Köpek Gibi Büyütülmüş Çocuk. (B.S. Haktanır, Trans.). Koridor Yayıncılık. [The Child Raised Like a Dog. (B.S. Haktanir, Trans.). Koridor Publishing].

Peterson, B. (2000). *Monarchs, missionaries and African intellectuals: African theatre and the unmaking of colonial marginality*. NYU Press.

Peters, S. J., & Engerrand, K. G. (2016). Equity and excellence: Proactive efforts in the identification of underrepresented students for gifted and talented services. *Gifted Child Quarterly, 60*(3), 159–171. doi:10.1177/0016986216643165

Peters, S. J., & Gentry, M. (2012). Group-specific norms and teacher-rating scales: Implications for underrepresentation. *Journal of Advanced Academics, 23*(2), 125–144. doi:10.1177/1932202X12438717

Phasha, N., Mahlo, D., & Dei, G. J. S. (Eds.). (2017). *Inclusive education in African contexts: A critical reader*. Springer. doi:10.1007/978-94-6300-803-7

Pianta, R. C. (1999). *Enhancing relationships between children and teachers*. American Psychological Association.

Pianta, R. C., & La Paro, K. (2003). Improving early school success. *Educational Leadership*, (April), 24–29.

Pianta, R. C., Stuhlman, M. W., & Hamre, B. K. (2002). How schools can do better: Fostering stronger connections between teachers and students. *New Directions for Youth Development*, *93*, 91–107.

Picower, B. (2012). Using their words: Six elements of social justice curriculum design for the elementary classroom. *International Journal of Multicultural Education*, *14*(1). https://go.gale.com/ps/i.do?p=AONE&sw=w&issn=19345267&v=2.1&it=r&id=GALE%7CA420198248&sid=googleScholar&linkaccess=abs. doi:10.18251/ijme.v14i1.484

Pinar, W. F. (1975). *Curriculum theorizing: The reconceptualists*. McCutchan Pub. Corp.

Pitts, D. (2005, March). Diversity, representation, and performance: Evidence about race and ethnicity in public organizations. *Journal of Public Administration: Research and Theory*, *15*(4), 615–631. doi:10.1093/jopart/mui033

Plessy v. Ferguson, 163 US 537 (1896)

Plucker, J. A., & Callahan, C. M. (2014). Research on giftedness and gifted education: Status of the field and considerations for the future. *Exceptional Children*, *80*(4), 390–406. doi:10.1177/0014402914527244

Polat, F. (2011). Inclusion in education: A step towards social justice. *International Journal of Educational Development*, *31*(1), 50–58. doi:10.1016/j.ijedudev.2010.06.009

Polat, S. (2020). Multicultural structure of schools and intercultural education. In *Empowering multiculturalism and peacebuilding in schools* (pp. 61–85). IGI Global.

Posti-Ahokas & Janhonen-Abruquah. (2021). Towards equity literacy: Exploratory enquiry with Finnish student teachers. *European Journal of Teacher Education*, ●●●, 1–19. doi:10.1080/02619768.2021.1952977

Pratt, S. (2008). Complex constructivism: Rethinking the power dynamics of "understanding.". *Journal of the Canadian Association for Curriculum Studies*, *6*(1), 113–132.

Price-Dennis, D., & Souto-Manning, M. (2011). (Re)Framing Diverse Pre-service Classrooms as Spaces for Culturally Relevant Teaching. *The Journal of Negro Education*, *80*(3), 223–238. Retrieved June 16, 2021, from https://www.jstor.org/stable/41341130

Pugach, M. C., Matewos, A. M., & Gomez-Najarro, A. (2021). Disability and the meaning of social justice in teacher education research: A precarious guest at the table? *Journal of Teacher Education*, *72*(2), 237–250. doi:10.1177/0022487120929623

Quadlin, N. (2018). The mark of a women's record: Gender and academic performance in hiring. *American Sociological Review*, *83*(2), 331–360. doi:10.1177/0003122418762291

Raftopoulos, B., & Mlambo, A. S. (2009). *The hard road to becoming national*. Department of History, University of the Western Cape.

Raines, T. C., Dever, B. V., Kamphaus, R. W., & Roach, A. T.Tara C. Raines; Bridget V. Dever; Randy W. Kamphaus; Andrew T. Roach. (2012). Universal screening for behavioral and emotional risk: A promising method for reducing disproportionate placement in special education. *The Journal of Negro Education*, *81*(3), 283. doi:10.7709/jnegroeducation.81.3.0283

Ramo, A. N., Karovska, R., Rashikj, A., & Canevska, O. (2020). Training and competencies of special educators in Turkey and other countries. *Turkish Studies -Education*, *15*(6), 4459-4473. doi:10.47423/TurkishStudies.4

Ratković, S., Kovačević, D., Brewer, C., Ellis, C., Ahmed, N., & Baptiste-Brady, J. (2017), *Supporting refugee students in Canada: Building on what we have learned in the past 20 Years.* https://torontolip.com/wp-content/uploads/2021/03/Supporting-Refugee-Students-in-Canada-Report.pdf

Raufelder, D., Neumann, N., Domin, M., Lorenz, R. C., Gleich, T., Golde, S., Romund, L., Beck, A., & Hoferichter, F. (2021). Do Belonging and Social Exclusion at School Affect Structural Brain Development During Adolescence? *Child Development*, *92*(6), 2213–2223. doi:10.1111/cdev.13613 PMID:34156088

Rausch, A., Joseph, J., & Steed, E. (2019, December 21). *DIS/ability critical race studies (DisCrit) for inclusion in early childhood education: Ethical considerations of implicit and explicit bias.* ZERO TO THREE. https://www.zerotothree.org/resource/dis-ability-critical-race-studies-discrit-for-inclusion-in-early-childhood-education-ethical-considerations-of-implicit-and-explicit-bias/

Ray, V. (2019). A theory of racialized organizations. *American Sociological Review*, *84*(1), 26–53. https://doi.org/10.1177/0003122418822335

Ready, D. D., & Wright, D. L. (2011). Accuracy and inaccuracy in teachers' perceptions of young children's cognitive abilities: The role of child background and classroom context. *American Educational Research Journal*, *48*(2), 335–360.

Redding, C. (2019). A Teacher Like Me: A Review of the Effect of Student–Teacher Racial/Ethnic Matching on Teacher Perceptions of Students and Student Academic and Behavioral Outcomes. *Review of Educational Research*, *89*(4), 499–535. https://doi.org/10.3102/0034654319853545

Redmond, G., Main, G., O'Donnell, A.W., Skattebol, J., Woodman, R., Mooney, A., Wang, J., Turkmanı, S., Thomson, C. & Brooks, F. (2022). Who excludes? Young People's Experience of Social Exclusion. *Jnl. Soc. Pol.*, 1–24. . doi:10.1017/S0047279422000046

Regional Equity Assistance Centers. (2017). *Equity Based Framework for Achieving Integrated Schooling: A Framework for School Districts and Communities for Designing Racially and Economically Integrated Schools.* IDRAEC. https://www.idraeacsouth.org/wp-content/uploads/2018/12/Equity-Based-Framework-for-Achieving-Integrated-Schooling-112718.pdf

Reimann, C. B. (2016). *District teacher hiring practices.* Michigan State University. https://www.proquest.com/docview/1868871917?pq-origsite=gscholar&fromopenview=true

Reis, S. M., & Peters, P. M. (2021). Research on the schoolwide enrichment model: Four decades of insights, innovation, and evolution. *Gifted Education International*, *37*(2), 109–141. doi:10.1177/0261429420963987

Renzulli, J. S. (1986). The three-ring conception of giftedness: A development model for creative productivity. In R. J. Sternberg and J. Davidson (Eds) Conceptions of Giftedness (pp.332–357). Cambridge University Press.

Renzulli, J. S. (1978). What makes giftedness? Reexamining a definition. *Phi Delta Kappan*, *60*(3), 180–261.

Renzulli, J. S., & Reis, S. M. (2012). A virtual learning application of the schoolwide enrichment model and high-end learning theory. *Gifted Education International*, *28*(1), 1. doi:10.1177/0261429411424382

Resta, P., & Laferrière, T. (2007). Technology in support of collaborative learning. *Educational Psychology Review*, *19*(1), 65–83. doi:10.100710648-007-9042-7

Riasati, M. J., & Mollaei, F. (2012). Critical pedagogy and language learning. *International Journal of Humanities and Social Science*, *2*(21).

Rigby, J. G. (2014). Three logics of instructional leadership. *Educational Administration Quarterly*, *50*(4), 610–644. doi:10.1177/0013161X13509379

Rivkin, S., Hanushek, E., & Kain, J. (2005). Teachers, schools, and academic achievement. *Econometrica*, *73*(2), 417–458. doi:10.1111/j.1468-0262.2005.00584.x

Robson, K., Anisef, P., Brown, R. S., & George, R. (2018). Underrepresented students and the transition to post-secondary education: Comparing two Toronto cohorts. *Canadian Journal of Higher Education*, *48*(1), 39–59. https://doi.org/10.47678/cjhe.v48i1.187972

Roche, S. (2016). Education for all: Exploring the principle and process of inclusive education. *International Review of Education*, *62*(2), 131–137. doi:10.100711159-016-9556-7

Rodgers, B. L., & Knafl, K. A. (2000). *Concept development in nursing. Foundation, techniques and applications* (2nd ed.). Saunders.

Rodgers, W. J., Weiss, M. P., & Ismail, H. A. (2021). Defining specially designed instruction: A systematic literature review. *Learning Disabilities Research & Practice*, *36*(2), 96–109. doi:10.1111/ldrp.12247

Rogoff, B. (2011). Developing destinies: a Mayan midwife and town. Oxford University Press. Retrieved November 2, 2022, from, https://doi.org/10.1093/acprof:oso/9780195319903.001.0001.

Rojas, L., & Liou, D. D. (2017). Social justice teaching through the sympathetic touch of caring and high expectations for students of color. *Journal of Teacher Education*, *68*(1), 28–41. doi:10.1177/0022487116676314

Rosenholtz, S. J. (1989). *Teachers' workplace: The social organization of schools*. Longman.

Rosenthal, J. O. (1957). Negro teachers' attitude toward desegregation. *The Journal of Negro Education*, *26*(1), 63–71. doi:10.2307/2293328

Ross, A. S., & Rivers, D. J. (2018). *The sociolinguistics of hip-hop as critical conscience: Dissatisfaction and dissent*. doi:10.1007/978-3-319-59244-2

Rothenbusch, S., Voss, T., Golle, J., & Zettler, I. (2018). Linking teacher and parent ratings of teacher-nominated gifted elementary school students to each other and to school grades. *Gifted Child Quarterly*, *62*(2), 230–250. doi:10.1177/0016986217752100

RSA (Republic of South Africa). (1996). *The Constitution, Act No. 108 of 1996*. Government Printer.

Rucinski, C. L., Brown, J. L., & Downer, J. T. (2018). Teacher–child relationships, classroom climate, and children's social-emotional and academic development. *Journal of Educational Psychology*, *110*(7), 992–1004. https://dx.doi.org/10.1037/edu0000240

Rueda, E. (2015). The benefits of being Latino: Differential interpretations of student behavior and the social construction of being well behaved. *Journal of Latinos & Education*, *14*(4), 275–290. doi:10.1080/15348431.2015.1025955

Russell, H. K. (2012). *The state of Southern Illinois: An illustrated history*. Southern Illinois University Press.

Ryan, G. W., & Bernard, H. R. (2000). Data management and analysis methods. In N. Denzin & Y. Lincoln (Eds.), Handbook of qualitative research (pp. 769–802). Sage.

Ryan, G. W., & Bernard, H. R. (2003). Techniques to identify themes. *Field Methods*, *15*, 85–109.

Ryan, J. (2006). Inclusive leadership and social justice for schools. *Leadership and Policy in Schools, 5*(1), 3–17. doi:10.1080/15700760500483995

Ryan, J., Pollock, K., & Antonelli, F. (2009). Teacher diversity in Canada: Leaky pipelines, bottlenecks, and glass ceilings. *Canadian Journal of Education, 32*(3), 591–617.

Sabnis, S., Castillo, J. M., & Wolgemuth, J. R. (2020). RTI, equity, and the return to the status quo: Implications for consultants. *Journal of Educational & Psychological Consultation, 30*(3), 285–313. doi:10.1080/10474412.2019.1674152

Sadioglu, O., Bilgin, A., Batu, S., & Oksal, A. (2013). Problems, expectations, and suggestions of elementary teachers regarding inclusion. *Educational Sciences: Theory and Practice, 13*(3), 1760–1765.

Sahin Asi, D. (2019). How Banking Time intervention works in Turkish preschool classrooms for enhancing student–teacher relationships. *ICEP, 13*(3). doi:10.1186/s40723-019-0059-4

Şahin, T. (2009). *Sosyal Dışlanma ve Yoksulluk İlişkisi.* [Yayınlanmamış sosyal yardım uzmanlık tezi. T.C.Başbakanlık Sosyal Yardımlaşma Ve Dayanışma Genel Müdürlüğü, Türkiye]. (*Relationship between Social Exclusion and Poverty.* [Unpublished social assistance dissertation, T.R. Prime Ministry General Directorate of Social Assistance and Solidarity, Turkey].].

Sakiz, H. (2016). Thinking change inclusively: Views of educational administrators on inclusive education as a reform initiative. *Journal of Education and Training Studies, 4*(5), 64–75.

Sakiz, H., & Woods, C. (2014). From thinking to practice: School staff views on disability inclusion in Turkey. *European Journal of Special Needs Education, 29*(2), 135–152. https://doi.org/10.1080/08856257.2014.882058

Sakiz, H., & Woods, C. (2015). Achieving inclusion of students with disabilities in Turkey: Current challenges and future prospects. *International Journal of Inclusive Education, 19*(1), 21–35. https://doi.org/10.1080/13603116.2014.902122

SAMHSA. (2022, April 22). *Understanding child trauma.* SAMHSA - Substance Abuse and Mental Health Services Administration. https://www.samhsa.gov/child-trauma/understanding-child-trauma

Samier, E. A. (2020). Missing non-western voices on social justice for education: A postcolonial perspective on traditions of humanistic marginalized communities. *Handbook on promoting social justice in education*, 105-126.

Samkange, W. (2013). Inclusive education at primary school: A case study of one primary school in Glen View/Mufakose education district in Harare, Zimbabwe. *International Journal of Social Sciences & Education, 3*(4), 953–963.

Santrock, J. W. (2015). İlk Çocuklukta Sosyoduygusal Gelişim. (A. Aslan, Trans.). Ergenlikte Sosyoduygusal Gelişim. (G. Yüksel, Trans). G. Yüksel (Trans Ed.). Yaşam Boyu Gelişim içinde (pp. 241-247; 382-396). Nobel Yayıncılık. [Socioemotional Development in Early Childhood. (A. Aslan, Trans.). Socioemotional Development in Adolescence. (G. Yuksel, Trans). G. Yuksel (Trans Ed.). In Lifetime Development (pp. 241-247; 382-396). Nobel Publishing].

Santrock, J. W. (2021). Sosyal duygusal Gelişim. A. Güre (Trans Ed.). (D.S. Atalar & Z. Çakmak, Trans). Çocuk Gelişimi içinde(pp. 278-383) Nobel Yayıncılık. [Social Emotional Development. A. Gure (Trans Ed.). (D.S. Atalar & Z. Cakmak, Trans). In Child Development. (pp. 278-383) Nobel Publishing].

Sarangapani, P. M. (2020). Chapter written for the section titled 'Teachers, Teaching and Teacher Education' Section, Padma M. Sarangapani and Yusuf Sayed in 'Handbook of Education Systems in South Asia'. Springer Major Reference Work, pp. 1-19

Sari, T., Nayir, F., & Kahraman, U. (2020). A Study on inclusive education. *Journal of Education and Future Year, 18,* 69-82.

Saskatchewan Ministry of Education. (2017, May). *Supporting reconciliation in Saskatchewan schools.* Government of Saskatchewan. https://www.edonline.sk.ca/webapps/blackboard/content/listContent.jsp?course_id=_3514_1&content_id=_129667_1&mode=reset

Saskatchewan Ministry of Education. (2022, March 9). *$140,000 in provincial funding help Saskatchewan schools support for Truth And Reconciliation.* Government of Saskatchewan. https://www.saskatchewan.ca/government/news-and-media/2022/march/09/140000-in-provincial-funding-help-saskatchewan-schools-support-truth-and-reconciliation

Saskatchewan Teachers' Federation. (2022). *Residential schools and reconciliation.* https://www.stf.sk.ca/professional-resources/emma-stewart-resources-centre/resources/related-links/residential-schools-and

Saunders, W. M., & Goldenberg, C. (2007). The effects of an instructional conversation on English language learners' concepts of friendship and story comprehension. In R. Horowitz (Ed.), *Talking texts: How speech and writing interact in school learning* (pp. 221–252). Erlbaum.

Sawchuk, P. (2010). Equity in organizations: Issues of gender, race, disability and class. In J. Bratton (Ed.), *Work and organizational behavior* (2nd ed., pp. 276–293). Palgrave Mcmillan.

Sawyer, R., & Norris, J. (2015). Duoethnography: A retrospective 10 years after. *International Review of Qualitative Research*, *8*(1), 1–4. https://doi-org.myaccess.library.utoronto.ca/10.1525/irqr.2015.8.1.1. doi:10.1525/irqr.2015.8.1.1

Scarface. (2017). Black still [Song]. On *Deeply Rooted: The Lost Files* [Album].

Schmidt, C. (2015). Herculean efforts are not enough: Diversifying the teaching profession and the need for systemic change. *Intercultural Education*, *26*(6), 584–592. doi:10.1080/14675986.2015.1109776

Schoemaker, N. K., Wentholt, W. G. M., Goemans, A., Vermeer, H. J., Juffer, F., & Alink, L. R. A. (2020). A meta-analytic review of parenting interventions in foster care and adoption. *Development and Psychopathology*, *32*(3), 1149–1172. doi:10.1017/S0954579419000798 PMID:31366418

Schuelka, M. J., & Engsig, T. T. (2020). On the question of educational purpose: Complex educational systems analysis for inclusion. *International Journal of Inclusive Education*, 1–18. https://doi.o doi:rg/10.1080/13603116.2019.1698062

Schugurensky, D. (2010). The heteronymous university and the question of social justice: In search of a new social contract. In J. Zajda (Ed.), *Globalization, education, and social justice.* Springer. doi:10.1007/978-90-481-3221-8_4

Schutte, V., Milley, P., & Dulude, E. (2022). The (in)coherence of Canadian refugee education policy with the United Nations'. *Education Policy Analysis Archives*, *30*(39–41), 1–59. doi:10.14507/epaa.30.6887

Scott, T. M., Gage, N. A., Hirn, R. G., Lingo, A. S., & Burt, J. L. (2019). An examination of the association between MTSS implementation fidelity measures and student outcomes. *Preventing School Failure*, *63*(4), 308–316. doi:10.1080/1045988X.2019.1605971

Scribner, S., & Cole, M. (1981). *The psychology of literacy.* Harvard University Press. doi:10.4159/harvard.9780674433014

Seidel, J., & Rokne, A. (2011). Picture books for engaging peace and social justice with children. *Diaspora, Indigenous, and Minority Education*, *5*(4), 245–259. doi:10.1080/15595692.2011.606007

Sen, A. (2011). *The idea of justice.* Harvard University Press.

Sensoy, Ö., & DiAngelo, R. (2017). "We are all for diversity, but...": How faculty hiring committees reproduce whiteness and practical suggestions for how they can change. *Harvard Educational Review*, *87*(4), 557–580. doi:10.17763/1943-5045-87.4.557

Shah, N., & Coles, J. A. (2020). Preparing teachers to notice race in classrooms: Contextualizing the competencies of preservice teachers with antiracist inclinations. *Journal of Teacher Education*, *71*(5), 584–599. https://doi.org/10.1177/0022487119900204

Shah, S. (2007). Special or mainstream: The views of disabled students. *Research Papers in Education*, *22*(4), 425–442. doi:10.1080/02671520701651128

Shim, J. M. (2017). Play of the unconscious in pre-service teachers' self-reflection around race and racism. *Journal of Curriculum Studies*, *49*(6), 830–847. https://doi.org/10.1080/00220272.2017.1320429

Shizha, E. (2007). Critical analysis of problems encountered in incorporating indigenous knowledge in science teaching by primary school teachers in Zimbabwe. *The Alberta Journal of Educational Research*, *53*(3), 302–319.

Shizha, E., & Kariwo, M. T. (2012). *Education and development in Zimbabwe: A social, political and economic analysis.* Sense Publishers.

Shor, R., & Bernhard, J. K. (2003). A comparative study of conflicts experienced between immigrant parents in Canada and in Israel, and professionals in educational institutions about appropriate responses to children's misbehavior. *Intercultural Education*, *14*(4), 385–396.

Shyman, E. (2012). Differentiated instruction as a pedagogy of liberation. *The International Journal of Critical Pedagogy*, *4*(1), 65–75.

Simpson, J. (2009). *Everyone belongs: A toolkit for applying intersectionality.* Canadian Research Institute for the Advancement of Women (CRIAW). https://also-chicago.org/also_site/wp-content/uploads/2017/03/Everyone_Belongs-A-toolkit-for-applying-intersectionality.pdf

Sinclair, M. (2014). Education: Cause and solution. *Manitoba Teacher*, *93*(3), 6–10. http://www.mbteach.org/pdfs/mbt/2014/Dec14_MBT.pdf

Singh, R. (2009). Meeting the challenge of inclusion—from isolation to collaboration. *Inclusive education across cultures: Crossing boundaries, sharing ideas,* 12-29.

Singhal, P. (2018, January 9). Open up selective schools for more 'inclusive' education, says Rob Stokes. *The Sydney Morning Herald.* https://www.smh.com.au/education/open-up-selective-schools-for-more-inclusive-education-says-rob-stokes-20180109-h0fk94.html#:~:text=Education%20Minister%20Rob%20Stokes%20says%20opening%20up%20selective,not%20%22create%20a%20rigid%2C%20separated%20public%20education%20system%22

Siziba, K., & Kaputa, T. M. (2022). Management of learners with conduct disorders in Nkayi rural district primary schools in Zimbabwe. *Journal of Research in Social Science and Humanities*, *3*(1), 19–24. doi:10.47679/jrssh.v3i1.38

Slee, R. (2001). Inclusion in practice: Does practice make perfect? *Educational Review*, *53*(2), 113–123. doi:10.1080/00131910120055543

Slee, R. (2001). Social justice and the changing directions in educational research: The case of inclusive education. *International Journal of Inclusive Education*, *5*(2–3), 167–177. doi:10.1080/13603110010035832

Slee, R. (2018). *Inclusive education isn't dead, it just smells funny.* Routledge. doi:10.4324/9780429486869

Sleeter, C. E. (2011). An agenda to strengthen culturally responsive teaching. *English Teaching, 10*(2), 7–23. https://education.waikato.ac.nz/research/files/etpc/files/2011v10n2art1.pdf

Sleeter, C. E. (2014). Deepening social justice teaching. *Journal of Language & Literacy Education, 42*(6), 512–535.

Sleeter, C. E. (2017). Critical race theory and the whiteness of teacher education. *Urban Education, 52*(2), 155–159. doi:10.1177/0042085916668957

Sleeter, C. E., & Grant, C. A. (2007). *Making choices for multicultural education: five approaches to race, class, and gender* (5th ed.). John Wiley & Sons.

Smagorinsky, P., Tobin, J., & Lee, K. (2019). Introduction. In P. Smagorinsky, J. Tobin, & K. Lee (Eds.), *Disability studies in education* (pp. 1–22). Peter Lang.

Smith, D. G. (1999). Globalization and education: Prospects for postcolonial pedagogy in a hermeneutic mode. *Interchange, 30*(1), 1–10.

Solórzano, D., & Bernal, D. (2001). Examining transformational resistance through a critical race and LatCrit framework: Chicana and Chicano students in an urban context. *Urban Education, 36*(3), 308–342.

Soriano, L. (2021). DepEd to teachers; be neutral in politics. *The Post.* Retrieved from https://thepost.net.ph/news/nation/deped-to-teachers-be-neutral-in-politics/

Sorkos, G., & Hajisoteriou, C. (2020). Sustainable intercultural and inclusive education: Teachers' efforts on promoting a combining paradigm. *Pedagogy, Culture & Society, 29*(4), 1–20. https://doi.org/10.1080/14681366.2020.1765193

Souto-Manning, M., & Mitchell, C. H. (2010). The Role of Action Research in Fostering Culturally Responsive Practices in a Preschool Classroom. *Early Childhood Education Journal, 37*, 269. https://doi.org/10.1007/s10643-009-0345-9

Sparkman, D. J., & Hamer, K. (2020). Seeing the human in everyone: Multicultural experiences predict more positive intergroup attitudes and humanitarian helping through identification with all humanity. *International Journal of Intercultural Relations, 79*, 121–134. doi:10.1016/j.ijintrel.2020.08.007

Spitz, R. A. (1951). The Psychogenic Diseases in Infancy. *The Psychoanalytic Study of the Child, 6*(1), 255–275. doi:10.1080/00797308.1952.11822915

Spolsky, B., & Shohamy, E. (2000). Language practice, language ideology, and language policy. *Language policy and pedagogy: Essays in honour of A. Ronald Walton*, 1–41.

St. Denis, V. (2011). Silencing Aboriginal curricular content and perspectives through multiculturalism: "There are other children here. *Review of Education, Pedagogy & Cultural Studies, 33*(4), 306–317.

Stanford, P., Crowe, M. W., & Flice, H. (2010). Differentiating with technology. *Teaching Exceptional Children Plus, 6*(4), 1–9.

Stangvik, G. (2010). Special education in society and culture: Comparative and developmental perspectives. *European Journal of Special Needs Education, 25*, 349-358. .2010.513539 doi:10.1080/08856257

Sternberg, R. J. (1999). Rising tides and racing torpedoes: Triumphs and tribulations of the adult gifted as illustrated by the career of Joseph Renzulli. *Journal for the Education of the Gifted, 23*(1), 67–74. doi:10.1177/016235329902300104

Stewart, J. (2017). A culture of care and compassion for refugee students. *Ed-Can Network*. https://www.edcan.ca/articles/a-culture-of-care-and-compassion-for-refugee-students/

Stewart, J., & Martin, L. (2018), *Bridging two worlds: Supporting newcomer and refugee youth. A guide to curriculum implementation and integration.* Toronto: CERIC. Canadian Education and Research Institute for Counselling (CERIC). https://ceric.ca/resource/bridging-two-worlds-supporting-newcomer-refugee-youth/

Stewart, J. (2011). *Supporting refugee children: Strategies for educators.* University of Toronto Press.

Sturgis, C., & Jones, A. (2017). In pursuit of equality: A framework for equity strategies in competency-based education. Vienna, VA: International Association for K–12 Online Learning United Nations. (2008). Convention on the rights of persons with disabilities. New York: UN.

Su, Y. L. (2005). *Understanding Teachers' Experiences Working with Young Children from Diverse Cultural and Linguistic Backgrounds* [Unpublished doctoral dissertation]. Virginia Polytechnic Institute and State University.

Substance Abuse and Mental Health Services Administration. (2014). *SAMHSA's concept of trauma and guidance for a trauma-informed approach.* (HHS Publication No. 14-4884). https://ncsacw.acf.hhs.gov/userfiles/files/SAMHSA_Trauma.pdf

Sullivan, A., Weeks, M., Kulkarni, T., & Goerdt, A. (2018). *Preventing disproportionality through nondiscriminatory tiered Services.* Great Lakes Equity. https://greatlakesequity.org/sites/default/files/20182706619_brief.pdf

Sullivan, A. L. (2011). Disproportionality in special education identification and placement of English language learners. *Exceptional Children, 77*(3), 317–334. doi:10.1177/001440291107700304

Sullivan, A. L., Miller, F. G., McKevett, N. M., Muldrew, A., Hansen-Burke, A., & Weeks, M. (2020). Leveraging MTSS to Advance, Not Suppress, COVID-Related Equity Issues. *Communique, 49*(1), 1–26.

Sullivan, A. L., & Proctor, S. (2016). The shield or the sword? Revisiting the debate on racial disproportionality in special education and implications for school psychologists. *School Psychology Forum, 10*(3), 278–288.

Suyatno, S., & Wantini, W. (2018). Humanizing the classroom: Praxis of full day school system in Indonesia. *International Education Studies, 11*(4), 115–125. doi:10.5539/ies.v11n4p115

Suzuki, T., Huss, J., Fiehn, B., & Spencer, R. M. (2015). Realities of war: Using picture books to teach the social effects of armed conflicts. *Multicultural Education, 22*, 54–58.

Szymanski, A., & Lynch, M. (2020). Educator perceptions of English language learners. *Journal of Advanced Academics, 31*(4), 436–450. doi:10.1177/1932202X20917141

Taie, S., & Goldring, R. (2020). *Characteristics of Public and Private Elementary and Secondary School Teachers in the United States: Results from the 2017-18 National Teacher and Principal Survey. First Look.* NCES 2020-142. National Center for Education Statistics. https://eric.ed.gov/?id=ED604223

Tana Charity Village. (2014, May 21). *Bias-free hiring: Interview questions not to ask.* https://charityvillage.com/bias_free_hiring_interview_questions_not_to_ask/

Tarnoto, N. (2016). Permasalahan-permasalahan yang dihadapi sekolah penyelenggara pendidikan inklusi pada tingkat SD. *Humanitas. Jurnal Psikologi Indonesia, 13*(1), 50–61.

Taylor, S. J., Bogdan, R., & Walker, P. (2000). Qualitative research. In A. E. Kazdin (Ed.), *Encyclopedia of psychology* (Vol. 6, pp. 489–491). American Psychological Association and Oxford University Press.

Tchatchoueng, J. (2014). Inclusive education in the classroom: Practical applications. In Schooling, society and inclusive education: An Afrocentric perspective (pp. 195-217). Oxford University Press.

Tekinarslan, I. C., Sivrikaya, T., Keskin, N. K., Ozlu, O., & Ucar Rasmussen, M. (2018). Determining the needs of parents with children in inclusive education. *Elementary Education Online, 17*(1), 82–101.

Terzi, L. (2008). Justice and equality in education: A capability perspective on disability and special educational needs. *Continuum*.

Terzi, L. (2014). Reframing inclusive education: Educational equality as capability equality. *Cambridge Journal of Education, 44*(4), 479–493.

The Education of Students with Refugee Backgrounds. (n.d). https://sites.google.com/view/educationofrefugees/home

The Refugee Experience. (n.d.) https://sites.google.com/view/educationofrefugees/refugee-experience

The Student Christian Movement of Zimbabwe. (2013). *Poor O-level results: A manifestation of a neglected generation.* http://kubatana.net

Theodore, S., Cummings, C., Silva, M. S., Flores, H., Urquiza, N., & Cramer, E. D. (2022). The healer: A model for culturally responsive trauma-informed practices in urban schools. In Hunter, W., Taylor, J., Scott, L., The mixtape volume 1: Culturally sustaining practices within MTSS featuring the everlasting mission of student engagement. Council for Exceptional Children.

Theoharis, G. T. (2007). Social justice educational leaders and resistance: Toward a theory of social justice leadership. *Educational Administration Quarterly, 43*(2), 221–258. doi:10.1177/0013161X06293717

Thijs, J., Westhof, S., & Koomen, H. (2012). Ethnic incongruence and the student–teacher relationship: The perspective of ethnic majority teachers. *Journal of School Psychology, 50*, 257–273.

Thurlow, M. L., Ghere, G., Lazarus, S. S., & Liu, K. K. (2020). *MTSS for all: Including students with the most significant cognitive disabilities.* National Center on Educational Outcomes/TIES Center. https://nceo.umn.edu/docs/OnlinePubs/NCEOBriefMTSS.pdf

Timucin, E. (1998). *Inclusion in Turkey, existing practices and what needs to be done to achieve inclusion* [Paper presentation]. *8th National Special Education Congress*, Edirne, Turkey.

Toldson, I. A., & Lemmons, B. P. (2013). Social demographics, the school environment, and parenting practices associated with parents' participation in schools and academic success among Black, Hispanic, and White students. *Journal of Human Behavior in the Social Environment, 23*(2), 237–255.

Tomasevski, K. (2004). *Manual on rights-based education: Global human rights requirements made simple.* UNESCO Bangkok. https://unesdoc.unesco.org/ark:/48223/pf0000135168

Tony Blaire Institute for Global Change. (2017). *Difficult dialogue in the classroom.* Available at https://institute.global/sites/default/files/inline-files/Difficult-Dialogue.pdf

Toohey, K. (2017). Tangled up with everything else: Toward new conceptions of language, teachers, and identities. In G. Barhuizen (Ed.), Reflections on Language Teacher Identity Research. Routledge/Taylor & Francis Group.

Toronto District School Board. (2017). *Enhancing equity task force.* https://www.tdsb.on.ca/Portals/0/community/docs/EETFReportPdfVersion.pdf

Toronto District School Board. (2021, May 31). *Tragic discover in British Columbia.* https://www.tdsb.on.ca/News/Article-Details/ArtMID/474/ArticleID/1653/Statement-Re-Tragic-Discovery-in-British-Columbia

Toronto District School Board. (2022a). *Equity, anti-racism and anti-oppression.* https://www.tdsb.on.ca/About-Us/Equity-Anti-Racism-and-Anti-Oppression

Toronto District School Board. (2022b). *Resources for Indigenous resources.* https://www.tdsb.on.ca/Community/Indigenous-Education/Resources

Torres-Harding, S., Baber, A., Hilvers, J., Hobbs, N., & Maly, M. (2018). Children as agents of social and community change: Enhancing youth empowerment through participation in a school-based social activism project. *Education, Citizenship and Social Justice, 13*(1), 3–18. doi:10.1177/1746197916684643

Towle, H. (2015). *Disability and inclusion in Canadian education.* desLibris.

Trenerry, B., & Paradies, Y. (2012). Organizational assessment: An overlooked approach to managing diversity and addressing racism in the workplace. *Journal of Diversity Management, 7*(1), 11–26.

Tropp, L. R., O'Brien, T. C., Gutierrez, R. G., Valdenegro, D., Migacheva, K., de Tezanos-Pinto, P., Berger, C., & Cayul, O. (2016). How School Norms, Peer Norms, and Discrimination Predict Interethnic Experiences Among Ethnic Minority and Majority Youth. *Child Development, 87*(5), 1436–1451. doi:10.1111/cdev.12608 PMID:27684397

Truth and Reconciliations Commission of Canada. (2015). *Truth and reconciliation commission of Canada: Calls to action.* https://www.trc.ca/websites/trcinstitution/File/2015/Findings/Calls_to_Action_English2.pdf

Turkish Ministry of Family and Social Services. (2022). *Services for Children.* AILE. https://www.aile.gov.tr/media/108736/kurumsal-istatistikler.pdf

Turnbull, A. P., & Turnbull, H. R. (1990). *Families, professionals, and exceptionality: A special partnership* (2nd ed.). Charles E. Merrill.

U. S. Census Bureau. (2021). *QuickFacts.* https://www.census.gov/quickfacts/fact/table/US/PST045221

Ugurlu, H. E. (2017). *Inclusion of students with learning and behavior problems: knowledge, attitudes, and inclusive practices in Turkey* [Unpublished master's thesis]. University of Massachusetts, Amherst, MA.

UK Department of Education. (2018). Children in Need of Help and Protection. *Assets.* https://assets.publishing.service.gov.uk/government/uploads/system/uploads/attachment_data/file/690999/Children_in_Need_of_help_and_protection_Data_and_analysis.pdf

Unal, R., & Aladag, S. (2020). Investigation of problems and solution proposals in the context of inclusive education practices. *Journal of Interdisciplinary Education: Theory and Practice, 2*(1), 23–42.

UNESCO. (1994). *The Salamanca Statement and Framework for Action on Special Needs Education.* Adopted by the World Conference on Special Needs Education; Access and Quality, Salamanca, Spain, 7–10 June 1994. UNESCO.

UNESCO. (1994). *The Salamanca Statement and Framework for Action on Special Needs Education*. Retrieved from http://www.unesco.org/education/pdf/SALAMA_E.PDF

UNESCO. (2009). *Policy Guidelines on Inclusion in Education*. Retrieved from http://www.inclusive-education-in-ction.org/iea/dokumente/up load/72074_177849e.pdf

UNESCO. (2011). *UNESCO and Education*. Retrieved from https://unesdoc.unesco.org/images/0021/002127/212715e.pdf

UNESCO. (2012). *Addressing exclusion in education: a guide to assessing education systems towards more inclusive and just societies*. UNESCO.

UNESCO. (2014). *Education for All Global Monitoring Report 2013/4: Teaching and Learning: Achieving Quality for All*. UNESCO.

UNESCO. (2015). *Education for All 2000-2015: achievements and challenges*. UNESCO.

UNESCO. (2016). *Global education monitoring report*. UNESCO.

UNESCO. (2017). *A guide for ensuring inclusion and equity in education*. UNESCO.

UNESCO. (2018). *Handbook on Measuring Equity in Education*. UNESCO Institute for Statistics.

UNESCO. (2020). *Towards inclusion in education: Status, trends and challenges. UNESCO Salamanca Statement 25 years on*. UNESCO.

Unicef (2022). *Convention on the Rights of the Child*. UNICEF. https://www.unicef.org/turkiye/%C3%A7ocuk-haklar%C4%B1na-dair-s%C3%B6zle%C5%9Fme

UNICEF. (2019). *Syrian children in Turkey*. Retrieved from https://www.unicefturk.org/yazi/acil-durum-turkiyedeki-suriy eli-cocuklar

United Nations Girls' Education Initiative (UNGEI) (2010). *Equity and Inclusion in education: A guide to support education sector plan preparation, revision and appraisal*. New York: UN

University of Ontario Institute of Technology. (2022). *Indigenous K-12 teacher resources*. https://guides.library.ontariotechu.ca/indigenous_k-12/textb ooks-curriculum

US Department of Health and Human Services & US Department of Education. (2015). Policy statement on inclusion of children with disabilities in early childhood programs. USDE. https://www2.ed.gov/policy/speced/guid/earlylearning/joint-statement-full-text.pdf

Uygur, M., Aycicek, B., Dogrul, H., & Yanpar Yelken, T. (2020). Investigating stakeholders' views on technology integration: The role of educational leadership for sustainable inclusive education. *Sustaniablity, 12*, 10354. doi:10.3390/su122410354

Van den Bergh, L., Denessen, E., Hornstra, L., Voeten, M., & Holland, R. W. (2010). The implicit prejudiced attitudes of teachers: Relations to teacher expectations and the ethnic achievement gap. *American Educational Research Journal, 47*(2), 497–527.

van der Galien, M. (2006). *Conservatives and education*. The Moderate Voice. Retrieved from https://themoderatevoice.com/conservatives-and-education/

Van Norman, E. R., Nelson, P. M., & Klingbeil, D. A. (2017). Single measure and gated screening approaches for identifying students at-risk for academic problems: Implications for sensitivity and specificity. *School Psychology Quarterly, 32*(3), 405–413. doi:10.1037pq0000177 PMID:27684539

Vanclay, F. (2020). Reflections on social impact assessment in the 21st century. *Impact Assessment and Project Appraisal, 38*(2), 126–131. doi:10.1080/14615517.2019.1685807

VanTassel-Baska, J. (2021). Curriculum in gifted education: The core of the enterprise. *Gifted Child Today, 44*(1), 44–47. doi:10.1177/1076217520940747

Vaughn, S. (2015). Building on past successes: Designing, evaluating, and providing effective treatment for persons for whom typical instruction is not effective. *Remedial and Special Education, 36*(1), 5–8. doi:10.1177/0741932514543928 PMID:25745278

Vaught, S. E., & Castagno, A. E. (2008). "I don't think I'm a racist:" Critical Race Theory, teacher attitudes, and structural racism. *Race, Ethnicity and Education, 11*(2), 95–113. https://doi.org/10.1080/13613320802110217

Verschueren, K., & Koomen, H. M. Y. (2012). Teacher–child relationships from an attachment perspective. *Attachment & Human Development, 14*(3), 205–211.

Vervaet, R., D'hondt, F., Van Houtte, M., & Stevens, P. A. J. (2016). The ethnic prejudice of Flemish teachers: The role of ethnic school composition and of teachability. *Cultural Diversity & Ethnic Minority Psychology, 22*(4), 552–562. https://doi.org/10.1037/cdp0000085

Villa, R. A., Thousand, J. S., & Chapple, J. W. (2000). Preparing educators to implement inclusive practices. In R. A. Villa & J. S. Thousand (Eds.), *Restructuring for caring and effective education: Piecing the puzzle together* (2nd ed., pp. 531–557). Paul H. Brookes.

Vural, D., Piskin, N. B., & Durmusoglu, M. C. (2021). Problems and practices experienced by preschool teachers in inclusive education. *International Journal of Curriculum and Instructional Studies, 11*(2), 287–308. https://doi.org/10.31704/ijocis.2021.014

Wade, R. C. (2007). Service-learning for social justice in the elementary classroom: Can we get there from here? *Equity & Excellence in Education, 40*(2), 156–165. doi:10.1080/10665680701221313

Waldock, T. (2019). Marginalized Children and Discrimination: A Focus on Child Welfare, Race, and Culture. *Carleton University.* https://ojs.library.carleton.ca/index.php/pcran/article/view/2371

Walker, J., & Zuberi, D. (2020). School-aged Syrian refugees resettling in Canada: Mitigating the effect of pre-migration trauma and post-migration discrimination on academic achievement and psychological well-being. *Journal of International Migration and Integration, 21*(2), 397–411. doi:10.100712134-019-00665-0

Walton, E., & Engelbrecht, P. (2022). Inclusive education in South Africa: Path dependencies and emergences. *International Journal of Inclusive Education,* 1–19. doi:10.1080/13603116.2022.2061608

Walton, E., & Lloyd, G. (2011). An analysis of metaphors used for inclusive education in South Africa. *Acta Academica, 43*(3), 1–31.

Ward, T., & Stewart, C. (2008). Putting human rights into practice with people with an intellectual disability. *Journal of Developmental and Physical Disabilities, 20*(3), 297–311. doi:10.100710882-008-9098-4

Warne, R. T. (2009). Comparing tests used to identify ethnically diverse gifted children: A critical response to Lewis, Decamp-Fritson, Ramage, McFarland, & Archwamety. *Multicultural Education, 17*(1), 48–48.

Wellman, D. (1993). Portraits of white racism (2nd ed.). Cambridge University Press. https://doi.org/doi:10.1017/CBO9780511625480.

Wells, A. S., Fox, L., & Cordova-Cobo, D. (2016). How racially diverse schools and classrooms can benefit all students. *Education Digest, 82*(1), 17.

Wenger-Trayner, E., & Wenger-Trayner, B. (2014). Learning in a landscape of practice: A framework. In E. Wenger-Trayner, M. Fenton-O'Creevy, S. Hutchinson, C. Kubiak, & B. Wenger-Trayner (Eds.), *Learning in landscapes of practice: Boundaries, identity, and knowledgeability in practice-based learning* (pp. 13–30). Routledge. doi:10.4324/9781315777122-3

Werner, N. E., & Hill, L. G. (2010). Individual and Peer Group Normative Beliefs About Relational Aggression. *Child Development, 81*(3), 826–836. doi:10.1111/j.1467-8624.2010.01436.x PMID:20573107

Westwood, P. (2013). *Inclusive and adaptive teaching: meeting the challenge of diversity in the classroom.* Routledge.

Wiggin, L. P. (2017). Demography in America: Gifted education for a growing population of English language learners. *Indiana Journal of Law and Social Equality, 5*(2), 1–13.

Williams, K. L., Russell, A., & Summerville, K. (2021). Centering blackness: An examination of culturally-affirming pedagogy and practices enacted by HBCU administrators and faculty members. *Innovative Higher Education, 46*(6), 733–757. doi:10.100710755-021-09562-w

Williford, A. P., & Pianta, R. C. (2020). Banking Time: A Dyadic Intervention to Improve Teacher-Student Relationships. In A. Reschly, A. Pohl, & S. Christenson (Eds.), Student Engagement. Springer. https://doi.org/10.1007/978-3-030-37285-9_13.

Willis, A. S. (2021). Teachers' cultural, social and emotional capabilities: How teacher compassion and humility is an antecedent to student confidence. *Pedagogy, Culture & Society.* Advance online publication. doi:10.1080/14681366.2021.1884122

Wise, A. E., Darling-Hammond, L., & Berry, B. (1987). *Effective teacher selection: From recruitment to retention* (R-3462-NIE/CSTP) [Report]. The RAND Corporation. https://www.rand.org/pubs/reports/R3462.html

Woodgate, R., & Busolo, D. S. (2021). African refugee youth's experiences of navigating different cultures in Canada: A "push and pull" experience. *International Journal of Environmental Research and Public Health, 18*(4), 2063. doi:10.3390/ijerph18042063 PMID:33672518

Woolard, K. A. (2020). Language ideology. In J. Stanlaw (Ed.), The International Encyclopedia of Linguistic Anthropology. doi:10.1002/9781118786093.iela0217

Wright, B. L., Ford, D. Y., & Young, J. L. (2017). Ignorance or indifference? Seeking excellence and equity for under-represented students of color in gifted education. *Global Education Review, 4*(1). https://link.gale.com/apps/doc/A544247889/AONE?u=txshracd2488&sid=AONE&xid=6fa3f2c4

Wright, W. E. (2002). The effects of high stakes testing in an inner-city elementary school: The curriculum, the teachers, and the English language learners. *The Curriculum, 5*(5), 1–23.

Wubbels, T., Den Brok, P., Veldman, I., & Van Tartwijk, J. (2006). Teacher interpersonal competence for Dutch secondary multicultural classrooms. *Teachers and Teaching, 12*(4), 407–433.

Wynter-Hoyte, K., Braden, E., Myers, M., Rodriguez, S. C., & Thornton, N. (2022). *Revolutionary love: Creating a culturally inclusive literacy classroom.* Scholastic.

Yaman, A. (2017). *Determining the opinions of classroom teachers on the development and implementation of individualized education programs for students educated with the inclusion model* [Unpublished master's thesis]. Necmettin Erbakan University, Konya, Turkey.

Yates, T. M., & Marcelo, A. K. (2014). Through race-colored glasses: Preschoolers pretend play and teachers' ratings of preschooler adjustment. *Early Childhood Research Quarterly, 29*, 1–11.

Yazcayir, G., & Gurgur, H. (2021). Students with Special Needs in Digital Classrooms during the COVID-19 Pandemic in Turkey. *Pedagogical Research, 6*(1), em0088. doi:10.29333/pr/9356

Yee, N., & Butler, D. (2020). Decolonizing possibilities in special education services. *Canadian Journal of Education, 43*(4), 1071–1103.

Yikmiss, A., Sahbaz, U., & Peker, S. (1998). *The effect of in-service training programs on teachers' attitudes towards inclusion* [Paper presentation]. *8th National Special Education Congress*, Edirne, Turkey.

Yildirim, E., & Merey, Z. (2020). Inclusive Education. In I. Kozikoglu (Ed.), *Current approaches in education* (pp. 1-16). Pegem. Retrieved from www.onceokuloncesi.com/.../9b084d96d5254342f0e3f88ae24e/4a3.doc

Yıldız, Y., Kaçar, M., Albayrak, E., Çalaboğlu, T., Çakmak, S., & Bayraktar, T. (2017). Çocuk İhmali Ve İstismarı Hakkında İlköğretim Öğretmenlerinin Bilgi Düzeylerinin Değerlendirilmesi. *Van Tıp Dergisi,* 24(4):303-309. (Evaluation of Primary Education Teachers' Knowledge Levels about Child Neglect and Abuse. *Van Medical Journal, 24*(4), 303–309. doi:10.5505/vtd.2017.99609

Yilmaz, E., & Batu, E. S. (2016). Opinions of primary school teachers from different branches about individualized education program, legal regulations and inclusion practices. *The Journal of Special Education, 17*(3), 247–268.

Yilmaz, E., & Melekoglu, M. A. (2018). Evaluation of the status of inclusive education in law and practice in Turkey and the European context. *Osmangazi Journal of Educational Research, 5*(1), 1–17.

Yolcuoğlu, İ. (2009). Türkiye'de Çocuk Koruma Sisteminin Genel Olarak Değerlendirilmesi. *Aile ve Toplum, 5*(18): 43-57. [General Evaluation of Child Protection System in Turkey. *Family and Society, 5*(18): 43-57].

Yörükoğlu, A. (2002). Çocuk Ruh Sağlığı. (25. Basım). Özgür Yayınları. [Child Mental Health. (25th Edition). Özgür Publications].

Yosso, T. J. (2005). Whose culture has capital? A critical race theory discussion of community cultural wealth. *Race, Ethnicity and Education, 8*(1), 69–91.

Young, L. (2014, March 28), *Coming Out From Shadows: A History of Gay and Lesbian Educators in the United States*. New Teaching and Learning Spaces.

Zakszeski, B., Rutherford, L., Heidelburg, K., & Thomas, L. (2021). In pursuit of equity: Discipline disproportionality and SWPBIS implementation in urban schools. *The School Psychologist, 36*(2), 122–130. doi:10.1037pq0000428

Zeichner, K. M. (2019). *The struggle for the soul of teacher education*. Routledge.

Zhang, Y., & Wildemuth, B. M. (n.d.). *Unstructured interviews*. Available at https://www.ischool.utexas.edu/~yanz/Unstructured_interviews.pdf

Zhang, Y., Goddard, J. T., & Jakubiec, B. A. (2018). Social justice leadership in education: A suggested questionnaire. *Research in Educational Administration and Leadership, 3*(1), 53–86. doi:10.30828/real/2018.1.3

Zimbabwe Ministry of Primary and Secondary Education (MoPSE). (2015). *Secretary's Circular Minute No. 13 of 2015: Guidelines on enrolment of Form 1 students*. Government Printers.

Zimmerman, B. J., & Dibenedetto, M. K. (2008). Mastery learning and assessment: Implications for students and teachers in an era of high-stakes testing. *Psychology in the Schools*, *45*(3), 206–216. doi:10.1002/pits.20291

Zullig, K. J., Collins, R., Ghani, N., Hunter, A. A., Patton, J. M., Huebner, E. S., & Zhang, J. (2015). Preliminary development of a revised version of the School Climate Measure. *Psychological Assessment*, *27*(3), 1072–1081. doi:10.1037/pas0000070 PMID:25642931

About the Contributors

Jonathan Chitiyo's teaching experience started in Zimbabwe and Malawi, where he served as a substitute high school teacher before moving to the USA to pursue graduate studies. His research interests include the implementation of different school-based practices (i.e., school-wide positive behavior support), inclusive education, factors affecting the education of vulnerable students, and the development of special education systems in developing countries.

* * *

Heidi R. Bacon is an Associate Professor of Language, Literacies, and Culture in the School of Education at Southern Illinois University Carbondale. A former high school teacher and K-12 reading specialist, she currently teaches courses in disciplinary literacies, diversity in education, practitioner research, and qualitative research methods. Her research focuses on literacy identities, disciplinary literacies in STEM education, culturally responsive and sustaining pedagogies, and home, school, and community engagement using narrative inquiry, discourse analysis, and critical theories and methods.

William A. Clark, D. Ed. is currently Assistant Professor of Secondary Education and was previously a Visiting Assistant Professor of Education at the University of Pittsburgh at Bradford. Prior to being appointed to the positions at Pitt at Bradford, Dr. Clark was the Executive Director of the Barber National Institute Bollinger Campus in Warren, superintendent of the Warren County School District, an Educational Consultant for the Solanco Area School District, Superintendent at Manheim Central and Milton Area School District. He earned a Bachelor of Science degree from Pennsylvania State University, a Master of Education degree from Shippensburg University and a Doctor of Education degree from Pennsylvania State University.

Elizabeth D. Cramer is a professor of special education and Graduate Program Director of Teaching and Learning at Florida International University. Her research is focused on the education of high-need children in inclusive urban settings. Her work explores opportunity and achievement gaps; the intersection of race, culture, language, poverty, and disability; collaboration with diverse family and faculty; data-based decision making; and placement issues and educational outcomes for minoritized learners.

Chauntea S. Cummings is a licensed school psychologist, special education doctoral student at Florida International University, and recipient of the Project INCLUDE fellowship, funded by the U.S. Department of Education Office of Special Education Programs (OSEP). Her research interests include improving educational outcomes for children with emotional/behavioral disorders, family collaboration in urban school settings, trauma-informed practices, culturally responsive pedagogy, and the intersectionality of race, gender, and poverty for young Black girls.

Helen Flores, Ed.S, is a Graduate Assistant for Project PATHWAYS at Florida International University (FIU). She is also a special education doctoral candidate at FIU and recipient of the Project INCLUDE fellowship, funded by the U.S. Department of Education Office of Special Education Programs (OSEP).

Antoinette Gagné has been a professor at the University of Toronto since 1989. Her research has focused on teacher education for diversity and inclusion in various contexts as well as the experiences of newcomers and their families in Canadian schools.

Özge Gümüş is an Assistant Professor of the School of Foreign Languages at Adiyaman University. Her research interests are language learning motivation, teacher training, English language education, teaching young learners and inclusive education.

Merry Ruth Morauda Gutierrez holds a full professor rank assigned as faculty of College of Graduate Studies and Teacher Education Research at PNU- Manila where she serves as Graduate Program Academic Adviser in Reading and Literacy.

Leanne Howell teaches full time in the online EdD program at Baylor University, Learning and Organizational Change.

Arlo Kempf, PhD, is an Assistant Professor at the Ontario Institute for Studies in Education, University of Toronto. Arlo's research interests include anti-racism and anticolonialism in K-12 and teacher education; (critical) whiteness and White supremacy in education; teachers' work and professional lives in critical perspective; and critical perspectives on neoliberalism in education. Arlo teaches in the areas of race and equity in education, and is Faculty Editor of the journal Curriculum Inquiry.

Shea Kerkhoff is an Assistant Professor of literacy and secondary education at the University of Missouri-St. Louis. She holds a Ph.D. from North Carolina State University in Curriculum and Instruction with a focus in literacy and language education. Dr. Kerkhoff utilizes mixed methods to investigate critical, digital, and global literacies. Her work has been published in Teaching and Teacher Education, Reading and Writing: An Interdisciplinary Journal, and Reading Research Quarterly. She taught high school English for seven years, including North Carolina and District of Columbia public schools. She is co-PI on a large statewide grant for comprehensive literacy instruction. She also serves as Going Global, Inc.'s Education Director. In 2018, she was named a Longview Foundation Global Teacher Educator fellow and currently serves as a mentor for the fellowship program.

Thursica Kovinthan Levi is a SSHRC Postdoctoral Fellow and lecturer at the Ontario Institute for Studies in Education (OISE), University of Toronto. Her current research focuses on trauma-informed pedagogies for integration and reconciliation in refugee education. She is also a teacher with the Toronto District School Board.

Lori Leibowitz, serving as the district administrator for Gifted and Talented programs in Norwalk, Connecticut, combines her knowledge of best practices in identifying gifted students, especially from underserved populations, with a passion for talent development and curriculum development. Lori was awarded the Gifted Coordinator Award in 2020 by the National Association of Gifted Children (NAGC) and is currently a doctoral candidate at Baylor University with an anticipated graduation date of May 2023.

Aniva Lumpkins is a clinical supervisor of school psychologists in a large urban school district and a doctoral student pursuing her PhD in Special Education at Florida International University. She has centered her research on early intervention efforts that support RELD children with or at risk for disruptive behavior disorders and early learning problems. With her recent work as the first Policy Intern for the Teacher Education Division of CEC, she has also explored how policy might best support efforts to shape practices which impact the quality and future of special education through a culturally responsive lens.

Ismail Hakki Mirici, full-time professor at Hacettepe University, is the ELP National Contact Person of the Turkish Ministry of Education in the Council of Europe. He is also the Past President (2011- 2013) of the World Council for Curriculum and Instruction (WCCI), and the Founder of the WCCI Turkish Chapter. He has about 20 books and more than 50 articles published in national and international academic journals. His main fields of studies are English Language Teaching, Teacher Training and Curriculum and Instruction.

Serap Öztürk graduated from Hacettepe University Child Development and Education Department undergraduate program in 1998. In 2015, she completed her master's degree at the Ankara University Institute of Health Sciences, Department of Social Work. She started working as a Child Developmentalist at the Social Services and Child Protection Agency in 1998 and currently working as a Child Developmentalist at the Ministry of Family and Social Services, General Directorate of Disabled and Elderly Services. Throughout her working life, she attended various courses, in-service training programs, symposiums, and panels related to his profession and social work. Organizations were organized to monitor the development of children in need of protection, working with children with special needs, community-based rehabilitation works, publication and documentation on social services, planning and preparation of the institution's budget, and personnel training. She carried out the coordination and secretariat services of the Social Services Advisory Board. It continues to carry out its duties, such as working on the disability health board regulations and the rights of the disabled.

Matthew Rice is a doctoral candidate at Baylor University. He lives with his partner and son in New Jersey. Matthew serves as an instructional coach for middle and high school for his local school district. He is happiest when he is working in intersectional equity advocacy in PreK–12 spaces. Matthew wrote his dissertation on supporting trans and non-binary teachers in K–12 education.

Selvinaz Saçan, after graduating from high school as a nurse, studied at the Hacettepe University Child Development and Education undergraduate program while working as a nurse in the Oncology Clinic of Sami Ulus Children's Hospital. She completed her MA in 2000 and Ph.D. in 2010 in Hacettepe University Health Sciences Institute Child Development and Education Department. She worked on determining the self-concept levels of adolescents in her master's program and examining the emotional and behavioral problems of children and adolescents aged 6-18 years under protection in her doctoral program. She took part in the "Foster Family Training Module" within the "Support the Strengthening of the Foster Care System Project" and "Evaluation Framework Guidelines for Professionals Working in the Field of Child Protection" within the scope of the "Strengthening Decision Support Mechanisms in Child Protection Services Project" supported by Unicef.

Juland D. Salayo is a research and language instructor at the University of Santo Tomas, Manila, the Philippines. His research interests include critical language pedagogy, critical discourse analysis, sociolinguistics, pragmatics, and language and culture. Most of his papers were presented and published in various local and international conferences and journals, respectively. He is now a Ph.D. Candidate in English Language Education at the Philippine Normal University in Manila.

Burcu Şentürk is an Assistant Professor of ELT at Bartin University Faculty of Education. Her research interests are teacher training, English language education, curriculum and instruction, inclusive education.

Lwazi Sibanda, PhD, is an Associate Professor in the Faculty of Science and Technology Education at the National University of Science and Technology in Zimbabwe. She is currently the Executive Dean in the Faculty of Science and Technology Education. She specialised in Education Management and is involved in teacher education. She teaches education courses (modules) to undergraduate and postgraduate students. She supervises undergraduate research projects and postgraduate dissertations and theses at Master's and Doctoral levels. Her research interest is on education management, leadership and supervision, inclusive education, teacher education, curriculum design, assessment, quality and equity in education, guidance and counselling, positive discipline and improving instructional delivery in all levels of education. She has published quite a number of journal articles and book chapters individually and collaboratively including book editing. She is a member of the journal editorial board and has reviewed various manuscripts from a number of journals and book chapters from international publishers.

Lena Shulyakovskaya is a PhD student in Adult Education and Community Development (with a collaborative specialization in Workplace Learning and Social Change) at the Ontario Institute for Studies in Education, University of Toronto. Lena's research interests include Critical Mixed-Race Studies, Critical Asian Studies, socialization, learning in life history, transformative learning, situated learning, workplace learning, emotional labour. Lena is also a public middle school teacher.

Alina Slapac is an Associate Professor of action research and curriculum and instruction at the University of Missouri-St. Louis (UMSL). Her research interests include teacher preparation and development with focus on global and multicultural education, culturally and linguistically responsive teaching, collaborative online international learning, and transformative pedagogy. She has been collaborating with educators from China, Norway, Romania, Spain, South Africa, and USA on research and teaching. Dr. Slapac has been an UMSL Global Fellow and an UMSL Inquiry Circles Fellow on global competency. Her two co-edited books are Handbook of Research on the Global Empowerment of Educators and Student Learning through Action Research (Slapac, Balcerzak & O'Brien, 2021, IGI Global) and Beyond Language Learning Instruction: Transformative Supports for Emergent Bilinguals and Educators (Slapac & Coppersmith, 2019) (IGI Global). Besides book chapters, she published articles in Journal of Research on Childhood Education, Educational Studies, Kappa Delta Pi Record,

Scholar-Practitioner Quarterly, Journal of Immersion and Content-Based Language Education, and Teacher Education and Practice, among others. She is currently working on a third co-editing book with Cristina A. Huertas-Abril, entitled Encouraging Transnational Learning through Telecollaboration in Global Teacher Education (IGI Global, forthcoming in 2023). She is also the recipient of three teaching awards and several service awards.

Matshidiso Taole holds a PhD degree in Curriculum Development from the North West University. She is a full professor at Unisa in the Department of Curriculum and Instructional Studies. She is presently involved in research supervision in the fields of Curriculum Studies, Multigrade teaching and Language Teaching and Learning. Her interests are rural education, multi-grade teaching, teacher professional development, teaching practice and inclusivity in education.

Sharde Theodore is a Graduate Assistant for Project PATHWAYS at Florida International University (FIU). She is also a special education doctoral candidate at FIU and a recipient of the Project INCLUDE fellowship, funded by the U.S. Department of Education Office of Special Education Programs (OSEP).

Nicholas Werse, serving as the Director of the Baylor University EdD Research and Writing Development Center, combines his love for writing with a passion for student development by supporting student research and writing development in the EdD in Learning and Organizational Change Program. Dr. Werse is both an instructor and a practitioner of the craft of writing, having published broadly in the fields of academic writing development and professional doctoral education.

Index

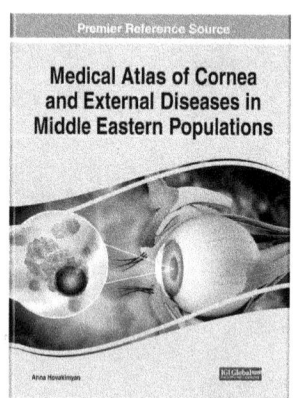

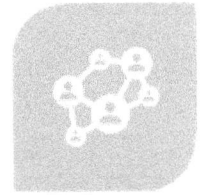

CPSIA information can be obtained
at www.ICGtesting.com
Printed in the USA
BVHW091221230123
656900BV00011B/330